Feibleman, James
Kern

An introduction
to the philosophy
of Charles S....

AN INTRODUCTION TO
THE PHILOSOPHY OF
CHARLES S. PEIRCE

by James K. Feibleman

Co-Author of

AN INTRODUCTION TO
THE PHILOSOPHY OF
CHARLES S. PEIRCE

Interpreted as a System

by
James K. Feibleman

With a Foreword by
Bertrand Russell

THE M.I.T. PRESS
Cambridge, Massachusetts, and London, England

ISBN 0 262 06035 3 (hardcover)
ISBN 0 262 56008 9 (paperback)
Library of Congress catalog card number: 71-97496

To

the memory of my father

Leopold Feibleman

CONTENTS

❮❮❮❮❭❯❯❯❯

FOREWORD

MR. FEIBLEMAN HAS PERFORMED A MOST VALUABLE WORK IN PRESENTING TO THE public a systematic exposition of Charles Peirce's philosophy. Peirce himself, like Leibniz, gave to the world only fragments of his system, with the result that he has been very thoroughly misunderstood, not least by those who professed to be his admirers. I am—I confess to my shame—an illustration of the undue neglect from which Peirce has suffered in Europe. I heard of him first from William James when I stayed with that eminent man in Harvard in 1896. But I read nothing of him until 1900, when I had become interested in extending symbolic logic to relations, and learnt from Schröder's "Algebra der Logik" that Peirce had treated of the subject. Apart from his work on this topic, I had until recently read nothing of him except the volume entitled by its editors "Chance, Love and Logic."

To those who only know Peirce through his admirers (other than Mr. Feibleman) it will, I think, come as a surprise to learn of his profound interest in scholastic philosophy, and of the great importance which he attached to realism (in the scholastic sense) as against nominalism. To many professional philosophers, Duns Scotus is scarcely more than a name, whereas Peirce felt towards him as if he were almost a contemporary, to be championed against the criticisms of William of Ockham. I think Peirce was right in regarding the realist-nominalist controversy as one which is still undecided, and which is as important now as at any former time.

Peirce's pragmatism (or pragmaticism, as he came to call it) is a very different doctrine from those of James and Schiller and Dewey, and one not open to the same criticisms. He has, in fact, two doctrines, not mutually inconsistent, one as to what truth is, the other as to how we discover it. He gives (I quote from Mr. Feibleman's account) two definitions of truth. One of them, quoted by Dewey, says: "Truth is that concordance of an abstract statement with the ideal limit towards which endless investigation would tend to bring scientific belief." The other, not quoted by Dewey, says: "Truth is the universe of all universes, and is assumed on all hands to be real." Pragmatism, for Peirce, was only a method; the truths which it sought to discover were absolute and eternal. He did not believe in the supremacy of action over thought. If pragmatism, he said, "really made Doing to be the Be-all and the End-all of life, that would be its death. For to say that we live for the mere sake of action, as action, regardless of the thought it carries out, would be to say that there is no such thing as rational purport." Peirce, in fact, was a rationalist, and had no sympathy with the irrationalist doctrines to which some of his opinions, unduly isolated, have been erroneously thought to give support.

Peirce was a man of tremendous energy, producing a multitude of ideas, good, bad, and indifferent. He reminds one of a volcano spouting vast masses of rock, of which some, on examination, turn out to be nuggets of pure gold. He holds—and I confess that an examination of scientific inference has made me feel the force of this view—that man is adapted, by his congenital constitution, to the apprehension of natural laws which cannot be proved by experience, although experience is in conformity with them. "The chicken you say pecks by instinct. But if you are going to think every poor chicken endowed with an innate tendency towards a positive truth, why should you think that to man alone this gift is denied?" This is an important question, to which I do not know the answer.

Peirce was undoubtedly a great philosopher, and it is important that he should receive the respect that he deserves. Much of his system will seem to most modern readers, as it does to me, unduly metaphysical on the one hand, and on the other hand too much influenced by evolutionary optimism. But even when his general system is discarded there remain very many suggestions that, in a receptive mind, are capable of giving rise to large developments of great importance. For having so greatly facilitated this process, Mr. Feibleman deserves the grateful thanks of all students of philosophy.

BERTRAND RUSSELL

INTRODUCTION

IN THE TWENTY-FOUR YEARS SINCE THIS BOOK WAS FIRST PUBLISHED A LARGE BODY
of literature about Peirce has grown up. He has been widely recognized as
the father of pragmatism, a precursor of symbolic logic, and a worker in the
field of the philosophy of science. Less well known are his contributions to
metaphysics, to ethics, to psychology, and to many other disciplines. He was
a thinker of the first rank, and it is not necessary to call him the American
Leibniz in order to acknowledge the force of his originality.

Peirce did not present his philosophy in a comprehensive system, although
he made plans to do so more than once. The question of whether he had a
system, in other words whether or not such a plan could have been carried
out, has been left open. Many investigators have supported the idea that
Peirce did have a system, while as many others have insisted that he did
not. Can the truth on this question be credited absolutely only on one side
or the other? There is a sense in which a system has a constrictive as well
as a liberative effect, and perhaps a man would be ill-advised to put the finish-
ing touches to such an enterprise until he was sure he had nothing more
to say. Those who consider systems of philosophy to be outdated and who
consequently would save Peirce from what they view as a false charge,
perhaps do not understand what they are admitting, for a system is only
another way of talking about consistency. It might be fair to ask why
empirical-minded philosophers feel on more secure grounds with piecemeal work, as though Rutherford had been an empiricist and Einstein not,
when the fact is that there is more than one way of doing science: the grand
theorist is as much a scientist as the patient investigator, and the same can
be said for philosophy.

The question probably hangs on whether Peirce in the course of his long
life abandoned his earlier ideas for later ones or merely developed the earlier
ideas. Very likely no clear case can be made for either. A man not only adds
to his work during the course of a long lifetime, he also develops it and in

the development significant changes may occur so that in the end his position has altered. Thus it has come about in Peirce's case that some scholars look for his system while others think it more important to follow the course of his development.

A thinker's reputation grows in proportion not only to the number of citations and references to his work in journal articles and books by his professional colleagues but also to the degree of divergence of the views of those who seek to derive from him, until it begins to appear almost as though fame consists in a sufficient number of misunderstandings. But the appearances in this instance could be wrong.

Certainly it can be said for Peirce that while all philosophers know about him and many have read his work his reputation still falls somewhat short of what it should be in the case of a full-scale figure. He is known to the members of his profession everywhere, but not so much outside it. The shortcomings can be softened somewhat if we remember that in the United States at the present time there is no such thing as a philosopher whose name is a household word. Not even our best novelists acknowledge philosophers as influences; Zen Buddhists perhaps but philosophers seldom if ever. The best known names in American philosophy are those of William James and John Dewey, but if we stop to consider them for a moment we can see that while both were professional philosophers, neither was known popularly for his philosophy. James made his reputation in psychology and Dewey in education.

It is a measure of the size of Peirce as an influence that both James and Dewey considered themselves his students. Certainly his shadow lay broadly across the American intellectual scene, and he still stands there, a large and powerful but lonely thinker, awaiting full recognition. It is discouraging to consider that had he been German there would by now be a Peirce *Gesellschaft* and a leading Peirceian scholar in every institution of higher learning. But all is not over and the best may yet be ahead. After all there is a journal, *Transactions of the Charles S. Peirce Society,* and, even if to stay afloat it has had to open its pages to the study of the work of other men, it does exist.

At the present time most American philosophers go to Europeans for guidance, to Wittgenstein's followers in England, to the memory of Kierkegaard and Husserl on the Continent, and in our own day to Heidegger and Sartre. The sin is one of omission rather than of commission: no one would want to make the chauvinistic point that productivity should begin at home and remain there, but at least it should be found at home, as in fact it was once in the days of Peirce and James, of Royce and Mead.

Philosophy is indeed the last of the great cultural enterprises in which we still look exclusively abroad. Culturally speaking, this is at best an unhealthy situation. Let us hope that it will not last. If we turn back to see the work of Peirce as a whole and try to understand the direction in which it points, we may find one kind of corrective, for Peirce was sure, if he was sure of anything, that the direction of philosophy was toward open-ended inquiry, with no absolutes to render it unnecessary and no preconceptions to bar the way. He refused to abandon metaphysics in order to gain empiricism because he thought that empiricism has its own metaphysics, and so he endeavored to explain empiricism and discover its metaphysics.

If we can feel inspiration in Peirce to locate the roots of a fresh philosophical enterprise in our own already impressive cultural achievement, even though what we emerge with might not resemble too closely his own ideas and values, it would still owe much to the spirit of his undertakings and in this sense continue what he so courageously started. Grounding research in Peirce's writings still leaves open the prospect of interpolation as well as extrapolation. There are fields in which he did not excel, such as aesthetics, and others with which he was not concerned, such as politics and economics. What would a Peirceian aesthetics be like? Could a Peirceian politics be constructed? Again, in those fields in which he did do important work his ideas could be extended. To the philosopher who possesses the ideal combination of a rigorous training and a flexible yet controlled imagination, the future is wide. It is probably the case that nothing has been done for the last time, and so very much not even for the first time.

But surely the greatest monument to Peirce that could be erected in these days of narrow if deep investigations and intense professional intolerances would be not only to say but to mean what he advocated, to leave all doors open to inquiry. One measure of a culture is the extent to which its leading advocates are able not only to welcome differences of opinion but even to encourage them and to assist in their promulgation. Unhappily, this is far from the case now.

Ours is the day of the preeminence of experimental science and of the fine arts and literature, but not of philosophy. Philosophy is a neglected field, and a neglected field is a shrinking field, in which everyone feels crowded and unhappy. Philosophers, like other people, need living space; but since it is a philosophical living space, they are the only ones who can provide it for each other. It was not something Peirce enjoyed in his own day but it was something he advocated with enthusiasm, and it can be counted among the good things he has left us. We will be doing him honor if we strike out with imagination in every hopeful direction in search of the truths which the cardinal axiom of his faith always assumed were there to be found.

Chilmark, Massachusetts
June, 1969

PREFACE

❮❮❮❰❱❯❯❯

THIS BOOK HAS TWO AIMS, THE FIRST OF WHICH IS TO OFFER AN INTRODUCTION to the general philosophy of Charles S. Peirce, who may fairly be described as one of the greatest philosophers America has thus far produced. A mere introduction is not sufficient for the understanding of work at once so complex and so suggestive. If the reader is carried by his interest in this book to the study of the six volumes of *Collected Papers* which have been published by the Harvard University Press, and, perhaps further, to an examination of the remaining manuscripts which repose in the Widener Library, the present effort will have served its primary purpose.

The second aim is to exhibit the system which seems to be inherent in Peirce's philosophy. Because of the random way in which he often presented his ideas, and the wanderings, repetitions, and general disorderliness of his scattered papers, some persons have been led to suppose that Peirce did not have a systematic philosophy. While these critics are busy attacking Peirce for not having been more orderly, others, again, claim him for that very reason. In either case, he has been considered an undisciplined thinker, gifted with occasionally brilliant insights; and this he most assuredly was. For instance, it was characteristic of him that he would start an essay on one topic and, in the course of proving it, stray off onto almost any other, before reaching a logical conclusion. Many versions of some papers exist, but only two books were ever completed.

Yet to assume that these shortcomings are the limits of Peirce's philosophy is to confuse the manner in which he presented his ideas with the ideas themselves, the psychological development of his thought with the logical value of the thoughts. Those who criticize him have been guilty of mistaking the lack of a systematic exposition for the lack of a systematic philosophy. However, his writings certainly were unorganized, even though his ideas were not. Because of his own psychological difficulties or perhaps because of the restraining force of adverse circumstances, but probably due to a combination of both causes, Peirce himself never formulated his system. His fault was one of method of presentation, not one of thought; in other words,

Peirce had a systematic philosophy which he set down unsystematically, as he said, in the form of "detached ideas." To read his scattered papers is to become more and more convinced that their sole purpose is to perfect an implicit system of philosophy. Thus what I have undertaken involves a refutation of the contention that Peirce's various dicta cannot be rendered consistent.

Peirce had many valuable ideas whose usefulness and validity will be more easily understood when they are placed in the context of his system. Therefore the emphasis of this presentation is positive rather than negative. The aim is neither to criticize Peirce nor to defend him. We shall not be concerned here with a detailed refutation of the opponents Peirce may have had in his day or may have developed in our own. Nor are we concerned with pronouncing any final judgment upon his worth. No doubt he is guilty of committing many fallacies; what great philosopher is not? Yet we shall seek merely to comprehend rather than to argue or to criticize his philosophy. Wherever possible we shall go along with him; hence the elaborate use of quotations from his own writings, which has followed a deliberate plan. We shall try as closely as possible to read Peirce's ideas in his own words. The novelty will appear in the organization and selection of material, and in the remarks that make up the bulk of the book. All comments on his work will be made in such a way as to reveal the implicit system which stood behind everything he wrote, but which somehow never got itself organized on paper. In the following pages Peirce's system will be displayed in the order of topics by chapter and by section. By means of footnotes which refer to passages above, the manner in which each topic is presumed to rest upon previous topics is shown. Footnotes referring to passages below are less common, and are intended only to be referential, an aid to the reader in grasping the outline.

Despite the orderliness of the system that is here discovered in Peirce's writings, these writings themselves contain many conflicting statements; and it would be no difficult task to draw up a calendar of contradictions on basic topics. But to show the conflict in each would only serve to emphasize the account of the struggles undergone by the philosopher in his efforts to arrive at a single and comprehensive point of view. Since the immediate purpose has been rather to concentrate upon that maturer position, the presentation of his philosophy as self-consistent has entailed a selection. The canon employed has consisted of those leading principles which he himself derived from reaction to certain philosophical antecedents and from agreement with others. Thus I have sought to arrange the details of Peirce's philosophy in terms only of his own leading principles. Where statements conflict (and this situation is not at all uncommon), a choice has been made of the one which is most consistent with his leading principles and the others abandoned; and the system itself has been constructed by such a method, just as a picture puzzle, after reaching a certain point, begins to suggest the easiest way to its own completion.

Since this work is devoted to the exposition of Peirce's philosophy, the emphasis will be placed—as he would have wished—on the ideas which he held rather than on the way in which he came to hold them. However, such was the ambitiousness of his plan that nothing can be safely overlooked which will serve in any fashion to aid the reader in thinking as Peirce himself might have thought. Accordingly, we shall begin with a subjective presentation, by seeking to show the chief influences which occasioned particular views. But we shall end with an objective one, by attempting to fit Peirce into the philosophical tradition as it led to him and as it has begun to lead from him.

Two books are needed in this connection where I have attempted only one. Not only an exposition of Peirce's system but also a commentary on that system is wanting. In this book I have endeavored to meet the first requirement; some day perhaps I may be able to understand the second. But even with the completion of the first half of this self-appointed task, I am conscious of my shortcomings. There are in existence two extremes which the student of a classical philosopher must painstakingly avoid. Abject discipleship is a betrayal of the master; but then the taking of part of a man's work for the whole because that part seems to bolster one side of a current controversy is also a betrayal. I am confident that my task has not been done too well, but at least the start has been made. If I have succeeded in demonstrating that the philosophy of Peirce is important, perhaps those who come after me will have more success in pointing out exactly where that importance lies.

If the unpublished writings of Peirce, which were planned to be Volumes VII to X of the *Collected Papers* but are now awaiting publication, are made available, it should be possible to improve my *Introduction*. Most of the improvement will be in Chapter I. In the meanwhile it remains my hope and persists in remaining also my conviction that the addition will need to consist only of a simple elaboration and not any drastic revision. There are many reasons for suspecting that such will be the case.

I wish to thank those who have aided me in my task, especially Dean Richard P. McKeon, Professor Paul Weiss, and Dr. Arthur W. Burks for their technical advice, Mr. Ordway Tead for his generous assistance, and Mr. Huntington Cairns for his general sympathy and encouragement in the matter of publication. They are not responsible for the point of view I have adopted, nor for its attendant errors.

Formal acknowledgment must be made of the permission to quote extensively from the *Collected Papers of Charles Sanders Peirce*, a permission that was purchased from the Harvard University Press. Neither the Harvard University Press nor, of course, the Department of Philosophy of Harvard University is in any way responsible for the use that is made here of this material, for which the author alone can be held accountable.

Certain portions of this book originally appeared as essays: part of Chapter I in the *American Journal of Economics and Sociology*, part of Chapter II in the *T'ien Hsia Monthly*; part of Chapter IV in the *Journal of Philosophy & Phenomenological Research*; part of Chapter IX in *Ethics*; part of Chapter X in *The Personalist*; and part of Chapter XIII in the *Journal of the History of Ideas*; to whose editors acknowledgment is due for permission to reprint. Part of Chapter XIV, entitled "The Influence of Peirce on Dewey's Logic," was read at the annual meeting of the Eastern Division of the American Philosophical Association held at Columbia University on December 29, 1939.

New Orleans,
January, 1939—December, 1945.

❮❮❮◇❯❯❯

TOWARDS AN UNDERSTANDING OF PEIRCE

CHAPTER I

The Historical Development of Peirce the Individual

PHILOSOPHY, AT LEAST IN THAT SENSE IN WHICH PEIRCE'S PHILOSOPHY WAS conceived and communicated, must represent the widest and most cosmical hypothesis of an unlimited universe of being, a view both devised and corrected in accordance with the requirements of logic and fact. It is thus an absorbing program, calling upon enormous funds of knowledge and keen insight gained through rigorous training and exclusiveness of interest.

Of the few individuals who, in an age of emphasis on science, try to be philosophers, fewer still are able to succeed. Philosophy being what it is, however, this goal, like all others worthy of the name, is ultimately unattainable. Although no ambition can be said to be higher than that of the truly ambitious philosopher, there are difficulties which always beset him and which in almost every case must eventually prove insurmountable. These difficulties are occasioned by the peculiarities of perspective to which life in a given date and place have committed him. Since men are of necessity limited creatures, they have at their disposal never more than a reasoning that is apt at times to be faulty and a spatial sequence of events that is sure to be brief in the extreme. In the judgment of any accomplishment, these shortcomings must be taken into account. We shall be obliged, therefore, as we consider Peirce's philosophy, to begin by devoting a few pages to his philosophical biography in order to show where and whence his special prejudices were derived and what his equipment was for the undertaking at hand.

The life of Peirce badly needs writing, for at the present moment no full account exists; but that is not the task of this chapter. We are here interested only in the abstract ideas set forth by Peirce, for what they are worth; our aim is merely to aid in the comprehension and interpretation of Peirce's systematic philosophy. As he himself said, "The reader has a right to know how the author's opinions were formed. Not, of course, that he is expected to accept any conclusions which are not borne out by argument. But in discussions of extreme difficulty, like these, when good judgment is a factor, and pure ratiocination is not everything, it is prudent to take every element into consideration." (1.3)[1] To assist in that labor it will be necessary to have some knowledge of the cultural occasion which gave rise to the man and hence in a sense also to the philosophy. In order to comprehend his work, as part of our equipment we must have perceived, if ever so crudely, the particular development of the thoughts in his mind which led to the written formulation of his philosophy, in the version in which we have it preserved. In short, it may help toward the understanding of Peirce's logical philosophy to have some acquaintance with his historical development.

A. THE HISTORICAL SETTING

i. THE CULTURE OF BOSTON

The history of Boston culture during the first half of the nineteenth century is the account of the New England promise—and why it was not fulfilled. It is true that a tiny corner of Massachusetts led the way toward the establishment of an indigenous American culture; led the way, faltered, and then finally came to an abrupt close. The tale of this brief beginning and its abortive termination explains to some extent how the New England environment could give rise at once to a great philosopher, certainly the greatest that America has yet produced, and also to a society that failed to appreciate him.

In a new world, peopled at first largely by English stock and using the English language exclusively, it was logical that English cultural influences should be strongly felt. But from the beginning the impact of a rude and powerful geographical environment upon the early Puritans did not allow the imitation of England to take a naïve start. In the trading centers of New England, which early developed a world-wide commercial intercourse, the parent English influences were unable to remain undiluted. Windjammers returned from every important seaport, in the East as well as in the West, bringing strange cargoes and the sound of unknown tongues. The merchants' "brave little sailing ships went to Canton, St. Petersburg, the Ile de France, and Bombay" and "they continued to pile up fortunes out of sea

[1] All numbers within parentheses in the body of the text throughout this book refer to volume and paragraph of the *Collected Papers of Charles Sanders Peirce*, edited by Charles Hartshorne and Paul Weiss (Cambridge, Harvard University Press, 1931-1935). Thus (1.3) indicates the third paragraph of the first volume.

trade from 1780 to 1850."[2] Culture does not always result from a prosperous commerce, but cannot occur without it. Boston, the chief seaport of the New World, tried to establish its independence from England by grafting international influences upon the agricultural beginnings of American life. Particularly was the novelty of the Orient invigorating. Bostonian sons who had gone to sea came home with Eastern books and stories, speaking dialects rarely heard before even in Europe. The air was filled with excitement. Unconsciously perhaps, but none the less surely, it was felt that here was the opportunity for a cultural birth rare in history.

A self-conscious passion for learning soon gripped the little area; it was determined to make use of its virgin environment, and to implant thereon a complex culture that would spread from its provincial location to the rest of America and perhaps as far as Europe. Thus without comprehending all the implications, Boston and its neighborhood aspired to repeat the tremendously successful adventure that was insular England. At first the experiment was amazing. Emerson developed his stilted yet penetrating and singularly fresh version of Oriental mysticism known as transcendentalism; Hawthorne, with this transcendentalism, interpreted the town life of New England while Thoreau performed the same task for the country life. In this way was initiated a culture which any land would have been proud to call its own. Viewed with a sufficiently narrow logic, there would appear to be no reason to suppose that such a start might not have led to consequences of tremendous importance.

But something happened which had not been taken into account in the calculations. There were major factors at work of which not even the New England authors dreamed. For, while they were writing, while their neighbors went on considering Boston the "hub" of a world to come, the frontier was expanding, and America was becoming of a magnitude never dreamed of in any philosophy, Eastern or Western. While the Boston writers were endeavoring to establish a little island culture which was to be all of a piece like that of England, America was growing and was beginning to constitute an influence on its own account. England had been separated by water from the remainder of the world. New England was separated only by ignorance of the potentialities of the unknown new territory lying to the west. But while the ignorance was to last, the potential became actual. Boston sent out waves of influences to the rest of the United States, much as England sent out influences to its colonies. But the colonies were remote and could not influence England in the same important way, whereas the

---

[2] Robert R. Mullen. "Poor Old Boston," in *The Forum*, 103 (1940), 232.

broad United States reacted on New England in a fashion that made Boston culture shrink in upon itself in fear and trembling.

There was still another difference. England did not acquire its important colonies until after it had become culturally mature. The great period of empire expansion followed the period of Elizabethan cultural renaissance. With the English conquerors went evidence of a robust culture which stood in no fear of being quelled whatever it had to meet. In New England, however, the cultural renaissance was not given enough time to get solidly established before a marching army of immigration was at its door and an advancing frontier carried the boundaries of its sphere of influence indefinitely away toward the west and south. "Into such a decorous, well-to-do, chilly, ornate society were suddenly dumped the roisterous, indecorous, emotional, warm, tumultuous, laughing Irish. For, just as Boston reached this nice, ever rising mid-nineteenth-century economic plane, Ireland experienced a potato famine. Nothing would grow. . . . This was the summer Cunard plastered the Emerald Isle with his steamship posters. The cheapest trip was from Queenstown to Boston. They came in droves."[3] In the period from 1830 to 1850 the population of New England rose only from 2,000,000 to 2,700,000. Considering that of this number 300,000 were foreign-born, chiefly Irish, New England must have lost an equal number, or an even greater one, to the new frontiers.[4] The challenge was more than the young arts of Boston were able to meet; they did not prove equal to it because they could not. The simple truth is that they were not prepared.

Cultures, like lesser organizations, have two choices, or, more rarely, three. They can advance or retreat, and occasionally they are allowed to stand still. Boston tried in vain to hold its gains without making any fresh efforts, and the result was a retrogression that shook the little society at every level of its activities. First of all, it lost its great seaport trade to the port of New York. As early as 1794, the tonnage shipped from the port of New York exceeded the shipments from Boston. By 1797, Boston was exporting only 84,259 tons against New York's 153,931 tons. Then it tried to supplant this loss by turning its energies over to manufacture. The Merrimac River was the scene of the new busy occupation, as mills sprang up everywhere, and Boston became the banking center for the region. Already in 1850, the value of New England manufactures, according to the national census, was $274,740,000, of which Massachusetts alone could claim over half.[5] "The Asiatic trade had already dropped away, and in 1868 the

[3] *Ibid.*, p. 233.
[4] Frederick Jackson Turner, *The United States: 1830-1850* (New York, Holt, 1935), p. 44.
[5] *Ibid.*, chap. III.

Cunard Line also shifted from Boston. The mail and passenger steamers from Europe made New York the main port of entry. Thus Boston was isolated, as compared with New York, both from the West and from Europe, although it grew richer and richer from the factory-system. It profited by the growth of the West, creating goods for the pioneers, who sent their own products to New York."[6] This made it dependent upon the areas producing raw materials, particularly upon southern cotton; so that it became involved in the issue of the Civil War. Twist and turn as it might, the days of its pretensions to isolation were past and they could not be recalled.

Boston lost its confidence; and it was soon evident that the promise of American life—so near in New England—was not to be fulfilled for a while. New Englanders themselves were aware of the new situation. Lowell wrote that he remembered Americans in an earlier day as having stood firmer on their feet; and the "furtive apology," as someone said in reference to Henry James, revealed a self-conscious effort to be noble that was sure to end in failure.[7] As Boston lost its leadership in trade to New York and its intellectual isolation to the whole continent of North America, it shrank culturally and endeavored to preserve the achievements with which it had started. Hence conservatism supplanted the beginnings of a brave new world, bringing puritanism, conformism, and the imitation of European models, particularly those of England, in its wake. The shift was unfortunate; for as Boston grew self-conscious about its earlier virtues it became evident that whatever these virtues had been they were not entirely those of the Calvinist. Values had existed, and terrific living; where now there was only retrenchment, and the abandonment of all that had been so desperately gained.

The new generation of the Boston of 1870 felt lost; it did not know its own ground as something safely under it, and looked elsewhere helplessly. "Then the values of England resumed their sway, as nature abhors a vacuum."[8] Symptomatic of the return was the literature produced by Henry James, excellent in craftsmanship yet none the less mere novels of British nostalgia written by a provincial expatriate. Boston slowly became what it has continued to be to the present day: a pioneer imitation of what it supposes England is. The prudish provincialism regained its influence, unrelieved when the scholars returned from Europe to reproduce what they had learned.

---

[6] Van Wyck Brooks, *New England: Indian Summer* (New York, Dutton, 1941), p. 95.

[7] See Van Wyck Brooks, *The Flowering of New England* (New York, Dutton, 1936), pp. 513-514.

[8] *Ibid.*, p. 514.

A hedge of stern disapproval was erected about those who did not behave in the way that seemed expected. The boisterous sensuality of an earlier period that had gone hand in hand with intellectual achievement was banished to give it air; but the sensitive plant of the New England intellectual rebirth died anyway.

The picture of Harvard as it was during the early years of its decline into reaction has been well expressed by Brooks. "The college was not for ladies, neither was it meant for men of genius, or any other sort of extravagant creature. For a thorough Boston lawyer, a merchant who desired a well-trained mind, a minister who did not indulge in raptures, Harvard had proved to be an adequate nest. It fostered polite, if not beautiful letters, it sent one back to Plutarch for one's models, it sharpened the reasoning faculties, it settled one's grounds for accepting a Christian faith that always knew where to draw the line."[9] Such was the Harvard in which the father of Charles Peirce worked and indeed flourished.

ii. PEIRCE'S FATHER

The Peirce family were the descendants of a weaver named John Pers of Norwich, England, who emigrated to the United States in 1637. Benjamin Peirce, the grandfather of the philosopher, graduated from Harvard College in the second year of the nineteenth century, served in the Massachusetts state senate and was before his death librarian of the college. His son, also named Benjamin, the father of Charles, was a Harvard graduate too, and remained all his life a teacher of mathematics at the same institution.[10] While holding this position, he was for a time superintendent of the U. S. Coast Survey, from 1867 to 1874.[11]

There is no space here in which to give a full account of the man who made so great an impression upon his associates and pupils. It is possible only to mention a few characteristics which were to appear in more exaggerated form in his son. These characteristics show on the debit as well as on the credit side of the ledger, for Charles Peirce was to acquire some of the bad features as well as some of the good ones of his father. On the credit side may be mentioned the tremendous generalizing power of his mind. Benjamin Peirce was never concerned merely with the operational aspects of the teaching of mathematics. He understood his task as that of advancing the frontiers of mathematics. Nor was he content with this. His

[9] *Ibid.*, p. 38.
[10] *Benjamin Peirce: 1809-1880*, by Various Hands (Oberlin, Open Court, 1925), p. 9.
[11] *Ibid.*, pp. 3, 11.

interests were wide, and it was never true even for a brief while that his appointment specified mathematics exclusively. His title, at first that of professor of mathematics and natural philosophy, was later changed to that of professor of astronomy and mathematics.

Pupils have paid tribute time and again to his generalizing power, to "the quality of his mind which tended to regard any mathematical theorem as a particular case of some more comprehensive one, so that," as one of them said, "we were led onward to constantly enlarging truths."[12] In the winter of 1878-1879, Professor Peirce "delivered a course of lectures at the Lowell Institute entitled 'Ideality of the Physical Sciences.' In the sixth and last of these lectures he made the statement that 'Ideality is preëminently the foundation of mathematics.' "[13] He believed indeed in mathematics as the equivalent of the essential truths of philosophy.[14] And he saw an affinity between the mind of man and the laws of nature. In particular, "he thought it most interesting that a calculus which so strongly appealed to the human mind by its intrinsic beauty and symmetry should prove to be especially adapted to the study of natural phenomena. The mind of man and that of Nature's God must work in the same channels."[15] The analogy of objective natural forces to the force of the will proved the existence of God, whose will must be the forces of nature.[16]

On the debit side of Benjamin Peirce's characteristics it is necessary to register a certain failure to commit to ordered writing such of his fruitful speculations as he threw out at random. He was a mathematical author of no mean accomplishment, it is true, yet at least one writer has seen fit to record of him that "it is interesting to speculate as to the possible publication harvest if Peirce had been able throughout his career constantly to meet his mathematical equals or peers, and if he had had a capable disciple always at hand to put his ideas on paper in a form suitable for publication."[17]

He was obviously a man of restless and active intellect who took very few things for granted. In the Harvard of his day that point of view was no virtue, yet for Benjamin Peirce, Harvard presented few difficulties; he was a mathematician, and innovations of any radical and revolutionary social nature are hard to detect in mathematics. He seems to have been a robust soul who had no trouble in keeping his excess of energy within

[12] *Ibid.*, pp. 4-5.
[13] *Ibid.*, p. 8.
[14] *Ibid.*, p. 5.
[15] *Ibid.*, p. 6.
[16] *Ibid.*, p. 6.
[17] *Ibid.*, pp. 18-19.

the proper channels. He was "a massive intellect" and "a profoundly inspiring teacher."[18] He succeeded in handing on to one of his children his own vitality and intelligence but in a restrictive social environment with which these gifts were hard to reconcile.

B. THE PREPARATION

i. HIS CHILDHOOD

Books have been written about the flowering of New England which do not even mention the birth of its greatest son, an event which occurred in Cambridge, Massachusetts, on September 10, 1839, "in a stone-colored wooden house in Mason Street." (2.663) The judgment of oblivion imposed by contemporary Harvard upon its supremest achievement has remained that of its historians. Surely no environment in America could have been more academic than that into which Peirce was born in 1839. To have Cambridge as a birthplace and Benjamin Peirce as a father marked the limits of the best of the intellectual life in the United States that could have been expected for any child.[19] His father supervised his education, giving it a special emphasis upon mathematics and philosophy. Peirce then, and also long after, placed great value upon the influence thus exercised upon him. Mathematical logic and philosophy itself became his chief preoccupations, and Peirce supplemented these studies with others of his own choosing, indeed with all other related studies so far as he was able. Peirce, like John Stuart Mill, was pushed by his father in the direction his interests would probably have taken him; for he had a distinctly abstract turn of mind. He has recorded that his earliest memories were of tracing labyrinths to amuse himself; (4.533) and indeed he showed an early interest in all kinds of puzzles, mathematical card tricks, and chess problems. But more than this: he has reported that when he was a very young child he had already found the notion of chance interesting. (1.366) At the age of eight he began to study chemistry of his own accord, and at twelve he had set up his own chemical laboratory. By thirteen he had not only read but studied intensively at least one treatise on logic.

Peirce belonged to what Brooks has described as "the younger generation of 1840," a generation dissatisfied with the retrenchment that had just begun

---

[18] President Emeritus Lowell, quoted in *Science*, 89 (1939), 21.

[19] For some of these biographical notes I am obligated to the article on Peirce by Paul Weiss in the *Dictionary of American Biography*, vol. xiv, p. 398.

to set in. The environment, physical and social, had ceased to please its members;[20] but instead of attempting to change it, they rebelled as our postwar liberals did: by turning inward on themselves. With most of them, any novelty was sufficient to justify a different way of life and a desperate reaching for permanent values; but then it was the self that became their dominant value. Only Peirce succeeded in distinguishing between what-is and what-ought-to-be in any rational manner; the realistic distinction was to lead him on toward a valid philosophy, whereas the others of his age were led by their mystic introspection to become an earlier "lost generation." In this atmosphere, Peirce was keen enough to understand that help must come from the outside. The interest in German learning, which had started some while before, was gaining in strength.[21] Seeking an escape from the materialism of Lockian sensationalism, Peirce was drawn at first into the subjective idealism that was as nominalistic as that error from which he had run. The period from Locke to Fichte was marked by no admirable advance in thought; but when his father taught him the philosophy of Kant, Peirce found a way out toward realism.

"The first strictly philosophical books that I read were of the classical German schools; and I became so deeply imbued with many of their ways of thinking that I have never been able to disabuse myself of them. Yet my attitude was always that of a dweller in a laboratory, eager only to learn what I did not yet know, and not that of philosophers bred in theological seminaries, whose ruling impulse is to teach what they hold to be infallibly true." (1.4) It was, perhaps, his father's instructions in the philosophy of Kant that had the profoundest effect upon him. "When I was a babe in philosophy my bottle was filled from the udders of Kant," (2.113) he wrote in 1860. Under the elder Peirce's guidance he "devoted two hours a day to the study of Kant's *Critic of the Pure Reason* for more than three years," until he "almost knew the whole book by heart." (1.4) It was in 1860, too, that he said he had studied Kant for four years but was familiar with the works of no other philosopher, (1.563) a limitation soon wholeheartedly corrected. That the young Charles did not become an abject Kantian is most likely due to the fact that his teacher was no hero-worshiper; the latter had pointed out to him grave lacunae in Kant's reasoning "which I should probably not otherwise have discovered." (1.560) The works of Kant meant to him a discipline rather than a revelation of the truth. It was this insight implanted in him by his father at his most impressionable

[20] Brooks, *The Flowering of New England*, pp. 180, 183 and 187.
[21] *Ibid.*, p. 191.

age which led him in later years to see that, since there were some relations between the categories which had not been listed by Kant among his particular set, a wider system than that established by Kant was demanded. (4.2)

As soon as the philosophy of Kant had become thoroughly absorbed, other philosophies were studied. From Kant, Peirce's father led him on to the classical philosophers, and he mentions the following in the order in which he became acquainted with them: Berkeley, Hume, Aristotle, St. Augustine, Abélard, John of Salisbury, Aquinas, Duns Scotus, and Ockham. (1.560) Of these, Peirce decided, two men, "Duns Scotus and William Ockham, are decidedly the greatest speculative minds of the middle ages, as well as two of the profoundest metaphysicians that ever lived," (1.29) the subtilest advocates of realism and nominalism, respectively. Even at this early date he appreciated the value of empathy to learning. In studying the metaphysical systems of classical writers, he was never satisfied until he felt that he was thinking about them "as their own advocates thought." (1.3) In 1866, De Morgan sent him an essay on logic, which much excited him (1.562) and probably started him on his path toward the study that was to receive the best labors of his life. The same year he recorded a refutation of the Kantian reduction of all deductive reasoning to the syllogism in Barbara. (4.2) The inclusive sweep of metaphysics was already being supplemented by the rigorous examination into the validity of logical postulates. Two years later he fell under the influence of Thomas Reid, who showed him how it was possible to react to Hume in a way entirely different from the way in which Kant had reacted; and from then on he remained to some extent a member of the realistic "common-sense" school.

In the light of what we can learn of the influence of Benjamin Peirce upon his son, it must be admitted that he seemed to have had a careful plan and some knowledge of how to apply it to the boy who, he had decided, must become a mathematician. The happy result, however, owes a great deal to the avidity with which Peirce himself followed all the leads indicated to him by the parental education. Training was not confined to abstract topics but was extended to include power in concentration and sensuous discrimination. (5.112) Carried to this point under guidance, Peirce took the hint and, for instance, became a connoisseur of wines on his own account, aided by a professional *sommelier*. He was not long in grasping the fact that in the development of a full human being every front must be carried forward. He knew what so many European philosophers before him had failed to realize, that philosophy must be the product of the influences of the environment upon the whole man and not merely upon his mind, even though it is his mind that in the end is the most important part.

ii. EDUCATION AND MARRIAGE

Peirce's formal education properly began at home. He was sent to private grammar schools and then to Cambridge High School. After a year of preparation for college at still another school, he entered Harvard in 1855. Once again his father was a prominent factor in his education, though now chiefly in mathematics. Despite his proficiency in this subject, when he was graduated in 1859 his only distinction was that he was one of the youngest members of his class. His ability did not at first show itself: he finished his undergraduate studies seventy-first out of a class of ninety-one. Like so many world-shaking geniuses, he had a slow development. His father wanted him to become a mathematical scientist, and after some hesitation, due to his greater concern with the problems of philosophy, he joined the staff of the United States Coast and Geodetic Survey in 1861, in which service he remained for some thirty years. In 1873 he was put in charge of the Coast Survey office. It so happened that one of his first assignments took him to the Gulf of Mexico; at the age of twenty-one he had been "surveying in the wilds of Louisiana" (5.64) when "Darwin's great work appeared." It had a profound effect upon him, opening up not only vistas of evolutionary theory, which awakened his early interest in the question of chance, but also the whole field of the biological sciences. He lost no time in studying the technique of classification with Agassiz (1.205) and added to botanical work a host of zoological problems.

In the six volumes of his papers which have been published, it is evident that Peirce ranged over a great number of topics. His curiosity was aroused by almost every fact and by every discipline with which he came into contact. Yet in all these writings there appears to be not one mention of the Civil War. He had gone to work for a government division when the war was just beginning; he was not unaware of the injustices of the economic system under which he lived (6.292); and he was sensitive to all the factors in his cultural environment. It may be concluded, therefore, that in some way he was indifferent to the conflict that shook his country. True, economics and politics were not his chief concerns; and yet there must be another explanation. Indifference may be read as shortsightedness; but it may also be due to an absorbing emphasis on something else. Extreme intensity of attention calls for the attitude of indifference toward all topics not being attended to. And the more intense the focus of attention the dimmer the periphery of indifference. Peirce was at the time a busy man; he was filling a full-time position and also was endeavoring to complete his studies in other fields. There is, of course, another possible explanation. Since Peirce could not have been unaware of the Civil War, his silence must have been an indication of his disapproval. Being so vigorously affirmative, so deeply concerned with all the positive manifestations of the human spirit, he might have failed to consider that negative action, and even the violent negative action of war, also is a manifestation of the human spirit.

In 1862 he obtained his M.A. degree from Harvard and the following year an Sc.B. *summa cum laude,* in chemistry, which was, incidentally, the first degree of its kind given by Harvard. William James wrote home to his mother describing Peirce at this time. "In last year's [class] there is a son of Prof. Peirce, whom I suspect to be a very 'smart' fellow with a great deal of character, pretty independent and violent though . . . "[22] The physical and biological sciences did not, however, abate his major interest in philosophy, and in lectures given at Harvard in 1864-1865 he combined what he knew of science with what he was thinking about philosophy by treating of the philosophy of science. Two years later he had already conceived the idea of a formal science of symbols, of speculative grammar dealing with the truth of symbols, and of rhetoric as the science of communication. (4.116) None of these, not even rhetoric, as he realized at once, had anything to do with psychology. He had in the same year outlined his theory of the three modes of reasoning, Abduction, Induction, and Deduction. (5.145) Deduction, he said, works from an hypothesis to an ideal conclusion; Induction, from fact to theory. But the only form of reasoning which contributes new ideas in science is Abduction, studying facts and "devising a theory to explain them." He proceeded on a tentative basis with this outline, however, for at the same time "various facts proved to me beyond a doubt that my scheme of formal logic was still incomplete." (4.4)

Looking back years later upon the period when his graduate studies were finished, Peirce admitted that he had done almost as much beyond the formal requirements of his education as he had done for them. "From the moment when I could think at all, until now, about forty years, I have been diligently and incessantly occupied with the study of methods

[22] Ralph Barton Perry, *The Thought and Character of William James* (2 vols.) (Boston, Little, Brown, 1935), vol. i, p. 211.

[of] inquiry, both of those which have been and are pursued and those which ought to be pursued. For ten years . . . I had been in training in the chemical laboratory. I was thoroughly grounded . . . in all that was then known of physics and chemistry. . . . I am saturated through and through with the spirit of the physical sciences. I have been a great student of logic, having read everything of any importance on the subject, devoting a great deal of time to medieval thought, without neglecting the works of the Greeks, the English, the Germans, the French, etc. . . . In metaphysics, my training has been less systematic; yet I have read and deeply pondered upon all the main systems." (1.3)

Marriage at this time was contracted with Harriet Fay, the daughter of a prominent New England family. Peirce's wife, who was three years his senior, was herself a person of some scientific ability. She worked with Peirce in the laboratory and did a little writing on miscellaneous topics. The marriage was short-lived, however, due, according to Peirce's own account, to his inability to exercise the proper moral self-control. In this respect, he complained, the parental teaching had been neglectful. We may presume that Peirce was not what would be considered a libertine except from the puritanical background of the Cambridge of his day. When in 1883 he obtained a divorce, he charged that desertion had taken place in 1876. The divorce was the occasion of much embarrassment for Peirce. His wife's popularity in Cambridge, together with her family connections, resulted in widespread sympathy for her. Peirce was viewed as something of a reprobate for his part in the quarrel, and evidently the result was that obstacles were put in the way of his academic career, already none too rosy because of his idiosyncratic inability to make the expected compromises with the powers that be. Before long, however, he was married again, this time to a French girl, Juliette Froisy, of Nancy. The marriage was successful and lasted until his death. According to Joseph Jastrow, the psychologist, who was one of Peirce's disciples at Johns Hopkins, the new Mrs. Peirce was entertained by the Pinchots of Pennsylvania when she was first brought to this country by her husband. When Peirce gave the Lowell Lectures, the Peirces stopped with the James family, and Mrs. Peirce was officially received by Charles Eliot Norton.

C. THE CAREER RIPENS

In 1869 and 1870 Peirce, together with Emerson and others, gave the university lectures in philosophy at Harvard. It was a "time when Emerson,

Hedge, and their friends were disseminating the ideas that they had caught from Schelling, and Schelling from Plotinus, from Boehm, or from God knows what minds stricken with the monstrous mysticism of the East. But the atmosphere of Cambridge held many an antiseptic against Concord transcendentalism; and I am not conscious," added Peirce, "of having contracted any of that virus." (6.102) Peirce was a Western rather than an Eastern mystic; he envisaged remote goals and impossible ideals not as objects of pure contemplation but as limits to the accomplishment possible of approach by means of the scientific method. Nevertheless, as he admitted later, "it is probable that some cultured bacilli, some benignant form of the disease" of transcendentalism may have been "implanted in my soul, unawares, and that . . . after long incubation, it comes to the surface, modified by mathematical conceptions and by training in physical investigations."

James wrote of Peirce in 1869: "The poor cuss sees no chance of getting a professorship anywhere, and is likely to go into the Observatory for good. It seems a great pity that as original a man as he is, who is willing and able to devote the powers of his life to logic and metaphysics, should be starved out of a career, when there are lots of professorships of the sort to be given in the country to 'safe' orthodox men. He has had good reason, I know, to feel discouraged about the prospect, but I think he ought to hang on. . . . "[23]

Peirce was an original, untouched by the irrational influences of his day, yet unable to conform to the requirements of a university which placed its emphasis on the self-conscious pursuit of culture and refinement. Harvard was a place for gentlemen and athletes, (1.650) not for rigorous and uncompromising thinkers. The misfortune for Peirce lay in the fact that the university was almost as well aware of this situation as was he. That same New England life which had made the scholar possible through its emphasis upon learning put a prohibition upon philosophical genius by discouraging untoward ways and ignoring spectacular invention. In so doing, the authorities were being more provincial and unintentionally imitative than they had ever dreamed. For England, too, had as often as not made possible and then disparaged and refused to recognize its own best men.

The lectures which Peirce gave at Harvard were on the early history of modern science. (5.604) "How few were the guesses," he observed, "that men of surpassing genius had to make before they rightly guessed the laws of nature." The following year he was the university lecturer on logic, and

---

[23] Quoted in Perry, *Thought and Character of William James*, vol. i, p. 292.

for the time logic chiefly occupied his thoughts. He now published his first memoir on the threefold division of symbols in logic and epistemology, three years after its discovery. (1.564) In 1870 he also published his first paper on the "logic of relatives," (3.646) in which he anticipated many of the leading ideas so prominent today in symbolic logic. He has recorded with what trepidation he pointed out to Professor De Morgan, then an old man, how much of the latter's work was superseded by the "immense superiority of the Boolian method," (4.4) and with what manliness and pathos the older man received the news. Peirce had an enormous sympathy for the human predicament, exceeded only by his inflexible fidelity to the cause of truth.

The "Metaphysical Club," which met from 1872 to 1874 in Peirce's or William James' study, was the scene of the birth of pragmatism. As early as 1871 Peirce held the idea of pragmatism without the name, but the definition as well as the name for it were developed in conversations at the Club. Nicholas St. John Green, a lawyer, had been urging upon his fellow members "the importance of applying Bain's definition of belief as 'that upon which a man is prepared to act.' From this definition pragmatism is scarce more than a corollary." (5.12) Wright, James, and F. E. Abbot were among the other members; Wright, "the strongest member," James, and Peirce assuming the attitude of British empiricists toward the metaphysical speculations of the others. Peirce drew up a paper setting forth the opinions he had been maintaining at the club. This was subsequently published in two issues of the *Popular Science Monthly*, for November, 1877 ("The Fixation of Belief"), and for January, 1878 ("How to Make Our Ideas Clear"), which marked the original appearance of the formulation of pragmatism in print.

Peirce intended pragmatism to be a maxim of procedure in theory, not a dogma of metaphysics in practice. Yet precisely the latter is what it became in the hands of his followers. Although endeavoring only to hold speculation down to what could be logically allowed by the factual evidence, he was interpreted as calling for its abolition altogether; and the result was a philosophical position just the opposite of the one which he himself held. Peirce's connection from that day on consisted in his efforts to correct the misinterpretations of his followers. The Peircian doctrine of pragmatism, according to which thought was intended to "*apply* to . . . conceived action," (5.402 n) was twisted by William James and F. C. S. Schiller to mean that "thought *consists* in acts," an anti-intellectual interpretation specifically refuted by Peirce when he said that he was "speaking in no other sense than that of *intellectual purport.*" For Peirce, pragmatism involved "strenuous insistence upon the truth of scholastic realism," (5.423) a rationalist point of view which made him stand aghast when "to the delight of the Pragmatist school" pragmatism was announced by Papini (6.482) to be incapable of definition! Indeed, he was further dismayed when pragmatism got "abused in the merciless way that words have to expect when they fall into literary clutches." (5.414)

One science after another received Peirce's concentrated attention; so that there was nothing in the scientific purview which could escape his later philosophical attention due to ignorance. From 1869 to 1872 he worked as an assistant astronomer at the Harvard Observatory for $2,500 a year, and from then until 1875 he made the astronomical observations contained in *Photometric Researches* (1878),[24] almost the only book Peirce succeeded in completing and the only one he was able to get published during his lifetime. Meanwhile he went on with his work at the Coast and Geodetic Survey Department. In 1871 he was in temporary charge of the office, and from the next year until 1884 he held the position of assistant. In 1873 he was made assistant computer for the nautical almanac and put in charge of all gravity research. In 1875 he went to Europe to make pendulum investigations and to be the first American delegate to the International Geodetic Conference. His originality in pendulum work and his acuity in detecting the inaccuracies of earlier investigations won him opposition at first but later received confirmation and a vote of approval. He worked also on weights and measures, both for the survey and as a member of an international commission. He was the first to try to use the wave length of a light ray as a unit of measure, thus anticipating Michelson. He continued his researches on gravity until 1891, when he left the survey's employment, each having become dissatisfied with the other's conception of what should be investigated and of how careful experimentation should be conducted. The precise reason for the termination of this connection has not yet been wholly brought to light; but at any rate it marked the end of his active scientific career.

We have a characteristic picture of him in Paris at this time, in letters sent home to the James family by Henry James. On November 18, 1875, he wrote: "Yesterday morning appeared Charles Peirce, who is wintering here and who had heard of me from William. He took me up very vigorously, made me dine with him at the Maison Dorée and spend the evening at his rooms which are very charming. He seems quite a swell (at least

[24] Leipzig, Wilhelm Engelmann.

from the point of view of that little house on the car-track where I last knew him)—has a secretary, etc."[25] Three days later, however, Peirce wrote in a different tone to William. "My Dear Willie," he wrote. "Your letter led me to look up your brother whose presence here is a great thing for me as I am lonely and excessively depressed."[26] Several months later Henry James mentioned Peirce again. He had seen "Charles Peirce, who wears beautiful clothes, etc. He is busy swinging pendulums at the Observatory, and thinks himself indifferently treated by the Paris scientists. We meet every two or three days to dine together; but though we get on very well, our sympathy is economical rather than intellectual."[27] A month later the mask was off even before Henry, who wrote home again about Peirce. "The only man I see here familiarly is C. Peirce, with whom I generally dine a couple of times a week. He is a very good fellow—when he is not in ill-humour; then he is intolerable. But, as William says, he is a man of genius, and in such, in the long run, one always finds one's account. He is leading here a life of insupportable loneliness and sterility—but of much material luxury, as he seems to have plenty of money. He sees, literally, not a soul but myself and his secretary."[28]

Although Peirce's father and brother were mathematicians by profession, and his early training was in mathematics as well as in philosophy, it was to logic rather than to mathematics that his interest turned. His mathematical work might have been of importance had he received the proper recognition for it in his own day. Sylvester, a leading mathematician, prophesied that Peirce would exceed his father. As it was, however, the work has been done over by others, so that, were it to be published now, it would make more of a stir among historians of mathematics than among mathematicians. Once again Peirce was able to combine two major interests. As he had done in the case of science and philosophy when he worked on problems in the philosophy of science, so he turned to logic with a mathematical cast and became one of the pioneers in mathematical logic, the study of the logical foundations of mathematics. As early as 1867, in a paper "Upon the Logic of Mathematics,"[29] he had clearly anticipated some of the notions that were embodied later in Whitehead's and Russell's *Principia Mathematica*.

As always, whenever Peirce had some philosophical interest in a topic,

[25] R. B. Perry, *Thought and Character of William James*, vol. i, pp. 361-362.
[26] *Ibid.*, vol. i, p. 536.
[27] *Ibid.*, vol. i, p. 362.
[28] *Ibid.*, vol. i, p. 536.
[29] *Proc. Am. Acad. Arts and Sciences*, 7, 402-412.

he made it his business to acquire an intimate and working knowledge of it. Or conversely, whenever he happened to gain a working knowledge of some activity, it invariably led to an interest in the philosophical aspects. From his years with the Coast and Geodetic Survey, a connection that was not terminated until 1891, we should expect that Peirce would either have become completely absorbed in the problems of practical technology or have revolted against them altogether. As a matter of fact he did neither. Although his chief interest was and remained one of pure theory, he was much concerned with the relation of theory to practice. Practice was of course a matter of philosophical import in Peirce's philosophy. He was a philosopher first and everything else afterward.

D. The Struggle

The more certainly Peirce found his place in life the more completely he lost his hold on his contemporaries. The latter half of his career is the record of an increasing devotion to specific problems in philosophy accompanied by decreasing recognition from the academic men who should have made up his public. The more he came to deserve a reputation the more it receded, as though mocking him. Yet he remained indifferent to this cosmic irony. The extraordinary thing about him was that he never complained. Earlier, Richard Henry Dana had said that no man could go on forever without some little response from the world about him,[30] but to Peirce the difficulties in the path of his achievement were—difficulties, sheer facts, and as such neither good nor evil. When he became irritated, as he did infrequently, it was in a vexed and interrupted but not in an injured way. His habit, on the whole, was to circumvent interruptions without comment and to get on with his work.

For almost fifty years, from 1866 until his death, Peirce was preoccupied with the study of logic. It was the topic to which he looked for the most enlightenment in philosophy. Almost unaided, he continued to lay the vast foundations for the logic of relatives, which, under its modern name of symbolic logic, has become recognized as representing the first enormous advance made in the field of logic since the work of Aristotle. He revised the Boolian algebra, making it available for propositions and relations. He invented the copula of inclusion, new systems of logical graphs, and he connected the logic of classes with the logic of propositions. His general work on the algebra of logic dates from 1883. (3.448) As early as 1867,

---

[30] Van Wyck Brooks, *The Flowering of New England*, p. 116.

however, he had tried to define cardinal numbers in terms of logic, and he did so again in 1881. Seven years later Dedekind, the mathematician, forced him to recognize that, although mathematics might be based on logic, there is still a genuine difference between the two fields. (4.239)

Accordingly, Peirce retreated into logic, and his researches in that topic were tremendous. He studied all the logic he could find and probably read more books on the subject than any other student of his day. Among these books were many medieval treatises; and they gradually led Peirce to discern that the "laws of thought" were apprehensions of the objective principles of logic, which are conditions of nature, and not the reverse. Aided by this method and by suggestions from other fields of investigation, he was able to rescue logic from its nineteenth century subordination to psychology.

In addition to original work in logic itself, the importance of his studies in logic is evident in the light which logic seemed to throw for him on other investigations. In March, 1878, again in the *Popular Science Monthly*, appeared Peirce's "Doctrine of Chances," an essay on ethics in which he demonstrated by the use of probability theory that self-interest must be illogical unless it is enlightened and spreads its interest outward in an ever-increasing periphery from the self through the family, the neighbors, and social organizations, until it includes the universe, finally surpassing "this geologic epoch" (2.654) and going "beyond all bounds," uniting at last with an "unlimited community" of interests. When self-interest becomes identified with anything less than the unlimited community, its illogical choice is proved by the cessation of its object of choice, since nothing has ever been known to last forever. As late as 1910 he still approved the main idea of his ethics, which had been published in almost final form some thirty-two years before. (2.661)

Peirce's teaching career was brief indeed. His longest single academic connection was with the Johns Hopkins University, where he lectured on logic from 1879 to 1884. He was rewarded by a small but eager group of interested students, some of whom continued his work as investigator and teacher. Among his friends at the University were Rowland, the physicist, and H. Newell Martin, the biologist. He edited a book, *Studies in Logic,* while there, and planned much experimental work in psychology with Christine Ladd-Franklin. He has been described at about that time as having blond hair and a blond beard, and wearing a flowing black tie. He was emphatic in manner, quick and even brusque, not sociable in general but fond of discussion with friends, and forever impatient of academic routine. Joseph Jastrow has said that Peirce was an inspiring teacher, and that he was surrounded by a number of students who were greatly influenced by him. This last fact must have had an important effect upon Peirce, for when, in 1887, he inherited some money it was used to buy a large plot of ground and to build a house, with an attic that was to be spacious enough to contain his many disciples. The house itself, of ambitious size, was never completed because of a shortage of funds, and the attic designed to accommodate the many disciples was, symbolically enough, never finished.[31] The Peirces occupied the house, but the attic only became a place in which to hide from creditors.

In the period between 1891 and 1893, Peirce wrote those articles for *The Monist* which constitute one of the best presentations of his cosmology, one from which could be deduced, he thought, "consequences capable of being compared with experience." (6.35) In a series of brilliant essays which are in many respects to be ranked with Peirce's finest work, he established as the fundamental categories for all philosophizing three ontological ultimates, broad groups into which, he maintained, all the elements of our experience could be divided. These are: love, or feeling or value; chance, or actuality or happenings; and logic, or law or rationality. (6.7-34) The continuum of feeling gives an indication of the generality and objectivity of law. (6.102-163) As opposed to the prevalent psycho-physical dualism, Peirce proposed that "a person is nothing but a symbol involving a general idea," (6.270) and further that "every general idea has the unified living feeling of a person." Through "man's glassy essence," in Shakespeare's phrase, it is possible to read beyond the individual to his social purpose. (6.238-271) The course of actuality itself tends to work toward an increase in order because of the tendency of natural chance happenings to take on habits. (6.288-317) It is chance, in other words, that occasions the tendency of love to work toward logic; this is what Peirce called "evolutionary love."

Toward the end of 1893, Peirce wrote that all his life he had been cruelly hampered by the inability to procure the necessary books. (4.118) One might add that he was equally hampered all his life by the failure to interest a publisher. The torrent of original speculation had to be put on paper somehow; but there was present no urgent necessity—represented by a publisher's contract, for instance—to organize the flow into a systematic work. Only two full-length works on philosophical subjects, one of which was *The Grand Logic*, were ever completed, despite the enormous bulk of Peirce's writings; but there were many plans, plans which fell through because of his inability to obtain the required backing. Typical of these was his un-

[31] Joseph Jastrow, "The Widow of Charles S. Peirce," in *Science,* 80 (1934), 440.

successful effort in this year to secure sufficient subscribers for a twelve-volume philosophical work, a project that had the approval of many prominent intellectuals but for which not enough subscribers could be found. This is of some significance since Peirce drew on all the published work of the philosophers not only for abstract and detached ideas but for continued vitality in his day. He objected to political partisanship in matters of philosophy, holding that the followers of Mill's logic had only the intent of a "party-reveil" (4.33) to offer, being always "in a passion about something." Yet Peirce too was frequently in a passion when he argued points of metaphysics with his friends and acquaintances. Dr. Carus, editor and publisher of *The Monist*, not only gave Peirce many chances to air his conceptions in print but often engaged in lively controversies with him. (6.558-618) Peirce himself was sufficiently aware of the vital interest of philosophical issues; he felt that all significant figures in the field of philosophy, regardless of place and date, were his philosophical contemporaries, warring with him for the settlement of burning problems.

E. The Successful Failure

i. the recording

We can see that as Peirce grew older his earlier work began to exercise a formative influence upon him. A man's ideas are frozen into their final pattern when his own earlier work joins other environmental conditions in molding whatever he sets about to do. His own past becomes, so to speak, a part of his present environment, at least so far as logical influences are concerned. It was so with Peirce beginning about 1893, when he began to put down some of his best writing. In that year he declared that an early paper on logic had been the strongest he had ever written. (4.85 n.) He recognized then, too, that it was because of his increasing estimation of the principle of pragmatism that he omitted the term from the *Century Dictionary*. Although it was his "own offspring, with which the world resounds," (5.13 n.) he recognized at the time that James's "exegesis" had "not been very deep." As a young man he had tossed off pragmatism as one among a number of leading principles not regarded as necessary to his philosophical salvation en route; and so he had not cared when James popularized the notion. However, much later in life his resentment toward James grew for this act, and in 1899 he recalled that James had "pushed this method to such extremes as must tend to give us pause. The doctrine appears to assume that the end of man is action [instead of *conceived* action]—a stoical maxim which, to the present writer at the age of sixty, does not recommend itself so forcibly as it did at thirty." (5.3) He became more bitter toward James as he got closer to his own doctrine of pragmatism and sought to attach to it many of his later conceptions.

Peirce's attitude toward himself and his work remained, however, uncompromising. Although he never succeeded in finding either a commercial publisher or a philanthropic foundation to issue his books, he continued to seek them out, and never relaxed for a moment his painstaking efforts toward perfection. The university in which he lectured in 1898 did not regard logic as one of the "topics of vital importance" (1.622) and asked him to change to something like ethics or economics. They asked this of "an Aristotelian and a scientific man, condemning with the whole strength of conviction the Hellenic tendency to mingle philosophy and practice," (1.618) for such Peirce said he was. It was rather James who found such an atmosphere of opinion congenial. Those philosophers who attain success in their own lifetime do so because in their original ideas they echo the unconscious presuppositions of the age in which they live and thus appear to it to have discovered the truth. But others who think for themselves with a power of abstraction that enables them to transcend their own date and place, and who refuse merely to abstract with their minds the ideas which their environment has incorporated in their bones, must wait for a later day for recognition, which, when it arrives, is ever stronger for having been delayed. Peirce belongs to this latter classification.

Peirce's reputation has suffered considerably from the fact that he never presented his theoretical system in any organized way. This was not entirely a matter of the failure it has always appeared. There are, after all, two methods of inquiry, and these correspond to the two directions of inquiry. The pursuit of the smallest part, commonly considered the method of the research scientist, leads to the writing of isolated papers or reports of experiments. The pursuit of the largest whole, traditionally the method of the speculative philosopher but lately also deemed to be that of the mathematical physicist, leads to the construction of theoretical systems. Peirce consciously determined to pursue the former method but to pursue it in philosophy— only to find that it led him finally to the necessity for concluding with the latter one. Implicit in his isolated papers is the outline of a system. The fact that he never got round to presenting his system explicitly does not mean that it is not present in his writings. He worked, unfortunately for him, against the method popular (and therefore understood) in his day; he was after something new, a novel and exact yet inclusive approach to philosophy.

He must have been more or less aware of that shortcoming, too, for he never gave up the struggle to get his finished ideas recorded on paper. His was the common fate of those who in their single-minded eagerness to tell the truth about something have gone largely against the grain of their own society. "Man is essentially a social animal: but to be social is one thing, to be gregarious is another." (1.11) Those who are martyrs to philosophy, like those who are martyrs to religion, almost seem to beg their martyrdom, as though they were conscious of its necessity for the fulfillment of their task. Peirce steadily declined to serve as a "bellwether," and ordered those who sought "philosophical soup-shops to find them on any corner." As a consequence, he had little academic success and met with no acceptance outside professional circles. Nevertheless, he remained throughout his lifetime optimistic concerning the eventual outcome of the effect of his work. A large part of Peirce's failure to gain a reputation was no doubt due to his inability to organize his writings. His ideas were highly organized, it is true, but they were never set down consecutively, according to some fixed plan of writing. He condemned the "pitchfork" method of bookmaking (1.179) by collecting essays into a volume, yet the only full-length work he ever completed was done in this fashion.

There is some tendency today to regard Peirce's unfortunate, interrupted, and even finally discontinued academic career as the natural and almost deserved result of personal idiosyncrasies and of the failure in general to conform. To some extent the truth of this account must be admitted. The connection is most often noted by those more fortunate who are engaged in the same profession today. However, the vicissitudes of Peirce's career throw an interesting light upon what contemporary conditions must have been. Think, for instance, of the dozens upon dozens of professional philosophers who did what seemed expected, were revered by their colleagues, lived out their careers in honor and respectability within the academic walls, yet contributed little if anything to the sum of human knowledge and are now wholly forgotten. Viewed in the light of this fact, Peirce's failure as a professor of philosophy in the prescribed sense appears more as a Socratic martyrdom than as a magnified eccentricity.

One of Peirce's ideas which was becoming increasingly central in his thought was that of the struggle between realism and nominalism, a classic issue which Peirce's friend, Abbot, had revived in early sessions at the Metaphysical Club in Boston, and later, in 1885, set forth in a book entitled

Scientific Theism. Peirce recognized that the philosophy of science was realistic despite its claim to nominalism; and yet he did not go to extremes in realism, either; because, as he noted, the extreme form of Platonic realism, in which universals have more value or more reality than actual particulars, is not realism at all but nominalism. In his lectures of 1898 Peirce returned to this controversy, and pointed out that nominalism had become so deeply the common view that the man in the street regarded realists as nothing less than demented. (4.1) He recalled at this date the discussions which as a young man he had enjoyed with Chauncey Wright, a follower of Mill, discussions which had helped to clarify his antagonism to the nominalism set forth in Mill's logical works. (5.64) Wright held many views which are to be found more elaborated and interconnected in Peirce's writings. Wright was much influenced by positivism without abandoning his emphasis on speculative metaphysics. The tendency of Peirce's association with Wright was to lead him away from Kantianism, to the notion that, for example, "the constitution of nature is written in its actual manifestations, and needs only to be deciphered by experimental and inductive research; that it is not a latent invisible writing, to be brought out by the magic of mental anticipation or metaphysical meditation."[32] Peirce came to hold the talks with Wright in high esteem for what they had done in turning him toward realism.

In the long struggle of his life in philosophy, Peirce was compelled to fight the indifference that confronted him on all sides. He was well aware that the neglect of his work did not spring from mere indifference on the part of the America which had produced him but rather from other positive interests with which that America was preoccupied. He termed "Americanism, the worship of business, the life in which the fertilizing stream of genial sentiment dries up or shrinks to a rill of comic tit-bits, or else on the other hand, to monasticism, sleepwalking in this world with no eye nor heart except for the other." (1.673) He characterized the nineteenth century as "the Economical Century; for political economy has more direct relations with all the branches of its activity than has any other science." (6.290) In such an atmosphere, it was possible to keep the magnificent hold which Peirce had on his philosophy only by answering the preoccupation of his times with the same indifference with which it met his own efforts. "The present writer," he declared roundly, "cares nothing about social matters, and knows not what such things mean." (4.33) So spoke the man who con-

[32] Chauncey Wright, *Philosophical Discussions* (New York, Holt, 1877), p. 131.

sidered the crying need of the day to be a criticism of ethics in terms of the new world created by science.[33]

ii. LAST YEARS

Peirce's later years did not witness the diminishing either of his energy or of his plans, despite the fact that he remained one "of whom critics have never found anything good to say." (1.10) He did not complete his existential system of graphs in form suitable for publication until 1897, and six years later he was still concerned about it. (4.422) Not until 1899 did he reach the conclusion that ethics is a normative science; and his important studies in ethics were dated no earlier than 1883. (5.129) In 1898 we find him recording that Husserl's logic was hopelessly involved in psychology. (4.7) Peirce never yielded an inch. He never grew softheaded or mystical in his regard for the favorite study of his whole life. Looking back upon an essay on the logic of probability published nineteen years earlier, he could say in 1902 that when the essay was first published he had been "an explorer upon untrodden ground." (2.102) He wrote the same year that he had refused to join the Psychical Research Society when it was started because "to do so would be to sanction a probable great waste of time, together with the placing of some men in a compromising position." (2.111)

But on the whole, at this period he was still looking forward rather than backward; and if it was in terms of the solutions by others of the problems which he saw so plainly, then it is safe to say that he did not recognize any discontinuity in this development. "It is," he said, "above all the normative sciences, esthetics, ethics, and logic, that men are in dire need of having severely criticized, in their relation to the new world created by science. Unfortunately, this need is as unconscious as it is great. . . . The needed new criticism must know whereon it stands; namely, on the beliefs that remain indubitable; and young Critical Common-sensists of intellectual force who burn for a task in which they can worthily sacrifice their lives without encouragement, reward, recognition, or a hearing (and I trust such men still live) can find in this field their heart's desire." (5.513)

The activity of Peirce's mind in these years is well illustrated by his struggles with the philosophy of Hegel. He found Hegel's ideas fascinating because they were so close to his own yet never the same. After due reflection on the subject, Peirce made up his mind; he said, "I reject his philosophy *in toto*." (1.368) But the Hegelian dialectic held his attention, as being

[33] See this chapter, F, ii.

to some extent a temporal formulation of his own triad of ontological categories, and so in 1896 we find him castigating Hegel for reaching "each category from the last preceding by virtually calling 'next'!" (1.453) Peirce could never bring himself to accept the determinism that is so essential a property of the Hegelian conception. Nine years later the estimate of Hegel had undergone a further revision, this time a drastic one, for the German had become "in some respects the greatest philosopher that ever lived." (1.524) This is particularly of interest in view of the fact that Peirce was not a facile thinker who can be said to have been addicted to frequent shifts of opinion. His intellectual honesty and vitality hardly ever deserted him.

For some years Peirce had given private instruction in logic in New York City; (1.668) but when he moved permanently to Milford, Pennsylvania, and built his house in the hills, his financial situation became increasingly worse. His last steady employment was the task of writing the articles on logic for J. M. Baldwin who edited his *Dictionary of Philosophy and Psychology* during the years 1901 to 1905. After that he lived on the edge of poverty. In 1902 he applied to the Carnegie Fund, proposing to write a number of memoirs on philosophical subjects, but the plan was rejected. In 1903 James succeeded in persuading the authorities at Harvard to authorize six lectures to be given by Peirce, who, in the same year, also gave a series of lectures at the Lowell Institute in Boston. James wrote to Schiller about the Harvard engagement. "Charles Peirce is now giving six public lectures on 'pragmatism' at Harvard, which I managed to get up for his benefit, pecuniary and professional. He is a hopeless crank and failure in many ways, but a really extraordinary intellect. I never knew a mind of so many different kinds of spotty intensity or vigor."[34] Through the efforts of William James, a sum of money was collected from friends of long standing and admiring students, and on the very small proceeds from this money Peirce and his wife lived. Peirce continued to write and to publish, but he was aging. The variety of his concern with philosophical matters went unaffected. In 1905 we find him corresponding with Dedekind and Cantor, the mathematicians to whom he was ready to "pay full homage." (4.331) He was in this year, although old and sick, still making ambitious plans for philosophy; he wanted to make a study of the "belief which men *betray* and not that which they *parade*," for which task he recognized that "a great range of reading is necessary." (5.444 n.) In the following year he called attention to the great merit of the works on logic of the Hungarian Catholic

[34] R. B. Perry, *Thought and Character of William James.* vol. ii, p. 375.

priest, Bernardo Bolzano, whose realistic philosophy, like that of Peirce himself, remains neglected to this day.[35]

The relation that existed between Peirce and James must have been a very strange one indeed; it certainly colored Peirce's entire career. It was, as we have seen, James and not Peirce who popularized the term "pragmatism" by which word the writings of both men are largely known. And yet Peirce repudiated the Jamesian version while retaining his love and gratitude for James. It remained true, however, that James had misinterpreted pragmatism, as had Schiller and others, and so in 1905 Peirce announced the birth of the word "pragmaticism," "which is ugly enough to be safe from kidnappers." (5.414) The change was made in order to keep his ideas clear of the misconceptions that had in a short while grown up around the term he had invented. Jamesian pragmatism had been exposed as nominalistic and irrational, whereas the meaning Peirce intended was both realistic (5.453) and rational. (5.412) In the next year he adopted the middle name of "Santiago" or St. James, (5.614) probably out of gratitude for James's many personal kindnesses.

As late in his life as 1911, when Peirce was no less than seventy-two years old, he was still wrestling with the conflicting influences of James the man, the perfect lover of truth, and James the misinterpreter of pragmatism and the hater of mathematics, (6.182) "he so concrete, so living; I a mere table of contents, so abstract, a very snarl of twine." (6.184) Yet Peirce was sure that he would not have wished to change places with James. Addressing a prospective audience in a proposed lecture, written just before the close of the nineteenth century, Peirce cautioned: "But should it happen to any of you to select for his life's explorations a region very little trodden, he will, as a matter of course, have the pleasure of making a good many discoveries of more fundamental importance than at all remain to be made in any ground that has long been highly cultivated. But on the other hand, he will find that he has condemned himself to an isolation like that of Alexander Selkirk. He must be prepared for almost a lifetime of work with scarce one greeting, and I can assure him that if, as his day is sinking, a rare good fortune should bring a dozen men of real intellect, some men of great promise, others of great achievement, together to listen to so much of what he has learned as his long habit of silence shall have left him the power of expressing in the compass of eight lectures, he will know then an almost untasted joy and will comprehend then what gratitude I feel at this

[35] See Eduard Winter, *Bernardo Bolzano* (Leipzig, Hegner, 1938).

moment." (6.213) The eight lectures were delivered at the residence of Mrs. Ole Bull on Brattle Street in Cambridge.

About this time we can begin to detect signs of the termination of a career. Peirce still respected the laboratory, still considered himself an experimentalist, (5.411) but he began to give indications also that he recognized his own life was to contain no more plans. He still continued to carry a pad in his pocket and to make notes of various descriptions on all sorts of philosophical topics that interested him, at the rate of some twenty-five a day, (5.611) but this was a habit of long standing. He had occasion to walk a mile each night on a deserted road over open fields, and he has reported that he spent much of his walk thinking of problems centering about God and religion, stimulated by the spectacle of the stars. (6.501) Logical problems still beset him, but in 1909, five years before his death, he admitted that it must be old logical problems and not new ones to which he would henceforth devote himself; "in order to get time to make what work I have done generally useful before extreme old age overtakes me, I must leave new problems or difficulties to another generation, however much they may tempt me." (4.653) It was characteristic of Peirce that he envisaged an uninterrupted continuum of work in logic, so that his own death could only mean that the new problems would have to be solved by others.

The last five years of his life were years of suffering. Compelled to take a grain of morphine daily because of the extreme pain caused by a cancer, he continued to revise his earlier work; and he managed to retain his intellectual composure to the very end. Even when he could do no more than sit in a glass-enclosed porch in the sun, it took all the efforts of his wife to keep him from trying to return to work. The will was still there when the instrument was no longer competent.

Peirce was very ambitious for his metaphysics and thought he had been accomplishing a most tremendous task. "The undertaking which this volume inaugurates," he wrote about 1898 in the Preface to a proposed work which was to be entitled *The Riddle of the Sphinx*, "is to make a philosophy like that of Aristotle, that is to say, to outline a theory so comprehensive that, for a long time to come, the entire work of human reason, in philosophy of every school and kind, in mathematics, in psychology, in physical science, in history, in sociology, and in whatever other department there may be, shall appear as the filling up of its details." (1.1) However, he enjoyed no external satisfaction from his achievements except "such slices of bread and butter as it might waft my way." (1.10) When the critics "could see no opportunity to injure me, they have held their peace," he said; and the only praise had come from one who had meant not to praise him but rather to accuse him of not being absolutely sure of his own conclusions, an accusation which Peirce always thought of as praise because he regarded fallibilism as the cornerstone of his philosophy. (1.13) Yet there was no word of complaint, no railing against fate, no cessation of interest or of work. "It is true that I have not received much credit either for pragmatism or any other part of my work. However, as it was not done for the sake of anything of that kind, I have no reason to complain. What I expected to gain when I did it, I have gained."[36] He labored to the end, and continued to write even when his hands trembled so much that he was compelled to hold one steady with the other. The man who writes for an audience that is to come in an indefinite future can never be absolutely sure in his lifetime that the neglect of his work is final. "The development of my ideas has been the industry of thirty years. I did not know as I ever should get to publish them, their ripening seemed so slow. But the harvest time has come, at last, and to me that harvest seems a wild one, but of course it is not I who have to pass judgment. It is not quite you, either, individual reader; it is experience and history." (1.12)

His death was uneventful to the world at large, for he had at the last no friends and no disciples to ease the oblivion to which the man as well as his work was finally brought—finally—but with a temporary finality, since the recovery of the philosophy of Peirce is a task that is almost certain to be accomplished in a future which will be made aware of its importance through the power of its influence for good. The last chapter of Peirce's life has not yet been completed. It is in the care of those who wish to devote themselves to the discovery of the truth and the gaining of some power for the human race without hope of reward for themselves. They could do worse than to build on Peirce's systematic work, or to take as a model for their own careers his selfless devotion to his ideal.

[36] *Journal of Philosophy, Psychology and Scientific Method*, 13:26 (1916, 718-719).

CHAPTER II

The Logical Development of Peirce's Thought

‹‹‹‹‹‹‹‹‹‹‹‹‹‹‹‹‹‹‹‹‹‹‹‹‹‹‹‹‹‹‹‹‹‹‹‹›››››››››››››››››››››››››››››››››

IN ORDER PROPERLY TO COMPREHEND THE DEVELOPMENT OF A PHILOSOPHER'S thought it is necessary to consider certain writers of previous generations as his contemporaries. The truly great philosopher is never limited in his interests to any one generation of persons simply because it happens to be the one in which he lives. According to the strictest philosophical view, life is only a location from which readings are taken. By the same logic, men long dead whose ideas the philosopher finds sympathetic become his friends, while those whose ideas seem inimical prove to be his opponents. Intellectual influences are no more limited to a certain date than they are to a certain place; although brought into evidence by individual thinkers, they are not owned by anybody. Thus the ideas which impressed themselves on Peirce will here be presented as they came to him in a particular connection, so that later on, with this accounting rendered, his system of ideas, although derived from his psychological history, can be evaluated as a logical affair, independent of its derivation.

From the unorganized welter of forces which confronted Peirce in the course of his intellectual coming of age, five main influences gradually emerged to give direction to the future of his thought. Many lesser influences existed, of course, but these, like everything that arises in the path of such a powerful intellectual development as that of Peirce, were eventually drawn into conformity with the central drive that had been imparted to his philosophy. The five main influences came from the stimulus of Kant, the practice of physical science, the adoption of Duns Scotus, the lesson of Darwin, and the revolt against Descartes.

A. THE STIMULUS OF KANT

Peirce's great interest in technical philosophy came with his study of the German metaphysicians, especially Kant. Although in Peirce's estimation wanting in both sensibility and energy,[1] Kant was a great metaphysician who had come to philosophy from physics. "As a scientific man beneath the skin," Peirce wrote in 1902, "Kant is comparatively free from the besetting fallacy of the philosophers, which may be described, without exaggeration, as consisting in producing arguments to prove a micron, at most, and in concluding a light-year, at least. Kant, perceiving in some measure this universal fault of the philosophers, was naturally led to his evident ambition to be the arbiter of philosophical disputes. But he could have exercised this office only in the weak manner of the Eclectics, allowing so much weight to this consideration and so much to another diametrically opposed to it, if he had not fortunately been gifted with a great strength in logical analysis, that enabled him at once to do full justice to the arguments and tendencies of both sides, and to make both contributory to a third unitary conception. Yet even his logical analysis would not have sufficed, if it had not been for a supereminent share in a characteristic that may be remarked in all the more powerful scientific intellects, the power of making use even of conceptions that resisted his logical analysis, and of drawing from them nearly the same conclusions as any clear mind would have done that had analyzed them. We cannot, in a few words, make our meaning very clear; but one might say that an ordinary intelligent mind has an upper layer of clear thought, underlaid by muddled ideas; while in Kant's mind there appears to be a pure solution down into those depths where daylight hardly penetrates. He thinks pretty correctly even when he does not think distinctly."[2]

Although more influenced by Kant than by any other philosopher encountered during his own period of development, Peirce did not emerge as a neo-Kantian. In this distinction is contained the key to the understanding of much in Peirce's whole position. The result of his devotion to classical German philosophy was that he came to consider it upon its constructive side as of little weight, (1.5) and leaned toward the meager but more scientific English tradition. German philosophy remained for him "a rich mine of philosophical suggestions."[3] In other words, he learned the desirability of constructing a massive system on the German model but wished to do it by the empirical method of the British.

Among the German philosophers, Kant alone seemed to him to have "possessed in a high degree all seven of the mental qualifications of a philosopher: the ability to discern what is before one's consciousness; inventive

---

[1] Review of Paulsen's *Kant* in *The Nation*, 75 (1902), 209 f.

[2] *Ibid., loc. cit.*

[3] Wherever a quotation from Peirce is not accompanied by a reference number, the reference will be presumed to be the last one cited.

originality; generalizing power; subtlety; critical severity and sense of fact; systematic procedure; energy, diligence, persistency, and exclusive devotion to philosophy." (1.522) Everywhere Kant seemed suggestive, and many of Peirce's conclusions may be said to have been stimulated by a study of the master. Yet seldom if ever does Peirce come to the same conclusion as that reached by Kant. Interest in a given problem was often stimulated by a reading of Kant, yet Peirce's own solution was almost always different, and often diametrically opposed to that of his teacher. Thus, while Peirce owed much in the formation of his philosophy to the influence of Kant, the result was not Kant's philosophy nor even that of a good Kantian.

At least two of Peirce's leading preoccupations were emphasized for him by his study of the Critical Philosophy. These were points raised in the philosophy of science, and in ethics. The *Critique of Pure Reason* turned his attention to the nature of scientific knowledge both in its method and in its aims. The *Critique of Practical Reason* probably was an important factor in turning his attention to the establishment of a logical basis for ethics. But this account by no means exhausts the extent of the influence of Kant upon him. Perhaps the greater part, though by no means all, of this influence may be discerned in the examination of his philosophical speculations both in their detail and as a system. It may be traced in the conclusions to which Peirce was led by his profound study of the Koenigsberg philosopher, under the following topics: the architectonic of philosophy; the logical basis of metaphysics; the limits of rationalism; the limits of empiricism; the unity of logic and experience; and the logical character of action.

i. THE ARCHITECTONIC OF PHILOSOPHY

The parallel between philosophy and architecture drawn by Kant was one which Peirce was able to accept. (1.176)[4] Philosophy ought not to have the precious, piquant, and semiprivate character which seems to be the property of minute and inconsequential works of art, "executed for a single patron by a single artist." It should rather be public and general, not shut up in a room but admired by all as the whole edifice. Further, it should be not only a building but "a great public building, meant for the whole people," erected by the exertions of an army of representatives, according to plans called forth from the architect's soul. Peirce was thus led by Kant to see that he could not consider philosophy in the English empirical or piecemeal

---

[4] *Kritik der Reinen Vernunft*, A 707, B 735, and what Peirce called "that splendid third chapter of the Methodology": A 832 ff., B 860 ff.

manner only, as a series of assorted subjects to be carefully approached. He must come to it in the grand manner of the best of the German meta-physicians: as a self-consistent body of knowledge, excluding nothing and applicable to everything.

But if a grand system of philosophy was to be developed, what, according to Kant, should be the method employed? A hint of the answer to this question is contained in the reference to Kant's observation that systematic philosophy had its method prescribed for it by the example of Euclidian geometry. "The conviction that any metaphysical philosophy is possible has been upheld at all times, as Kant well says, by the example in geometry of a similar science." (1.400) To this suggestion Peirce himself adds a further one. The cosmological, or, as he preferred to call it, the secular, character of philosophy demands that philosophy grow "by the fission of minute parts and not by accretion." (1.177) Such a scheme for the development of a system would be feasible only if the whole system were to be planned from the very beginning. "Every person who wishes to form an opinion con-cerning fundamental problems should first of all make a complete survey of human knowledge," (6.9) drawing on the results made available both by the sciences and by common-sense experience. Thus it was not allowed that a man's thought could wait for development until he had formulated his system; the necessary logical preparation must be taken in advance. This preparation Peirce conceived as the replacement in the mind of everything particular by something general. Man is by nature intensely individualistic; he has original ideas and instincts, which are racial ideas. These must be replaced by a "deliberate logical faculty," (1.178) "and the sole function of this logical deliberation is to grind off the arbitrary and the individualistic character of thought."

From the philosopher whose aim was critical rather than constructive,[5] Peirce learned how to erect his own system. Prerequisite for its unity was a plan; for its actualization, adequate building materials. Thus pragmatism was developed, as Kant would have said, "architectonically." The "inde-composable concepts" (5.5) needed for its construction were tested as a civil engineer would test his materials before erecting a bridge. Nowhere was Peirce willing to say that he had hold of the final truth. The engineer bears always in mind that, despite the excellence of his bridge, later develop-ments will see better bridges constructed. Peirce enlarged Kant's under-

---

[5] *Ibid.*, A 12, B 25: "It should be called a critique, not a doctrine, of pure reason. Its utility, in speculation, ought properly to be only negative, not to extend, but only to clarify our reason." See also Peirce's understanding of this point in his review of Paulsen's *Kant*, in *The Nation*, 75 (1902), 209 f.

standing of the definition of hypothesis,[6] and refused to consider even the possibility of attaining to absolute certainty. (1.141; 5.587) The *belief* of some philosophers that they have hold of the ultimate truth does not *prove* that they have it. (6.50) Even of that sphere in which Kant placed so much faith, namely, in the possibility of arriving at something finally dependable by mathematics, Peirce said that "it is only in a Pickwickian sense that mathematical reasoning can be said to be perfectly certain." (6.595) Unfortunately, Peirce did not succeed altogether in "grinding off the arbitrary and the individualistic character of thought" any more than did Kant, although Peirce made a brave attempt. Probably no one can do so altogether.

ii. THE LOGICAL BASIS OF METAPHYSICS

Having accepted the necessity for a systematic metaphysics, Peirce was next confronted with the question of what should be its foundations. Philosophy cannot begin with nothing. Something must always be postulated from which to make a start: a revealed faith, a philosophic authority, or a set of ideas accepted as given. Here Kant was to prove of enormous help. Peirce observed that "Kant's whole philosophy turns upon his logic," (1.35) as does that of Aristotle and all metaphysicians of the first rank. (2.121) This, Peirce thought, was as it should be, for the converse could not be true: a metaphysics not founded on logic would prove "shaky and insecure, and altogether unfit for the support of so important a subject as logic." (2.36) But where Kant's ambition for logic (not entirely fulfilled) had been to render his philosophy chiefly critical, it became Peirce's plan to set up a positive constructive metaphysics upon logic. The "Kantian principle that metaphysical conceptions mirror those of formal logic" (3.487) could be used in the case of a positive as well as of a negative metaphysics. Logic wears a critical dress only where its propositions are considered negatively. But the propositions of logic can also serve as premises from which to deduce a systematic philosophy. Although Peirce did not allow the proof of his metaphysics to rest altogether on such deducibility, he yet hoped that by this method "exact logic will prove a stepping-stone to 'exact' metaphysics." (3.454) Peirce's entire philosophy is in one regard the measure of the success of this attempt.

From Benjamin Peirce's emphasis on Kant, perhaps more than from Duns Scotus or any other source, Peirce gained an intense interest in logic, so much so that it became for a long while his chief preoccupation. If Kant's

---

[6] *Ibid.*, A 770, B 798.

logic had been perfect in Peirce's eyes, there would have been no task left except to deduce a metaphysics from that logic. But Peirce found flaws, (3.641)[7] and it may have been the discovery of these flaws that occasioned certain of his studies in logic, studies which led finally to the logic of relatives, in anticipation of much subsequent mathematical or symbolic logic. Kant's regulative principle[8] meant, according to Peirce, (6.169 ff.) that every instance of regularity calls for explanation, and it was in terms of the completeness of this explanation that he had endeavored to construct his logic. But Kant had overlooked the medieval logicians (1.560) whose list of categories was larger than his own, (2.345-346) and as a consequence had allowed his logic to become entirely an affair of psychology. (2.157)[9] He could not have read the schoolmen, and then termed all propositions and principles "judgments" as he persisted in doing.[10] Peirce lost no time in correcting the error, but in this way was obliged to combine the best of the two developments of logic he had learned: those of Kant and those of the scholastics.

The escape from Kant lay in the attack upon the limitations of his logic. So many places were discovered where gaps in the categories were in evidence that Peirce said he found himself "blindly groping among a deranged system of conceptions." (1.563) The only method of correcting the system was the one whereby it had been constructed. Peirce accordingly attacked the problem from the side of formal logic. The result was the complete objectification of the Kantian system.

Kant taught that the most fundamental conceptions stem from a system of logical forms, which if examined very closely will prove to be three elementary and primary conceptions of all objects and domains. (3.422)[11] In making the transition from logic to metaphysics, Kant naturally took his subjectivism along with him: he thought his categories of knowledge to be essentially psychological. (1.374)[12] However, Peirce in correcting the Kantian excesses of subjectivity did not seek to enlarge upon the number of the fundamental conceptions; (1.350) he simply transformed them into objective

---

[7] E.g., he held that the Kantian distinction (Kant, *ibid.*, B 9 ff.) between analytical and synthetical judgments is invalid.

[8] Kant, *Kritik der Reinen Vernunft*, A 508 ff., B 536 ff.

[9] Despite his dictum in A 53, Kant considered reason to be an affair of the understanding, which is the ground for all *a priori* rational knowledge: *ibid.*, A 15-6, B 29-30. ". . . form must lie ready for the sensations *a priori* in the mind": *ibid.*, A 20, B 34 (Norman Kemp Smith, trans.). Logic is "the science of the rules of the understanding in general": *ibid.*, A 52, B 76.

[10] *Ibid.*, A 132 ff., B 171 ff., and A 150 ff., B 190 ff.

[11] *Ibid.*, A 94-95.

[12] *Ibid.*, A 97.

categories (1.300) where their explanatory value seemed to expand. Increase in the number of categories was still a matter reserved for logic, (1.563) while in this connection Peirce was concerned chiefly with metaphysics. Yet there can be no doubt that Peirce's whole ontology, which is constructed upon the three fundamental categories, grew out of his logic, in imitation of the Kantian postulate that logic is ontologically prior to metaphysics.[13]

iii. THE LIMITS OF RATIONALISM

With regard to at least two aspects of the philosophy of science, Peirce's conclusions were in direct opposition to those of Kant, despite the fact that he reached them only after a prolonged investigation into the validity of Kant's arguments. The first of these conclusions has to do with the limits of dogmatic rationalism. Kant who was, as he himself said, wakened from his dogmatic slumbers by Hume, advanced the thesis that metaphysics (or ontology) is impossible. By making a breach between knowledge derived from the senses and rational knowledge ("synthetic judgments *a priori*") Kant brought about a difficulty[14] which he himself was forever hopelessly trying to eliminate.[15] Although endeavoring to establish the certainty of the grounds for such knowledge as we do have, Kant was suspicious of the systematic ontologists, and condemned cosmology on the assumption that it consisted of antinomies forever incapable of resolution.

Thus in a sense Kant's whole labors were devoted to preparing the ground for the construction of an ontology which he did not conceive, in the last analysis, to be possible.[16]

Most persons, according to Peirce, would agree with Descartes in assigning the locus of the mind to the pineal gland, but, he added, by those who have studied Kant carefully no such conclusion can possibly be reached. (5.128) Kant said that our conceptions do not pass beyond the reach of possible experience. But this would be to "pronounce our whole knowledge of the past to be mere delusion!" (6.108) Kant himself, after positing the things-in-themselves as unknowable by reason of the subjectivity of time, space, and the categories,[17] comes to treat them as external and objective yet know-

---

[13] Cf., vol. i, bk. iii.

[14] The antinomies of pure reason are functions of pure reason alone, and, logically enough, their resolution without any empirical reference is found to be impossible.

[15] Witness his attempt to resolve the antinomies of the pure reason by appealing to the distinction between phenomena and noumena, Kant, *Kritik der Reinen Vernunft*, A 249 ff., B. 306.

[16] A hint of this is contained in the beginning of Section II of the Introduction and in the overtones of scattered passages throughout the *Kritik der Reinen Vernunft*.

[17] *Ibid.*, B 118.

able.[18] Kant meant that "our knowledge of things-in-themselves is relative" but that of them "we do have direct experience," (6.95) and moreover that all such "experience and knowledge is of that which is independent of its being represented."

Such was the burden of the third moment of Kant's thought, Peirce said, and it was made prominent only in the second edition of the *Critique of Pure Reason*, "an idea in which Kant's mind was so completely immersed that he failed to see the necessity for making an explicit statement of it, until Fichte misinterpreted him." This being the case, Peirce felt that he would have been justified by Kant when he added to the subjective, negative strictures on the experiential limits of rational knowledge, which Kant had given to him, the need for a positive system of realistic philosophy whose objects should correspond to objective things-in-themselves. Kant, Peirce maintained, "seeks to show that the only way we can apprehend our own flow of ideas, binding them together as a connected flow, is by attaching them to an immediately perceived persistent externality." (1.39) Although there remained in Peirce's mind some doubt as to whether or not in the Kantian system (6.95) the things-in-themselves were available to direct experience, it was certain that in the Peircian system they were. Peirce interpreted the emphasis on the realistic phases of Kantian thought[19] in the second edition of the *Critique* as self-correction, as leaning on that position toward which Peirce himself was already inclined.

Peirce's assiduous cultivation of the empirical sciences as aids in the construction of a systematic philosophy is evidence that he had taken to heart the lesson he had learned early in life. For Kant, who had been at pains to show that a valid metaphysics cannot be constructed on reason alone, had by his logical condemnation of rational dogmatism[20] driven Peirce to seek for a constant suggestion and allowance of the elements of his metaphysics from among the body of evidence offered by the empirical sciences. The unity of reason and empiricism, which Kant had categorically insisted upon but methodologically departed from, was at long last employed by Peirce in the construction of his own metaphysical system. By giving objectivity to Kant's subjective principles, Peirce succeeded in doing for Kant's point of view what the Critical Philosopher himself had failed to accomplish.

Kant's strictures upon systematic metaphysics thus failed to have the effect upon Peirce which they exercised upon some later philosophers, of

[18] *Ibid.*, B 276-278.
[19] See, for example, *Col. Pap.*, 5.525.
[20] Kant, *Kritik der Reinen Vernunft*, p. 382.

preventing the postulation of an ontological system. Modern logical positivists believe with Kant that ontology by nature is dogmatic and unconnected with anything empirical, and therefore according to scientific
standards impossible[21]—a view held in part by at least one of Peirce's friends
and followers, James.[22] But Peirce took Kant's views in this regard merely
as a caution not to be too absolutistic and insistent in the formulation of a
metaphysics; to set up systems as tentative merely, and as necessitating a
later empirical checking. For Peirce, metaphysics is a broad science which
must of necessity answer to scientific method and include the other sciences
as special branches. Thus, though he started from Kant's position, he came
round finally to a far different conclusion.

iv. THE LIMITS OF EMPIRICISM

The second aspect of the philosophy of science in which Peirce learned a
good deal from Kant has to do with the limits of empiricism. Kant maintained that genuine knowledge is universal and necessary,[23] and here Peirce
gave his assent. He agreed also with Kant that universal and necessary
knowledge concerns the order of ideas. Where Kant had found some relations between the categories, Peirce sought others. (4.2) The difference
came with the understanding of the term "ideas." An idea (*idee*) for Kant
was "a concept formed from notions and transcending the possibility of
experience,"[24] or in other words, a subjective affair. Peirce, on the other hand,
defined an idea as "the definition of a real class," (1.214) a completely objective affair. (1.217) For Kant all true knowledge is half mental, in that
we can have no knowledge of things-in-themselves. But for Peirce, the ideas,
or, as he called them, the generals, have an external and objective existence.
The generals did not have to be actual; they could also be possible; but the
possibility was that of an objective actualization. Such generals were capable
of being as well as of being known. Following Kant's principle that "all our
knowledge begins with experience,"[25] Peirce concluded that the generals of
which we gain knowledge must have been suggested by our actual experience, that is, by our experience with the actuals which exemplify logical
possibility.

In this way Peirce seized upon the rational aspect of Kant's thought to

[21] E.g., Rudolph Carnap, *Philosophy and Logical Syntax* (London, 1935), pt. i.
[22] *The Will to Believe* (New York, 1923), pp. 39, 67 ff.
[23] Kant, *Kritik der Reinen Vernunft*, A 2.
[24] *Ibid.*, B 377 (Norman Kemp Smith trans.).
[25] *Ibid.*, B 1.

prevent his own development from leading to that radical empiricism according to which no generalizations are possible beyond those contained in the immediate data at hand. Kant himself had offered a warning against empirical dogmatism, following a counterblast to the rational dogmatism represented by one variety of Platonism. If it is true that reason cannot proceed without experience, it is equally true that experience cannot proceed without reason. The contradictory of the latter assumption, namely, that experience can proceed without reason, constitutes the excess of empirical dogmatism. Peirce was aware that all scientific experimentation involves some tacitly assumed laws of logic. He saw philosophy degenerating into dogmatic psychology in the hands of Kantians who maintained the critical school's preoccupation with the problem of knowledge. He saw, further, that the criterion of knowledge is not to be found in epistemology itself but rather in a logical examination of the presuppositions of empirical research, a theoretical reason which is at one with its practical applications. And he was led on from this to the study of logic and to the proclamation of its affinity with mathematics.[26] Thus once more Peirce began with Kant but ended with a position diametrically opposed to that of Kant. Starting from Kant's denial of the ability of science to reach any valid conclusions without the aid of the understanding of rational (i.e., subjective) principles, he moved away from Kant almost at once in the effort to find objective grounds for those principles.

V. THE UNITY OF LOGIC AND EXPERIENCE

Let us go back, said Peirce, and seek in the work of Kant some suggestions as to the unity of logic and experience. The leading question of Kant's great work was, "How are synthetical judgments *a priori* possible?" (5.348) Peirce has told us that *a priori* means universal, and that synthetic means relating to experience. Thus in Peirce's terms Kant's question would read, How are universals related to experience, or rather, how can we justify (i.e., explain) the relations of universal propositions to the world of actual particulars? This question cannot be answered until we understand the relation of reasoning to experience. (2.690 ff.) Kant offered a solution in the doctrine of the combination of percepts and concepts, since, he said, neither the intuition of objects nor the *a priori* understanding can function alone;[27] but Kant in a sense himself rejected this solution when he posited the

[26] Peirce, 2.215; 2.76.

[27] Kant, *Kritik der Reinen Vernunft*, A 51, B 75: "The understanding can intuit nothing, the senses can think nothing. Only through their union can knowledge arise." Cf. also *supra*.

truistic and circular nature of analytical reasoning.[28] He condemned all
analytical reasoning to the limitations inherent in the *petitio principii*; he
held "that the conclusion is thought in the premisses although indistinctly."
(4.51) He distinguished between things known immediately (the three
angles of a triangle) and things inferred (their sum equals two right
angles).[29] But he confused the theorem of graphic geometry with the census
theorem of topology, Peirce maintained. (4.51) The geometric inference
depends upon other factors, such as the criterion of measurement adopted.
Thus what Kant said is known is demonstrable, but what he said is
demonstrable is not so.

It is probable that in Kant's understanding of the syllogism, the element
of time was a factor.[30] The understanding of premises as antecedents and
of the conclusion as a consequent exemplifies one type of syllogism, namely,
the existential syllogism, but is by no means applicable to the syllogism in
general, since most types are possible or necessary and thus independent of
the temporal order. The confusion in Kant's mind may have resulted from
his prejudice against the scholastic method of attempting to answer questions relating to actuality by making logical distinctions. The error led
Kant to assume that the conclusion of a syllogism is *thought* in the premises,
and thus involved him in a reversion to subjectivism. (4.52)[31] But the truth
of Fermat's theorem, for example, cannot be discovered by considering the
premises of the theory of numbers, as Peirce pointed out. Peirce's criticism
of Kant is both keen and constructive. The conclusion of a syllogism may
be *contained* in the premises, but it is never *thought* in it. Peirce declared
that it not only follows *after* it, but also follows *from* it. (4.53)

Thus was Peirce led through his criticism of the shortcomings of Kant's
logic to the view that while the syllogism may be a truism it is also an
instrument of discovery. Only one short step remained from this statement
to the next, namely, that deductive reasoning has valid application to experience. In another place, Peirce worked out from Kant's "Transcendental
Aesthetic," particularly from the assertion that universality and necessity in
scientific inductions are the analogues of philosophic universality and necessity, a conclusion which refutes Kant's own statement that universal and
necessary propositions are not given in experience. (5.223 n.2)[32] For Kant
had a second principle, which asserted that the truth of universal and neces-

---

[28] *Ibid.*, A 7 ff., B 11 ff.

[29] *Ibid.*, A 303; cf. A 716, B 744.

[30] *Ibid.*, B 360, B 387.

[31] *Ibid.*, A 154.

[32] *Ibid.*, "Transcendental Doctrine of Elements," First Part, Transcendental Aesthetic.

sary propositions is dependent upon the conditions of the possibility of experience, which, as Peirce said, "is no more nor less than the principle of Induction."

Thus by taking both experience and reason as the starting point, Peirce deduced from Kant's original position the conclusion that logic and experience (or experiment) are interdependent in any and every instance of valid knowledge.[33] This was a conclusion which was to have an all-important effect upon basic propositions in Peirce's whole metaphysical outlook. Peirce was to build important principles upon certain postulates implicit in Kant's assumptions, by a chain of reasoning which Kant himself had failed to carry to its logical conclusion.

vi. THE LOGICAL CHARACTER OF ACTION

It was in the effort to demonstrate the relatedness of logic and experience that Peirce succeeded where Kant had failed. The two *Critiques*, of *Pure* and *Practical Reason*, fell apart, as many subsequent critics have observed. Kant himself was aware that the attempt to deduce the Categorical Imperative from pure reason presented its own peculiar difficulties.[34] The Categorical Imperative never did entirely justify itself in connection either with the "Transcendental Aesthetic" or with the "Transcendental Logic." Kant was forced to make a leap from his critical philosophy to his leading principles of ethics which seemed quite unjustified. But Peirce was no Kantian; he was instead a student of Kant. He saw the shortcomings as well as the merits of his teacher. In attempting to close the gap between pure reason and practical action which Kant, although fully aware of the necessity, had never succeeded in doing properly, Peirce found the formula for satisfactorily tying up ethics with the philosophy of science. The transition is, in fact, typical of the influence of Kant on the development of Peirce's ideas.

Kant saw the unity of pure reason and empirical knowledge *in the mind*, but never succeeded in making it hold because of his postulation of an essentially unknowable real world. "Thoughts without content are empty, intuitions without concepts are blind," he said;[35] but the percepts originated

[33] Kant evidently despaired of ever finding the origins of this interdependence, for he set up *sensibility* (i.e., experience) and the *understanding* (i.e., logic) as "two stems of human knowledge which perhaps spring from a common, but to us unknown, root": *op. cit.*, A 15, B 29.

[34] Immanuel Kant, *Critique of Practical Reason*, T. K. Abbot trans. (London, Longmans, Green, 1898), p. 136.

[35] Kant, *Kritik der Reinen Vernunft*, Norman Kemp Smith trans., A 51.

in sensations of an actual phenomenal world, whereas the concepts were an *a priori* product. Such a union could never be productive because the breeds were too far apart. Kant was never able to explain satisfactorily how the "understanding," which is itself the "source of the laws of nature"[36] and of space, time, and the categories as well,[37] could produce conceptions whose "distinguishing feature consists in just this, that they relate to their objects without having borrowed from experience anything that can serve in the representation of those objects."[38] Peirce's improvement was to maintain the same unity *outside the mind*, in an external, objective, and knowable real world. The union became for Peirce not one of percepts and concepts, or of pure reason and practical action, but rather of generals and forces, generals and "reactions," as he called them. Generals and reactions inhabit one region of existence, and are two sides of the same coin. Generals are apprehended by the mind in acts of cognition; reactions take place in an objective real world where they illustrate generals.

Through the effort to point out the difference between Kant's conception of this relation and his own interpretation, Peirce's doctrine of pragmatism was born.[39] "Consider," he said, "what effects, that might conceivably have practical bearings,[40] we conceive the object of our conception to have. Then, our conception of these effects is the whole conception of the object." (5.402) In other words, the objective and external effect which a conception has in the world is the meaning of the conception. This was only another way of saying that Kant's percepts and concepts are the mental counterparts of reactions and generals. "A premiss," said Peirce, "is something we hope is true," and we find out whether it is or not by exhausting the experiential meaning of the premise. Thus pragmatism was a child born of the union of logic and experience. Kant had suggested that logic and experience[41] were united by the mind, in which they became incapable of further analysis, but Peirce supposed them to constitute a unity quite apart from and independent of the examining mind.

Once having established pragmatism as a procedure based upon the external unity of logic and experience, Peirce turned his attention to the prob-

---

[36] *Ibid.*, A 127.

[37] *Ibid.*, B 118.

[38] *Ibid.*, A 86. Cf. also B 118.

[39] Peirce mentions many precursors for pragmatism, especially Kant, Berkeley, and Spinoza. (5.412) It was clearly the study of Kant, however, that had the most to do with furnishing the occasion for Peirce's enunciation of the doctrine.

[40] The phrase "practical bearings" does not reintroduce subjectivism, since it may refer to some*thing* as well as to some*body's* actual or possible experience.

[41] I.e., in Kant's terminology "the understanding" and "sensibility."

lem of uniting ethics with this doctrine. Here again he went beyond Kant, who had in this field of endeavor met with failure. In Kant's terms the Categorical Imperative failed to rest, as it was supposed to, on the grounds established for the pure reason.[42] The whole Kantian orientation of ethics in terms of the individual, from which Kant had tried unsuccessfully to get away,[43] is illustrated in the "hypothetical imperative" of the end of happiness as the purpose of human beings.[44] Self-love is the usual spring of most men's actions, as Kant had observed,[45] but Peirce was able to detect in the direction of human endeavors based on self-love another sort of end altogether. The demands of logic would require us to identify our interests, since we are selfish, with those actual things which persist the longest. For we do not wish to have the objects of our interests perish and so see the interests themselves defeated. But through the use of Peirce's experimental logic we are enabled to discover that there is nothing actual which can reasonably be supposed to persist forever. Loved ones, friends, neighbors, social groups, states, humanity, even the geologic universe, in the enormous mathematics of transience must finally cease to exist. We are thus driven, if we would be logical, to the apparent paradox of identifying our selfish interests with what must persist the longest, namely, with an unbroken order of brief-lived things: an unlimited community. (2.645-655) For Kant's "kingdom of ends"[46] Peirce substituted a hierarchy of means and ends, such that every-thing is both relative means and absolute end in a series. Thus ethics rests on logic and experience, and both reason and the practical world are shown to make a unity with moral action.

Peirce was able to exhibit a consistency where Kant, because of a funda-mental contradiction between the realism of the second edition of the *Critique of Pure Reason* and the nominalism of his subjective *a priori* reason in the first edition, could not. In order to develop the proper ethics, Kant had had to abandon his metaphysics and fall back upon an instinctive feel-ing for what is right. But although Peirce produced a more self-consistent philosophy, it was Kant who had demonstrated the necessity. From the Kantian attempt to support the moral law upon reason directly and not through mediation of the field of the normative sciences as a whole, Peirce had learned a lesson. The latter's improvement was to discover that self-consistency between metaphysics and ethics could be gained not by the

---

[42] As Kant himself saw, *Critique of Practical Reason*, T. K. Abbot trans., p. 84.

[43] Kant, *ibid.*, p. 27, n. 1.

[44] Kant, *ibid.*, "Fundamental Principles of the Metaphysics of Morals," p. 32.

[45] *Ibid.*, p. 24.

[46] *Ibid.*, p. 51.

mediation of certain rules for the normative sciences but rather by subor-
dinating ethics to a general doctrine of practice as well as to one of metaphysics.[47] The broadening of ethics resulted in a general normative doctrine that included natural scientific method in its sweep of application and
thus bridged the gap between the normative and the empirical.

Both pragmatism and the ethics of the unlimited community, as well as
the more purely rational and empirical elements of Peirce's philosophy, owe
much to Kant. It should not be surprising that the ethical doctrines of both
men eventually appeal to an implicit principle of ultimate unity—Kant in
the assumed basis for the unity of pure *a priori* reason and practical action;
Peirce in the integrating principle of the unlimited community—which
proves to be the ground whereby action can be moral at all.

B. The Practice of Physical Science

When Peirce turned from the study of Kant to actual experimental work
in the physical sciences, he was faced with the necessity of reconciling his
new occupation with his old one. Before setting up a system of his own, in
the hope that the new philosophy might include all that he had learned, he
felt obliged to explore the methods and laws of the empirical sciences inside
the laboratories. This he proceeded to do with intense application and great
thoroughness. The influence of physical science upon him may be examined
under the following topics: the relation of science to metaphysics; the logical
method of science; the realistic character of science; the science of philosophy; the relation of science to religion; science as process; and the aim of
science.

i. THE RELATION OF SCIENCE TO METAPHYSICS

The result of any prolonged concentration upon the ideas of Kant must
be a reaction away from metaphysics and toward the empirical sciences.
Most of those who have followed such a course have ended by embracing
the positivistic denial of the validity of metaphysics as perfectly valid, and
by accepting the operational procedure of science as its own justification.
Whether or not it was Kant who led Peirce to enter the laboratory, the fact
remains that there Peirce halted, refusing to follow the usual development.

---

[47] "The present writer was a pure Kantist until he was forced by successive steps into Pragmaticism," Peirce wrote. (5.452) Pragmaticism was a later and more realistically formulated
version of pragmatism.

For what he learned of the sciences compelled him to reject positivism[48] as a doctrine out of keeping with the true situation in science. The lessons he gained in the laboratory had to do with the postulates, method and conclusions of science in a general way rather than with more special problems.

He discovered, above all, that "the special sciences are obliged to take for granted a number of most important propositions, because their ways of working afford no means of bringing these propositions to the test. In short, they always rest upon metaphysics." (1.129) Since "there is no escape from the need of a critical examination of 'first principles,' " it is to the philosopher and not to the scientist that we must look, for "the philosopher alone is equipped with the facilities for examining such 'axioms' and for determining the degree to which confidence may safely be reposed in them." Philosophy cannot be avoided by the ostrich attitude, and it is therefore more cautious to be critical of the philosophy which is accepted implicitly in science than it is to turn a deaf ear to those who wish to make it explicit.

Thus Peirce was led to retain a belief in the validity of metaphysics and to seek to tie up metaphysics with science. The doctrine, learned from a study of Kant, of the unity of logic and experiment, was of relevancy here, and Peirce was brought to the conclusion that science through its empirical method was seeking the utmost generalizations allowable by resort to experience. Science proved to be not a study of facts in and for their own sake but a search for the laws demanded by the facts and inclusive of them.

ii. THE LOGICAL METHOD OF SCIENCE

Science, Peirce discovered, cannot be pursued without imagination. Since science sprang from magic, only those people who had allowed their fancies some rein could have scientific ability. (1.46-48) But, on the other hand, uncontrolled imagination never led to science. Rather was it a special kind of imagination that was required. For "the scientific imagination dreams of explanations and laws." There is a sensuous quality to the scientific imagination, but the method of science very soon transcends mere sense experience. In so doing it abstracts from experience a generality that is nonsubjective. The search for laws allows for the operation of scientific method in fields where sense experience may be wanting. "Men colour blind have more than once learnedly discussed the laws of colour-sensation, and have made interesting deductions from those laws." (6.435)

In scientific method the direction is from the qualitative to the structural and the quantitative. "All the great steps in the method of science in every department have consisted in bringing into relation cases previously [observed only as] discrete." (1.359) From the discreteness of cases to the generality of relations involves progress in the method of abstracting the quantitative from the qualitative. "It is a common observation that a science first begins to be exact when it is quantitatively treated." (2.645) The exact sciences are the mathematical ones. "Admirable as the work of research of the special sciences—physical and psychical—is, as a whole, the reasoning [employed in them] is of an elementary kind except when it is mathematical." (4.425)

Scientific investigation may be described as an interrogation of nature. Peirce quoted Stöckhardt to the effect that an experiment is a question put to nature. (5.168) It is necessary first of all to know what question is to be asked. The selection of the question to be put must satisfy certain fundamental requirements. One of these is logical consistency, which rests upon the postulate of continuity, "the leading conception of science." (1.62) Given the condition that any answer to the question put will have to prove continuous with the method and findings of the science, the next requirement is the one formulated in Ockham's Razor, which is a "sound maxim of scientific procedure," (5.60) to the effect that the hypothesis selected must be the simplest one which will suffice. Only so can scientific method advance the knowledge of the special sciences toward the effort to show the interrelations between the sciences. For the doctrine that all the sciences form a system, (1.256) those which are more special (i.e., the empirical sciences) drawing their principles from those which are more general (i.e., logic and mathematics), (2.119) is a fundamental postulate in all science.

iii. THE REALISTIC CHARACTER OF SCIENCE

The understanding of science as the search for laws gets rid once for all of the subjective interpretation of science. The method abstracts from sense experience (from which it assuredly must take its start) to a knowledge of laws. Thus the field of operations of the scientific method is the objective field of nature, and, as Peirce observed, "belief proper has nothing to do with science." (1.239 n.) The sudden recollection that the laws of science are not final formulations but are susceptible to change by means of later operations of scientific method should not be taken to mean that subjectivity is reintroduced. The established truths of science merely mean "propositions to which no competent man today demurs" (1.635) until further applications of scientific method give him reason to do so.

The correspondence between the reasoning of human beings and the logic of nature is what makes scientific method possible. Nature is not a subjective conception merely; nor is the mind merely a physical mechanism, as solipsism and behavioristic psychology respectively would have us believe. (6.465) The explanation of reasoning as the "movements of neurites that strictly obey certain physical laws" does not "explode the theory that my neighbor and myself are governed by reason." Thus when we are reasoning according to scientific method, i.e., checking our reasoning by experimentation, we are investigating the reason in nature. "Every scientific explanation of a natural phenomenon is a hypothesis that there is something in nature to which the human reason is analogous." (1.316) The "natural and anthropomorphic metaphysics" (2.713) is quite correct when it makes us, as it usually does, "conceive Nature to be perpetually making deductions in *Barbara.*"

The conclusions concerning the rationality of nature and the nonsubjective character of a scientific method which seeks to apprehend natural laws led Peirce to what became the central and dominating conception of his whole philosophy. This conception was brought upon him by the thought that if the part of nature with which science is concerned consists of regularity or laws, (4.1) then these laws must be what metaphysics termed universals. Peirce's pragmatic followers, William James (6.482) and F. C. S. Schiller, (5.552) had inclined toward positivism. But Peirce expressly saw that the error lay in not wanting to take seriously the applicability of laws or universals to actuality where such application had not yet taken place. Peirce observed that Schiller "does not wish us to devote any attention to the effects of conditions that do not occur," (5.537) and responded by saying that "such talk shows great ignorance of the conditions of science."

The inevitable conclusion to which Peirce was led was that "science has always been at heart realistic, and always must be so." (1.20) A work by F. E. Abbot entitled *Scientific Theism* (4.50) convinced Peirce that his own inclinations were correct. The Church had been realistic; therefore the new empiricists in revolting against Church restrictions had established experimental science as nominalistic. But in fact the nominalistic features of science are "merely superficial and transient," and science itself stands out as realistic. For the search for universals, or laws independent of experience and applying equally to those conditions which do occur and to those which do not, requires at least the postulate that such universals exist to be applied.

Here Peirce left Kant behind him and took up a position sharply opposed to him, for Kant was a nominalist, as Peirce very clearly saw, (6.590)[49] one who had derived his nominalism from Leibniz and Wolf. Peirce had become a pronounced realist. Peirce preferred to call his universals generals in order to show that he did not mean them to be anything absolute or final, an advance over Kant as well as over Abbot. In other ways, also, he went beyond Abbot. For although Abbot had furnished the clue to scientific realism, the elaboration was Peirce's own. He was the first modern philosophical advocate of the realistic character of science possessing sufficient technical knowledge to be able to defend the position.

iv. THE SCIENCE OF PHILOSOPHY

The first lesson that Peirce learned from physical science had to do with the philosophy of science; the second lesson had to do with the science of philosophy. For despite his objections to what he called modern philosophy, Peirce did believe in the scientific character of the philosophic field. Upon this topic he was very explicit. "Philosophy, as I understand the word," he said, "is a positive theoretical science, and a science in an early stage of development." (5.61) It has "no more to do with belief than [has] any other science." Elsewhere he asserts that it is a branch of theoretical science, capable of having immense consequences. "A philosophical or other scientific error may be fraught with disastrous consequences for the whole people. It might conceivably bring about the extirpation of the human race." (1.663)

However, it was not of modern philosophy that Peirce was speaking. What he had in mind was something nearer the logical philosophy of the scholastics, which he found had more in common with science than the philosophy of his own day. For instance, authority, which we usually identify with the philosophic method of the scholastics, actually attaches more to science than to modern philosophy. (1.32) Scientists have some faith in the validity of an hypothesis which has been tried and tested by a number of competent scientists, but modern philosophers do not accept each other's statements to that extent. Of course, authority has its limitations both in science and in philosophy; we cannot go very far with the scholastics in this respect. Although "science and philosophy seem to have been changed in their cradles" (1.44) in that the philosopher is a man with a system to defend and the scientist is only a man burning with a desire to learn, nevertheless true science and true philosophy are never very far apart.

---

[49] See this chapter, A, iii.

Peirce accepted the definition of science in Lewes's work on *Aristotle*,[50] that science consists in verification. For the scientist in the laboratory and in the field is *not* engaged in "passive perception unassisted by thought," (1.34) but rather is "perceiving by the aid of analysis—and testing suggestions of theories." But this is just what the scholastic philosophers were doing also. "Now this same unwearied interest in testing general propositions is what produced those long rows of folios of the schoolmen." The tests which they employed were of limited validity because they were not unhampered; yet their spirit was the same as that which pervades scientists. Both scholastic philosophy and modern science differ from modern philosophy. The latter must be reformed so that its proper scientific nature can function unrestricted by the antiphilosophical spirit of those contemporary philosophers "who have called themselves empirical."

V. THE RELATION OF SCIENCE TO RELIGION

Peirce found that science and scholastic philosophy have much in common, although the scholastics were subject in their researches to restrictions which do not confine the scientists. Once having rejected modern philosophy in favor of the scholastics, who as it happened were theologians as well as metaphysicians, Peirce felt obliged to indicate the dividing line between science and religion. Now, curiously, Peirce thought that the difference between science and religion concerned the question of practice. Theology, Peirce maintained, inflames men with the desire to amend the lives of themselves and others, while science animates them with the pure search for truth. (1.620)[51] Philosophy has failed because in this respect it has leaned toward theology rather than toward science. (1.619) If philosophy is to be of any eventual practicality at all, it must be, like science, strictly divorced from practice. The Greeks mingled philosophy and practice, but the scientific cast of thought will not mingle the two, but will seek to develop an abstract theory which can be of practical value in its applications. In other words, it is just the nature of science as the pure search for truth, and the remoteness of scientific investigation from practice, that in time produces such important scientific practice.

Theology rests upon faith in miracles, and leads to practical morality. Contrary to the usual understanding, which supposes that science denies the miracles which theology asserts, Peirce held that science must reserve its opinion. For if science consists of the testing of hypotheses, it cannot

---

[50] *Aristotle: A Chapter from the History of Science* (London, 1864).

[51] Duns Scotus, *Opus Oxoniense*, Prol. q. 4-5; *Disputationes subtilissimae*, 30.

treat of any hypothesis not available to the ordinary scientific procedures. Therefore "science can no more deny a miracle than it can assert one." (1.90) As to morality, Peirce felt more forthright on this score. For morality is naturally conservative, and "conservatism about morals leads to conservatism about manners and finally conservatism about opinions of a speculative kind." (1.50) Hence it is that "an exaggerated regard for morality is unfavorable to scientific progress."

Peirce learned from the sciences to assume the attitude which he called fallibilism. This is the caution that all formulations are subject to error, and that even the most mathematical of the sciences must state their laws in terms of high probability, (1.9) there being no absolute certainty possible short of logical and mathematical tautologies. Fallibilism led him to hold that the demonstrations of the metaphysicians were "all moonshine." (1.7) Philosophy ought to consist of critical common sense as well as of construction. (5.451) The best that metaphysicians can offer, he said, are hypotheses, capable of an indefinitely remote future verification or refutation. Of himself in this connection he implied that he did not ever wish to be absolutely sure of his own conclusions. (1.10)

Infallibilism, or the claim to the absolute and dogmatic assertion of "truths," he unqualifiedly condemned, claiming that it existed only in religion, and there only as a practical affair. (1.8) With astonishing acumen, however, he detected traces of infallibilism among certain classes of scientific men; among those who regarded their sciences as manufactures of "creeds" and "homilies," and among those who, having acquired their knowledge of science from reading, regarded scientific method as involving the possession of knowledge rather than its pursuit. All propositions in philosophy must be held tentatively, (6.181) in the same way that scientific hypotheses are held, that is to say, always ready to be abandoned whenever the evidence of reason or of fact demands that they should be.

vi. SCIENCE AS PROCESS AND AIM

Science is a "living process" which is "busied mainly with conjectures, which are either getting framed or getting tested." (1.234) The dictionary defines science as systematized knowledge (1.232) but science is a "pursuit of living men" and "the life of science is in the desire to learn" (1.235) rather than "the desire to prove the truth of a definite opinion." From the point of view of the men engaged in science, its genetic origins may be traced back to the two instincts of *feeding and breeding*. From feeding we get an "elementary knowledge of mechanical forces, space, etc." (1.118) of the external world in which our food is contained and found. From breeding we get an "elementary knowledge of psychical motives, of time, etc." "Thus, then all science is nothing but an outgrowth from these two instincts." (6.500) As such science can claim to be an inevitable result of the development of the human organism, the later stages of an inquiry whose first objective lay in determining ways and means for perpetuating the organism's self-existence.[52]

From the above considerations certain conclusions flow. It follows that science is radical rather than conservative, since there is always held out the possibility of change. Nothing is safe from change, not even the classification of the sciences themselves, which will have to be altered if it is to keep up with developments in scientific inquiry. (1.203) What in science are called established truths are nothing more than "propositions into which the economy of endeavor prescribes that, for the time being, futher inquiry shall cease." (5.589) Science is radical in "the eagerness to carry consequences to their extremes. Not the radicalism that is cocksure, however, but the *radicalism that tries experiments*." (1.148) It follows too that in science we can never have anything more certain than extreme probabilities. "There is not a single truth of science upon which we ought to bet more than about a million of millions to one," (1.150) not even upon the prediction that the sun will rise tomorrow!

The influence of science on Peirce may be summed up in a certain general viewpoint toward the meaning of science that emerges from his studies. Fundamental to this viewpoint is the distinction between the theoretical sciences and their practical applications. "I recognize two branches of science," he announced, "Theoretical, whose purpose is simply and solely knowledge of God's truth; and Practical, for the uses of life." (1.239) Theoretical science started with a spirit that is the urge to learn, so that the method of science "is itself a scientific result." (6.428) Not even knowledge constitutes science, but only a certain method of learning, of experimentally testing hypotheses. "That which constitutes science, then, is not so much correct conclusions as it is a correct method."

"Science is from its procedure confined to the investigation of the ordinary course of nature." (1.87) Science studies the "utterly useless" (1.75) in order to arrive at immensely practical conclusions. But it is practical rather than theoretical science that is concerned with these conclusions. The aim of theoretical science is to seek out the eternal verities, and indeed

[52] See this chapter, D, i.

"the only end of science, as such, is to learn the lesson that the universe has to teach it." (5.589) Moreover, every scientific investigation tends toward but one solution. "All the followers of science are animated by a cheerful hope that the processes of investigation, if only pushed far enough, will give one certain solution to each question to which they apply it." (5.407) "This great hope is embodied in the conception of truth and reality. The opinion which is fated to be ultimately agreed to by all who investigate, is what we mean by the truth, and the object represented in this opinion is the real. This is the way I would explain reality." Fate itself means nothing more than "that which is sure to come true." Thus, finally, the aim of science is the discovery of the regularity of that which is sure to come true, in order that human beings may learn something of their fate, an ambition which is itself in turn fated never to be entirely fulfilled.

C. The Adoption of Duns Scotus

The realistic nature of science is a doctrine that must be found to rest eventually upon some realistic formulation of metaphysics. Kant had served his turn; his formulations clearly would not do for the purpose now in hand in Peirce's development. "Kant," Peirce remarked, "was a nominalist; although his philosophy would have been rendered compacter, more consistent, and stronger if its author had taken up realism, as he certainly would have done if he had read Scotus." (1.19) Peirce was led by science to a study of the realistic philosophers. In this connection one would logically expect him to turn to the Greeks. But to Peirce, who was no aesthetician, Plato's poetic and dramatic presentation of realism did not make the proper appeal. Aristotle was important for logic, and, in a certain suggestiveness, for the sciences also, but Aristotle's name had been too roundly taken by the nominalists; he was not by himself[53] a sufficient advocate of the realism required.

Who else, then, was to be considered? The custom in Peirce's day was to jump from classical Greek philosophy to the Renaissance writers, ignoring the intervening periods. The nineteenth century still felt the influence of the Renaissance too strongly to allow any validity to the scholastic philosophers. But here again Peirce took the lead. He was in fact one of the first modern philosophers to return to the scholastics, and to discover that, quite apart from theological and religious questions, there was much

---

[53] See 5.77 n.: "I should call myself an Aristotelian of the scholastic wing, approaching Scotism, but going much further in the direction of scholastic realism."

of logical and metaphysical value in their work. The philosophers who were contemporaries of Peirce had abandoned ontology for epistemology; conceding problems of being to science, they had taken refuge in the puzzles of the knowledge process, only to discover that the scientific attempts to solve these were furnished by psychology. This was a logical development, and followed from nominalistic presuppositions.

But Peirce was a newly born realist. He felt obliged to reopen the study of being to philosophy, and sought in the writings of the scholastic philosophers for suggestions leading to the proper ontology. It might be added that this too was a logical development, and followed from explicitly held realistic postulates. The writer Peirce found of most interest was Duns Scotus. For Peirce, William of Ockham "was beyond question the greatest nominalist that ever lived; while Duns Scotus, another British name, it is equally certain is the subtilest advocate of the opposite opinion." (1.29) In Peirce's view, "the metaphysics of Aquinas, a modified Aristotelianism, had been immensely elaborated and deeply transformed by the vast logical genius of the British Duns Scotus," (2.166) who was "one of the greatest metaphysicians of all time." (4.28) Curiously, although Scotus was a Platonist, Peirce gave little acknowledgment to Plato, while Aristotle came in for a huge share. The realism which Peirce had learned was true from physical science he found most fully developed in Scotus. Peirce did not become a slavish follower, however, but developed realism along his own lines. Later, he acknowledged an obligation to Duns Scotus but did not hesitate to criticize him. (1.560)

He was well aware of the necessity for caution in addressing the principles discovered in one period to the altogether different problems of another. "In calling himself a Scotist, the writer does not mean that he is going back to the general views of 600 years back; he merely means that the point of metaphysics upon which Scotus chiefly insisted and which has since passed out of mind, is a very important point, inseparably bound up with the *most* important point to be insisted upon today." (4.50) Thus, "If his [Duns Scotus'] logic and metaphysics, not slavishly worshipped, but torn away from its mediaevalism, be adapted to modern culture, under continual wholesome reminders of nominalistic criticisms, I am convinced that it will go far toward supplying the philosophy which is best to harmonize with physical science." (1.6)

There is no way in which it is possible absolutely to discriminate, among the ideas to be found in a man's reading, those which have occasioned in him the holding of certain beliefs. Peirce acknowledged the influence of

Duns Scotus but may himself have been mistaken in tracing specific doctrines to their origins in suggestions found in the Scottish philosopher. We are limited finally in such studies to logical similarities—the rest is speculation. There are several elements in the philosophy of Duns Scotus which in all probability must have had a bearing on the development of Peirce's thought. In some cases the influence is more obvious than it is in others, and we shall consider only the main parts of it. These are the pursuit of philosophy as a separate science; the support of reason by faith; the doctrine of universals; the substitution of individuality for matter; and the freedom of the will.

i. PHILOSOPHY AS A SEPARATE SCIENCE

Peirce may have learned from Duns Scotus that philosophy can be pursued as a separate science. Aquinas had maintained that philosophy is the handmaiden of theology, an opinion contradicted by the view of Duns Scotus.[54] Kant had done philosophy the same disservice, although from another side, by limiting philosophy to its critical and epistemological departments. In so doing, both Aquinas and Kant had pointed the way toward the eventual abandonment of philosophy, a course easily open to Peirce when he went into the physical laboratory. The tradition of scientists who had grown to be protective in their attitude toward science dictated that philosophy could neither be a science nor have anything to say about it. The scientists relegated philosophy to its old status of *a priori* dogmatism, and continued to insist upon the fact that it must continue to be a mere appendage to theology. Thus the new Kantian attitude actually continued the old tradition of the impotence of constructive philosophy, merely substituting science for theology as the source of all dependable knowledge of the truth.

Although Peirce was a scientist as well as a philosopher, he did not follow in philosophy the lead of the scientists, but rather went back to take a fresh start from the Middle Ages. The importance of Duns Scotus in this connection was that he proclaimed the independence of philosophy from theology, and thus pointed the way toward the establishment of an independent science of philosophy. Logically, his preoccupation could not have been with epistemology, to which philosophy on the other alternative was reduced, but rather with logic and ontology. The modern problems of epistemology for the most part disappear in one or another of the

---

[54] The notion that theology is practical while philosophy is theoretical or speculative was perhaps suggested to Peirce by Duns Scotus. See the latter's *Quaestiones quodlibetales*, q. 14; and his *Opus Oxoniense*, Prologus, q. 4, n. 13 and n. 31. See also this chapter, B, v.

divisions of logic which Peirce learned from Duns Scotus, (3.430) chiefly between speculative grammar, (2.206)[55] or the study of propositions, and "pure rhetoric," (2.229) or the study of communication.

For Duns Scotus, the study of philosophy as an independent science meant merely the pursuit of philosophy as a separate rational enterprise. But for Pierce, living in the late nineteenth century, the problem was more complicated. What the study of philosophy as an independent science in his day meant included an emphasis on the word "science," which had by then acquired a more precise meaning. It meant that there were two studies to reconcile: philosophy and science. Peirce thus was led to speculate upon the philosophical aspects of science and, as we have already noted, also upon the scientific aspects of philosophy. The only scientific philosophy available to him was one reputedly derived from science, and this was the nominalistic philosophy, which inevitably led to a divorce between science and philosophy in the name of science.

But to bring about the establishment of the proper relations between science and philosophy, a philosophy was demanded which could support them both, a demand which nominalism was unable to meet. This demand Peirce found adequately supplied by the realistic philosophy of Duns Scotus. From Abbot's work Peirce had learned that science was realistic rather than nominalistic; but, as Peirce himself said, it was Duns Scotus who had showed him exactly what kind of realism was conformable with science.

ii. THE SUPPORT OF REASON BY FAITH

Duns Scotus showed that not everything can be proved. There is a sphere in which reason is not competent to enter, and that sphere is the theological. Logic does not apply to the infinite where black becomes white and two plus two is equal to five, a failure to which all mathematicians will bear witness. Reason must leave certain things to faith; things it requires of faith if there is to be reason at all. The establishment of philosophy as an independent science involved assigning reason to the service of philosophy and faith to the service of theology. But the division was not complete and was not meant to be. Reason requires certain assumptions which cannot be proved, and these Duns Scotus found in theology. The movement initiated by Aquinas to guard theological questions against the encroachment of reason was participated in by Duns Scotus in almost its orthodox form.

But the distinction between reason and faith had quite another meaning

[55] Originally due to Thomas of Erfurt.

for Peirce. He understood it to imply that philosophy and science as applications of reason must take for granted certain assumptions or postulates radically incapable of proof (1.654) and demonstrable only on grounds of the validity of the conclusions drawn from them. Deductive logic does not select the postulates upon which it operates, nor does it prove them once they have been selected. It merely accepts them, and uses them as its starting point. From the axioms of mathematical systems to the intuited givens of ethics, reason can only accept what it is asked to accept and can only question what there is reason to call into question.[56] But the fact that rational systems of philosophy are unable to demonstrate the truth of postulates does not indicate, as has so often been supposed, that reason is at bottom irrational. The unproved postulates of reason are not proved irrational; they are merely not proved rational, which is quite another thing. What does emerge from such a situation is the lesson that a rational system is a limited system, and that the limits of rational proof are also the limits of the system. That Peirce believed the universe rational is shown in many passages, as, for example, by his dictum that "Nature syllogizes from one grand major premise." (6.66)

To base reason on faith no more makes reason irrational than it makes faith rational. They can function together only by being different. But Peirce's version of this relation differed from that of Scotus in that Peirce's faith was—faith in reason, and in other faculties only in so far as they aided and abetted reason.

iii. THE DOCTRINE OF UNIVERSALS

Another influence which came from Duns Scotus had to do with the doctrine of universals. The extent and importance of this particular factor in Peirce's thought can hardly be underestimated. Peirce had learned to reject nominalism in favor of realism from a study of science in its theory and practice. But to discover realism is one thing and to decide just how far to go with it is another. Extreme realism, as more than one realist has discovered,[57] is not realism but a variety of objective nominalism. Idealism is at bottom only another form of nominalism, since it assigns reality to the mind alone and denies it to objective universals.

[56] In a later section we shall see the force of this argument directed against the first principle of Descartes's metaphysics. See this chapter, E, i.

[57] M. de Wulf, *History of Mediaeval Philosophy*, vol. i, p. 165; and Morris R. Cohen, *Reason and Nature*, p. 75. What Wulf condemns as "exaggerated realism" is what Cohen designates as not realism at all but "crypto-materialism."

The idealists have always maintained that universals have a mental existence that is either exclusive of or superior to any other form of existence. The Aristotelians, at the other extreme, admit the existence of universals only in actual things. But the realism of Duns Scotus is different; and it is clear enough to make misunderstanding on the fundamental issue all but impossible. For Scotus asserted time and again that universals are not intellectual fictions, that they are not mental although they have mental counterparts, and that they exist objectively in the reality of nature.[58] The universal is predicated of many individuals yet its unity is not exclusively of the mind, for it has its own objective unity;[59] it is an integral part of the reality of the natural world.

Probably the correct way to approach realism is by going through nominalism first, just as "Dante first saw hell before the divine ascent." To suppose that universals are things somehow actually existing is to disbelieve in the world of sense experience, an extreme form of realism made untenable by the nominalistic caution. Enough of the caution of nominalism therefore should remain to ensure that realism will be moderate. It was when Peirce had first become a realist that he discovered Duns Scotus, and Scotian realism was moderate.

The controversy over the status of universals, the conflict between realism and nominalism, was solved by the Arabian philosopher, Avicenna, and it was his solution that was adopted by Albert, Aquinas, and Duns Scotus. Do universals exist in things, before things, or after things? The nominalists held uncompromisingly to the first view, extreme realists to the second, and conceptualists, who sought a middle ground, to the third. Duns Scotus agreed that in a sense all three were true.[60] Universals exist *ante res* in the mind of God, *in rebus* as the essence of things, and *post res* as abstract concepts in human minds. Making due allowance for the language of the schol .stics, *ante res* became for Peirce the logical possibility of ontology; *in reb .s* became the knowledge relation of epistemology; and *post res* became the mental concepts of psychology. But the solution was not confined to the level of metaphysical problems only; it became a leading canon for Peirce and stands implicit behind all his other writings. For by scholastic realism Peirce understood that "general principles are really operative in nature." (5.101)

---

[58] E.g., *Theoremata*, iv; *Reportata Parisiensia* II, dist. xii, q. 5, n. 12.
[59] *Rep. Par.* II, dist. xii, q. 5, n. 11.
[60] *Quaestiones in Meta. Arist.*, VII, q. 18, n. 10.

iv. INDIVIDUALITY VERSUS MATTER

From Aristotle to Aquinas, matter conceived either as substance or as the basis of individuality had remained a leading principle in philosophy. For Aquinas, matter was the *principium individuationis*; but not so for Duns Scotus. The subtle doctor asserted that the species plus the individual difference accounts for the existence of the singular. "*Hic et nunc* is the phrase perpetually in the mouth of Duns Scotus, who first elucidated individual existence." (1.458) The *haecceitas*, or, in a later terminology, the *thisness*, is the medium whereby universals become singular. (1.405) The *haecceitas* is the essence of the individual and is emphatically not universal.[61] "As M. de Wulf has pointed out,[62] to the medieval thinker knowledge was essentially a matter of the general and universal; the particular [i.e., the singular] so much despised by the realist, seemed to elude altogether the grasp of the mind. Duns Scotus, however, tries hard to rehabilitate the individual[63] in a position of epistemological respectability, and his more scientific insistence on the concrete nature of reality gives to his thinking a distinctively modern flavour.[64]

An understanding of the relevance of this change to general problems of philosophy and science was urged upon Peirce in all probability by his general inclination to apply the metaphysics of Duns Scotus to current philosophical issues. Peirce came to challenge the legitimacy of substance as a logical category, (5.500) and asserted that it meant nothing more than the present in general. (1.547) For Peirce the change was instrumental in supporting the realistic metaphysics. More specifically, it meant the necessity of substituting for the primacy of matter the primacy of relations. For Scotus, first among the scholastics, "the singular is *per se intelligible* . . . to the human mind."[65] For Peirce a singular was not a substantial piece of matter having qualities, attributes or characteristics, but rather a set of relations constituting a singular by virtue of their assemblage in an individual. Things were not static substances but rather dynamic relations. If the mode of existence is individual, then each individual depends for its existence not upon its identity merely but also upon its difference from

---

[61] *Reportata Parisiensia* II, dist. xii, q. 5, n. 13.

[62] *Philosophy and Civilization in the Middle Ages*, pp. 183-184.

[63] C. R. S. Harris, *Duns Scotus* (Oxford, 1927), vol. ii, pp. 23-24.

[64] Peirce distinguished between singular, as meaning "one in number from a particular point of view" (3.93), and individual, as meaning "absolutely indivisible," but admitted that they had come to be used in much the same sense.

[65] C. R. S. Harris, *Duns Scotus*, vol. ii, p. 24, quoting Duns Scotus, *Opus Oxoniense*, II, dist. iii, q. 6, n. 17.

other individuals. Thus "the mode of being of the individual thing is existence; and existence lies in opposition merely." (1.458)[66] This opposition is what Peirce later termed secondnesss or reaction. The same general line of reasoning also proved consistent with Peirce's innovation of symbolic logic, the "logic of relatives" or relations.

V. PRIMACY OF THE WILL

The last point we shall touch upon in trying to trace the influence of Duns Scotus on Peirce has to do with the Scotian doctrine of the primacy of the will. Peirce raised the element of chance in existence to an eminence it has seldom achieved. He considered it one of the fundamental and ultimate categories. True, the will is a subjective conception, whereas Peirce assumed that chance had an objective and natural status. But is not chance in this connection only a generalized will? At the level of less self-determinative creatures, will as the primacy of choice, always governed to some extent by chance, becomes a purely chance affair, and the difference disappears. Peirce here, as usual, went further than his sources. He did not assign a very important role to the will in his philosophy, but he did to feeling (or firstness), and he did assert the equivalence of subjective feeling and objective chance. Such an interpretation is in keeping with Peirce's lack of emphasis on subjective categories and also with his way of objectifying whatever influences came to him from subjectivistic elements in classical philosophy.

For Peirce never succeeded in finding a philosopher who was not tinged somewhat with subjectivism. Although he had learned from his earliest experiences with Kant to read subjective notions objectively, and thereby to uncover some neglected insights, yet he found that this method of discovery has its limitations. And eventually he was always forced to go off, so to speak, on his own, to think for himself, and to develop his own special way of looking at the nature of things. He always acknowledged his profound debt to Duns Scotus; but in the end criticized him because he "inclines too much toward nominalism." (1.560) Scotus took Peirce out of the excessive rationalism of Kant, which his intensive study of the limits of the pure reason had forced on him, by showing that the will is

---

[66] Duns Scotus's "Individual" and Peirce's "reaction" are more in keeping with the findings of modern physics than is the older substance-predicate notion of Aristotle. Scotus substituted the individual for matter; Peirce discovered that the individual consists in dynamic reaction. This dynamic reaction is what in effect modern physics, and some modern philosophers, have termed an "event."

superior to the reason, and as such in itself reasonable. But Peirce learned from Scotus not only how to proceed in certain cases but also how not to proceed in others. (6.361)

D. THE LESSON OF DARWIN

i. THE MEANING OF DARWINISM

When Darwin's *Origin of Species* first appeared it exercised a profound effect upon Peirce, just as it did upon all the progressive thinkers of his generation. The uncovering of the importance of evolution as a serious factor controlling all forms of life appeared to Peirce and to most of his contemporaries to be an event that must mark a turning point in the history of science. But Peirce stood more alone, perhaps, with respect to the other, and to some extent unique, lessons which the theory of natural selection taught him. For while everyone else was concerned with the biological and theological implications of the Darwinian hypothesis, Peirce was struck by its logical, metaphysical, and cosmological meanings.

"The theory of Darwin was that evolution had been brought about by the action of two factors: first, heredity, as a principle making offspring nearly resemble their parents, while yet giving room for 'sporting' or accidental variations—for very slight variations often, for wider ones rarely; and, second, the destruction of breeds or races that are unable to keep the birth rate up to the death rate." (6.15) These two factors are termed by Darwin "the Unity of Type" and the "Conditions of Existence,"[67] or "variation" and "natural selection."[68] In this theory, Peirce professed to detect three factors: "to wit: first, the principle of individual variation or sporting; second, the principle of hereditary transmission, which wars against the first principle; and third, the principle of the elimination of unfavorable characters." (1.398)

The meaning of Darwinism is immediately broadened by Peirce to the dimensions of a larger problem. "Whether the part played by natural selection and the survival of the fittest in the production of species be large or small there remains little doubt that the Darwinian theory indicates a real cause, which tends to adapt animal and vegetable forms to their environment.[69] A remarkable feature of it is that it shows how merely fortuitous variations of individuals together with merely fortuitous

---

[67] *Origin of Species*, ch. VI.
[68] *Ibid.*, ch. XV.
[69] *Ibid.*, chap. V.

mishaps to them would, under the action of heredity, result, not in mere irregularity, nor even in a statistical constancy, but in continual and indefinite progress toward a better adaptation of means to ends." (1.395)[70] "Now the adaptation of a species to its environment consists, for the purposes of natural selection, in a power of continuing to exist,[71] that is to say, in the power of one generation to bring forth another; for as long as another generation is brought forth the species will continue and as soon as this ceases it is doomed after one lifetime." (1.397)

The problem is here turned over by Peirce to a continuity of causality between life and its inanimate environment, and to a continuity of ontological existence. In connection with the first, Peirce observed that Darwinian evolution, in contradistinction to the other varieties, takes place by a series of insensible single steps, (6.17)[72] a point destined for further elaboration. In connection with the second, he observed that "not man merely, but all animals derive by inheritance (presumably by natural selection) two classes of ideas which adapt them to their environment." (2.753) These are: mechanical ideas of force, matter, space and time; and ideas of "what sort of objects their fellow-beings are, and of how they will act on given occasions," that is to say, dynamical ideas. Human intuitions in particular are ascribed by Peirce to natural selection. (5.341)

In the next sections we shall see how these implications of Darwinism were taken over into the fields of philosophy. Of course, Peirce was not alone in seeing such implications. The best-known philosopher of evolution was Herbert Spencer. But Spencer followed Darwin slavishly and uncritically, and modeled all his theories after that of evolution. To Peirce, Spencer was no great philosopher. "The followers of Herbert Spencer, for example, cannot comprehend why scientific men place Darwin so infinitely above Spencer, since the theories of the latter are so much grander and more comprehensive. They cannot understand that it is not the sublimity of Darwin's theories which makes him admired by men of science, but that it is rather his minute, systematic, extensive, strict, scientific researches which have given his theories a more favorable reception." (1.33) Peirce was a scientific man and as such more prepared to retain his equilibrium in fitting the Darwinian theory into its background. He saw its immense value for general philosophy, yet he did not lose his sense of proportion.

[70] *Ibid.*, chap. XV.
[71] *Ibid.*, chap. III.
[72] *Ibid.*, chap. V.

ii. THE MODIFICATION OF ARISTOTELIANISM

The launching of Darwinism was accepted by Peirce's contemporaries as a direct attack upon the authority of the Church. Peirce was here more discriminating, for he distinguished within the Church dogma certain errors which the Darwinian theory upset; he was much more specific in detecting the true nature of the conflict. The official philosophy of the later scholastics was founded upon Aristotelianism, and Aristotelianism meant a belief in fixed forms and natural classes which exist irrevocably. It meant an absolute logic which is equally final, and, in short, a modified realism which had come to be accepted as the ultimate truth. These were the tenets of a doctrine which evolutionism came to upset. Let us see what it had to say on these specific issues.

Aristotelianism holds to a theory of fixed forms, universals infrangibly established for once and all in the beginning of time, unadaptive and unalterable forever. Since the mode of their being is *in re,* the transition from one form to another becomes almost ruled out by definition. In Peirce's view, this theory was upset by the theory of evolution. For "natural selection is the theory of how forms come to be adaptive, that is, to be governed by a *quasi* purpose. It suggests a machinery of efficiency to bring about the end—a machinery inadequate perhaps—yet which must contribute some help toward the result." (1.269) This is not to say that forms have no validity and that the whole thing is in a hopeless state of flux. The meaning is made somewhat clearer in the case of natural classes. "What is meant by a true and natural class? A great many logicians say there is no such thing; and, what is strange, even many students of taxonomic sciences not only follow this opinion but allow it a great part in determining the conclusions of botany and zoölogy. The cause of their holding this opinion has two factors; first, that they attach a metaphysical signification to the term *natural* or *real class,* and secondly, that they have embraced a system of metaphysics which allows them to believe in no such thing as that which they have defined a real or natural class to be. . . . A *class,* of course, is the total of whatever objects there may be in the universe which are of a certain description. What if we try taking the term 'natural,' or 'real class' to mean a class of which all the members owe their existence as members of the class to a common final cause? . . . In the case of natural classes the final cause remains occult . . . The doctrine of evolution refrains from pronouncing whether forms are simply fated or whether they are providential; but that definite ends are worked out none of us today any longer deny." (1.204)

Although Aristotle had not entirely overlooked probability,[73] it was not so with his scholastic followers. Now, "The Darwinian controversy is, in large part, a question of logic. Mr. Darwin proposed to apply the statistical method to biology." (5.364)[74] "This Darwinian principle [of natural selection] is plainly capable of great generalization. Wherever there are large numbers of objects having a tendency to retain certain characters unaltered, this tendency, however, not being absolute but giving room for chance variations, then, if the amount of variation is absolutely limited in certain directions by the destruction of everything which reaches those limits, there will be a gradual tendency to change in directions of departure from them. Thus, if a million players sit down to bet at an even game, since one after another will get ruined, the average wealth of those who remain will perpetually increase.

"Here is indubitably a genuine formula of possible evolution, whether its operation accounts for much or little in the development of animal and vegetable species." (6.15) But the character of survival "plainly is one of those which has an absolute minimum, for no animal can produce fewer offspring than none at all and it has no apparent upper limit, so that it is quite analogous to the wealth of those players. It is to be remarked that the phrase 'survival of the fittest' in the formula of the principle does not mean the survival of the fittest individuals, but the survival of the fittest types;[75] for the theory does not at all require that individuals ill-adapted to their environment should die at an earlier age than others, so long only as they do not reproduce so many offspring as others; and indeed it is not necessary that this should go so far as to extinguish the line of descent, provided there be some reason why the offspring of ill-adapted parents are less likely than others to inherit those parents' characteristics." (1.397)

No absolute logic can survive a doctrine of gradualism which rests upon a basis of facts, provided the two theories claim the same grade of being. Other thinkers saw in the conflict a genuine contradiction, and so inclined, and continue to incline today, toward the abandonment of the Aristotelian logic.[76] But Peirce was keen enough to discern that the contradiction was an apparent one merely; and so he retained both the absoluteness of the Aristotelian formulation, for the realm of being, and the probability theory, for the realm of existence; thus avoiding the fallacy of nominalism into

[73] See Ernest Nagel, *Principles of the Theory of Probability* (Chicago, University of Chicago Press, 1939), p. 5.

[74] Oddly enough, Aristotle had touched on the statistical approach only in a biological problem.

[75] See this chapter, D, i.

[76] See, for example, the work of Count Korzybskie.

which the greater part of his contemporaries were led through their mis-understanding of the Darwinian conception. To put the matter in another way, Darwin had destroyed Aristotelian realism, for the exhaustion of universals in things was no longer tenable once Darwin had demonstrated that biological species come into existence as a development from other species in time. The issue was forced to a choice between Platonic realism and nominalism. Peirce chose Platonic realism.

iii. THE SHORTCOMINGS OF NOMINALISM

Darwin was interpreted nominalistically by Peirce's contemporaries, as indicating the unreality of universals, which must be neither independent of nor external to the human mind. Chauncey Wright, one of Peirce's friends, in particular was "all enthusiasm for Darwin, whose doctrines appeared to him as a sort of supplement to those of Mill," (5.64) the archnominalist. But Peirce observed that the ideas of development would be the vine that would in time kill the tree of associationism, since "Mill's doctrine was nothing but a metaphysical point of view to which Darwin's, which was nourished by positive observation, must be deadly." For "the real science that Darwin was leading men to was sure some day to give a death-blow to the sham-science [and the "nominalism"] of Mill." (6.297)

The error of nominalism and the corresponding realism implied by the Darwinian theory are brought into high relief by the various subjective theories combated by evolution. Let us consider, for example, the problem of knowledge and its acquirement. Is it not that here, "besides ordinary experience which is dependent on there being a certain physical connection between our organs and the thing experienced, there is a second avenue of truth dependent only on there being a certain intellectual connection between our previous knowledge and what we learn in that way? Yes, this is true. Man has this faculty, just as opium has a somnific virtue; . . . How is the existence of this faculty accounted for? In one sense, no doubt, by natural selection. Since it is absolutely essential to the preservation of so delicate an organism as man's, no race which had it not has been able to sustain itself." (5.341) And the fitting of man into his natural environment, which we have seen is also the outcome of natural selection,[77] likewise accounts in part for the validity of sense experience: the doctrine of immediate perception is sustained through the "certain connection between our organs and the thing experienced."

[77] See this chapter, D, i.

Much the same criticism is made of the arbitrariness of belief. Although "there is no more striking characteristic of [the] dark ages, when thought was little developed, than the prevalence of a sentiment that an opinion was a thing to be chosen because one liked it . . . [yet]. Natural selection is against it; and it breaks down." (2.149) Presumably, the slow change evolved by cumulative facts is undeniable and unavoidable, not susceptible to will, whim, or fancy.

The doctrine that belief is not arbitrary but requires a cause was destined to play a sizable role in the development of Peirce's philosophy, and particularly in his psychology and studies of method. The Darwinian theory, as we have in fact already noted, was not alone in giving Peirce a turn away from nominalism and toward realism, but it was of substantial assistance in this regard.

iv. THE EXTENSION OF NATURAL SELECTION

According to natural selection theory, living things are adapted to a slowly changing environment, on a principle that itself either does not change or changes less slowly. Thus animals and plants are adapted "precisely" to their environment and kept in adaptation. (2.86) "Natural selection, as conceived by Darwin, is a mode of evolution in which the only positive agent of change in the whole passage from moner to man is fortuitous variation. To secure advance in a definite direction chance has to be seconded by some action that shall hinder the propagation of some varieties or stimulate that of others. In natural selection, strictly so called, it is the crowding out of the weak." (6.296)

In extending the application of Darwinism, great care must be taken to make the right interpretation. For instance, a literal reading of natural selection in ethics would produce exactly the gospel of greed according to which the modern politico-economic system works: by cut-throat competition. This has been the usual interpretation. But it is indeed possible that the derivation is the other way round, and that "The *Origin of Species* of Darwin merely extends politico-economical views of progress to the entire realm of animal and vegetable life. The vast majority of our contemporary naturalists hold the opinion that the true cause of those exquisite and marvelous adaptations of nature for which . . . men used to extol the divine wisdom, is that creatures are so crowded together that those of them that happen to have the slightest advantage force those less pushing into situations unfavorable to multiplication or even kill them before they reach the age of reproduction. Among animals, the mere mechanical individualism is vastly reinforced as a power making for good by the animal's ruthless greed. As Darwin puts it on his title-page, it is the struggle for existence; and he should have added for his motto: Every individual for himself, and the Devil take the hindmost! Jesus in his sermon on the Mount, expressed a different opinion." (6.293)

Clearly, then, a different interpretation of natural selection must be made for both ethics and cosmology, if the Darwinian theory is to be extended to other fields. We can account neither for the responsibility of the human being nor for the organization of the actual universe by the devil-take-the-hindmost hypothesis. Let us see, then, what other interpretation Peirce was able to put upon Darwin's work and what lesson he was finally able to draw from it.

In the first place, Darwin's theory and his means of arriving at it suggested a new importance for an old branch of logic, that described by Aristotle as *apagoge,* or, as Peirce preferred to call it, abduction or retroduction: an induction based on conjecture derived from experience. (2.755) "We are, doubtless, in the main logical animals, but we are not perfectly so. Most of us, for example, are naturally more sanguine and hopeful than logic would justify. We seem to be so constituted that in the absence of any facts to go upon we are happy and self-satisfied; so that the effect of experience is continually to contract our hopes and aspirations. Yet a lifetime of the application of this corrective does not usually eradicate our sanguine disposition. Where hope is unchecked by any experience, it is likely that our optimism is extravagant. Logicality in regard to practical matters (if this be understood, not in the old sense, but as consisting in a wise union of security with fruitfulness of reasoning) is the most useful quality an animal can possess, and might, therefore, result from the action of natural selection." (5.366)

Natural selection was responsible in large part for the emphasis Peirce came to place upon the ideas of evolution, growth, and chance. (6.613) We shall see in later chapters how much these ideas came to be central in his systematic philosophy. One of Peirce's most brilliantly original conceptions was suggested to him by the Darwinian hypothesis; namely, the idea that chance begets order. (6.297) Moreover, ideas of "time, space and force, even to the lowest intelligence, are such as to suggest that they are the results of natural selection." (6.418)

With the hard teachings of Kant, the discipline of the laboratory, and the sympathetic viewpoints of Duns Scotus and Darwin now behind him,

Peirce was ready to come to the fullness of his own philosophy by meeting the opposition of well-established proponents of contradictory views. He was ready to face the clearest and at the same time the most subtle of adversaries. His final development was to be achieved through the dialectical refutation of a philosophical position fundamentally contradictory to his own.

E. THE REVOLT AGAINST DESCARTES

It was Peirce's way to be far more concerned with the logical than with the temporal order. He chose his influences where he found them, deeming all historical figures alike with regard to their proponence of doctrine, despite considerations of chronology. Thus if Kant was his Teacher, and Duns Scotus his Friend, Descartes became his Adversary.

We now have the spectacle of a philosopher who started as a Kantian but who had come to realism through the influence of physical science and had found a permanent formulation suggested by the realistic philosophy of Duns Scotus. The final challenge to Peirce's position was to come from a study of the work of Descartes. Having surmounted that obstacle, the remainder of his labors was to consist in a consolidation and elaboration of his realistic metaphysics. Peirce was helped toward the development of his metaphysics by a complete rejection of the Cartesian philosophy. Peirce found himself in sympathy with almost nothing that Descartes had pronounced. "Descartes was a nominalist," (1.19)[78] for whom Peirce did not have even the respect he had for other nominalists, such as Ockham. (4.1) Descartes was a philosopher with a much exaggerated reputation. Much of the work with which Descartes has been credited is really due to the labors of Malebranche. (2.38) Especially does this hold true of logic. Despite the success attending Descartes's efforts in the field of geometry, he had abandoned that study because he deemed it useless. (1.75)

It is interesting to observe the similarities in the reactions of Vico and Peirce toward the Cartesian innovations. Vico was an eighteenth century thinker who saw the importance of the new empiricism without wishing to abandon what was valid in the scholastic philosophy.[79] But where Vico

---

[78] On the whole this is a fair accusation, and the Cartesian philosophy is fundamentally nominalistic on the subjective side. See, for instance, the statement that universals are "simply modes of thought," *Principles*, I, LVIII. But Descartes himself often inconsistently defended realism against other nominalists. See, for instance, his defense against the materialistic nominalism of Hobbes in the latter's attack upon Descartes's assumption of real universals in the *Third Set of Objections*, Obj. XIV. *Philosophical Works of Descartes*, trans. by Haldane and Ross (2 vols.) (Cambridge, 1934), vol. ii, pp. 76-77.

[79] See my "Toward the Recovery of G. Vico," in *Social Science*, 14 (1939), 31.

had endeavored to reconcile Descartes with the scholastics by borrowing from each what was of value, Peirce challenged the right of Descartes to speak for physical science and sought to deny his claims altogether in order to reconcile the scholastic philosophy with the philosophy of science. Important, then, in Peirce's development was a refutation of Descartes.

The gravamen of Peirce's charges against Descartes may be considered under the following topics: (i) false skepticism; (ii) the primacy of consciousness; (iii) the mystery of faith; (iv) the method of single inference. These Peirce emphasized by contrasting them with corresponding views of the scholastics.

i. AGAINST FALSE SKEPTICISM

Cartesianism "teaches that philosophy must begin with universal doubt;[80] whereas scholasticism had never questioned fundamentals." (5.264) Descartes considered that there are no absolutely certain ideas which prime consciousness, and hence established the fact of his own complete doubt as the most fundamental in all existence. He sought, following Augustine, to establish his metaphysics from this indubitable beginning. But, Peirce argued, Descartes's doubt is not really doubt, for "genuine doubt does not talk of *beginning* with doubt" (6.498) but rather *is* doubt itself. How can genuine doubt be self-conscious and yet be an all-embracing doubt? So Descartes does not start with doubt, as he supposes, but with self-consciousness; "there is one thing he will find himself unable to doubt, and that is, that he does doubt." (5.382 n.)

But that is not all. Descartes "professes to doubt the testimony of his memory"; (4.71) but "to make believe one does not believe anything is an idle and self-deceptive pretence." Further, Descartes pretended to doubt everything; but common sense cannot be doubted. There were some things which in fact Descartes pretended to doubt but could not. "You think that your *logica utens* is more or less unsatisfactory. But you do not doubt that there is *some* truth in it. Nor do I; nor does any man," said Peirce. (2.192) Doubt cannot be applied absolutely to ordinary knowledge in which one is convinced there reside partial truths. The last attack upon the doctrine of doubt as a beginning in philosophy has to do with the question of doubting that of which we know nothing. Peirce maintained that we must have a positive reason to doubt; (5.265) hence that which is not cognized is not subject to doubt.

In other words, the universal doubt which Descartes required for his

[80] *Meditations* I, *Principles* I, I.

first principle of inquiry in metaphysics is limited, first, by its inability to be applied to itself, secondly, by its inability to be applied to that of which there is some positive knowledge, and, thirdly, by its inability to be applied to that of which there does not exist any positive knowledge. This, the first part of Peirce's refutation, is logical; universal doubt is contradictory.

The second part of Peirce's refutation is psychological. Feigned skepticism, he maintained, is a false attitude; we must begin our philosophy "with all the prejudices which we actually have when we enter upon the study of philosophy" (5.265) for "these prejudices are not to be dispelled by a maxim." The situation reveals that our beliefs actually go much deeper than Descartes thought; for we do not truly doubt a thing by assuming an intellectually skeptical attitude toward it. "Let us not pretend to doubt in philosophy what we do not doubt in our hearts." Doubt must start where beliefs are held, if the doubt is to be genuine. But to pretend doubt where it does not exist is not to get anywhere with first principles. For "no one who follows the Cartesian method will ever be satisfied until he has formally recovered all those beliefs which in form he has given up."

ii. AGAINST THE PRIMACY OF CONSCIOUSNESS

Doubt is a mental act; whatever doubts must think, and the thinking thing must exist, at least while it thinks.[81] Descartes, again following Augustine, regarded his *cogito, ergo sum*[82] as "the first and most certain knowledge." "But," said Peirce, "what he means is that when one considers that one thinks, one at once perceives thereby that one exists. He thus makes the knowledge of one's existence an effect of the knowledge that one thinks."[83] Mathematics, the most exact of the sciences, begins with self-evident truths, or axioms; here, then, was the self-evident starting point for metaphysics. Against this avowed position of Descartes, Peirce strongly inveighed. Cartesianism "teaches that the ultimate test of certainty is to be found in the individual consciousness; whereas scholasticism had rested on the testimony of sages and of the Catholic Church." (5.264) Descartes followed the admirable purpose of seeking "to discard the practice of the schoolmen of looking to authority as the ultimate source of truth." (5.391) But in thinking that he had found "a natural fountain of true principles . . . in the human mind" he had jumped out of the frying pan and

[81] *Principles* I, VII; *Discourse*, IV.
[82] *De civitate Dei*, XI, 26.
[83] Review of William Turner, *History of Philosophy*, in *The Nation*, 79 (1904), 15.

landed in the fire. For rationality does not have to be apprehended by a mind in order to exist. Logic "is not obliged even so much as to *suppose* that there is consciousness." (2.66) Now to imagine "that there is any such objective entity as Rationality would be to break away from all modern thought from Descartes down." (2.157) Nevertheless, rationality does not consist in being known but rather "is [itself] being governed by final causes." (2.66)

Descartes, the instigator of psychophysical parallelism, had provided no natural bridge between *res cogitans* and *res extensa*.[84] Having found himself on the *res cogitans* side, Descartes was led, as Peirce noted, to deny the validity of the doctrine of immediate perception. (5.56) But "ordinary ideas of perception, which Descartes thought were most horribly confused, have nevertheless something in them . . . 'Seeing is believing' says the instinct of man." (5.593) Having started with consciousness, the result was pure subjectivism. Peirce said that Descartes was "aiming at a kind of truth which saying so can make to be so" (5.382 n.) and hence "attributed to the human mind the miraculous power of originating a category of thought that has no counterpart at all in Heaven or Earth." (5.63) To assert that whatever one is clearly convinced of is true is to abandon all tests of certainty beyond individual opinion. The assertion would lead the philosophers to agree that metaphysics is the most advanced science because they are the most certain scientists, but would lead them to agree on little else. (5.265)

Descartes appealed to *a priori* metaphysical principles, (1.624) "to the universality of certain truth as proving that they are not derived from observation," (2.370) another way of deriving them from consciousness. For the claim of *a priori*ty is only another way of saying that truths exist inalienably in consciousness, and that, as Descartes in fact does say, they come to consciousness from God. "Descartes and others have endeavored to bolster up the light of reason by make-believe arguments from the 'veracity of God' and the like. They had better not have pretended to call that in question which they intended to prove, since the proofs, themselves, call for the same light to make them evident." (2.28) God is called in as evidence to prove the existence of God, so that in turn His existence can make it possible for consciousness itself to account for the content of consciousness. God proves the only hope of those who would seek an objective justification for an extremely subjective position. Instead of the irrational ground of rationality, He is asked to become the rational ground of irrationality.

---

[84] *Meditations*, VI; *Principles*, I, VIII, and I, XLVIII.

The last argument of Descartes on this score is that for the criterion of the clarity and distinctness of ideas as a test of their truth.[85] It was not one that could fool Peirce, who discerned in it merely another costume in which to disguise the appeal to the *a priori* mental status of those subjective conceptions which Descartes wished to foster. A distinction of Duns Scotus proved apt in this regard. "Scotus distinguishes between conceiving confusedly and conceiving the confused." (2.392) Descartes, in Peirce's opinion, was clearly conceiving the confused.[86] "The celebrated criterion of clearness and distinctness, proposed by Descartes . . . was, as Hamilton says, 'nothing new,' since it was no more than an utterly unsuccessful attempt to define the old 'self-evidence' of the axioms of reason." (2.28)

Peirce concluded that the "old dualistic notion of mind and matter so prominent in Cartesianism, as two radically different kinds of substance, will hardly find defenders today." (6.24) Opposition to Descartes had thrown light upon the epistemological problem and indeed upon the whole mind-matter relation. Peirce could see that "There is nothing then, to prevent our knowing outward things as they really are." (5.311)

iii. AGAINST THE MYSTERY OF FAITH

The denial of immediate perception "led Cartesians to the utterly absurd theory of divine assistance." (5.56) "Scholasticism had its mysteries of faith, but undertook to explain all created things. But there are many facts which Cartesianism not only does not explain but renders absolutely inexplicable, unless to say that 'God makes them so' is to be regarded as an explanation." (5.264)

There is no causation in Descartes's philosophy except divine causation. Thus the objective religious infallibilism which reason ought to supplant (1.8) was supplanted in the Cartesian philosophy by a surreptitious objective religious infallibilism in subjective dress. True reasoning is not

[85] *Discourse*, IV; *Meditations*, III and IV; *Principles*, I, XXX, and I, XLIII. See the objections urged also by P. Gassendi against the validity of clarity and distinctness as criteria of truth, *Fifth Set of Objections*, Relative to Meditation III, 1, *Philosophical Works of Descartes*, vol. ii, pp. 151-152.

[86] Peirce held that Descartes's own theories violated the Cartesian canon since "They were not *clear and distinct*. Worse than that—for that, in itself, would not have been fatal—they were not capable of being made clear and distinct. Like the works of many other philosophers, at first glance they seemed beautifully sharp-outlined, but, when closely studied, they were found to be a composite of nebulae which no scrutiny could resolve. They wanted that fundamental perspicuity to which so few writers except mathematicians attain, which consists in this, that, unintelligible as they may seem at first reading, yet when they are closely studied they are seen to be based upon the distinctions which were pertinent to the problem"—Review of *Method and Results*, Thomas H. Huxley, in *The Nation*, 58 (1894), 34.

subjective altogether; it rather consists in reasoning from signs.[87] And reasoning from signs leads to conclusions which explain facts. But Descartes's divine causation only serves to render facts inexplicable. Descartes came forward to offer to men disgusted with scholasticism a new authority, that of reason. But by rendering reason subjective, he kept the dictation of principles arbitrary, and concealed within subjectivism the same unquestioning appeal to deity which his philosophy had ostensibly come to supplant. (6.542)

Descartes's argument runs somewhat as follows. After establishing the fact that we *are* because we *think*, the question arises as to what else we can know. Obviously, nothing else, so long as we are confronted with the notion of a deceiving God.[88] Since we are imperfect beings but have the notion of a perfect God, the notion cannot have been originally ours but must have been placed in us by God.[89] Therefore, a perfect God exists. "Descartes," Peirce quietly observed at this point, "makes God easier to know than anything else; for whatever we think He is, He is." (5.382 n.)[90] Now, since God cannot be a deceiver, since there really is a God, whatever we think is clear and distinct must be true. But again Peirce destroyed the argument by a simple logical acceptance of the general position. Very well, he said, but men have considered that theory, and thought it to be nonsense, and so it must be nonsense since they must be right! The whole refutation of the Cartesian theory of divine causation is nothing more or less than a refutation of the subjectivistic interpretation of reason. Reasoning may be a subjective process, but it has to do always with objective things. If there were no rational order to the universe, there would be nothing for men to reason about and consequently there would be no reason. But Descartes is wrong, and an objective rational order, concerning which we reason, does exist.

iv. AGAINST THE METHOD OF SINGLE INFERENCE

Even on the question of philosophical method, Peirce took Descartes to task. "The multiform argumentation of the middle ages is replaced [in Descartes] by a single thread of inference depending often upon inconspicuous premisses." (5.264) It will be recalled that the acceptance of

[87] Psychology rests on logic (3.432) and logic is the science of signs (1.559).

[88] *Meditations*, I.

[89] *Discourse*, IV.

[90] Descartes asserted that the knowledge of all other things depends on the knowledge of God (*Principles*, I, XIII), which would "make God easier to know than anything else." But Descartes did not draw the inference from his own argument, which Peirce saw was inherent in it.

Descartes's doubt left us with nothing but "a vague indescribable idea," (4.71) and an idea all off by itself is less than nothing at all. Relatedness is of the essence of truth; the meeting of an idea consists in its relations with other ideas. The first test of a scientific hypothesis is to show it to be noncontradictory with fact, but the final one consists in showing it to be self-consistent with the system of principles in science. "We never can attain absolute certainty; but such clearness and evidence as a truth can acquire will consist in its appearing to form an integral unbroken part of the great body of truth."

Scientific method resembles the scholastic rather than the Cartesian method in that the scientific method is dependent upon a great number of proofs rather than upon any one.[91] The image is not one of a chain no stronger than its weakest link but rather of a cable whose fibers are numerous and intimately connected. (5.265) The entire Cartesian position rests upon the strength of a single argument, but philosophy, following the example set by the schoolmen and scientists, should "trust rather to the multitude and variety of its arguments than to the conclusiveness of any one." (5.265) The weakness of the Cartesian method taught Peirce that what he had found the scientists doing was foreign to the pseudo-scientific philosophy of the nominalistic Descartes, but had much in common with the greater rationality of the realistic scholastics.

V. THE GENERAL SCHEME

In the foregoing sections we have noted just how and in what order Peirce's ideas developed, and just what were the chief influences upon him. In this and the preceding chapter we have not attempted to set forth any except the most important leading references. The system we shall be exhibiting from this point on is a logical, not a historical or psychological, affair. For the purposes of the system, the question of how Peirce came to his ideas is totally irrelevant: he could, for instance, have reached the same conclusions through other channels. Part One, which we have just succeeded in completing, is intended to aid only in the *understanding* of Peirce and his system. The remainder of this book will be devoted to the exposition of the philosophy that represents Peirce's attempt to get his ambition

---

[91] The assertion that a system should be dependent upon a great number of proofs rather than upon any one does not conflict with the earlier assertion (see this chapter C, ii) that systems hang upon a single premise. The latter point deals with the *structure* of systems; the former with their *proof*. There is nothing contradictory in the fact that a system which is structurally monistic may yet require a pluralistic proof.

fulfilled. Since we shall be leaving the personal aspects behind us with the present chapter, it may be well to point some of them out here for the last time.

Peirce emerged from his training as a full-blown philosopher with a gigantic philosophical ambition and a terrific personal humbleness. He greeted his reader, knowing him to be "one out of millions," (1.2) and thanked him for his wisdom and patience. For himself, he said he expected nothing, inasmuch as "he who would affect the future cannot paint the ground in front of him." Peirce wanted his philosophy to become a power in the world, and he well knew that "ideas utterly despised and frowned upon have an inherent power of working their way to the governance of the world, at last." (2.149) He was aware that he had done nothing except lay down certain lines of inquiry the pursuit of which must be the work of later generations; but then "it is not for an individual, nor for an age, to pronounce upon a fundamental question of philosophy. That is a task for a whole era to work out." (6.102) Of his own development he said that his ideas had been the industry of thirty years. (1.12) "I did not know as I ever should get to publish them, their ripening seemed so slow. But the harvest time has come, at last, and to me that harvest seems a wild one."

So indeed it was. Philosophy in Peirce's day had traveled a long way and was in a parlous state. It had, as he remarked, paid the usual tax upon inheritances from revolutions, having gone through the Renaissance, the Reformation, and the Copernican Revolution. "It has been a derelict on a vast ocean of surmise, drifting hither and thither, driven by storms, wrecked, shattered, its pieces dispersed even to opposite poles. Jetsam only is now occasionally cast up on the beaches of solid science, fraught with no cargo of wisdom except the one sad lesson of the issues of loose thinking." (2.13) As a consequence, Peirce's philosophical plans, like his great house, remained to the end "a lumber heap of unfulfilled ambitions."[92] The ideas, daring and original, were far-flung, but were never organized to show that self-consistent whole which they do indeed form.

In general Peirce described his philosophy as "the attempt of a physicist to make such conjecture as to the constitution of the universe as the methods of science may permit, with the aid of all that has been done by previous philosophers." (1.7) By the use of certain elementary ideas he endeavored to ground a cosmical theory, and from it to deduce a considerable number of consequences capable of being compared with experience. (6.35) It has been said by someone that all philosophies are suggested by either physical

[92] Jastrow, *op. cit.*

science or biological science; for, although Peirce did not neglect biology, physics was the starting point. As against leaning too heavily upon the findings of any one science, however, he offered the caution of fallibilism and the emphasis on method rather than on enshrined results. (1.13-14) He did not want to be followed blindly, for it is not individuals we should follow but rather the truths discovered by them. Peirce thus declined to "serve as bellwether." (1.11)

Despite the overwhelming modesty of this disavowal of personal leadership, his ambition was high. He viewed the social world that he lived in quite correctly as Aristotelian. Aristotle builded upon a few deliberately chosen concepts—such as matter and form, act and power—very broad, and in their outlines vague and rough, but solid, unshakable, and not easily undermined; and thence it has come to pass that Aristotelianism is babbled in every nursery, that "English Common Sense," for example, is thoroughly peripatetic, and that ordinary men live so completely within the house of the Stagyrite that whatever they see out the windows appears to them incomprehensible and metaphysical. (1.1) Yet, although Peirce insisted that the Aristotelian philosophy is thus responsible for perhaps the greater part of modern Western civilization, it does not any longer meet the requirements of new knowledge and advancing practice. "The old structure will not do for modern needs."

Peirce's general scheme, then, was nothing less than to supplant Aristotle, to furnish a new system of philosophy, comprised under a new set of categories, far-reaching enough to include both the truths of the Aristotelian philosophy and the new knowledge which has arisen since that work ceased to be entirely valid and broad. "Philosophy ought to be deliberate and planned out"; (1.179) the most fitting conclusion to this chapter will be to offer Peirce's plan as set forth in his own words. "The undertaking which this volume inaugurates is to make a philosophy like that of Aristotle, that is to say, to outline a theory so comprehensive that, for a long time to come, the entire work of human reason, in philosophy of every school and kind, in mathematics, in psychology, in physical science, in history, in sociology, and in whatever other department there may be, shall appear as the filling up of its details. . . . To erect a philosophical edifice that shall outlast the vicissitudes of time, my care must be, not so much to set each brick with nicest accuracy, as to lay the foundations deep and massive. . . . The first step toward this is to find simple concepts applicable to every subject." (1.1)

How well Peirce fulfilled this ambition is what we shall attempt to discover in the following chapters.

PART TWO

❮❮❮❮❯❯❯❯

A SYSTEM OF PEIRCE'S PHILOSOPHY

CHAPTER III

Logic

A. The Foundations of Logic

MORE THAN ONE SCHOLAR HAS OBSERVED THAT, ALTHOUGH LOGIC WAS PEIRCE'S favorite study, his conclusions on this topic do not constitute a system. Peirce was not unaware of this difficulty, for he once said that although his thoughts on logic consisted of "outcroppings here and there of a rich vein . . ." and "most of it has been written down; no human being could ever put together the fragments, I could not myself do so."[1] Most of the technical aspects of his logical work were of a pioneer nature. The accomplishment was a brilliant one, but Peirce has in general been surpassed in this field by later logicians. His symbols have not been generally adopted, although many of his conceptions remain, in another dress, in the work of other men. However, in the services rendered to philosophy by logic we find that Peirce's contribution is inestimable and has in no wise been superseded. "The chief advantages of the new systems of formal logic" are the "broad and philosophical aperçus" that they make possible, as Peirce himself remarked.[2] Therefore, in dealing with the logic from a broad philosophical point of view, we have the justification that Peirce's own ultimate interest lay in the same direction.

i. CLASSICAL THEORIES

Before establishing his own theory of the foundations of logic, Peirce felt obliged to consider and to give sufficient arguments for rejecting certain of the classical theories of logic which found defenders in his own day. The twelve theories which Peirce rejected held that logic is founded on subjective feeling, on the natural light of reason, on philosophy, on psychology, on the data of psychology, on epistemology, on philology, on the order of society,

---

[1] *Collected Papers*, vol. ii, p. xii.
[2] Review of Jevons, *Studies in Deductive Logic*, in *The Nation*, 32 (1881), 227, quoted by Buchler.

on the authority of the Church, on the history of science, on individual experience, and on facts reasoned about.

Against Sigwart and Schröder, Peirce argued that logic is not founded on subjective feeling. (2.19) Even if rationality *rested* on feelings, that would not mean that it *consisted* of feelings, any more than the Pope's *ex cathedra* pronouncements of what is pleasing to God are supposed to mean that God's being pleased has no other reality than the Pope's pronouncements. (2.158) Feelings are good or bad, while reasoning is perfect or imperfect. There are no false feelings, and reasoning is not good or bad. (2.151) Hegel traced logic back to thought, thus overlooking what the English logicians knew as Fact. (2.157) But "no judgment can judge itself to be true, and no reasoning can conclude that it is itself sound." (5.86) Arguments have to be weighed "by recognizable marks into those which have different orders of validity, and has to afford means for measuring the strength of arguments." (2.203) "In all reasoning, therefore, there is a more or less conscious reference to a general method." (2.204)

Against the Aristotelians, Peirce argued that logic is not founded upon the natural light of reason. The light of reason proves to be another name for self-evidence. (2.26) But self-evidence requires a retrogression to "a first demonstration reposing upon an indemonstrable premiss." (2.27) To call upon the veracity of God to bolster self-evidence, as Descartes does, is to "call that in question which they intended to prove, since the proofs, themselves, call for the same light to make them evident." (2.28) Reason cannot challenge its own pronouncements. Thus the criterion of inconceivability, proposed for ascertaining whether or not a proposition is necessarily true, consists in trying whether or not its denial is inconceivable. As Mill says, "the history of science teems with inconceivabilities which have been conquered." (2.29) The denial comes not from the light of reason but from fact.

Against "some writers," Peirce argued that logic is not founded upon a philosophical basis. If logic were founded upon metaphysics, metaphysics could not be founded upon logic, and "a metaphysics not founded on the science of logic is of all branches of scientific inquiry the most shaky and insecure, and altogether unfit for the support of so important a subject as logic." (2.36)[3] Thus, since "metaphysics ought to be founded upon logic," (2.168) logic cannot be founded upon metaphysics.

Against Wolf and Mill, Peirce argued that logic is not founded upon

[3] See further, this chapter, A, ii.

psychology. Logic arises from the temporal circumstances of thinking (2.710) but cannot be held down to the sequence of thoughts. To suppose this a "shallow" doctrine (5.28) assumes that "how we *ought* to think can be ascertained in no other way than by reflection upon those psychological laws which teach us how we *must needs* think." (2.47) "But because there is nothing to be said against our thinking in a certain way, in subconscious thought, when we cannot do otherwise, it does not, at all, follow that we ought to think in that way when we have our choice between several ways of thinking." But if Mill means conscious thought, then he is appealing to a category in which the criterion of clarity, which reduces back to that of inconceivability, plays an important role. The conclusion of the syllogism, if Sortes is a man, and all men are mortal, then Sortes must be mortal, does not conclude that "Sortes *ought to be thought* mortal. . . . Mill's *Logic* certainly says no such thing. What [the treatises on logic] all say is that Sortes must *be* mortal. Logical treatises never say anything about what 'ought to be thought'." (2.50; 2.52) "At any rate, a knowledge of the processes of thinking, even if it were at hand, would be entirely irrelevant to that sort of knowledge of the nature of our reasonings which it is incumbent upon us to have in order that we may give them our deliberate approval." (2.185) "All the psychology in the world will leave the logical problem just where it was" (5.172) for there is a sharp distinction between reasoning and the relations between the facts from which reasoning starts and the facts it infers. (2.599)

Against other authors, Peirce argued that logic is not founded upon the data of psychology. The data of psychology with respect to this problem consists in self-observation of how we think. But "logic is not the science of how we *do* think; but, in such sense as it can be said to deal with thinking at all, it only determines how we *ought* to think . . . in order to think what is true." (2.52) Herbart is right when he says that "a *thought*, in the sense in which alone logic deals with thoughts, is not a thinking but that which a thinking brings before the mind." (2.53) Further, it must be admitted that "numerical computation is reasoning," yet there are machines that perform such computation without having any data of psychology to offer. (2.56-59) And again, "a syllogism in *Barbara* virtually takes place when we irritate the foot of a decapitated frog." (2.711)

Against Wundt and Erdmann, Peirce argued that logic is not founded upon epistemology. Epistemology is concerned with whether or not we have knowledge of reality. But "whether or not there is, at all, any such thing as Reality, the logician need not decide. He cannot hide from himself, any more than another man can, that objects very nearly like real things there are; and he cannot pretend to doubt it." (2.64) For "logic is obliged to suppose (it need not assert) that there is knowledge embodied in some form, and that there is inference, in the sense that one embodiment of knowledge affects another." The theory of cognition is concerned with consciousness, while logic "is not obliged even so much as to *suppose* that there is consciousness." (2.66)

Against Steinthal and Sayce, Peirce argued that logic is not founded upon philology. Logicians have been in the habit of considering propositions only when these have been expressed in standard forms. But the standard forms chosen have been suggested by a narrow class of languages. (2.669-670) Those who would found logic upon language have in mind a small group of closely similar languages: the European. (2.68) Others who contend that to change language means also to change logic are indicating certain psychological necessities and tendencies, with which logic has already been shown to have nothing to do. (2.338)

Against Pearson, Peirce argued that logic is not founded upon the existing order of society. Here all the previous objections apply, as well as "some others" not given. (2.71) For instance, in Pearson's sense of society as an aggregate of individuals, the objections to the data of psychology, already raised above, apply *mutatis mutandis* to social psychology. Then again, Peirce probably had in mind that, since the character, profound as well as superficial, of existing society is something that undergoes a rapid process of change, it would not be able to support a relatively stable logic.

Against the medieval logicians, Peirce argued that logic is not founded upon the authority of the Church. The Church argues that what seems absurd cannot really be so, since the Church declares it to be true. (2.72) "Authority, from the nature of things, cannot *advance* knowledge." (2.73; 5.358 ff.)

Against Whewell, Peirce argued that logic is not founded upon the history of science. "We also have to ask," he says, "whether the facts are sufficiently numerous to lend any great certainty to an induction." (2.74) If logic is to be based on probable reasonings, then the history of science will "have great weight"; but it will not if we mean by logic the demonstration that its reasoning from initial assumptions must be accepted. (2.213)

Against Abbé Gratry, Peirce argued that logic is not founded upon direct individual experience. But if every inference "be due to a direct inspiration of the Holy Spirit . . . consistency would require us to grant that the admission of a logical principle, which covers an infinity of possible inferences, is also a mystical experience," (2.21) and we would be no further than we were before. Moreover, some experiences are those which we resist having. What we may take at first to be a shadow on the floor of the barn may turn out to be a large black snake. "Were Gratry right, then, every inductive reasoning which passes from observation of the finite and the discrete to belief in the infinite or the continuous ought to be accompanied by the sense that that belief was forced upon me, whether I will or no." (2.22) Logic may start from direct experience but is founded on something else.

Finally, against Read,[4] Peirce argued that logic is not founded upon "facts concerning the things reasoned about. There is certainly this to be said in favor of the last opinion, namely, that the question of the validity of any kind of reasoning is the question how frequently a conclusion of a certain sort will be true when premisses of a certain sort are true; and this is a question of fact, of how things are, not of how we think. But, granted that the principles of logic are facts, how do they differ from other facts? For facts, in this view, should separate themselves into two classes, those of which logic itself takes cognizance and those which, if needed, have to be set up in the premisses. It is just as if we were to insist that the principles of logic were facts; in that case we should have to distinguish between the facts which the court would lay down and those which must be brought out in the testimony. What, then, are the facts which logic permits us to dispense with stating in our premisses? Clearly those which may always be taken for granted: namely, those which we cannot consistently doubt, if reasoning is to go on at all: for example, all that is implied in the existence of doubt and of belief, and of the passage from one to the other, of truth and falsehood, of reality, etc. Mr. Read, however, recognizes no such distinction between logical principles and other facts."[5]

ii. PEIRCE'S THEORY

"Everyday experience, such as presses in upon every man, at every hour of his life, is open to no other doubt than that it may not have been correctly formulated in general terms. This must be the main source of what little matter of fact logic has occasion to assert." (2.75) The "positive, categorical truth" (5.39) which logic does assert rests upon "certain facts of experience" (5.110) which are themselves positive.[6] But if logic is to take its

---

[4] Carveth Read, *The Theory of Logic* (London, 1878).

[5] *Ibid.*, reviewed by Peirce in *The Nation*, 28 (1879), 234.

[6] Letter to Francis C. Russell, quoted by Paul Carus in *The Monist*, 20 (1910), 45. In one place Peirce argued that logic is only "an explanation of the *suppositio communis*." (5.320) But logic cannot be based upon *logica utens*, or the "general idea" which "every reasoner has . . . of what good reasoning is," (2.186) unless reasoning was never bad. But the badness of some reasoning in everyone argues for the necessity of a "*logica docens*," or scientific system of logic. (2.204-205) And the *logica docens* cannot be based on the *suppositio communis*.

start from positive-fact and endeavor to formulate that fact in general terms, the generality must be elicited from the fact. Peirce provided the method. "If a given habit, considered as determining an inference, is of such a sort as to tend toward the final result, it is correct; otherwise not. Thus inferences become divisible into the valid and the invalid; and thus logic takes its reason of existence." (3.161) By habit here is meant not merely psychological habit but the evidence of regularity in all things. The regularity is as irreducible as any single fact, and must be reckoned with as itself a fact. "That belief gradually tends to fix itself under the influence of inquiry is, indeed, one of the facts with which logic sets out." (2.693)

Logic, then, takes its start in stubborn fact; but its nature is akin to mathematics. Although "the boundary between some parts of logic and pure mathematics in its modern treatment is almost evanescent," (2.215) "the chief source of logical truth, though never recognized by logicians . . . must be the same as the source of mathematical truth." (2.76) There is no conflict between these two aspects of logic, for even "in mathematical reasoning there is a sort of observation" (2.216) of the relations which, for instance, a diagram reveals.

But if logic is obtained from fact and resembles mathematics, we should expect it to be close to ontology, for these relationships could both prevail only in a study occupied with the widest possible categories. Actually, the question of which comes first, logic or some other branch of philosophy, such as ontology—considered either logically or philosophically—was one Peirce was never able finally to decide. Sometimes he was sure that "*logic is based on phenomenology,*[7] as when he states that logic ought to be the science of thirdness in general"; (1.539)[8] and again when he states that logic starts with what-is but seeks what-ought-to-be, (5.39) while at other times he was equally sure that the opposite is true. "Metaphysics [i.e., ontology (1.192)] consists in the results of the absolute acceptance of logical principles not merely as regulatively valid, but as truths of being"; (1.487) "the metaphysical conceptions . . . are merely adapted from those of formal logic, and therefore can only be apprehended in the light of a minutely accurate and thorough-going system of formal logic." (1.625) Elsewhere he is doubtful of the importance of the distinction, holding that the extent of the application of logic to metaphysics is secondary to the selection of the proper conceptions in logic. (1.301) In his classification of the sciences, Peirce

---

[7] See the argument in this chapter, A, i, against "some writers."
[8] Thirdness is one of the three principal ontological categories of Peirce. See chap. IV, B, iii.

decided that logic is a subdivision of normative science, normative science being on a par with metaphysics. (1.186; 1.191)

If we confine our consideration for the moment to Peirce's own logic and ontology, it becomes clear that ontologically there is no reason for distinguishing between the two topics, but that logically there is. From the point of view of logic, the categories of being involve an application of logic, they are not the presuppositions of logic; ontology is merely one of many fields to which logic can be applied. From the point of view of ontology, the theory of signs and illative relations involves a part of ontological being rather than the mere application of ontology; the subject matter of logic is one of the three exhaustive and mutually exclusive fields into which all being can be divided.

But if there is no distinction between logic and ontology in any but a logical sense, then logic presupposes an objective truth, for ontology in Peirce's sense does so; and the study of logic shows that there must be at least one answer to every question, "one answer which is decidedly right, whatever people may think about it." (2.135) Truth is objective, and objective truth is of two kinds: propositions concerning possible conditions and propositions concerning positive fact. "There is such a thing as a proposition correct whatever may be opinions about it"; (2.137) as to any question of fact, "experience alone can settle it." But in either case, "the essence of truth lies in its resistance to being ignored." (2.139) Reasoning deals with propositions rather than with facts, since facts belong to the past and present, while "all conclusions of reasoning partake of the general nature of expectations of the future." (2.145)[9] "The past is actual fact. But a general (fact) cannot be fully realized. It is a potentiality; and its mode of being is *esse in futuro*. The future is potential, not actual." (2.148) Thus the logical ground of reasoning is nothing other than the objectivity of truth plus the assumption that nothing in the future will refute it, that, in short, there is a logic which is independent both of reasoning and of fact.

Since logic is independent of reasoning and fact, we should not expect it to start with axioms based on reasoning nor to rely on reasonings containing facts. Nor does it. "The fundamental principles of formal logic are not properly axioms, but definitions and divisions; and the only *facts* which it contains relate to the identity of the conceptions resulting from those processes with certain familiar ones." (3.149) We may, then, proceed to an exposition of the definitions and divisions of logic. These, Peirce held, revolve around the functions of signs.

[9] See below, chap. VI, D, iii.

"A sign," says Peirce, "is something which stands to somebody for something in some respect or capacity." (2.228) Since all logic, in one way or another, treats of signs as so defined, logic in Peirce's sense is "the science of the general necessary laws of signs," (1.191; 2.93) "the science of . . . true representation;" (1.539) it is "only another name for *semiotic* (σημειωτική), the quasi-necessary, or formal doctrine of signs." (2.227)[10] It operates as the "study of the theory of inquiry," (2.106) as "the theory of *right* reasoning, of what reasoning ought to be, not of what it is," (2.7) and therefore as "the theory of the conditions which determine reasonings to be secure." (2.1) Peirce has named three subdivisions of logic to cover the three references of the sign (i.e., in some *respect* for *something* to *somebody*). These are: Speculative Grammar (following Duns Scotus, 2.206; 1.444) or "the general theory of the nature and meaning of signs; Critical Logic (following Kant, 2.205), which classifies arguments and determines the validity of each kind;" and finally Speculative Rhetoric or Methodeutic, which "studies the methods that ought to be pursued in the investigation, in the exposition, and in the application of truth." (1.191)[11] Speculative Grammar deals with the general theory of *signs*; Critical Logic, or Critic, with the relevancy of arguments to *truth*; and Speculative Rhetoric with the *communication* of reasoning and the discovery of truth.

Of this threefold division of logic, chiefly the first and second parts treat of the traditional, or "Aristotelian," logic: the form of the syllogism, and the types and degrees of the validity of reasoning, including deduction and induction. The first division, with the old name revived for it by Peirce, embraces, besides terms and propositions, the study of signs in so far as they bear the meanings of relations. Together with the second division, it includes the field of what is now called symbolic or mathematical logic. Peirce has widened the second division to include the study of necessary implication and probable inference. The third division carries an old name also, the name for an old study which it was Peirce's intention to resuscitate and revitalize: the study of Speculative Rhetoric. It is concerned with "the laws by which . . . one sign gives birth to another," (2.229) with the power inherent in ideas of working themselves out in fact. It includes modern semantics, pragmatics, and scientific method, or the logic of discovery.

"Each division," Peirce tells us, "depends on that which precedes it." (1.192) Properly, then, we shall begin with an examination of Speculative Grammar.

---

[10] Following Locke, *Essay*, IV, xxi, 4.
[11] See also 1.559, 2.93, and 2.229.

B. Speculative Grammar

Speculative Grammar is, as we have seen, the first and most fundamental of Peirce's three main divisions of logic. All logic has to do with the "reference of symbols in general to their objects," (1.559) and Speculative Grammar treats particularly of the meaning of signs or symbols, "that is, of the reference of symbols in general to their grounds," "the formal conditions of symbols having meaning." (4.116)

i. THE FORMAL DOCTRINE OF SEMIOTIC

Logic in general is the science of signs, and the science of signs is, Peirce tells us—in an effort to show that he means something exact by the use of the term "science" in this connection, an observational one. To Peirce, all the sciences, and even mathematics, are observational. Signs as such are products of abstraction; and "as to that process of abstraction, it is itself a sort of observation." (2.227) The researcher constructs in his imagination the sort of ideal which he seeks, "a sort of skeleton diagram or outline sketch," and considers "what modifications the hypothetical state of things would require to be made in that picture" and then "examines it, that is, observes what he has imagined." The process is the same for all sciences, despite its effort to discover "what must be and not merely what is in the actual world."

A sign is "anything which determines something else (its *interpretant*) to refer to an object to which itself refers (its *object*)." (2.303) A sign, called the *representamen*, in every case is used to "stand for an object independent of itself." (1.538) It stands for something, its *object*. It stands for an object to somebody (or something) in whom it arouses a more developed sign, the *interpretant*. And, finally, a sign stands for an object to an interpretant in some respect, that is, it represents the "common characters" of the object, (2.418) and this respect is called the *ground*. A representamen can only stand for an object where there is some capacity for the interpretant. Otherwise there is no representation; for the object of direct acquaintance is something which is never conveyed by logic. The representamen, or sign, stands for the object only where the intrinsic element is taken for granted respecting the object. "The sign can only represent the object and tell about it. It cannot furnish acquaintance with or recognition of that object; for that is what is meant in this volume by the object of a sign; namely, that with which it presupposes an acquaintance in order to convey some further information concerning it." (2.231)

Representamen, object, interpretant, and ground are names to explain the semiotic function or relation of significance. This relation is triadic, (2.233) and depends primarily on representamen, object, and interpretant. According to Peirce, triadic relations of signs are the most basic kind; the dyadic relations themselves presuppose the triadic relation. "To exemplify what is meant, the dyadic relations of logical *breadth* and *depth*, often called denotation and connotation, have played a great part in logical discussions, but these take their origin in the triadic relation between a sign, its object, and its interpretant sign." (3.608) We are more familiar with dyadic relations, but these depend upon triads. "To give a good and complete account of the dyadic relations of concepts would be impossible without taking into account the triadic relations which, for the most part, underly them." The point is that the dyadic relations of logic are dyadic relations among signs which are themselves triads.

There are three divisions of triadic relations. These are: (*a*) "triadic relations of comparison," or logical possibilities, based on the kind of sign; (*b*) "triadic relations of performance," or actual facts, based on the kind of ground; and (*c*) "triadic relations of thought," or laws, based on the kind of object. (2.234)

(*a*) The first trichotomy of signs gives us the *qualisign*, "a quality which is a sign"; (2.244) the *sinsign*, "an actual existent thing or event which is a sign"; (2.245) and the *legisign*, "a law that is a sign." (2.246) The qualisign "cannot actually act as a symbol until it is embodied; but the embodiment has nothing to do with its character as a sign." (2.244) Since a sinsign, the sign of "being only once," is an actual thing or event "and can only be so through its qualities, it involves a qualisign or qualisigns." (2.245) Similarly, legisigns act as signs through their applications; "thus every legisign requires sinsigns." (2.246)

(*b*) The second trichotomy of signs consists of the *icon*, a sign which refers to an object by virtue of characters of its own which it possesses whether the object exists or not (2.247); the *index*, "a sign which refers to the object that it denotes by virtue of being really affected by that object"; (2.248) and the *symbol*, "a sign which refers to the object that it denotes by virtue of a law, usually an association of general ideas, which operates to cause the symbol to be interpreted as referring to that object." (2.249)

The icon is a sign "by virtue of characters which belong to it in itself as a sensible object, and which it would possess just the same were there no object in nature that it resembled, and though it never were interpreted as a sign." (4.447) "That is, a quality that it has *qua* thing renders it fit to be a representamen. Thus, anything is fit to be a *substitute* for anything that it is like." (2.276) "The icon has no dynamical connection with the object it represents; it simply happens that its qualities resemble those of that object," (2.299) and so it represents a mere relation between sign and thing signified. (1.372) "Unless there really is such an object, the icon does not act as a sign, but this has nothing to do with its character as a sign" (2.247) for it "would possess the character which renders it significant even though its object had no existence." (2.304) But despite this independence of the icon from its object, "Anything whatever . . . is an icon of anything, in so far as it is like that thing and used as a sign of it." (2.247) The functioning of an icon as a sign is dependent upon its capability of similarity of structure.

The index "is a real thing or fact which is a sign of its object by virtue of being connected with it as a matter of fact." (4.447) A genuine index and its object must be existent individuals (whether things or facts) and its immediate interpretant must be of the same character. The index refers to its object "by virtue of being really affected by that object . . . In so far as the index is affected by the object, it necessarily has some quality in common with the object, and it is in respect to [this] that it refers to the object." (2.248) Hence "the index is physically connected with its object" (2.299) and "they make an organic pair." An index "is a sign which would, at once, lose the character which makes it a sign if its object were removed, but would not lose that character if there were no interpretant." (2.304) Indices have three characteristics which distinguish them from other signs. They "have no significant resemblance to their objects . . . they refer to individuals . . . they direct the attention to their objects by blind compulsion." (2.306) "A rap on the door is an index. Anything which focuses the attention is an index. Anything which startles us is an index, in so far as it marks the junction between two portions of experience." (2.285)

"Because compulsion is essentially *hic et nunc*, the occasion of the compulsion can only be represented to the listener by compelling him to have experience of that same occasion. Hence it is requisite that there should be a kind of sign which shall act dynamically upon the hearer's attention [although the latter need have only a problematical existence (2.334)] and direct it to a special object. Such a sign I call an index" (2.336) and the whole event is an assertion. To distinguish the reference of a sign from the fictitious world to the real world an index is needed. (2.337) Thus "one index, at least, must form a part of every assertion." An index, of course, need not be a noun or even a part of spoken or written language; "it may be a mere look or gesture." (2.338) But in any case, the index serves by force to assert the existence of that to which it refers. Assertion, which is present in **every** index, points by compulsion to something real in the actual world.

The symbol is "a representamen whose representative character consists precisely in its being a rule that will determine its interpretant." (2.292) The symbol is a sign whose nature ensures that it will be interpreted as a sign. (2.308) Its "fitness to represent just what it does represent lies in nothing but the very fact of there being a habit, disposition, or other effective general rule that it will be so interpreted." (4.447) The symbol has a triple reference to its object. It refers directly to its object; indirectly to its ground through its object; and to its interpretant through its object. (2.418) "The symbol is connected with its object by virtue of the . . . symbol-using mind, without which no such connection would exist." (2.299) It should be well understood, however, that "symbol-using mind" is not to be taken as equivalent to "human mind." Such minds are not confined to human beings theoretically, since it is conceivable that a higher animal, or even a machine, could be made to respond to certain symbols. Moreover, "symbol-using mind" is not to be construed subjectively, since the mind is a factor in the life of the symbol but not its creator. The symbol "is a law, or regularity of the indefinite future." (2.293) It denotes a "kind of thing" (2.301) rather than any particular thing. "Symbols grow;" (2.302) "they come into being by development out of other signs, particularly from icons" but they lead a life of their own.[12]

In order to illustrate the relation between the three classes of signs which Peirce has determined as grounds, let us consider the icon, index, and symbol in a single relationship or signification. The ground of a sign may "consist in the sign's having some character in itself, or in some existential relation to that object, or in its relation to an interpretant." (2.243) More particularly, "Take, for instance, 'it rains.' Here the icon is the mental composite photograph of all the rainy days the thinker has experienced. The index is all whereby he distinguishes *that day*, as it is placed in his experience. The symbol is the mental act whereby [he] stamps that day as rainy." (2.438) It may be necessary to emphasize that not all symbols are mental any more than all icons have actual objects which they resemble.

(*c*) The third trichotomy of signs consists of the *rheme*, a sign which represents a possible object, (2.250) the *dicent* (or *dicisign*), a sign which represents an actual object, (2.251) and the *argument*, a sign which represents a legal object. (2.252)

The rheme is "a sign which, for its interpretant, is a sign of qualitative

[12] For other explanations of icon, index, and symbol, see 4.531 and 6.471.

possibility, that is, is understood as representing such and such a kind of possible object." (2.250)[13] A rheme may afford information although it is not so interpreted. Another name for rheme is "seme." (4.538)

The dicisign, or proposition, is "a sign which, for its interpretant, is a sign of actual existence." (2.251) One characteristic of the dicisign is that it "*conveys* information, in contradistinction to a sign [such as an icon] from which information may be derived." (2.309) But perhaps "the readiest characteristic test showing whether a sign is a dicisign or not is that a dicisign is either true or false, but does not directly furnish reasons for its being so." (2.310) Another name for dicisign is "pheme." (4.538)

The argument is "a sign which, for its interpretant, is a sign of law." (2.252) It "represents the interpretant, called its *conclusion*, which it is intended to determine." (2.95) "An argument is a sign whose interpretant represents its object as being an ulterior sign through a law, namely, the law that the passage from all such premisses to such conclusions tends to the truth." (2.263)

Using the three trichotomies of signs, Peirce proceeded to construct, by combination, ten classes of signs. He discovered that these could be so arranged in a table that their possible valid combinations would be evident. Writing the three trichotomies in vertical columns, we get[14]

	Sign	*Ground*	*Object*
First	qualisign (1)	icon (4)	rheme (7)
Second	sinsign (2)	index (5)	dicisign (8)
Third	legisign (3)	symbol (6)	argument (9)

From these nine signs, ten possible valid combinations can be obtained by observing two simple rules. These are: (*a*) no sign may be combined with any sign in the same column and (*b*) no sign may be combined with any sign to the right and below it.

The ten classes of signs are: 369, 368, 367, 358, 357, 347, 258, 257, 247, and 147. They may be illustrated as follows: an argument symbolic legisign (369) by a syllogism; a dicent symbol legisign (368) by a proposition; a

[13] In modern symbolic logic, a propositional function.
[14] I owe this table to Professor Paul Weiss.

rhematic symbol legisign (367) by a logical term; a dicent indexical legisign (358) by a street cry; a rhematic indexical legisign (357) by a demonstrative pronoun; a rhematic iconic legisign (347) by a diagram, apart from its factual individuality; a dicent indexical sinsign (258) by a weathercock; a rhematic indexical sinsign (257) by a spontaneous cry; a rhematic iconic sinsign (247) by an individual diagram; and a rhematic iconic qualisign (147) by a feeling of "red." (2.254-263)

Peirce himself showed the combinations between these ten classes in the following diagram. The "heavy boundaries between adjacent squares are appropriated to classes alike in only one respect. All other adjacent squares pertain to classes alike in two respects. Squares not adjacent pertain to classes alike in one respect only, except that each of the three squares of the vertices of the triangle pertains to a class differing in all three respects from the classes to which the squares along the opposite side of the triangle are appropriated. The lightly printed designations are superfluous." (2.264)

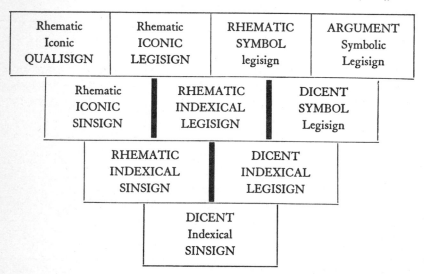

From the individual trichotomies, together with additional rules, Peirce developed ten trichotomies and sixty-six classes of signs. (2.243 n.) The fact is that anything which can be isolated and then interpreted in its connections with other things can be considered in its capacity as a sign. Since this is true of all things, anything can be a sign. In Peirce's system of logic, there are many signs, but the chief trichotomic sets are established with a definite purpose. We shall see one set—the representamen, its object, and interpretant—become the basis of logic. Another group—the qualisign, sinsign, and legisign—suggests the primary categories of ontology.[15] A third—the icon, index, and symbol—will be developed into the leading notions in epistemology.[16] And a fourth—the rheme, dicisign, and argument—will be used in psychology.[17] Thus we see confirmed in practice Peirce's theory that logic is itself logically primary, the first philosophical study. What the combined signs lead to will be developed in later sections of this chapter, and, to a greater extent, in later chapters of this book.

The objective and independent nature of signs, so far as the question of knowledge is concerned, is likewise confirmed in Peirce's system, since the representation of an object by a sign in no wise depends upon its being known. Where human consciousness, or awareness, is involved in the recognition of representation by a sign, that consciousness is one kind of exemplification of a process to which it is, however, not essential.[18]

ii. SIGNS AND TERMS

"A term," says Peirce, "is a sign which leaves its object, and *a fortiori* its interpretant, to be what it may." (2.95) "The logical term, which is a class-name, is a seme" (4.538) or rheme. "Any symbol which may be a direct constituent of a proposition is called a *term*." (2.328) Terms are "symbols which directly determine only their *grounds* or imputed qualities." (1.559) Predicates are terms, as are class-names. (2.341)

"What is a 'term' or 'class-name,' supposed to be? It is something which signifies, or . . . 'connotes' certain characters, and thereby denotes whatever possesses those characters." (2.341) The most important "factors of the import of a term" (2.391) are those of comprehension (i.e., connotation) and extension (i.e., denotation). Peirce regarded this distinction,[19] as "the turning

[15] See chap. IV, B.

[16] See chap. V, A.

[17] See chap. VI, A.

[18] "Every thought is a sign" (1.538; 5.253) but not every sign is a thought. Subjectivism or psychologism is easily avoided in Peirce's logic in that the category of signs is greatly wider than that of thoughts. Of a legisign Peirce says, "This law is usually established by men." (2.246) Usually—but not always or necessarily. Again, the interpretant is a second "and more developed" sign created by the representamen in the mind of "somebody." (2.228) It is clear that Peirce's emphasis is on the arousal of a sign by a sign, and that "somebody" means anybody, or anything, capable of receiving a sign. Where the semiotic relation becomes a series, the "interpretant becoming in turn a sign," (2.303) "no doubt, intelligent consciousness must enter into the series," since nothing else, as far as we have been able to discover, is capable of receiving such developed signs as the hierarchy of representation produces; yet even here participation by intelligent consciousness is only an element in the relation and not its determining factor.

[19] Derived from the *Port Royal Logic*.

point of logic." (2.400 n.2) Comprehension (usually now called intension) is equivalent to the logical definition or meaning of a term, while extension is equivalent to its range of application or inclusion. Peirce accepted the law of the inverse proportionality of extension and comprehension, and stated it as follows: "If a and b are logical terms so related that $a = bx$, then also $b = a + y$ and conversely." (2.400 n.1)

Another notion which Peirce considered important in connection with the understanding of terms is that of *information*. Since "logic treats of the reference of symbols in general to their objects," (2.418) "a symbol, in its reference to its object, has a triple reference": these are "to its object, or the real things which it represents"; "to its ground through its object, or the common characters of those objects"; and "to its interpretant through its object, or all the facts known about its object. What are thus referred to, so far as they are known, are: First, the informed *breadth*[20] of the symbol [i.e., its extension]; Second, the informed *depth* of the symbol [i.e., its intension]; and Third, the sum of synthetical propositions in which the symbol is subject or predicate, or the *information* concerning the symbol." Peirce in this last category has thus endeavored "to make out a third quantity of terms" (2.364) called "information," defined in logic as "the measure of predication." (2.418 n.)

For extension and comprehension, Peirce thus uses *breadth* and *depth* respectively. (2.407)[21] In addition to the *informed*, Peirce set up the *essential* and the *substantial*. (2.409) The *informed breadth* of a term is "all the real things of which it is predicable, with logical truth on the whole in a supposed state of information." (2.407) The *essential breadth* of a term is "those real things of which, according to its very meaning, a term is predicable." (2.412) The *"substantial breadth* is the aggregate of real substances of which alone a term is predicable with absolute truth." (2.414) The *informed depth* of a term is "all the real characters (in contradistinction to mere names) which can be predicated of it (with logical truth on the whole) in a supposed state of information, no character being counted twice over knowingly in the supposed state of information." (2.408) The *essential depth* of a term is "the really conceivable qualities predicated of it in its definition." (2.410) The *"substantial depth* is the real concrete form which belongs to everything of which a term is predicable with absolute truth." (2.414) Breadth and depth unqualified mean informed breadth and depth. (2.419) The information involved may be termed the *area*, so that breadth × depth = area.

[20] For breadth and depth see this chapter, B, i, quoting 3.608.
[21] Following Hamilton. Peirce pointed also to John of Salisbury's distinction between *nominat* and *significat*. (5.471)

In order fully to understand the term, it will be necessary to proceed to the study of the proposition; for terms, Peirce held, are rudimentary or incomplete propositions. A term, or class-name, Peirce said, is nothing but a proposition with its indices or subjects left blank or indefinite. Peirce left "the *is* as an inseparable part of the class-name." (2.328) To exemplify the function of the term in a proposition, he said "take the idea of 'buying by — of — from — in exchange for —.' This has four places where hecceities, denoted by indexical words, may be attached." (3.461) Each of the four is a term. Terms contain elements of assertion, as we should expect to find, seeing that terms are abbreviated propositions; in fact, "rudimentary assertions—assertions in form with no substance—precisely express the meanings of logical terms." (2.342)

iii. SIGNS AND PROPOSITIONS

The "argument" contains for Peirce the "fundamental logical relation, that of illation, expressed by ergo." (3.440) The other parts of the traditional logic, terms and propositions, are fragments of arguments. "A proposition . . . is but an argumentation divested of the assertoriness of its premiss and conclusion. In like manner, a 'term' or class-name, is nothing but a proposition with its indices or subjects left blank, or indefinite." We shall see later that Peirce's logic of relatives (symbolic logic) also stemmed from certain changes which he made in the traditional analysis of the proposition. First, however, let us place the proposition where it belongs in Peirce's own system of symbols.

Propositions are defined by Peirce as "symbols which [directly determine their grounds and] also independently determine their objects by means of other term or terms, and thus, expressing their own objective validity, become capable of truth or falsehood." (1.559) The proposition is "a sign which distinctly indicates the object which it denotes, called its subject, but leaves its interpretant to be what it may." (2.95) Elsewhere he says that a proposition is a dicent symbolic legisign (2.262; 2.2.64), "a dicisign that is a symbol" (2.320)—the dicisign, it will be remembered, being a sign that represents an actual object. A dicisign is always either true or false, but "does not directly furnish reasons for its being so" since it "must profess to refer or relate to something as having a real being independently of the representation of it as such." (2.310) Thus there is a brute and irreducible resistance involved in the reference of a dicisign; rationality is ruled out and existence reveals its stubborn nature. "But the only kind of sign whose object is necessarily existent is the genuine index," and "consequently a dicisign represents itself to be an index" of its object. The dicisign for this purpose is defined as "a representamen [i.e., sign] whose interpretant represents it as an index of its object." (2.312) In other language, a proposition presents itself as a general, bearing a necessary one-to-one relation to the relevant facts of actuality.

Now, a dicisign so defined contains two parts. One is the *subject*, the other is the *predicate*. Every proposition is a dicisign. "A proposition is equivalent to a sentence in the indicative mood," (2.315) in one language or another, and it must be either meaningless or have a genuine reference to some actual thing as its object. But if every proposition is a dicisign, the analysis of the proposition must correspond to the analysis of the dicisign; and indeed such is the case. Every proposition must have a subject and a predicate. (2.318) The function of the subject is the "characteristic function of an index, that of forcing the attention upon its object." (2.357) When a baby points at a flower and says, "Pretty"—"the pointing arm . . . is the subject of this proposition." "Every subject of a proposition, unless it is either an index (like the environment of the interlocutors, or something attracting attention in that environment, as the pointing finger of the speaker) or a sub-index (like a proper name, personal pronoun or demonstrative) must be a *precept*, or symbol, not only describing to the interpreter what is to be done, by him or others or both, in order to obtain an index of an individual (whether a unit or a single set of units) of which the proposition is represented as meant to be true, but also assigning a designation to that individual, or, if it is a set, to each single unit of the set." (2.330) Thus the subject term of a proposition is to be called a precept. There is a "distinction between that which [the] subject denotes and that which [the] predicate asserts." (5.471) "The predicate is always necessarily an iconic sumisign" or rheme; (2.317) it always represents a possible object or possibility. Predication, defined as "the joining of a predicate to a subject so as to increase logical breadth without diminishing the logical depth," (2.359) is an essential part of every proposition. (2.360) The copula is the actual syntax which the proposition must have, disguised as a third part of the proposition. The copula does not completely fulfill the need for syntax; "it is merely the accidental form that syntax may take." (2.319)

The fact that "an index may be a dicisign" (2.320) is sufficient to prevent logic from becoming exclusively a verbal or linguistic affair. In believing that logic is exhausted neither by its application to language nor by its place in psychology, Peirce departed sharply from the nineteenth century tradition; yet he was clear enough about his meaning. "A man's portrait with a man's name written under it is strictly a proposition, although its syntax is not that of speech." A proper name is an informational index, and so is a photograph. Thus, obviously, there can be nothing subjective about the proposition. Peirce is explicit on this point. He says that the accord of propositions is "quite irrespective of their being asserted or assented to." (2.321) The argument thus supports Peirce's contention that whatever indicates something actual is a proposition. Since any dicisign which represents itself to be an index is capable of indicating something actual, the conclusion to which we are led is that any proposition must be a dicisign.

iv. THE NATURE OF PROPOSITIONS

Following Petrus Hispanus,[22] Peirce divided propositions into the *de inesse* and the *modal*. "A proposition *de inesse* contemplates only the existing state of things," (2.323) whereas "a model proposition takes account of a whole range of possibility." Modal propositions are either possible or impossible, contingent or necessary. "The simplest account of modality is the scholastic, according to which the necessary (or impossible) proposition is a sort of universal proposition; the possible (or contingent, in the sense of not necessary) proposition, a sort of particular proposition." (2.382)

The subjects of propositions are either particular or universal, (2.271) resulting in definite kinds of propositions as opposed to indefinite, following Apuleius. "The quantity of a proposition," said Peirce, (2.364) "is that respect in which a universal proposition is regarded as asserting more than the corresponding particular proposition." "A particular proposition is one which gives a general description of an object and asserts that an object to which that description applies occurs in the universe of discourse, without asserting that it applies to the whole universe or to everything in the universe of a specified general description; as some dragons breathe fire." (2.373) A particular proposition is singular and asserts the existence of something; (2.456) it indicates a "fact of existence." (2.271) "It is singular if it indicates an otherwise known individual." (2.324) "Every proposition refers to some index: universal propositions to the universe, through the environment common to speaker and auditor, which is an index of what the speaker is talking about. But the particular proposition asserts that, with sufficient means, in that universe would be found an object to which the subject term would be applicable, and to which further examination would prove that the

---

[22] The *Summulae Logicales*, "after Boethius, the highest authority for logical terminology" (*Col. Pap.*, 2.323 n. 1).

image called up by the predicate was also applicable." (2.369) A universal proposition is "a proposition *de omni*, said to be true without exception, whatever there may be of which the subject term is predicable." (2.369) It indicates "a real law." (2.271) "Leibnitz rightly insists that a universal proposition does not assert, or imply, the existence of its subject," (2.369)[23] and Peirce agrees with him rather than with Aristotle. (2.456) A universal proposition "applies to whatever individual there is in the universe or to whatever there *may be* of a general description without saying that there is any." (2.324) A general subject is either universal or particular. Peirce regarded "quantities as belonging to propositions . . . as well as to terms." (2.364) He saw that besides universal (all), particular (some), and singular (one), there were other quantities of propositions intermediate. "At least 2 A's are B's" or "All the A's but one are B's, etc., *ad infinitum*." (1.354)

Propositions are hypothetical, categorical, and relative. (2.325) A hypothetical proposition is defined as "any proposition compounded of propositions." (2.271) Hypothetical propositions apply to actual conditions, but "the peculiarity of the hypothetical proposition is that it goes out beyond the actual state of things and declares what *would* happen were things other than they are or may be." (3.374) But all hypothetical propositions involve predication in that they presuppose some background of reference. (2.360) "A hypothetical proposition, generally, is not confined to stating what actually happens, but [like the modal proposition] states what is invariably true throughout a universe of possibility." (3.366) Thus it is the broadest classification of propositions, applying to all possibility. "Hypothetical propositions embrace all propositions," (2.355) except perhaps those denoting class membership or inclusion. Hypothetical propositions are subdivided into the disjunctive and the copulative. The third common subdivision of the conditional is invalid, since the "conditionals are really only a special kind of *disjunctives*." (2.316 n.) All hypothetical propositions represent possibilities, but these are generally negative, whereas the disjunctive hypothetical represents a positive possibility. (2.347)

The categorical proposition is given no definition since Peirce holds it to be the same as the hypothetical: that is, "essentially the same as *compound propositions*." (2.351) "The categorical proposition, 'every man is mortal,' is but a modification of the hypothetical proposition, 'if humanity, then mortality'." (2.710) This is illustrated in some languages, old Egyptian, for instance, where the simplest assertions which we make in categorical form take hypothetical forms. (2.354) The relative proposition "is concerned

[23] *Nouveaux Essais*, bk. IV, chap. 9.

with the identity of more than one individual"; the nonrelative is not concerned with the identity of more than one. (2.271) "Whether a proposition is to be regarded as non-relative or relative depends on what use is to be made of it in argument. But it does not follow that the distinction is merely one of outward guise; for the force of the proposition is different according to the application that is to be made of it."

Propositions differ as to quality according as they are affirmative or negative. Affirmative propositions imply the existence of the subject; negative propositions do not. (4.44) "The universal affirmative is the type of all propositions." (2.510) "Prefixing *non-* to a term converts the proposition from a negative to an *affirmative* or so-called *infinite* proposition," a process called by Abélard[24] infinition. (2.326) "The relation of negation may be regarded as defined by the principles of contradiction and excluded middle ... That is an admissible, but not a necessary, point of view," (2.379) since "almost any two" of the "conceptions of non-relative deductive logic" will accomplish the same purpose. "Of two contradictory propositions each is said to result from the *negation* of the other." "Two propositions involving selective expressions may be contradictories; but in order to be so, each selective has to be changed from indicating *a suitable selection* to indicating *any selection that may be made,* or vice versa." In the more modern terminology of symbolic logic this would mean, for instance,

$$(\exists x) \, \phi \times \; = \, \sim (x) \sim \phi \times$$

There is no difficulty in showing that the affirmative proposition can be defined in terms of the hypothetical; but Peirce insisted that the negative proposition can also.

$$a \,\text{—}\!\!< \, a \,\text{—}\!\!< \, a \,\text{—}\!\!< \, a \,\text{—}\!\!< \, a \,\text{—}\!\!< \, a \,\text{—}\!\!< \, a \,\text{—}\!\!< \, a \,\text{—}\!\!<$$

without end, where —< is the "sign of inclusion," (2.356) is a "series of antecedents without a final consequent" and "may be seen to be equivalent to the denial of a.[25] Thus, without the introduction of any other sign, but merely by the idea of an endless sequence, after we already have the idea of successive sequence, we reach the idea of negation." Thus, as a recent reviewer observed, "A negation [in Peirce's view] is an infinitely iterated hypothetical; 'not p,' where p is a proposition, means 'p implies that p implies that p implies that ... without end'."[26]

---

[24] *Opera Hactenus Inedita*, p. 225. See also Peirce, *Col. Pap.*, 2.551.
[25] The editors of the *Collected Papers* point out that "it is equivalent to: not-a or not-a or not-a ..."
[26] W. V. Quine, review of vol. ii of the *Collected Papers* in *Isis*, 19 (1933), 223.

Lastly, propositions can be divided into those which are true and those which are false. A proposition "is false if any proposition could be legitimately deduced from it, without any aid from false propositions, which would conflict with a direct perceptual judgment, could such be had. A proposition is true if it is not false." (2.327) The truth of a proposition consists in the relation of the "outward expression" of a proposition to that to which it refers "just as any possibility is related to its actualization." (5.424 n.1) Peirce mentions both this "descriptive," or absolute, division and the "metric conception," which "would be that every proposition is more or less false and that the question is one of amount." (3.365) But he adopts the former view as the guiding one, and hence, remembering that a proposition is true only if it is not false, he asserts that "an entirely meaningless form of proposition is to be classed along with true propositions." (2.327) But "the self-contradictory proposition . . . is not meaningless; it means too much." (2.352)

From the broadest point of view, the proposition "signifies that an eternal fitness, or truth, a permanent conditional force, or law, attaches certain hecceities [i.e., certain actual references] to certain parts of an idea." (3.461) Hence it follows that the universe required for logic "is that of determinate states of things that are admissible hypothetically," (3.621) a universe of possibilities. Thus the true proposition represents a real relation of the universe, of which it is a sign. And logic, fundamental to philosophy, implies a view of the universe which is already implicitly philosophical.

V. ARISTOTLE'S THREE LAWS

Allowing for certain criticisms and limitations as well as for changes in interpretation, Peirce was committed to the validity of Aristotle's three laws of logic. Let us glance at his comments upon the laws.

"The principle of identity, expressed by the formula 'A is A,' states that the relation of subject to predicate is a relation which every term bears to itself." (3.407) "To say that things are identical is to say that every predicate is true of both or false of both." (3.398) "Identity is the relation that everything bears to itself: Lucullus dines with Lucullus." (1.365) Thus "identity is essentially a dual relation." (1.446) "*Equality* is a relation of which identity is a species." (3.42) In short, identity is defined as that species of equality which consists in the relation that everything bears to itself. Two characteristics of identity may be noted. "Otherness . . . is the inseparable spouse of identity: wherever there is identity there is necessarily otherness;

and in whatever field there is true otherness there is necessarily identity."
(1.566) Finally, identity is close to opposition. "Throughout all vicissitudes
its oppositions to other things remain intact, although they may be accidentally modified; and therein is manifest the positive character of identity."
(1.461)

The principle of contradiction, "*A* is not not-*A*," (2.593) can also be
stated, "*A* is other than whatever is other than whatever is *A*." (2.597) Contradiction, which ought to be called the Principle of Consistency, (2.600)
"is a reciprocal relation," (2.477) and may be understood in the sense "that
any term is in the relation of negation to . . . its own converse"; (3.407)
from which it follows "that no term is in the relation of negation to itself"
and also "that every term is in the relation of negation to everything but
itself." The relation of contradiction is not limited to propositions, as, for
instance, inconsistency is; (2.611) contradiction is also inherent in events.
(1.493) "The principle of contradiction may be regarded as a formalistic
result" (6.231) of the truth expressed by saying "The now is one, and but
one." It is a valid principle, and Peirce so employed it. (2.352)

The principle of excluded middle, "often called *principium exclusi tertii*,"
(2.581) states that "everything is either *A* or not-*A*." (2.593) It may be
understood as meaning "that every term, *A*, is predicable of anything that
is in the relation of negation to a term which is in the same relation to it";
(3.407) from which it follows "that the objects of which any term, *A*, is
predicable together with those of which the negative of *A* is predicable
together make up all the objects possible," and also "that every term, *A*,
is predicable of whatever is in the relation of negation to everything but *A*."
The principle of excluded middle means "that the individual is determinate
in regard to every possibility, or quality, either as possessing it or as not
possessing it," (1.434) "that [of] an affirmative and its corresponding negative predicate—as 'black' and 'not-black'— . . . one or the other must be
true of any *single individual*."[27] Indeed, "the principle of excluded middle
only applies to an individual." (6.168) "The principle . . . does not belong
to the so-called 'traditional' logic, since, although it occurs in Aristotle as
a definition of the kind of opposition called contradiction, and in other
passages in dissent from a statement of Plato's, yet it plays no important
part in Aristotle's system, and was first made a fundamental principle by
Wolf."[28] It is closely related to De Morgan's law which affirms that "any

---

[27] Review of J. G. Hibben, *Hegel's Logic*, in *The Nation*, 66 (1903), 419.
[28] *Ibid.*

collection of objects whatsoever possess[es] universally some character which belongs to no other object at all." (1.450)

Despite the strength of the attacks that have been launched upon the validity of the principle, Peirce's use of it would imply that he regarded it as valid, for he appealed to it, both implicitly (1.27) and explicitly. (2.352) He asserted that the principle of excluded middle and the principle of contradiction "may be regarded as together constituting the definition of the relation expressed by 'not,' yet they also imply that whatever exists consists of individuals." (3.612) Elsewhere, he admits, however, that the use of the principle of excluded middle is possible but not necessary in connection with the definition of negation, (2.379) though he evidently preferred so to employ it. (2.595)

Despite the fact that the three laws have been known for some time as the "laws of thought," they are not "sufficient laws of all thought or of all reasoning." (2.593) Many things remain obscure, as, for instance, the question of whether the copula involves existence. (2.594) But the insistence upon the existential reference of the three laws gets rid of many of the contemporary objections to their validity. For example, the fact that the proposition "It is raining" may be true today and false tomorrow, and that its truth or falsity may change as many times as it is uttered, does not refute the fact that "It is raining" and "It is not raining" are contradictory propositions when they have the same references to date and place. Peirce's arguments for the validity of the law of excluded middle, as set forth in the above paragraphs, defend it by anticipation on the very points on which it has since been held vulnerable, almost as though he knew exactly where the attack would come. It has, for instance, been maintained that contradiction defines negation, rendering the excluded middle principle unnecessary for this purpose; and it has in addition been held that excluded middle does not apply to existence. On the former point, it is asserted that excluded middle adds nothing to contradiction but is merely a restatement of it. Peirce dissents, as it were, from this in holding that it is the application of a predicate or its denial to all objects possible, together with the principle of contradiction itself, that makes up negation. On the latter point, it is asserted, for instance, that one drop of water may make not two drops of water but only one (larger) drop, the principle or law of excluded middle expressly fails to apply to the existential world, and thus, while theoretically true, has no sure applicability. Peirce dissents, as it were, also from this in holding that every individual is determinate with respect to every quality in either having it or not having it. The strong point of the principle of excluded middle Peirce believed to be its definition of the individual, which is the very essence of actual existence.

Within limits, it appears to be Peirce's view that all three laws are in many respects fundamental and necessary.

vi. THE LOGIC OF RELATIVES

"The great difference between the logic of relatives and ordinary logic is that the former regards the form of relation in all its generality and in its different possible species while the latter is tied down to the matter of the single relation of similarity." (4.5) The logic of relatives was Peirce's commonest name for the mathematical treatment of abstract relations which has since come to be known as symbolic logic. He defined it as "logic . . . treated by means of a special system of symbols." (4.372) The purpose of symbolic logic, Peirce held, is not "to aid the drawing of inferences" (4.373) but rather to further "the investigation of the theory of logic," to "help the study of logical principles." (3.485) Considerations of space as well as of interest make a technical discussion of the logic of relatives impossible here. Our concern is rather with the implications of Peirce's discoveries to the more general problems of philosophy. Peirce was one of the pioneers in the development of symbolic logic; although in some cases not Peirce's work but that of other men was followed. However, Peirce's formulation was the one which influenced his own philosophy; and it is his philosophy we are endeavoring to present. We shall proceed, then, to consider those items in Peirce's logic of relatives which had the most bearing on his philosophical doctrines, regardless of their place in the history of symbolic logic.

The attempt to find "an indisputable theory of reasoning by the aid of mathematics" (3.618) led by unbroken steps from Peirce's studies in the traditional logic. It issued in three broad conclusions, which are the essential ones to be drawn from the logic of relatives, in so far as that logic affected his general philosophical viewpoint. These three conclusions are: (*a*) that everything logical reduces to relations; (*b*) that the knowledge of relations is a product of observation; and (*c*) that inclusion is a fundamental logical relation. Each of these conclusions involves a host of lesser points, in the exposition of which the transition from the traditional logic to the logic of relatives will be made clear.

(*a*) That everything logical reduces to relations is a proposition which must be exhibited in its several subdivisions. But before we can show every kind of item to be a relation we must first explain what Peirce meant by the word "relation." It will be recalled that a rheme is "a sign which represents a possible object."[29] The relation, or "relative,"[30] is the brief name for a "relative rhema," (3.636) socalled because a relative is nothing more than a rheme.[31] "A *relation* . . . consist[s] in . . . the possibility of a fact which could be precisely asserted by filling the blanks of a corresponding relative rheme with proper names." (4.354) A relative is that which can be represented by an expression which becomes a sentence when its blanks are filled in. (3.466) The degree of the relative is indicated by the number of the blanks. (3.465) "A *relationship*, or *fundamentum relationis*, is a fact relative to a number of objects, considered apart from those objects, as if, after the statement of the fact, the designations of those objects had been erased. A *relation* is a relationship considered as something that may be said to be true of one of the objects, the others being separated from the relationship *yet kept in view*.[32] Thus, for each relationship there are as many relations as there are blanks." (3.466) That there is nothing exclusively verbal or linguistic about the nature of the relation is borne out by the analogy of a relation which Peirce offers. The chemical atom is like a relative; its loose ends or "unsaturated bonds" correspond to the blanks of the relative. (3.469) A relation, then, is "a fact relative to a number of objects, considered apart from those objects." (3.466) It is thus a universal, and has no necessary reference to any particular.[33] "Every relative . . . is general; its definition describes a system in general terms." (3.220) But although relatives are "without attachments to experience, without 'a local habitation and a name'," they yet have "indications of the need of such attachments." (3.459)

Now that we have some understanding of Peirce's use of the idea of relation, we may proceed to analyze what his definition does to some of the traditional conceptions of logic.

All terms are to be interpreted as relations. Proper nouns may stand, but the demarcation of common nouns from verbs becomes indefensible. It will be recalled that Peirce left "the *is* as an inseparable part of the class-

---

[29] See chap. II, B, i.

[30] Peirce lived to regret that he had changed the name, "logic of relations," employed by his "master, Augustus de Morgan, to 'the logic of relatives'." (3.574 n. 2) Obviously, it was "the logic of relations" (3.574) that Peirce intended, but his own term had come into general use by 1903, and although his "thoughtless act" was a "bitter reflection" to him, he considered it too late to correct the error.

[31] The "relative rhema," or relation, is what in current symbolic logic is termed the propositional function. For Peirce's derivation of the symbolic formulation of the relation corresponding to the propositional function, see 3.636. Cf. also 2.95 n.

[32] Italics mine.

[33] "A non-relative term may be called a term of *singular reference*." (3.219)

name,"[34] and he now declares again that a "class-name is nothing but a proposition with its indices or subjects left blank or indefinite." (3.440; 3.636) But a proposition with its indices, i.e., proper nouns, left blank is one that features its verb: e.g., —————— gives —————— to —————.
Thus Peirce would assert that the meaning of nouns in his logic of relatives, like that of verbs, lies in possible action. (2.330) One way to make this clear is to substitute relative terms for all absolute terms. This is a comparatively simple affair, since "the absolute term 'man' is really exactly equivalent to the relative term 'man that is —————', and so with any other"; (3.73) "any absolute term may be thus regarded as a relative term." Another way is of course to employ the nouns themselves as verbs: substantive verbs or verbal nouns. Peirce regarded nouns as reified verbs. The "signification" of a verb is "the agreement between its several manifestations." (3.460) This is what the nominalists call "a *mere* name" and the realists assert "*is* real." Strike out the "mere" and . . . "substitute for 'is' *may be*," and leave the judgment to "experience and reason," and you have something near the truth. But the logic of relatives even so cannot hang upon terms. Although "the best treatment of the logic of relatives will dispense altogether with class-names and only use verbs" (3.459), the verbs themselves exist in the abstract only as incomplete propositions, propositions with verbs and blanks. For the proposition, and not the class-name or the verb, is the fundamental logical form.[35]

We have seen conditional propositions reduced to disjunctive, and both disjunctive and categorical propositions reduced to hypothetical propositions.[36] Here we shall see the categorical as well as the hypothetical proposition embraced by a still more fundamental relation, that of implication, contained in the symbolic expression A—<B. (3.175)[37] "Thus, to say that all men are mortal is the same as to say that if any man possesses any character whatever then a mortal possesses that character. To say, 'if A, then B' is obviously the same as to say that from A, B follows, logically or extralogically. By thus identifying the relation expressed by the copula with that of illation,[38] we identify the proposition with the inference,[39] and the term with the proposition."[40] Thus what is true of term, proposition, or inference is true of all three.

---

[84] See chap. II, B, iv.
[85] See chap. II, B, iv.
[86] See chap. II, B, iii. For the same reductions in terms of the logic of relatives, see 3.140 and 3.366.
[87] I.e., A implies B.
[88] See chap. II, B, v.
[89] See chap. II, C, i.
[40] See chap. II, B, iv.

But the implicative relation of A—<B includes not only all three types of abstract relation but facts and operations as well. We have already noted[41] that although relatives are unattached to experience, they need such attachment. The proposition with its indices left blank is an abstract verbal affair until the blanks are supplied with indices, so that the proposition in a sense compels attachment to the terms substituted for the blanks. In the example already quoted, the expression "____ gives ____ to ____" compels some kind of term to be substituted for the blanks in order to complete the expression. Thus *John* gives *his book* to *Tom* completes the expression in terms of indices, but *quantity* gives *form* to *quality* completes the expression also. Peirce says that "in the expression of a fact we have a considerable range of choice as to how much we will denote by the indexical and how much signify by iconic words." (3.462) The incomplete expression, with its blanks, is therefore a mere possibility, to be made into a complete expression by filling in the blanks with indices or actual facts. "The relation, by itself, is, therefore an *ens rationis* and mere logical possibility; but its subsistence is of the nature of a fact. When the quality of the fact concerning two objects is considered, without reference to any distinction between these subjects other than that which this fact establishes, its possibility is termed by the author a *"relationship."* (3.571) It follows that "a *relation* is a fact about a number of things"; (3.416) and, since there are no actual things which do not stand in some reactive relation with other things, "in reality, every fact is a relation" or a set of relations.

(*b*) The second conclusion to which we are led by the logic of relatives in our effort at the understanding of Peirce's philosophy is that the knowledge of relations is a product of observation.[42] It has surprised many persons, says Peirce, that mathematics has led to so many discoveries; but the truth is that "all deductive reasoning, even simple syllogism, involves an element of observation." (3.363) Mathematical relations between relations are discovered through the observation of icons. Now, logic, like mathematics, involves observation; and in the same way, for "it is by the observation of diagrams that the reasoning proceeds in such cases." (3.641) The method of discovery in mathematics is, according to Kant, the use of what is called in geometry a "construction." "Such a construction is formed according to a precept furnished by the hypothesis. Being formed, the construction is submitted to the scrutiny of observation, and new relations are discovered among its parts, not stated in the precept by which it was formed." (3.560) Kant's shortcoming was that he denied the same conditions to logic, where,

[41] See chap. II, B, v.
[42] See this chapter, A, ii.

in fact, they do exist. Deduction elicits not only what was implicitly thought in the premises (3.641) but relations which were not formerly known at all. "Take the syllogistic formula

$$\text{All } M \text{ is } P$$
$$S \text{ is } M$$
$$\therefore S \text{ is } P$$

This is really a diagram of the relations of S, M, and P. The fact that the middle term occurs in the two premises is actually exhibited . . . " (3.363) Other more complex arguments can be constructed to illustrate logical discovery and deduction through observation. (3.418) "Such a method of forming a diagram is called *algebra*," and the logic of relatives simply employs this logical algebra as a formal method but "with greater freedom" than is usual in the symbolic representation of relations.

(*c*) The fact that inclusion is a fundamental logical relation is made evident by the exhibition of other logical copulas or connectives as subclasses of inclusion. Peirce demonstrated that the relations of identity, equality and implication, for example, are special cases of the relation of inclusion.

Identity is what Peirce termed "the first icon of [logical] algebra." (3.376) Let us suppose that the token 1 expresses identity, and we write 1*ij*. (3.398) But this relation of identity has two properties. "The first is that if i and j are identical, whatever is true of i is true of j . . . The other property is that if everything which is true of i is true of j, then i and j are identical." Thus, "to say that things are identical is to say that every predicate is true of both or false of both," or, in other words, to assign an equality to them.

In fact, Peirce said, it will be recalled that equality is a relation of which identity is a species.[43] But "all equality is inclusion in, but the converse is not true; hence inclusion is a wider concept than equality." (3.47 n.1) And thus inclusion includes identity. Similarly, implication is a wider concept than equality. (3.173 n.2) Identity, too, is attributed to implication as one example of it; $x \!-\!\!<\! x$ is an identification directly by means of the sign of implication. (3.373) But implication, too, is contained in the notion of inclusion. The implication, $A \!-\!\!<\! B$, means that every C which includes A is a C which includes B. (3.165)[44] Thus implication, as well as identity

[43] See this chapter, B, v, quoting 3.42.

[44] Peirce speaks of illation as fundamental in logic (2.444 n. 1; 3.472), but in most cases does not seem to have distinguished between illation and inclusion. For instance, in 3.175 the sign $-\!\!<$ represents illation, and illation is defined as meaning implication, "P, $\therefore$ C, where $\therefore$ is the sign of illation," (3.162) whereas in 2.356 the same sign is explicitly defined as the sign of inclusion. There is good evidence for believing, however, that Peirce regarded illation as contained in the relation of inclusion, and considered the latter more fundamental. In 3.165 Peirce makes it clear that inclusion as the leading principle of implication is superior to it in generality.

and equality, are included in inclusion. Inclusion, which is in effect the whole-part relation, is a basic one for logic.

C. CRITICAL LOGIC

Critical logic is the second of Peirce's three main divisions of logic. Having outlined in Speculative Grammar, the theory of the *meaning* of symbols, we turn now to an examination of their *truth*. Critical Logic treats of "the formal conditions of the truth of symbols." (1.559; 4.116)

i. SIGNS AND THE SYLLOGISM

Having examined the term and the proposition, we come now to the third and more complex of the divisions of logic: the argument, or syllogism. "The chief business of the logician is to classify arguments; for all testing clearly depends on classification. The classes of the logicians are defined by certain typical forms called syllogisms." (2.619) It will be recalled that Peirce considered the argument as the fundamental logical form, and derived both the term and the proposition from it. Just as a term was a proposition with indices left blank, so now a syllogism is a proposition with assertiveness added.[45] In Critical Logic, where the proposition is developed past the notion of mere meaning to that of truth, the syllogism is taken as central, and the single proposition becomes "nothing more nor less than an argumentation whose propositions have had their assertiveness removed." (2.356) But before investigating the implications of this statement, let us see how the syllogism is related by Peirce to the general system of semiotic, the formal doctrine of signs.

The syllogism is an argument symbolic legisign, (2.263-264) or "a sign whose interpretant represents its object as being an ulterior sign through a law, namely, the law that the passage from all such premisses to such conclusions tends to the truth." We have seen that symbols which directly determine only their *grounds* are terms,[46] and that those which independently determine their *objects* by means of other terms are propositions.[47] But there are "symbols which also independently determine their *interpretants*, and thus the minds to which they appeal, by premissing a proposition or propositions which such a mind is to admit. These are *arguments*" (1.559) or syllogisms.

---

[45] See this chapter, B, iii.
[46] See this chapter, B, ii, quoting 1.559.
[47] See this chapter, B, iii, quoting 1.559.

The syllogism, or argument,[48] "is a representamen which does not leave the interpretant to be determined as it may by the person [or thing] to whom the symbol is addressed, but separately represents what is the interpreting representation that it is intended to determine." (5.76) A syllogism "is a sign which distinctly represents the interpretant, called its *conclusion*, which it is intended to determine." (2.95) The syllogism "must, therefore, be a symbol, or sign whose object is a general law or type. It must involve a dicent symbol, or proposition, which is termed its premiss: for the argument can only urge the law by urging it in an instance. . . . As for another proposition, called the conclusion, often stated and perhaps required to complete the argument, it plainly represents the interpretant, and likewise has a peculiar force, or relation to the interpretant." (2.253) The determination of the interpreting representation, the "peculiar force," is the assertiveness of the syllogism.

Assertion is present as an element in the term and proposition but is fully developed only in the syllogism. Endowing the members of a proposition with assertiveness "will convert it into a process of *argumentation*." (2.355) When an assertion is made, there is always a deliverer who makes signals to the receiver. (3.433) The receiver may be "upon a different planet, an æon later" or it may be the receiver himself "as he will be a second after." The receiver, in fact, "need have only a problematical existence, as when during a shipwreck an account of the accident is sealed in a bottle and thrown upon the water." (2.334) Some of the signals (or at least one of them) "are supposed to excite in the mind of the receiver familiar images, pictures . . . or *dreams* . . . now quite detached from the original circumstance of their first occurrence, so that they are free to be attached to new occasions." (3.433)

The assertion consists in evidence furnished by the deliverer to the receiver that he "finds a certain idea to be definitely compulsory on a certain occasion." (2.335) In every assertion there are three parts. These are: "a

---

[48] By "argument" Peirce did not mean "reason*ing*" but rather reason. "Reasoning moves in first intentions [i.e., formal abstraction], while the forms of logic are constructions of second intentions [i.e., abstracted forms]." (2.599) Argument denotes merely "a body of premisses considered as such," (2.461) where "the term 'premiss' will refer exclusively to something laid down . . . and also exclusively to that part of what is laid down which is (or is supposed to be) relevant to the conclusion." In other words, what is ordinarily called an argument, as when one person reasoning logically endeavors to convince another of the truth of something, is a dynamic and special case, or cases, of the static condition laid down by the triadic relation which Peirce has technically defined as an "argument." The syllogism, in other words, does not necessarily represent a piece of reasoning; it represents a relationship which holds between three propositions; and this relationship may be employed in reasoning, and certainly must be followed if the reasoning is to be sound.

sign of the occasion of the compulsion, a sign of the enforced idea, and a sign evidential of the compulsion affecting the [deliverer] in so far as he identifies himself with the scientific intelligence." "Because compulsion is essentially *hic et nunc*, the occasion of the compulsion can only be represented to the [receiver] by compelling him to have experience of that same occasion. Hence it is requisite that there should be a kind of sign which shall act dynamically upon the [receiver's] attention and direct it to a special object or occasion." (2.336) Such a sign Peirce had called an index. Thus "one index, at least, must form a part of every assertion." (2.337)

What is asserted by the syllogism is, of course, the truth. Peirce understood by truth the correspondence between a proposition or set of propositions as sign and that possibility or actuality to which as a sign it refers. (2.541; 5.553; 6.350) The argumentation as an exemplification of the syllogism "belongs to a class of reasonings, few or none of which lead from truth to falsity." (2.446) Following this definition, and in opposition to Aristotle, Peirce accepted as the premise and conclusion of an argument any two propositions, regardless of whether or not the one seems to follow directly from the other. (2.448)

$$2+2=4,$$
$$\therefore \text{ Lightning is an electrical phenomenon}$$

would have been accepted by Peirce as a valid argument, (2.447) a contention having important implications to ontology.[49] "My reason is, that such things are of no practical importance whatever—for as long as reasoning does not lead us astray, the whole purpose of logic is fulfilled—and to admit these reasonings as sound simplifies very considerably the whole doctrine of syllogism." (2.448) Of course, a syllogism does not have to assert the truth in order to be a syllogism. An invalid syllogism is also a syllogism, for "an argument which is false can in some conceivable case lead to absurdity" and "as soon as we admit the idea of absurdity, we are bound to class the rejection of an argumentation among argumentations." (2.356)[50]

ii. ELEMENTS OF THE SYLLOGISM

The method whereby the syllogism asserts the truth (or attempts to) is that of inclusion.[51] Although the distinction between logical breadth and

---

[49] See chap. II. The logical point is a clear anticipation of later logicians.
[50] Cf. the statement that self-contradictory propositions are propositions, this chapter, B, iv, quoting 2.352.
[51] See this chapter, B, vi (c).

depth holds of the argument also, in that there is a "distinction between the state of things in which its premisses are true and the state of things which is defined by the truth of its conclusion." (5.471)[52] "It can be mathematically proved," Peirce said, "that every possible necessary inference from two premisses, both having the same form as the conclusion, must depend upon a relation of *inclusion*." (2.558) "To say that an inference is correct is to say . . . that every possible state of things in which the premisses should be true would be included among the possible states of things in which the conclusion would be true. We are thus led to the copula of inclusion." (2.710) Inclusion in the syllogism analyzes into some six factors. These are (*a*) leading principle, (*b*) premise, or premises, (*c*) colligation, (*d*) involvement, (*e*) inference, and (*f*) conclusion. We may give them each a separate word.

(*a*) The leading principle is described as follows: "Every inference involves the judgment that, if *such* propositions as the premisses are are true, then a proposition related to them, as the conclusion is, must be, or is likely to be, true. The principle implied in this judgment, respecting a genus of argument, is termed the *leading principle* of the argument." (2.462) The leading principle is whatever is required by the true premises of a syllogism if a true conclusion is to follow. "The leading principle contains, by definition, whatever is considered requisite besides the premisses to determine the necessary or probable truth of the conclusion." (2.465) "Each premiss must, in fact, be equivalent to a subsumption under the leading principle" and "matter can be transferred from the premisses to the leading principle, and *vice versa*," and only so is elimination from either possible. A perfect syllogism is one in which "no part of the leading principle can be stated as a premiss and so eliminated from the leading principle." (2.576)

The leading principle may be compared with two other logical notions. It is the defining principle of a class of arguments and it determines a subclass in the universe of discourse. As the defining principle of a class of arguments its antecedent must "describe all possible premisses upon which it could operate, while the consequent should describe how the conclusion to which it would lead would be determinately related to those premisses." (2.588) But the defining principle of a class is closely related to the attempt to give precise definition to that peripheral reference to that "collection of individuals or of possibilities, which cannot be adequately described, but

---

[52] For this distinction between logical breadth and depth applied to terms, see this chapter, B, ii.

can only be indicated as something familiar to both speaker and auditor," which is indicated by the term "universe of discourse." (2.536) The universe of discourse is a name for the connotations of that which is denoted by the leading principle. "A rhetorical argumentation," said Peirce, is "one not depending upon logical necessity, but upon common knowledge as defining a sphere of possibility. Such an argument is rendered logical by adding as a premiss that which it assumes as a leading principle." (2.449 n.) It is difficult to see how anything which was familiar to both speaker and auditor could fail to be common knowledge. And can we not, then, identify this "common knowledge as defining a sphere of possibility" with the "collection of . . . possibilities, which cannot be adequately described, but can only be indicated as something familiar to both speaker and auditor"? (2.536) If so, then, since even a perfect syllogism having two expressed premises still requires a leading principle, (2.576) a perfect syllogism must be a rhetorical argument whose universe of discourse substitutes in the leading principle for the common knowledge which premises do not express. There is, no doubt, a sense in which every syllogism, however exact, contains rhetorical elements, and every argumentation, however rhetorical, contains elements of exactitude.

The last statement reveals the character of a highly important distinction made by Peirce in the leading principle. Peirce distinguished between the logical (or formal) and the factual (or material) leading principle. "Any leading principle whose truth is implied in the premisses of every inference which it governs is called a 'logical' (or, less appropriately, *formal*) leading principle; while a leading principle whose truth is not implied in the premisses is called a 'factual' (or *material*) leading principle." (2.589) Nothing in the formal leading principle can be eliminated, and it produces complete (as opposed to enthymematic) arguments. (2.466) The material leading principle, however, can be eliminated to some extent by transferring that which is in the leading principle over to the premises. The material leading principle is employed in arguments which consider "a logical universe having peculiar properties." (2.549) "Since it can never be requisite that a fact stated should also be implied in order to justify a conclusion, every *logical principle* considered as an assertion will be found to be quite empty. The only thing it really enunciates is a rule of inference." (2.467) Thus the leading principle acts as the formal element in a material inference, and as the material element in a formal implication.

(*b*) The premise is "a proposition, the consideration of which has logically affected, or contributed to the determination of, a conclusion of reasoning." (2.582) Arguments are usually regarded as containing two premises; "every argument of more than two premisses can be resolved into a series of arguments of two premisses each." (2.470) "It is usual with logicians to speak of the premisses of an argument, instead of the premiss. But if there are more premisses than one, the first step of the argumentation must be to colligate them into one copulative proposition: so that the only simple argument of two premisses is the argument of colligation. . . .[53] For that reason, it seems more proper in general to speak of the 'premiss' of an argument than of its 'premisses'." (2.253) "Three propositions which are related to one another as though major premiss, minor premiss, and conclusion of a syllogism of the first figure will be termed respectively *rule, case,* and *result.*" (2.479) A major premise, or rule, as its name implies, must be of the utmost generality, and must hold without exception. (2.453) The minor premise, or case, is a more particular proposition under the rule. The case, as its name implies, often refers to an actual thing or event, but not necessarily so. It may be a general proposition, only less general than the rule, and therefore particular in relation to the rule which subsumes it. "A syllogism in the first figure argues from a *rule,* and the subsumption of a *case,* to the *result* of that rule in that case." (2.794) The result is the conclusion of the syllogism and it follows from the premises. There is no such thing as a so-called suppressed premise. Premises are always present as operative in every valid syllogism, no matter how elliptically that syllogism may be expressed. (2.582)

(c) Colligation, or the bringing of the two premises together, is a difficult part of the syllogism, but an essential one. (2.451) The step is ordinarily not expressed but is there none the less in every valid instance. Thus the syllogism

> All men are mortal,
> All patriarchs are men;
> ∴ All patriarchs are mortal,

really consists of these two steps:

> All men are mortal,
> All patriarchs are men;
> ∴ All men are mortal, and all patriarchs are men;
> ∴ All patriarchs are mortal.

"The operation . . . which consists in bringing the different premisses together and applying them, the one to another, or to a repetition of itself, in a particular way" (2.553) is called colligation, following Whewell.[54]

---

[53] See this chapter, C, ii, (c).
[54] *Novum Organum Renovatum*, II, iv.

(*d*) The involvement of the conclusion in the premises is a necessary part of the syllogism. "The fact inferred [in the conclusion] shall be involved in the very being of the facts premissed, regardless of the manner in which those premissed facts may have become known." (2.553)

(*e*) The heart of the syllogism is inference. Of much importance for the syllogism is the middle term and its distribution. Of all the generalizations which have been made concerning the syllogism, "the only such canon that really holds is that in order that there should be a, syllogistic conclusion there must be two premisses containing a middle term 'distributed' in one, but not in the other, and the conclusion will be drawn by compounding the two premisses in such a way that this middle term may be dropped upon the same principle upon which it is dropped in *Barbara*." (2.529) Inference carries the necessity of the syllogism. The unavoidable implication of the conclusion by the premisses taken together is the result of the inference. "If *such* propositions as the premisses are are true, then a proposition related to them, as the conclusion is, must be, or is likely to be, true." (2.462)

(*f*) Beyond the fact that the conclusion is involved in the premises lies the status of the conclusion itself. The conclusion is "of the nature of an insertion; that is to say, the conclusion is super-added to the premisses; since the premisses remain true." (2.555) But if the premises remain true, so does the conclusion, which is, as Peirce says, an insertion. It has an independent status, since, although it follows from the premises, it is a statement which differs from both of them taken either separately or together.

iii. DEDUCTION, INDUCTION, AND ABDUCTION

From the point of view of the arrangement of propositions, there are three kinds of syllogism. "An argument is always understood by its interpretant to belong to a general class of analogous arguments, which class, as a whole, tends toward the truth. This may happen in three ways, giving rise to a trichotomy of all simple arguments into deductions, inductions, and abductions [or hypotheses]." (2.266)

Deduction is analytic or explicative; induction and abduction are synthetic or ampliative. (2.623) Inductive syllogisms differ from the deductive variety in that in induction "the facts summed up in the conclusion are not among those stated in the premisses." (2.680) Using the same three propositions, the differences between deduction, induction and abduction may be illustrated as follows:

DEDUCTION

Rule.—All the beans from this bag are white.
Case.—These beans are from this bag.
∴ Result.—These beans are white.

INDUCTION

Case.—These beans are from this bag.
Result.—These beans are white.
∴ Rule.—All the beans from this bag are white.

HYPOTHESIS (ABDUCTION)

Rule.—All the beans from this bag are white.
Result.—These beans are white.
∴ Case.—These beans are from this bag. (2.623)

The same three propositions in different arrangements are thus made to illustrate the three kinds of syllogism. It is important to note that all three forms, though they need not be expressed in syllogistic form, are presented as forms of the syllogism, and not merely as forms of human reasoning. As has already been pointed out,[55] Peirce regarded even reasoning as something wider than human reasoning, since it could be performed by machines. Deduction, induction, and abduction are forms of argument, fixed abstractions which reasoning exemplifies.

(*a*) *Deduction.* "A deduction is an argument whose interpretant represents that it belongs to a general class of possible arguments precisely analogous which are such that in the long run of experience the greater part of those whose premisses are true will have true conclusions." (2.267) It is "an argument representing facts in the premiss, such that when we come to represent them in a diagram we find ourselves compelled to represent the fact stated in the conclusion." (2.96) In other words, "the conclusion is drawn in acknowledgement that the facts stated in the premiss constitute an index of the fact which it is thus compelled to acknowledge. All the demonstrations of Euclid are of this kind." The deductive argument always starts from one general premise. The minor premise may also be a general proposition. Deduction is "the only kind of argument which is compulsive."

In deduction, "the warrant is that the facts presented in the premisses could not under any imaginable circumstances be true without involving the truth of the conclusion, which is therefore accepted with necessary modality. But though it be necessary in its modality, it does not by any means follows that the conclusion is certainly true. When we are reasoning about purely hypothetical states of things, as in mathematics, and can make

---

[55] See this chapter, A, i, quoting 2.56-59.

it one of our hypotheses that what is true shall depend only on a certain kind of condition—so that, for example, what is true of equations written in black ink would certainly be equally true if they were written in red— we can be certain of our conclusions, *provided no blunders have been committed.* . . . It is to ideal states of things alone—or to real states of things as ideally conceived, always more or less departing from the reality—that deduction applies." (2.778)

"Deductions are either *necessary* or *probable.* Necessary deductions are those which have nothing to do with any ratio of frequency, but profess (or their interpretants profess for them) that from true premisses they must invariably produce true conclusions. A necessary deduction is a method of producing dicent symbols by the study of a diagram. It is either *corollarial* or *theorematic.* A corollarial deduction is one which represents the conditions of the conclusion in a diagram and finds from the observation of this diagram, as it is, the truth of the conclusion. A theorematic deduction is one which, having represented the conditions of the conclusion in a diagram, performs an ingenious experiment upon the diagram, and by the observation of the diagram, so modified, ascertains the truth of the conclusion." (2.267)

"Probable deductions, or more accurately, deductions of probability, are deductions whose interpretants represent them to be concerned with ratios of frequency. They are either *statistical deductions* or *probable deductions proper.* A statistical deduction is a deduction whose interpretant represents it to reason concerning ratios of frequency, but to reason concerning them with absolute certainty. A probable deduction proper is a deduction whose interpretant does not represent that its conclusion is certain, but that precisely analogous reasonings would from true premisses produce true conclusions in the majority of cases, in the long run of experience." (2.268)

The deductive syllogism is the basic type of syllogism. It is the most compelling kind, since its conclusion is necessary; and other types of syllogism must presuppose it, being themselves in effect composed of rearrangements of its elements. *Barbara* is the typical deductive syllogism. "*Barbara* is, in fact, nothing but the application of a rule.[56] The so-called major premiss lays down this rule; as, for example, *All men are mortal.* The other or minor premiss states a case under the rule; as *Enoch was a man.* The conclusion applies the rule to the case and states the result: *Enoch is mortal.* All deduction is of this character." (2.620) Peirce is careful to point out, however, that "because all inference may be reduced in some way to *Bar-*

[56] See this chapter, C, iii.

bara, it does not follow that this is the most appropriate form in which to represent every kind of inference. . . . Inductive, or synthetic reasoning, being something more than the mere application of a general rule to a particular case, can never be reduced to this form."

(*b*) *Induction.* "An induction is a method of forming dicent symbols concerning a definite question," (2.269) of which method the interpretant represents that if it be persisted in, "it will in the long run yield the truth, or an indefinite approximation to the truth, in regard to every question." "Induction may be defined as an argument which proceeds upon the assumption that all the members of a class or aggregate have all the characters which are common to all those members of this class concerning which it is known, whether they have these characters or not; or, in other words, which assumes that this is true of a whole collection which is true of a number of instances taken from it at random. This might be called statistical argument. In the long run, it must generally afford pretty correct conclusions from the true premisses." (5.275) If from a bag of beans we draw a handful at random and find 2/3 of the beans in the handful white, and then conclude that 2/3 of those in the bag are white, "we are rowing up the current of deductive sequence, and are concluding a *rule* from the observation of a *result* in a certain *case*." (2.622)[57] In induction, the argument runs from two particular premisses to a general conclusion. Only the conclusion is of great generality, so that in a sense induction verifies the generals which are the rules which deduction proposes to apply. But the verification of the rules which deduction proposes to apply is not part of the deductive process, which can proceed equally well without it. It belongs rather to induction and abduction.

Induction is divided by Peirce into three valid kinds: (1) crude, (2) quantitative, and (3) qualitative.

(1) Crude induction, "the first and weakest kind . . . is that which goes on the presumption that future experience as to the matter in hand will not be utterly at variance with all past experience. *Example*: 'No instance of a genuine power of clairvoyance has ever been established: So I presume there is no such thing'." (2.756) Crude induction is the most common way of arriving at universal propositions regarding the general run of future experience. But "the undipped heel of crude induction is that if its conclusion be understood as indefinite, it will be of little use, while if it be taken definitely, it is liable at any moment to be utterly shattered by a single experience." (2.757) Another name for crude induction

---

[57] Italics mine.

is the "pooh-pooh" argument. "A pooh-pooh argument is a method which consists in denying that a general kind of event ever will occur on the ground that it never has occurred. Its justification is that if it be persistently applied on every occasion, it must ultimately be corrected in case it should be wrong, and thus will ultimately reach the true conclusion." (2.269) The pooh-pooh argument makes the conduct of daily life possible; we invite friends for dinner and make plans for a summer vacation on the assumption that there will be no world cataclysm to interfere in the next few months because there have been none in the past few years. But wars do come, and diseases: men are killed in accidents and struck by lightning. Also the pooh-pooh argument is the weapon used by conservatism against the innovation of change.

(2) Quantitative induction is the second kind of induction and also the strongest. If we want to determine whether an individual member of the S class has the character of P, we do so by taking a "fair sample" of the S's, and by estimating that the value of the proportion among them of those that are P probably approximates, within a certain limit of approximation, to the value of the P-ness of the whole class of S's. (2.758) This quantitative method of induction, the most exact, is developed more fully in that branch of mathematics called probability theory.[58] It is the variety of induction most favored in the method of science.[59]

Quantitative induction employs the argument from a random sample. "An argument from a random sample, is a method of ascertaining what proportion of the members of a finite class possess a predesignate, or virtually predesignate, quality, by selecting instances from that class according to a method which will, in the long run, present any instance as often as any other, and concluding that the ratio found for such a sample will hold in the long run." (2.269) Two rules must be observed for the most successful results by the method of random sampling. "The first of these is that the sample must be a random one," (1.95) selected without prejudice or preconception. All depends upon the absolute arbitrariness of the choice with which we select our sample. The other rule is that the character to be sought for in the sample must be chosen in advance. "We must first decide for what character we propose to examine the sample, and only after that decision examine the sample." The last rule is termed predesignation.[60] The predesignate quality "must be decided upon in advance of the

[58] See this chapter, C, iv.
[59] See chap. VIII, C, iii.
[60] Following W. Hamilton, *Lectures on Logic*, xiii.

examination of the sample," (2.736) or, in other words, that "the character for which the samples are to be used as inductive instance must be specified independently of the result of that examination." (2.790) "If in sampling any class, say the M's, we first decide what the character P is for which we propose to sample that class, and also how many instances we propose to draw, our inference is really made before these latter are drawn." (2.737) Predesignation acknowledges the generality present in every particular instance of sampling, as the purpose in terms of which there is sampling at all.

(3) Midway between crude induction and quantitative induction stands the qualitative variety. Crude induction may be termed the induction of common experience, quantitative the induction of experimentation, while qualitative is the induction of enlightened common sense, the verification of a general prediction. Crude inductions are made from "experience in one mass," (2.759) while at the other extreme quantitative inductions rest "upon a collection of numerable instances of equal evidential values." Intermediate between them, qualitative inductions are drawn from "a stream of experience in which the relative evidential values of different parts of it have to be estimated according to our sense of the impressions they make upon us." Qualitative induction thus lies between the other varieties and contains elements of both, being "alike in respect to security and to the scientific value of its conclusions."

"A verification of a general prediction is a method which consists in finding or making the conditions of the prediction and in concluding that it will be verified about as often as it is experimentally found to be verified. Its justification is that if the prediction does not tend in the long run to be verified in any approximately determinate proportion of cases, experiment must, in the long run, ascertain this; while if the prediction will, in the long run, be verified in any determinate, or approximately determinate, proportion of cases, experiment must in the long run, approximately ascertain what that proportion is." (2.269)

(c) *Abduction.* An "abduction is an argument which presents facts in its premiss which present a similarity to the fact stated in the conclusion, but which could perfectly well be true without the latter being so . . . and thus we are not led to assert the conclusion positively but are only inclined toward admitting it as representing a fact of which the facts of the premiss constitute an icon." (2.96) "Hypothesis [or abduction] may be defined as an argument which proceeds upon the assumption that a character which is known necessarily to involve a certain number of others, may be probably predicated of any object which has all the characters which this character is known to involve." (5.276) "An abduction is [thus] a method of forming a general prediction." (2.269) But this prediction is always in reference to an observed fact; indeed, an abductive conclusion "is only justified by its *explaining* an observed fact." (1.89) If we enter a room containing a number of bags of beans and a table upon which there is a handful of white beans, and if, after some searching, we open a bag which contains white beans only, we may infer as a probability, or fair guess, that the handful was taken from this bag. This sort of inference is called making an hypothesis or abduction. "It is the inference of a *case* from a *rule* and a *result*." (2.712)

An abduction or "hypothesis is really a subsumption of a case under a class," (2.629) where we start with the class and upon discovering the case, make the hypothesis that the case is really a case under the class. "Fossils are found; say, remains like those of fishes, but far in the interior of the country. To explain this phenomenon, we suppose the sea once washed over this land." (2.625) The abduction is a weak kind of argument which must be put as a question. (2.634)

The character of abduction may best be explained, perhaps, by comparing it with induction. Behind both inductions and abductions Peirce assumed an "explaining syllogism" which must be deductive, and if the inductive or abductive syllogism is to be valid, the explaining syllogism must be valid. In the case of both inductive and abductive syllogisms these are composed of the elements of the deductive syllogism, "one of whose premisses is inductively or hypothetically inferred from the other and from its conclusion." (2.511) As distinct from the deductive syllogism, however, "the conclusion [of an inductive or hypothetical syllogism] is not to be held as absolutely true, but only until it can be shown" to be so. As we may see by comparing the syllogisms,[61] induction runs from specific case to general rule while abduction runs from general rule to specific case. "Just as induction may be regarded as the inference of the major premiss of a syllogism, so hypothesis may be regarded as the inference of the minor premiss, from the other two propositions." (5.276) "The great difference between induction and hypothesis [i.e., abduction] is, that the former infers the existence of phenomena such as we have observed in cases which are similar, while hypothesis supposes something of a different kind from what we have directly observed, and frequently something which it would be impossible for us to observe directly." (2.640) "Induction is where we generalize from a number of cases of which something is true, and infer that the same thing is true of a whole class. . . . Hypothesis is where we find some very curious circumstance, which would be explained by the supposition that it was a case of a certain general rule, and thereupon adopt that supposition." (2.624) "By induction, we conclude that facts, similar to observed facts, are true in cases not examined. By hypothesis, we conclude the existence of a fact quite different from anything observed, from which, according to known laws, something observed would necessarily result. The former, is reasoning from particulars to the general law; the latter, from effect to cause." (2.636)

We may conclude this brief survey of deduction, induction, and abduction by a brief comparison of the three types.

There are: one kind of abduction, two kinds of deduction, and three kinds of induction. "Abduction is the process of forming an explanatory hypothesis. It is the only logical operation which introduces any new idea; for induction does nothing but determine a value, and deduction merely evolves the necessary consequences of a pure hypothesis."[62]

"Deduction proves that something *must* be; induction shows that something *actually is* operative; abduction merely suggests that something *may be.*

"Its [i.e., abduction's] only justification is that from its suggestion deduction can draw a prediction which can be tested by induction, and that, if we are ever to learn anything or to understand phenomena at all, it must be by abduction that this is to be brought about." (5.171)

iv. PROBABILITY

The key to the understanding of the logical theory of probability is to be found, according to Peirce, in the nature of the inductive process itself.[63] Indeed, Peirce declared that probability is part of all synthetic or ampliative inference. The marvel of the inductive process is its tendency to correct itself through repetition. (5.575-576) For any induction it is true that "the probability of its conclusion only consists in the fact that if the true value of the ratio sought has not been reached, an extension of the inductive process will lead to a closer approximation." (2.729)

Let us see what definition of probability Peirce is able to discover from this derivation, what follows from the definition, and then how antecedent understandings of the topic differ.

"The theory of probabilities is simply the science of logic quantitatively

---

[62] Cf. 6.475: "Deduction explicates; induction evaluates."
[63] See this chapter, C, iii.

treated. There are two conceivable certainties with regard to any hypothesis, the certainty of its truth and the certainty of its falsity. The numbers *one* and *zero* are appropriated, in this calculus, to marking these extremes of knowledge; while fractions having values intermediate between them indicate, as we may vaguely say, the degrees in which the evidence leans toward one or the other. The general problem of probabilities is, from a given state of facts, to determine the numerical probability of a possible fact. This is the same as to inquire how much the given facts are worth, considered as evidence to prove the possible fact." (2.647) Probability, then, "is the science of the laws of irregularities." (2.769) It is "a statistical ratio," (5.21) "the ratio of the favorable cases to all the cases," (2.675) "a fraction whose numerator is the frequency of a specific kind of event, while its denominator is the frequency of a genus embracing that species." (2.747)[64] Probability thus marks the frequency with which the relevant formal principle[65] is supported by the favorable cases. Put otherwise, "an objective probability is the ratio in the long run of experience of the number of events which present the character of which the probability is predicated to the total number of events which fulfill certain conditions often not explicitly stated, which all the events considered fulfill." (2.785) This is in accord with the "materialistic" view, so named by Venn, but proposed before him by Bolzano and Cournot,[66] and even by Aristotle, called by Peirce the "objective" view.

Between this understanding of the probability of events and the probability contained in arguments, or syllogisms, of the inductive or abductive varieties, there is no irreconcilable difference. From the point of view of inference, "probability is the proportion of arguments carrying truth with them among those of any genus." (2.669) Both event and argument are contained in the view of probability as relative frequency. Thus "probability depends solely upon the relative frequency of a specific event (namely, that a certain kind of argument yields a true conclusion from true premisses) to a generic event (namely, that that kind of argument occurs with true premisses)." (3.19) Thus, "probability never properly refers immediately to a single event, but exclusively to the happening of a given kind of event on any occasion of a given kind." (2.661) The point may be made clearer by comparing probability with analogy. "Probability is wholly an affair of

---

[64] Peirce said he was following Venn, *Logic of Chance*, see *Col. Pap.*, 2.651. But see also George Boole, *The Laws of Thought* (Chicago, Open Court, 1940), pp. 258 ff. Peirce's doctrine is substantially that of Boole purged of all subjectivism.

[65] See this chapter, C, ii, (a).

[66] M. Cournot, *Exposition de la théorie des chances*.

approximate, not at all of exact, measurement; so that when the class sampled is very large, there is no need of considering whether objects can be drawn more than once or not. But in what is known as 'reasoning from analogy' the class sampled is small, and no instance is taken twice." (2.733) Probability is the only form of argument which gains accuracy through repetition, a property which gives it great importance as a method of investigating the nature of occurrences.

From Peirce's definition of probability certain corollaries follow as to the relation of probability theory to the deductive syllogism and also the question of belief. Three theories of probability were current in Peirce's day; probability was held to rest on deducibility, belief, and relative frequency. Peirce accepted the third view, but was at pains to show how the limited truths of the first two were not inconsistent with his own. Let us see, then, how he regarded the theories of (*a*) deducibility and (*b*) belief.

(*a*) It will be recalled that, although Peirce insisted that synthetic forms of inference of both inductive and abductive varieties contain an additional logical principle that is not to be found in Barbara,[67] he was equally clear about the conformation of the inductive and abductive logic to the syllogistic form.[68] "The logic of probability is related to ordinary syllogistic as the quantitative to the qualitative branch of the same science. Necessary syllogism recognizes only the inclusion or non-inclusion of one class under another; but probable inference takes account of the proportion of one class which is contained under a second." (2.696) In the light of this knowledge, let us look at inductive and abductive probabilities, syllogistically expressed.

All beans considered will be beans from these bags.
The more beans selected the closer they will approximate to being ⅔ white.
∴. All beans from bags are approximately ⅔ white.

This is the inductive probability. The abductive runs:

All beans from these bags are approximately ⅔ white.
The more beans selected the closer they will approximate to being ⅔ white.
∴. All beans being considered must be beans from bags.

The repetition of synthetic reasoning is fruitful in that it leads to closer approximation of truth concerning fact, whereas the repetition of analytic reasoning changes nothing and so leads no further. Thus, it is the former which is the chief center of interest.[69]

[67] See this chapter, C, iii.
[68] See this chapter, C, iii.
[69] See this chapter, C, iv.

Since probability, then, takes the syllogistic form, and every syllogistic inference depends upon the relation of inclusion,[70] we should expect that there would be a deductive as well as an inductive and abductive variety of probability. Indeed, Peirce tells us that probability is expressed also by the deductive syllogism. In comparison with the singular syllogism in Barbara, which runs (2.695):

> Every M is a P,
> S is an M;
> Hence, S is a P

we have the "simple probable deduction":

> The proportion ρ of the M's are P's;
> S is an M;
> It follows, with probability ρ, that S is a P.

"A probable deduction proper is a deduction whose interpretant does not represent that its conclusion is certain, but that precisely analogous reasonings would from true premises produce true conclusions in the majority of cases." (2.268)[71] Bearing in mind the form of the probable deductive syllogism, consider the following:

The beans in this bag are ⅔ white.
This bean has been drawn in such a way that in the long run the relative number of white beans so drawn would be equal to the relative number in the bag.
∴ This bean has been drawn in such a way that in the long run it would turn out white ⅔ of the time. (2.621)

Compare this syllogism with the inductive and abductive examples given on the preceding page. It is a valid deductive probability even though as an instrument of discovery its usefulness is proscribed for it by the major premise. In all deductive probable inference the predesignation is obvious and overweighing. (2.790)[72] In deductive probability the "relative frequency of certain events" is given, "and we perceive that in these facts the relative frequency of another event is given in a hidden way. This being stated makes the solution. . . . Mere explicative reasoning . . . is evidently entirely inadequate to the representation of synthetic reasoning, which goes out beyond the facts given in the premises." (2.681)

(*b*) Many of Peirce's predecessors in logical theory had held that probability is *exclusively* deductive. This was the conceptualist theory, held for

---

[70] See this chapter, C, ii.
[71] For a further account of probable deduction, see 2.785.
[72] See this chapter, C, iii.

the most part by those who wished to confine the syllogism to the representation of the subjective laws of thought. (2.673) Since deductive syllogisms start from premises which are already part of knowledge, and do not present any new knowledge which was not contained in the premises, probability on the deductive view would be confined to the exploration of what is known. This theory went further to assert the implication that since deduction is exclusively a mental process, probability must be equivalent to degree of belief. Peirce insisted that there was no real distinction between the view which held probability to be *exclusively* deductive and that which held it to be a matter of belief.[73] De Morgan was prominent among those in Peirce's day who held the conceptualist view.[74]

The validity of the subjectivist position which endeavored to equate probability with degree of belief is "that the conjoint probability of all the arguments in our possession, with reference to any fact, must be intimately connected with the just degree of our belief in that fact." (2.676) Nevertheless, "probability, to have any value at all, must express a fact. It is, therefore, a thing to be inferred upon evidence." (2.677) Probability thus expresses fact on evidence, not on belief. The chief advocate of the subjective view was Laplace, and many followed him in maintaining "that it is possible to draw a necessary conclusion regarding the probability of a particular determination of an event . . . based on nothing." (2.764) But, Peirce argued, to know nothing is to have no inclination at all toward one of a number of alternatives, any more than a mathematical point can incline toward a compass direction.[75] Peirce rejected the view that a state of "ignorance is denoted by the probability 1/2." (2.747)

Following Locke, Peirce pointed out that the foundation of degree of assent could indicate the probability of an occurrence without necessarily resting it upon any subjective basis. Peirce found the key to this interpretation of probability in a passage in which Locke discussed the nature of assent. Locke pointed out that to assent to an inference is to "receive it for true. In which case the foundation of assent is the probability, the proof being such as, for the most part, carries truth with it." (2.649)[76] But, as Peirce did not fail to see, "There is an allusion in this passage [of Locke's] to the fact that a probable argument is always regarded as belonging to a *genus* of arguments." (2.696) "The validity of an inference does not depend on any tendency of the mind to accept it, however strong such tendency

[73] J. M. Keynes and certain mathematicians continue to support these views.
[74] In his *Formal Logic*.
[75] The argument against Laplace is presented in more detail in 2.762.
[76] *Essay Concerning Human Understanding*, bk. IV, chap. 15, §1.

may be; but consists in the real fact that when premisses like those of the argument in question are true, conclusions related to them like that of this argument are also true." (2.649) There is a relation between probability and belief, but it rests upon the previous harmony between belief and fact. And since fact is the basis too for probability, the objective nature of the latter as independent of belief does not rule out the tendency toward an agreement between belief and probability. It remains true, and is illustrative, that insurance companies do not rest their hopes for success upon probabilities based on belief but rather upon probabilities based on fact. (6.534) For Peirce the subjective, or "conceptualist," view of probability was "only an absurd attempt to reduce synthetic to analytic reasoning" (2.685) in which way "no definite solution is possible."

D. Speculative Rhetoric

Speculative Rhetoric is the third of Peirce's three main divisions of logic. It is the "highest and most living branch of logic." (2.333) Having outlined in Speculative Grammar the *meaning* of symbols and examined in Critical Logic the *truth* of symbols, we now turn to the question of their *force*. Speculative Rhetoric "would treat of the formal conditions of the force of symbols," (1.559; 4.116) had Peirce amplified it in the systematic fashion which he surely intended to do. All that remain, however, are certain suggestive passages. We shall try to discover from these what topics the third division of logic was planned to comprise.

It becomes evident, then, that Speculative Grammar and Critical Logic are concerned with the theory of pure logic, while Speculative Rhetoric occupies itself with the theory of applied logic. We have noted in the two foregoing sections how general ideas can be represented symbolically as terms, propositions, and arguments or syllogisms. In the present section we shall be introduced to the broad topic of the activities of these symbols. As Peirce says, "now we have to examine . . . whether there be a life in signs, so that—the requisite vehicle being present—they will go through a certain order of development, and if so, whether this development be merely of such a nature that the same round of changes of form is described over and over again whatever be the matter of the thought or whether, in addition to such a repetitive order, there be also a greater life-history that every symbol furnished with a vehicle of life goes through, and what is the nature of it." (2.111) We shall learn how such symbolic representation can be effective (i) in the relations between symbols, e.g., as they take place in minds (communication); (ii) in the relations of symbols to facts, e.g., in practice (pragmatism); and (iii) in the relations of facts to symbols, e.g., in the discovery of general ideas and the demonstration of their validity (scientific method).

i. THE PROCESS OF COMMUNICATION

It will be recalled[77] that a sign is defined as a representamen which on some ground determines an interpretant to refer to an object to which it itself refers. Communication, then, in logical terms deals with the arousal of representamen in interpretants. In one place Peirce emphasized the role of the interpretant in a definition of Speculative Rhetoric. He said that "it is the doctrine of the general conditions of the reference of symbols and other signs to the interpretants which they aim to determine." (2.93)

Thus far in the development of his logic Peirce succeeded in treating logic altogether without the aid of psychology. At this point, however, he introduced the psychological *person*, but was still concerned with him only in his *logical* aspects. That is, he was concerned with minds only in so far as they contained signs. "In coming to Speculative Rhetoric, after the main conceptions of logic have been well settled, there can be no serious objection to relaxing the severity of our rule of excluding psychological matter," (2.107) remembering always of course that the psychological matter comprises the psychological aspects of "a purely logical doctrine." For "it would be a mistake, in my opinion, to hold [Speculative Rhetoric] to be a matter of psychology." (4.116) Peirce defined a sign in one place as "anything which is so determined by something else, called its object, and so determines an effect upon a person, which effect I call its interpretant, that the latter is thereby mediately determined by the former."[78] Note that the *effect* on the person, and not the *person*, is the interpretant. Elsewhere the analysis is even more exact. A sign "has an *object* and an *interpretant,* the latter being that which the sign produces in the quasi-mind that is the interpreter by determining the latter to a feeling, to an exertion, or to a sign, which determination is the interpretant." (4.536) Peirce distinguished in this passage between interpreter and interpretant, an important distinction indeed. For his chief concern is with the interpretant, which proves to be equivalent

[77] See this chapter, B, i.

[78] Letter of 1908 to Lady Welby, quoted in C. K. Ogden and I. A. Richards, *The Meaning of Meaning* (New York, Harcourt, Brace, 1927), p. 288. Peirce added, "My insertion of 'upon a person' is a sop to Cerberus, because I despair of making my own broader [i.e., entirely logical] conception understood."

to a second sign aroused in the interpreter by the latter's recognition of the reference of the first sign to its object.

The interpreter, in whom the interpretant is determined, does not, in point of fact, have to be a mind and may not even be a sentient human being. Of course, the interpreter may be the mind of a human being, and frequently is; but emphatically it does not have to be. It may be anything sufficiently sentient to receive the impression of a sign and entertain an interpretant. For the interpretant of a sign is always itself a sign. Thus the apprehension of sense impressions and of relations in the knowledge process of human beings is one example of the arousal of interpretants in interpreters. But more is involved than the lack of necessity for the interpreter to be a human being; for the actual existence of the interpretant itself may be only a possibility. "It is not necessary that the interpretant should actually exist. A being *in futuro* will suffice." (2.92) Thus since interpretant as well as interpreter may have only a problematic existence for the purposes of significance, it becomes clear that the relation of a sign to its object is the fundamental one in semiotic; and that communication, or the arousal of one sign by means of another sign, depends upon this fundamental relation.

The principal logical notion in the understanding of communication is that of assertion.[79] Now, an assertion is nothing more than a proposition[80] considered in its relation to communication. As such it is a rudimentary form of argument;[81] it seeks to convince a possible interpreter of some truth. Just as an interpreter was shown to be not necessarily a mind[82] and a proposition not necessarily a verbal or linguistic affair[83] so the assertion, too, is not necessarily a matter of words. It may consist in any significant communication.

We may distinguish in every communication a speaker and a listener. (2.334) The listener, like the interpreter, may have the status of possible existence only. Moreover, the speaker and the listener may exist in the same person, as in the mental registering of an act of judgment. Although "thought is an *action*," it "consists in a *relation*." (5.399) It is important to repeat in this connection that "the assertion consists in the furnishing of evidence by the speaker to the listener that the speaker believes something,

[79] Every term and proposition, as well as every argumentation (see this chapter, C, i) involves assertion of a rudimentary and implicit variety. But the assertion involved becomes explicit only in communication.

[80] See this chapter, B, iii.

[81] See this chapter, C, i.

[82] See this chapter, D, i.

[83] See this chapter, B, iii.

that is, finds a certain idea to be definitively compulsory on a certain occasion. There ought, therefore, to be three parts in every assertion, a sign of the occasion of the compulsion, a sign of the enforced idea, and a sign evidential of the compulsion affecting the speaker . . . " (2.335) "The occasion of the compulsion can only be represented to the listener by compelling him to have experience of that same occasion." (2.336) Hence, as we have seen, the sign of the occasion of compulsion is an index.[84] Hence "one index, at least, must form part of every assertion," (2.337) although it must be remembered that "the index . . . may be a mere look or gesture" (2.338) as well as a linguistic term. The "sign of the enforced idea" is the mental image stimulated in the mind of the possible listener. The sign "draws the attention to an idea, or mental construction, or diagram, of something possessing [certain] characters." (2.341) The sign evidential of the compulsion affecting the speaker is the retention "of those characters . . . in the foreground of consciousness. What does that mean unless that the listener says to himself 'that which is *here* (before the attention) possesses such and such characters'?" Again, "when a listener hears the term 'light' he proceeds to *create* in his mind an image thereof"; and "until this process is performed, the name excites no meaning in the mind of the listener."

The relation of speaker to potential listener involves the notion of meaning, and this notion, too, is cast by Peirce in logical terms. That which conveys meaning is an icon. Since we can communicate only by means of icons, and assertion is the logical essential in communication, every assertion must contain an icon. (2.278) Meaning is defined by Peirce as "the translation of a sign into another [sign or] system of signs." (4.127) "The meaning of a sign is the sign it has to be translated into." (4.132) But since a sign may be either a term, a proposition, or an argument,[85] "by the *meaning* of a term, proposition or argument, we understand the entire general intended interpretant." (5.179) Meaning is essentially general. (5.429) But the entire general intended interpretant cannot be exhausted by examples of interpretants in the past or future, since these must be less than the total and, more, must be denumerable, and the general interpretant is inexhaustible in its examples and therefore innumerable. Thus meaning so defined must be "a law, or regularity of the indefinite future." (2.293) For nothing less than an indefinite future would be required to meet the demand for "every obvious necessary deduction," which, Peirce said, the meaning of a proposition embraces. (5.165) Meaning, then, "denotes the intended interpretant of a symbol,"

[84] See this chapter, B, i.
[85] See this chapter, B and C.

(5.175) or sign. Since every communication involves an interpretant, communication is dependent upon meaning; but on the other hand, since meaning is independent of assertion, (2.252) meaning is independent of communication.

We have said that communication according to Peirce consists in the arousal of representamen in interpretants.[86] We may now see, from our examination of what Peirce meant by this, that the arousal of representamen in interpretants is the active or practical version of the process of communication, which analyzes logically to the way in which an index relates an icon to a symbol.[87]

ii. THE FORCE OF MEANING

We have seen that communication logically has to do with the arousal of signs in interpretants; and, as meaning, in the relation of signs to other signs. In this section we shall examine the force of the relation between signs and their objects, and the notion of meaning will be extended to include the determination of signs by their objects.[88]

The analysis of meaning yielded as an end product the "entire general intended interpretant."[89] First of all, "the idea of *meaning* is such as to involve some reference to a purpose.[90] But meaning is attributed to representamens alone, and the only kind of representamen who has a definite professed purpose is an 'argument.'[91] The professed purpose of an argument is to determine an acceptance of its conclusion, and it quite accords with general usage to call the conclusion of an argument its meaning." (5.175) Peirce's justification for the introduction of the term "meaning" as a technical term of logic is that he had "a new conception to express," namely, "that of the conclusion of an argument as its intended interpretant."

But this notion is itself capable of further analysis. Clearly, what is intended by the entire generality of the interpretant is some conception which shall be sufficiently inclusive, and this conception is contained in the notion of "ultimate." What is the ultimate meaning of a sign? (5.179) At this stage in the development of Speculative Rhetoric, a further distinction is required. Corresponding to the determination of the interpretant to a feel-

[86] See this chapter, D, i.
[87] See this chapter, B, i, (*b*).
[88] See this chapter, D, i.
[89] See this chapter, D, i.
[90] See 5.166.
[91] See this chapter, C, i.

ing, an exertion or another sign.[92] Peirce distinguished between the *immediate*, the *dynamical*, and the *final* interpretant. In the preceding section, we dealt with the immediate interpretant, that is, with "the interpretant as it is revealed in the right understanding of the sign itself." (4.536) But the ultimate meaning of a sign will have to include all meanings of interpretant. In this section, then, we shall concern ourselves with the final interpretant "which refers to the manner in which the sign tends to represent itself to be related to its object," leaving the dynamical interpretant for the following section.

"All dynamical action, or action of brute force . . . takes place between two subjects" or is the result of such action; (5.484) it is essentially a dyadic relation. But there is such a thing as "action . . . which is, or involves, a coöperation of *three* subjects, such as a sign, its object, and its interpretant, this tri-relative influence not being in any way resolvable into actions between pairs." This triadic relation is that of semiosis. We may observe its operation upon the interpreter, who, it must be remembered, is often but not necessarily a human being.[93] The first proper effect of a sign is a feeling, (5.475) and in this capacity the sign is called an emotional or immediate interpretant. "If a sign produces any further significate effect, it will do so through the mediation of the emotional interpretant, and such further effect will always involve an effort." This is the energetic or dynamical interpretant. The third effect of a sign is the logical or final interpretant, a mental sign or thought. (5.476) It has its effect in the arousal of a general concept or a habit-change, "meaning by a habit-change a modification of a person's tendencies toward action."

We live, according to Peirce, in two worlds: an inner world and an outer world. (5.474) The inner world "exerts a comparatively slight compulsion upon us . . . while the other world, the outer world, is full of irresistible compulsions." The vast majority of determinations are external; and all external determinations come from signs. That the signs may constitute propositions which yet need not be verbal is a truth which cannot be too often emphasized. Peirce is clear on this issue; for, as he said, the pointing arm may be the subject of a proposition (2.357) and a mere look or gesture may act as a noun. (2.338)

In terms of the anticipation of the possible triad of effects of the sign, it is essential to discover the meaning of signs. Before we can decide upon the power of any particular sign, we must have a method of verifying significant

[92] See this chapter, D, i, quoting "Prolegomena to an Apology," etc.
[93] See this chapter, D, i.

determination. Now, signs are determined by their objects; "that thing which causes a sign as such is called the *object* ... the sign is determined to some species of correspondence with that object." (5.473) Signs themselves, as we have seen,[94] arouse other signs, and this is their meaning. The signs which they arouse may be the actions which follow from them. In terms of effect, then, the meaning of a sign may now be said to "consist in how it might cause us [or any thing capable of apprehending a sign] to act." (5.135) In terms of action, or possible action, as we have noted, "the *meaning* of a proposition embraces every obvious necessary deduction from it." (5.165)

The exploration of the possible effects of signs, or propositions, consists, then, in the anticipation of possible deductions from them. This gives us leave at the outset to omit those propositions which cannot yield valid deductions. The remainder have the status of hypotheses; and "any hypothesis, therefore, may be admissible in the absence of any special reasons to the contrary, provided it be capable of experimental verification." (5.197) This doctrine is called by Peirce pragmatism: the extension of the doctrine of meaning to effect and verification of (possible) effect. Pragmatism is "a method of ascertaining the meanings, not of all ideas, but only of ... 'intellectual concepts', that is to say, of those upon the structure of which, arguments concerning objective fact may hinge." (5.467) Pragmatism in this sense is nothing more than a maxim of procedure, although such an understanding of it does not exhaust its meaning. If such and such an hypothesis is true, the operation of it will have such and such a result. (5.483)[95] By "calling a thing *hard*," for example, we mean that "it will not be scratched by many other substances." (5.403)

"Intellectual concepts, however—the only sign-burdens that are properly denominated 'concepts'—essentially carry some implication concerning the general behavior either of some conscious being or of some inanimate object, and so convey more, not merely than any feeling, but more, too, than any existential fact, namely, the 'would-acts', 'would-dos' of habitual behavior; and no agglomeration of actual happenings can ever completely fill up the meaning of a 'would-be.' (5.467) The meanings of signs are powers which we can hope to understand, and perhaps partially to control. But ideas, whether acting as intellectual concepts or as habits in things, have "more or less [the] power of working [themselves] out into fact" (2.149) and "ideas utterly despised and frowned upon have an inherent power of working their way to the governance of the world, at last."

---

[94] See this chapter, D, i.
[95] "And conversely." See this chapter, D, iii.

iii. THE METHOD OF DISCOVERY

We have seen that pragmatism is a check upon those ideas which go beyond existential fact to the "would-be" of habitual behavior.[96] The method of discovery is, in a sense, the reverse of pragmatism. Pragmatism says that ideas work themselves out in facts; the method of discovery says that ideas may be discovered through facts. Pragmatism says that if such and such an hypothesis is true, the operation of it ought to have such and such a result.[97] The method of discovery says that if such and such is a fact, it ought to be the effect of such and such a law, and this supposition is then framed as an hypothesis for testing by means of prediction.

"The order of the march of suggestion," then, says Peirce, "is from experience to hypothesis." (2.755) Indeed, this direction has confused logicians, so that they have supposed abstraction to be entirely a question of psychology. Abstraction, in the logical "sense in which an abstract noun marks an abstraction," (4.235) has been confused with "that operation of the mind by which we pay attention to one feature of a percept to the disregard of others. The two things are entirely disconnected." Logic is concerned only with the former, which Peirce termed "*hypostatic* abstraction,[98] the abstraction which transforms 'it is light' into 'there is light here'."[99] Hypostatic abstraction is the direction of the logic of discovery, the first step in scientific method. But scientific method includes more than "the discovery of laws"; (2.713) it includes also "the discovery of causes" and "the prediction of effects."[100] Speculative Rhetoric includes among its topics only that step of scientific method which is the discovery of causes.

Let us consider the logic of the method of discovery. Logical discovery is in terms of the *dynamical* interpretant.[101] The dynamical interpretant is the actual effect which the sign determines. (4.536) The relation of a sign to its object is not a mental association but an absolute necessity and an ineradicable one. (3.361) When we attempt to learn through the actual effect of a sign, or its dynamical interpretant, what the sign is which has determined it, we are embarked upon the process of discovery. Thus the method of discovery is the search among actual effects for indications of its determining representamen. The representamen so discovered is termed an hypothesis, and

[96] See especially this chapter, D, ii.
[97] See this chapter, D, ii.
[98] In contrast with psychological, or "precisive," abstraction.
[99] It is by means of symbols that we make abstractions. (4.531)
[100] For a treatment of the whole of scientific method, including all three steps, see chap. VIII, C, iii.
[101] See this chapter, D, iii.

the logical process involved is termed induction.[102] Where the hypothesis chosen is broader and more inclusive than the facts strictly warrant, that is, where "the existence of a fact quite different from anything observed" (2.636) is concluded, the process involved is termed abduction.[103] Facts may be about one object, two objects, or a number of objects greater than two, (1.371) and the importance of the discovery of the hypothesis is in proportion to the number of objects included in its degree of generality. But hypotheses inferred from facts about objects do not have to be absolutely general, or universal, in order to be valid propositions. Moreover, such is the tentative nature of discovery that they do not have to be certain in order to enjoy a status in the logic of discovery. Propositions of the form "*S* may be *P*" are valid propositions. (2.383)

We have seen that induction, although tentative by nature, in the long run must approximate to the truth. (1.67)[104] We have seen, too, that the strongest kind of induction is quantitative induction, such as is comprised in the theory of probability. (2.758)[105] Induction informs us of the ratio of the probability that *S* may be *P*. We must not lose sight, either, "of the constant tendency of the inductive process to correct itself. This is of its essence. The probability of its conclusion only consists in the fact that if the true value of the ratio sought has not been reached, an extension of the inductive process will lead to a closer approximation." (2.729)

Here the question may well be asked, a "closer approximation" to what? Peirce is ready with the answer, that "if inductive and hypothetic premises lead to true oftener than to false conclusions, it is only because the universe happens to have a certain constitution." (2.749) When we abstract from particular fact to general law, we make continuity "the leading conception of science" (1.62) because we hold that it is also the leading principle of the natural order. The number of good inductions made by those familiar with the deductive system of some science suggests a "tendency toward an agreement between the ideas which suggest themselves to the human mind and those which are concerned in the laws of nature." (1.81) Such a *tendency* is itself a vivid manifestation of the force of truth.

The quantitative exactness of inductive probability and the tendency of truth to suggest itself to the mind leads Peirce to a further insight. Logical abstraction "is a necessary inference whose conclusion refers to a subject not referred to by the premiss[es]." (4.463) The method of abstraction is one

[102] See this chapter, C, iii.
[103] See this chapter, C, iii, (*c*).
[104] See this chapter, C, iii.
[105] See this chapter, C, iv.

which can be repeated, but unlike the method of strict induction, it is not self-corrective in terms of a given hypothesis but it is self-corrective in the sense that it leads to more and more refined generalizations, which are qualitatively different from the original material from which the abstractive process may have taken its start. At every step, the result of abstraction is considered as material for the further application of the process of abstraction. This is particularly true in mathematics, for "the mathematician conceives an operation as something itself to be operated upon." (1.83) Thus there occurred to Peirce the possibility of an exact and abstract science which would attempt to specify "those general conditions under which a problem presents itself for solution and those under which one question leads to another." (3.430) Such a science would be one of "the logical study of the theory of inquiry," (2.106) and its first task would be a "method of discovering methods." (2.108)[106]

The method of discovery is akin to the method of mathematics which, Peirce asserted,[107] is the study of diagrams or graphs. (3.556) This relationship is evidenced by the fact that the generalization of the method of studying graphs leads back to the logic of relatives, i.e., the algebra of logic. (3.499)[108] The graphic representation of facts is iconic, (3.641) and hence one must learn to think *in* graphs *about* the facts they represent. (4.475) The merit of the graph "springs from its being veridically iconic, naturally analogous to the thing represented, and not a creation of conventions." (4.368) A diagram or "system of diagrammatization" (4.530) is that "by means of which any course of thought can be represented with exactitude." "Theorematic reasoning invariably depends upon experimentation with individual schemata." (4.233) Moreover, "operations upon diagrams, whether external or imaginary, take the place of the experiments upon real things that one performs in chemical and physical research," for instance. For just as experimentation can be described as "the putting of questions to Nature," so "experiments upon diagrams are questions put to the Nature of the relations concerned."

The puzzle of how mathematics can be "purely deductive in its nature" (3.363) and yet "present as rich and apparently unending a series of surprising discoveries as any observational science" is solved by the fact that mathematical deduction is based on observation. Deduction proceeds by the observation of diagrams. (3.641) The "deduction consists in constructing an

---

[106] See also 3.454. Also Plato, *Charmides*, 169.
[107] Following Kant, *Kritik der Reinen Vernunft*, I, I, 1.
[108] See this chapter, B, vi, (*b*).

icon or diagram the relations of whose parts shall present a complete analogy with those of the parts of the object." (3.363)[109]

There are four steps, or stages, in Peirce's iconic method.[110] In the first stage, the formation of the icon takes place. "We form in the imagination some sort of diagrammatic, that is, iconic, representation of the facts, as skeletonized as possible . . . . [This diagram is] constructed to represent intuitively or semi-intuitively the same relations which are abstractly expressed in the premises." (2.778) In the second stage, there is observation on and experimentation with the icon. "Such a construction is formed according to a precept furnished by the hypothesis. Being formed, the construction is submitted to the scrutiny of observation, and new relations are discovered among its parts, not stated in the precept by which it was formed, and are found, by a little mental experimentation, to be such that they will always be present in such a construction." (3.560) In the third stage, the conclusion is reached and stated. "We observe the result of [the] experiment, and that is our deductive conclusion." (5.579) This conclusion consists, as Burks pointed out,[111] in a formulation of the relations found in the modified icon. The fourth, and last, stage is that in which the universal validity of the conclusion is established. "A few mental experiments—or even a single one, so expert do we become at this kind of experimental inquiry—satisfy the mind that the one icon would at all times involve the other, that is, suggest it in a special way. . . . Hence the mind is not only led from believing the premiss to judge the conclusion true, but it further attaches to this judgment another —that *every* proposition *like* the premiss, that is having an icon like it, *would* involve, and compel acceptance of, a proposition related to it as the conclusion then drawn is related to that premiss. Thus we see, what is most important, that every inference is thought, at the time of drawing it, as one of a possible class of inferences." (2.444)

"Thus the necessary reasoning of mathematics is performed by means of observation and experiment." (3.560) However, in drawing conclusions from the observation of diagrams it must be remembered that we are concerned not with the relation of the diagram to the facts which it represents but only with the diagram itself employed as a premise. (3.559) Thus necessary reasoning is independent of actual facts, although conclusions discovered by reasoning must be checked against such facts. Peirce's theory is

---

[109] For a more extended discussion of deductive observation, see 2.778.

[110] For a full and excellent discussion of Peirce's iconic method, as well as of other points in his logic, see Arthur W. Burks's doctoral dissertation, *The Logical Foundations of the Philosophy of Charles Sanders Peirce* (Ann Arbor, Mich., June, 1941), especially chap. II, sec. 2.

[111] *Ibid.*, p. 60.

that graphic assertions are about an "arbitrarily hypothetical universe. . . . Thus conformity to an existing, that is, entirely determinate universe does not make necessity, which consists in what always *will* be, that is, what is determinately true of a universe not yet entirely determinate." (4.431)

Graphs begin at the elementary level of simple syllogism; but they "lead more directly to the ultimate analysis of logical problems than any algebra yet devised." (3.619) Peirce conceived of an advanced theory of graphs which would be exceedingly complex and would treat of the whole universe of logical possibility. (4.512)[112] The method of "abstractive observation," (2.227) or "ideal experimentation" (3.528), must consist, in part at least, of the observation of diagrams at the high abstractive level where the transformation of sets of propositions into other sets is required.

Such a method, the discovery of which was set forth by Peirce as the task of Speculative Rhetoric, (2.107) was to operate at the high abstractive level of formal propositions, which had already been found by means of the scientific method. "We frame a system of expressing propositions—a written language—having a syntax to which there are absolutely no exceptions. We then satisfy ourselves that whenever a proposition having a certain syntactical form is true, another proposition definitely related to it—so that the relation can be defined in terms of the appearance of the two propositions on paper—will necessarily also be true. We draw up our code of basic rules of such illative transformations, none of these rules being a necessary consequence of others. We then proceed to express in our language the premisses of long and difficult mathematical demonstrations and try whether our rules will bring out their conclusions." (4.481)

Ideal experimentation, Peirce's iconic method of deductive reasoning, is observational and experimental. We observe graphs, which is "just as much an operation of *observation* as is the observation of bees. This observation leads us to make an *experiment* upon the graph. Namely, we first duplicate portions of it; and then we erase portions of it, that is, we put out of sight part of the assertion in order to see what the rest of it is. We observe the result of this experiment, and that is our deductive conclusion." (5.579) All necessary reasoning whatsoever proceeds by constructions; and the only difference between mathematical and philosophical [i.e., logical] necessary deductions is that the latter are so excessively simple that the construction attracts no attention and is overlooked. The construction exists in the simplest syllogism in Barbara. "Why do the logicians like to state a syllogism

---

[112] See in this connection, *Col. Pap.*, vol. iv, chaps. V and VI.

by writing the major premiss on one line and the minor below it, with letters substituted for the subject and predicates? It is merely because the reasoner has to notice that relation between the parts of those premisses which such a diagram brings into prominence. If the reasoner makes use of syllogistic in drawing his conclusion, he has such a diagram or construction in his mind's eye, and observes the result of eliminating the middle term." (3.560) Thus deduction is a logical method involving observation and experimentation. Peirce in fact defined one kind of deduction, "theorematic deduction," as "one which, having represented the conditions of the conclusion in a diagram, performs an ingenious experiment upon the diagram, and by the observation of the diagram, so modified, ascertains the truth of the conclusion." (2.267) "Deduction is really a matter of perception and experimentation, just as induction and hypothetic inference are; only, the perception and experimentation are concerned with imaginary objects instead of with real ones." (6.595) In a "certain universe of logical possibility, certain combinations occur while others do not occur. Of those which occur in the ideal world some do and some do not occur in the real world; but all that occur in the real world occur also in the ideal world. For the real world is the world of sensible experience, and it is a part of the process of sensible experience to locate its facts in the world of ideas." (3.527)

By this method, and starting from the observation of graphs, Peirce hoped to work from the "lesser environment of the utterer and interpreter" (5.506) of each particular "proposition that actually gets conveyed, to which that proposition more particularly refers and which is not general," to "the truth, which is the universe of all universes." This is what Peirce conceived of as "ideal experimentation." It was necessary, Peirce felt, to generalize his conception of the methods employed by mathematicians and scientific men (2.110) in order to discover the "purely logical doctrine of how discovery must take place." (2.107) Men who have prepared themselves with the proper training in the logic of scientific method will then be putting themselves in the way of discovery; their minds will be in a condition to serve as vehicles for the occupancy of important ideas. For it is true that "ideas are not all mere creations of this or that mind, but on the contrary have a power of finding or creating their vehicles, and having found them, of conferring upon them the ability to transform the face of the earth." (1.217)[118] As the final task of Speculative Rhetoric, Peirce conceived the necessity of finding out how to cope with the force of true ideas with which in the future we may have to be concerned.

[118] See this chapter, D, i.

iv. SUMMARY OF THE CHAPTER

Peirce rejected the theories of the foundations of logic offered by other workers in the field in his day. He denied that logic is founded upon subjective feeling, individual experience, the natural light of reason, philosophy, psychology, the data of psychology, epistemology, language, society, authority, the history of science, or common experience.

Against these alternatives, Peirce proposed his own, namely, that logic takes its start in stubborn fact and is akin to mathematics. It presupposes an objective truth, and is close to ontology. Logic is the theory of signs. Accordingly, there are three grand divisions of logic: Speculative Grammar, Critical Logic, and Speculative Rhetoric.

Speculative Grammar deals with the reference of symbols to their grounds. A sign or representamen determines something else to refer to an object to which itself refers. It stands for its object to an interpretant. There are nine fundamental kinds of signs: qualisign, sinsign, and legisign; icon, index, and symbol; and rheme, dicisign, and argument; and these yield ten valid trichotomies. In the light of these distinctions, anything can be considered in its capacity as a sign.

The syllogism is the typical logical form. The smallest element of the syllogism is also the simplest to explain as a sign; this is the *term*. Terms are symbols which directly determine their imputed qualities,[114] denoting the possession of certain characters. Terms have depth, or intension, and breadth, or extension. They are parts of propositions

Propositions are parts of arguments, which last express the fundamental logical relation of illation. Propositions determine their objects by means of other terms and thus express their own validity. Propositions are not exclusively linguistic; they do not depend upon their assertion. Propositions may express existing states of things (*de inesse*) or a whole range of possibility (*modal*). Of the various types of proposition, the hypothetical embraces the others.

The three basic propositions, or principles, known as Aristotle's three laws—identity, contradiction, and the excluded middle—are, despite the criticisms made of them, within limits valid. Much criticism is answered successfully when the laws are considered to have an existential reference. The laws, however, are not merely "laws of thought," as they have been called. They are also valid and necessary conditions of existence.

[114] With the possible exception of indexes.

The last department of Speculative Grammar is the logic of relatives. The logic of relatives implies three conclusions. These are: that everything logical reduces to relations; that relations are products of empirical observation; and that inclusion is a fundamental logical relation.

Critical Logic, the second of Peirce's grand divisions, deals with the formal conditions of the truth of symbols by means of the argument, or syllogism. The syllogism consists in the proposition with assertiveness added. Assertion is the determination of the interpreting representation; what is asserted is the truth. The syllogism involves six elements: leading principle, premise, colligation, inference, involvement, and conclusion.

There are three kinds of syllogism: abductive, deductive, and inductive. The abductive is the predictive type; it consists in arriving at an hypothesis from observed facts. There is only one kind of abduction. The deductive is the necessary type; it consists in the fact that the premises involve the conclusion. There are two kinds of deduction: necessary and probable, or absolute and frequentative. The inductive is the statistical type; it consists in arguing from some members of a class to all members of that class. There are three kinds of induction: crude, quantitative, and qualitative, or weak, exact, and common-sense induction.

Probable inference or probability is a branch of induction. Probability is defined as the relative frequency with which the relevant formal principle is supported by the favorable cases. The other definitions of probability which would equate it with deducibility or degree of belief, while untrue, can be subsumed by the relative frequency theory.

Speculative Rhetoric, the third of Peirce's grand divisions, deals with the communication, meaning, and discovery of symbols. Communication is the arousal of one sign by another, of a representamen in the interpretant; it involves a possible interpretant, and does not require an actual one. The speaker asserts something to a possible (or actual) listener, conveying to him the occasion of a compulsion.

Meaning has to do with the force of the relation between signs and their objects. There are three kinds of effects upon interpretants: the immediate, the dynamical, and the final, corresponding to feeling, action, and thought. Of these, only the final refers to the relation from sign to object. This direction indicates the possible action indicated by the sign.

The discovery of symbols involves a direction from experience to hypothesis, such that the effects of general laws are predicted. It involves the first step in scientific method. Ideal experimentation is both deductive and experimental in that it draws necessary conclusions from the observation of and experiment with diagrams and graphs. Logical discovery is in terms of the dynamical interpretant, and employs all three forms of argument.

We have reached the end of our exposition of Peirce's logic. This topic has been placed first in the chapters devoted to the exposition of Peirce's philosophy not only because logic was a leading interest, but also because his work in other departments was based upon his logic.[115] He, himself, had occasion to remark of one part of his logic that "if deeply pondered [it] will be found to enwrap an entire philosophy. Kant taught that our fundamental conceptions are merely the ineluctable ideas of a system of logical forms; nor is any occult transcendentalism requisite to show that this is so, and must be so. Nature only appears intelligible so far as it appears rational. (3.422)

Peirce defined logic "in its narrower sense" (1.444) as "the science of the necessary conditions of the attainment of truth." It follows that in so far as he was able to attain to truth in other branches of philosophy it was because the "necessary conditions" dictated by logic were adhered to. "Questions of philosophy," he said, "ought to be decided upon logical principles." (3.425) Thus the postulate upon which the following chapters are based is that Peirce's philosophy is consistent with his logic. The effort to maintain this consistency may have led him at times to indulge in a certain amount of exaggeration and distortion; but where the logic is valid, and the derivation of the philosophy from it such that the denial of the latter involves the denial of the former, it will be shown that there is no doubt of the fact that the discovery of relations of vast philosophical import has been accomplished.

[115] See this chapter, A, i.

CHAPTER IV

Metaphysics

<<<<<<<<<<<<<<<<<<<<<<<<<<<<<<<<<<<<<<>>>>>>>>>>>>>>>>>>>>>>>>>>>>>>>>>>>

A. Phenomenology

THIS IS THE FIRST OF TWO CHAPTERS IN WHICH IS PRESENTED PEIRCE'S SYSTEM
of metaphysics. Why ontology precedes epistemology will become obvious
in the course of the development of these studies. The closeness of logic
and ontology has already been indicated,[1] an affinity so complete that the
distinction between the two topics is of no interest to ontology.[2] Peirce
asserted that "when we come to philosophical questions . . . it becomes
necessary to examine the principles of logic in order to discover a general
method of proving that a given hypothesis involves no contradiction. . . .
Unfortunately, philosophy cannot choose its first principles at will, but has
to accept them as they are." (4.176) Logic is the "key of philosophy."
(3.455)[3] "We should expect to find metaphysics . . . to be somewhat more
difficult than logic, but still on the whole one of the simplest of sciences,
as it is one whose main principles must be settled before very much progress
can be gained. . . . "(6.4) "Metaphysics consists in the results of the absolute
acceptance of logical principles not merely as regulatively valid,[4] but as
truth of being." (1.487) And "'exact' logic will prove a stepping-stone to
'exact' metaphysics." (3.454) Although logic is more general than experience
and fact, it rests upon them.[5] Thus if metaphysics rests on logic, from which
it is at times indistinguishable, and logic rests on experience and fact, it
follows that metaphysics must be, indirectly at least, an observational discipline. But it is also an observational discipline directly. "Metaphysics, even
bad metaphysics, really rests on observations, whether consciously or not;
and the only reason that this is not universally recognized is that it rests

---

[1] See chap. III, A, ii.

[2] See chap. III, A, ii.

[3] "My philosophy, and all philosophy worth attention, reposes entirely upon the theory of logic."
Letter of December 26, 1897, to William James. Quoted in Ralph Barton Perry, *The Thought and
Character of William James* (Boston, Little, Brown, 1935), vol. ii, p. 419.

[4] In opposition to Kant, *Kritik der Reinen Vernunft*, A 179-180, B 222-223.

[5] See chap. III, A. ii.

upon kinds of phenomena with which every man's experience is so saturated that he usually pays no particular attention to them." (6.2) It was Peirce's idea that the foundations of metaphysics would be better understood if this dependence of metaphysics on observation were to be generally known. Hence phenomenology must be the first topic in the exposition of metaphysics.

i. PURPOSE AND DEFINITION

The purpose of "Phenomenology, or the Doctrine of Categories,[6] . . . is to unravel the tangled skein [of] all that in any sense appears, and wind it into distinct forms; or in other words, to make the ultimate analysis of all experiences the first task to which philosophy has to apply itself." (1.280) Phenomenology is a "preliminary inquiry," "a science that does not draw any distinction of good and bad in any sense whatever, but just contemplates phenomena as they are, simply opens its eyes and describes what it sees; not what it sees in the real as distinguished from figment—not regarding any such dichotomy—but simply describing the object, as a phenomenon, and stating what it finds in all phenomena alike." (5.37) The business of phenomenology, then, is "to draw up an inventory of appearances without going into any investigation of their truth." (2.120) "It simply scrutinizes the direct appearances, and endeavors to combine minute accuracy with the broadest possible generalization." (1.287) By "describing individual phenomena and endeavoring to explain them," (1.180) "Phenomenology ascertains and studies the kinds of elements universally present in the phenomenon; meaning by the *phenomenon* whatever is present at any time to the mind in any way." (1.186) To the question *"when* and to *whose* mind," (1.284) Peirce replied that he had "never entertained a doubt" that those features of the phenomena which he had found in his mind "are present at all times and to all minds." "There can be no psychological difficulty in determining whether anything belongs to the [phenomena] or not; for whatever seems to be before the mind *ipso facto* is so." (1.288)

The phenomenologist does not have an easy task. He must "look well at the phenomenon and say what are the characteristics that are never wanting in it, whether that phenomenon be something that outward experience forces upon our attention, or whether it be the wildest of dreams, or whether it be the most abstract and general of the conclusions of science." (5.41) For this task three faculties are required: first, "the faculty of seeing what stares one in the face," (5.42) which is "the faculty of the artist"; secondly,

[6] See *Col. Pap.*, vol. i, bk. iii.

the faculty of "resolute discrimination which fastens itself like a bulldog upon the particular feature that we are studying, follows it wherever it may lurk, and detects it beneath all its disguises"; and finally, the faculty which consists in "the generalizing power of the mathematician who produces the abstract formula that comprehends the very essence of the feature under examination purified from all admixture of extraneous and irrelevant accompaniments."

"Phenomenology treats of the Universal Qualities of Phenomena in their immediate phenomenal character, in themselves as phenomena." (5.122) "'Phenomenon' is to be understood in the broadest sense conceivable; so that phenomenology might rather be defined as the study of what seems than as the statement of what appears. It describes the essentially different elements which seem to present themselves in what seems"; (2.197) so that "in Phenomenology there is no assertion except that there are certain seemings; and even these are not, and cannot be asserted, because they cannot be described." They are merely pointed to or indicated, but as such they constitute the "facts of phenomenology." (5.126)

Peirce's alternative name for phenomenology is "phaneroscopy" (1.284) and for phenomena the "phaneron." We may proceed now to a description of the nature of the phaneron, the subject matter of phaneroscopy.

ii. THE PHANERON

"Phaneroscopy is that study which, supported by the direct observation of phanerons and generalizing its observations, signalizes several very broad classes of phanerons; describes the features of each; shows that although they are so inextricably mixed together that no one can be isolated, yet it is manifest that their characters are quite disparate; then proves, beyond question, that a certain very short list comprises all of these broadest categories of phanerons there are; and finally proceeds to the laborious and difficult task of enumerating the principal subdivisions of those categories." (1.286) "Phaneroscopy . . . is occupied with the formal elements of the phaneron." (1.284)

After a careful analysis, Peirce came to the conclusion that at least three and only three categories would be necessary to describe the basic elements of what was contained in his experience. "The three categories are supposed to be the three kinds of elements that attentive perception can make out in the phenomenon."[7]

---

[7] Letter of June 8, 1903, quoted in Perry, *Thought and Character*, chap. ii, p. 429.

At this point Peirce took an important step. Although the phaneron includes everything that is experienced, we want to consider, he said, "not everything in the phaneron, but only its indecomposable elements, that is, those that are logically indecomposable, or indecomposable to direct inspection." (1.288) The indecomposable elements of the phaneron must be sorted out "into their different kinds according to their real characters." There are only two such classifications: the first, "according to the form or structure," and a second, "according to their matter." The first classification is the one adopted, for Peirce wrote that he had failed miserably in his attempt to "ascertain something for certain about the latter." As to the difficulty of how indecomposable elements could have differences of structure, Peirce replied that "of internal logical structure it would be clearly impossible. But of external structure, that is to say, structure of its possible compounds, limited differences of structure are possible." (1.289) Since "a category is an element of phenomena of the first rank of generality," (5.43) we should expect "the universal categories [to] belong to every phenomenon, one being perhaps more prominent in one aspect of that phenomenon than another but all of them belonging to every phenomenon."

Here we find that both the raw experience and the logic upon which ontology draws come together to yield the first tentative hints of the basic phenomenological distinctions. Phenomenology is seeking indecomposable elements and has found them to have a kind of "external structure." This structure is first indicated in the relation between signs and their logical objects. "There is no *a priori* reason," said Peirce, "why there should not be indecomposable elements of the phaneron which are what they are regardless of anything else, each complete in itself; provided, of course, that they be capable of composition." (1.295) This is the same notion described in logic as the *immediate* or emotional interpretant of a sign,[8] in which "the whole universe of phenomena appears to be made up of nothing but sensible qualities." (1.424) Quality is that "part of the phenomenal world" which is "presented to the observer" "regardless of its parts." (1.429) It is that in which we attend to each part as it appears in itself, in its own suchness, while we disregard the connections. Red, sour, toothache, are each *sui generis* and indescribable. In themselves that is all there is to be said about them.

"The first [category of elements of phenomena] comprises the qualities of phenomena, such as red, bitter, tedious, hard, heartrending, noble; and there are doubtless manifold varieties utterly unknown to us. Beginners in

[8] See chap. III, D, ii.

philosophy may object that these are not qualities of things and are not in the world at all, but are mere sensations. Certainly, we only know such as the senses we are furnished with are adapted to reveal; and it can hardly be doubted that the specializing effect of the evolutionary process which has made us what we are has been to blot the greater part of the senses and sensations which were once dimly felt, and to render bright, clear, and separate the rest. But whether we ought to say that it is the senses that make the sense-qualities or the sense-qualities to which the senses are adapted, need not be determined in haste. It is sufficient that wherever there is a phenomenon there is a quality; so that it might almost seem that there is nothing else in phenomena. The qualities merge into one another. They have no perfect identities, but only likenesses, or partial identities. Some of them, as the colors, and the musical sounds, form well-understood systems. Probably, were our experience of them not so fragmentary, there would be no abrupt demarcations between them, at all. Still, each one is what it is in itself without help from the others. They are single but partial determinations." (1.418).

"*In secundo,* there is no *a priori* reason why there should not be inde-composable elements which are what they are relatively to a second but independently of any third. Such, for example, is the idea of otherness." (1.296) This is the same notion described in logic as the *dynamical,* or energetic, interpretant of a sign.[9] In order to perceive this second aspect of phenomena we must attend to two of its features: "first, that which the logicians call the *contingent,* that is, the accidentally actual, and second, whatever involves an unconditional necessity, that is, force without law or reason, *brute* force." (1.427) These two features, combined in the coinci-dental, are what Peirce called fact. All facts are " 'coincidences', a name which implies that our attention is called in them to the coming together of two things. Two phenomena, and but two, are required to constitute a coincidence." (1.429) Thus fact involves dependence. "Whenever we come to know a fact, it is by its resisting us. A man may walk down Wall Street debating within himself the existence of an external world; but if in his brown study he jostles up against somebody who angrily draws off and knocks him down, the sceptic is unlikely to carry his scepticism so far as to doubt whether anything beside the ego was concerned in that phenome-non. The resistance shows him that something independent of him is there." (1.431)

"The second category of elements of phenomena comprises the actual

[9] *Ibid.*

facts. The qualities, in so far as they are general, are somewhat vague and potential. But an occurrence is perfectly individual. It happens here and now. A permanent fact is less purely individual; yet so far as it is actual, its permanence and generality only consist in its being there at every individual instant. Qualities are concerned in facts but they do not make up facts. Facts also concern subjects which are material substances. We do not see them as we see qualities, that is, they are not in the very potentiality and essence of sense. But we feel facts resist our will. That is why facts are proverbially called brutal. Now mere qualities do not resist. It is the matter that resists. Even in actual sensation there is a reaction. Now mere qualities, unmaterialized, cannot actually react. So that, rightly understood, it is correct to say that we immediately, that is, directly perceive matter. To say that we only infer matter from its qualities is to say that we only know the actual through the potential. It would be a little less erroneous to say that we only know the potential through the actual, and only infer qualities by generalization from what we perceive in matter. All that I here insist upon is that quality is one element of phenomena, and fact, action, actuality is another." (1.419)

"*In tertio* there is no *a priori* reason why there should not be indecomposable elements which are what they are relatively to a second and a third, regardless of any fourth. Such, for example, is the idea of *composition*." (1.297) This is the same notion described in logic as the *final*, or logical, interpretant of a sign.[10] This third aspect of the phaneron is called law. There can be no law without generality. (1.476) Law is not in the world of quality and of fact yet it governs the world. (1.478) Genuine law "is separated entirely from those worlds and exists in the universe of *representations*." (1.480)

"The third category of elements of phenomena consists of what we call laws when we contemplate them from the outside only, but which when we see both sides of the shield we call thoughts. Thoughts are neither qualities nor facts. They are not qualities because they can be produced and grow, while a quality is eternal, independent of time and of any realization. Besides, thoughts may have reasons, and indeed, must have some reasons, good or bad. But to ask why a quality is as it is, why red is red and not green, would be lunacy. If red were green it would not be red; that is all. And any semblance of sanity the question may have is due to its being not exactly a question about quality, but about the relation between two qualities, though even this is absurd. A thought then is not a quality. No more

[10] *Ibid.*

is it a fact. For a thought is general. I had it. I imparted it to you. It is general on that side. It is also general in referring to all possible things, and not merely to those which happen to exist. No collection of facts can constitute a law; for the law goes beyond any accomplished facts and determines how facts that *may be,* but *all* of which never can have happened, shall be characterized. There is no objection to saying that a law is a general fact, provided it be understood that the general has an admixture of potentiality in it, so that no congeries of actions here and now can ever make a general fact. As *general,* the law, or general fact, concerns the potential world of quality, while as *fact,* it concerns the actual world of actuality. Just as action requires a peculiar kind of subject matter, which is foreign to mere quality, so law requires a peculiar kind of subject, the thought, or, as the phrase in this connection is, the *mind,* as a peculiar kind of subject foreign to mere individual action. Law, then, is something as remote from both quality and action as these are remote from one another." (1.420)

"We find then *a priori* that there are three categories of indecomposable elements to be expected in the phaneron: those which are simply positive totals, those which involve dependence but not combination, and those which involve combination." (1.299) "The metaphysical categories of quality, fact, and law being categories of the matter[11] of phenomena," (1.452) "it is *a priori* impossible that there should be an indecomposable element which is what it is relatively to a second, a third, and a fourth. The obvious reason is that that which combines two will by repetition combine any number. Nothing could be simpler; nothing in philosophy is more important." (1.298) Thus "our division of the elements of phenomena into the categories of quality, fact, and law may not only be true, but also have the utmost possible value, being governed by those same characteristics which really dominate the phenomenal world." (1.427)

Peirce called the indecomposable elements of the phenomena, as these are laid bare in the phaneron, quality, fact (or reaction), and law (or representation). They are also known in his writings as monad, dyad, and triad, (1.293) or, more commonly, firstness, secondness, and thirdness. (5.121) These are the categories that form the basis of his philosophy.

iii. LOGICAL IMPLICATIONS

Peirce's systematic philosophy is so constructed that each grand division can be exhibited to rest directly upon matters of fact and also upon the

---

[11] "Matter" evidently is employed here in a metaphorical sense.

previous divisions. Thus logic, being the first grand division, rests exclusively upon matters of fact the knowledge of which is derived from experience,[12] and ontology, being the second, must rest upon matters of fact and also upon logic. Phenomenology draws upon fact and logic but not upon any positive science. (5.39) All other divisions, as we shall see, rest upon fact and upon all those divisions which precede them. In the first two sections of this chapter we observed in what way ontology rests directly upon fact; and we became acquainted with the subject matter of phenomenology. And we have already noted that only logic is interested in the distinction between logic and ontology.[13] Therefore in the present section we shall note the partial identity and the consistency of ontology with logic. Something of this has been shown already.[14] But the evidence will be extended by a demonstration of how the ontological categories of quality, fact, and law (or firstness, secondness, and thirdness) are in certain instances roughly in agreement with, and in others more precisely deducible from, the categories and divisions of logic, established in the foregoing chapter.

The broad divisions of semiotic are derived from the three references of the sign, which stands "in some respect or capacity for something to somebody,"[15] and the three general topics of logic—Speculative Grammar, Critical Logic, and Speculative Rhetoric—cover these three references of the sign. There is an obvious similarity between these semiotic references and the ontological categories. Quality is the "respect or capacity," fact is the "something," and law is the "somebody" (or relation between some bodies, represented by a universal). The similarity is more evident when we recall that Speculative Grammar deals with relations, Critical Logic with truth, and Speculative Rhetoric with communication. We can see the connection between quality and its relations, between fact and its truth, and between law and its communication.

So much for the similarity between the ontological categories and the whole of logic. There are other and more specific similarities. It may be said of Peirce's three phenomenological categories of quality, fact, and law that they came as a conjecture of the most primitive kind. Like "every general proposition of the great edifice of science," "these ideas are the *first logical interpretants* of the phenomena that suggest them, and which, as suggesting them, are signs, of which they are the (really conjectural) interpretants." (5.480) There is at least a family resemblance between quality

---

[12] See chap. III, A, ii.
[13] See this chapter, A, ii.
[14] See this chapter, A, ii.
[15] See chap. III, A, ii.

and the qualisign,[16] fact and the sinsign, and law and the legisign. There can be little, if any, difference between "a quality which is a sign" (2.244) and a quality considered as a sign of the category of quality; and so *passim*.

In the definitions of the second trichotomy of sign—icon, index, and symbol—Peirce left no doubt as to their correspondence with the three phenomenological categories. In the more complex definitions of these signs, their phenomenological character is explicitly set forth. "An *Icon*," said Peirce, "is a Representamen whose Representative Quality is a Firstness of it as a First." (2.276) "An *Index* is a Representamen whose Representative character consists in its being an individual second." (2.283) And "a *Symbol* is a Representamen whose Representative character consists precisely in its being a rule that will determine its Interpretant." (2.292) In the last definition, since a rule is a general statement or law, thirdness must be intended.

Another way in which Peirce identifies the ontological with the logical categories is through the three varieties of the rheme, the sign which "represents a possible object."[17] It will be recalled that the relative rhema can be singular, dual, or plural, (3.421) depending upon how many blanks it has which must be filled in to make a sentence.[18] Now, said Peirce, "it follows that if we find three distinct and irreducible forms of rhemata, the ideas of these should be the three elementary conceptions of metaphysics," (3.422) an inference already involved, however, in certain preconceptions regarding the similarity of semiotic categories with ontological ones,[19] and therefore probably not so strong as the resemblance noted in the preceding paragraph.

Another way in which the three categories are involved already in the divisions of logic is exhibited by the three syntactical distinctions of term, proposition, and argument. (1.515) "The monad has no features but its suchness, which appears in logic . . . as the signification of the verb. This already receives embodiment in the lowest of the chief forms of logic, the *term*.[20] The dyad introduced a radically different sort of element, the subject, which first shows itself in the *proposition*." (1.515)[21] "The conception of *being* arises upon the formation of a proposition." (1.551) But its definition rests upon the logical relation of class-inclusion, which it nevertheless transcends. "Being . . . may be defined, for example, as that which is common to the objects included in any class, and to the objects not included

---

[16] See chap. III, B, i, (*a*).
[17] See chap. III, B, i, (*c*).
[18] See chap. III, B, vi, (*a*).
[19] See chap. VIII, A, ii,.and IX, A, ii.
[20] See chap. III, B, iv.
[21] See chap. III, B, iii.

in the same class." (5.294)[22] "The triad brings a third sort of element, consisting of a colligation of two propositions . . . This reason first emerges in the *syllogism*."[23]

The last parallel between the logical categories and the phenomenological or ontological ones has to do with the three divisions of reasoning. Peirce raised this question explicitly. "Why should there be three principles of reasoning [i.e., deduction, induction, and abduction] and what have they to do with one another? This question, which was connected with other parts of my schedule of philosophical inquiry that need not be detailed, now came to the front. . . . The recurrence of triads in logic was quite marked, and must be the croppings out of some fundamental conceptions. I now undertook to ascertain what the conceptions were. This search resulted in what I call my categories. . . . Quality, Reaction, and Representation. . . . For scientific terms, Firstness, Secondness, and Thirdness are to be preferred as being entirely new words without any false associations whatever. How the conceptions are *named* makes, however, little difference." (4.3)

The point is that the study of logic, as derivable from experience, and the setting up of logical divisions led to the notion of a triad of phenomenological categories, which thus sprang from logic but which experience of the phenomenal world served to confirm. Our next task is to examine these categories in some detail, and then to trace the implications from them to other ontological topics. Before embarking upon this task, it may be illustrative to compare Peirce's phenomenology with those of Kant and Hegel. Peirce acknowledged Kant as his source rather than Hegel, although Hegel's philosophy, too, rested upon a triad of phenomenological categories, as Peirce often pointed out. The comparison will exhibit fundamental differences as well as marked similarities between the systems.

It should be noted, then, first of all, that Peirce's categories grew out of a study of Kant and not out of Hegel. (1.300) It was Kant who founded philosophy upon a strict acceptance of logic, and Peirce followed him in this.[24] There are, to be sure, vast differences in the philosophies of the two men. Peirce made no such distinction as did Kant between phenomena and noumena.[25] Kant's phenomena do not comprehend all appearances; Peirce's do.[26] Peirce made no such distinction between things "represented as they

---

[22] See chap. III, B, vi.
[23] See chap. III, C, i.
[24] See chap. II, A, ii.
[25] *Kritik der Reinen Vernunft*, A 249.
[26] See this chapter, A, ii.

are" and "known only as they appear."[27] However, we may note the source of Peirce's phenomenological categories in "the three regulative laws of logic," (1.449) set forth in the Appendix to the "Transcendental Dialectic."[28] These are "*homogeneity, specification,* and *continuity* of forms." It will become clear, as the development of Peirce's categories proceeds in this chapter, that quality is homogeneous, reaction specific, and representation continuous.

Peirce felt "strongly drawn" (4.50) to Hegel but could not decide to call himself a Hegelian. Although Hegel is "in some respects the greatest philosopher that ever lived," (1.524) Peirce "reject[ed] his philosophy *in toto,*" (1.368) chiefly because Hegel, like all the Germans, had a "tendency to look at everything subjectively," (5.160) a tendency which was of course opposed to Peirce's own. His philosophy "resuscitates Hegel, though in a strange costume." (1.42) Although he took the term "phenomenology" from Hegel, (5.37) "it would be historically false to call [Peirce's method] a modification of Hegel's." (1.544) Peirce felt that if he named his work "objective logic," (1.444) that would indicate the similarity sufficiently, and would call attention to the fact that his three categories "agree substantially with Hegel's three moments." (2.87) "Most of what is true in Hegel," however, "is a darkling glimmer of a conception which the mathematicians had long before made pretty clear." (6.31) Hegel's ignorance of mathematics was thus fatal to his phenomenology. (5.40)

According to Peirce's analysis, Hegel made phenomenology his starting point, (5.37) but employed a spurious method. "Hegel begins by assuming whatever appears most evident to an utterly unreflecting person, and sets it down. The only difference between the unreflecting person and Hegel, as he is in this mood, is that the former would consider the subject exhausted, and would pass to something else; while Hegel insists upon harping on that string until certain inevitable difficulties are met with. Hegel at once embraces these objections with the same good faith (for it is good faith, notwithstanding his being able, if he chooses, to see further) with which he assumed the original position. He pushes his objection for all it is worth—for more than it is worth, since the original position has something to say for itself, in reply. Hegel is anxious not to allow any 'foreign considerations' to intervene in the struggle which ensues—that is to say, no suggestions from a more advanced stage of philosophical development. [But] I cannot see that it would conflict with the spirit of the general method to allow

[27] *Kritik der Reinen Vernunft,* A 250.
[28] *Ibid.,* A 658, B 686.

suggestions from experience, provided they are such as would be inevitable, and such as would be within the grasp of the thought which for the moment occupies the theatre." (2.32)

Hegel "restricted himself to what *actually* forces itself on the mind," (5.37) without regard for possible impressions, a "fatally narrow" restriction "in which the worst of the Hegelian errors have their origin." Peirce, in contrast, refused to restrict phenomenology "to the observation and analysis of *experience*" but instead extended it "to describing all the features that are common to whatever is *experienced* or might conceivably be experienced or become an object of study in any way direct or indirect." Hegel traced everything to one principle: thought. (2.157) In Peirce's terms, he held phenomena to consist in quality and representation while omitting resistance altogether. Hence he believed "the syllogism to be the fundamental form of real being." (2.386) This kind of subjectivism is entirely alien to Peirce's phenomenology. For Peirce, the three categories were equally important; whereas Hegel "usually overlooked external Secondness, altogether. In other words, he has committed the trifling oversight of forgetting that there is a real world with real actions and reactions." (1.368)

While secondness was omitted altogether, firstness was recognized but, so to speak, denatured. When Hegel said that the simplest character of firstness was its immediacy, or presentness, he was quite right; but when he insisted that it was also abstract, he was involved in glaring falsity. "Go out under the blue dome of heaven and look at what is present as it appears to the artist's eye. The poetic mood approaches the state in which the present appears as it is present. The present is just what it is regardless of the absent, regardless of past and future. Consequently, it cannot be *abstracted* (which is what Hegel means by the abstract) for the abstracted is what the concrete, which gives it whatever being it has, makes it to be." (5.44) All actuality is thus removed both from secondness and from firstness.

Thirdness alone, then, is held to be the real category in the Hegelian system, and "the other two are only introduced in order to be *aufgehoben*." (5.79) Yet thirdness involves firstness and secondness and must have them to build upon. (5.90) Thirdness "can have no concrete being without action, as a separate object on which to work its government." (5.436) Having reduced firstness and secondness to thirdness, Hegel took the next inevitable step, a step we should expect him to take from our knowledge of his subjectivistic position. Thirdness itself is allowed to have no external and objective reality but is "degraded to a mere stage of thinking." Thus Hegel invalidated his own initial insight into the triune nature of the phenomenon by "regarding the first two stages with his smile of contempt" and reducing the third to the status of a mental affair. Although Peirce felt that Hegel's initial viewpoint had been one which resembled his own, it is clear that with the Hegelian categories finally reduced to the conditions by which we now understand them Peirce's set could have little in common.

Having distinguished Peirce's categories from those of Hegel, we may now proceed to examine the former as a necessary first step in the exposition of the metaphysics.

B. THE PHENOMENOLOGICAL CATEGORIES

i. FIRSTNESS

The first of Peirce's three fundamental ontological categories is that of firstness. "Category the First is the idea of that which is such as it is regardless of anything else. That is to say it is a *Quality* of Feeling." (5.66) "Imagine me," said Peirce, "to wake and in a slumbrous condition to have a vague, unobjectified, still less unsubjectified, sense of redness or of salt taste, or of an ache, or of grief or joy, or of a prolonged musical note. That would be, as nearly as possible, a purely monadic state of feeling." (1.303) But the idea of firstness "is much nearer an object than it is to a conception of self." Hence, "in order to convert that psychological or logical conception into a metaphysical one, we must think of a metaphysical monad as a pure nature, or quality, in itself without parts or features, and without embodiment." The clue to the understanding of the transition from the psychological idea of feeling to the metaphysical idea of quality lies in the notion of the isolation of feeling, which is quite separate from the person feeling and the thing felt. In what way does redness without end or beginning, a perpetual whistle, or a permanent thrill of delight, differ from a substance? (1.305) None of the conditions on which we suppose such qualities to depend—such as the flow of time, the physical substratum, etc.—"are either seen in the color, heard in the sound, or felt in the visceral sensation. Consequently, there can be no logical difficulty in supposing them to be absent." Thus, "an idea of feeling is such as it is within itself, without any elements or relations." (4.157)

Two opinions prevail among philosophers with regard to the relation of qualities to the sense experience which makes the qualities known to us. The nominalists have always maintained that quality does not exist without sense. The realists, among whom we may number Peirce, have always denied this, and even maintained the opposite. "That quality is dependent upon sense is the great error of one branch of nominalists known as the conceptualists. That it is dependent upon the subject in which it is realized is the great error of all the nominalistic schools." (1.422) "That the quality of red depends on anybody actually seeing it, so that red things are no longer red in the dark, is a denial of common sense." But "a realist fully admits that a sense quality is only a possibility of sensation"; only, "he thinks a possibility remains possible when it is not actual." "The mode of being a *redness*, before anything in the universe was yet red, was nevertheless a positive qualitative possibility." (1.25) "The sensation is requisite for its apprehension; but no sensation nor sense-faculty is requisite for the possibility which is the being of the quality." (1.422) The abstract may be "what the concrete makes it to be," as Peirce had maintained in his arguments against Hegel,[29] but it is also something more, since the abstract is possibility of concrete actuality, and possibility of concretion is not itself concrete, yet it is not nothing. It is the absolute terms, whose "logical form involves only the conception of quality, and which therefore represent a thing only as 'a——.' These discriminate objects in the most rudimentary way, which does not involve any consciousness of discrimination. They regard an object as it is in itself as *such* (*quale*)." (3.63) "A quality is a mere abstract potentiality; and the error of those [nominalistic] schools lies in holding that the potential, or possible, is nothing but what the actual makes it to be." (1.422) Thus quality is an external thing, independent of the mind. (6.327) It is a possibility which sense experience may or may not actualize, (1.426) but which is in any case independent of such actualization.

Since firstness neither derives from nor leads to anything else, it is both original and free. "The origin of things, considered not as leading to anything, but in itself, contains the idea of First." (6.32) It is marked by the "positive internal characters of the subject in itself." (5.469) "*Originality* is being such as that being is, regardless of aught else." (2.89) "Although Originality is the most primitive, simple, and original of the categories, it is not the most obvious and familiar." (2.90) "Now the world is full of this element of irresponsible, free, Originality. Why should the middle part of the spectrum look green rather than violet? There is no conceivable reason for it nor compulsion in it. Why was I born in the nineteenth century on Earth rather than on Mars a thousand years ago? Why did I today sneeze just five hours, forty-three minutes and twenty-one seconds after a certain man in China whistled (supposing this did happen)? We know

[29] See this chapter, B, iii.

perhaps why a meteorite should fall to the earth, if it gets in the Earth's way; but why should the arrangements of nature be such that this particular meteorite was in the Earth's way? All these are facts which are as they are simply because they happen to be so." (2.85)

"The idea of First is predominant in the ideas of freshness, life, freedom. The free. is that which has not another behind it, determining its actions; but so far as the idea of the negation of another enters, the idea of another enters; and such a negative idea must be put in the background, or else we cannot say that the Firstness is predominant. Freedom can only manifest itself in unlimited and uncontrolled variety and multiplicity." (1.302) First-ness is both "peculiar and idiosyncratic."

The next thing about firstness to which attention should be called is its status with regard to generality. Of course, "the quality-element of experience" (1.425) has no generality, being exactly what it is without anything else. (1.357) But qualities reflected upon reveal themselves general. Quality, in effect, "is the monadic element of the world. Anything whatever, however complex and heterogeneous, has its quality *sui generis,* its possibility of sensation, would our senses only respond to it." (1.426) The complexity and heterogeneousness of the phenomenon makes "no particular difference in the quality." (1.425) It only serves to make it more general. The seeming contradiction between the particularity of a particular quality and its generality when reflected on, is resolved when we understand that although quality can only occur under particular determinations, it "is, in itself, general." (1.447)

ii. SECONDNESS

"Category the Second is the Idea of that which is such as it is as being Second to some First, regardless of anything else. . . . That is to say, it is *Reaction* as an element of the Phenomenon." (5.66) "Second is the conception of being relative to, the conception of reaction with, something else." (6.32) It is the "brute actions of one subject or substance on another." (5.469) It may otherwise be defined as "force in its widest sense," (1.487) "the object of experience as a reality." (1.342) To these definitions may be added a certain description, as well as some of the inferences which follow from them.

To regard the object of experience as a reality means to regard the individual thing as in existence, and "qualities of the individual thing . . . neither help nor hinder its identical existence." (1.458) Thus secondness is another category from that of firstness, or quality. "The genuine second suffers and yet resists, like dead matter, whose existence consists in its inertia." The idea of "second is eminently hard and tangible. It is very familiar, too; it is forced upon us daily; it is the main lesson of life. In youth, the world is fresh and we seem free; but limitation, conflict, constraint, and secondness generally, make up the teaching of experience." (1.358) Secondness "blindly forces a place for itself in the universe, or wilfully crowds its way in." (1.459)

There is only one kind of firstness, which has already been described.[30] But there are two kinds of secondness, and three kinds of thirdness.[31] We shall next consider the two kinds of secondness.

The distinction between two kinds of secondness is involved in the very idea of secondness. The dyad contains two subjects and some sort of union between them. (1.326) "The dyad has two sides according to which subject is considered as first." (1.326) Every dyad has "a suchness of monoidal character" resulting from one of its subjects considered as a monad or firstness; and it has "a suchness peculiar to it as a dyad. The dyad brings the two subjects together, and in so doing imparts a character to each of them." There is "a distinction between two kinds of Secondness; namely, the Secondness of genuine seconds, or matters, which I call genuine Secondness, and the Secondness in which one of the seconds is only a Firstness, which I call degenerate Secondness." (1.528)

Genuine secondness is what Peirce also termed "obsistence." "Obsistence . . . is that wherein secondness differs from firstness; or, is that element which taken in connection with Originality [or firstness],[32] makes one thing such as another compels it to be." (2.89) Genuine secondness concerns subjects which are nonmonadic. In this kind of dyad, at least one of its subjects must have a "mode of being over and above what its mere inward suchness involves." (1.456) That is, "it must have a mode of being gained by its opposition to another." That opposition imparts to it a special quality of its own, which marks it a genuine secondness. In genuine secondness, the general aspect of the quality of the subjects is not considered; only their individuality. (2.91)

Degenerate secondness is the weaker form, and need only be relatively degenerate. The secondness in this form need not belong to the secondness in its own right through the quality of the pair, although this is also in-

[30] See this chapter, B, i.
[31] See this chapter, B, ii and iii.
[32] See this chapter, B, i.

volved, but belongs to it only in respect to the quality of its two subjects in their own right. (5.69) "The degenerate dyad . . . is a proposition whose two subjects are mere qualities." (1.516) "When scarlet and red are contemplated together, the former as first, the latter as second, a certain aspect *sui generis* presents itself, like that which presents itself when toothache and ache are contemplated together." (1.455) This kind of secondness Peirce termed *essential,* because it is the only kind of secondness which can be composed of firstnesses alone, i.e., without a notion of their union as a separate and determinate affair. "It cannot be regarded as a *fact* that scarlet is red. It is a *truth.*" (1.452) Degenerate secondness "really amounts to nothing but this, that a subject, in its being a second, has a Firstness, or quality." (1.528)

There are a number of ways in which secondness is subdivided.[33] The most obvious one to consider is that of secondness regarded (*a*) as an individual thing and (*b*) as a field of individual things. Peirce referred to the individual thing as a fact, and to the field of individual things as either existence or actuality. We may consider each of these before taking up the other subdivisions.

(*a*) Secondness regarded as an individual thing is termed a fact. There are, according to Peirce, twelve separate and distinct characteristics of fact. These are set forth as follows: (1) "Fact has distinct features," (1.435) indeed "having a structure" it "must present a variety of features." (1.445) It can never be sufficiently described by one feature alone. (2) "Facts are either accidentally actual or involve brute force," (1.435) they are "contingent," and they "involve an unconditional necessity." (1.427) "Facts resist our will. That is why facts are proverbially called brutal." (1.419) The individuality of fact is partly a result of its bruteness. "When we speak of a fact as *individual* . . . we mean to attribute to it . . . the character . . . [of] having fighting force or self-assertion." (1.434) (3) "Every fact has a here and now." (1.435) "It is not pretended that what is here termed fact is the whole phenomenon, but only an element of the phenomenon—so much as belongs to a particular place and time." (1.428) Thus a particular reference to time and space: the date and place of an occurrence is a characteristic of fact. (4) "Fact is intimately associated with the dyad." (1.435) And the dyad "consists of two *subjects* brought into oneness. . . . The dyad is not the subjects; it has the subjects as one element of it." (1.326) In bringing the two subjects together it "imparts a character to each of them," and has itself "two sides according to which subject is considered as first." (5)

"Every fact is the sum of its consequences." (1.435) We may learn of a fact indirectly, by some physical effect of it. "Thus . . . the physical effects of a fact can take the place of experience of the fact by a witness." (1.431) "There can hardly be a doubt that the existence of a fact does consist in the existence of all its consequences." (1.432) All the consequences must consist in more than merely physical effects, since "it is the sum of *all* its consequences." (1.436) (6) "The existence of facts consists in fight." (1.435) "If, for example, something supposed to be a hard body acts in every respect like such a body, that constitutes the reality of that hard body." (1.432) "This may be expressed by saying that the fact fights its way into existence; for it exists by virtue of the oppositions which it involves." "What we call a Thing is a cluster or habit of reactions, or, to use a more familiar phrase, is a centre of forces." (4.157)

Continuing with the characteristics of fact, we have (7) "Every fact is determinate in reference to every character." (1.435) We have seen that every fact is individual[34] but "individuality implies another [property], which is that the individual is determinate in regard to every possibility, or quality, either as possessing it or as not possessing it." (1.434) Of second-ness, "every quality whatever is either true or false." (1.436) There is no limit to determination. (1.449) (8) "Every fact . . . has two subjects; for the fact concerns two things. One of these two subjects, at least, is a thing itself of the nature of fact." (1.436) This subject is a *thing*. Its existence . . . consists in its reacting against the other things in the universe," each one of which must be a fact. A fact, however, is not two subjects but rather one object containing two subjects in a certain relation. A married couple is neither a man nor a woman nor a man and a woman. "It is a third object, to whose constitution, which is its nature, and therefore to its existence, too, a man is requisite and a woman is requisite." (1.442) (9) "Every fact is connected with a reciprocal fact, which may or may not, be inextricably bound up with it. If one body strike upon another, the second body reciprocally strikes upon it; and the two facts are inseparable. But if one body is hard, there must be a second body of some degree of hardness for the former to resist. Yet the annihilation of the second body would [not] destroy the hardness of the first." (1.437) (10) The "natural classification [of fact] takes place by dichotomies." (1.438)[35] (11) If fact "involves any variation in time, this variation consists in a change in the qualities of its subjects, but never the annihilation or production of those subjects." (1.439)

[34] In this chapter, B, ii, (*b*).
[35] This has been illustrated in (9) above.

It consists in being a second to any object taken as first. It is not time and space that produce this character. It is rather this character which for its realization calls for something like time and space. But "the subjects of facts generally, are permanent and eternal." (1.439) (12) Fact "is accidental." (1.440) "It is something which *happens*." "It is . . . an adventitious circumstance that [a] particular unit [of the universe] is embraced under [some determinate] monad." (1.451)

(*b*) Secondness regarded as the field of individual things is termed existence, or actuality. The field of actuality is also that of activity, as Aristotle described it,[36] and "activity implies a generalization of *effort;* and effort is a two-sided idea, effort and resistance being inseparable, and therefore the idea of Actuality has also a dyadic form." (4.542) Of course, actuality, being the field of individual things, takes on the characteristics of individual things. "The actuality of the [thing or] event seems to lie in its relations to the universe of existents," (1.24) and such relations, so far as secondness is concerned, consist in struggle and opposition. Actuality is the ground of all opposition. (1.432) "Existence is that mode of being which lies in opposition to another. To say that a table exists is to say that it is hard, heavy, opaque, resonant, that is, produces immediate effects upon the senses, and also that it produces purely physical effects, attracts the earth (that is, is heavy), dynamically reacts against other things (that is, has inertia), resists pressure (that is, is elastic), has a definite capacity for heat, etc. . . . A thing without oppositions *ipso facto* does not exist." (1.457) "The mode of being of the . . . thing is existence; and existence lies in opposition merely." (1.458)[37]

"There are different kinds of existence. There is the existence of physical actions, there is the existence of psychical volitions, there is the existence of all time, there is the existence of the present, there is the existence of material things, there is the existence of the creations of one of Shakespeare's plays, and, for aught we know, there may be another creation with a space and time of its own in which things may exist. Each kind of existence consists in having a place among the total collection of such a universe. It consists in being a second to any object in such a universe taken as first." (1.433)

Actuality, or existence, is, like individual things, brute. "Actuality is something *brute*. There is no reason in it. I instance putting your shoulder against a door and trying to force it open against an unseen, silent, and

[36] Action = ἐνέργεια (1.325). Aristotle, *Metaphysica*, 1048a, 25 ff.
[37] Cf. William James, *Essays in Radical Empiricism* (New York, Longmans, Green, 1938) pp. 167-168

unknown resistance. We have a two-sided consciousness of effort and resistance, which seems to me to come tolerably near to a pure sense of actuality. On the whole, I think we have here a mode of being of one thing which consists in how a second object is." (1.24) "For example, an existent particle . . . is nothing for itself; whatever it is, it is for what it is attracting and what it is repelling: its being is actual, consists in action, is dyadic. That is what I call *existence*." (6.343) Brute opposition requires that everything in the field of actuality shall be individual. "*Hic et nunc* is the phrase perpetually in the mouth of Duns Scotus, who first elucidated individual existence. It is a forcible phrase if understood as Duns did understand it, not as describing individual existence, but as suggesting it by an example of the attributes found in this world to accompany it." (1.458)

There is one characteristic of actuality which is characteristic also of individual things but which somehow is inseparable from the field itself. The *activity* of existent things has already been mentioned; but such activity must have some regularity about it. "The existence of things consists in their regular behavior. If an atom had no regular attractions and repulsions, if its mass were at one instant nothing, at another a ton, at another a negative quantity, if its motion instead of being continuous, consisted in a series of leaps from one place to another without passing through any intervening places, and if there were no definite relations between its different positions, velocities and directions of displacement, if it were at one time in one place and at another time in a dozen, such a disjointed plurality of phenomena would not make up any existing thing." Moreover, "not only substances, but events, too, are constituted by regularities. The flow of time, for example, is itself a regularity." (1.411)

Before closing the exposition of secondness, it may be useful to say a word concerning the relation of secondness to firstness, in order to show the way in which the first two categories are intermingled in every existing thing.

In order to have a secondness, "we need not, and must not, banish the idea of the first from the second; on the contrary, the second is precisely that which cannot be without the first." (1.358) There must be a firstness with its quality for the secondness to resist, if there is to be a secondness at all.[38] Secondness is inseparable from the idea of dependence (3.422)—dependence on firstness. "The idea of second must be reckoned as an easy one to comprehend. That of first is so tender that you cannot touch it without spoiling it . . . With what firstness

[38] See this chapter, B, ii, (9).

'The scarfed bark puts from her native bay;'

with what secondness

'doth she return,

With overweathered ribs and ragged sails'." (1.358)

We have already seen that when you have a pair, besides the pairness itself there are two units. (1.530)[39] "Thus Firstness is an essential element of Secondness." But the reverse is not true; for secondness is not part of firstness. Firstness is absolutely simple, whereas secondness exhibits a degree of complication. This complication consists in the opposition of a second subject to the quality of a first subject. Thus firstness is independent of secondness, but secondness is dependent upon firstness to be the secondness that it is.

iii. THIRDNESS

"Category the Third is the Idea of that which is such as it is as being a Third, or Medium, between a Second and its First. That is to say, it is *Representation* as an element of the Phenomenon." (5.66) "Thirdness is nothing but the character of an object which embodies Betweenness or Mediation in its simplest and most rudimentary form." (5.104) "Continuity represents Thirdness almost to perfection." (1.337) It is that character "whereby a first and second are brought into relation." (6.32) It "mediates between the two subjects and brings about their connection"; thus it is the "process intervening between the causal act and the effect," (1.328) and "is what it is owing to things between which it mediates." (1.356) Thus thirdness involves the idea of "composition" (1.297) or combination. "A combination is something which is what it is owing to the parts which it brings into mutual relationship." (1.363) This makes it both "complex and simple, at the same time! It is complex in the sense that different features may be discriminated in it, but the peculiar idea of *complexity* that it contains, although it has complexity as its object, is an unanalyzable idea." (5.88) Thirdness is a "conception of complexity," (1.526) which is not to say, however, that it is a complex conception.

There are three grades of genuine thirdness and two degenerate forms. The first grade of genuine thirdness is a "positive qualitative possibility, in itself nothing more." (1.536) It consists in "laws of quality." (1.482) "The laws of quality are all of one type. Namely, they all simply detemine sys-

[39] See this chapter, B, ii, (8).

tems of qualities, of which Sir Isaac Newton's law of color-mixture with Dr. Thomas Young's supplement thereto, is the most perfect known example." Laws of quality may concern single qualities, pairs of qualities or triads of qualities. "Every quality is perfect and in itself such as it is." (1.484) Two qualities may be independent of one another, or one may be a "further determination of the other." Third qualities may be the qualities in respect to which "compared qualities agree or differ." They may agree or differ with respect to "the quality of the quality," e.g., hue or salt and sugar taste; with respect to "the absolute intensity of the quality," e.g., loudness in sound or luminosity in color; and with respect to "purity, or the relative intensity of the strongest elements," e.g., "bright colors tend toward yellow, dim colors toward violet," or "very faint sounds tend toward a certain pitch."

The second grade of genuine thirdness "is an existent thing without any mode of being less than existence, but determined by that first." (1.536) It consists in "laws of fact." (1.483) "If two forces are combined according to the parallelogram of forces, their resultant is a real third" (1.366) of the second grade. "Laws of fact divide themselves . . . into laws *logically necessary* and laws *logically contingent*." (1.483) "Of laws logically contingent the most universal are of such a kind that they must be true provided every form which by logical necessity must be thought of a given subject is also a form of its real being. Calling this kind of necessity, metaphysical necessity, we may divide laws logically contingent into laws *metaphysically necessary* and laws *metaphysically contingent*."

The third grade of thirdness is a "mode of being which consists in the Secondnesses that it determines, the mode of being of a law." (1.536) It is marked by regularity. "A law never can be embodied in its character as a law except by determining a habit. . . . A law is how an endless future must continue to be," and "consists in the fact that future facts of Secondness will take on a determinate general character." (1.26) Laws of regularity may be either monadically definite, in that "every subject is existentially determinate with respect to each predicate"; (1.485) dyadically determinate, in that "the possibilities are two at least and . . . that they are two at most," each subject with respect to each predicate being either positive or negative; or triadically true, in that the idea or predicate, the fact or subject, and the relation between them are recognized as being together.

In addition to the three grades of genuineness, there are two degrees of degeneracy. The first degree of degeneracy is "where there is in the fact itself no Thirdness or mediation, but where there is true duality." (1.366)

"The First degree of Degeneracy is found in an Irrational Plurality which, as it exists, in contradistinction [to] the form of its representation, is a mere complication of duality." (5.70) "That orange color is intermediate between red and yellow is a monoidally degenerate triad," (1.473) and could be expressed in a qualitative syllogism. (1.516) Or, again, "a pin fastens two things together by sticking through one and also through the other: either might be annihilated, and the pin would continue to stick through the one which remained. A mixture brings its ingredients together by containing each. We may term these accidental thirds." (1.366)

The second degree of degeneracy "is where there is not even true Secondness in the fact itself." (1.366) "The most degenerate Thirdness is where we conceive a mere Quality of Feeling, or Firstness, to represent itself to itself as Representation. Such, for example, would be Pure Self-Consciousness, which might be roughly described as a mere feeling that has a dark instinct of being a germ of thought." (5.71) "In portraiture, photographs mediate between the original and the likeness. In science, a diagram or analogue of the observed fact leads on to a further analogy. . . . Philadelphia lies between New York and Washington. Such thirds may be called intermediate thirds or thirds of comparison." (1.367)

Genuine thirdness, like logic itself, may be defined as representation, (5.105)[40] or combination. (1.515)[41] Without "the psychological or accidental human element, in genuine Thirdness we see the operation of a sign." (1.537) The relation of representation or meaning, carried by sign, object, and interpretant, (1.339) is essentially a relation of thirdness, and is so defined. (1.541) As an example of the triad we may instance icon, index, and symbol. "Of these three genera of representamens, the *Icon* is the Qualitatively degenerate, the *Index* the Reactionally degenerate, while the *Symbol* is the relatively genuine genus." (5.73) As we have seen, triadic relations of signs are the most basic kind,[42] and in addition to the three fundamental trichotomies of signs many others of a like nature are discernible.[43] The representation of relations is expressed by the combination or "colligation" of two propositions.[44] This relation of two propositions consists of a third which can be elicited, as is illustrated in the form of the syllogism itself. (1.369) The syllogism, it will be recalled, is one of the semiotic triads, namely, an Argument Symbolic Legisign,[45] in itself perfectly general. (1.340)

[40] See chap. III, B, i, quoting 1.539.
[41] See this chapter, B, iii.
[42] See chap. III, B, i.
[43] *Ibid.*
[44] See chap. III, C, ii, (c).
[45] See chap. III, C, i.

"The general is essentially *predicative* and therefore of the nature of a representamen." (5.102) It is by definition nonindividual, but such generality can also be exemplified in actual experience. For instance, "we seldom, probably never, desire a single individual thing." (1.341) When we desire an apple pie, "what we want is something which shall produce a certain pleasure of a certain kind," and that something goes unspecified, for it is no particular apple pie that we want; not this or that apple pie but simply and generally —apple pie. Now, said Peirce, "no triad which does not involve generality, that is, the assertion of which does not imply something concerning *every possible* object of some description can be a genuine triad." (1.476)

In noting the relation between thirdness and the other two categories, it is clear that both firstness and secondness are involved in every triad. There can be no reaction without a quality against which the reaction can take place, nor any representation without a quality and a reaction taken together. (5.90) "Not only does Thirdness suppose and involve the ideas of Secondness and Firstness, but never will it be possible to find any Secondness or Firstness in the phenomenon that is not accompanied by Thirdness." But, on the other hand, it is equally true that thirdness cannot be reduced to firstness and secondness, or to both. (1.345) Every triadic relation involves a meaning, and a quality taken by itself is obviously not a meaning. Further, no number of dyadic relations will constitute a triadic relation. Therefore thirdness, although it includes firstness and secondness, is something more.

The relation of thirdness to firstness, then, is that of inclusion. "Firstness is an essential element of . . . Thirdness." (1.530) Any attempt to relate entities without reference to thirdness must meet with failure. Even "qualities cannot resemble one another nor contrast with one another unless in respect to a third quality; so that the resemblance of qualities is triadic." (1.462) "To express the Firstness of Thirdness, the peculiar flavor or color of mediation, we have no really good word. *Mentality* is, perhaps, as good as any, poor and inadequate as it is." (1.533)

Secondness, too, is included in Thirdness, as an essential element, (1.530). Every triad involves dyads; (1.474) for "where you have a triplet you have three pairs." (1.530) Thus thirdness requires but transcends secondness.

Why stop at three categories? "Why not go on to find a new conception in four, five, and so on indefinitely?[46] The reason is that while it is impossible to form a genuine three by any modification of the pair, without introducing something of a different nature from the unit and the pair, four, five, and every higher number can be formed by mere complications of

[46] See Aristotle, *Physica*, 189.

threes." (1.363) "A tetradic, pentadic, etc., relationship is of no higher nature than a triadic relationship; in the sense that it consists of triadic relationships and is constituted of them." (6.323) "Analysis will show that every relation which is *tetradic, pentadic*, or of any greater number of correlates is nothing but a compound of triadic relations. It is therefore not surprising to find that beyond the three elements of Firstness, Secondness, and Thirdness, there is nothing else to be found in the phenomenon." (1.347) Thus, far from being mere logical and mathematical conceptions devoid of richness in combination, we find that the three categories are responsible for all the others. "So prolific is the triad in forms that one may easily conceive that all the variety and multiplicity of the universe springs from it." (4.310)

"A man must be wedded to a system of metaphysics not to see the philosophical importance of the fact that these ideas thus insist upon intruding where we have done our best to bolt and bar the doors against them." (4.317) But it is impossible to deal with a triad without being forced to recognize "a triad of which one member is positive but ineffective, another is the opponent of that, a third, intermediate between these two, is all-potent." "Other examples, however, should not be neglected. The first is agent, the second patient, the third is the action by which the former influences the latter." (1.361) Again, quality can be considered in its aspect of reference to a ground; relation, reference to a correlate; and representation, reference to an interpretant. (1.555) In further chapters of this work the triad will be exhibited as constituting an important part of the logico-ontological framework on which the various other theories are constructed.

Meanwhile, we must turn not forward but backward, and this time once more to logic, in order to shed some of the light which the later development of ontology has made clear upon one of the fundamental divisions of logic. As we have seen time and again, the distinction between logic and ontology is not an absolute one, and logic is the prior study. When we come to develop our ontological triads, we find that the categories which are fundamental to every other topic have not been omitted in logic. The subject matter of logic is treated in three formal divisions: Speculative Grammar, Critical Logic, and Speculative Rhetoric. The doctrine of signs sets forth three sets of three signs each. The elements of the syllogism consist in the term, the proposition, and the syllogism itself. There are three kinds of argument: deduction, induction, and abduction. Speculative Rhetoric yields three broad divisions: communication, meaning, and discovery. A number of other triads in the logic could be cited.

The triad of categories calls for the interrelations of all things. Whatever is not firstness is secondness or thirdness, and whatever is not secondness must be one of the others, and so for thirdness. No two things can be absolutely disconnected, if this is true. There is of course relative disconnection. But "to say that two things are disconnected is but to say that they are connected in a way different from the way under contemplation. For everything is in some relation to each other thing." (4.319) This does not mean, of course, that all things are on the same level with regard to their value. The three categories, into which all things fit in one way or another, are equally "applicable to being," (1.300) but they are not of the same value. (6.324) These identities and differences among the categories have further ontological meaning which will be shortly explored.

C. METAPHYSICS

Metaphysics in a broad sense includes ontology and epistemology; in a narrower sense, ontology alone. "Metaphysics," says Peirce, "is the science of reality." (5.121) "Its business is to study the most general features of reality and real objects." (6.6) "We should expect to find metaphysics . . . to be somewhat more difficult than logic, but still on the whole one of the simplest of sciences, as it is one whose main principles must be settled before very much progress can be gained either in psychics or in physics." (6.4) We shall try to distinguish first between the true and the false metaphysics; then, after discussing what the nature of the true metaphysics is, set forth the metaphysical categories in terms of which the further exposition of the philosophical topics is conducted.

i. REALISM VERSUS NOMINALISM

We have seen that the source of the matter of fact which logic has occasion to assert consists in everyday experience, and that such experience was "open to no other doubt than that it may not have been correctly formulated in general terms."[47] But since laws are general terms, and logic itself is the "science of general necessary laws,"[48] the question of the reality of general terms becomes of paramount importance. Now, Peirce discovered that the most prevalent philosophical conceptions of his day were based upon the doubt of the reality of general terms. The question was explicitly at least as old as Duns Scotus and Thomas Aquinas. "You know what the question

---

[47] See chap. III, A, ii.
[48] See chap. III, A, ii.

was. It was whether *laws* and general *types* are figments of the mind or are real." (1.16) The question was that of nominalism versus realism, exhaustive and mutually exclusive doctrines. Nominalism consists in the denial of the reality of general terms. It has two parts. The first part consists in the denial of the reality of general terms independent of objective facts or things. The second part consists in the denial of the reality of general terms independent of the processes of the mind.

Realism consists simply in the assertion of the reality of general terms or laws, a reality equal to that of objective things and subjective minds. As to the first part, Peirce defined nominalism as "the question of which is the best, the laws or the facts under those laws," (4.1) where the decision is in favor of the facts. Or, conversely, "the question of realism and nominalism . . . means the question how far real facts are analogous to logical relations, and why." (4.68) Here a problem of logic merges into one of metaphysics, for, as we have noted, "metaphysics consists in the results of the absolute acceptance of logical principles not merely as regulatively valid, but as truths of being."[49]

The problem had been set forth and argued explicitly in the Middle Ages by the scholarly doctors of the Church. "The metaphysics of Aquinas, a modified Aristotelianism, had been immensely elaborated and deeply transformed by the vast logical genius of the British Duns Scotus." (2.166) Scotus, the realist, was opposed by William of Ockham, the nominalist. "Nominalism was rendered a respectable opinion by the halting realism of Scotus and by the extravagant unpragmatism of his followers." (6.175) "The great argument for nominalism is that there is no man unless there is some particular man. That, however, does not affect the realism of Scotus; for although there is no man of whom all further determination can be denied, yet there is a man, abstraction being made of all further determination. There is a real difference between man irrespective of what the other determinations may be, and man with this or that particular series of determinations, although undoubtedly this difference is only relative to the mind and not *in re*.[50] Such is the position of Scotus." (5.312)

"Notwithstanding a great outburst of nominalism in the fourteenth century which was connected with politics, the nominalists being generally opposed to the excessive powers of the Pope and in favor of civil govern-

---

[49] See chap. III, A, ii.
[50] Peirce attributed "the nominalistic position [which was, after Scotus] soon adopted by several writers, especially by the celebrated William of Ockham" to the fact that Scotus himself "was separated from nominalism only by the division of a hair."—Review of A. C. Fraser, *The Works of George Berkeley*, in the *North American Review*, 113 (1871), 449.

ment, a connection that lent to the philosophical doctrine a factitious following, the Scotists, who were realists, were in most places the predominant party, and retained possession of the universities. At the revival of learning they stubbornly opposed the new studies; and thus the word *Duns*, the proper name of their master, came to mean an adversary of learning. The word originally further implied that the person so called was a master of subtle thought with which the humanists were unable to cope. But in another generation the disputations by which that power of thought was kept in training had lost their liveliness; and the consequence was that Scotism died out when the strong Scotists died. It was a mere change of fashion." (1.17)

"As matters went, Ockhamism derived its chief strength from its political alliance. (2.167) So this is the way in which modern philosophy became pushed into Ockhamism." (2.168) "The humanists were weak thinkers," (1.18) "incapable of the subtle thought that would have been necessary for any adequate discussion of the question. They accepted nominalistic views upon the most superficial grounds. The question soon became buried and put out of sight by new questions which overlaid it, like new papers on an encumbered study table. In that way it has happened that the question has never attracted general, acute attention among modern metaphysicians." (2.168)

But the more the question of nominalism became one of implicit acceptance rather than of explicit controversy, the more prevalent it became. "In short, there was a tidal wave of nominalism. Descartes was a nominalist. Locke and all his following, Berkeley, Hartley, Hume,[51] and even Reid, were nominalists. Leibniz was an extreme nominalist.... Kant[52] was a nominalist. ... Hegel was a nominalist of realistic yearnings. ... Thus, in one word, all modern philosophy has been nominalistic." (1.19)

Although "truth is rather on the side of the scholastic realists," (6.348) "modern thought has been extravagantly Ockhamistic." "The nominalistic *Weltanschauung* has become incorporated into what I will venture to call the very flesh and blood of the average modern mind." (5.61) The extremity of the acceptance of nominalism in modern times is made possible by the fact that "modern nominalists are mostly superficial men, who do not know, as the more thorough Roscellinus and Occam did, that a reality which has no representation is one which has no relation and no quality." (5.312)

As early as 1871,[53] Peirce had "declared for realism." (1.20) Since then he

[51] See also 6.605.
[52] Cf. F. E. Abbot, *Scientific Theism*, p. 3.
[53] See the long review of Fraser's *Berkeley*, in the *North American Review*, 113 (1871), 449, for an excellent account of the history and doctrines of realism and nominalism.

"very carefully and thoroughly revised" his philosophical opinions "more than half a dozen times," and indeed had "modified them more or less on most topics"; but he had "never been able to think differently on that question of nominalism and realism."

"The heart of the dispute," he felt, "lies in this. The modern philosophers —one and all, unless Schelling be an exception—recognize but one mode of being, the being of an individual thing or fact, the being which consists in the object's crowding out a place for itself in the universe, so to speak, and reacting by brute force of fact, against all other things." (1.21) This was Peirce's "existence," or secondness. "Aristotle, on the other hand, whose system, like all the greatest systems, was evolutionary, recognized besides, an embryonic kind of being, like the being of a tree in its seed, or like the being of a future contingent event. . . . In a few passages Aristotle seems to have a dim *aperçu* of a third mode of being in the *entelechy*. The embryonic being for Aristotle was the being he called matter, which is alike in all things, and which in the course of its development took on form." (1.22) The efforts of the scholastics were confined to the "attempt to mould this doctrine of Aristotle into harmony with Christian truth." Thus they were concerned only with two modes of being.

Peirce felt that there are three modes of being. "We can directly observe them in elements of whatever is at any time before the mind in any way. They are the being of positive qualitative possibility, the being of actual fact, and the being of law that will govern facts in the future." (1.23)[54] Peirce recognized the authority of Ockham's Razor, which, he felt, had validity despite the nominalistic sponsorship of its author. Thus the necessity for giving "an account of the universe with the fewest and simplest possible categories" (5.78) was justifiable also on the basis of realism. Certainly the theory of the reality of universals which requires that phenomenon be subsumed by them does not deny that no more universals than necessary should be supposed to subsume a given phenomenon. He was convinced, however, that three categories were the least possible number for the purpose. All varieties of nominalism proved to be the results of efforts to render the universe explicable on the basis of only one or two categories.

There have been attempts to explain the universe by means of only one category. For instance, Condillac and the associationalists, the nihilists and idealistic sensualists, accept only the category of firstness, (5.79) ignoring the fact that quality is not dependent upon the subject in which it is realized, (1.422) and thus also the fact that at least two categories are required. The

[54] See this chapter, A, ii.

next hypothesis is that of "the corpuscularians, Helmholtz and the like, who would like to explain everything by means of mechanical force [or second-ness], which they do not distinguish from individual reaction." (5.79) "Hegel . . . regards Category the Third as the only true one."

Other efforts have been made to explain the universe by means of two categories. For instance, "the more moderate nominalists who nevertheless apply the epithet *mere* to thought and to representamens may be said to admit Categories First and Second and to deny the third." (5.81) But since "reality [itself] is an affair of . . . mediation between Secondness and First-ness," (5.121) it cannot be omitted. The Berkeleians admit qualities of feel-ing, or firstness, by "ideas in the souls," and rationality, or thirdness, by "Divine Creative Influence," (5.81) but deny secondness. "In the idea of reality, Secondness [too] is predominant; for the real is that which insists upon forcing its way to recognition as something *other* than the mind's creation." (1.325) The Cartesians, together with Leibniz, Spinoza, and Kant, "admit Categories Second and Third as fundamental and . . . deny the First." (5.81) But since quality is dependent neither upon thought nor "upon the fact that some material thing possesses it," (1.422) it is wholly explained neither by representation nor by reaction.

The final alternative, given only three categories, is the attempt to account for the universe in terms of all three: ". . . the metaphysics that recognizes all the categories. It ought to be subdivided. . . . It embraces Kantism, Reid's Philosophy, and the Platonic Philosophy of which Aristotelianism is a spe-cial development." (5.79) The demonstration that all varieties of nominalism are equally unsuccessful results of the endeavor to account for the universe with less than the three necessary categories, is in effect an argument against nominalism. But before proceeding to an exposition of the philosophy that Peirce found to be consequent upon the acceptance of all three categories, which is a kind of Aristotelianism "of the scholastic wing, approaching Scotism, but going much further in the direction of scholastic realism," it will be well to mention briefly Peirce's arguments against nominalism.

The arguments against nominalism fall roughly into four classifications, according as they are taken (*a*) from logic, (*b*) from metaphysics, (*c*) from psychology, and (*d*) from science. These are very rough divisions, for the arguments shade off almost imperceptibly into one another. Peirce gave many others, in either partial or complete form, but we shall confine our-selves to these.

(*a*) We may select one or two arguments from logic. The first has to do with identity and similarity. "Now, upon the nominalistic theory, there is not only no absolute or numerical identity, but there are not even any real agreements or likenesses between individuals; for likeness consists merely in the calling of several individuals by one name, or (in some systems) in their exciting one idea." (6.593) This is consistent with the other nominalistic view, which would keep the secondary qualities unreal but makes the "dynamical relations" of primary qualities real. The theory that denies real agreement or likeness shuts off all reasoning and communication; if true, it would make all human discourse, which is based on identity and difference, impossible and would prohibit all planning. It is denied by the very existence of successful reasoning, communication, discourse, and planning.

The second has to do with the reality of abstractions. The citadel of nominalism can be taken easily by those who have scaled the height of the logic of relatives. (4.1) "The logic of [relatives or] relations shows that the introduction of abstractions—which nominalists have taken such delight in ridiculing—is of the greatest service in necessary inference." (4.611) If everything logical reduces to abstract relations[55] which are yet products of empirical observation,[56] then nominalism is wrong in asserting that there can be any infringement of their reality, a reality which *ipso facto* must be as great as that of anything else.

"It is very easy to laugh at the old physician who is represented as answering the question, why opium puts people to sleep, by saying that it is because it has a dormative virtue. It is an answer that no doubt carries vagueness to its last extreme. Yet, invented as the story was to show how little meaning there might be in an abstraction, nevertheless the physician's answer does contain a truth that modern philosophy has generally denied: it does assert that there really is in opium *something* which explains its always putting people to sleep. This has, I say, been denied by modern philosophers generally. Not, of course, explicitly; but when they say that the different events of people going to sleep after taking opium have really nothing in common, but only that the mind classes them together—and this is virtually to say in denying the reality of generals—they do implicitly deny that there is any true explanation of opium's generally putting people to sleep." (4.234) "The protest of nominalism against such hypostatisation . . . is simply a protest against the only kind of thinking that has ever advanced human culture." (3.509)

(*b*) The next argument against nominalism is taken from metaphysics. This consists in establishing the independent being of ideas, by showing that they are independent both of minds and of the objective world of events.

---

[55] See chap. III, B, vi, (*a*).
[56] See chap. III, B, vi, (*b*).

In order to divorce the being of ideas from their apprehension by minds, the attack is launched upon the postulation of an unknowable. "The Unknowable is a nominalistic heresy. The nominalists in giving their adherence to that doctrine which is really held by all philosophers of all stripes, namely, that experience is all we know, understand experience in their nominalistic sense as the mere first impressions of sense. These 'first impressions of sense' are hypothetical creations of nominalistic metaphysics." (6.492) Peirce denied their existence, but insisted that "even if they exist, it is not in them that experience consists. By experience must be understood the entire mental product." And the entire mental product includes ideas; so that if ideas are experienced they could not have been created in the mind, since that would be to argue that the mind both creates ideas and experiences them. Nominalism, in supposing that ideas are created by the mind is guilty of attributing to it the "power of originating a kind of ideas the like of which Omnipotence has failed to create as real objects," (5.62) and which have "no counterpart at all in Heaven or Earth." (5.63) "But, in fact, a realist is simply one who knows no more recondite reality than that which is represented in a true representation." (5.312)

Ideas are no more dependent upon the objective flow of history than they are upon minds. The argument here consists in a demonstration that the continuity of time is dependent upon ideas. "How can a past idea be present?" Peirce asked. (6.107) Not vicariously, since "then the question would arise how the past idea can be related to its vicarious representation." Not in consciousness, since the only consciousness that contained it was a past consciousness. The past "cannot be wholly past; it can only be going, infinitesimally past, less past than any assignable past date. We are thus brought to the conclusion that the present is connected with the past by a series of real infinitesimal steps." (6.109) The conclusion could be drawn that the past must be connected with the present by ideas which are held over from the past to the present. In this sense it is not ideas that are dependent upon the sequence of past and present, but rather the sequence is dependent upon ideas. But if the sequence of past and present is dependent upon ideas, the ideas must be somehow independent of the sequence.

(c) The third argument against nominalism is taken from psychological considerations. In an attack upon the position of the nominalist, Karl Pearson, Peirce observed that it was Pearson and not his opponents who had not "thoroughly assimilated the truth that everything we can in any way take cognizance of is purely mental. . . . Repeatedly, when he has proved the content of an idea to be mental, he seems to think he has proved its object to be of human origin. He goes to no end of trouble to prove in various ways, what his opponent would have granted with the utmost cheerfulness at the outset, that laws of nature are rational; and, having got so far, he seems to think that nothing more is requisite than to seize a logical maxim as a leaping pole and lightly skip to the conclusion that the laws of nature are of human provenance. If he had thoroughly accepted the truth that all realities, as well as all figments, are alike of purely mental composition, he would have seen that the question was, not whether natural law is of an intellectual nature or not, but whether it is of the number of those intellectual objects that are destined to be exploded from the spectacle of our universe, or whether, as far as we can judge, it has the stuff to stand its ground in spite of all attacks."[57]

The answer is that it has. "All human thought and opinion contains an arbitrary, accidental element, dependent on the limitations in circumstances, power, and bent of the individual; an element of error, in short. But human opinion universally tends in the long run to a definite form, which is the truth. Let any human being have enough information and exert enough thought upon any question, and the result will be that he will arrive at a certain definite conclusion, which is the same that any other mind will reach under sufficiently favorable circumstances."[58] Everything that we can know is mental, yet what is known by the mind originates not in the mind where it is known but in an objective world. Thus, the relations, or universals, of which we have knowledge, like the qualities we sense, exist independently, as is evidenced by their stubbornness and intractability.

(*d*) The fourth group of arguments against nominalism comes from the evidence of science. In the introduction to *Scientific Theism* published in 1885, F. E. Abbot showed conclusively that, contrary to an early opinion held by Peirce, science has always been and must be realistic. (1.20)[59] "Physical science," Peirce unhesitatingly declared, "gives its assent . . . to scholastic realism." (6.361) "After physical science has discovered so many general principles in Nature, nominalism becomes a disgraceful habitude of thought." (6.175)

Nominalism fails to distinguish between regularity and law. It supposes that "a law [is] nothing more than a regularity, a regularity nothing less than a law." (6.273) But law cannot be reduced to mere uniformity, and not every uniformity is a law. "Let a law of nature—say the law of gravitation—

---

[57] Review of Karl Pearson, *The Grammar of Science*, in the *Popular Science Monthly*, 48 (1901), 296.

[58] Review of Fraser's *Berkeley* in the *North American Review*, 113 (1871), 449.

[59] See also 4.50, 5.423. Peirce was a realist in 1871 but did not comprehend the realism of science until Abbot pointed it out to him.

remain a mere uniformity—a mere formula establishing a relation between terms—and what in the world should induce a stone, which is not a term nor a concept but just a plain thing, to act in conformity to that uniformity? All other stones may have done so, and this stone too on former occasions, and it would break the uniformity for it not to do so now. But what of that?" (5.48) "Thus, a nominalist may admit that there is in the events themselves an agreement consisting in the uniformity with which all stones dropped from the hand fall to the ground; but if he admits that there is anything at all, except the mere fact that they happen to do so, that should in any sense *determine* the different stones to fall every time they are dropped, he ceases to be a good nominalist and becomes a mediaeval realist." (6.377)

Just as ideas, by connecting the past with the present, were seen to be independent of time,[60] so laws can demonstrate their reality by relating the present with the future. The future of an event is part of that event now. "The future necessary consequent of a present state of things is as real and true as that present state of things itself." (6.368) The nominalists say that an idea or law is a *mere* name. "Strike out the 'mere,' and this opinion is approximately true." (3.460) Laws are only names, but they are names for something real: real possibilities.[61]

Nominalism marks out an area which, following Comte, it terms *metaphysical*, and it holds that propositions in this area are unverifiable. To accept this description as a sufficient explanation "would be to block the road of inquiry." (6.273) The nominalistic metaphysics is "the most blinding of all systems . . . because it deprives the mind of the power to ask itself certain questions, as the habit of wearing a confining dress deprives one's joints of their suppleness." (5.499) Now, any metaphysics which deliberately blocks the road of inquiry is, as everyone must admit, inconsistent with the premises, the aim, and the method of science. "It is one of the peculiarities of nominalism that it is continually supposing things to be absolutely inexplicable," (1.170) whereas science in order to proceed at all must suppose that explanation is at least possible, if not readily attainable. Thus science is inconsistent with nominalism.

ii. THE NATURE OF REALITY

Despite Peirce's familiarity with the history of philosophy, he did not understand philosophical issues to be bound down to the dates and places in

---

[60] See this chapter, C, i, (*b*).
[61] See the definition of the rheme, chap. III, B, i, (*c*).

which they were discovered. Thus, while he had declared himself to be a Scotist, and gave Duns Scotus credit for having invented the word "reality," (4.28) he did not feel that this derivation in any way obligated him to return to the whole complex of medieval philosophy. Genuine philosophical problems are always contemporary. "In calling himself a Scotist," Peirce wrote, "the writer does not mean that he is going back to the general views of 600 years back; he merely means that the point of metaphysics upon which Scotus chiefly insisted and which has since passed out of mind, is a very important point, inseparably bound up with the *most* important point to be insisted upon today." (4.50) That point is the opposition of nominalism and realism. We have just learned how Peirce refuted nominalism. We may now turn to an examination of his own theory of realism. This will consist, first, in an introduction to the nature of reality, and, secondly, in another two sections on the metaphysical categories.

There are indications from the ground which we have already surveyed of what Peirce's theory of reality must be. If the remainder of his philosophy is to be consistent with his logic, then he has already committed himself to a theory of reality. We have been given the quality which is a sign, the thing or event which is a sign, and the law which is a sign, as the primary triad of significant relations,[62] and we have already decided that these are to form the basis of the ontology. We have learned from the logic of relatives that everything reduces to relations, that relations are products of empirical observation, and that the fundamental logical relation is that of inclusion.[63] It follows that if everything is relations, real things must be relations also, and further that these real things are products of empirical observation. Thus reality must consist in objective relations. But these objective relations must themselves be related in terms of the fundamental relation of inclusion. Thus we conclude that an integrated set of objective relations is the picture of reality according to the logic of relatives. As if in support of this thesis, Speculative Rhetoric arrives independently at similar conclusions. We have learned that all true propositions are implicative,[64] and since "that which any true proposition asserts is *real*, in the sense of being as it is regardless of what you or I may think about it," (5.432) the universe must have a certain constitution.[65] Peirce asserted that a system of metaphysics was to be determined by applying those underlying principles which are supposed by Speculative Rhetoric. (2.117) In addition to the ideal constitution which we

---

[62] See chap. III, B, i, (a).
[63] See chap. III, B, vi, (a), (b) and (c).
[64] See chap. III, i, (c).
[65] See chap. III, D, iii.

have seen Speculative Rhetoric presupposes for the universe, it suggests an ideal method for attaining to the knowledge of it.[66] Reality, Peirce concluded, is the object of this final investigation. (2.693) We shall note other obligations to logic, and some to phenomenology, as we proceed.

Peirce very bluntly asserts the being of an "ideal[67] world of which the real world is but a fragment." (3.527)[68] The real is composed of the potential and actual *together*."[69] "Of those [combinations] which occur in the ideal world some do and some do not occur in the real world; but all that occur in the real world occur also in the ideal world, for the simple reason that the real world is a part of the ideal world." (3.527) "From this point of view we must suppose that the existing universe . . . is an off-shoot from, or an arbitrary determination of, a world of ideas, a Platonic world." (6.192) Those ideas which are undetermined have a "mere potential being, a being *in futuro*," (1.218) which is yet not "utter nothingness."[70] While accepting Platonic realism, Pierce took occasion to warn against the danger of nominalism which lurks in too great an enthusiasm for the Platonic ideas. The point is that the Platonic ideas of the ideal world are real, but they are no more real than the things and events of the actual world. The Platonic ideas may be considered the wholes of which actual things are fragments, but to suppose them to be absolute exemplars is to hold the kind of Platonism which "has been held by the extremest nominalists." (5.470)

Peirce called his Platonic ideas sometimes universals but more usually generals. Although "generality is an indispensable ingredient of reality" on the grounds that "actuality without any regularity whatever is a nullity,"[71] absolute universality is impossible of attainment. (1.141) Absolutes are inexplicable, so that to maintain that generals are subject to growth is to render them somewhat more explicable. (1.175) A universal or general, of course, refers to something real: the regularity of a common relationship; it is neither exclusively actual nor an invention of men. (1.27 n.1) The reality of generals is not a proposition that brings with it the necessity for regarding any and every general as real. The difficulty is to determine not whether generals can be real but which generals are real. (5.430)

---

[66] See chap. III, D, iii.

[67] By an ideal, Peirce meant "the limit which the possible cannot attain." (5.311 n.)

[68] For "real" in this passage, we should read "existent." In the light of all that has gone before, Peirce cannot be accused of subscribing to the ontology according to which the existent alone is real. See, e.g., this chapter, C, i.

[69] Letter of January 23, 1903, quoted in Perry, *Thought and Character of William James*, vol. ii, p. 426.

[70] A possible concrete nothing is the logical contradictory of a concrete being. (6.619)

[71] See this chapter, B, ii, and D, ii.

We have already learned in this section that logic suggests the nature of real generals. They must be either qualities, facts, or laws,[72] a triad which has already been shown to be phenomenologically evident.[73] According to Peirce's scheme, qualities are general, events, or reactions, both general and particular, and laws, or relations, general.

Qualities are general (1.422) but none is more general than another. (1.425) Indeed, the whole study of phenomenology was set up to treat of the "universal qualities of phenomena." (5.122) "In the idea of being, Firstness is predominant, not necessarily on account of the abstractness of that idea, but on account of its self-containedness." (1.302)

Reaction, too, has its aspect of generality. The existence of a fact consists in its consequences, (1.432) some of which at least are general. (1.436) "Whatever reacts is *ipso facto* real," (5.96) but reaction involves at least two things and a general relation between them. For "the being [of a thing] consists in some other fact." (4.463) Thus "it is the brute Irrational insistency that forces us to acknowledge the reality of what we experience." (6.340)

But if qualities and reactions are general, relation is of the very essence of generality. Reality is an affair of mediation between quality and reaction. (5.121) Any two things are connected in some way, "for to say that two things are disconnected is but to say that they are connected in a way different from the way under contemplation. For everything is in some relation to each other thing." (4.319) This leads us to the conclusion that all truths form a system, the proposition of total relatedness. (2.447-448) There is no doubt that "general principles are really operative in nature." (5.101) Leibniz's principle of sufficient reason, that "whatever exists has a *reason* for existing, not a blind cause" (4.36) is superfluous. "Existing things do not need supporting reasons; for they *are* reasons, themselves."

From the idea of relations, then, we come to the basic notion of reality. "There are ideas in nature which determine the existence of objects." (1.231) It is impossible to escape the conclusion that general principles be real, at least as real as actual objects; and this is the controlling tenet of realism. "Reality . . . is a special mode of being, the characteristic of which is that things that are real are whatever they really are, independently of any assertion about them." (6.349) "The great realists . . . showed that the general is not capable of full actualization in the world of action and reaction but is of the nature of what is thought, but that our thinking only apprehends

---

[72] See this chapter, B, i, ii, and iii.
[73] See this chapter, A, ii.

and does not create thought, and that that thought may and does as much govern outward things as it does our thinking." (1.27) "Ideas[74] utterly despised and frowned upon have an inherent power of working their way to the governance of the world, at last." (2.149)

We have tried to set forth briefly but essentially what Peirce's theory of reality is. Reality, however, is not merely internal to metaphysics but external to it also in the sense of having implications from metaphysics to other topics. Other chapters coming both before and after this one will carry the full weight of such implications. Here we can only suggest Peirce's answers to some of these other metaphysical problems, and indicate the topics to which they more properly belong.

The first implications from reality are those which revert back to logic. Since the method of attaining to reality is that of an indefinitely prolonged series of inductions, so that "a sufficiently long succession of inferences from parts to whole will lead men to a knowledge of it," (5.351)[75] it follows that reality is "something which is constituted by an event indefinitely future," (5.331) "a real fact which corresponds to the idea of probability." (2.650) Reality is thus something which is hypothetical;[76] there are real possibilities in the realm of being. (4.547; 4.580)

The second implication from reality bridges the gap between phenomenology and epistemology. The preliminary inquiry, which consists in contemplating phenomena, in opening its eyes and describing what it sees,[77] carries the assumption that what it sees is real. It would follow, as a primary postulate of epistemology, that "there is nothing, then, to prevent our knowing outward things as they really are," (5.311) and it would further follow from the probabilistic and hypothetical nature of reality stated just above, that "it is most likely that we do know them [i.e., things as they really are] in numberless cases, although we can *never be absolutely* certain of doing so in any special case." (5.311) This uncertainty of knowledge does not mean, however, that reality is a subjective affair. Although "the real world cannot be distinguished from a fictitious world by any description," (2.337) "we may define the real as that whose characters are independent of what anybody may think them to be." (5.405; 5.430)

Reality is not only wider than opinion; it is also wider than truth. To

---

[74] It should no longer be necessary to point out that by "ideas" Peirce here means mentally apprehended generals or universals.

[75] See chap. III, C, iii.

[76] See chap. III, B, iv.

[77] See this chapter, A, i.

make reality independent of opinion is also to make it wider than truth. For the question of truth, the real may be defined as "the immediate object of that which is true." (6.393) But this can never be a sufficient definition of reality, since reality is wider than truth. It so happens that "that which any true proposition asserts is *real*," (5.432) but a false proposition would have to be admitted to be a proposition[78] also. Thus there is a reality for which there is no corresponding truth, namely, the reality of falsity. Falsity is real in the sense that there exists real falsity. The idea of reality is more occult than that of truth. (1.578)

The implications of the theory of reality to the study of psychology are enormous, and in a way revolutionary. If "reality is that mode of being by virtue of which the real thing is as it is, irrespectively of what any mind or any definite collection of minds may represent it to be," (5.565) then the psychology which is consistent with such a definition would have to be set up on the principle that the reality which the mind contains came to it from the outside; and its own structure would have to be studied in the light of this basic fact. Objective theoretical and factual propositions would have to be the center toward which the mind is oriented. "The only effect which real things have is to cause belief," (5.406) so that the mind must become an instrument for the acceptance of belief as true or the rejection of it as false. Those which are true are a result of the orientation of the mind toward objective truths deeply held. We shall see that to Peirce this deduction is followed to the point where "a person is only a particular kind of general idea." (6.270)[79]

For theology, the implications of the definition of reality render a deeper reality for God than for his creatures. Things are almost real, but perhaps God alone is absolutely real. Only in terms of the infinite being of God does Peirce admit degrees of reality. (2.532) All things are equally real except God, who is perhaps a little more so. At least, God is made the ideal of reality, the limit to which real things approach.[80]

There are particular questions "commonly reckoned as metaphysical, and which certainly are so, if by metaphysics we mean ontology." (5.496) "These are, for example, What is reality? Are necessity and contingency real modes of being? Are the laws of nature real?[81] Can they be assumed to be immutable or are they presumably results of evolution?[82] Is there

---

[78] See chap. III, B, iv.
[79] See chap. VI.
[80] See chap. XII.
[81] See chap. VIII.
[82] See chap. XI.

any real chance, or departure from real law?"[83] We have just seen the answer to the first of these questions. We must now turn to the solution which Peirce proposed to the second.

D. The Metaphysical Categories

i. the modes of being

Using the theory of reality which has been established in the last two sections, it is possible to perceive, from certain distinctions which were made in the logic and certain requirements which appear in the phaneron, what the metaphysical categories must be. These metaphysical categories are established in this section and the next. But before we discuss them let us return to their presence in the previous topics.

At the outset of the chapter on logic, Peirce was quoted as saying that "a general fact cannot be fully realized. . . . The future is potential, not actual."[84] In the section on the nature of propositions, this distinction is represented by the terms, *de inesse* and *modal*, into which propositions are divided. *De inesse* propositions take account only of "the existing state of things," whereas *modal* propositions "take account of the whole range of possibility."[85] The distinction between actuality and possibility is required throughout the logic and phenomenology, and finally is revealed as the basic metaphysical categories. It should be sufficient if we indicate the presence of these categories behind a few more terms in logic. We find it in the distinction between universal and particular propositions; the particular asserts the existence of its subject, the universal does not.[86] Universal propositions are therefore possible, while particular ones are existential, or actual. Again, the hypothetical proposition, while applicable to real happenings, is more relevant to possibility.[87] "A hypothetical proposition, generally, is not confined to stating what actually happens, but states what is invariably true throughout a universe of possibility." (3.366) The distinction between formal and material, accepted by Peirce for the leading principle, is once more dependent upon possibility and actuality. The formal is a reference to the possible, while the material is one to the actual, in this comparison.[88]

---

[83] See chap. XI.
[84] See chap. III, A, ii.
[85] See chap. III, B, iv.
[86] See chap. III, B, iv.
[87] *Loc. cit.*, also 3.178, 3.374.
[88] See chap. III, C, ii.

In an earlier division of the logic, however, Peirce has demarked not two but three distinctions with regard to possibility and actuality. This occurs in the doctrine of signs, where the last three sets of signs are established. The rheme represents a possible object; the dicent an actual existent; and the argument a law.[89] Three modes of being are in fact what Peirce endeavored to establish.

From certain passages in the phenomenology, we can detect the presence of the metaphysical categories which we have already noted in the logic.

We have already seen quality denoted as a possibility which may or may not be actualized,[90] a positive qualitative possibility independent of the mind. Indeed, quality, firstness, and possibility are equated (1.527) in many places in Peirce's writings.[91] One aspect of the universe of possibility is that of qualities.

Secondness is termed actuality as the field of opposition and reaction.[92] This may be the opposition of qualities, as "when scarlet and red are contemplated together," (1.455) or it may be a more violent physical opposition, as when something reacts dynamically against other things.[93]

The third category of the phaneron is termed law, and since a law is "how an endless future must continue to be,"[94] Peirce terms it destiny. Destiny as law is divided into laws necessary and laws contingent.[95] Necessary laws are associated with determinism; contingent laws, with freedom.

The metaphysical categories of possibility, actuality, and destiny are not absolutely identical with the phenomenological categories of firstness, secondness, and thirdness, (4.545) else there would be nothing gained by according them separate treatment. (4.549) We shall see the phenomenological categories develop more closely into the second set of metaphysical categories.[96] What distinguishes the metaphysical from the phenomenological categories is the overlay of generality which pervades all three of the metaphysical categories. (1.476) They are the ultimate and irreducible broad divisions into which the phenomenological categories fall.

In order to note the distinction made here between the metaphysical and the phenomenological categories, let us indicate a few differences.

Possibility differs from firstness in two ways. Possibility is absolutely

---

[89] See chap. III, B, i.
[90] See this chapter, B, i.
[91] See, for example, 1.475, 1.310.
[92] See this chapter, B, ii, (b).
[93] See *loc. cit.*
[94] See this chapter, B, iii.
[95] See this chapter, B, iii.
[96] See this chapter, D, ii.

general; firstness is not. Quality "lends itself readily to generalization but is not itself general," (6.205) but "the idea of a general involves the idea of possible variations which no multitude of existent things could exhaust but would leave between any two not merely *many* possibilities, but possibilities absolutely beyond all multitude." (5.103) Again, "the word *possibility* fits [firstness], except that possibility implies a relation to what exists while Universal Firstness is the mode of being of itself." (1.531)

Actuality differs from secondness in that secondness imparts actuality to the possibility of firstness (1.327-328) by introducing a field of reaction and opposition. "The mode of being of the quality is that of Firstness. That is to say, it is a possibility. It is related to the matter accidentally; and this relation does not change the quality at all, except that it imparts *existence*, that is to say, this very relation of inherence, to it. But the *matter*, on the other hand, has no being at all except the being a subject of qualities. This relation of really having qualities constitutes its *existence*." (1.527)

Destiny differs from thirdness, in that thirdness is confined to law,[97] whereas destiny concerns both what is within and what is without law. Freedom from law is as much destiny as law itself. (4.549) Therefore destiny proves to be the wider category.

The phenomenological categories are, as their name implies, modes of phenomena; the metaphysical categories are modes of being. Peirce's formal statement of the latter is perfectly clear. "My view," he says, "is that there are three modes of being. I hold that we can directly observe them in elements of whatever is at any time before the mind in any way. They are the being of positive qualitative possibility, the being of actual fact, and the being of law that will govern facts in the future." (1.23) Undoubtedly, being itself is the widest category of all; even nothing is not exempt from it. The attempt to prove that being is nothing leads to the proof that nonbeing is being, a contradiction which Peirce followed Avicenna in accepting. (6.620-622) There seems no reason to believe that nonbeing, or nothing, has no determination. Nonbeing is a form of being. Being in this broad sense has meaning only with reference to the *summum bonum*. (2.116) The modes of being "are elements of coöperation toward the *summum bonum*." (2.118)

We are now in a position to discuss the metaphysical categories by themselves and in their relation to each other. We shall deal briefly first with (*a*) possibility, then (*b*) the relation of possibility to actuality, (*c*) actuality,

[97] See this chapter, B, iii.

(*d*) the relation of possibility and actuality to destiny, and finally (*e*) destiny.

(*a*) The understanding of the notion of possibility starts with the idea of the independence of qualities from sense experience.[98] Possibility is both real and objective; (5.527) it is a positive affair and hence must be distinguished from negative possibility. Negative possibility *is* subjective and ignorantial; (2.347) "The special kind of possibility here called subjective is that which consists in ignorance. If we do not know that there are not inhabitants of Mars, it is subjectively possible that there are such beings." (4.573) Thus negative possibility is a category of knowledge, while positive possibility is a category of being. But if possibility is not to be understood negatively, neither is it to be equated with potentiality. Potential being is being *in futuro*, (1.218) and while future contingency is as real as the present, (6.368) possibility is not exclusively concerned with the future. It is not a time category in that sense at all, but is closer to what Mill nominalistically described as a "permanent possibility." (1.487) There are some existing ostriches, which means that there are potentially some in the future. But the possibility of ostriches in no wise depends upon their existence in the present.

Potentiality means "indeterminate yet capable of determination in any special case," (6.185) while metaphysical possibility means rather "possibility by supernatural power," (6.371)[99] so that the latter is "nearly a potentiality" but not quite. Potentiality "connotes some inherent tendency to actuality, which, if not thwarted, leads to final completeness of being," (6.365) whereas possibility has no such tendency. Possibility is the more inclusive term, of which potentiality is the subspecies. Metaphysical possibility must be distinguished also from real possibility. Real possibility means possibility in the thing. With regard to possibility, there is no distinction between there being an ostrich in this room and there being no actual ostrich at all, since both are possible; but with regard to probability the difference is great indeed.

It is not necessary, however, to distinguish too sharply between metaphysical and logical possibility: they are equivalent. Logical possibility means simply "freedom from all contradiction," (2.538) while metaphysical possibility means "possibility of existence." (6.371) But that is possible of existence which is free from contradiction. To the extent to which there is nothing contradictory in the idea of an ostrich ostriches are possible. All

[98] See this chapter, B, i.
[99] See *loc. cit.* for other meanings of possibility.

existing things are partially contradictory, but their existence depends upon their having been positively possible to some extent at least, and not upon their contradictoriness. Possibility denotes exactly what is denoted by the term, *posse*, can be. (6.365) It is that indetermination which can be determined (1.468) but which never is absolutely so in any special case.

(*b*) Before considering actuality by itself, it will be necessary to establish just what the relation is between possibility and actuality. "Possibility implies a relation to what exists." (1.531) Possibility is more than the actual, for "a possibility remains possible when it is not actual," (1.422) while an actual cannot remain actual if it is not possible. The "possibility evolves the actuality" (1.453) in that *only* what is possible may be assumed to be actual. "It is impossible, 'in the nature of things,' as we say, that is, is logically impossible, that all that ever will have happened should at any time actually have happened." (3.580) Existence is a matter of degree. (1.175) Not all possibles can exist; actuality is a selection of them. "In order to represent to our minds the relation between the universe of possibilities and the universe of actual existent facts, if we are going to think of the latter as a surface, we must think of the former as three-dimensional space in which any surface would represent all the facts that might exist in one existential universe." (4.514) Although the actual world cannot contain pure possibility, it is governed by it. (1.478) The actual world is in fact an offshoot of the Platonic world which is the world of possibility.[100]

If, instead of looking at the relation between possibility and actuality from the viewpoint of possibility, we look at the relation from the viewpoint of actuality, we see much the same conclusions prevailing. "No reaction among individual things can create one of those things nor destroy it; for before its existence or after it there would not be anything to react. So that the fountain of existence must be sought elsewhere." (1.460) "The existence of things," moreover, "consists in their reguar behavior," (1.411) and regularity is an affair of generality. "All that we perceive or think, or that exists, is general," (3.93 n.) and although it is also "infinitely determinate," it could not exist at all without the generality which it possesses. Thus its existence is dependent upon its generality, which is only another name for possibility. Actuality considered alone ignores "the distinction of essence and existence"[101] and so is guilty of the fallacy of nominalism. (5.37)

(*c*) Peirce learned from Kant that "no general description of existence

---

[100] See this chapter, C, ii, quoting 6.192.

[101] Following Peirce's practice, existence has been employed as a synonym for actuality. The corresponding synonym of essence for possibility is less frequently employed. But the distinction between essence and existence is closely related to the possibility-actuality distinction.

is possible." (1.35) Actuality is the activity of the real. (1.325) It is very close to what we have already described as the field of individual things.[102] Existence "is an affair of blind force. . . . No law determines any atom to exist." (1.329) The passive condition of capability of action which consists in the function of reaction or resistance is actuality. To be actual is to be the subject of qualities, to be stimulated to action by some "object's crowding out a place for itself in the universe." (1.21) "Effort supposes resistance" (1.320) and vice versa. "Existence lies in the possibility of an identical opposite, or of being indeterminately over against itself alone, with a determinate opposition, or over-againstness, besides." (1.447) Since "that which gives actuality is opposition," (1.432) "the existence of a fact does consist in the existence of all its consequences." But since "acts are the most perfectly individual objects there are," (5.529) no *explanation* of facts in terms of consequences is possible. Thus "no congeries of actions here and now can ever make a general fact." (1.420) Any complete description of actuality must appeal beyond actuality to the field of generality or possibility.

(*d*) "The unsophisticated conception is that everything in the Future is either *destined*, i.e., necessitated already, or is *undecided*, the contingent future of Aristotle. In other words, it is not Actual . . . but is either Necessary or Possible"; (5.459) necessary, if only one state of things satisfies the conditions, possible when there is more than one. (5.454) But in actuality there is both necessity and real freedom, so that destiny is required to distinguish these from both actuality and possibility.

(*e*) Destiny has two parts. Unlike actuality and possibility, it is subdivided. There is destiny as necessity, or determinism, and there is destiny as freedom. Destiny as freedom may be described as "Freedom from Destiny," (4.549) since the affirmation or negation of this mode of being is equally relevant to it. (4.547) Thus both destiny and freedom from destiny are aspects of destiny. We shall, following Peirce, refer to the former as necessity and to the latter as freedom.

"Philosophical necessity is a special case of universality." (6.592) Destiny as necessity is what is "sure to come true." (4.547) "I do not see," said Peirce, "by what confusion of thought anybody can persuade himself that he does not believe that tomorrow is destined to come. The point is that it is today really true that tomorrow the sun will rise; or that, even if it does not, the clocks or *something* will go on. . . . We are too apt to confound destiny with the impossibility of the opposite. I see no impossibility

[102] See this chapter, B, ii, (*b*).

in the sudden stoppage of everything." Necessity itself is subdivided into possible and actual necessity. Possible (or logical) necessity is universal and tautological truth. For instance, it would not be necessary to know "whether there was or was not such an animal as a *basilisk*, or whether there are any such things as serpents, cocks, and eggs" in order to "know that every basilisk there may be has been hatched by a serpent from a cock's egg." (4.67)

Actual necessity is termed fate. "*Fate* is that special kind of *destiny* by which events are supposed to be brought about *under definite circumstances* which involve no necessitating cause for those occurrences." (4.547 n.1) "It is a superstition to suppose that a certain sort of events are ever fated, and it is another to suppose that the word fate can never be freed from its superstitious taint. We are all fated to die." (5.407 n.1) Fate, or actual necessity, proves to be blind destiny. It is this variety which is mistakenly thought to be absolute: "the common belief that every single fact in the universe is precisely determined by law"; (6.36) that "the state of things existing at any time, together with certain immutable laws, completely determine the state of things at every other time." (6.37) But the truth is that even Epicurus, the arch victim of this point of view, "in revising the atomic doctrine and repairing its defenses, found himself obliged to suppose that atoms swerve from their course by spontaneous chance," (6.36)[103] and, in much the same way, Lucretius following Democritus admitted that "the atoms swerve from the paths to which the laws of mechanics would confine them," (1.132) deviating fortuitously from their rectilinear trajectories.[104]

Freedom shares with actual necessity the control of actuality, and it is in this province that the absolute sway of logical, or possible, necessity is interrupted. It is in the discrepancy between law and real fact that freedom is discovered. "We observe that phenomena approach very closely to satisfying general laws; but we have not the smallest reason for supposing that they satisfy them precisely." (1.132) "We enormously exaggerate the part that law plays in the universe. It is by means of regularities that we understand what little we do understand of the world, and thus there is a sort of mental perspective which brings regular phenomena to the foreground." (1.406) But, understanding this, "uniformity is seen to be really a highly exceptional phenomenon. But we pay no attention to irregular relationships, as having no interest for us." "The universe is *not* a mere mechanical result

---

[103] For a detailed exposition of absolute actual necessity, or fate, and the arguments against it, see *Col. Pap.*, vol. vi, chap. II.

[104] *De Rerum Natura*, bk. ii, pp. 216-293.

of the operation of blind law." (1.162) Diversity is as primitive as law. Freedom consists in uncontrolled variety; (1.302) in freshness, spontaneity, originality, and novelty. (1.357) For this aspect of reality, too, is destiny of a definite sort.

ii. THE MODES OF EXISTENCE

We have seen that one of the metaphysical categories of the modes of being, namely, actuality, or existence, is "an affair of blind force."[105] Blind force, in its phenomenological aspect of secondness, we had already learned, is an effort of resistance, of opposition, of reaction.[106] But the repetition of such effort in the course of actuality leads to certain patterns which can be detected. For resistance can only be effected, opposition conducted, and reaction exerted in terms of further categories, which the repetition compels them to reveal. These categories are the modes of existence. Peirce described them as (*a*) chance, (*b*) law, and (*c*) habit. "Three elements are active in the world: first, chance; second, law; and third, habit-taking." (1.409) They are closely related to the phenomenological categories;[107] "Chance is First, Law is Second, the tendency to take habits is Third." (6.32) We may treat them in this order.

(*a*) Chance is the first category of existence. Aristotle, Peirce reminded us, often said that "some things are determined by causes while others happen by chance." (1.403)[108] Chance is subsidiary to Thirdness. (6.202)[109] It is, in a way, the same as freedom. (6.200)[110] Chance is only "a mathematical term to express with accuracy the characteristics of freedom or spontaneity." (6.201) Uniformity is a "highly exceptional phenomenon." (1.406) "Conformity to law exists only within a limited range of events and even there is not perfect, for an element of pure spontaneity or lawless originality mingles . . . with law everywhere." (1.407) "When we gaze upon the multifariousness of nature, we are looking straight into the face of a living spontaneity." (6.553) Trace the causes of "irregular departures from the law . . . back far enough and you will be forced to admit they are always due to arbitrary determination, or chance." (6.46)

---

[105] See this chapter, D, i, (*c*).
[106] See this chapter, B, ii.
[107] See this chapter, B.
[108] E.g., in the *Physica*, 195f., 31-198a, 13. Peirce's definition of chance corresponds more to what Aristotle means by spontaneity than to what he means by chance. See *Physica*, 197^{b}15 rather than 197^{a}5. See also Plato, *Laws*, IV, 709.
[109] See this chapter, B, iii.
[110] See this chapter, D, ii.

Chance, then, "or irregularity—that is, the absence of any coincidence, is that diversity and variety of things and events which law does not prevent." (6.612) "Chance itself pours in at every avenue of sense: it is of all things the most obtrusive." This obtrusive character of the universe is its variety; (6.64) "variety is a fact which must be admitted; and the theory of chance merely consists in supposing this diversification does not antedate all time." (6.65)[111] The "infinite diversity of the universe, which we call chance, may bring ideas into proximity which are not associated in one general idea." (6.143)

Before Peirce, chance had usually been considered to be a subjective affair. It is still so considered by many. On this view, chance is a product of human ignorance: were all known, there would be no chance. But, consistently with the remainder of his philosophy, Peirce transformed chance from a subjective to an objective category. Chance, according to him, is a genuine constituent of the actual world. The chance component of an event may be reduced somewhat but it can never be altogether eliminated. This means that everything that happens happens at least partly by chance, since actuality itself is essentially a chance affair. Our knowledge of chance, then, comes to us from the objective and actual world; we know, subjectively, about the existence of objective chance. But we do not by our knowing put chance into the objective world, for indeed it is already there.

(*b*) Law is the second category of existence. There are many kinds of law, according to Peirce, but we shall be concerned here only with metaphysically contingent law.[112] "Law as an active force is second but order and legislation are third" (1.337) and it is law as second that is meant by metaphysically contingent law. (1.483 ff.) Law and chance are correlatives; (2.684) law is not explicable in terms of chance alone. (5.172) On the other hand, laws cannot always have been what they are, and they cannot have sprung into being by a sudden fiat. These explanations make the laws of nature "blind and inexplicable." (1.175) An alternative solution is that the laws of nature may "have naturally grown up." "*Nature* is an inheritance." (1.214) This would give rise to "a natural history of the laws of nature," (1.354) for no law is great enough to escape the overriding law of evolution. (1.348) Peirce wished "to make the laws themselves subject to law. For that purpose that law of laws must be a law capable of developing itself. Now the only conceivable law of which that is true

---

[111] According to William James, Chauncey Wright used to say "if there be no essential chaos . . . an anti-chaotic νους is superfluous."—William James, *Collected Essays and Reviews* (London, Longmans, 1920), p. 24.

[112] Cf. phenomenological law as thirdness. This chapter, A, ii, and B, iii.

is an evolutionary law. We therefore suppose that all law is the result of evolution, and to suppose this is to suppose it to be imperfect." (6.91)[113]

The discrepancy between the absolute generality which we might suppose law to have and the limited generality of actual law is accounted for by the fact that law is not a mere uniformity but a compulsion. "Let a law of nature—say the law of gravitation—remain a mere uniformity . . . and what in the world should induce a stone . . . to act in conformity to that uniformity"? (5.48) "A law which never will operate has no positive existence." (5.545) Hence genuine laws are those which will "govern facts in the future," (1.23) and this gives them their significance, for "the future necessary consequent of a present state of things is as real and true as that present state of things itself." (6.368) Thus, since "a law is how an endless future must continue to be," it follows that "a law never can be embodied in its character as a law except by determining a habit." (1.536) The examination of habit must complete the understanding of law.

(*c*) Habit is the third category of existence. In some ways, it is the most important, since it both characterizes existence and gives it a direction. Habit may be found in logic, in the notion of a symbol.[114] "A Symbol incorporates a habit, and is indispensable to the application of any *intellectual* habit, *at least*." (4.531)[115] Habit derives from chance. There is a "logical process which we may suppose takes place in things, in which the generalizing tendency builds up new habits from chance occurrences." (6.206) When "accident acquires some incipient staying quality, some tendency toward consistency," (6.204) then "some beginning of a *habit* has been established." Almost in the earliest state of spatial extension, changes are undergone; "and habits will be formed of passing from certain states to certain others." (1.413) Thus "pairs of states will begin to take habits." (1.414)

What is the meaning of habit, according to Peirce? Not the ordinary psychological meaning of the term, but one very much broader. "Let us use the word 'habit,' throughout this book, not in its narrower, and more proper sense, in which it is opposed to a natural disposition (for the term *acquired habit* will perfectly express that narrower sense), but in its wider and perhaps still more usual sense, in which it denotes such a specialization, original or acquired, of the nature of a man, or an animal, or a vine, or a crystallizable chemical substance, or anything else, that he or it will behave, or always tend to behave, in a way describable in general terms

---

[113] See also 6.13.
[114] See chap. III, B, i, (*b*).
[115] See also 4.464.

upon every occasion (or upon a considerable proportion of the occasions) that may present itself of a generally describable character." (5.538) Thus habits are characteristic of all actual things, inanimate as well as animate. "Empirically, we find that some plants take habits. The stream of water that wears a bed for itself is forming a habit. . . . Habits in themselves are entirely unconscious, though feelings may be symptoms of them." (5.492) Also, since habits of feelings and habits of actions can both be acquired by all actual things, there are two worlds of habit: an inner world, the world of Platonic forms; and an outer world, the world of existence. (4.157) "All things have a tendency to take habit." (1.409)[116] Defining a habit means "describing the kind of behavior in which the habit becomes actualized." (2.666) "The performance of a certain line of behavior, throughout an endless succession of occasions, without exception, very decidedly *constituted* a habit." (2.667)

The laws to which we find no exception seem to be the results of long periods of habit-taking. (6.97) "Uniformities in the modes of action of things have come about by their taking habits. At present, the course of events is approximately determined by law. In the past that approximation was less perfect: in the future it will be more perfect. The tendency to obey laws has always been and always will be growing." (1.409) The growth of habit-taking together with the element of chance accounts for law. (6.297) "Meantime, if law is a result of evolution, which is a process lasting through all time, it follows that no law is absolute. That is, we must suppose that the phenomena themselves involve departures from law analogous to errors of observation." (6.101) Yet "habits produce statistical uniformities," and when these are high enough in number "there are at least no departures from the law that our senses can take cognizance of."[117] "It is clear that nothing but a principle of habit, itself due to the growth by habit of an infinitesimal chance tendency toward habit-taking, is the only bridge that can span the chasm between the chance medley of chaos and the cosmos of order and law." (6.262)

Before Peirce did his work on the topic, habit was almost exclusively a psychological category. Habits were entirely human affairs, and the term had no meaning outside the human province. Peirce did not deny the psychological validity of the category of habit. But he added to habit as a psychological category the conception of habit as a cosmological one.

---

[116] Also 6.101.

[117] There exists an objective ground for that marvelous ability of the inductive process to correct itself through repetition. See chapter III, C, iii.

Instead of being merely a function of the higher organisms, habit was shown also to be characteristic of the objective and actual world; and this is one of Peirce's chief contributions to philosophy. Peirce performed the same task for habit as for chance in that he made both validly objective as well as subjective conceptions. There is, however, no hidden anthropomorphism in his conception of the meaning of these terms. Physical events repeated sufficiently reveal a tendency to take habits, whether there are human beings to observe and to know it or not; and the fact that the habits of actual physical events bear an analogy to the habits of psychological events in no wise makes the physical habits psychological. Habit, for Peirce, is an authentic, ontological category.

iii. SUMMARY OF THE CHAPTER

Metaphysics, as the science of reality, rests on the absolute acceptance of logical principles as the truths of being, and also on experience and fact. The purpose of the preliminary metaphysical inquiry, which is phenomenology, is to make an ultimate analysis which will hold for all experience. Pursuant with this purpose, phenomenology reveals the existence of three fundamental categories of the phaneron: quality, fact, and law. These are the indecomposable elements, and they agree with the categories of logic as well as with the facts of experience. In logic they correspond to the three references of the sign. There is an obvious comparison to be made between the three phenomenological categories thus established and the well-known categories of Hegel. Superficial similarities there are, but, also, profound differences are revealed. Peirce's categories are wholly objective.

The phenomenological categories examined under the names of firstness, secondness, and thirdness prove to have many subtle appearances and meanings. These in turn require the setting up of further subdivisions, in order to keep the various distinctions clear.

In a discussion of general metaphysics, nominalism is attacked and rejected. Nominalism is considered to be the most prevalent metaphysical error. Arguments against it are offered from logic, from metaphysics, from psychology, and from science. Realism is then established as the metaphysics which best accords with the conditions of the world. Reality consists in an ideal world of Platonic ideas, of which the actual world is but a fragment albeit a genuine one. A number of metaphysical problems are held over for later chapters.

From the theory of reality already established certain metaphysical categories follow. These are divided into modes of being and modes of existence. The modes of being are: possibility, actuality, and destiny. The modes of existence are: chance, law, and habit.

In the following chapters, Peirce's theories in other philosophical fields may be seen to follow from experience, from logic, and also from metaphysics, as established in the preceding chapter, in this one, and in the next.

CHAPTER V

Epistemology

‹‹›››››››››››››››››››››››››››››››

A. THE FOUNDATIONS OF KNOWLEDGE

NEXT TO ONTOLOGY IN IMPORTANCE IS THE TOPIC OF EPISTEMOLOGY. PEIRCE defined epistemology as "the broadest positive truths of the psycho-physical universe—positive in the sense of not being reducible to logical formulae." (5.496) "It considers, for example, in what sense and how there can be any true proposition and false proposition, and what are the general conditions to which thought or signs of any kind must conform in order to assert anything." (2.206) It is what the Germans meant by *Erkenntnisstheorie*, "the investigation of the sense in which knowledge is possible." (2.62)

"Knowledge," we are told, "can only be furthered by the real desire for it." (2.635) Fortunately, the desire is a very deep-rooted one, for "all human knowledge, up to the highest flights of science, is but the development of our inborn animal instincts." (2.754) "The instinct of *feeding* brought with it elementary knowledge of mechanical forces, space, etc., and the instinct of *breeding*, brought with it elementary knowledge of psychical motives, of time, etc." (1.118) "Man has thus far not attained to any knowledge that is not in a wide sense either mechanical or anthropological in its nature, and it may be reasonably presumed that he never will." (2.753) We have from birth some notion of fairly correct mechanical ideas and some notion of what sort of objects our fellow beings are. The appeal which Galileo made to the natural light of reason, *il lume naturale*, (1.80) is really an appeal to instinct. (1.630) "Unless man have a natural bent in accordance with nature's, he has no chance of understanding nature at all." (6.477) The fact that there is some understanding of nature would argue that the human mind, being part of nature, would have some natural affinity for its truths.

"Every person who wishes to form an opinion concerning fundamental problems should first of all make a complete survey of human knowledge." (6.9) This task includes an examination of the method and findings of the separate sciences as well as of the various branches of philosophy itself. But before we can undertake it, we must try to discover the answer to a prior problem, which is that of the grounds of knowledge itself: how is knowledge possible? In the following sections we shall inquire into the foundations of knowledge, for although epistemology, like every branch of philosophy, is a separate study, having a separate field and special investigations of its own, we shall find that in the three previous chapters, Peirce has already committed himself to certain propositions involving questions of knowledge, of the process of knowing and of truth. We may therefore begin by setting forth these commitments, as we find them in logic, in phenomenology, and in ontology.

i. FROM LOGIC TO KNOWING

Logic, we saw,[1] is not founded on epistemology, since epistemology is forced to certain assumptions which logic does not have to make. Among these are reality and knowing. The logician does not have to decide questions of reality nor does he depend upon minds, whereas in epistemology these are necessary assumptions. On the other hand, epistemology owes much to logic, and depends to some extent upon logical findings. (1.625)

We have seen that the reference of propositions is to truth and falsity.[2] Generals and facts are true; they cannot be false, for they are what they are. Thus truth has relevance to propositions, generals, and facts, while falsity has relevance only to propositions. But despite the fact that objective truth is both general and particular, experience alone can settle it.[3] Peirce accepted the correspondence theory of truth, i.e., that to the extent to which there is a correspondence between a proposition and that to which it refers, to that extent the proposition is said to be true.[4] Propositions, it will be recalled, "independently determine their objects by means of other terms, and thus, expressing their own objective validity, become capable of truth or falsehood."[5] Since "we may say that the purpose of signs—which is the purpose of thought—is to bring truth to expression," (2.444 n.) it will be well to refer again to the peculiar nature of signs considered as leading to knowing, that is in their aspect of the awareness of truth.

The expression of truth consists, according to Peirce, in the assertion of a proposition, through the second triad of signs: icon, index, and symbol.[6]

---

[1] See chap. III, A, i.
[2] See chap. III, B, iii.
[3] See chap. III, A, ii.
[4] See chap. III, C, ii.
[5] Quoted in chap. III, B, iii.
[6] See chap. III, B, i, (*b*).

These are the leading notions of epistemology.[7] The knowing person, for the purposes of understanding the logical framework for the existence of knowledge, is simply a mind, in which interpretants are aroused by signs (propositions), thus allowing communication to take place. "A sign which denotes a thing by forcing it upon the attention is called an *index*." (3.434) Propositions are asserted by means of a certain force which inheres in indices.[8] "The assertion represents a compulsion which experience, meaning the course of life, brings upon the deliverer to attach the predicate to the subjects as a sign of them taken in a particular way." (3.435) Thus the stubbornness of experience furnishes the compulsion which signs exert upon the arousal of interpretants in minds. Of course, the connection between icons, indexes, and symbols and the objects to which they refer is so direct that the relation is not felt in the compulsion *as* a relation. Especially does this hold for facts. "A real thing or fact . . . is a sign of its object by virtue of being connected with it as a matter of fact and by also forcibly intruding upon the mind, quite regardless of its being interpreted as a sign." (4.447)

Thus far we have been considering the process of knowing from the implications in which logic has already involved it. Epistemology, from the standpoint of logic, is simply one of the most important subdivisions of Speculative Rhetoric,[9] a further distinction in communication to show how meaning is forced upon minds. Logic, from the standpoint of epistemology, however, is simply that division of a process which explains it from the outside. Logic views the knowledge process from the standpoint of the symbols themselves, and from this coign of vantage the mind appears as an interpretant mechanism which signs have the capacity to arouse. But the process of knowledge is obviously not exhausted by such an analysis, for it can be viewed from either end: either from that which is known (symbols) or from the knower himself. In epistemology proper we are obliged to include the view of knowledge from the knower, since that is the position in which we find ourselves ordinarily. Yet we must take such a position, and extend its implications only within the limits allowed to us by the logical assumptions of the semiotic view.

ii. FROM PHENOMENOLOGY TO EXPERIENCE

The knowledge relation is not, according to Peirce's view, one of the necessary relations of objects, since objects can exist with all their logical

---

[7] See chap. III, B, i.
[8] See chap. III, D, ii.
[9] See chap. III, D.

relations, available for experience, without there being any knowledge of them. Hence phenomenology, like logic, was established as a prior field independent of epistemology. But, continuing the analogy, the reverse is not true, for epistemology is dependent upon the findings of phenomenology and must work with its data.

Communication is made possible by a universe held in common through experience. (2.357)[10] Phenomenology "draws up an inventory of appearances without going into any investigation of their truth"[11] and "studies the kinds of elements universally present in the phenomenon; meaning by the phenomenon whatever is present at any time to the mind in any way." In epistemology, the investigation of their truth is conducted, but this is possible only by drawing on the elements of the phenomenon. Thus experience is a reaction to the phaneron. "Direct experience is neither certain nor uncertain, because it affirms nothing—it just *is*. There are delusions, hallucinations, dreams. But there is no mistake that such things really do appear, and direct experience means simply the appearance." (1.145)[12] The concept of experience is phenomenology's contribution to epistemology.

Although Peirce meant nothing more by experience, seen epistemologically than "the course of life," (1.426) he was careful to define the term again and again, and to contrast his definition with some of those of classical philosophy. The "forcible modification of our ways of thinking" by "the brutal inroads of ideas from without" makes up experience. (1.321) Experience is *"esse in praeterito,"* (2.84) "that determination of belief and cognition generally which the course of life has forced upon a man." (2.138) Again, experience is "the resultant ideas that have been forced upon us." (4.318) Peirce, looking over the traditional definitions of experience, passed over Aristotle's, that experience is a knowledge of singulars,[13] in favor of Locke's, that "all the materials of reason and knowledge" come "from *experience*: in that all our knowledge is founded, and from that it ultimately derives itself. Our observation employed either about *external sensible objects, or about the internal operations of our minds, perceived and reflected on by ourselves, is that which supplies our understanding with all the materials of thinking."* (5.611)

"Experience," Peirce said, "is our only teacher." (5.50) And yet he did not believe in a *tabula rasa*. For "all [our] knowledge comes to us by observation. A part is forced upon us from without and seems to result from

---

[10] Cf. the opening sentence of Kant's *Kritik der Reinen Vernunft.*
[11] Quoted in chap. IV, A, i.
[12] See chap. IV, A, ii.
[13] *Metaphysics*, A.

Nature's mind; a part comes from the depths of the mind as seen from within, which by an egotistical anacoluthon we call *our* mind." (2.444) All notions of general principle "spring from the power of the human mind to originate ideas that are true. But this power, for all it has accomplished, is so feeble that . . . truths are almost drowned in a flood of false notions; and that which experience does is gradually, and by a sort of fractionation, to precipitate and filter off the false ideas, eliminating them and letting the truth pour out its mighty torrent." (5.50) The action of experience takes place by a series of surprises. The teaching of experience is by a series of "practical jokes mostly cruel." (5.51) Experience says,

> Open your mouth and shut your eyes
> And I'll give you something to make you wise.

The action of experience, therefore, takes place by altering the expected, and yet it cannot be conceived entirely as producing its effect upon a passive subject. For there must be an awareness of experience, too. Peirce's appeal here is to observation—"observation that each of you must make for yourself." (5.52) Thus there takes place an active as well as a passive aspect of experience. Experience contains an element which is forceful and unavoidable, and yet requires an act of attention to appreciate fully. The complete appreciation of experience, then, comprises the forceful effect of some external object upon a subject which is internally aware, and which accumulates *in praeterito* the products of experience and rolls them up into habits. "An 'Experience' is a brutally produced conscious effect that contributes to a habit, self-controlled, yet so satisfying, on deliberation, as to be destructible by no positive exercise of internal [i.e., mental] vigour." (6.454)

iii. FROM ONTOLOGY TO KNOWLEDGE

We have already seen that the knowledge relation is not an ultimately prior one, (1.455)[14] whereas reality, which is the subject matter of ontology, consists in objective relations which are what they are regardless of what we may think about them.[15] Undoubtedly, "the realist defends his position only by assuming that the immediate object of thought in a true judgment is real."[16] Thus ontology does not depend upon epistemology, whereas the reverse does hold. For what we know is knowledge gained from the real world, and hence epistemology does depend to some extent upon ontology.

[14] See this chapter, A, i.
[15] See chap. IV, C, ii.
[16] Review of Fraser's *Berkeley* in the *North American Review*, 103 (1871), 449.

The reality of our knowledge can be verified only by means of a prior reality of the world of which we have knowledge.

In metaphysics, we find additional support for Peirce's doctrine of the knowledge process, which thus far has proved to be an affair involving the awareness of compulsion. In this awareness of compulsion, which we may now begin to call perception, character and otherness are already given. (5.194) Not the thirdness of inference, perhaps, but the firstness of character and the secondness of otherness are thus already present. The vagueness and irrationality in which otherness appears to the subject is a natural kind of nominalism which is inescapably part of the process of cognition. (4.344) Thus negative possibility is a kind of subjective ignorance, and is dependent upon the positive possibility of being.[17] Ignorance is marked by the absence of thirdness, or inference, in the dyadic relation of the knowledge process.

Truth and ignorance take their place side by side in the mind, and confusion makes it difficult to separate them, but that does not alter the fact that there are "cognitions whose objects are *real* and those whose objects are *unreal*." (5.311)[18] Sense experience reports qualities. (1.422) "The colors of objects of human experience" (6.327) are "relative to the sense of sight," for example, but "not *mental*."[19] "There is a difference between a color and a sensation of color. For a color is a quality of a thing which remains the same whether it be exposed to one kind of illumination or another, and whether it be seen by a normal or a color-blind eye."

It is important to remember that epistemological considerations all stem from the process of knowing, which involves a dualism of knower and known. It is always offset by the immobile monism of being. Thus the necessity for separating the real from the unreal, the clear from the confused, the true from the false, the changing from the unchanging, which is always a procedural affair.[20] Consider for a moment the epistemological import of the essence-existence distinction. We have already seen how this distinction applies to ontology.[21] In epistemology, however, essence is defined as "that

---

[17] See chap. IV, D, i.

[18] See chap. IV, C, i.

[19] The mentalistic epistemologies of nominalism are in direct contradiction to Peirce's theory. A statement of Abbot's well expresses Peirce's position on the question: "The triumph of Nominalism did indeed force upon thought a new problem in the question of the 'origin of knowledge'; but great is the delusion of the two schools [i.e., the *a priori* school based on Descartes' *cogito ergo sum* and the *a posteriori* school based on Locke's "sensation"] which imagine the solution of that question to lie with one of themselves."—F. E. Abbot, *Scientific Theism*, Introduction, p. 35.

[20] See chap. IV, C, i, quoting 6.492.

[21] See chap. IV, D, i and ii.

intelligible character which truly defines what a general or indefinite . . . predicate primarily asserts, so that all else that it asserts is the necessary consequence of this epistemological essence." (6.337) "When a new image, optical, acoustical, or other, appears in the mind, one subjects it to various tests in order to ascertain whether it be of internal or of external provenance." (6.333) If external, it is validated as existential. "All to which the senses normally testify without room for critical reasoning is usually and properly said to be 'experienced'; and all that is truly experienced is, in the epistemological sense, *existent*." (6.335) Thus images which are centrally aroused are of internal provenance and have no existential status in epistemology.[22]

What is the nature of this externally real object which is experienced in perception? Peirce said that it is thirdness that we perceive: "All that we perceive . . . is general." (3.93 n.) Perception is a process of apprehending generals,[23] and moreover one which does so directly. (5.209) The generals that we apprehend exert a force upon us just as they do in the actual world in which we perceive them, for "every idea has in some measure . . . the power to work out physical and psychical results. They have life, generative life." (1.219) Thus beliefs are forced on us through the compulsion which is an integral part of our apprehension of ideas. The study of perception is much facilitated by the premise of the objective reality of knowledge. The mind has the ability to overcome gradually its own susceptibility to error since it is aided by its affinity for truth. Peirce proclaimed that all his philosophy grew out of a "contrite fallibilism, combined with a high faith in the reality of knowledge." (1.14)

B. THE PROCESS OF KNOWING

i. NATURE OF THE KNOWABLE

In deriving the foundations of knowledge from logic and ontology, we started with the process of knowing and with the interaction that is experience, and came to a discussion of the status of knowledge. Now, however, in building up Peirce's theory of epistemology as a systematic affair, it will be well to reverse the order, and to give attention, first, to the examination of that which can be known, following this with a discussion of the method by which knowledge is gained.

Peirce's theory of the knowable turns upon a refutation of Kant's views in the *Critique of the Pure Reason*, or, more accurately, upon a reinterpreta-

[22] They have, however, in psychology. See chap. VI, B, iii.
[23] See chap. IV, C, i.

tion of it which differs from the classical interpretation. "The first moment of Kant's thought is to recognize that all our knowledge is, and forever must be, relative to human experience and to the nature of the human mind. That conception being well digested, the second moment of the reasoning becomes evident, namely, that as soon as it has been shown concerning any conception that it is essentially involved in the very forms of logic or other forms of knowing, from that moment there can no longer be any rational hesitation about fully accepting that conception as valid for the universe of our possible experience." (6.95) The implications of the second moment limit those of the first, if they do not actually reverse them. "The idealistic argument turns upon the assumption that certain things are absolutely 'present', namely what we have in mind at the moment, and that nothing else can be immediately, that is, otherwise than inferentially known." (1.37) But Kant "seeks to show that the only way we can apprehend our own flow of ideas, binding them together as a connected flow, is by attaching them to an immediately perceived persistent externality." (1.39)

The problem of knowledge for Peirce is, how can we advance from the merely subjective to a knowledge of the independently real? "All our knowledge may be said to rest upon *observed facts*." (6.522) The point is that any element of thought which is irreducible must have come from environing nature. (1.344) "There is nothing, then, to prevent our knowing outward things as they really are,[24] and it is most likely that we do thus know them in numberless cases, although we can never be absolutely certain of doing so in any special case." (5.311) Peirce frankly preached "immediate perception" (5.56) according to which there is "direct perception of the external world." (5.539)

At all events, "we feel facts resist our will," (1.419) so that "it is correct to say that we immediately, that is, directly perceive matter." "But observed facts relate exclusively to the particular circumstances that happened to exist when they were observed. They do not relate to any future occasions upon which we may be in doubt how we ought to act. They, therefore, do not, in themselves, contain any practical knowledge. Such knowledge must involve additions to the facts observed." (6.523) What are those additions? The answer is that "there is a reason operative in experience to which our own can approximate." (5.160) An objective rationality as well as an objective factuality exists to be known, and indeed furnishes "the only possibility of any knowledge." We can know the potential only through the actual,[25] the

---

[24] See chap. IV, A, ii.
[25] See chap. IV, A, ii.

whole only through its parts. But that the possible can be known contains one tremendous implication, which is, so to speak, the very ground and bedrock upon which the acquisition of knowledge rests. The implication is that that which has being is also that which can be known. "Ignorance and error can only be conceived as correlative to a real knowledge and truth, which latter are of the nature of cognitions. Over against any cognition, there is an unknown but knowable reality; but over against all possible cognition, there is only the self-contradictory. In short, *cognizability* (in its widest sense) and *being* are not merely metaphysically the same, but are synonymous terms." (5.257)

ii. PERCEPTUAL JUDGMENT

It is possible that in psychology there is an interest in levels below that of perception; but this cannot be true of epistemology. For it is with perception, and not with sensation or feeling, that the knowledge process *qua* knowledge process properly begins. Peirce raised the question of a lower level, but immediately referred it to logic. "Is there any law about the mode of the peripheral excitations?" he asked, (3.161) and himself replied, "The logician maintains that there is, namely, that they are all adapted to an end, that of carrying belief, in the long run, toward certain predestinate conclusions which are the same for all men." The process involves repetition: "the spontaneous development of belief is continually going on within us, fresh peripheral excitations are also continually creating new belief-habits.[26] Thus, belief is partly determined by old beliefs and partly by new experience.

"We have no power of introspection, but all knowledge of the internal world is derived by hypothetical reasoning from our knowledge of external facts." (5.265) We do, however, have direct knowledge. "The knowledge which you are compelled to admit is that knowledge which is directly forced upon you, and which there is no criticizing." (2.141) These are the "evidence of the senses," the percepts. "Anything . . . has . . . its possibility of sensation, would our senses only respond to it." (1.426) The percept, "although not the first impression of sense, is a construction with which my will has had nothing to do." The only part which is remembered is the *perceptual fact*, or "the intellect's description of the evidence of the senses" in which the will participates. (2.141) Perceptual facts are not wholly like the percept and may be untrue to it. It is certainly a fact, in all events, that we can immediately know more than what is present to the mind. (1.38) However, "the Imme-

[26] See chap. IV, D, ii, (c).

diate Object of all knowledge and all thought is, in the last analysis, the Percept." (4.539)

"Nothing is more indispensable to a sound epistemology than a crystal-clear discrimination between the Object and the Interpretant of knowledge."[27] "Even with regard to perceptual facts, or the immediate judgments we make concerning our single percepts, the same distinction is plain. The percept is the reality. It is not in propositional form. But the most immediate judgment concerning it is abstract." (5.568) "That we are conscious of our Percepts is a theory that seems to be beyond dispute; but it is not a fact of Immediate Perception. A fact of Immediate Perception is not a Percept, nor any part of a Percept; a Percept is a Seme [or rheme], while a fact of Immediate Perception, or rather the Perceptual Judgment of which such fact is the Immediate Interpretant, is a Pheme [or dicisign],[28] that is the direct Dynamical Interpretant of the Percept, and of which the Percept is the Dynamical Object." Although the perceptual judgment is different from the percept, the percept nevertheless leads inevitably to perceptual judgment.

We come now to the nature of the perceptual judgment itself, the central conception of Peirce's epistemology. By a perceptual judgment, Peirce said that he meant "a judgment asserting in propositional form what a character of a percept directly present to the mind is." (5.54) He explained it in this way: "Even after the percept is formed there is an operation which seems to me to be quite uncontrollable. It is that of judging what it is that the person perceives. A judgment is an act of formation of a mental proposition combined with an adoption of it or act of assent to it. A percept on the other hand is an image or moving picture or other exhibition. The perceptual judgment, that is, the first judgment of a person as to what is before his senses, bears little resemblance to the percept. . . ." (5.115) It is not possible to "exercise any control over that operation[29] or subject it to criticism. If we can criticize it at all, as far as I can see, that criticism would be limited to performing it again and again and seeing whether, with closer attention, we get the same result." Experience furnishes the percept; previously accepted belief, the judgment. They are equally uncontrollable. The perceptual judgment would appear to be the uncontrollable first judgment of a percept.

An example or two may serve to make the notion of perceptual judgment clearer. "You look at something and say, 'It is red.' Well, I ask you what justification you have for such a judgment. You reply, 'I *saw* it was red.'

[27] See chap. III, B, i.
[28] See chap. III, B, i.
[29] See also 4.541.

Not at all. You saw nothing in the least like that. You saw an image. There was no subject or predicate in it. It was just one unseparated image, not resembling a proposition in the smallest particular. It instigated you to your judgment, owing to a possibility of thought; but it never told you so. Now in all imagination or perception there is such an operation by which thought springs up; and its only justification is that it subsequently turns out to be useful." (1.538) "Now let us take the perceptual judgment, 'This wafer looks red.' It takes some time to write this sentence, to utter it, or even to think it. It must refer to the state of the percept at the time that it, the judgment, began to be made. But the judgment does not exist until it is completely made. It thus only refers to a memory of the past; and all memory is possibly fallible and subject to criticism and control. The judgment, then, can only mean that so far as the character of the percept can ever be ascertained, it will be ascertained that the wafer looked red." (5.544)

"Every perception is more or less unexpected." (1.332) Perceptual judgments belong to the same class of operations as insights. (5.173) Experience, which confronts us with sudden changes of perception, is therefore broader than perception. (1.336) The experience of phenomena surprises the ego with the nonego. (5.52) Indeed, perceptual judgments might be described as intellectual intuitions. (5.341) Apart from "original (i.e., indubitable because uncriticized) beliefs of a general and recurrent kind" (5.442) and "indubitable acritical inferences," there is perceptual judgment. Perceptual judgment has already been shown to involve firstness and secondness. Firstness is involved in perception in that perception is the experience of a quality.[30] Secondness is involved in the surprise, or in the resistance which such surprise entails, as has just been noted. As for thirdness, there is no doubt that "perceptual judgments contain general elements." (5.182)[31] The perceptual judgment does not require that in awareness the actually present be in any way transcended in order to include thirdness, for the relational as well as the qualitative exists objectively to the perceiving subject. "Thirdness pours in upon us through every avenue of sense," (5.157) "in our very perceptual judgments." (5.150) This is illustrated extremely well by some phenomena. Let us draw a serpentine line which, when completely drawn, appears to be a stone wall. "The point is that there are two ways of conceiving the matter. [It can be conceived as a serpentine line or as a stone wall.] Both, I beg you to remark, are *general ways of classing the line*, gen-

[30] See this chapter, A, iii.
[31] See also 5.166.

eral classes under which the line is subsumed.[82] But the very decided
preference of our perception for one mode of classing the percept shows
that this classification is contained in the perceptual judgment." (5.183)
There is little doubt that "perception attains a virtual judgment [for] it
subsumes something under a class, and not only so, but virtually attaches to
the proposition the seal of assent—two strong resemblances to inference."[33]

Peirce interpreted Aristotle's dictum, that there is nothing in the mind
which was not first in sense,[34] somewhat differently from the way in which
Aristotle intended it. By mind, he understood any representation. By the
phrase, *in sensu*, he understood "*in a perceptual judgment*, the starting point
or first premiss of all critical and controlled thinking." (5.181) The proposition expressing a perceptual judgment involves generality in its predicate.
(5.151) Universal propositions are deducible from perceptual judgments in
the same way that particular propositions are inferred from universal ones.
(5.181) "Abductive inference shades into perceptual judgment without any
sharp line of demarcation between them." "Perceptual judgments are to be
regarded as an extreme case of abductive inferences." In fact, "it is a characteristic of perceptual judgments that each of them relates to some singular
to which no other proposition relates directly, but, if it relates to it at all,
does so by relating to that perceptual judgment." (5.153)

"All our knowledge rests upon perceptual judgments. These are necessarily
veracious in greater or less degree according to the effort made, but there is
no meaning in saying that they have any other truth than veracity, since a
perceptual judgment can never be repeated. At most we can say of a perceptual judgment that its relation to other perceptual judgments is such as
permit a simple theory of the facts." (5.142) But since knowledge consists
in more than simple theories of the facts, a further explanation of the process
is required. This is contained in the function of cognition.

iii. THE FUNCTION OF COGNITION

In contrast to the brevity and immediateness of the perceptual judgment,
the function of cognition reveals itself as a process involving a longer period
of time and a greater amount of experience. "There is no absolutely first
cognition of any object, but cognition arises by a continuous process."
(5.267) From the point of view of the knowledge process, "*experience* means

[82] This is a realistic interpretation of the meaning of the *gestalten* phenomena of the contemporary psychological school of Wertheim and Kohler.
[33] Review of William James, *The Principles of Psychology* in *The Nation*, 53 (1891), p. 32.
[34] Aristotle, *de Anima*, bk. III, chap. 8.

nothing but just that of a cognitive nature which the history of our lives has forced on us. It is *indirect*, if the medium of some other experience or thought is required to bring it out. Duality, thought abstractly, no doubt requires the intervention of reflection; but that upon which this reflection is based, the concrete duality, is there in the very experience itself." (5.539) The cognition emerges from the perceptual judgment by imperceptible stages or degrees. "At any moment we are in possession of certain information, that is, of cognitions which have been logically derived by induction and hypothesis from previous cognitions which are less general, less distinct, and of which we have a less lively consciousness. These in their turn have been derived from others still less general, less distinct, and less vivid," until the idea of singulars beyond consciousness is reached. (5.311) The cognitive process does not begin with doubt, as Descartes asserted; (5.265) it begins with cognitions, that is, with knowledge. All "cognitions not judgments may be determined by previous cognitions," (5.213) and indeed all are so determined.

"We must begin, then, with a *process* of cognition, and with that process whose laws are best understood and most closely follow external facts. This is no other than the process of valid inference, which proceeds from its premiss, A, to its conclusion, B, only if, as a matter of fact, such a proposition as B is always or usually true when such a proposition as A is true. It is a consequence, then, of the first two principles whose results we are to trace out, that we must, as far as we can, without any other supposition than that the mind reasons, reduce all mental action to the formula of valid reasoning. (5.267)

"But does the mind in fact go through the syllogistic process? It is certainly very doubtful whether a conclusion—as something existing in the mind independently, like an image—suddenly displaces two premisses existing in the mind in a similar way. But it is a matter of constant experience, that if a man is made to believe in the premisses, in the sense that he will act from them and will say that they are true, under favorable conditions he will also be ready to act from the conclusion and to say that that is true. Something, therefore, takes place within the organism which is equivalent to the syllogistic process." (5.268)[35]

The final step, and the most important, in the knowledge process proves to be reasoning, or the development of concepts from other concepts. Thus beginning with the relation of semiotic and the bare phenomena, we have seen how Peirce developed his theory of the process of knowledge as far as

[35] See chap. III, C, i.

the limits of modern scientific knowledge allowed. It is easier to explain the function of perceptual judgment than to account for what happens inside the organism when a conclusion is drawn from premises. But there was no doubt in Peirce's mind that all the evidence of experience pointed toward such an event as reasoning, exactly in accordance with the syllogistic plan, taking place in the mind. Ignorance of the mechanism that makes possible mental syllogistic inference is no argument against the existence of such a mental process, and Peirce regarded its occurrence as a fact.

C. TRUTH AND FALSITY

i. THE STATUS OF KNOWLEDGE

The term "knowledge" is used to describe not only an act of cognition but the cognition itself. In the latter sense, Peirce sets three conditions for the perfect cognition: it must "hold for true a proposition that really is true," (5.605) it must be "self-satisfied and free from the uneasiness of doubt," and "some character of this satisfaction" must be "such that it would be logically impossible that this character should ever belong to satisfaction in a proposition not true." "Suppose our opinion with reference to a given question to be quite settled, so that inquiry, no matter how far pushed, has no surprises for us on this point. Then we may be said to have attained *perfect knowledge* about that question." (4.62) "Perhaps we have already attained to perfect knowledge about a number of questions; but we cannot have an unshakable opinion that we have attained such perfect knowledge about any given question. That would be not only perfectly to know, but perfectly to know that we do perfectly know, which is what is called *sure knowledge*." (4.63)

The distinction between perfect knowledge and sure knowledge admits of human fallibilism and of what Peirce described as the meaning of the phrase "the relativity of knowledge." "Thus, that an object is blue consists of the peculiar regular action of that object on human eyes." (3.416) Relative knowledge is better described as relational knowledge. "A *relation* is a fact about a number of things. Thus the fact that a locomotive blows off steam constitutes a relation." "Not only is every fact really a relation, but your thought of the fact *implicitly* represents it as such. Thus when you think 'this is blue,' the demonstrative 'this' shows you are thinking of something just brought up to your notice; while the adjective shows that you recognize a familiar idea as applicable to it. Thus, your thought when explicated, develops into the thought of a fact concerning this thing and concerning the character of blueness. Still, it must be admitted that, antecedently to the unwrapping of your thought, you were not actually thinking of blueness as a distinct object, and therefore were not thinking of the relation as a relation. There is an aspect of every relation under which it does not appear as a relation. Thus, the blowing off of steam by a locomotive may be regarded as merely an action of the locomotive, the steam not being conceived to be a thing distinct from the engine. This aspect we enphrase in saying, 'the engine blows'." (3.417)

"The past is the storehouse of all our knowledge." (5.460) "But," Peirce added, "I may be asked what I have to say to all the minute facts of history, forgotten never to be recovered, to the lost books of the ancients, to the buried secrets.

> 'Full many a gem of purest ray serene
>   The dark, unfathomed caves of ocean bear;
> Full many a flower is born to blush unseen,
>   And waste its sweetness on the desert air.'

Do these things not really exist because they are hopelessly beyond the reach of our knowledge? And then, after the universe is dead (according to the prediction of some scientists), and all life has ceased forever, will not the shock of atoms continue though there will be no mind to know it? To this I reply that, though in no possible state of knowledge can any number be great enough to express the relation between the amount of what rests unknown to the amount of the known, yet it is unphilosophical to suppose that, with regard to any given question (which has any clear meaning), investigation would not bring forth a solution to it, if it were carried far enough." (5.409) Everything is cognizable, but all never is cognized. (5.330) Nevertheless, the goal of the knowledge process is the cognition of everything. The tendency of knowledge is to increase, and of the ultimately irreducible fallibilism to be reduced. Thus does perfect knowledge become surer, if not absolutely sure. For "the opinion which is fated to be ultimately agreed to by all who investigate, is what we mean by the truth." (5.407)

ii. FALSITY

"It ought to be assumed that all our knowledge has some error in it—even our knowledge that there is something real." (2.532) The conception of error is a human and adult conception; moreover, it is one which is very advanced. "Probably it will not be doubted that every child in its mental development necessarily passes through a stage in which he has some ideas, but yet has never recognized that any idea may be erroneous; and a stage that every child necessarily passes through must have been formerly passed through by the race in its adult development. It may be doubted whether many of the lower animals have any clear and steady conception of falsehood; for their instincts work so unerringly that there is little to force it upon their attention. Yet plainly without a knowledge of falsehood no development of discursive reasoning can take place." (3.488) And without discursive reasoning there can be no advance in knowledge. Hence error serves as the indicator that such knowledge as we do have is incomplete, a service which assigns it a most important place in the knowledge process.

In addition to indicating the incompleteness of knowledge, error even makes us aware of the existence of the knower as a separate being capable of knowing. "A child hears it said that the stove is hot. But it is not, he says; and, indeed, that central body is not touching it, and only what that touches is hot or cold. But he touches it, and finds the testimony confirmed in a striking way. Thus, he becomes aware of ignorance, and it is necessary to suppose a *self* in which this ignorance can inhere." (5.233) "Ignorance and error are all that distinguish our private selves from the absolute *ego* of pure apperception," (5.235) all that call us back from the illusory possession of *"paradisaical logic* . . . the state of Man's cognition before the Fall." (3.488) Thus Peirce gave falsity credit both for the increase in knowledge and for the knower's awareness of the limitations of his knowledge. It is truth that we seek and falsity that we seek to avoid; but the stimulus to the pursuit of truth comes from falsity, so that we are obliged to the error of our knowledge for the suggestion that the truth is something that we do not necessarily possess and that is to be sought.

iii. THE TRUTH

The final goal of all inquiry is the discovery of truth, and the determination of the status of truth is the guiding factor in all epistemological inquiry. First we shall quote Peirce's definition of the truth, and then his attempts to clarify his definition by distinguishing it from others.

"All propositions refer to one and the same determinately singular subject, well-understood between all interpreters and utterers; namely, to the Truth, which is the universe of all universes, and is assumed on all hands to be real." (5.506) Truth, then, is the reference of all propositions to the universe, (5.153) and as such is endowed with eternal life. (1.219) The ontological definition of truth is static; epistemologically, yet with full consistency, truth may be defined as a process. "Truth is that concordance of an abstract statement with the ideal limit towards which endless investigation would tend to bring scientific belief, which concordance the abstract statement may possess by virtue of the confession of its inaccuracy and onesidedness, and this confession is an essential ingredient of truth." (5.565)

Truth must be distinguished first from fact. The existence of truth is not the only fact, although it is a fact; and the existence of fact is not the only truth, although it is a truth. "Whether or not there be any such thing as truth is a question of fact," (1.247) yet, for example, "it cannot be regarded as a *fact* that scarlet is red. It is a *truth*; but it is only an essential truth." (1.452) To be more than an essential truth, that is, to be a factual truth, it would have to refer to some particular and actual object having these qualities. Truth and fact are overlapping categories; they are in no wise mutually exhaustive. The category of truth that is not fact is larger than the category of truth that is. This may seem to require some explanation. Corresponding to every fact there is a possible proposition for which it is the truth, and corresponding to every truth there is a possible fact which would render it true. But the reference of truth to possibility and actuality makes it a wider category than fact, which belongs to actuality and does not, properly speaking, refer to possibility at all. In this sense "the possibility evolves the actuality." (1.453) The distinction is the same one which Peirce approved in Leibniz:[86] the distinction between "truths of reason" and "truths of fact." (6.366)

"*That* truth consists in a conformity to something *independent of his thinking it to be so*" (5.211) distinguishes truth also from that which is subjective. We have no "power of eliciting truth by inward meditation." (1.55) Truth is definitely something objective; "there is *something* that is SO, no matter if there be an overwhelming vote against it"; (2.135) "there is such a thing as a proposition correct whatever may be opinions about it." (2.137) "The very opinion entertained by those who deny that there is any Truth, in the sense defined, is that it is not force, but their inward freedom which determines their experiential cognition. But this opinion is flatly contradicted by their own experience. They insist upon shutting their eyes to the element of compulsion, although it is directly experienced by them." (2.138)

Truth is to be distinguished from what is verifiable, and Peirce argued against Comte and the positivists of his day that to make truth identical

---

[86] *Monadology*, 33.

with what is verifiable is to resort to another form of the theory according to which truth is subjective. (5.597) "The field of Thought, in its turn, is in every thought, confessed to be a sign of that great external power, that Universe, the Truth. We all agree that we refer to the same real thing when we speak of the truth, whether we think aright of it, or not. But we have no cognition of its essence that can, in strictness, be called a *concept* of it: we only have a direct perception of having the matter of our Thought forced upon it from outside our own control. It is thus, neither by immediate feeling, as we gaze at a red color, that we mean what we mean by the Truth; for Feeling tells of nothing but itself. Nor is it by the persuasion of reason, since reason always refers to two other things than itself." (4.553 n.2) "That truth and justice are great powers in the world is no figure of speech, but a plain fact to which theories must accommodate themselves." (1.348)

The reference of truth in the metaphysical sense, a sense which includes epistemology, must be distinguished from truth in the syntactical sense. Truth in the syntactical sense is what Peirce termed complex truth. Complex truth is the correspondence of predicate to subject, (5.553) and is thus wholly internal to propositions. (5.570) What is called simple truth is "more complex than propositions," (5.573) since it refers both to propositions and to the things to which the propositions themselves refer. Simple truth, which is the truth given in Peirce's definitions at the outset of this section, is "the conformity of things to their essential principle." (5.572)

iv. SUMMARY OF THE CHAPTER

Epistemology has a well-defined field of its own but also is dependent to some extent upon logic, phenomenology, and ontology. Logic forces upon epistemology the distinction between knower and object known. Phenomenology leads to the concept of experience as the course of life which compels us to certain determinations. Ontology furnishes the grounds for the validity of real knowledge.

The problem of knowledge is to advance from the subjective to the independently real. We experience the universe by observing facts; what has being is also cognizable.

The knowledge process begins with perception. What is remembered is the perceptual fact, the evidence of the senses. A perception presented to the mind is immediately an abstraction and is termed a perceptual judgment. The perception cannot be made without the judgment, although we do have immediate experience in the percept. The perceptual judgment is as uncontrollable as experience. It is the foundation of all knowledge.

The function of cognition involves the perceptual judgment in longer time and more experience. The process of cognition is analogous to the syllogistic process; the organism does make inferences. The last stage in the series, from perception to perceptual judgment to cognition, is reasoning, which develops concepts from previous concepts.

The aim of cognition is toward the attainment of knowledge. Knowledge is relative only because human fallibilism prevents the attainment of perfect knowledge. The tendency of knowledge is to increase.

Error indicates that the knowledge we do have is incomplete. It also acquaints us with the knower as a separate being in which error resides.

The goal of all inquiry, however, is the truth. The truth is the universe of all universes. Truth is wider than fact; it is independent of opinion; it is not absolutely susceptible to verification. It is the conformity of things to their principles.

CHAPTER VI

Psychology

A. PHILOSOPHY AND PSYCHOLOGY

FROM EPISTEMOLOGY TO PSYCHOLOGY IS NOT A FAR STEP. INDEED, THE FIELDS of the two studies adjoin. We have seen that epistemology treats of the relations of mind and the world, or the external relations of mind. Psychology is concerned with the mind as a whole, with its internal relations. Since metaphysical realism, unlike certain varieties of nominalism, does not admit that the mind possesses any more reality than does any other natural phenomenon, it is a philosophy for which psychology sets peculiar problems. Psychology has always been the stumbling block of realists, and it should be interesting, therefore, to learn what Peirce's system of psychology involves.

Peirce did not hold psychology to be a primary study, upon which logic and so much else depend, as did many of the philosophers of the nineteenth century. "Under an appeal to psychology is not meant every appeal to any fact relating to the mind. For it is, for logical purposes, important to discriminate between facts of that description which are supposed to be ascertained by the systematic study of the mind, and facts the knowledge of which altogether antecedes such study, and is not in the least affected by it." (2.210) On the contrary, psychology, in Peirce's view, depends largely upon other divisions of knowledge. He was well aware of the helpless dependence of psychology upon other fields, and sometimes wondered whether there is after all "any such thing as psychology, apart from logic on the one hand and physiology on the other." (2.428)

The fundamental conceptions of psychology have made a great advance since 1890, Peirce wrote in 1901; "they are not by any means thoroughly clear, even yet; but probably nobody would now propose, as James did then, to write a psychology altogether uninfluenced by any metaphysics. As Ladd well names it, the 'clandestine' metaphysics which such an attempt inevitably brings with it, is all the more dangerous from its lying in ambush."[1] "On the contrary, it is now generally admitted that psychology, like general physics, necessarily takes for granted a *Weltanschauung* or outline system of metaphysics."[2] Modern psychology, again, made "an admirable beginning," (2.42) but developed a "tendency to turn upon its axis, without making any great advance. Matters of brain-physiology and matters of consciousness elbow one another in unsympathetic juxtaposition, in a way which can only be transitional." Certainly "no very deep biology" is needed by the psychologist. (1.264)

As a tentative definition, Peirce proposed that psychology be considered "the positive, or observational, science of the mind, or of consciousness," (1.310) but decided, when he came to subdividing its branches according to the method employed: Introspectional, Experimental, Physiological, and Child, that "only . . . parts of psychology . . . investigate the general phenomena of mind." (1.199) But before we proceed to an examination of what psychology as a whole investigates, let us look back over the previous chapters, in order to determine whether Peirce has not already committed himself to certain presuppositions in psychology. In the first section, then, we shall indicate what Peirce's psychology owes to other topics, specifically to logic, ontology and epistemology. The derivation will only be suggestive, however. Other derivations from these same fields will be indicated from time to time throughout the chapter, in the course of the development of the ideas which are peculiar to psychology.

i. FROM LOGIC TO PSYCHOLOGY

We have seen that the categories of psychology are not basic to logic.[3] Despite the fact that from one point of view "logic may be defined as the science of the laws of the stable establishment of beliefs," (3.429) logic does not rest upon either feeling, direct individual experience, the data of psychology, or psychology itself. To base logic upon psychology is to place it above logical criticism or support. (2.210) On the contrary, Peirce stated baldly that "psychology must depend in its beginnings upon logic"; (2.51) he repeated again and again that "the only sound psychology . . . ought itself to be based upon a well-grounded logic," (3.432) and indeed is, "of

---

[1] Review of *Psychology: Empirical and Rational*, by Michael Maher, in *The Nation*, 73 (1901), 267. See also *Col. Pap.*, 1.250.

[2] Review of *Ethics: Descriptive and Explanatory*, by Sidney Edward Mezes, in *The Nation*, 73, (1901), 325.

[3] See chap. III, A, i. See also 2.39 ff.

all the special sciences, the one which stands most in need of appeal to a scientific logic." (2.210) Instead of interpreting logical categories by means of psychology, Peirce interpreted psychological categories by means of logic. Yet the relation between certain logical and psychological categories "does not spring from considerations of formal logic, but from those of psychology." (5.329)

The central theory of logic is the formal doctrine of semiotic. This, we saw, is the function of a sign, which on some ground determines an interpretant to refer to an object to which it itself refers.[4] In the performance of this function the psychological subject plays the part of the capacity for receiving determinations of the interpretant. The psychological subject was, in fact, said to be only one exemplification of the field of the interpretant and in no wise essential to it, since being, represented in this case by the semiotic relation, does not depend on knowing, represented in this case by the human consciousness.[5] But, conversely, the ground, object and interpretant of the representamen are essential to psychology, and furnish its basis.[6]

We begin to understand why this triad occurs only toward the end of the exposition of the logic, in the section devoted to Speculative Rhetoric,[7] where for the first time considerations of psychology are introduced. There we find the distinction between the person and the effect on the person (the interpretant),[8] leading to the further distinction between the interpretant and the interpreter (the person), such that an interpretant can have one of three effects upon the interpreter.[9] The effects are: the arousal of a feeling, an exertion, or a sign. These three were destined to become the three chief divisions of psychology, under the names of feelings, sensations of reaction, and general conceptions. We live in an Inner World described by psychology, and an Outer World which is brought to us through the relations set forth under the topic of epistemology. While it is the latter, as Peirce said, from which most irresistible compulsions come,[10] still there are irresistible compulsions in the former too, and their explanation is perhaps the most important problem of psychology.

[4] See chap. III, B, i.
[5] See chap. III, B, i.
[6] See chap. III, B, i.
[7] See chap. III, D.
[8] See chap. III, D, i.
[9] See chap. III, D, i.
[10] See chap. III, D, ii.

ii. FROM ONTOLOGY

The triad of categories—feelings, sensations of reaction, and general conceptions—which we saw to be derived from the categories of semiotic, accord equally well with the categories of phenomenology. "A man cannot conceive of a one-subject fact otherwise than as vaguely analogous to a feeling of his own. He cannot conceive of a two-subject fact otherwise than as analogous to an action of his own. A three-subject fact is comprehensible and is analogous to an utterance, a speech, a thought." (6.323) In other words, "in psychology Feeling is First, Sense of Reaction Second, General Conception Third." (6.32)[11] Or, in more generally suggestive terms, "the first is thought in its capacity as mere possibility; that is, mere *mind* capable of thinking, or a mere vague idea. The *second* is thought playing the role of a Secondness, or event. That is, it is of the general nature of *experience* or *information*. The third is thought in its role as governing Secondness. It brings the information into the mind, or determines the idea and gives it body. It is informing thought, or *cognition*." (1.537) We have to do with that which is present to the mind, that with which the mind must struggle, and that which the mind knows. (5.44 ff.)

It is clear from these distinctions that the mental categories were for Peirce established according to the nature of the problems which exist for the mind. The problems differ according as they oblige the mind to confront a quality, deal with a fact, or grasp a law.[12] But these three problems are established for the mind by the external world in its three chief phases, and not arbitrarily chosen by the mind itself. "Instead of the familiar division of . . . Kant which makes pleasure-pain, cognition and volition the three categories of mental phenomena, we have feeling or quality, the action of opposition, and synthetic thought." (1.350)[13] Kant, as Peirce had seen, was a nominalist,[14] and the reasoning of nominalists leaves much to be desired, (1.165) particularly when it allows the psychological category to swallow the whole of experience and thus renders any explanation of experience impossible. Reality, even in the psychological field, comes from the outside,[15] and consists in an integrated set of objective relations.[16] This

[11] See chap. IV, B, i, ii and iii.
[12] See chap. IV, A, ii.
[13] Cf. the subjective cast of the three mental categories of "apprehension, reproduction and recognition," as explained by Kant, *Kritik der Reinen Vernunft*, A 97.
[14] See chap. IV, C, i.
[15] See chap. IV, C, ii.
[16] See chap. IV, C, ii.

will mean a study of the mind as tropistically oriented toward the truth, as attracted toward theoretical and factual propositions.

iii. FROM EPISTEMOLOGY

Although the subject matter of psychology will have to treat of the mind as related to the propositions of an external world, it is not the relation between the mind and the propositions that concerns us now. For that is a purely epistemological question. Psychology proper treats not of the mind in its external relations to the world but rather of the mind in its internal relations as they are affected by the external world. Thus psychology is the level of study adjoining epistemology; and although their fields of interest are close they are distinctly different studies and do not overlap.

Experience, it will be recalled,[17] takes place by a series of surprises. (5.51) "Our own existence . . . is proved by the occurrence of ignorance and error." (5.283) The child who hears that a stove is hot and does not believe it has "the testimony confirmed in a striking way" (5.233) when he touches it. "Thus, he becomes aware of ignorance, and it is necessary to suppose a *self* in which this ignorance can inhere. So testimony gives the first dawning of self-consciousness."[18] "In short, *error* appears, and it can be explained only by supposing a *self* which is fallible," (5.234) since there must be some utility in which error can inhere. Ignorance and error make us aware not only of the limitations of our knowledge, but also of the fact that it is ourselves who have this knowledge. In addition to the outer world of experience, there is also an inner experience, a personal history. (4.91) In this way, the gaps in our knowledge, the shortcomings in the process of knowing, call for the existence of a psychological realm which is to some extent autonomous, and for which knowledge can be increased. Inner experience takes its place beside outer experience and innate ideas, as one of the three sources of knowledge. (4.92) Kant asked, "How are synthetical judgments *a priori* possible?"[19] "The true question for him should have been 'How are universal propositions relating to experience to be justified?'" The question arises from the epistemological field; the answer can only be furnished by an examination of the functioning of psychological processes.

[17] See chap. V, A, iii and C, ii.
[18] See this chapter, B, ii.
[19] See chap. II, A, iii.

iv. THE NATURE OF MIND

The inner world is distinguished from the outer in many ways. The inner world can be controlled to a greater extent than the outer, while, on the other hand, satisfactory experiments can be made in the outer in abundance but are difficult to contrive for the inner. "Phenomena that inward force puts together appear *similar*; phenomena that outward force puts together appear *contiguous*. The difference seems to be one of degree. But nothing could be more extravagant than to jump to the conclusion that because the distinction between the Inward and the Outward is merely one of how much, therefore it is unimportant; for the distinction between the unimportant and the important is itself purely one of little and much. Now, the difference between the Inward and the Outward worlds is certainly very, very great, with a remarkable absence of intermediate phenomena." (4.87) "Certainly psychology has no dealings with objects out of the mind." (2.64)

What, then, is the mind? Peirce defined it as the widest possible truth-function of logic. "In one of the narrowest and most concrete of its logical meanings, a Mind is that Seme [or rheme] of The Truth, whose determinations become Immediate Interpretants of all other Signs whose Dynamical Interpretants are dynamically connected." (4.550) The editors of the *Collected Papers* interpret this statement as follows. "Mind is a propositional function of the widest possible universe, such that its values are the meanings of all signs whose actual effects are in effective interconnection." (4.550 n.) Mind functions within actuality, yet somehow reaches beyond it.

It must at once be obvious that such a definition of mind is consonant with the remainder of Peirce's philosophical system, in that mind itself becomes not a subjective conception but rather a function of the real external world. In being consonant with Peirce's realism, however, it is put in opposition to the prevailing view. For "modern philosophy has never been able quite to shake off the Cartesian idea of the mind, as something that 'resides' . . . in the pineal gland. Everybody laughs at this nowadays, and yet everybody continues to think of mind . . . as something within this person or that." (5.128) But Peirce insisted that "We can admit no statement concerning what passes within us except as a hypothesis necessary to explain what takes place in what we commonly call the external world." (5.266)

The universal law of mind is that all action takes place by final causation or purpose, (1.269) and nothing has itself for a final purpose. "Now it is precisely action according to final causes which distinguishes mental from mechanical action; and the general formula of all our desires may be taken as this: to remove a stimulus. Every man is busily working to bring to an end that state of things which now excites him to work." (1.392) Thus the purpose of mental action is always something outside the mind; but that is not all. Mental actions themselves are in a sense due to the nonmental characters of the content of mind. "Under this universal law of mind . . . there is, first of all, the great law of association" (1.270) of ideas, that "Every state of mind, acting under an overruling association, produces another state of mind." (6.70) The sight of the morning newspaper made Peirce think of the sinking of the *Maine*. This he explained not as an internal function exclusively but rather as "an attraction between ideas." (1.270) The fact is that "everything in the psychical sciences is inferential. Not the smallest fact about the mind can be directly perceived as psychical. An emotion is directly felt as a bodily state, or else it is only known inferentially. That a thing is agreeable appears to direct observation as a character of an object, and it is only by inference that it is referred to the mind." (1.250)

Keeping this fundamental conception of the mind and its function in view, we may now turn in the following sections to a development of the three chief divisions of psychology: the feelings, the sensations of reaction, and the general conceptions, with a final section devoted to the broadest considerations and conclusions regarding the mental function as a whole.

B. Feelings

i. THE BASIS OF FEELING

The first category of psychology, according to Peirce, is feeling. Logic, as we have seen,[20] does not rest on feeling, but feeling to some extent is determined by logic. "The first proper significate effect of a sign is a feeling produced by it." (5.475) "There is no feeling which is not also a representation, a predicate of something determined logically by the feelings which precede it." (5.292) Those feelings which are not predicates are emotions, and even emotions have objective subjects. The metaphysical category of firstness gives rise to the oneness of feeling. "So far as feelings have any continuity, it is the metaphysical nature of feeling to have a *unity*." (6.229) The secondness of the struggle between qualities occasions the contrast of

[20] See chap. III, A, i.

feelings. Qualities are the objective facts which occasion feelings, and the differences between qualities make us aware of them.[21] "If a man is blind to the *red* and *violet* elements of light and only sees the *green* element, then all things appear of one color to him. . . . Yet since all things look alike in this respect, it never attracts his attention in the least." (6.222) "Empirical psychology has established the fact that we can know a quality only by means of its contrast with or similarity to another." (1.552)

Quality is transmitted into feeling through effort. "Effort is a phenomenon which only arises when one feeling abuts upon another in time, and which then always arises." (1.320) This sense of struggle "is present even in such a rudimentary fragment of experience as a simple feeling. For such a feeling always has a degree of vividness, high or low; and this vividness is a sense of commotion, an action and reaction, between our soul and the stimulus." (1.322) As to thirdness, "instantaneous feelings flow together into a continuum of feeling, which has in a modified degree the peculiar vivacity of feeling and has gained generality. And in reference to such general ideas, or continua of feeling, the difficulties about resemblance and suggestion and reference to the external cease to have any force." (6.151)

Another approach to the understanding of feeling is through the category of chance and the physical categories: the world of actuality. Chance is indeed very close to the function of feeling; "in fact, chance is but the outward aspect of that which within itself is feeling." (6.265)[22] "Consider a gob of protoplasm, say an amoeba or a slime-mold. It does not differ in any radical way from the contents of a nerve-cell, though its functions may be less specialized. There is no doubt that this slime-mold, or this amoeba, or at any rate some similar mass of protoplasm, feels. That is to say, it feels when it is in its excited condition. But note how it behaves. When the whole is quiescent and rigid, a place upon it is irritated. Just at this point, an active motion is set up, and this gradually spreads to other parts. In this action, no unity nor relation to a nucleus, or other unitary organ can be discerned. It is a mere amorphous continuum of protoplasm, with feeling passing from one part to another. Nor is there anything like a wave-motion. The activity does not advance to new parts just as fast as it leaves old parts. Rather, in the beginning, it dies out at a slower rate than that at which it spreads. And while the process is going on, by exciting the mass

[21] In one place, Peirce described quality itself as perhaps a kind of "sleeping consciousness." (6.221)

[22] Cf. Descartes, *The Passions of the Soul*, I,I: "That what in respect of a subject is passion, is in some other regard always action." Peirce's chance is an objective category. See chap. IV, D, ii.

at another point, a second quite independent state of excitation will be set up. In some places, neither excitation will exist, in others each separately, in still other places, both effects will be added together. Whatever there is in the whole phenomenon to make us think there is feeling in such a mass of protoplasm—*feeling*, but plainly no *personality*—goes logically to show that that feeling has a subjective, or substantial, spatial extension, as the excited state has." (6.133) Feeling, in other words, "may be supposed to exist wherever a nerve-cell is in an excited condition. The disturbance of feeling, or sense of reaction, accompanies the transmission of disturbance between nerve-cells, or from a nerve-cell to a muscle-cell, or the external stimulation of a nerve-cell." (6.22) "Feeling . . . arises in an active state of nerve-cells." (1.386)

Peirce defended the blind man who asked whether scarlet was not something like the blare of a trumpet, and was almost ready to "hazard a guess that the form of the chemical oscillations set up by this color in the observer will be found to resemble that of the acoustical waves of the trumpet's blare." (1.312) All feeling is, in fact, accompanied by movement. "There is some reason to think that, corresponding to every feeling within us, some motion takes place in our bodies." (5.293) "Feeling . . . is without any doubt dependent upon the extreme complexity of the protoplasmic molecule, if the word molecule can be applied to so intricate, unstable, and ununified a system. But it is the law of high numbers that extreme complication with a great multitude of independent similars results in a new simplicity. . . . It is the property by which any state of high cohesiveness tends to spread through the albuminoid matter. We usually call the property contractility." (1.351)

Feeling has always been considered to be of two kinds: pleasure and pain. This is the usual psychological understanding of the term. But, according to Peirce, feeling overlaps with pleasure and pain but they are by no means the same. "Pleasure and pain can only be recognized as such in a judgment; they are general predicates which are attached to feelings rather than true feelings." (1.376) We can arrive at this position by a separate analysis of pleasure and of pain. "In beginning to perform any series of acts which had been determined upon beforehand, there is a certain sense of joy, an anticipation and commencement of a relaxation of the tension of need, which we now become more conscious of than we had been before. In the act itself taking place at any instant, it may be that we are conscious of pleasure; although that is doubtful. Before the series of acts are done, we already begin to review them, and in that review we recognize the pleasurable character of the feelings that accompanied those acts." (1.595) *Pain,* on the other hand, "would seem to be a good deal more positive than pleasure." (5.112) It is not possible to "recognize with confidence any quality of feeling common to all *pains.*"

Pleasure and pain "are secondary feelings or generalizations of such feelings; that is, of feelings attaching themselves to, and excited by, other feelings.[23] A toothache is painful. It is not pain but pain *accompanies* it; and if you choose to say that pain is an ingredient of it, that is not far wrong. However, the quality of the feeling of toothache is a simple, positive feeling, distinct from pain; though pain accompanies it. . . . The feeling of pain is a symptom of a feeling which repels us; the feeling of pleasure is the symptom of an attractive feeling." (5.552) "But perhaps pleasure and pain are nothing more than names for the state of being attracted and that of being repelled by present experience. Of course, feelings would accompany them, but under the latter hypothesis no feeling would be common to all pleasures, and none to all pains." (1.333) Peirce further suggested that pleasure and pain might have contrasting constitutions, "pleasure arising upon the forming or strengthening of an association by resemblance, and pain upon the weakening or disruption of such a habit or conception." (6.462)

He did not think that "unadulterated feeling, if that element could be isolated, would have any relation to pain or to pleasure." (1.333) Feeling is further independent of the mind which feels, of the changes which take place, and of the physical substratum in which the feeling takes place. The feeling of redness, the sound of a whistle, the thrill of joyous delight—"none of them are either seen in the color, heard in the sound, or felt in the visceral sensation." (1.305) There can be neither logical nor psychological difficulty in supposing them to be absent.

From the psychological level purely, feeling appears as the interval between sensations. Sensation is "the initiation of a state of feeling; — for by state of feeling I mean nothing but sensation *minus* the attribution of it to any particular subject. . . . When an ear-splitting, soul-bursting locomotive whistle starts, there is a sensation, which ceases when the screech has been going for any considerable fraction of a minute; and at the instant it stops there is a second sensation. Between them there is a state of feeling." (1.332) Feeling, then, is absolutely simple. (1.311) "A feeling is a state of mind having its own living quality, independent of any other state of mind." (6.18) "In short, a pure feeling can be nothing but the total unanalyzed impression of the *tout ensemble* of consciousness," (6.345) and we may now

[23] Cf. Plato, *Republic,* IX, 584.

give a more developed definition of feeling as "that mode of consciousness whose being lies wholly in itself and not in any relation to anything else."[24]

ii. CONSCIOUSNESS AND INTROSPECTION

There is hardly any difference recognized in Peirce's system between feeling and consciousness. "Consciousness alone—i.e. feeling—is the only distinctive attribute of mind." (5.492) The difference in feelings corresponds to the occasions of consciousness. "The whole content of consciousness is made up of qualities of feeling, as truly as the whole of space is made up of points or the whole of time of instants." (1.317) "Contemplate anything by itself—anything whatever that can be so contemplated. Attend to the whole and drop the parts out of attention altogether. One can approximate nearly enough to the accomplishment of that to see that the result of its perfect accomplishment would be that one would have in his consciousness at the moment nothing but a quality of feeling. . . . To be conscious is nothing else than to feel." (1.318) Consciousness, like feeling,[25] contains an element of semiotic relatedness. (1.532) "All that we can find out by directly watching consciousness are the qualities of feeling, and those, not as they are felt, but as, after being felt, they are grouped." (2.184) Yet it is a hopeless undertaking to try to realize what consciousness would be without the element of representation. "The interpretant is, at least, in all cases, a sufficiently close analogue of a modification of consciousness to keep our conclusion pretty near to the general truth." (5.485)

In logical terms, consciousness may be defined as "that congeries of non-relative predicates, varying greatly in quality and in intensity, which are symptomatic of the interaction of the outer world—the world of those causes that are exceedingly compulsive upon the modes of consciousness, with general disturbance sometimes amounting to shock . . . —and of the inner world. . . ." (5.493) In metaphysical terms, "The most degenerate thirdness is where we conceive a mere Quality of Feeling, or Firstness, to represent itself to itself as Representation. Such, for example, would be Pure Self-Consciousness." (5.71) Consciousness "is a sort of public spirit among the nerve-cells," (1.354) but "we never can be immediately conscious of finiteness, or of anything but a divine freedom that in its own original firstness knows no bounds." (1.358) Thus the physiological organism furnishes the occasion for an awareness of feeling which is by its very nature unlimited.

---

[24] See also 1.306.
[25] See this chapter, B, i.

Since "the brain shows no central cell," (6.229) we must argue that "the unity of consciousness is not of physiological origin." It can only be metaphysical.[26]

The next degree of complication in the psychic life takes us from consciousness to self-consciousness or introspection.[27] "Self-consciousness, as the term is here used, is to be distinguished both from consciousness generally, from the internal sense, and from pure apperception. Any cognition is a consciousness of the object as represented; by self-consciousness is meant a knowledge of ourselves.[28] Not a mere feeling of subjective conditions of consciousness, but of our personal selves." (5.225) The question, Peirce said, comes down to one of whether the inner world is known by inference from the outer, or not. "In a certain sense, there is such a thing as introspection; but it consists in an interpretation of phenomena presenting themselves as external percepts.[29] We first see blue and red things. It is quite a discovery when we find the eye has anything to do with them, and a discovery still more recondite when we learn that there is an *ego* behind the eye, to which these qualities properly belong."[30]

By introspection, therefore, he meant "a direct perception of the internal world, but not necessarily a perception of it *as* internal," (5.244) actually "any knowledge of the internal world not derived from external observation." Properly speaking, "we have no power of Introspection," (5.265)[31] "nor can we gain knowledge of any feeling by introspection, the feeling being completely veiled from introspection . . . for the very reason that it is our immediate consciousness." (1.310) The fact is that "consciousness may be set down as one of the most mendacious witnesses that ever was questioned. But it is the only witness there is; and all we can do is to put it in the sweat-box and torture the truth out of it, with such judgment as we can command." (1.580)

Aside from the proposition that "we are more certain of our own existence than of any other fact," (5.237) a proposition with dubitable value,[32] an examination of introspection and its claims reveals that "the only way of

---

[26] See the same point as applying to the aspect of feeling, this chapter, B, i.

[27] See "Evolution of Self-Consciousness" in Chauncey Wright, *Philosophical Discussions* (New York, Holt, 1877), pp. 199 ff.

[28] William James described the self as "the *active* element in all consciousness."—*The Principles of Psychology* (2 vols.) (New York, Holt, 1931), vol. i, p. 297.

[29] See this chapter, B, iii.

[30] Review of Karl Pearson, *The Grammar of Science*, in the *Popular Science Monthly*, 58 (1901), 296.

[31] Cf. G. E. Moore, *Philosophical Studies* (London, Kegan Paul, 1922), p. 25.

[32] See the rejection of self-consciousness as the cardinal metaphysical premise of the Cartesian philosophy, in chap. II, E, ii.

investigating a psychological question is by inference from external facts."
(5.249) It is unnecessary "to suppose an unknown cause" (5.226) in the
face of "known faculties under conditions known to exist." There is no
evidence of self-consciousness in extremely young children. (5.227) "On
the other hand, [they] manifest powers of thought much earlier." (5.228)
"A very young child may always be observed to watch its own body with
great attention. There is every reason why this should be so, for from the
child's point of view this body is the most important thing in the universe."
(5.229) Yet "no one questions that, when a sound is heard by a child, he
thinks, not of himself as hearing, but of the bell or other object as sounding.
How when he wills to move a table? Does he then think of himself as
desiring, or only of the table as fit to be moved?" (5.230) "There is one
sense in which any perception has an internal object, namely, that every
sensation is partly determined by internal conditions. Thus the sensation
of redness is as it is, owing to the constitution of the mind; and in this
sense it is a sensation of something internal. Hence, we may derive a knowledge of the mind from a consideration of this sensation, but that knowledge
would, in fact, be an inference from redness as a predicate of something
external." (5.245)

"On the other hand, there are certain other feelings—the emotions, for
example—which appear to arise in the first place, not as predicates at all,
and to be referable to the mind alone. It would seem, then, that by means
of these, a knowledge of the mind may be obtained, which is not inferred
from any character of outward things. The question is whether this is
really so." "Although introspection is not necessarily intuitive, it is not
self-evident that we possess this capacity; for we have no intuitive faculty
of distinguishing different subjective modes of consciousness. The power,
if it exists, must be known by the circumstance that the facts cannot be
explained without it." (5.246) "It is to be concluded, then, that there is
no necessity of supposing an intuitive self-consciousness, since self-consciousness may easily be the result of inference." (5.237) "Everything in the
psychical sciences is inferential. Not the smallest fact about the mind can
be directly perceived as psychical. An emotion is directly felt as a bodily
state, or else it is only known inferentially." (1.250) "Introspection is wholly
a matter of inference. One is immediately conscious of his Feelings, no
doubt; but not that they are feelings of an ego. The *self* is only inferred.
There is no time in the present for any inference at all, least of all for
inference concerning that very instant. Consequently the present object
must be an external object, if there be any objective reference in it." (5.462)

The only way in which we can describe self-consciousness at all is as "Pure Self-Consciousness, which might be roughly described as a mere feeeling that has a dark instinct of being a germ of thought." (5.71)

iii. PURE PERCEPTION

The most fundamental and bare content of consciousness, and, according to Peirce, even of introspection,[33] is the percept considered quite simply and by itself. "That we are conscious of our percepts is a theory that seems to be beyond dispute." (4.539) We wish to know "what is the content of the *percept*," (5.53) but this is not so easy to answer. The ideal situation of course would be to have all ultimate premises as percepts and all ultimate logical principles as clear as the principle of contradiction. (6.497) But we can be mistaken about the indubitableness of logical principles, and "it is quite possible for perception to deceive us." We must be wary of accepting the evidence of perception alone, and feel our way tentatively.

Let us consider as an example of the way in which Peirce regarded the phenomenon of sensation his description of the sensation of light. "When a point is emitting unpolarized and homogeneous undulations equally in all directions, its state may be defined by two numbers; as, for instance by the wave-length of the undulations and their amplitude at a certain distance from the point. If the light is not homogeneous, indefinitely more numbers will be required to define it. But when a point upon the retina is illuminated, just three numbers are in every case requisite to define the sensation produced. In other words, light is a triple sensation.

"Since we have not yet succeeded in getting a clear general conception of any relation between different sensations, except that of more or less, it follows that when we have said that the sensation of light has three elements (arbitrarily taken as primary) we have gone as far toward describing that sensation as the present state of our ideas enables us to do."[34]

To begin with, it is clear that "we have no images even in actual perception. It will be sufficient to prove this in the case of vision; for if no picture is seen when we look at an object, it will not be claimed that hearing, touch, and the other senses, are superior to sight in this respect. That the picture is not painted on the nerves of the retina is absolutely certain, if, as psychologists inform us, these nerves are needle-points pointing to the light and at distances considerably greater than the *minimum visible*. The

---

[33] See this chapter, B, ii, quoting 5.245.

[34] C. S. Peirce, *Photometric Researches* (Leipzig, Wilhelm Engelmann, 1878), chap. I.

same thing is shown by our not being able to perceive that there is a large blind spot near the middle of the retina. If, then, we have a picture before us when we see, it is one constructed by the mind at the suggestion of previous sensations. Supposing these sensations to be signs, the understanding by reasoning from them could attain all the knowledge of outward things which we derive from sight, while the sensations are quite inadequate to forming an image or representation absolutely determinate. If we have such an image or picture, we must have in our minds a representation of a surface which is only a part of every surface we see, and we must see that each part, however small, has such and such a color. If we look from some distance at a speckled surface, it seems as if we did not see whether it were speckled or not; but if we have an image before us, it must appear to us either as speckled, or as not speckled. Again, the eye by education comes to distinguish minute differences of color; but if we see only absolutely determinate images, we must, no less before our eyes are trained than afterwards, see each color as particularly such and such a shade. Thus, to suppose that we have an image before us when we see, is not only a hypothesis which explains nothing whatever, but is one which actually creates difficulties which require new hypotheses in order to explain them away." (5.303)

"Our logically initial data are percepts. These percepts are undoubtedly purely psychical, altogether of the nature of thought. They involve three kinds of psychical elements, their qualities of feeling, their reactions against my will, and their generalizing or associating element.[35] But all that we find out afterward. I see an inkstand on the table: that is a percept. Moving my head, I get a different percept of the inkstand. It coalesces with the other. What I call the inkstand is a generalized percept, a quasi-inference from percepts, perhaps I might say a composite photograph of percepts. In this psychical product is involved an element of resistance to me, which I am obscurely conscious of from the first. Subsequently, when I accept the hypothesis of an inward subject for my thoughts, I yield to that consciousness of resistance and admit the inkstand to the standing of an external object."[36]

Peirce held that "continuity is given in perception; that is, that whatever the underlying psychical process may be, we seem to perceive a genuine flow of time, such that instants melt into one another quite without separate individuality." (5.205) He went on to describe percepts in terms of his

---

[35] See chap. IV, B, i, ii and iii.
[36] Review of Karl Pearson, *The Grammar of Science,* in the *Popular Science Monthly,* 58 (1901), 296 ff.

own personal experience. "For example, here I sit at my table with my inkstand and paper before me, my pen in my hand, my lamp at my side. It may be that all this is a dream. But if so, that such dream there is, is knowledge. But hold: what I have written down is only an imperfect description of the percept that is forced upon me. I have endeavored to state it in words. In this there has been an endeavor, purpose—something not forced upon me but rather the product of reflection. I was not forced to this reflection. I could not hope to describe what I see, feel, and hear, just as I see, feel, and hear it. Not only could I not set it down on paper, but I could have no kind of thought adequate to it or any way like it." (2.141)

"Hundreds of percepts have succeeded one another while I have been setting down these sentences. I recognize that there is a percept or flow of percepts very different from anything I can describe or think. What precisely that is I cannot even tell myself. It would be gone, long before I could tell myself many items; and those items would be quite unlike the percepts themselves. In this thought there would always be effort or endeavor. Whatever is the product of effort might be suppressed by effort, and therefore is subject to possible error. I am forced to content myself not with the fleeting percepts, but with the crude and possibly erroneous thoughts, or self-informations, of what the percepts were. The science of psychology assures me that the very percepts were mental constructions, not the first impressions of sense. But what the first impressions of sense may have been, I do not know except inferentially and most imperfectly. Practically, the knowledge with which I have to content myself, and have to call 'the evidence of my senses,' instead of being in truth the evidence of the senses, is only a sort of stenographic report of that evidence, possibly erroneous. In place of the *percept,* which, although not the first impression of sense, is a construction with which my will has had nothing to do, and may, therefore, properly be called the 'evidence of my senses,' the only thing I carry away with me is the *perceptual facts,*[37] or the intellect's description of the evidence of the senses, made by my endeavor. These perceptual facts are wholly unlike the percept, at best; and they may be downright untrue to the percept. But I have no means whatever of criticizing, correcting, or recomparing them, except that I can collect new perceptual facts relating to new percepts, and on that basis may infer that there must have been

[37] For Peirce, the percept is a fleeting and indescribable experience. He therefore resorts to the use of the term only as an adjective, in such phrases as "perceptual fact." For another example of such usage see the description of "perceptual judgment" in chap. V, B, ii.

some error in the former reports, or on the other hand I may in this way persuade myself that the former reports were true. The perceptual facts are a very imperfect report of the percepts; but I cannot go behind that record.[38] As for going back to the first impressions of sense, as some logicians recommend me to do, that would be the most chimerical of undertakings." (2.141)

"The percepts, could I make sure what they were, constitute experience proper, that which I am forced to accept." (2.142)[39] But "the data from which inference sets out and upon which all reasoning depends are the *perceptual facts*," (2.143) which are "strictly memories of what has taken place in the recent past." (2.145) Such is "the doctrine of Immediate Perception which is upheld by Reid, Kant, and all dualists who understand the true nature of dualism," (5.56)[40] a doctrine that is necessary for the cognition of relations. "We are continually bumping up against hard fact . . . and perception [is where the modification of other things] on us is overwhelmingly greater than our effect on them." (1.324) "The quality of redness and the quality of blueness differ without differing in any essential character which one has but the other lacks. The otherness of them is as irrational as the qualities themselves, if not more so. It appears to consist in a mutual war between them, in our taste." (4.344)

The operations involved in perception "are utterly beyond our control and will go on whether we are pleased with them or not." (5.55) "Examine the Percept in the particularly marked case in which it comes as a surprise. Your mind was filled [with] an imaginary object that was expected. At the moment when it was expected the vividness of the representation is exalted, and suddenly, when it should come, something quite different comes instead. I ask you whether at that instant of surprise there is not a double consciousness, on the one hand of an Ego, which is simply the expected idea suddenly broken off, on the other hand of the Non-Ego, which is the strange intruder, in his abrupt entrance." (5.53)[41]

"When a man is surprised he knows that he is surprised. Now comes a dilemma. Does he know he is surprised by direct perception or by inference? First try the hypothesis that it is by inference. This theory would

---

[38] Cf. William James's "present to sense" in his definition of perception, *The Principles of Psychology*, vol. ii, p. 76.

[39] See chap. V, A, ii.

[40] Those who detect here a return to topics already treated in epistemology (chap. V, especially B, ii) will recall the distinction discussed in the opening pages of the present chapter, in which it was pointed out that psychology treats of the knowledge relation only from the perspective of the *inner world* of the knower.

[41] See also 5.52, and chap. V, A, ii.

be that a person (who must be supposed old enough to have acquired self-consciousness) on becoming conscious of that peculiar quality of feeling which unquestionably belongs to all surprise, is induced by some reason to attribute this feeling to himself. It is, however, a patent fact that we never, *in the first instance*, attribute a Quality of Feeling to ourselves. We . . . attribute it to ourselves when irrefragable reasons compel us to do so. Therefore, the theory would have to be that the man first pronounces the surprising object a *wonder*, and upon reflection convinces himself that it is only a wonder in the sense that he is *surprised*. That would have to be the theory. But it is in conflict with the facts which are that a man is more or less placidly *expecting* one result, and suddenly finds something in contrast to that forcing itself upon his recognition. A duality is thus forced upon him: on the one hand, his expectation which he had been attributing to Nature, but which he is now compelled to attribute to some mere inner world, and on the other hand, a strong new phenomenon which shoves that expectation into the background and occupies its place. The old expectation, which is what he was familiar with, is his inner world, or *Ego*. The new phenomenon, the stranger, is from the exterior world or *Non-Ego*." (5.57) Undoubtedly, "this direct perception presents an *Ego* to which the smashed expectation belonged, and the *Non-Ego*, the sadder and wiser man, to which the new phenomenon belongs." (5.58)

In the pure percept there is no element of thought. But we shall see in the following sections how the data of perception is worked over by the mind in increasing degrees of complexity, by means of the process of inference. The transformation of percepts in the inner world is slow at first, consisting of various degrees of reaction, but ends finally in thoroughgoing cognition. For Peirce mainained that "every sort of modification of consciousness—Attention, Sensation, and Understanding—is an inference." (5.298)

C. SENSATIONS OF REACTION

"Besides Feelings, we have Sensations of reaction; as when a person blindfold suddenly runs against a post, when we make a muscular effort, or when any feeling gives way to a new feeling. Suppose I had nothing in my mind but a feeling of blue, which were suddenly to give way to a feeling of red; then, at the instant of transition, there would be a shock, a sense of reaction, my blue life being transmuted into red life. If I were further endowed with a memory, that sense would continue for some time, and there would also be a peculiar feeling or sentiment connected with it.

This last feeling might endure (conceivably, I mean) after the memory of the occurrence and the feelings of blue and red had passed away. But the *sensation* of reaction cannot exist except in the actual presence of the two feelings blue and red to which it relates. Wherever we have two feelings and pay attention to a relation between them of whatever kind, there is a sensation of [reaction]." (6.19) The point is that "even in actual sensation there is a reaction." (1.419)

Logically, "a sensation is a simple predicate taken in place of a complex predicate; in other words, it fulfills the function of an hypothesis." (5.291) Ontologically, sensations of reaction belong with secondness.[42] There is struggle, and effect of agent on patient. (5.45) "The main distinction between the Inner and the Outer Worlds is that inner objects promptly take any modifications we wish, while outer objects are hard facts that no man can make to be other than they are. Yet tremendous as this distinction is, it is after all only relative. Inner objects do offer a certain degree of resistance and outer objects are susceptible of being modified in some measure by sufficient exertion intelligently directed." In sensation, however, secondness is weak. (5.69)

The sensation of reaction has, of course, a physiological basis or occasion. "The sense of action and reaction, or the polar sense . . . is plainly connected with the discharge of nervous energy through the nerve-fibres." (1.386) "The disturbance of feeling, or sense of reaction, accompanies the transmission of disturbance between nerve-cells, or from a nerve-cell to a muscle-cell, or the external stimulation of a nerve-cell." (6.22) "In the case of a sensation the manifold of impressions which precede and determine it are not of a kind, the bodily motion corresponding to which comes from any large ganglion or from the brain, and probably for this reason the sensation produces no great commotion in the bodily organism." (5.293) "The sense of effort . . . seems to be a sensation which somehow arises when striped muscles are under tension. But though this is the only way of stimulating it, yet an imagination of it is by association called up, upon the occasion of other slight sensations, even when muscles are uncontracted; and this imagination may sometimes be interpreted as a sign of effort." (5.539) Psychologically, the sensation of reaction derives from "consciousness of an interruption into the field of consciousness, sense of resistance, of an external fact, of another something." (1.377) "*Red* is relative to sight, but the fact that this or that is in that relation to vision that we call being red is not *itself* relative to sight; it is a real fact." (5.430)

[42] See chap. IV, B, ii.

Thus, in Peirce's view, psychological events, at any and every level of happening in the inner world, are reactions to stimuli of external provenance, and can be accounted for satisfactorily only in this way.

i. HABIT

We have already discussed habit in its broadest sense as one of the ontological categories of actuality.[43] There we found it to be a characteristic of all actual things, of rivers as well as of animals, of plants as well as of crystalline substances. We found, too, that there are two worlds of habit: an inner world and an outer world. It is the inner world that Peirce had in mind in his category of psychological habit, and moreover a particular kind of inner world: the inner world of the mind.

The psychological meaning of habit may be explained as follows: " . . . multiple reiterated behaviour of the same kind, under similar combinations of percepts and fancies, produces a tendency—the *habit*—actually to behave in a similar way under similar circumstances in the future." (5.487) A habit or disposition is a "general principle working in a man's nature to determine how he will act." (2.170) "Let us recall the nature of a sign[44] and ask ourselves how we can know that a feeling of any sort is a sign that we have a habit implanted within us." (5.371 n.1) "A habit is involuntarily formed from the consideration of diagrams, which process when deliberately approved becomes inductive reasoning." (2.170) "We can understand one habit by likening it to another habit. But to understand what any habit is, there must be some habit of which we are directly conscious in its generality." (5.371 n.1)

Physiologically, Peirce accounted for psychological habit by the fact "that protoplasm is chilled by liquefaction, and that this brings it back to the solid state, when the heat is recovered. This series of operations must be very rapid in the case of nerve-slime and even of muscle-slime, and may account for the unsteady or vibratory character of their action. Of course, if assimilation takes place, the heat of combination, which is probably trifling, is gained. On the other hand, if work is done, whether by nerve or by muscle, loss of energy must take place. In the case of the muscle, the mode by which the instantaneous part of the fatigue is brought about is easily traced out. If when the muscle contracts it be under stress, it will contract less than it otherwise would do, and there will be a loss of heat.

[43] See chap. IV, D, ii, (c).
[44] See chap. III, B, i.

It is like an engine which should work by dissolving salt in water and using the contraction during the solution to lift a weight, the salt being recovered afterwards by distillation. But the major part of fatigue has nothing to do with the correlation of forces. A man must labor hard to do in a quarter of an hour the work which draws from him enough heat to cool his body by a single degree. Meantime, he will be getting heated, he will be pouring out extra products of combustion, perspiration, etc., and he will be driving the blood at an accelerated rate through minute tubes at great expense. Yet all this will have little to do with his fatigue. He may sit quietly at his table writing, doing practically no physical work at all, and yet in a few hours be terribly fagged. This seems to be owing to the deranged sub-molecules of the nerve-slime not having had time to settle back into their proper combinations. When such sub-molecules are thrown out, as they must be from time to time, there is so much waste of material." (6.259)

"In order that a sub-molecule of food may be thoroughly and firmly assimilated into a broken molecule of protoplasm, it is necessary not only that it should have precisely the right chemical composition, but also that it should be at precisely the right spot at the right time and should be moving in precisely the right direction with precisely the right velocity. If all these conditions are not fulfilled, it will be more loosely retained than the other parts of the molecule; and every time it comes round into the situation in which it was drawn in, relatively to the other parts of that molecule and to such others as were near enough to be factors in the action, it will be in special danger of being thrown out again. Thus, when a partial liquefaction of the protoplasm takes place many times to about the same extent, it will, each time, be pretty nearly the same molecules that were last drawn in that are now thrown out. They will be thrown out, too, in about the same way, as to position, direction of motion, and velocity, in which they were drawn in; and this will be in about the same course that the ones last before them were thrown out. Not exactly, however; for the very cause of their being thrown off so easily is their not having fulfilled precisely the conditions of stable retention. Thus, the law of habit is accounted for, and with it its peculiar characteristic of not acting with exactitude." (6.260)[45]

Such is the way in which habits are formed. But we also have to consider "the operation of the environment, which goes to break up habits destined to be broken up and so to render the mind lively." (6.301) "Now

---

[45] For further on the physiology of habit, see 1.390 and 1.393-394.

the manner in which habits generally get broken up is this. Reactions usually terminate in the removal of a stimulus; for the excitation continues as long as the stimulus is present. Accordingly, habits are general ways of behaviour which are associated with the removal of stimuli. But when the expected removal of the stimulus fails to occur, the excitation continues and increases, and non-habitual reactions take place; and these tend to weaken the habit." (6.264)[46] "Everybody knows that the long continuance of a routine of habit makes us lethargic, while a succession of surprises wonderfully brightens the ideas. Where there is a motion, where history is a-making, there is the focus of mental activity, and it has been said that the arts and sciences reside within the temple of Janus, waking when that is open, but slumbering when it is closed. Few psychologists have perceived how fundamental a fact this is. A portion of mind, abundantly commissured to other portions, works almost mechanically. It sinks to a condition of a railway junction. But a portion of mind almost isolated, a spiritual peninsula, or *cul-de-sac*, is like a railway terminus. Now mental commissures are habits. Where they abound, originality is not needed and is not found; but where they are in defect spontaneity is set free." (6.301)

At the psychological level, feelings are symptoms of habits.[47] "Habits are either habits about ideas of feelings or habits about acts of reaction. The ensemble of all habits about ideas of feeling constitutes one great habit which is a World." (4.157) Thus psychological sensations of reaction are habits of feeling. But it is true of the individual that "he not merely has habits, but also can exert a measure of self-control over his future actions." (5.418) "Every man exercises more or less control over himself by means of modifying his own habits; and the way in which he goes to work to bring this effect about in those cases in which circumstances will not permit him to practice reiterations of the desired kind of conduct in the outer world shows that he is virtually well-acquainted with the important principle that *reiterations in the inner world—fancied reiterations—if well-intensified by direct effort, produce habits*,[48] just as do reiterations in the outer world; *and these habits will have power to influence actual behaviour in the outer world*; especially if each reiteration be accompanied by a peculiar strong effort that is usually likened to issuing a command to one's future self." (5.487)

[46] The physiological explanation of psychological habit "has a certain value as an addition to our little store of mechanical examples of actions analogous to habit." (6.261) See the whole of this paragraph and the next, also my chapter IV, D, ii, (c).

[47] See chap. IV, D, ii, (c), quoting 5.492.

[48] Cf. James's law of mental association in *The Principles of Psychology*, vol. i, p. 561.

The inner world of psychology and the outer world of nonpsychological existence interact, "the interaction of these two worlds chiefly consisting of a direct action of the outer world upon the inner and an indirect action of the inner world upon the outer through the operation of habits." (5.493) But, if this is true, then "how otherwise can a habit be described than by a description of the kind of action to which it gives rise, with the specification of the conditions and of the motive?" (5.491) "The identity of a habit depends on how it might lead us to act." (5.400) Peirce described "the modification of a person's tendencies toward action" (5.476) as a "habit-change." "Habits have grades of strength varying from complete dissociation to inseparable association. These grades are mixtures of promptitude of action, say excitability and other ingredients not calling for separate examination here. The habit-change often consists in raising or lowering the strength of a habit. Habits also differ in their endurance (which is likewise a composite quality). But generally speaking, it may be said that the effects of habit-change last until time or some more definite cause produces new habit-changes. It naturally follows that repetition of the actions that produce the changes increases the changes." (5.477)

ii. BELIEF AND DOUBT

From a habit to a belief is not a far step. "The feeling of believing is a more or less sure indication of there being established in our nature some habit which will determine our actions." (5.371) "The essence of belief is the establishment of a habit; and different beliefs are distinguished by the different modes of action to which they give rise." (5.398) "A belief is an intelligent habit upon which we shall act when occasion presents itself." (2.435) Habit in this connection may be described as "a rule active in us." (2.643) "There can, of course, be no question that a man will act in accordance with his belief so far as his belief has any practical consequences. The only doubt is whether this is *all* that belief is, whether belief is a mere nullity so far as it does not influence conduct." (5.32) "A proposition that could be doubted at will is certainly not *believed*.[49] For belief, while it lasts, is a strong habit, and as such, forces the man to believe until some surprise breaks up the habit. The breaking of a belief can only be due to some novel experience, whether external or internal." (5.524)

[49] "For, what is proved by valid argument or is recounted as credible, is believed by us whether we will or no."—*The Philosophical Works of Descartes,* Haldane and Ross trans. (Cambridge, University Press, 1934), vol. ii, Objections III (of Hobbes), p. 75.

"A belief [then] is a habit," (5.510) "but it is a habit of which we are conscious," (5.242) and "a deliberate, or self-controlled, habit is precisely a belief." (5.480) "Now to be deliberately and thoroughly prepared to shape one's conduct into conformity with a proposition is neither more nor less than the state of mind called Believing that proposition, however long the conscious classification of it under that head be postponed." (6.467) But objective action, however it be dictated by belief, does not exhaust it; and it is the result of no ordinary kind of habit. "A cerebral habit of the highest kind, which will determine what we do in fancy as well as what we do in action, is called a *belief*." (3.160) Belief has a physiological basis; "for the analogue of belief, in the nervous system, we must look to what are called nervous associations—for example, to that habit of the nerves in consequences of which the smell of a peach will make the mouth water." (5.373) The "peripheral excitations . . . are all adapted to an end, that of carrying belief, in the long run, toward certain predestinate conclusions which are the same for all men." (3.161)

"There are, besides perceptual judgments,[50] original (i.e. indubitable because uncriticized) beliefs of a general and recurrent kind, as well as indubitable acritical inferences." (5.442)[51] "What is properly and usually called a *belief* . . . is the adoption of a proposition as a κτῆμα ἐς ἀεί," (1.635) a property for ever. Hence "belief gradually tends to fix itself under the influence of inquiry." (2.693)[52] "Our belief ought to be proportional to the weight of evidence." (2.676) To define truth in this connection as "a finally compulsory belief," (2.29) then, is not to indicate that belief is a matter of arbitrary choice. Belief is based on reason.[53] Subjective belief is a result of objective truth.[54] Truth from the psychological point of view is simply "a state of belief unassailable by doubt." (5.416) The compulsion must come from without, for we are not free to believe whatever we wish to believe; we can believe only what we must.[55]

Peirce divided beliefs into practical and theoretical varieties. Belief as habit is practical belief, for "a practical belief may be described as a habit

---

[50] See chap. V, B, ii.

[51] An acritical inference is "a belief that has been determined by another given belief." (5.441) When we are unaware of such determination, it is called "associational suggestions of belief."

[52] See chap. I, A, ii.

[53] Cf. John Locke, *Essay Concerning Human Understanding*, bk. iv, chap. xvii, sec. 24. Also Thomas Reid, *Essays on the Intellectual Powers of Man*, II, x.

[54] See chap. V, C, iii.

[55] The same thing is true of belief that is true of doubt. (5.265) See chap. II, E, i and ii. Cf. Plato, *Republic*, VII, 536.

of deliberate behavior." (5.538) A theoretical belief is an expectation, or almost an expectation. (5.539) While theoretical beliefs, or expectations, do not involve muscular effort, as practical beliefs do, they yet consist "in the stamp of approval, the act of recognition as one's own, being placed by a deed of the soul upon an imaginary anticipation of experience." (5.540) "As to purely theoretical beliefs not expectations, if they are to mean anything, they must be somehow expectative." (5.541) "It now begins to look strongly as if perhaps all belief might involve expectation as its essence." (5.542) For "every belief is belief in a proposition. Now every proposition has its predicate which expresses *what* is believed, and its subjects which express *of what* it is believed."

In the province of theoretical belief not everything is perfect, for there is usually an element of doubt along with the belief.[56] "Nevertheless, in every state of intellectual development and of information, there are things that seem to us sure, because no little ingenuity and reflection is needed to see how anything can be false which all our previous experience seems to support; so that even though we tell ourselves we are *not* sure, we cannot clearly see *how* we fail of being so. Practically, therefore, life is not long enough for a given individual to rake up doubts about everything; and so, however strenuously he may hold to the doctrine of catalepsy, he will practically treat one proposition and another as certain. This is a state of *practically perfect belief.*" (4.64)[57]

That which keeps belief from being absolutely perfect is doubt. "Doubt is a state of mind marked by a feeling of uneasiness;[58] but we cannot from a logical, least of all from a pragmaticistic point of view, regard the doubt as consisting in the feeling." (5.510) Both doubt and the struggle of the mind to escape from it are facts. (2.210) "A man in doubt is usually trying to imagine how he shall, or should, act when or if he finds himself in the imagined situation. He supposes himself to have an end in view, and two different and inconsistent lines of action offer themselves. His action is in imagination (or perhaps really) brought to a stop because he does not know whether (so to speak) the righthand road or the lefthand road is the one that will bring him to his destination; and (to continue the figure of speech) he waits at the fork for an indication, and kicks his heels. His pent up

---

[56] "It is possible to construct a true scale for the measurement of belief." (4.143)

[57] Cf. "sure knowledge," chap. V, C, i.

[58] Although ontological categories can in no wise be said to depend, ontologically, upon psychological categories, psychology can in certain cases offer supporting evidence for ontology. Thus the fact of doubt requires reality. "Nobody can really doubt that there are Reals, for, if he did, doubt would not be a source of dissatisfaction." (5.384)

activity finds vent in feeling, which becomes the more prominent from his attention being no longer absorbed in action. A true doubt is accordingly a doubt which really interferes with the smooth working of the belief-habit." (5.510) "We generally know when we wish to ask a question and when we wish to pronounce a judgment, for there is a dissimilarity between the sensation of doubting and that of believing." (5.370)

"Doubt [then] is an uneasy and dissatisfied state from which we struggle to free ourselves and pass into the state of belief;[59] while the latter is a calm and satisfactory state which we do not wish to avoid, or to change to a belief in anything else." (5.372) "Among the inner shapes which binarity assumes are those of the *doubts* that are forced upon our minds. The very word 'doubt' or 'dubito,' is the frequentative of 'duhibeo'—i.e. *duo habeo*, and thus exhibits its binarity. If we did not struggle against doubt, we should not seek the truth." (2.84) Doubt is a product of falsity.[60] "The irritation of doubt is the only immediate motive for the struggle to attain belief. It is certainly best for us that our beliefs should be such as may truly guide our actions so as to satisfy our desires; and this reflection will make us reject every belief which does not seem to have been so formed as to insure this result. But it will only do so by creating a doubt in the place of that belief. With the doubt, therefore, the struggle begins, and with the cessation of doubt it ends." (5.375) "All doubt is a state of hesitancy about an imagined state of things. . . . It is anticipated hesitancy about what I shall do hereafter, or a feigned hesitancy about a fictitious state of things. It is the power of making believe we hesitate, together with the pregnant fact that the decision upon the merely make-believe dilemma goes toward forming a bona fide habit that will be operative in a real emergency." (5.373 n.1)

Doubt, then, although it is a negative affair, bridges the gap between the habit of belief and the incentive to thought. Doubt "is not a habit, but the privation of a habit. Now a privation of a habit, in order to be anything at all, must be a condition of erratic activity that in some way must get superseded by a habit." (5.417) But "as it appeases the irritation of doubt, which is the motive for thinking, thought relaxes, and comes to rest for a moment when belief is reached. But since belief is a rule for action, the application of which involves further doubt and further thought, at the same time that it is a stopping-place, it is also a new starting-place for thought." (5.397) Belief "is the demi-cadence which closes a musical phrase in the symphony of our intellectual life. We have seen that it has just three

[59] Peirce added that "for the sake of the pleasures of inquiry, men may like to seek out doubts. Yet, for all that, doubt essentially involves a struggle to escape it." See chap. II, E, i.
[60] See chap. V, C, ii.

properties: First, it is something that we are aware of; second, it appeases the irritation of doubt; and, third, it involves the establishment in our nature of a rule of action, or, say for short, a *habit*." "Thus both doubt and belief have positive effects upon us, though very different ones. Belief does not make us act at once, but puts us into such a condition that we shall behave in some certain way, when the occasion arises. Doubt has not the least such active effect, but stimulates us to inquiry until it is destroyed." (5.373)

iii. INSTINCT

The antagonism which Peirce felt toward the whole Cartesian mode of thought[61] was so strong in him that it led him to question the role of intuition and its first cousin, instinct. "We have no power of Intuition," he asserted, "but every cognition is determined logically by previous cognitions." (5.265) Yet he was obliged to give it a place in his system, referring it to "the same general class of operations to which Perceptive Judgments[62] belong." (5.173)

Although it is not a simple matter to distinguish between intuitions and mediate cognitions, the fact remains that intuitions, or instincts, really exist. (2.171) We have seen that the scientific guide to knowledge, which Galileo referred to as *il lume naturale*,[63] is nothing more than instinctive judgment. (1.80) "It is certain that the only hope of retroductive [i.e., abductive] reasoning ever reaching the truth is that there may be some natural tendency toward an agreement between the ideas which suggest themselves to the human mind and those which are concerned in the laws of nature." (1.81) "Thus reason, for all the frills it customarily wears, in vital crises, comes down upon its marrow-bones to beg the succour of instinct." (1.630) The perceptual judgment, in fact, is an abductive inference[64] which comes like an insight. (5.181) "This faculty is at the same time of the general nature of Instinct, resembling the instincts of the animals in its so far surpassing the general powers of our reason and for its directing us as if we were in possession of facts that are entirely beyond the reach of our senses. It resembles instinct too in its small liability to error; for though it goes wrong oftener than right, yet the relative frequency with which it is right is on the whole the most wonderful thing in our constitution." (5.173) Man, he admitted, "has a certain Insight . . . into . . . the general elements of Nature."

---

[61] See chap. II, E.
[62] See chap. V, B, ii.
[63] See chap. V, A.
[64] See chap. III, C, ii, (c).

"But little as we know about instincts, even now, we are much better acquainted with them than were the men of the eighteenth century. We know, for example, that they can be somewhat modified in a very short time." (5.445) They can be modified because they have come into existence as modifications. "An instinct, in the proper sense of the word, is an inherited habit, or in more accurate language, an inherited disposition." (2.170) Instinct, however, can be described in terms of origins but not defined in such a way. The definition must depend upon what it is essentially, and not upon how it came to be what it is.

An intuition Peirce defined as "a cognition not determined by a previous cognition of the same object, and therefore so determined by something out of the consciousness. . . . *Intuition* here will be nearly the same as "premiss not itself a conclusion"; the only difference being that premises and conclusions are judgments, whereas an intuition may, as far as its definition states, be any kind of cognition whatever. But just as a conclusion (good or bad) is determined in the mind of the reasoner by its premise, so cognitions not judgments may be determined by previous cognitions; and a cognition not so determined directly by the transcendental object, is to be termed an *intuition*. (5.213) Undoubtedly, "besides ordinary experience which is dependent on there being a certain physical connection between our organs and the thing experienced, there is a second avenue of truth dependent only on there being a certain intellectual connection between our previous knowledge and what we learn in that way." (5.341) There is an intellectual intuition, which can never be explained on the basis of an examination of the human mind alone. It depends, in a sense, upon the "validity of induction." (5.349) [65]

"Now, it is plainly one thing to have an intuition and another to know intuitively that it is an intuition, and the question is whether these two things, distinguishable in thought, are, in fact, invariably connected, so that we can always intuitively distinguish between an intuition and a cognition determined by another." (5.214) In so far as cognitions are self-validating, so that "the determination or nondetermination of the cognition by another may be a part of the cognition," we would seem to have the faculty of so distinguishing. But, on the other hand, "there is no evidence that we have this faculty, except that we seem to *feel* that we have it." But then we cannot feel the origins of our feelings; we do not know from our feeling whether it is the result of "education, old associations, etc., or whether it is an intuitive cognition." The feelings are not infallible.

[65] See chap. III, C, ii, (*b*).

"In the middle ages, reason and external authority were regarded as two coördinate sources of knowledge, just as reason and the authority of intuition are now." (5.215) Only, in those days, all authorities were not considered infallible, or essentially indemonstrable. "The credibility of authority was regarded by men of that time simply as an ultimate premiss, as a cognition not determined by a previous cognition of the same object, or, in our terms, as an intuition. . . . Now, what if our *internal* authority should meet the same fate, in the history of opinions, as that external authority has met? Can that be said to be absolutely certain which many sane, well-informed, and thoughtful men already doubt?" The unreliability of the senses suggests that "it is not always very easy to distinguish between a premiss and a conclusion, that we have no infallible power of doing so." (5.216) From this and other similar evidence Peirce concluded that "we have no intuitive faculty of distinguishing intuitive from mediate cognitions," (5.224) even though the existence of some such function as that of intuition or instinct is undeniable.

iv. DESIRE AND VOLITION

"It is . . . action according to final causes," Peirce maintained, "which distinguishes mental from mechanical action; and the general formula of all our desires may be taken as this: to remove a stimulus." (1.392) Thus "a purpose is an operative desire." (1.205)

"Now a desire is always general; that is, it is always some *kind* of thing or event which is desired. . . . Thus desires create classes, and extremely broad classes. But desires become, in the pursuit of them, more specific." (1.205)[66] "Let us examine the idea of generality. Every cook has in her recipe-book a collection of rules, which she is accustomed to follow. An apple pie is desired. Now, observe that we seldom, probably never, desire a single individual thing. What we want is something which shall produce a certain pleasure of a certain kind. To speak of a single individual pleasure is to use words without meaning. We may have a single experience of pleasure; but the pleasure itself is a quality. Experiences are single; but qualities, however specialized, cannot be enumerated. . . . An apple pie, then, is desired—a good apple pie, made of fresh apples, with a crust moderately light and somewhat short, neither too sweet nor too sour, etc. But it is not any particular apple pie; for it is to be made for the occasion; and the only particularity about it is that it is to be made and eaten today. For that, apples are wanted; and remembering that there is a barrel of apples in the

[66] See also 2.696.

cellar, the cook goes to the cellar and takes the apples that are uppermost and handiest. That is an example of following a general rule. She is directed to take apples. Many times she has seen things which were called apples, and has noticed their common quality. She knows how to find such things now; and as long as they are sound and fine, any apples will do. What she desires is something of a given quality; what she has to take is this or that particular apple. From the nature of things, she cannot take the quality but must take the particular thing. . . .[67] But desire has nothing to do with particulars; it relates to qualities. Desire is not a reaction with reference to a particular thing; it is an idea about an idea, namely, the idea of how delightful it would be for me, the cook's master, to eat an apple pie. . . . Throughout her whole proceedings she pursues an idea or dream without any particular thisness or thatness—or, as we say, *hecceity*—to it, but this dream she wishes to realize in connection with an object of experience, which, as such, does possess hecceity." (1.341)

"Closely connected with the fact that every desire is general, are two other facts which must be taken into account in considering purposive classes. The first of these is that a desire is always more or less variable, or vague. For example, a man wants an economical lamp. Then if he burns oil in it, he will endeavor to burn that oil which gives him sufficient light at the lowest cost. But another man, who lives a little further from the source of supply of that oil and a little nearer the source of a different oil may find that different oil to be the better for him. So it is with the desires of one individual. The same man who prefers veal to pork as a general thing, may think that an occasional spare rib is better than having cold boiled veal every day of his life. In short, variety is the spice of life for the individual, and practically still more so for a large number of individuals; and as far as we can compare Nature's way with ours, she seems to be even more given to variety than we." (1.206)

"But not only is desire *general* and *vague*, or indeterminate; it has besides a certain longitude, or *third* dimension. By this I mean that while a certain ideal state of things might most perfectly satisfy a desire, yet a situation somewhat differing from that will be far better than nothing; and in general, when a state is not too far from the ideal state, the nearer it approaches that state the better. Moreover, the situation of things most satisfactory to one desire is almost never the situation most satisfactory to another. A brighter lamp than that I use would perhaps be more agreeable to my eyes; but it would be less so to my pocket, to my lungs, and to my sense of heat.

[67] See chap. IV, B, iii.

Accordingly, a compromise is struck; and since all the desires concerned are somewhat vague, the result is that the objects actually will cluster about certain middling qualities, some being removed this way, some that way, and at greater and greater removes fewer and fewer objects will be so determined. Thus, clustering distributions will characterize purposive classes." (1.207)

"Though 'desire' implies a tendency to volition, and though it is a natural hypothesis that a man cannot *will* to do that which he has no sort of desire to do, yet we all know conflicting desires but too well, and how treacherous they are apt to be; and a desire may perfectly well be discontented with volition, *i.e.* with what the man *will* do." (1.331) There is a point at which "the element of will, which is always exercised upon an individual object upon an individual occasion, becomes so predominant as to overrule the generalizing character of desire." (1.205) "One great psychologist has said that the will is nothing but the strongest desire. I cannot grant that; it seems to me to overlook that fact which of all that we observe is quite the most obtrusive, namely, the difference between dreaming and doing." (1.380)

In the psychology of willing, secondness is strong. (5.69) "Volition is through and through dual. There is the duality of agent and patient, of effort and resistance, of active effort and inhibition, of acting on self and on external objects." (1.332) Polarity, of course, exists in the physical world. "Yet for the much smaller universe of psychology, polar distinctions abound, most of them referring to volition. Thus, pleasure is any kind of sensation that one immediately seeks, pain any that one immediately . . . shuns.[68] Right and wrong are expressly volitional." (1.330) Volition has a physiological basis; "the sense of action and reaction, or the polar sense . . . is plainly connected with the discharge of nervous energy through the nerve-fibres. External volition, the most typical case of it, involves such a discharge into muscle-cells." (1.386) "In regard to the doctrine that volition consists in, or is an aspect of, muscular contraction or inhibition, it is to be considered that considerable time elapses during the passage of the motor impulse down the nerve. During this interval we seem to be aware of a striving, like that of a nightmare. At any rate, something has taken place in which the muscle had no part. The muscle might even be amputated before the impulse reached it. But if a motor impulse can thus be communicated to a nerve fibre to be transmitted over it, how can we be sure that this latter may not abut against a nerve cell instead of against a muscle cell?"[69]

[68] See this chapter, B, i.
[69] Review of Th. Ribot, *The Psychology of Attention*, in *The Nation*, 50 (1890), 292.

At the level of psychology, however, "the consciousness of willing does not differ, at least not very much, from a sensation. The sense of hitting and of getting hit are nearly the same, and should be classed together. The common element is the sense of an actual occurrence, of actual action and reaction. There is an intense reality about this kind of experience, a sharp sundering of subject and object. While I am seated calmly in the dark, the lights are suddenly turned on, and at that instant I am conscious, not of a process of change, but yet of something more than can be contained in an instant. I have a sense of a *saltus*, of there being two sides to that instant. A consciousness of polarity would be a tolerably good phrase to describe what occurs. For will, then, as one of the great types of consciousness, we ought to substitute the polar sense." (1.380)

"Willing subdivides into Active Willing and Inhibitive Willing, to which last dichotomy nothing in Sensation corresponds." (5.69) "The will to produce a change is active, the will to resist a change is passive." (1.334) "Moreover, there is active volition and passive volition, or inertia, the volition of reform and the volition of conservatism." (1.332) "It is [the] special field of experience to acquaint us with events, with changes of perception. Now that which particularly characterizes sudden changes of perception is a *shock*. A shock is a volitional phenomenon." (1.336) "That shock which we experience when anything particularly unexpected forces itself upon our recognition (which has a cognitive utility as being a call for explanation of the presentment) is simply the sense of the volitional inertia of expectation, which strikes a blow like a water-hammer when it is checked; and the force of this blow, if one could measure it, would be the measure of the energy of the conservative volition that gets checked." (1.332)

"The past affects the senses, and more and more strongly the nearer it is; our will can affect the future, and more and more strongly the nearer it is." (6.387) Another name for the "volitional inertia of expectation" is self-control, which is also an exercise of the will. "Self-control seems to be the capacity for rising to an extended view of a practical subject instead of seeing only temporary urgency." (5.339 n.1) The will, in being directed toward the future, leads away from sensations of reaction and toward the psychological categories of ratiocination.

V. IMAGINATION AND MEMORY

Images are characteristic of imagination and memory, and do not occur in pure perception.[70] "For example, you look at something and say, 'It is red.'

---

[70] See this chapter, B, iii.

Well, I ask you what justification you have for such a judgment. You reply, 'I *saw* it was red.' Not at all. You saw nothing in the least like that. You saw an image. There was no subject or predicate in it. It was just one unseparated image, not resembling a proposition in the smallest particular." (1.538) Physiologically, "Certain stimuli, commonly visceral in their origin, throw the brain into an activity which stimulates the effect of peripheral excitations of the senses. The reactions from such stimuli have the same internal character; an inward action removes the inward stimulus. A fancied conjecture leads us to fancy an appropriate line of behaviour." (6.286) For the metaphysical realist, the importance of a sense-image is intimately connected with its logical status. The understanding of images, in Peirce's view, takes us back to semiotic.

"This is a real thing or fact which is a sign of its object by virtue of being connected with it as a matter of fact and by also forcibly intruding upon the mind, quite regardless of its being interpreted as a sign.[71] It may simply serve to identify its object and assure us of its existence and presence. But very often the nature of the factual connexion of the index with its object is such as to excite in consciousness an image of some features of the object, and in that way affords evidence from which positive assurance as to truth of fact may be drawn. A photograph, for example, not only excites an image, has an appearance, but, owing to its optical connexion with the object, is evidence that that appearance corresponds to a reality." (4.447) An image is an icon,[72] and "an icon has such being as belongs to past experience. It exists only as an image in the mind." "The value of an icon consists in its exhibiting the features of a state of things regarded as if it were purely imaginary." (4.448)

"Any material image, as a painting, is largely conventional in its mode of representation; but in itself, without legend or label it may be called a *hypoicon*." (2.276) "Hypoicons may be roughly divided according to the mode of Firstness[73] of which they partake. Those which partake of simple qualities, or First Firstnesses, are images." (2.277)

"An expectation is a habit of imagining. . . . An imagination is an affection of consciousness which can be directly compared with a percept in some special feature, and be pronounced to accord or disaccord with it. Suppose for example that I slip a cent into a slot, and expect on pulling a knob to see a little cake of chocolate appear. My expectation consists in,

[71] See chap. III, B, i, (*b*).
[72] See chap. III, B, i, (*b*).
[73] See chap. IV, B, i.

or at least involves, such a habit that when I think of pulling the knob, I imagine I see a chocolate coming into view. When the perceptual chocolate comes into view, my imagination of it is a feeling of such a nature that the percept can be compared with it as to size, shape, the nature of the wrapper, the color, taste, flavor, hardness and grain of what is within." (2.148) "We now know that the same action—the same in quality, if not equal in intensity—that is performed when we really act, is also performed when we vividly imagine we act; only, in the latter case, we add to the exertion an opposite exertion inhibiting it."[74]

The importance of imagination is made clear when we recall that the method of discovery involves imagination.[75] "Those which represent the relations, mainly dyadic, or so regarded, of the parts of one thing by analogous relations in their own parts, are *diagrams.*" (2.277) Now, "the actual world cannot be distinguished from a world of imagination by any description." (3.363) "So in contemplating a painting, [for example] there is a moment when we lose the consciousness that it is not the thing, the distinction of the real and the copy disappears, and it is for the moment a pure dream—not any particular existence, and yet not general. At that moment we are contemplating an *icon.*" (3.362) "People who build castles in the air do not, for the most part, accomplish much, it is true; but every man who does accomplish great things is given to building elaborate castles in the air and then painfully copying them on solid ground. Indeed, the whole business of ratiocination, and all that makes us intellectual beings, is performed in imagination. Vigorous men are wont to hold mere imagination in contempt; and in that they would be quite right if there were such a thing. How we feel is no matter; the question is what we shall do. But that feeling which is subservient to action and to the intelligence of action is correspondingly important; and all inward life is more or less so subservient. Mere imagination would indeed be mere trifling; only no imagination is *mere.* 'More than all that is in thy custody, watch over thy phantasy,' said Solomon, 'for out of it are the issues of life'." (6.286)

Closely related to imagination is memory. We have already discussed perceptual facts,[76] and perceptual facts are involved in involuntary memories. (2.145) When direct experience "comes up to be criticized it is past, itself, and is represented by *memory.*" (1.146) Though memory is a representation of past experience, it is itself "an articulated complex and worked-

[74] Review of Thomas Marshall, *Aristotle's Theory of Conduct* in *The Nation,* 83 (1906), 226.
[75] See chap. III, D, iii.
[76] See this chapter, B, iii.

over product which differs infinitely and immeasurably from feeling. Look at a red surface, and try to feel what the sensation is, and then shut your eyes and remember it. No doubt different persons are different in this respect; to some the experiment will seem to yield an opposite result, but I have convinced myself that there is nothing in my memory that is in the least like the vision of the red. When red is not before my eyes, I do not see it at all. Some people tell me they see it faintly—a most inconvenient kind of memory, which would lead to remembering bright red as pale or dingy. I remember colors with unusual accuracy, because I have had much training in observing them; but my memory does not consist in any vision but in a habit by virtue of which I can recognize a newly presented color as like or unlike one I had seen before. But even if the memory of some persons is of the nature of an hallucination, enough arguments remain to show that immediate consciousness or feeling is absolutely unlike anything else." (1.379)

"But it must be admitted that a feeling experienced in an outward sensation may be reproduced in memory. For to deny this would be idle nonsense. For instance, you experienced, let us say, a certain color sensation due to red-lead. It has a definite hue, luminosity, and chroma. These [are] three elements—which are not separate in the feeling, it is true, and are not, therefore, in the feeling at all but are said to be in it, as a way of expressing the results which would follow, according to the principles of chromatics, from certain experiments with a color disk, color box, or other similar apparatus. In that sense, the color sensation which you derive from looking at the red-lead has a certain hue, luminosity and chroma which completely define the quality of the color. The *vividness*, however, is independent of all three of these elements; and it is very different in the memory of the color a quarter of a second after the actual sensation from what it is in the sensation itself, although this memory is conceivably perfectly true as to hue, luminosity, and chroma, which truth constitutes it an exact reproduction of the entire quality of the feeeling." (1.308) Thus while memory differs from feeling, feeling can yet be reproduced in memory. Memory depends upon continuity, since if time consisted of discrete instants, "all but the feeling of the present instant would be utterly non-existent," (4.641) but there is little other distinguishable order. "It is important to remember that we have no intuitive power of distinguishing between one subjective mode of cognition and another; and hence often think that something is presented to us as a picture, while it is really constructed from slight data by the understanding. This is the case with dreams, as is shown by the frequent impossibility of giving an intelligible account of one without adding something which we feel was not in the dream itself. Many dreams of which the waking memory makes elaborate and consistent stories, must probably have been in fact mere jumbles of these feelings of the ability to recognize this and that." (5.302)

vi. EMOTION

Emotions, like feelings, are reactions to signs. Logically, emotions are represented by "emotional interpretant[s]," (5.475)[77] that is, by the arousal of signs in interpreters.[78] The emotional interpretant involves much more than feeling, and usually leads to effort, called by Peirce the "energetic interpretant." Ostensibly, in the case of an emotion, the action of the energetic interpretant is at least partially inhibitive.

"Now, when our nervous system is excited in a complicated way, there being a relation between the elements of the excitation, the result is a single harmonious disturbance which I call an emotion. Thus, the various sounds made by the instruments of an orchestra strike upon the ear, and the result is a peculiar musical emotion, quite distinct from the sounds themselves. This emotion is essentially the same thing as an hypothetic inference, and every hypothetic inference involves the formation of such an emotion." (2.643)

"An emotion . . . comes much later in the development of thought [than a sensation][79]—I mean further from the first beginning of the cognition of its object—and the thoughts which determine it already have motions corresponding to them in the brain, or the chief ganglion; consequently, it produces large movements in the body, and independently of its representative value, strongly affects the current of thought. The animal motions to which I allude, are, in the first place and obviously, blushing, blenching, staring, smiling, scowling, pouting, laughing, weeping, sobbing, wriggling, flinching, trembling, being petrified, sighing, sniffing, shrugging, groaning, heartsinking, trepidation, swelling of the heart, etc. To these may, perhaps, he added, in the second place, other more complicated actions, which nevertheless spring from a direct impulse and not from deliberation." (5.293)

"Everything in which we take the least interest creates in us its own particular emotion, however slight this may be. This emotion is a sign and

---

[77] See chap. III, D, ii.
[78] See chap. III, D, i.
[79] See this chapter, C.

a predicate of the thing." (5.308) For example, "if a man is angry, his anger implies, in general, no determinate and constant character in its object. But, on the other hand, it can hardly be questioned that there is some relative character in the outward thing which makes him angry, and a little reflection will serve to show that his anger consists in his saying to himself, 'this thing is vile, abominable, etc.', and that it is rather a mark of returning reason to say, 'I am angry.' In the same way any emotion is a predicate concerning some object." (5.247) Emotion, then, is an energetic reaction to some outward object, or to some quality of an outward object, which is capable of arousing an energetic interpretant.

D. General Conceptions

"Very different from both feelings and from reaction-sensations or disturbances of feeling are general conceptions." (6.20) By general conceptions Peirce meant the rational processes of the mind. "The cloudiness of psychological notions may be corrected by connecting them with physiological conceptions," (6.22) and this is no less true of the higher psychological functions than it is of the lower. "General conceptions arise upon the formation of habits in the nerve-matter, which are molecular changes consequent upon its activity and probably connected with its nutrition." One physical property of protoplasm is that it takes habits, (6.254)[80] and another is that it feels.[81] "It not only feels but exercises all the functions of mind." (6.255) "Intellectual power is nothing but facility in taking habits and in following them in cases essentially analogous to, but in nonessentials widely remote from, the normal cases of connections of feelings under which those habits were formed." (6.20)

"The one primary and fundamental law of mental action consists in a tendency to generalization. Feeling tends to spread; connections between feelings awaken feelings; neighboring feelings become assimilated; ideas are apt to reproduce themselves. These are so many formulations of the one law of the growth of mind. When a disturbance of feeling takes place, we have a consciousness of gain, the gain of experience; and a new disturbance will be apt to assimilate itself to the one that preceded it. Feelings, by being excited, become more easily excited, especially in the ways in which they have previously been excited. The consciousness of such a habit constitutes a general conception." (6.21)

[80] See this chapter, C, i.
[81] See this chapter, B, i.

But if mental action has a physiological basis, it is also autonomous at its own level; the higher mental functions can also be given a psychological explanation. The mechanism of psychological reactions may be physiological, "but the starting-point of all our reasoning is not in [the] sense-impressions,[82] but in our percepts.[83] When we first wake up to the fact that we are thinking beings and can exercise some control over our reasonings, we have to set out upon our intellectual travels from the home where we already find ourselves. Now, this home is the parish of percepts. It is not inside our skulls, either, but out in the open. It is the external world that we directly observe. What passes within we only know as it is mirrored in external objects."[84] It is not merely in these external objects, or "generalized percepts,"[85] that general conceptions consist; it is rather in certain aspects of them, their formal properties. General conceptions are the supreme functions of the mind, and "all supremacy of mind is of the nature of Form." (4.611)

i. IDEAS: JUDGMENT AND COGNITION

The order of dependence in the cognitive process reads: (*a*) ideas, (*b*) judgment, and (*c*) cognition. There can be no judgment without ideas, and there can be no cognition without judgment. We shall treat of them, therefore, in that order.

(*a*) All general conceptions involve ideas. By ideas, Peirce meant something akin to the Platonic ideas and the Aristotelian forms: universals independent of the mind and apprehended by the mind as concepts, or, as he termed them, the real relations of the external world, the ideal being of a world of possibility.[86] "Now every simple idea is composed of one of three classes" (5.7) or "elements" (6.135); "and a compound idea is in most cases predominantly of one of those classes." (5.7) "The first is its intrinsic quality as a feeling. The second is the energy with which it affects other ideas. . . . The third element is the tendency of an idea to bring along other ideas. with it." (6.135)

"As an idea spreads, its power of affecting other ideas gets rapidly reduced; but its intrinsic quality remains nearly unchanged. It is long years

---

[82] Peirce did not distinguish between sense impressions and feeling. See this chapter, B, i.
[83] See this chapter, B, iii.
[84] Review of Karl Pearson, *The Grammar of Science,* in *Popular Science Monthly,* 58 (1901), 296.
[85] *Ibid.*
[86] See chap. IV, C, ii.

now since I last saw a cardinal in his robes; and my memory of their color has become much dimmed. The color itself, however, is not remembered as dim." (6.136) "A finite interval of time generally contains an innumerable series of feelings; and when these become welded together in association, the result is a general idea."(6.137)[87]

"The first character of a general idea so resulting is that it is living feeling. A continuum of this feeling, infinitesimal in duration, but still embracing innumerable parts, and also, though infinitesimal, entirely unlimited, is immediately present. And in its absence of boundedness a vague possibility of more than is present is directly felt." (6.138)

"Second, in the presence of this continuity of feeling, nominalistic maxims appear futile.[88] There is no doubt about one idea affecting another, when we can directly perceive the one gradually modified and shaping itself into the other. Nor can there any longer be any difficulty about one idea resembling another, when we can pass along the continuous field of quality from one to the other and back again to the point which we had marked." (6.139) When one idea affects another, "the affected idea is attached as a logical predicate to the affecting idea as subject. So when a feeling emerges into immediate consciousness, it always appears as a modification of a more or less general object already in the mind." (6.142)

"Third, consider the insistency of an idea. The insistency of a past idea with reference to the present is a quantity which is less the further back that past idea is, and rises to infinity as the past idea is brought up into coincidence with the present. . . . We must extend the law of insistency into the future . . . for it is the present that affects the future." (6.140) It is "habit, by virtue of which an idea is brought up into present consciousness by a bond that had already been established between it and another idea while it was still *in futuro*." (6.141)[89] It happens that, "wherever ideas come together they tend to weld into general ideas; and wherever they are generally connected, general ideas govern the connection; and these general ideas are living feelings spread out." (6.143)

Peirce concluded from this that "general ideas are not mere words, nor do they consist in this, that certain concrete facts will every time happen under certain descriptions of conditions; but they are just as much, or rather far more, living realities than the feelings themselves out of which they are concreted." (6.152)

---

[87] See this chapter, B, i.
[88] See chap. IV, C, i.
[89] See this chapter, C, i.

Having an understanding of what Peirce meant by the relations of ideas, as these occur in the mind, we may now turn to the physiological and psychological functions in terms of which ideas are entertained.

"When two ideas resemble one another, we say that they have something in common; part of the one is said to be identical with a part of the other. In what does that identity consist? Having closed both eyes, I open first one and then shut it and open the other, and I say that the two sensations are alike. How can the impressions of two nerves be judged to be alike? It appears to me that in order that that should become possible, the two nerve-cells must probably discharge themselves into one common nerve-cell. [Or, in other words,] two ideas are alike so far as the same nerve-cells have been concerned in the production of them. In short, the hypothesis is that resemblance consists in the identity of a common element, and that that identity lies in a part of the one idea and a part of the other idea being the feeling peculiar to the excitation of one or more nerve-cells." (1.388)[90]

Psychologically, there exists the power of the human mind to *originate* ideas that are true. "It seems incontestable that the mind of man is strongly adapted to the comprehension of the world; at least, so far as this goes, that certain conceptions, highly important for such a comprehension, naturally arise in his mind; and, without such a tendency, the mind could never have had any development at all." (6.417) This is not so unusual a conception, after all. "The chicken you say pecks by instinct. But if you are going to think every poor chicken endowed with an innate tendency toward a positive truth, why should you think that to man alone this gift is denied?" (5.591)

By the human mind in this connection Peirce did not mean the conscious mind; he meant a sort of general function in the *psyche*. Conception, or active thought, is individual. "We are accustomed to speak of ideas as reproduced, as passed from mind to mind, as similar or dissimilar to one another, and, in short, as if they were substantial things; nor can any reasonable objection be raised to such expressions." (6.105) But we must take "the word 'idea' in the sense of an event in an individual consciousness"—at least, when we are discussing the psychological apprehension of ideas. For there can be no doubt that Peirce firmly believed in the being of ideas independent of minds, and in fact of all psychological functioning.[91] The function of active thought introduces reason into the consideration of ideas. "The elements of every concept enter into logical thought at the gate of perception and make their exit at the gate of purposive action." (5.212) In other words, ideas are originated by the human mind, as suggested by the elements of perception, and they are tested by experience[92] and by reason in the process of thought.

We are now in a position to understand judgment and then cognition.

(*b*) "A judgment is an act of consciousness in which we recognize a belief." (2.435) "The actual calling to mind of the substance of a belief, not as personal to ourselves, but as holding good, or true, is a *judgment*." (4.53) Judgment, then, turns on belief,[93] and "The representation to ourselves that we have a specific habit of this kind is called a *judgment*." (3.160)

"A question often put is: What is the essence of a Judgment? A judgment is the mental act by which a judger seeks to impress upon himself the truth of a proposition. It is much the same as an act of asserting the proposition, or going before a notary and assuming formal responsibility for its truth, except that those acts are intended to affect others, while the judgment is only intended to affect oneself." (2.252) "Do we not all perceive that *judgment* is something very closely allied to *assertion*? That is the view that ordinary speech entertains. A man or woman will be heard to use the phrase, 'I says to myself.' That is, *judgment* is held to be either no more than an *assertion to oneself* or at any rate something very like that." (5.29)[94] In a judgment, the speaker and the listener are the same person. Psychologically, assertion is the assumption of responsibility for the truth of a proposition, where some evil consequences would attend the demonstration of its falsity. (5.31) "A mental judgment or inference must possess some degree of veracity." (5.141) Judgment is nothing more than the psychological aspect, or act, of assertion. (5.547)[95]

"Every new concept first comes to the mind in a judgment." (5.546) There is certainly no conception without judgment. (5.307) With this understanding of conception, we may turn to the broader problem of cognition.

(*c*) In a sense, cognition is the most complex of the three broad psychological functions of feeling, having sensations of reaction and cognizing. "In the first place every kind of consciousness enters into cognition. Feelings, in the sense in which alone they can be admitted as a great branch of mental phenomena, form the warp and woof of cognition, and even in

---

[92] See chap. V, A, ii.
[93] See this chapter, C, ii.
[94] See chap. II, D, i.
[95] See chap. III, C, i.

the objectionable sense of pleasure and pain, they are constituents of cognition. The will, in the form of attention, constantly enters, and the sense of reality or objectivity, which is what we have found ought to take the place of will, in the division of consciousness, is even more essential yet, if possible. But that element of cognition which is neither feeling nor the polar sense, is the consciousness of a process, and this in the form of the sense of learning, of acquiring, of mental growth is eminently characteristic of cognition. This is a kind of consciousness which cannot be immediate, because it covers a time, and that not merely because it continues through every instant of that time, but because it cannot be contracted into an instant. It differs from immediate consciousness as a melody does from one prolonged note. Neither can the consciousness of the two sides of an instant, of a sudden occurrence, in its individual reality, possibly embrace the consciousness of a process. This is the consciousness that binds our life together. It is the consciousness of synthesis." (1.381)

"Every cognition involves something represented, or that of which we are conscious, and some action or passion of the self whereby it becomes represented. The former shall be termed the objective, the latter the subjective, element of the cognition. The cognition itself is an intuition of its objective element, which may therefore be called, also, the immediate object. The subjective element is not necessarily immediately known." (5.238) Cognition occurs in terms of logic, more particularly, in terms of the propositions of a syllogism. "The cognition of a rule is not necessarily conscious, but is of the nature of a habit, acquired or congenital. The cognition of a case is of the general nature of a sensation; that is to say, it is something which comes up into present consciousness. The cognition of a result is of the nature of a decision to act in a particular way on a given occasion." (2.711)[96]

Cognition is dependable: we know outward things as they really are.[97] There is also the cognition of relations, (5.56)[98] in particular of the illative relation.[99] This is the element that is found in common in "learning, acquisition, memory and inference, synthesis." (1.376) The cognition of the illative relation, arising by a continuous process, is what is called thought. or reasoning. (5.267)

[96] For rule, case and result, see chap. III, C, I, (*b*).
[97] See chap. IV, C, ii.
[98] See this chapter, B, iii.
[99] See chap. III, C, i.

ii. THOUGHT

Peirce treated of thought in general, as a function of mentality, and then of reasoning in particular. We shall, in this section, consider thought as a function of mentality, but before we can do so we must remember that thought is not peculiarly mental. "Thought is not necessarily connected with a brain. It appears in the work of bees, of crystals, and throughout the purely physical world; and one can no more deny that it is really there, than that the colors, the shapes, etc., of objects are really there." (4.551) " . . . all thoughts are interconnected. The field of Thought, in its turn, is in every thought, confessed to be a sign of that great external power, that Universe, the Truth." (4.553 n.2)[100] But there is thought in the organic world, as well as in the inorganic. Not only is thought in the organic world, but it develops there. In fact, "the organism is only an instrument of thought," (5.315) for ". . . thoughts are *determinations* of the mind." (4.582) In other words, whereas mind is not essential to thought, thought is certainly essential to mind.

By logical reflection, Peirce meant "the observation of thoughts in their expressions." (3.490) "We have no power of thinking without signs," (5.265) and in fact "all thought must necessarily be in signs," (5.251) since "every thought must be interpreted in another." (5.253) The very meaning of a sign is that it is at least capable of being known. (5.254-8) Just "as there cannot be a General without Instances embodying it, so there cannot be thought without Signs." (4.551) ". . . Whenever we think, we have present to the consciousness some feeling, image, conception, or other representation, which serves as a sign. But it follows from our own existence (which is proved by the occurrence of ignorance and error)[101] that everything which is present to us is a phenomenal manifestation of ourselves. This does not prevent its being a phenomenon of something without us, just as a rainbow is at once a manifestation both of the sun and of the rain. When we think, then, we ourselves, as we are at that moment, appear as a sign. Now a sign has, as such, three references: first, it is a sign *to* some thought which interprets it; second, it is a sign *for* some object to which in that thought it is equivalent; third, it is a sign, *in* some respect or quality, which brings it into connection with its object." (5.283)[102]

"Let us ask what the three correlates are to which a thought-sign refers."

[100] See chap. V, C, iii.
[101] See chap. V, C, ii.
[102] See chap. III, B, i.

"When we think, to what thought does that thought-sign which is ourself address itself? It may, through the medium of outward expression, which it reaches perhaps only after considerable internal development, come to address itself to thought of another person. But whether this happens or not, it is always interpreted by a subsequent thought of our own. If, after any thought, the current of ideas flows on freely, it follows the law of mental association. In that case, each former thought suggests something to the thought which follows it, i.e., is the sign of something to this latter. Our train of thought may, it is true, be interrupted. But we must remember that, in addition to the principal element of thought at any moment, there are a hundred things in our mind to which but a small fraction of attention or consciousness is conceded. It does not, therefore, follow, because a new constituent of thought gets the uppermost that the train of thought which it displaces is broken off altogether. On the contrary, from our second principle, that there is no intuition or cognition not determined by previous cognitions, it follows that the striking in of a new experience is never an instantaneous affair, but is an *event* occupying time, and coming to pass by a continuous process. Its prominence in consciousness, therefore, must probably be the consummation of a growing process; and if so, there is no sufficient cause for the thought which had been the leading one just before, to cease abruptly and instantaneously. But if a train of thought ceases by gradually dying out, it freely follows its own law of association as long as it lasts, and there is no moment at which there is a thought belonging to this series, subsequently to which there is not a thought which interprets or repeats it. There is no exception, therefore, to the law that every thought-sign is translated or interpreted in a subsequent one, unless it be that all thought comes to an abrupt and final end in death." (5.284)

"The next question is: For what does the thought-sign stand—what does it name—what is its *suppositum*? The outward thing, undoubtedly, when a real outward thing is thought of. But still, as the thought is determined by a previous thought of the same object, it only refers to the thing through denoting this previous thought. Let us suppose, for example, that Toussaint is thought of, and first thought of as a *negro*, but not distinctly as a man. If this distinctness is afterwards added, it is through the thought that a *negro* is a *man*; that is to say, the subsequent thought, *man*, refers to the outward thing by being predicated of that previous thought, *negro*, which has been had of that thing. If we afterwards think of Toussaint as a general, then we think that this negro, this man, was a general. And so in every case the subsequent thought denotes what was thought in the previous thought." (5.285)

"The thought-sign stands for its object in the respect which is thought; that is to say, this respect is the immediate object of consciousness in the thought, or, in other words, it is the thought itself, or at least what the thought is thought to be in the subsequent thought to which it is a sign." (5.286) That is as far as logic can go in the explication of the mental processes of thought. We know that formal logic must be taken for granted, and we shall see that no facts of the mind and its operation can controvert those of formal logic. Nevertheless, "the syllogism is not intended to represent the mind, as to its life or deadness, but only as to the relation of its different judgments concerning the same thing. And it should be added that the relation between syllogism and thought does not spring from considerations of formal logic, but from those of psychology." (5.329)

From the point of view of ontology, and more particularly of phenomenology, thought is thirdness. It is a definite element of things as well as of minds, and as such is not reducible to firstness, secondness, or both. (5.208)[103] Thoughts are neither qualities nor facts, since they are general; they have another side which makes them into what may be termed general facts. Epistemologically, thought is entirely dependent upon truth. Only true thinking is thinking. "A fallacy is . . . a supposititious thinking, a thinking that parades as a self-development of thought but is in fact begotten by some other sire than reason. . . . " For "thinking ceases to be Thought when true thought disowns it. A self-development of Thought takes the course that thinking will take that is sufficiently deliberate, and is not truly a self-development if it slips from being the thought of one object-thought to being the thought of another object-thought. It is, in the geological sense, a 'fault'—an incomformability in the strata of thinking." (4.10)

Physiologically speaking, "Thinking, as cerebration, is no doubt subject to the general laws of nervous action. When a group of nerves are stimulated, the ganglions with which the group is most intimately connected on the whole are thrown into an active state, which in turn usually occasions movements of the body. The stimulation continuing, the irritation spreads from ganglion to ganglion (usually increasing meantime). Soon, too, the parts first excited begin to show fatigue; and thus for a double reason the bodily activity is of a changing kind. When the stimulus is withdrawn, the excitement quickly subsides. It results from these facts that when a nerve

[103] See chap. IV, A, ii.

is affected, the reflex action, if it is not at first of the sort to remove the irritation, will change its character again and again until the irritation is removed; and then the action will cease.

"Now, all vital processes tend to become easier on repetition. Along whatever path a nervous discharge has once taken place, in that path a new discharge is the more likely to take place. Accordingly, when an irritation of the nerves is repeated, all the various actions which have taken place on previous similar occasions are the more likely to take place now, and those are most likely to take place which have most frequently taken place on those previous occasions. Now, the various actions which did not remove the irritation may have previously sometimes been performed and sometimes not; but the action which removes the irritation must have always been performed, because the action must have every time continued until it was performed. Hence a strong habit of responding to the given irritation in this particular way must quickly be established. A habit so acquired may be transmitted by inheritance." (3.155-158)[104]

"One of the most important of our habits is that one by virtue of which certain classes of stimuli throw us at first, at least, into a purely cerebral activity. Very often it is not an outward sensation but only a fancy which starts the train of thought. In other words, the irritation instead of being peripheral is visceral. In such a case the activity has for the most part the same character; an inward action removes the inward excitation. A fancied conjuncture leads us to fancy an appropriate line of action. It is found that such events, though no external action takes place, strongly contribute to the formation of habits of really acting in the fancied way when the fancied occasion really arises." (3.158-159) The development from judgment to belief-habit "begins by being vague, special, and meagre; it becomes more precise, general, and full, without limit. The process of this development, so far as it takes place in the imagination, is called *thought*." (3.160)

We have now considered thought from the standpoint of logic, phenomenology and physiology. It remains only to consider its relations to lower psychological levels before proceeding to a consideration of it on its own footing, namely, as reasoning.

"Sensation and the power of abstraction or attention may be regarded as, in one sense, the sole constituents of all thought." (5.295) "Thought is a thread of melody running through the succession of our sensations." (5.395) "By the force of attention, an emphasis is put upon one of the ob-

---

[104] For the physiology of habit, upon which this account depends, see this chapter, C, i. See also 6.278 ff.

jective elements of consciousness. This emphasis is, therefore, not itself an object of immediate consciousness; and in this respect it differs entirely from a feeling. Therefore, since the emphasis, nevertheless, consists in some effect upon consciousness, and so can exist only so far as it affects our knowledge; and since an act cannot be supposed to determine that which precedes it in time, this act can consist only in the capacity which the cognition emphasized has for producing an effect upon memory, or otherwise influencing subsequent thought. This is confirmed by the fact that attention is a matter of continuous quantity; for continuous quantity, so far as we know it, reduces itself in the last analysis to time. Accordingly, we find that attention does, in fact, produce a very great effect upon subsequent thought. In the first place, it strongly affects memory, a thought being remembered for a longer time the greater the attention originally paid to it. In the second place, the greater the attention, the closer the connection and the more accurate the logical sequence of thought. In the third place, by attention a thought may be recovered which has been forgotten. From these facts, we gather that attention is the power by which thought at one time is connected with and made to relate to thought at another time; or, to apply the conception of thought as a sign, that it is the *pure demonstrative application* of a thought-sign." (5.295) Thus synthetic consciousness, "binding time together" yields the sense of learning and of thought. (1.377)

The purpose of thought lies in things beyond itself. "Herbart made a statement very nearly correct when he said that a *thought* (*Begriff*), in the sense in which alone logic deals with thoughts, is not a thinking but that which a thinking brings before the mind." (2.53) The function of thought is "the production of belief" (5.394)[105] and "habits of action." (5.400) " . . . We may say that the purpose of signs—which is the purpose of thought—is to bring truth to expression. . . . It might be objected that to say this is to say that the production of *propositions*, rather than that of *inferences*, is the primary object. But the *production* of propositions is of the general nature of inference, so that inference is the essential function of the cognitive mind." (2.444 n.)

iii. REASONING

We come now to an examination of reasoning. Peirce frankly admitted that he did not believe that "in the present state of psychology, anybody

[105] See this chapter, C, ii.

knows much about the operations of the mind in reasoning. There is no easy way in which such knowledge can be had." (2.184) The instinct, Peirce steadily maintained, is more dependable than the power of reasoning, and his overwhelming interest in the latter seemed to depend upon the potentialities of reasoning rather than its accomplishments; for, unlike instinct, reasoning is susceptible of improvement. Peirce adduced Hume and F. H. Bradley as witnesses to the truth of the assertion that "reason is a mere succedaneum to be used where instinct is wanting." (6.500) "Every race of animals is provided with instincts well adapted to its needs, and especially to strengthening the stock. It is wonderful how unerring these instincts are. Man is no exception in this respect; but man is so continually getting himself into novel situations that he needs, and is supplied with, a subsidiary faculty of *reasoning* for bringing instinct to bear upon situations to which it does not directly apply. This faculty is a very imperfect one in respect to fallibility; but then it is only needed to bridge short gaps. Every step has to be reviewed and criticized." (6.497)

The faculty which man possesses of reasoning is "so called from its embodying in some measure Reason, or Νους, as a something manifesting itself in the mind, in the history of mind's development, and in nature." (1.615) "Reasoning cannot possibly be divorced from *logic*; because, whenever a man reasons, he thinks that he is drawing a conclusion such as would be justified in every analogous case. He therefore cannot really *infer* without having a notion of a class of possible inferences, all of which are logically *good*. That distinction of *good* and *bad* he always has in mind when he infers." (5.108) "The object of reasoning is to find out, from the consideration of what we already know, something else which we do not know," (5.365) "to proceed from the recognition of the truth we already know to the knowledge of novel truth." (4.476) Consequently, "reasoning is good if it be such as to give a true conclusion from true premisses, and not otherwise." (5.365)[106] But we are concerned in this chapter only with the psychological aspects of reasoning, and for this there is a special set of presuppositions, or first principles, "for the justification of which we have to make a last appeal to instinctive thought." (4.475)

"We can never really reason without entertaining a logical theory. This is called our *logica utens*." (4.476) "Every reasoner has some general idea of what good reasoning is. This constitutes a theory of logic: the scholastics

---

[106] "Thus, the question of validity is purely one of fact and not of thinking." (5.365) In Peirce's understanding, the psychological process of reasoning presupposes the whole of logic. See chap. III.

called it the reasoner's *logica utens*. Every reasoner whose attention has been considerably drawn to his inner life must soon become aware of this." (2.186) "Reasoning is a process in which the reasoner is conscious that a judgment, the conclusion, is determined by other judgment or judgments, the premises, according to a general habit of thought, which he may not be able precisely to formulate, but which he approves as conducive to true knowledge . . .[107] Without this logical approval, the process, although it may be closely analogous to reasoning in other respects, lacks the essence of reasoning." (2.773)

"The data from which inference sets out and upon which all reasoning depends are the *perceptual facts*, which are the intellect's fallible record of the *percepts*, or 'evidence of the senses.'[108] It is these percepts alone upon which we can absolutely rely, and that not as representative of any underlying reality other than themselves." (2.143) "Reasoning does not begin until a judgment has been formed; for the antecedent cognitive operations are not subject to logical approval or disapproval, being subconscious, or not sufficiently near the surface of consciousness, and therefore uncontrollable. Reasoning, therefore, begins with premises which are adopted as representing percepts, or generalizations of such percepts. All the reasoner's conclusions ought to refer solely to the percepts, or rather to propositions expressing facts of perception." (2.773) Although Peirce said that he was willing to take the psychologist's word for it that inferences could not be *perceived*, yet he maintained nevertheless that he did not see "that the logician can do better than to say that he *perceives* that when a copulative proposition is given, such as 'A is a horse and A has a bay color', any member of the copulation may be omitted without changing the proposition from true to false." (5.164) Inference is not only perceptual; it is emotional. For "when a thing resembling this thing is presented to us, a similar emotion arises; hence, we immediately infer that the latter is like the former." (5.308)[109]

"The first step of inference usually consists in bringing together certain propositions which we believe to be true, but which, supposing the inference to be a new one, we have hitherto not considered together, or not as united in the same way. This step is called *colligation*." (2.442)[110] "In inference one belief not only follows *after* another, but follows *from* it." (4.53) "If a belief is produced for the first time directly after a judgment or colligation of judg-

---

[107] *Logica utens*, then, merely employs the syllogism as a rule of thumb. See chap. III, C, i.
[108] See this chapter, B, iii.
[109] See this chapter, C, vi.
[110] See chap. III, C, ii.

ments and is suggested by them, then that belief must be considered as the result of and as following from those judgments. The idea which is the matter of the belief is suggested by the idea in those judgments according to some habit of association, and the peculiar character of believing the idea really *is* so, is derived from the same element in the judgments. Thus, inference has at least two elements: the one is the suggestion of one idea by another according to the law of association, while the other is the carrying forward of the *asserting* element of judgment, the holding for true, from the first judgment to the second." (4.55) In other words, "A judgment is formed; and under the influence of a belief-habit this gives rise to a new judgment, indicating an addition to belief. Such a process is called an *inference*." (3.160)

All psychological reasoning involves abstraction. We have already seen hypostatic abstraction described as part of the method of discovery in logic.[111] Precisive abstraction is part of the psychological process. (2.428) "The terms 'precision' and 'abstraction', which were formerly applied to every kind of separation, are now limited not merely to mental separation, but to that which arises from *attention to* one element and *neglect of* the other." (1.549)[112] In this sense "it is applied to a psychological act by which, for example, on seeing a theatre, one is led to call up images of other theatres which blend into a sort of composite in which the special features of each are obliterated. Such obliteration is called precisive abstraction." (4.463)

The abstractive process, psychologically considered, cannot be arbitrary. "For reasoning is essentially a voluntary act, over which we exercise control." (2.144) "We are, so to speak, responsible for the correctness of our reasonings. That is to say, unless we deliberately approve of them as rational, they cannot properly be called reasonings. But for this purpose, all that is necessary is that we should, in each case, compare premisses and conclusion, and observe that the relation between the facts expressed in the premisses involves the relation between facts implied in our confidence in the conclusion. What we call a reasoning is something upon which we place a stamp of rational approval. In order to do that, we must know what the reasoning is. In that sense it must be a conscious act." (2.183) Consequently, "to say that an operation of the mind is controlled is to say that it is, in a special sense, a conscious operation; and this no doubt is the consciousness of reasoning." (5.441) Inference, in this light, may be defined as "the con-

---

[111] See chap. III, D, iii.
[112] See also 2.428.

scious and controlled adoption of a belief as a consequence of other knowledge." (2.442)

"In all reasoning, there is a more or less conscious reference to a general method." (2.204) The governance of reasoning by logic has its effect from the level of physiology as well as at the higher psychological levels. "All cerebration depends upon movements of neurites that strictly obey certain physical laws, and thus all expressions of thought, both external and internal, receive a physical explanation." (6.465) Logical inference centers about the syllogism,[113] and Peirce's theory thus would call for a psychological correspondence of some sort for the syllogism. "But does the mind in fact go through the syllogistic process? It is certainly very doubtful whether a conclusion—as something existing in the mind independently, like an image—suddenly displaces two premises existing in the mind in a similar way. But it is a matter of constant experience, that if a man is made to believe in the premisses, in the sense that he will act from them and will say that they are true, under favorable conditions he will also be ready to act from the conclusion and to say that that is true. Something, therefore, takes place within the organism which is equivalent to the syllogistic process." (5.268) "There are . . . three fundamentally different kinds of reasoning, Deduction . . . Induction . . . and Retroduction [or] abduction." (1.65) We may give a word to each of these, beginning with a word for each of the propositional elements of the syllogism.

First, then, the leading principle in reasoning.[114] "When the inference is first drawn, the leading principle is not present to the mind, but the habit it formulates is active in such a way that, upon contemplating the believed premiss, by a sort of perception the conclusion is judged to be true." (3.164) "Though the leading principle itself is not present to the mind, we are generally conscious of inferring on some general principle." (3.164 n.1) "The particular habit of mind which governs this or that inference may be formulated in a proposition whose truth depends on the validity of the inferences which the habit determines; and such a formula is [in psychology] called a *guiding principle* of [that] inference." (5.367)

The premise[115] consists in the judgment which under the influence of a belief-habit gives rise to a new judgment. (3.160)

The conclusion[116] "is a general idea to which at the suggestion of certain

[113] See chap. III, C, i.
[114] See chap. III, C, ii, (*a*).
[115] See chap. III, C, ii, (*b*).
[116] See chap. III, C, ii, (*f*).

facts a certain general habit of reasoning has induced us to believe that a realization belongs." (2.146)

The psychological operation of deduction "consists in constructing an icon or diagram the relations of whose parts shall present a complete analogy with those of the parts of the object of reasoning, of experimenting upon this image in the imagination, and of observing the result so as to discover unnoticed and hidden relations among the parts." (3.363) "In deduction the mind is under the dominion of a habit or association by virtue of which a general idea suggests in each case a corresponding reaction. . . . That is the way the hind legs of a frog, separated from the rest of the body, reason, when you pinch them. It is the lowest form of psychical manifestation." (6.144) In the highest form of conscious mentality, "*Deduction* is that mode of reasoning which examines the state of things asserted in the premisses, forms a diagram of that state of things, perceives in the parts of that diagram relations not explicitly mentioned in the premisses, satisfies itself by mental experiments upon the diagram that these relations would always subsist, or at least would do so in a certain proportion of cases, and concludes their necessary, or probable, truth." (1.66)[117]

The psychological operation of induction "takes place when the reasoner already holds a theory more or less problematically (ranging from a pure interrogative apprehension to a strong leaning mixed with ever so little doubt); and having reflected that if that theory be true, then under certain conditions certain phenomena ought to appear (the stranger and less antecedently credible the better), proceeds to *experiment*, that is, to realize those conditions and watch for the predicted phenomena." (2.775) "By induction, a habit becomes established. Certain sensations, all involving one general idea, are followed each by the same reaction; and an association becomes established, whereby that general idea gets to be followed uniformly by that reaction." (6.145) "Induction, therefore, is the logical formula which expresses the physiological process of formation of a habit." (2.643)[118]

The psychological operation of abduction "is the process of forming an explanatory hypothesis." (5.171) Hypothetic inference is associated with emotion[119] "and every hypothetic inference involves the presence of such an emotion." (2.643) "Upon finding himself confronted with a phenomena unlike what he would have expected under the circumstances, he [the reasoner] looks over its features and notices some remarkable character or

---

[117] For a further elaboration of psychological deduction, see also 5.161 and 2.778.
[118] For a further elaboration of psychological induction, see also 1.67 and all of 2.775.
[119] See this chapter, C, vi.

relation among them, which he at once recognizes as being characteristic of some conception with which his mind is already stored, so that a theory is suggested which would *explain* (that is, render necessary), that which is surprising in the phenomena." (2.776)[120]

Such are the various psychological varieties of reasoning, and we can see that they depend upon logic, on the one hand, and lead to knowledge and to action, on the other. "The object of reasoning is to find out, from the consideration of what we already know, something else which we do not know." (5.365) "The purpose of reasoning is to proceed from the recognition of the truth we already know to the knowledge of novel truth." (4.476) ". . . the whole function of thought is to produce habits of action." (5.400) and "all conclusions of reasoning partake of the general nature of expectations of the future." (2.145) "The genuine synthetic consciousness, or the sense of the process of learning, which is the preëminent ingredient and quintessence of the reason, has its physiological basis quite evidently in the most characteristic property of the nervous system, the power of taking habits."[121] But at the higher level of psychology, the level of conscious mentality, "The interest which the uniformities of Nature have for an animal measures his place in the scale of intelligence." (6.406)

iv. UNCONSCIOUS THOUGHT AND THE SOUL

When we have done with our analysis of conscious and controlled reasoning, we have not completed the examination of reasoning. "Most of us are in the habit of thinking that consciousness and psychic life are the same thing and otherwise greatly to overrate the functions of consciousness." (6.489)[122] "There are," said Peirce, "mental operations which are as completely beyond our control as the growth of our hair," (5.130) and the "subconscious feelings . . . *are* unified so far as they are brought into *quate-*consciousness at all." (6.228) "That step of thought, which consists in interpreting an image by a symbol, is one of which logic neither needs nor can give any account, since it is subconscious, uncontrollable, and not subject to criticism. Whatever account there is to be given of it is the psychologist's affair. But it is evident that the image must be connected in some way with a symbol if any proposition is to be true of it." (4.479)

The fact is that "thinking no more needs the actual presence in the mind

---

[120] For further on psychological induction, see also 1.68.

[121] See this chapter, C, i.

[122] Peirce observed here that the "negative reply" given to the question, "Does 'Consciousness' Exist [William James, *Essays in Radical Empiricism*, chap. I], is, in itself, no novelty."

of what is thought than knowing the English language means that at every instant while one knows it the whole dictionary is actually present to his mind." (4.622) Thought goes on in the subconscious mind, and there is "subconscious reasoning—by which I mean an operation which would be a reasoning if it were fully conscious and deliberate." (2.172) "There are, I am prepared to maintain, operations of the mind which are logically exactly analogous to inferences excepting only that they are unconscious and therefore uncontrollable and therefore not subject to criticism." (5.108)

Peirce's contentions were in opposition to "the old psychology which identified the soul with the ego, declared its absolute simplicity, and held that its faculties were mere names for logical divisions of human activity. This was all unadulterated fancy. The observation of facts has now taught us that the ego is a mere wave in the soul, a superficial and small feature, that the soul may contain several personalities and is as complex as the brain itself, and that the faculties, while not exactly definable and not absolutely fixed, are as real as are the different convolutions of the cortex." (1.112) "It is the instincts, the sentiments, that make the substance of the soul. Cognition is only its surface, its locus of contact with what is external to it." (1.628)

Similarly, the older logicians "imagine that an idea has to be connected with a brain, or has to inhere in a 'soul.' This is preposterous: the idea does not belong to the soul; it is the soul that belongs to the idea. The soul does for the idea just what the cellulose does for the beauty of the rose; that is to say, it affords it opportunity." (1.216) It is possible, in other words, for ideas to be ensouled as well as embodied. (1.218)

Although Peirce failed to elaborate his notions of the role of the subconscious mental life, he held significant views as to its importance. Conscience, for example, was classified by him not with the data of ethics or of religion but with psychology; he held it to be a psychological problem. (1.577) Moreover, it was a special psychological problem in that it was asserted to be part of the subconscious. "Conscience really belongs to the subconscious man, to that part of the soul which is hardly distinct in different individuals, a sort of community-consciousness, or public spirit, not absolutely one and the same in different citizens, and yet not by any means independent in them. Conscience has been created by experience just as any knowledge is; but it is modified by further experience only with secular slowness." (1.56)[123]

---

[123] Peirce's understanding of the subconscious mind anticipates the Freudian school in many respects.

E. GENERAL CONCLUSIONS

There are many inferences to be made from the various topics discussed in this chapter, inferences of enormous suggestibility both to psychology and to other fields; but these threads Peirce left to others to follow. The conclusions which Peirce himself drew from his studies in psychology concern the highest functions in the psychological field: namely, the elusive property called personality, and that property of ideas which, in this connection, he named the law of mind.

i. PERSONALITY

In demonstrating the spatial extensity of feeling, Peirce admits that protoplasm has feeling, but "plainly no *personality*." (6.133) " . . . Each personality is based upon a 'bundle of habits'." (6.228) "The consciousness of a general idea has a certain 'unity of the ego' in it, which is identical when it passes from one mind to another. It is, therefore, quite analogous to a person; and, indeed, a person is only a particular kind of general idea. (6.270) What is necessary "to the existence of a person is that the feelings out of which he is constructed should be in close enough connection to influence one another." (6.271) For "personality is some kind of coördination or connection of ideas. . . . This personality, like any general idea, is not a thing to be apprehended in an instant. It has to be lived in time; nor can any finite time embrace it in all its fullness. Yet in each infinitesimal interval it is present and living, though specially colored by the immediate feelings of that moment. Personality, so far as it is apprehended in a moment, is immediate self-consciousness." (6.155)

"What distinguishes a man from a word? There is a distinction doubtless. The material qualities, the forces which constitute the pure denotative application, and the meaning of the human sign, are all exceedingly complicated in comparison with those of the word. But these differences are only relative." (5.313) The important difference, perhaps, is "that a person is not absolutely an individual. His thoughts are what he is 'saying to himself,' that is, saying to that other self that is just coming into life in the flow of time." (5.421) Reasoning, even within the self, is dualistic in that it involves the logical speaker and the logical listener,[124] even though these may be combined in the same person. A word, however, is absolutely individual in that it is a sign.[125] In comparing a personality with a word,

---

[124] See chap. III, D, i.
[125] See chap. III, B, ii.

Peirce did not mean that there was anything elusive or vague about personality. On the contrary, it is exceedingly concrete and easily recognizable. This fact is brought out by the contact between two personalities. "The recognition by one person of another's personality takes place by means to some extent identical with the means by which he is conscious of his own personality. The idea of the second personality, which is as much as to say that second personality itself, enters within the field of direct consciousness of the first person, and is as immediately perceived as his ego, though less strongly. At the same time, the opposition between the two persons is perceived, so that the externality of the second is recognized." (6.160)

Lastly, there is character. "The character of a man . . . consists in the ideas that he will conceive and in the efforts that he will make, and which only develops as the occasions actually arise. Yet in all his life long no son of Adam has ever fully manifested what there was in him." (1.615) The co-ordination or connection of ideas, which we have already mentioned, "implies a teleological harmony in ideas, and in the case of personality this teleology is more than a mere purposive pursuit of a predeterminate end; it is a developmental teleology. This is personal character. A general idea, living and conscious now, it is already determinative of acts in the future to an extent to which it is not now conscious." (6.156) Character, then, is a question of how we are prepared to face the future.

ii. THE LAW OF MIND

The field of psychology is of necessity incomplete in itself. The habit of reasoning leads to the expectation of law. (2.146) The study of psychology is a detour, albeit an important one, from the facts of actuality and the theories of logic and ontology and back again to them. Nothing subjective is self-validating, but all inward activity calls for an outward reference. The idealist denies this, and places all his faith in the dependability of consciousness for the purposes of desire, judgment and reasoning. "The answer to all such arguments is that no desire can possibly desire its own satisfaction, no judgment can judge itself to be true, and no reasoning can conclude that it is itself sound. For all these propositions stand on the same footing and must stand or fall together." (5.86) For example, consider the case of judgment. "If any judgment judges itself to be true, all judgments—or at least all assertory judgments—do so likewise; for there is no ground of discrimination between assertory judgments in this respect. Either therefore the judgment, J, and the judgment 'I say that J is true' are the same for all judgments or for none. But if they are identical, their denials are identical. But their denials are respectively, 'J is not true' and 'I do not say that J is true', which are very different. Consequently, no judgment judges itself to be true."[126] The mental, or psychological, factor is dependent upon something objective and outside consciousness to be genuine.

It is clear, then, that the mind is oriented toward objective propositions.[127] The conclusion toward which Peirce's psychology has led is not in the true sense a psychological proposition at all, but rather one which lies in the field of logic, more specifically in Speculative Rhetoric.[128] "Logical analysis applied to mental phenomena shows that there is but one law of mind, namely, that ideas tend to spread continuously and to affect certain others which stand to them in a peculiar relation of affectibility. In this spreading they lose intensity, and especially the power of affecting others, but gain generality and become welded with other ideas." (6.104) In other words, "an idea can only be affected by an idea in continuous connection with it. By anything but an idea, it cannot be affected at all." (6.158) "The psychological phenomena of intercommunication between two minds has been unfortunately little studied. . . . But the very extraordinary insight which some persons are able to gain of others from indications so slight that it is difficult to ascertain what they are is certainly rendered more comprehensible by the view here taken." (6.161)

Lastly, there is the relationship of mind and the future. There is every reason to believe that we have our feelings in common not only with other human beings but also with the lower animals, such as the bull and the dog. (1.314) Yet we have one great advantage over all other animals, and this advantage holds within it the possibility of mental progress. This advantage is the making of mistakes. It is a truth well worthy of rumination that all the intellectual development of man rests upon the circumstance that all our action is subject to error. *Errare est humanum* is of all commonplaces the most familiar. Inanimate things do not err at all; and the lower animals very little. Instinct is all but unerring; but reason in all vitally important matters is a treacherous guide. This tendency to error, when you put it under the microscope of reflection, is seen to consist of fortuitous variations of our actions in time. But it is apt to escape our attention that on such fortuitous variation our intellect is nourished and grows. For without such fortuitous variation, habit-taking would be impossible; and intellect consists in a plasticity of habit." (6.86)

"Instinct is capable of development and growth——though by a move-

---

[126] For the proof of Peirce's contention, see the remainder of the quoted paragraph.
[127] See chap. IV, C, ii.
[128] See chap. III, D, above.

ment which is slow in the proportion in which it is vital; and this development takes place upon lines which are altogether parallel to those of reasoning. And just as reasoning springs from experience, so the development of sentiment arises from the soul's Inward and Outward Experiences. Not only is it of the same nature as the development of cognition; but it chiefly takes place through the instrumentality of cognition. The soul's deeper parts can only be reached through its surface. In this way the eternal forms, that mathematics and philosophy and the other sciences make us acquainted with, will by slow percolation gradually reach the very core of one's being; and will come to influence our lives; and this they will do, not because they involve truths of merely vital importance, but because they are ideal and eternal verities." (1.648)

iii. SUMMARY OF THE CHAPTER

Psychology has a well-defined field of its own but is dependent to some extent upon logic, ontology and epistemology. Logic introduces the capacity of interpreter and the distinction between interpreter and interpretant. The logical triad of categories, together with the ontological triad, leads to the psychological divisions of feelings, sensations of reactions, and general conceptions. Epistemology requires that experience be employed as a key to the psychological subject from the external world. From these suggestions, the mind may be regarded as the widest truth-function of logic, a function of the external world.

Feeling, the first psychological category, may be approached as a sign in the subject of chance in the world. It is the simple impression of consciousness. To be conscious is to feel, which is all that consciousness means. Self-consciousness is a knowledge of ourselves presented as external. Introspection is a matter of inference. The content of consciousness is the percept. It is experience proper; what we are forced to accept.

Sensations of reaction, the second psychological category, involve a feeling of effort. They involve the subject's response to stimuli of external provenance. Habit has a physiological basis in molecular fatigue and derangement. Habit requires that the effect of the inner upon the outer world shall be indirect. A practical belief is a habit of which we are conscious. Belief is based on reason; we can believe only what we must. A theoretical belief is an expectation. Doubt is an uncomfortable state of struggle, bridging the gap between the ease of belief and the incentive to thought. Instinct, or intuition, is a natural tendency toward the truth.

They all depend upon the validity of induction, and can be modified. But they are difficult to distinguish from mediated cognitions. The purpose of desire is to remove stimuli. Desire is general and unspecified. It is vague but implies a tendency toward volition. Volition is almost pure duality, felt as a sensation or a polar sense. Shock and self-control are species of will. The will is directed toward the future, hence away from reaction and toward ratiocination. An image is a sign, imagining is an expectation. Imagination is inhibited action or the opposite exertion of action. Memory involves worked-over images and other sensations, indistinguishable from outward manifestations by vividity or similar criteria. Emotions are reactions to signs, a harmonious disturbance of the nervous system. An emotion is a predicate of some object, the energetic reaction to it.

General conceptions, the third psychological category, depend upon rational processes, the tendency to generalization. Ideas tend to involve other ideas. They are living feelings, having continuity and insistency. The general function of the psyche has the power to initiate general ideas. A judgment is an act of consciousness in which a belief is recognized. The judger impresses upon himself the truth of a proposition. Cognition is the most complex mental function, involving the others. It involves the complex consciousness of synthesis. Thought is a function of mentality but is not subjective and not necessarily connected with a brain. Thought is thirdness, using the organism as an instrument. The field of thought is the truth. Reasoning sets out from percepts but consists in an instinct for following the logical forms of the syllogism. Not all higher mental functioning is conscious, however. Some mental operations are beyond our control. Subconscious thought is that which would be reasoning were it deliberate; it is uncontrolled inference. Thought is the surface of the soul, and the soul is a complex function of the psyche. The ego is a wave in the soul. Conscience belongs to the subconscious.

The psychology concludes with certain broad and suggestive observations. The personality is a bundle of habits, the immediate self-consciousness of a co-ordination of ideas. Words are more individual than persons. Character is how we are prepared to face the future. All psychological investigation takes off from extrapsychological topics, like logic and ontology, and detours back to their theories and facts. Psychology is not self-validating. The mind is oriented toward objective propositions and directed toward the future. We differ from the higher animals only in thought: to err is human. Intellect consists in a plasticity of habit-taking. Instincts, the soul's deeper parts, grow, but can be reached only through its surface.

CHAPTER VII

Methodology

A. PHILOSOPHICAL METHOD IN GENERAL

THE QUESTION OF WHETHER METHOD OR SYSTEM IS HISTORICALLY FIRST IN philosophy is a difficult one to answer. Certainly, from a logical point of view, the system is prior, but, viewed historically, it is probably true that the method can claim priority. Be that as it may, it is clear that Peirce's system includes his method. We have already seen the establishment of the fundamental branches of his philosophy, and now we shall examine the problems of philosophical method before proceeding to the remaining branches. The justification for such a treatment is the topical arrangement, both logical and historical, into which Peirce's philosophy naturally falls.

We shall, then, undertake to discuss the problem of method, in its broad and general aspects as well as in the more particular and specific form which Peirce discovered for it. We shall be concerned with the method which he claimed followed from the construction of his own philosophy, since it is also the one which he advocated for the pursuit of philosophy by others. It will be necessary to discuss the general aspects first, in order to gain some insight into the direction in which the particular aspects will take us.

i. THE APPROACH TO PHILOSOPHY

The broadest purpose of philosophy "is to study the most general features of reality and real objects." (6.6) The "lock upon the door of philosophy" is the answer to the general problem of "how synthetical judgments in general, and still more generally, how synthetical reasoning is possible at all." (5.348)[1] But the very form in which the principal question is phrased sets up the conditions for its answer. We can go back of our method only by accepting certain systematic assumptions; we can go back of our system only by accepting the assumptions implied by our method. In either case,

[1] Cf. chap. VI, A, iii.

something definite is assumed at the start; and the fact that our philosophical investigations yield us anything valid at all is evidence that we started from truths of relatively permanent validity. The unity of the method we employ and the system we seek suggests that human reasoning is not a stranger to nature. In this way, philosophy begins to make us acquainted with eternal forms. (1.648)

Philosophy, admittedly, is a most difficult study, "presenting more pitfalls for the uninformed than almost any, which a mere amateur at it would be foolish to fancy that he could escape." (1.204) Those who feel themselves incompetent or (it comes to the same thing) contemptuous of philosophy, but who nevertheless think profoundly on other topics, are indulging in unconscious metaphysics, which is the most dangerous kind. (1.229) The subject matter of philosophy is so universal that it seems commonplace, yet it manages to remain elusive. The "observational part of philosophy" (1.134) is "not particularly laborious" but also not "easy." It "deals with positive truth, indeed, yet contents itself with observations such as come within the range of every man's normal experience, and for the most part in every waking hour of his life. Hence Bentham calls this class, *coenoscopic*.[2] These observations escape the untrained eye precisely because they permeate our whole lives, just as a man who never takes off his blue spectacles soon ceases to see the blue tinge. Evidently, therefore, no microscope or sensitive film would be of the least use in this class. The observation is observation in a peculiar, yet perfectly legitimate, sense. If philosophy glances now and then at the results of special sciences, it is only as a sort of condiment to excite its own proper observation." (1.241)

The recognition of the commonplace is difficult, and hence "How often do we hear it said that the study of philosophy requires *hard thinking*! But I am inclined to think a man will never begin to reason well about such subjects, till he has conquered the natural impulse to make spasmodic efforts of mind. In mathematics, the complexity of the problems renders it often a little difficult to hold all the different elements of our mental diagrams in their right places. In a certain sense, therefore, hard thinking *is* occasionally requisite in that discipline. But metaphysical philosophy does

---

[2] " . . . from two Greek words, one of which signifies *common*—things belonging to others in common; the other *looking to*. By *coenoscopic ontology*, then, is designated that part of the science which takes for its subject those properties which are considered as possessed in common by all the individuals belonging to the class which the name *ontology* is employed to designate, i.e. by *all* individuals." *The Works of Jeremy Bentham*, Edinburgh, 1843, vol. viii, p. 83 n. Coenoscopic is in contrast with Bentham's *idioscopic*, or looking to peculiar things, a term employed by Peirce for the special sciences, (1.241) following Bentham.

not present any such complications, and has no work that *hard thinking* can do. What is needed above all, for metaphysics, is thorough and mature thinking." (3.406)

We may conclude, then, that "philosophy is, or should be, an exact science,"[3] a "*positive science,* in the sense of discovering what really is true; but it limits itself to so much of truth as can be inferred from common experience." (1.184) "Philosophy is a department of pure Heuretic Science." (5.517) It is "a positive theoretical science, and a science in an early stage of development." (5.61) Peirce said that he wished philosophy to be "a strict science, passionless and severely fair. I know very well that science is not the whole of life, but I believe in the division of labor among intellectual agencies. The apostle of Humanism says that professional philosophists 'have rendered philosophy like unto themselves, abstruse, arid, abstract, and abhorrent.'[4] But I conceive that some branches of science are not in a healthy state if they are *not* abstruse, arid, and abstract. . . . " (5.537)

One of the difficulties, of course, is that philosophers have been in the practice of preferring to defend corners rather than to pursue philosophy. "When philosophy began to awaken from its long slumber, and before theology completely dominated it, the practice seems to have been for each professor to seize upon any philosophical position he found unoccupied and which seemed a strong one, to intrench himself in it, and to sally forth from time to time to give battle to the others. Thus, even the scanty records we possess of those disputes enable us to make out a dozen or more opinions held by different teachers at one time concerning the question of nominalism and realism. Read the opening part of the *Historia Calamitatum* of Abelard, who was certainly as philosophical as any of his contemporaries, and see the spirit of combat which it breathes. For him, the truth is simply his particular stronghold." (5.406) Philosophy is, "in its present condition . . . even more than the other branches of coenoscopy, a puny, rickety, and scrofulous science. It is only too plain that those who pretend to cultivate it carry not the hearts of true men of science within their breast. Instead of striving with might and main to find out what errors they have fallen into, and exulting joyously at every such discovery, they are scared to look Truth in the face. They turn tail and flee her. Only a small number out of the great catalogue of problems which it is their business to solve have they ever taken up at all, and these few most feebly." (6.6) There are,

---

[3] Perry, *Thought and Character,* vol. ii, p. 438.
[4] *Humanism, Philosophical Essays,* XVI (1903).

however, some few students of philosophy "who deplore the present state of that study, and who are intent upon rescuing it therefrom and bringing it to a condition like that of the natural sciences, where investigators, instead of contemning each the work of most of the others as misdirected from beginning to end, coöperate, stand upon one another's shoulders, and multiply incontestable results." (5.413)

ii. PHILOSOPHICAL BEGINNINGS

Where does philosophy obtain its first principles? It is easy to answer this question for the philosophers of the Middle Ages. "The most striking characteristic of medieval thought is the importance attributed to authority. It was held that authority and reason were two coördinate methods of arriving at truth, and far from holding that authority was secondary to reason, the scholastics were much more apt to place it quite above reason. . . . Next to sacred authorities—the Bible, the church and the fathers—that of Aristotle of course, ranked the highest. It could be denied, but the presumption was immense against his being wrong on any particular point." (1.30) The explanation of why authority was held in such veneration is that "the human mind [was] at that time in so uneducated a state that it could not do better than follow masters, since it was totally incompetent to solve metaphysical problems for itself. . . . " (1.31) But while we have to a certain extent placed more reliance upon reason, we still have our authority, albeit not the same one. "In the middle ages, reason and external authority were regarded as two coördinate sources of knowledge, just as reason and the authority of intuition are now." (5.215)

We have already seen that to a certain extent the current claims of intuition to be the authority to supplement reason in philosophical method were validated by Peirce.[5] But intuition alone is not sufficient to supplant the authorities of the medieval hierarchy, for this would imply that the faith which is required in addition to reason to furnish philosophy with its first principles is a matter of arbitrary choice. "We cannot begin with complete doubt.[6] We must begin with all the prejudices which we actually have when we enter upon the study of philosophy. These prejudices are not to be dispelled by a maxim, for they are things which it does not occur to us *can* be questioned." (5.265) Philosophical possibilities are "perplexing from [their] seemingly irresoluble mistiness. . . . Unfortunately, philosophy

[5] See chap. VI, C, iii, quoting 1.630.
[6] See chap. II, E, i.

cannot choose its first principles at will, but has to accept them as they are." (4.176) Its first principles have to be the product of that common experience[7] which forces the categories of phenomenology upon us.[8] Since we must have a faith, let it be faith in reason herself; let authority stem from no other indubitable than semiotic.[9] "Every unidealistic philosophy supposes some absolutely inexplicable, unanalyzable ultimate; in short, something resulting from mediation itself not susceptible of mediation. Now that anything *is* thus inexplicable can only be known by reasoning from signs. But the only justification of an inference from signs is that the conclusion explains the fact. To suppose the fact absolutely inexplicable, is not to explain it, and hence this supposition is never allowable." (5.265)

"Philosophy ought to imitate the successful sciences in its methods, so far as to proceed only from tangible premisses which can be subjected to careful scrutiny, and to trust rather to the multitude and variety of its arguments than to the conclusiveness of any one. Its reasoning should not form a chain which is no stronger than its weakest link, but a cable whose fibers may be ever so slender, provided they are sufficiently numerous and intimately connected." (5.265) A philosophy cannot be constructed on a single fruitful idea, although it is interesting to watch the attempt, which is one that has most frequently been tried. (6.7) Since it is in mathematics that we find a dependable method developed at an early date, we can surmise that philosophy owes much to mathematics historically in the matter of method. "Metaphysical philosophy may almost be called the child of geometry," (1.400) since it "depends in great measure on the idea of rigid demonstration from first principles. . . . Moreover, the conviction that any metaphysical philosophy is possible has been upheld at all times, as Kant well says, by the example in geometry of a similar science." Metaphysics has indeed "always been the ape of mathematics." (6.30) Science has led philosophy away from the seminary attitude and toward the attitude of the laboratory. Mathematics has taught philosophy many lessons with respect to particular philosophical questions, (e.g., 6.30, 1.401) but perhaps the most important lesson has to do with method of research. "One thing the laboratory-philosophers ought to grant: that when a question can be satisfactorily decided in a few moments by calculation, it would be foolish to spend much time in trying to answer it by experiment." (4.69)

The primary method of philosophy is that of analysis and synthesis. "The

[7] See this chapter, A, i; chap. III, A, ii; and chap. IV, A, i.
[8] See chap. IV, A, ii.
[9] See chap. III, B, i.

first problems to suggest themselves to the inquirer into nature are far too complex and difficult for any early solution, even if any satisfactorily secure conclusion can ever be drawn concerning them. What ought to be done, therefore, and what in fact is done, is at first to substitute for those problems others much simpler, much more abstract, of which there is a good prospect of finding probable solutions. Then, the reasonably certain solutions of these last problems will throw a light more or less clear upon more concrete problems which are in certain respects more interesting." (1.63)

"This method of procedure is that Analytic Method to which modern physics owes all its triumphs. . . . It is reprobated by the whole Hegelian army who think it ought to be replaced by the 'Historic Method', which studies complex problems in all their complexity, but which cannot boast any distinguished successes." (1.64) Peirce's "whole method will be found to be in profound contrast with that of Hegel." (1.368) Hegel attributed too much to originality. He was deficient in mathematics and hence accused the philosophers of failing to take thirdness into account,[10] not realizing that "the mathematical analysts had in great measure escaped this great fault, and that the thorough-going pursuit of the ideas and methods of the differential calculus would be sure to cure it altogether. Hegel's dialectical method is only a feeble and rudimentary application of the principles of the calculus to metaphysics."

Synthesis supplements analysis. "What really happens is that something is presented which in itself has no parts, but which nevertheless is analyzed by the mind, that is to say, its having parts consists in this, that the mind afterward recognizes those parts in it. Those partial ideas are not really in the first idea, in itself, though they are separated out from it. It is a case of destructive distillation. When, having thus separated them, we think over them, we are carried in spite of ourselves from one thought to another, and therein lies the first real synthesis." (1.384)

"Hegel . . . formulates the general procedure in too narrow a way, making it use no higher method than dilemma, instead of giving it an observational essence. The real formula is this: a conception is framed according to a certain precept, [then] having so obtained it, we proceed to notice features of it which, though necessarily involved in the precept, did not need to be taken into account in order to construct the conception. These features we perceive take radically different shapes; and these shapes, we find, must be particularized, or decided between, before we can gain a more perfect grasp of the original conception. It is thus that thought is urged on

[10] Peirce had accused him of failing to take secondness into account. See chap. IV, A, iii.

in a predestined path. This is the true evolution of thought, of which Hegel's dilemmatic method is only a special character which the evolution is sometimes found to assume. The great danger of the evolutionary procedure lies in forcing steps that are not inevitable, in consequence of not having a sufficiently distinct apprehension of the features of the conception in hand to see what it is that must immediately succeed it. The idea of time must be employed in arriving at the conception of logical consecution; but the idea once obtained, the time-element may be omitted, thus leaving the logical sequence free from time. That done, time appears as an existential analogue of the logical flow." (1.491)

"Philosophy tries to understand. In so doing, it is committed to the assumption that things are intelligible, that the process of nature and the process of reason are one. Its explanation must be derivation." (6.581) "*Explanation*, however, properly speaking, is the replacement of a complex predicate, or one which seems improbable or extraordinary, by a simple predicate, from which the complex predicate follows on known principles." (6.612)[11] "Explanation, derivation, involve suggestion of a starting point— starting-point in its own nature not requiring explanation nor admitting of derivation. Also, there is suggestion of goal or stopping-point, where the process of reason and nature is perfected. A principle of movement must be assumed to be universal. It cannot be supposed that things ever actually reached the stopping-point, for there movement would stop and the principle of movement would not be universal; and similarly with the starting-point." (6.581) Considerations of method in philosophy invariably bring us to the borderline where philosophical principles are postulated.

The chief tool that is employed by philosophy, and indeed by all thought, is language. ". . . the woof and warp of all thought and all research is symbols, and the life of thought and science is the life inherent in symbols; so that it is wrong to say that a good language is *important* to good thought, merely; for it is of the essence of it." (2.220) Definition is the primary requisite of the proper use of language by any special science, such as philosophy aims to be. To fail in this regard with respect to any important term is to treat "a verbal definition as a doctrine." (5.533) The secondary requisite is the use of new terms. ". . . the philosophist must be encouraged—yea, and required—to coin new terms to express such new scientific concepts as he may discover, just as his chemical and biological brethren are expected to do"; (5.13) "he who introduces a new conception into philosophy is under an obligation to invent acceptable terms to express it . . . furthermore . . .

[11] See 2.690, 2.716, and my chapter III, C, ii.

once a conception has been supplied with suitable and sufficient words for its expression, no other *technical* terms denoting the same things, considered in the same relations, should be countenanced." (5.413) "For in order that philosophy should become a successful science, it must, like biology, have its own vocabulary." (5.611)

Of course, technical terms will tend to deprive philosophy of something of its literary charm. But "if philosophy is ever to stand in the ranks of the sciences, literary elegance must be sacrificed—like the soldier's old brilliant uniforms—to the stern requirements of efficiency." (5.13) "Metaphysicians are a slow-thinking breed; but they seem duller than ordinary not to perceive that a literary style in philosophy is an incongruity whose days are numbered."[12] No study can become a science unless its "vocables have no such sweetness or charms as might tempt loose writers to abuse them—which is a virtue of scientific nomenclature too little appreciated" (5.413):[13] "In order to be deep it is requisite to be dull." (5.17)

In philosophy, "A good style is one which approximates as closely as possible to a self-explaining diagram or a tabular array of familiar symbols."[14] Philosophical method resembles scientific method in that ". . . language is but a kind of algebra. It would, certainly, in one sense be extravagant to say that we can never tell what we are talking about; yet, in another sense, it is quite true. The meanings of words ordinarily depend upon our tendencies to weld together qualities and our aptitudes to see resemblances, or, to use the received phrase, upon associations by *similarity*; while experience is bound together, and only recognizable, by forces acting upon us, or, to use an even worse chosen technical term, by means of associations by contiguity." (3.419)[15] In order to avoid all ambiguities and confusions, philosophy, like science, must aim at "an ideal philosophical terminology and system of logical symbols." (2.221) "The ideal terminology will differ somewhat for different sciences. The case of philosophy is very peculiar in that it has positive need of popular words in popular senses—not as its own language (as it has too usually used those words), but as objects of its study. It thus has a peculiar need of a language distinct and detached from common speech, such a language as Aristotle, the scholastics, and Kant endeavored to supply, while Hegel endeavored to destroy it. It is good

---

[12] Review of Baldwin's *Dictionary of Philosophy and Psychology* in *The Nation*, 76 (1903), 482.

[13] See also Ralph Barton Perry, *Thought and Character*, vol. ii, p. 432.

[14] *Ibid.*

[15] Cf. David Hume, *Treatise of Human Nature*, bk. I, pt. iii, sec. VIII.

economy for philosophy to provide itself with a vocabulary so outlandish that loose thinkers shall not be tempted to borrow its words." (2.223)

iii. INQUIRY

The method of inquiry, whereby philosophical truths are discovered, is defined by Peirce in terms of belief and doubt, as the movement from the latter to the former. "The irritation of doubt causes a struggle to attain a state of belief. I shall term this struggle *inquiry*." (5.374)[16] It is preoccupied with the appeasement of uncertainty, for "the settlement of opinion is the sole end of inquiry." (5.375)

"Every inquiry whatsoever takes its rise in the observation, in one or another of the three Universes, of some surprising phenomenon, some experience which either disappoints an expectation, or breaks in upon some habit of expection of the *inquisiturus;* and each apparent exception to this rule only confirms it." (6.469) In other words, inquiry begins with the observation of something unexpected in one of the three phenomenological fields.[17] "The inquiry begins with pondering these phenomena in all their aspects, in the search of some point of view whence the wonder shall be resolved. At length a conjecture arises that furnishes a possible Explanation, by which I mean a syllogism exhibiting the surprising fact as necessarily consequent upon the circumstances of its occurrence together with the truth of the credible conjecture, as premisses.[18] On account of this Explanation, the inquirer is led to regard his conjecture, or hypothesis, with favor. As I phrase it, he provisionally holds it to be 'Plausible'; this acceptance ranges in different cases—and reasonably so—from a mere expression of it in the interrogative mood, as a question meriting attention and reply, up through all appraisals of plausibility, to uncontrollable inclination to believe. The whole series of mental performances between the notice of the wonderful phenomenon and the acceptance of the hypothesis, during which the usually docile understanding seems to hold the bit between its teeth and to have us at its mercy, the search for pertinent circumstances and the laying hold of them, sometimes without our cognizance, the scrutiny of them, the dark laboring, the bursting out of the startling conjecture, the remarking of its smooth fitting to the anomaly, as it is turned back and forth like a key in a lock, and the final estimation of its Plausibility, I reckon as composing

---

[16] See chap. VI, C, ii.
[17] See chap. IV, B, i, ii, and iii.
[18] See chap. III, C, ii.

the First Stage of Inquiry. Its characteristic formula of reasoning I term Retroduction, i.e. reasoning from consequent to antecedent." (6.469)[19]

"Retroduction does not afford security. The hypothesis must be tested. This testing, to be logically valid, must honestly start, not as retroduction starts, with scrutiny of the phenomena, but with examination of the hypothesis, and a muster of all sorts of conditional experiential consequences which would follow from its truth. This constitutes the second state of inquiry. For its characteristic form of reasoning our language has, for two centuries, been happily provided with the name deduction." (6.470)

"Deduction has two parts. For its first step must be by logical analysis to Explicate the hypothesis, *i.e.* to render it as perfectly distinct as possible. . . . Explication is followed by demonstration. . . . Its procedure is best learned from Book I of Euclid's *Elements,* a masterpiece which in real insight is far superior to Aristotle's *Analytics*; and its numerous fallacies render it all the more instructive to a close student. . . . It usually, too, needs 'indexes,' or signs that represent their objects by being actually connected with them. But it is mainly composed of 'symbols', or signs that represent their objects essentially because they will be so interpreted." (6.471) It invariably needs something like a diagram, that is to say, an Icon; it usually, too, needs indexes; but is mainly composed of symbols.[20] "Demonstration should be *corollarial* when it can. An accurate definition of Corollarial Demonstration would require a long explanation; but it will suffice to say that it limits itself to considerations already introduced or else involved in the Explication of its conclusion; while *Theorematic* Demonstration resorts to a more complicated process of thought."[21]

"The purpose of Deduction, that of collecting consequents of the hypothesis, having been sufficiently carried out, the inquiry enters upon its Third Stage, that of ascertaining how far those consequents accord with Experience, and of judging accordingly whether the hypothesis is sensibly correct, or requires some inessential modification, or must be entirely rejected. Its characteristic way of reasoning is induction. This stage has three parts. For it must begin with Classification which is a . . . kind of Argument by which general Ideas are attached to objects of Experience; or rather by which the latter are subordinated to the former. Following this will come the testing-argumentations, the Probations; and the whole inquiry will be wound up with the Sentential part of the Third Stage, which, by Inductive

---

[19] I.e., abduction. See chap. III, C, iii.
[20] See chap. III, B, i.
[21] See 2.267.

reasonings, appraises the different Probations singly, then their combinations, then makes self-appraisal of these very appraisals themselves, and passes final judgment on the whole result." (6.472)

"The probations, or direct inductive argumentations, are of two kinds. The first is that which Bacon ill described as *'inductio illa quae procedit per enumerationem simplicem.'* So at least he has been understood. For an enumeration of instances is not essential to the argument that, for example, there are no such beings as fairies, or no such events as miracles. The point is that there is no well-established instance of such a thing. I call this crude induction.[22] It is the only induction which concludes a logically universal proposition. It is the weakest of arguments, being liable to be demolished in a moment, as happened toward the end of the eighteenth century to the opinion of the scientific world that no stones fall from the sky. The other kind of gradual induction,[23] which makes a new estimate of the proportion of truth in the hypothesis with every new instance; and given any degree of error there will *sometime* be an estimate (or would be if the probation were persisted in) which will be absolutely the last to be infected with so much falsity. Gradual Induction is either Qualitative or Quantitative and the latter either depends on measurements, or on statistics, or on countings." (6.473)

Philosophical method, then, consists in certain well-defined logical steps, which must be followed disinterestedly, and without appeal to any mental categories. "It is far better to let philosophy follow perfectly untrammeled a scientific method, *predetermined* in advance of knowing to what it will lead. If that course be honestly and scrupulously carried out, the results reached, even if they be not altogether true, even if they be grossly mistaken, cannot but be highly serviceable for the ultimate discovery of truth. Meantime, sentiment can say, 'Oh well, philosophical science has not by any means said its last word yet; and meantime I will continue to believe *so and so*." (1.644) Of this much we can be certain, that "Inquiry properly carried out will reach some definite and fixed result or approximate indefinitely toward that limit." (1.485) What is sought, of course, is sure knowledge[24] and perfect belief,[25] on the grounds that there exist eternal truths to be known. (1.219) Philosophical method, as we have just seen, relies chiefly on reasoning, and since "All positive reasoning is of the nature of judging the proportion of something in a whole collection

---

[22] See chap. III, C, iii, (*b*).
[23] See chap. III, C, iii, (*b*).
[24] See chap. V, C, i.
[25] See chap. VI, C, ii.

by the proportion found in a sample," (1.141)[26] "we cannot in any way reach perfect certitude nor exactitude." (1.147) Peirce concluded that "there is no tenable opinion regarding human knowledge which does not lead legitimately to this corollary." In this way, "every proposition which we can be entitled to make about the real world must be an approximate one; we can never have the right to hold any truth to be exact. Approximation must be the fabric out of which our philosophy has to be built." (1.404) To this doctrine of the tentative nature of all philosophical speculations, which are of necessity approximative only of those eternal truths which have their being apart from and independent of all efforts to reach them, Peirce gave the name fallibilism. "For fallibilism is the doctrine that our knowledge is never absolute but always swims, as it were, in a continuum of uncertainty and of indeterminacy." (1.171)

iv. CLASSIFICATION AND SYSTEM

"Science and philosophy," observed Peirce, "seem to have been changed in their cradles. For it is not knowing, but the love of learning, that characterizes the scientific man; while the 'philosopher' is a man with a system which he thinks embodies all that is best worth knowing." (1.44)

"Of the fifty or hundred systems of philosophy that have been advanced at different times of the world's history, perhaps the larger number have been, not so much results of historical evolution, as happy thoughts which have accidentally occurred to their authors. An idea which has been found interesting and fruitful has been adopted, developed, and forced to yield explanations of all sorts of phenomena." (6.7) This kind of method has not developed the most comprehensive systems, but it has shown us something about the ideas involved and taught many valuable lessons about the construction of philosophical systems, since "one idea'd philosophies are exceedingly interesting and instructive and yet are quite unsound." "The remaining systems of philosophy have been of the nature of reforms, sometimes amounting to radical revolutions, suggested by certain difficulties which have been found to beset systems previously in vogue; and such ought certainly to be in large part the motive of any new theory. This is like partially rebuilding a house." (6.8) But this is makeshift work, since some old faults may go unnoticed, and the new additions may not be brought into harmony.[27]

[26] Also 1.404.
[27] See chap. IV, C, i.

These are the wrong ways of constructing philosophical systems. The right way involves a great deal more caution. To begin with, 'studies preliminary to the construction of a great theory should be at least as deliberate and thorough as those that are preliminary to the building of a dwelling house." "That systems ought to be constructed architectonically has been preached since Kant, but I do not think the full import of the maxim has by any means been apprehended. What I would recommend is that every person who wishes to form an opinion concerning fundamental problems should first of all make a complete survey of human knowledge, should take note of all the valuable ideas in each branch of science, should observe in just what respect each has been successful and where it has failed, in order that, in the light of the thorough acquaintance so attained of the available materials for a philosophical theory and of the nature and strength of each, he may proceed to the study of what the problem of philosophy consists in, and of the proper way of solving it." (6.9) The task of preparing for the construction of a philosophical system is of the utmost importance, and Peirce wished "to give emphasis to one special recommendation, namely, to make a systematic study of the conceptions out of which a philosophical theory may be built, in order to ascertain what place each conception may fitly occupy in such a theory, and to what uses it is adapted."

The first step in the ordering of philosophy itself is the proper classification of philosophy among the other studies, and of the departments in philosophy. In the view of the scientific man, "the classification he is so painfully trying to find out is *expressive of real facts*."[28] Classification is the first step because classification is rudimentary system. "For example, a class consisting of a lot of things jumbled higgledy-piggledy must now be seen to be but a degenerate form of the more general idea of a *system*." (3.454)

To begin with, then, it is clear that philosophy underlies the special sciences, since the universal experiences with which philosophy deals must be taken into account by every special science "before it begins work with its microscope, or telescope, or whatever special means of ascertaining truth it may be provided with." (1.246)[29] That is to say, the first principles of philosophy, or metaphysics, underlie the empirical sciences as presuppositions and as implied by scientific method. But the most developed form of philosophy in its final conclusions, or cosmology, must draw not only on common experience but also on the findings of the special sciences. Philoso-

[28] Review of Thomas H. Huxley, *Method and Results*, in *The Nation*, 58 (1894), 34.
[29] See also 1.278.

phy "whose business it is to find out all that can be found out from those universal experiences which confront every man in every waking hour of his life," (1.246)[30] is philosophy *qua* philosophy. But there is also philosophy *qua* science, and this branch of philosophy, "while it rests and can only rest, as to the bulk of it, upon universal experience, yet for certain special yet obtrusive points is obliged to appeal to the most specialized and refined observations, in order to ascertain what minute modifications of everyday experience they may introduce." (1.273)

Philosophy falls, generally, into three main divisions. These are: Phenomenology, Normative Science, and Metaphysics. (1.186) We have already treated phenomenology at some length.[31] Normative Science "studies what ought to be" (1.281) and "investigates the universal and necessary laws of the relation of Phenomena to *Ends*." (5.121)[32] "Normative Science rests largely on phenomenology and on mathematics. (1.186) It has "three widely separated divisions: Esthetics,[33] Ethics,[34] Logic." (1.191)[35] We have already treated logic; ethics and aesthetics will be considered later. The third main division is that of "metaphysics, whose attitude toward the universe is nearly that of the special sciences (anciently, *physics* was its designation), from which it is mainly distinguished, by its confining itself to such parts of physics and of psychics as can be established without special means of observation." (1.282) "Metaphysics seeks to give an account of the universe of mind and matter." (1.186)[36] It "endeavors to comprehend the Reality of Phenomena";[37] it rests largely "on phenomenology and on normative science." (1.186) It may be divided into General Metaphysics, or Ontology;[38] Psychical, or Religious, Metaphysics;[39] and Physical Metaphysics.[40] "The second and third branches," adds Peirce, "appear at present to look upon one another with supreme contempt." (1.192)

"So then the division of Philosophy into these three grand departments, whose distinctness can be established without stopping to consider the contents of Phenomenology (that is, without asking what the true categories

---

[30] See chap. IV, A.
[31] See chap. IV, A and B.
[32] In addition to the references in this paragraph, see also for the normative sciences especially 1.573 ff., 2.120-122, 5.125 ff.
[33] See chap. IX.
[34] See chap. X.
[35] See chap. III.
[36] See chap. XI.
[37] See chap. IV, A and B.
[38] See chap. IV.
[39] See chap. XII.
[40] See chap. VIII.

may be), turns out to be a division according to Firstness, Secondness, and Thirdness,[41] and is thus one of the very numerous phenomena I have met with which confirm this list of categories." (5.121) Peirce's system of philosophy, which has a warp as well as a woof, can hardly be said to hang from a single thread.

V. THEORY AND PRACTICE

In all studies Peirce recognized two branches: "Theoretical, whose purpose is simply and solely knowledge of God's truth; and Practical, for the uses of life." (1.239) In philosophy, this meant for Peirce that the development of philosophical theory and the applications of such theories to practice, while closely related, should be maintained as two separate and distinct departments of philosophical activity. He insisted upon "condemning with the whole strength of conviction the Hellenic tendency to mingle philosophy [as theory] with practice," (1.618) on the grounds that such a confusion would be detrimental to both theory and practice. But, besides the application of philosophy to practice, there is another kind of relation, and this consists in the application of theory to practice purely for the purpose of verifying or validating theory. "The peculiarity of my philosophy," said Peirce, "is that it leads to positive predictions comparable with observation."[42] Instead of utility, there is the theoretical end of aiding the understanding. (2.1)

Of course, "a theory cannot be sound unless it be susceptible of applications, immediate or remote, whether it be good economy so to apply it or not." (2.7) But the business of philosophers, or at least of that class of philosophical theorists who are engaged upon the task of enlarging the frontiers and validating the theories of philosophy, lies in the domain of theory rather than in that of practice. "No doubt a large proportion of those who now busy themselves with philosophy will lose all interest in it as soon as it is forbidden to look upon it as susceptible of practical applications. We who continue to pursue the theory must bid *adieu* to them. But so we must in any department of pure science." (1.645)

Peirce's position with regard to the independence of theory from practice is perhaps best illustrated in his refutation of the contentions of the positivists. "Auguste Comte . . . would condemn every theory that was not 'verifiable.' Like the majority of Comte's ideas, this is a bad interpretation of a *truth*. An explanatory hypothesis, that is to say, a conception which

---

[41] See chap. IV, B.
[42] Quoted in Ralph Barton Perry, *Thought and Character*, vol. ii, p. 415.

does not limit its purpose to enabling the mind to grasp into one a variety of facts, but which seeks to connect those facts with our general conceptions of the universe, ought, in one sense, to be *verifiable*; that is to say, it ought to be little more than a ligament of numberless possible predictions concerning future experience, so that if they fail, it fails. Thus when Schliemann entertained the hypothesis that there really had been a city of Troy and a Trojan War, this meant to his mind among other things that when he should come to make excavations at Hissarlik he would probably find remains of a city with evidences of a civilization more or less answering to the descriptions of the Iliad, and which would correspond with other probable finds at Mycenae, Ithaca, and elsewhere. So understood, Comte's maxim is sound. Nothing but that *is* an explanatory hypothesis. But Comte's own notion of a *verifiable* hypothesis was that it must not suppose anything that you are not able directly to observe.[43] From such a rule it would be fair to infer that he would permit Mr. Schliemann to suppose he was going to find arms and utensils at Hissarlik, but would forbid him to suppose that they were either made or used by any human being, since no such beings could ever be detected by direct percept. He ought on the same principle to forbid us to suppose that a fossil skeleton had ever belonged to a living ichthyosaurus. This seems to be substantially the opinion of M. Poincaré at this day.[44] The same doctrine would forbid us to believe in our memory of what happened at dinnertime today. . . . Of course with memory would have to go all opinions about everything not at this moment before our senses. You must not believe that you hear me speaking to you, but only that you hear certain sounds while you see before you a spot of black, white, and flesh color; and those sounds somehow seem to suggest certain ideas which you must not connect at all with the black and white spot. A man would have to devote years to training his mind to such habits of thought, and even then it is doubtful whether it would be possible. And what would be gained? If it would alter our beliefs as to what our sensuous experience is going to be, it would certainly be a change for the worse, since we do not find ourselves disappointed in any expectations due to common sense beliefs. If on the other hand it would not make any such difference, as I suppose it would not, why not allow us the harmless convenience of believing in these

---

[43] *Cours de philosophie positive*, 28me leçon.
[44] That Poincaré was a positivist, there can be no doubt; see his *Introduction to the Value of Science*. The viewpoint has, however, despite its obvious fallaciousness, survived. Many scientists and philosophers stanchly cling to it. See e.g., P. W. Bridgman, *The Logic of Modern Physics*.

fictions, if they be fictions? Decidedly we must be allowed these ideas, if only as cement for the matter of our sensations. At the same time I protest that such permissions would not be at all enough. Comte, Poincaré, and Karl Pearson take what they consider to be the first impressions of sense, but which are really nothing of the sort, but are percepts that are products of psychical operations,[45] and they separate these from all the intellectual part of our knowledge, and arbitrarily call the first *real* and the second *fictions*. These two words *real* and *fictive* bear no significations whatever except as marks of *good* and *bad*. But the truth is that what they call *bad* or *fictitious*, or *subjective*, the intellectual part of our knowledge, comprises all that is valuable on its own account, while what they mark *good*, or *real*, or *objective*, is nothing but the pretty vessel that carries the precious thought." (5.597)

Peirce differed from the positivists in his regard for the reality of hypothesis; he did not seek the least hypothetical of propositions but the most. He said, "if I had the choice between two hypotheses, the one more ideal and the other more materialistic, I should prefer to take the ideal one upon probation, simply because ideas are fruitful of consequences, while mere sensations are not so; so that the idealistic hypothesis would be the *more verifiable*, that is to say, would *predict more*, and could be put the more thoroughly to the test." (5.598) He held that "there must be a *petitio principii* in any argument which, resting merely on common sense, concludes the exact truth of any matter of fact." (2.614) "Positivism, apart from its theory of history and of the relations between the sciences, is distinguished from other doctrines by the manner in which it regards hypotheses." (2.511 n.) Let us consider "a common statement of it; namely, 'that no hypothesis is admissible which is not capable of verification by direct observation.' The positivist regards an hypothesis, not as an inference, but as a device for stimulating and directing observation. But I have shown above that certain premisses will render an hypothesis probable, so that there is such a thing as legitimate hypothetic inference. . . . [46] Moreover, an hypothesis in every sense is an inference, because it is adopted for some reason, good or bad, and that reason, in being regarded as such, is regarded as lending the hypothesis some plausibility. . . . That the maxim of the positivists is superfluous or worse, is shown, first, by the fact that it is not implied in the proof that hypothetic inference is valid; and next, by the absurdities to which it gives rise when strictly applied to history, which is entirely hypothetical, and is absolutely incapable of verification by direct

---

[45] See chap. V, B, ii, and chap. VI, B, iii.
[46] 2.508-511. See also chap. III, C, iii.

observation. To this last argument I know of but two answers; first, that this pushes the rule further than was intended, it being considered that history has already been so verified; and second, that the positivist does not pretend to know the world as it absolutely exists, but only the world which appears to him. To the first answer, the rejoinder is that a rule must be pushed to its logical consequences in all cases, until it can be shown that some of these cases differ in some material respect from the others. To the second answer, the rejoinder is double: first, that I mean no more by 'is' than the positivist by 'appears' in the sense in which he uses it in saying that only what 'appears' is known, so that the answer is irrelevant; second, that positivists, like the rest of the world, reject historic testimony sometimes, and in doing so distinguish hypothetically between what is and what in some other sense appears, and yet have no means of verifying the distinction by direct observation." (2.511 n.)

It is the viewpoint of the positivists that Peirce had in mind when he attacked the criterion of inconceivability. "Philosophers there have been who have said that such [and such] a thing is inconceivable; but it is perfectly conceivable to a mind which takes up intelligently and seriously the task of forming the conception. Men who are ready to pronounce a thing impossible before they have seriously studied out the proper way of doing it, and especially without having submitted to a course of training in making the requisite exertion of will, merit contempt. When a man tells us something is inconceivable, he ought to accompany the assertion with a full narrative of all he has done in these two ways to see if it could not be conceived. If he fails to do that, he may be set down as a trifler." (1.274) We are forced to the conception of anything which we discover in practice; and to assert *a priori* that anything is inconceivable and hence not in accordance with practice is contrary to the true spirit of inquiry.

In all of Peirce's theories he was more concerned with theory than with practice, since he was interested in the development rather than in the applications of philosophy; and this was true even of his theories of practice. In order to show this, we must turn next to a consideration of the doctrine of methodology in particular, called pragmatism, wherein he occupied himself specifically with the theory of practice.

B. PHILOSOPHICAL METHOD IN PARTICULAR: PRAGMATISM

In this section we shall treat of philosophical method in particular, named pragmatism. Pragmatism, contrary to the supposition of many persons, is for Peirce not a philosophy but only a method in philosophy. "The study of philosophy consists . . . in reflexion, and *pragmatism* is that method of reflexion which is guided by constantly holding in view its purpose and the purpose of the ideas it analyzes." (5.13 n.1) Pragmatism is "a wonderfully efficient instrument." (5.14) We must treat it as a more special case of that methodology which we have already discussed.

i. FROM LOGIC TO THE PRINCIPLE OF CONDUCT

Peirce's name for philosophical method is "methodeutic," a name that is defined in a way which shows it to be a continuation of logic, at least in one direction. *"Methodeutic"* is what Peirce "formerly called Speculative Rhetoric." (4.9)[47] It "studies the methods that ought to be pursued in the investigation, in the exposition, and in the application of truth." (1.191)

The doctrine of pragmatism was intended by Peirce to be "a Maxim of Logic," (5.14)[48] a "logical rule," (5.465) a "logical doctrine," a "theory of logical analysis, or true definition," (6.490) and resulted from the study of the formal laws of signs.[49] Clearly, he envisaged pragmatism as resting on logical grounds, and indeed he understood it as "one of the propositions of logic."[50] There are a number of different logical points in which we can detect the seeds of the notion of pragmatism, and these will be taken up in order.

The first point to be recalled is that logic rests upon everyday experience,[51] and, a further refinement, that relations are products of empirical observation.[52] Pragmatism will treat of this function as the relation of hypothesis to the course of experience. But instead of the historical derivation, an emphasis upon the logical features of the function will be held primary.

If we were to consider the whole chapter on logic, and all that it contains, to be that part of the subject which is termed *formal* logic, then pragmatism might be described as that part of the same subject which is termed *material* logic. The syllogism purports to assert the truth,[53] but the truth of the syllogism, provided its conclusion follows from its premises (which it is the business of pure logic to discover), depends upon the truth of its premises, and premises, until they are proved true, are nothing more than hypotheses. Now, if pragmatism is dedicated to testing the va-

---

[47] See 2.93. Also my chap. III, D.
[48] Also 5.18.
[49] Letter to Ladd-Franklin in the *Journal of Philosophy,* 13 (1916), 720.
[50] Quoted in Perry, *Thought and Character,* vol. ii, p. 427.
[51] See chap. III, A, ii.
[52] See chap. III, B, i.
[53] See chap. III, C, i.

lidity of hypotheses, it is also testing premises. Thus we are justified in describing pragmatism as Peirce's material logic, supplementary to his formal logic, which throughout this volume we have described simply as logic.

Pragmatism is the logic of induction. All questions of the validity of induction necessarily involve pragmatism.[54] For "the validity of induction depends upon the necessary relation between the general and the singular. It is precisely this which is the support of Pragmatism." (5.170) But pragmatism itself Peirce described as the logic of abduction, (5.206)[55] the reasoning from effect to cause.[56]

Lastly, pragmatism is the theory of meaning, in which connection it is an extension of Speculative Rhetoric, particularly concerned with the interpretant of a sign. It will be recalled that the meaning of a sign lies in the interpretant,[57] and that the analysis of meaning yields as its product the entire interpretant.[58] Pragmatism may be considered a method of determining the *dynamical* interpretant, and is thus a development of that special department of Speculative Rhetoric which has to do with the logic of discovery,[59] or how symbols become effective in the relations between minds and facts. " . . . the ultimate meaning of any sign consists either in an idea predominantly of feeling or in one predominantly of acting and being acted on." (5.7) "But pragmatism does not undertake to say in what the meanings of all signs consist, but merely to lay down a method of determining the meanings of intellectual concepts, that is, of those upon which reasonings may turn." (5.8)

ii. FROM METAPHYSICS

Since pragmatism is a method concerned with the proper relations of theory and practice, and since phenomenology is so closely occupied with empirical observation, it might be supposed that pragmatism is closely derived from phenomenology. But Peirce insisted that pragmatism "is not definable as 'thorough-going phenomenalism,' although the latter doctrine may be a kind of pragmatism. The *richness* of phenomena lies in their sensuous quality. Pragmatism does not intend to define the phenomenal equivalents of words and general ideas, but, on the contrary, eliminates

[54] See chap. III, C, iii.
[55] See chap. III, C, iii.
[56] 2.636, quoted in *loc. cit.*
[57] See chap. III, B, i.
[58] See chap. III, D, ii.
[59] See chap. III, D, iii.

their sential element, and endeavors to define the rational purport, and this it finds in the purposive bearing of the word or proposition in question." (5.428)

The task of pragmatism, which is to discover the relation of hypotheses to the field of actuality,[60] has in a sense already been given in ontology, where it was asserted that "the existence of a fact does consist in the existence of all its consequences."[61] It has been given also in connection with ontological habit, of which Peirce asserted that there is "no other way of defining a habit than by describing the kind of behavior in which the habit becomes actualized." (2.666)[62]

In epistemology we can detect the note of pragmatism in the usefulness of the perceptual judgment which stimulates thought, and whose "only justification is that it subsequently turns out to be useful."[63] Usefulness, in Peirce's meaning, however, usually proves to mean some step which aids in the discovery of truth. Indeed, it would not be misleading to regard pragmatism as nothing more than the method that complements the correspondence theory of truth.[64] For if truth would be that verification (or contradiction) of our hypotheses which endless investigation would bring, then pragmatism is simply a name for the pursuit of verification.

iii. FROM PSYCHOLOGY

Pragmatism is independent of psychology in that the relations of hypotheses to the actual occurrences which exemplify them have a nonmental existence. But since such relations are frequently routed through the mind of experiencing individuals, it will be helpful to show the psychological implications. We have already seen that habit, for instance, in its wide ontological sense, is defined by the kind of behavior which it calls for.[65] In the narrower sense of psychology, "the identity of a habit depends on how it might lead *us* to act."[66] Similarly, "the essence of a belief is the establishment of a habit; and different beliefs are distinguished by the different modes of action to which they give rise." (5.398) Belief is a matter of preparing "to shape one's conduct into conformity with a propo-

---

[60] See chap. IV, B, ii, (*b*).
[61] See chap. IV, D, i, (*c*), quoting 1.432.
[62] See chap. IV, D, ii, (*c*).
[63] See chap. V, B, ii, quoting 1.538.
[64] See chap. V, C, iii.
[65] See this chapter, B, ii.
[66] See chap. VI, C, i, quoting 5.400. (Italics mine.)

sition,"[67] and, again, the purpose of thought lies in things beyond itself[68] —that is to say, to activities in the actual world which eventually tend to exemplify generals, for "a fancied conjuncture leads us to fancy an appropriate line of action."[69] Lastly, we may cite an instance of the chain of systematic construction in Peirce's system by observing the workings of logical principles through psychology to pragmatism. In the section devoted to cognition, Peirce said that "The cognition of a result [i.e., the cognition of the conclusion of a deductive syllogism] is of the nature of a decision to act in a particular way on a given occasion."[70] Psychology shows the workings of the logical laws according to the pragmatic method on the mind and actions of the individual person. "There can, of course, be no question that a man will act in accordance with his belief so far as his belief has any practical consequences. The only doubt is whether this is *all* that belief is, whether belief is a mere nullity so far as it does not influence conduct." (5.32) Thus the question of the meaning of belief lies to a certain extent outside the domain of psychology and in that of methodology.

iv. THE DEFINITION AND EXPLANATION OF PRAGMATISM

Special importance attaches to Peirce's doctrine of pragmatism, for the notoriety as well as for the fame the term has acquired. In an attempt to clarify meaning, Peirce offered a number of definitions, some of which, for purposes of comparison, may be given here.

The first definition, described as a "maxim for obtaining clearness of apprehension," is as follows: "Consider what effects, that might conceivably have practical bearings, we conceive the object of our conception to have. Then, our conception of these effects is the whole of our conception of the object."(5.2)[71]

The second definition states the same maxim in slightly altered form: "In order to ascertain the meaning of an intellectual conception one should consider what practical consequences might conceivably result by necessity from the truth of that conception; and the sum of these consequences will constitute the entire meaning of the conception." (5.9)

The third definition states the maxim in terms of grammar: "Pragmatism

[67] See chap. VI, C, ii, quoting 6.467.
[68] See chap. VI, D, ii.
[69] See chap. VI, D, ii, quoting 3.159.
[70] See chap. VI, D, i, (c), quoting 2.711.
[71] See also 5.402, and the French version, 5.18.

is the principle that every theoretical judgment expressible in a sentence in the indicative mood is a confused form of thought whose only meaning, if it has any, lies in its tendency to enforce a corresponding practical maxim expressible as a conditional sentence having its apodosis in the imperative mood." (5.18)

The fourth definition states the maxim, somewhat tortuously, in terms of experience. It asserts "that the *total* meaning of the predication of an intellectual concept is contained in an affirmation that, under all conceivable circumstances of a given kind (or under this or that more or less indefinite part of the cases of their fulfillment, should the predication be modal) the subject of the predication would behave in a certain general way—that is, it would be true under given experiential circumstances (or under a more or less definitely stated proportion of them, *taken as they would occur*, that is in the same order of succession, *in experience*)." (5.467)

The fifth definition states the maxim in terms of meaning: "The entire intellectual purport of any symbol consists in the total of all general modes of rational conduct which, conditionally upon all the possible different circumstances and desires, would ensue upon the acceptance of the symbol." (5.438)

The sixth definition states the maxim in terms of conduct. According to it, "the true meaning of any product of the intellect lies in whatever unitary determination it would impart to practical conduct under any and every conceivable circumstance, supposing such conduct to be guided by reflection carried to an ultimate limit." (6.490)

The seventh, and last, definition states the maxim in terms of experimentation, following the definition in terms of conduct. Thus, "since obviously nothing that might not result from experiment can have any direct bearing upon conduct, if one can define accurately all the conceivable experimental phenomena which the affirmation or denial of a concept could imply, one will have therein a complete definition of the concept, and *there is absolutely nothing more in it.*" (5.412)

The clearest of these statements of the pragmatic maxim, and the one closest to the meaning which accords best with Peirce's other writings, would appear to be the second of those listed above. He went on to explain the maxim at some length.

"*Pragmatism* is not a *Weltanschauung* but is a method of reflexion having for its purpose to render ideas clear." (5.13 n.) "There are two functions which we may properly require that Pragmatism should perform. . . . Namely, it ought, in the first place, to give us an expeditious riddance of all ideas essentially unclear. In the second place, it ought to lend support, and help to render distinct, ideas essentially clear, but more or less difficult of apprehension; and in particular, it ought to take a satisfactory atttitude toward the element of thirdness." (5.206) Pragmatism thus aims at achieving that clarity and distinctness which Descartes had established as the goal of knowledge.[72] For "after all pragmatism solves no real problem. It only shows that supposed problems are not real problems."[73] It "is expected to bring to an end those prolonged disputes of philosophers which no observations of facts could settle, and yet in which each side claims to prove that the other side is in the wrong. Pragmatism maintains that in those cases the disputants must be at cross-purposes. They either attach different meanings to words, or else one side or the other (or both) uses a word without any definite meaning. What is wanted, therefore, is a method for ascertaining the real meaning of any concept, doctrine, proposition, word, or other sign." (5.6) "All pragmatists will . . . agree that their method of ascertaining the meanings of words and concepts is no other than that experimental method by which all the successful sciences . . . have reached the degrees of certainty that are severally proper to them today." (5.465)

Pragmatism, however, is "a method of ascertaining the meanings, not of all ideas, but only of what I call 'intellectual concepts,' that is to say, of those upon the structure of which, arguments concerning objective fact may hinge." . . . "Intellectual concepts, however—the only sign-burdens that are properly denominated 'concepts'—essentially carry some implication concerning the general behavior either of some conscious being or of some inanimate object, and so convey more, not merely than any feeling, but more, too, than any existential fact, namely, the 'would-acts', 'would-dos' of habitual behavior; and no agglomeration of actual happenings can ever completely fill up the meaning of a 'would-be'." (5.467)

"Let us illustrate this rule [i.e., pragmatism] by some examples; and, to begin with the simplest one possible, let us ask what we mean by calling a thing *hard*. Evidently that it will not be scratched by many other substances. The whole conception of this quality, as of every other, lies in its conceived effects. There is absolutely no difference between a hard thing and a soft thing so long as they are not brought to the test. . . . Let us seek next a clear idea of weight. This is another very easy case. To say that a body is heavy means simply that, in the absence of opposing force, it

---

[72] See 5.388 ff.
[73] Perry, *Thought and Character*, vol. ii, p. 430.

will fall. This (neglecting certain specifications of how it will fall, etc., which exist in the mind of the physicist who uses the word) is evidently the whole conception of weight. It is a fair question whether some particular facts may not *account* for gravity; but what we mean by the force itself is completely involved in its effects." (5.403)

Peirce asked the question, "Whether a sign can have any meaning, if by its definition it is the sign of something absolutely incognizable," (5.253) and answered it by saying that "It would seem that it can, and that universal and hypothetical propositions are instances of it. Thus, the universal proposition, 'all ruminants are cloven-hoofed,' speaks of a possible infinity of animals, and no matter how many ruminants may have been examined, the possibility must remain that there are others which have not been examined. In the case of a hypothetical proposition, the same thing is still more manifest; for such a proposition speaks not merely of the actual state of things, but of every possible state of things, all of which are not knowable, inasmuch as only one can so much as exist." (5.254) On the other hand, all our conceptions are derived by abstraction from experience, and we are not likely to have conceptions of something absolutely incognizable since nothing of the sort occurs in experience. (5.255) However, so long as our meanings refer beyond the actual state of things, and cannot be verified, the fact remains that meanings unverified are yet meanings, and thus meaning is not the same as verification.

Another corollary from the above argument is that the meaning of a proposition does not necessarily demand that the action denoted by the proposition be carried out. But how is this true when it is said that "the sum of the experimental phenomena that a proposition implies makes up its entire bearing upon human conduct"? (5.427) The answer is that pragmatism "makes thought ultimately *apply* to action exclusively—to *conceived* action. But between admitting that and either saying that it makes thought, in the sense of the purport of symbols, to consist in acts, or saying that the true ultimate purpose of thinking is action, there is much the same difference as there is between saying that the artist-painter's living art is applied to dabbing paint upon canvas, and saying that that art-life consists in dabbing paint, or that its ultimate aim is dabbing paint. . . . I did not, therefore, mean to say that acts, which are more strictly singular than anything, could constitute the purport, or adequate proper interpretation, of any symbol. . . . I was speaking of meaning in no other sense than that of *intellectual purport*." (5.403 n.3) If pragmatism "really made Doing to be the Be-all and the End-all of life, that would be its death. For to say that we live for the mere sake of action, as action, regardless of the thought it carries out, would be to say that there is no such thing as rational purport." (5.429)

The relation to actuality of propositions bearing some truth is dependent upon the existence in actuality of some truth. This observation is consistent with pragmatism, for "the *whole* meaning of an intellectual predicate is that certain kinds of events would happen, once in so often, in the course of experience, under certain kinds of existential conditions—provided it can be proved to be true." (5.468) Thus pragmatism implies realism. As Paul Weiss has observed, "the pragmatic theory entails the doctrine that universals are real, that ideas are embodied in things. Since you cannot get meaning for an idea by referring it to that which has no meaning, experience can test an idea and give it meaning only so far as experience has some meaning of its own."[74] The pragmatic test, in other words, is the verification of a one-to-one relation between the meaning conveyed by an hypothesis, and the meaning which that hypothesis predicts is to be found in actual fact. Failure in the effort to obtain the correspondence disallows the hypothesis; success entails the conviction that the same reality which is a property of actuality is also a property of some propositions. "Indeed," said Peirce, "it is the reality of some possibilities that pragmatism[75] is most concerned to insist upon. . . . Pragmatism makes the ultimate intellectual purport of what you please to consist in conceived conditional resolutions, or their substance; and therefore, the conditional propositions, with their hypothetical antecedents, in which such resolutions consist, being of the ultimate nature of meaning, must be capable of being true; that is, of expressing whatever there be which is such as the proposition expresses, independently of being thought to be so in any judgment, or being represented to be so in any other symbol of any man or men. But that amounts to saying that possibility is sometimes of a real kind." (5.453)

V. HISTORY OF THE PRAGMATIC IDEA

The idea of pragmatism, if not the name, Peirce held to be a very old affair. "Socrates bathed in these waters"; (5.11) indeed, it "appears to have been virtually the philosophy of Socrates." (6.490) "Aristotle rejoices when he can find them." (5.11) "Substantially the same way of dealing with

---

[74] "Charles Sanders Peirce: 1839-1914" in the *Sewanee Review* for October, 1941.

[75] Pragmatism and pragmaticism are interchangeable terms. On the use of pragmaticism, see this chapter, C.

ontology seems to have been practised by the Stoics." (5.3) Pragmatism, said Peirce, "is only an application of the sole principle of logic which was recommended by Jesus; 'Ye may know them by their fruits,'[76] and it is very intimately allied with the ideas of the gospel." (5.402 n.2) Another suggestion for the idea of pragmatism came to Peirce from the writings of Duns Scotus.[77] "The logical upshot of the doctrine of Scotus is that real problems cannot be solved by metaphysics, but must be decided according to the evidence. As he was a theologian, that evidence was, for him, the dicta of the church. But the same system in the hands of a scientific man will lead to his insisting upon submitting everything to the test of observation." (4.28) The waters of pragmatism "run, where least one would suspect them, beneath the dry rubbish-heaps of Spinoza. Those clean definitions that strew the pages of the *Essay concerning Humane Understanding* . . . had been washed out in these same pure springs. It was this medium, and not tar-water, that gave health and strength to Berkeley's earlier works, his *Theory of Vision* and what remains of his *Principles*." (5.11)

"Berkeley on the whole has more right to be considered the introducer of pragmatism into philosophy than any other one man, though I was more explicit in enunciating it."[78] From it the general views of Kant derive such clearness as they have, for "Kant . . . is nothing but a somewhat confused pragmatist." (5.525) "Auguste Comte made still more—much more—use of this element; as much as he saw his way to using. Unfortunately, however, both he and Kant, in their rather opposite ways, were in the habit of mingling these sparkling waters with a certain mental sedative to which many men are addicted—and the burly business men very likely to their benefit, but which plays sad havoc with the philosophical constitution. I refer to the habit of cherishing contempt for logic." (5.11) "But although [pragmatism] is 'an old way of thinking,' in the sense that it was practised by Spinoza, Berkeley, and Kant, I am not aware of its having been definitely formulated, whether as a maxim of logical analysis or otherwise, by anybody before my publication of it in 1878." (6.490) The studies Peirce made of Berkeley and Kant in particular led him to realize that an abstract formulation of the pragmatic maxim was a necessity. (6.481) He asserted that he had been "a pure Kantist until he was forced by successive steps into Pragmaticism." (5.452)

[76] St. Matthew, 7:20.

[77] It is probable that no great figure in the history of philosophy has failed to make some statement which can be shown to contain a hint, at least, of the pragmatic maxim, and, more frequently, an appeal to it. See e.g., Thomas Aquinas, *Summa Theologica*, pt. ii, Q. 18, art. 1.

[78] Peirce, quoted in Ralph Barton Perry, *Thought and Character*, vol. ii, p. 425.

"So much for the past. The ancestry of pragmatism is respectable enough; but the more conscious adoption of it as a *lanterna pedibus* in the discussion of dark questions, and the elaboration of it into a method in aid of philosophical inquiry came, in the first instance, from the humblest *souche* imaginable. It was in the earliest seventies that a knot of us young men in Old Cambridge, calling ourselves, half-ironically, half-defiantly, 'The Metaphysical Club'—for agnosticism was then riding its high horse, and was frowning superbly upon all metaphysics—used to meet, sometimes in my study, sometimes in that of William James. It may be that some of our old-time confederates would today not care to have such wild-oats-sowings made public, though there was nothing but boiled oats, milk, and sugar in the mess. Mr. Justice Holmes, however, will not, I believe, take it ill that we are proud to remember his membership; nor will Joseph Warner, Esq. Nicholas St. John Green was one of the most interested fellows, a skillful lawyer and a learned one, a disciple of Jeremy Bentham. His extraordinary power of disrobing warm and breathing truth of the draperies of long worn formulas, was what attracted attention to him everywhere. In particular, he often urged the importance of applying Bain's definition of belief as 'that upon which a man is prepared to act.'[79] From this definition, pragmatism is scarce more than a corollary; so that I am disposed to think of him as the grandfather of pragmatism. Chauncey Wright, something of a philosophical celebrity in those days, was never absent from our meetings. I was about to call him our corypheus; but he will better be described as our boxing-master whom we—I particularly—used to face to be severely pummelled. He had abandoned a former attachment to Hamiltonianism to take up with the doctrines of Mill, to which and to its cognate agnosticism he was trying to weld the really incongruous ideas of Darwin. John Fiske and, more rarely, Francis Ellingwood Abbot, were sometimes present, lending their countenances to the spirit of our endeavours, while holding aloof from any assent to their success. Wright, James, and I were men of science, rather scrutinizing the doctrines of the metaphysicians on their scientific side than regarding them as very momentous spiritually. The type of our thought was decidedly British. I, alone of our number, had come upon the threshing-floor of philosophy through the doorway of Kant, and even my ideas were acquiring the English accent." (5.12)

"Our metaphysical proceedings had all been in winged words (and swift ones, at that, for the most part) until at length, lest the club should be dis-

---

[79] Cf. *The Emotions and the Will*, chap. 11, p. 505, 3rd ed. (1875).

solved, without leaving any material *souvenir* behind, I drew up a little paper expressing some of the opinions that I had been urging all along under the name of pragmatism. This paper was received with such un-looked-for kindness, that I was encouraged, some half dozen years later, on the invitation of the great publisher, Mr. W. H. Appleton, to insert it, somewhat expanded, in the *Popular Science Monthly* for November, 1877 and January, 1878, not with the warmest possible approval of the Spencerian editor, Dr. Edward Youmans. The same paper appeared the next year in a French redaction in the *Révue Philosophique*." (5.13)[80]

C. PRAGMATICISM AND CRITICAL COMMON-SENSISM

i. SOME SUBSEQUENT MISUNDERSTANDINGS

After Peirce's enunciation of the doctrine of pragmatism, it achieved a certain amount of recognition. However, in Peirce's opinion, it immediately began to be misunderstood and transformed, by his friends as well as by others. The chief offenders were his close associate, James, the Italian, Papini, and F. C. S. Schiller, but these were not all. Peirce had intended his doctrine to be "a mere maxim of logic" while they had transformed it into "a sublime principle of speculative philosophy." (5.18) "I sent forth my statement in January, 1878; and for about twenty years never heard from it again. I let fly my dove; and that dove has never come back to me to this very day. But of late quite a brood of young ones have been fluttering about, from the feathers of which I fancy that mine had found a brood. To speak plainly, a considerable number of philosophers have lately written as they might have written in case they had been reading either what I wrote but were ashamed to confess it, or had been reading something that some reader of mine had read. For they seem quite disposed to adopt my term *pragmatism*. I shouldn't wonder if they were ashamed of me. What could be more humiliating than to confess that one has learned anything of a logician?" (5.17)[81] "Toward the end of 1890, when this part of the Century Dictionary appeared, he did not deem that the word had sufficient status to appear in that work." (5.414 n.1)

Since James was closer to Peirce than any other pragmatist, and also since pragmatism is in the public mind if not in the minds of all phi-

---

[80] See also 6.482.

[81] James wrote to Peirce in 1894, confessing that "I have never given you sufficient public credit for all that you have taught me"—quoted in Perry, *Thought and Character*, vol. ii, p. 414, a statement that James intended for circulation by Peirce.

losophers associated with the name of James, it will be illustrative of the misunderstandings of the doctrine that began immediately upon its enunciation if we give some picture of James's version.

A close student of James, Professor Perry, has put the matter correctly. "Perhaps," he says, "it would be correct, and just to all parties, to say that the modern movement known as pragmatism is largely the result of James's misunderstanding of Peirce."[82] James had written as early as 1866 that he had been "to C. S. Peirce's lecture, which I could not understand a word of, but rather enjoyed the *sensation* of listening to for an hour."[83] But the fact that James could not understand Peirce did not give him pause; he went straight ahead with the formulation of his misunderstanding. "In 1897 Professor James remodelled the matter [i.e., pragmatism], and transmogrified it into a doctrine of philosophy, some parts of which I highly approved, while other and more prominent parts I regarded, and still regard, as opposed to sound logic." (6.482)[84] In a letter thanking James for the dedication, Peirce observed that "much has led me to rate higher than ever the individual deed as the only real meaning there is in the concept; and yet at the same time to see more sharply than ever that it is not the mere arbitrary force in the deed, but the life it gives to the idea that is valuable."[85] Professor James, according to Peirce himself, "took hold of the old thing, dignified it by calling it by its name in print (which I had never done even when I was in charge of the philosophical part of the *Century Dictionary*), furbished it up, and turned it into a philosophical doctrine." (6.490) This was in 1898.[86]

Peirce was concerned with the practicality of consequences to bear out intellectual concepts, but, as Perry sees, James was more concerned with *particularity* of consequences.[87] James wrote that "To attain perfect clearness in our thoughts of an object . . . we need only consider . . . what sensations we are to expect from it, and what reactions we must prepare . . . [88] The ultimate test for us of what a truth means is indeed the conduct it dictates or inspires. But it inspires that conduct because it first foretells some particular turn to our experience which shall call for just that conduct from us."[89] A comparison of this definition offered by

---

[82] Ralph Barton Perry, *Thought and Character,* vol. ii, p. 409.
[83] Quoted in Perry, *Thought and Character*, vol. i, p. 231. (Italics mine.
[84] Cf. *The Will to Believe,* published in 1897 and dedicated to Peirce.
[85] Quoted in Perry, *Thought and Character*, vol. ii, p. 222.
[86] Cf. *Collected Essays and Reviews* (1920), pp. 406-437.
[87] Perry, *Thought and Character*, vol. i, p. 458.
[88] James, *Collected Essays and Reviews*, p. 411.
[89] *Ibid.,* p. 412.

James with the definitions of Peirce will reveal profound differences. James's outlook is that of the nominalistic psychologist; Peirce's that of the realistic logician. James was concerned chiefly with the effect of thoughts on the individual and his particular acts; Peirce was concerned chiefly with the clarification of ideas. James was concerned with sensation; Peirce with conduct.

James wrote in 1902 that pragmatism is "the doctrine that the whole 'meaning' of a conception expresses itself in practical consequences, consequences either in the shape of conduct to be recommended, or in that of experiences to be expected, if the conception be true," (5.2) and in the following year his expressed failure to understand Peirce, from whom he got "only the sense of something dazzling and imminent in the way of truth,"[90] is amply confirmed some three years later by Peirce. "Between this [i.e., James's definition] and mine there certainly appears to be no slight theoretical divergence." (5.466)[91] Already in 1904, Peirce had written to James protesting against the latter's statement that Peirce had meant that the serious meaning of a concept lies in the concrete difference to some one which its being true will make. " . . . I do not think I have often spoken of the 'meaning of a concept' whether 'serious' or not. I have said that the concept itself 'is' *nothing more* than the concept, not of any concrete difference that *will* be made to someone, but is nothing more than the *conceivable* practical applications of it."[92] As early as 1902, Peirce had already written to James on this aspect. He pointed out that "Pragmatism is correct doctrine only in so far as it is recognized that material action is the mere husk of ideas. The brute element exists, and must not be explained away, as Hegel seeks to do.[93] But the end of thought is action only in so far as the end of action is another thought."[94]

"You and Schiller carry pragmatism too far for me,"[95] Peirce wrote to James in 1904. In the same year he observed to James that "Your mind and mine are as little adapted to understanding one another as two minds could be,"[96] and although Peirce graciously added that "therefore I always feel that I have more to learn from you than from anybody," this com-

[90] Quoted in Perry, *Thought and Character,* vol. ii, p. 427.

[91] In 1905 Peirce had written: "Although James calls himself a pragmatist, and no doubt he derived his ideas on the subject from me, yet there is a most essential difference between his pragmatism and mine."—Quoted in Perry, *Thought and Character,* vol. ii, p. 409.

[92] Quoted in Perry, *Thought and Character,* vol. ii, pp. 432-433.

[93] See my chap. IV, A, iii.

[94] Quoted in Perry, *Thought and Character,* vol. ii, pp. 424-425.

[95] Quoted in *ibid.,* vol. ii, p. 430.

[96] Quoted in *ibid.,* vol. ii, p. 431.

pliment evidently referred more to a beautiful friendship than to abstract philosophy, particularly in the matter of pragmatism. For illustration, if more are needed, we may cite some passages in James's volume entitled *Pragmatism* which contain remarks on other philosophical topics related to the general question of pragmatism. James was substance-minded; Peirce, relations-minded—a divergence fatal to any agreement about the nature of truth. James maintained that truth depends upon practical meaning,[97] whereas for Peirce practical meaning depends upon truth.[98] James said that "True ideas are those we can validate, corroborate and verify. False ideas are those that we cannot."[99] But for Peirce, only falsity is a subjective category.[100] Truth he defined as "the universe of all universes."[101] For James, truth is a matter of belief,[102] and refers to "relations among mental ideas," and that alone constitutes its "eternality." For Peirce, truth is endowed with eternal life[103] and as such is quite independent of belief.[104] For James, "Realities mean either concrete facts, or abstract kinds of things and relations perceived intuitively between them."[105] Compare this definition with Peirce's definition of reality. While Peirce would have admitted the reality of James's categories, he also insisted upon the reality of his own, which he considered to be far wider. The chief category of reality for Peirce lay in the being of universals or generals.[106] The actual world, for Peirce, a world which, by the way, includes all of James's real categories, is only a fragment of the ideal world of being.[107] Peirce was a classical realist, and fought constantly against the nominalistic error.[108] James, despite protestations to the contrary,[109] could go no further in the direction of a "reality independent of either of us" than that "taken from ordinary social experience."[110] No man could be called a realist legitimately who had made the assertion that "Truth *ante rem* means only verifiability,"[111] a proposition that holds the being of universals down to actual physical

[97] William James, *Pragmatism* (New York, Longmans, 1907), p. 44.
[98] See chap. V, C, iii. Also this chapter, B, ii, and B, v.
[99] James, *Pragmatism*, p. 201.
[100] See chap. V, C, ii.
[101] See chap. V, C, iii, quoting 5.506.
[102] James, *Pragmatism*, pp. 209-210.
[103] See chap. V, C, iii, quoting 1.219.
[104] See chap. V, C, iii, quoting 5.211, 2.135, and 5.137.
[105] James, *Pragmatism*, p. 212.
[106] See chap. IV, C, ii.
[107] See chap. IV, C, ii, quoting 3.527.
[108] See chap. IV, C, i, above.
[109] William James, *The Meaning of Truth* (New York, Longmans, 1909), p. 217.
[110] *Ibid.*, pp. 217-218.
[111] James, *Pragmatism*, p. 220.

particulars: the very definition of nominalism, since, it will be recalled, James emphasized particularity rather than action or conduct.

The final, and in some ways the most devastating, difference between Peirce and James lay in their views of the relations of logic to psychology. James insisted, against criticism, that there is no important difference. The point is important enough to justify quoting the paragraph from James. "A favorite way of opposing the more abstract to the more concrete account is to accuse those who favor the latter of 'confounding psychology with logic'. Our critics say that when we are asked what truth *means*, we reply by telling only how it is *arrived-at*. But since a meaning is a logical relation, static, independent of time, how can it possibly be identified, they say, with any concrete man's experience, perishing as this does at the instant of its production? This, indeed, sounds profound, but I challenge the profundity. I defy anyone to show any difference between logic and psychology here. The logical relation stands to the psychological relation between idea and object only as saltatory abstractness stands to ambulatory concreteness. Both relations need a psychological vehicle; and the 'logical' one is simply the 'psychological' one disemboweled of its fulness, and reduced to a bare abstractional scheme."[112] Now let us compare this statement with the position of Peirce. Against many other philosophers, Peirce contended that logic is founded neither upon psychology nor upon the data of psychology.[113] On the contrary, he insisted, when he came to write upon the subject of psychology, that psychology itself must be founded upon logic.[114]

After James, other men took up pragmatism, and impressed Peirce equally as having misunderstood his doctrine. Peirce was sure that his own position was "a very different position from that of Mr. Schiller and the pragmatists of today." (6.485) Schiller seemed to Peirce to occupy ground intermediate between that of James and himself. (5.466) Of Schiller and other pragmatists, Peirce said that "Their avowedly undefinable position, if it be not capable of logical characterization, seems to me to be characterized by an angry hatred of strict logic, and even some disposition to rate any exact thought which interferes with their doctrines as all humbug. . . . It seems to me a pity they should allow a philosophy so instinct with life to become infected with seeds of death in such notions as that of the unreality of all ideas of infinity[115] and that of the mutability of

---

[112] James, *Meaning of Truth*, pp. 152-153.
[113] See chap. III, A, i.
[114] See chap. VI, A, i; quoting 3.432.
[115] Cf. F. C. S. Schiller, *Humanism* (London, 1903), p. 314 n., and *Studies in Humanism* (London, 1907), p. 295.

truth." (6.485)[116] The last ignominy which the doctrine of pragmatism had to suffer was at the hands of Papini. Pragmatism "did not shine with its present effulgence until Professor Papini made the discovery that it cannot be defined—a circumstance which, I believe, distinguishes it from all other doctrines, of whatsoever natures they may be, that were ever promulgated." (6.490)[117]

How could it be shown that truth is practicable, "in the teeth of Messrs. Bradley, Taylor, and other high metaphysicians, on the one hand, and of the entire nominalistic nation, with its Wundts, its Haeckels, its Karl Pearsons, and many other regiments, in their divers uniforms, on the other?" (5.468) ". . . at present, the word begins to be met with occasionally in the literary journals, where it gets abused in the merciless way that words have to expect when they fall into literary clutches. Sometimes the manners of the British have effloresced in scolding at the word as ill-chosen —ill-chosen, that is, to express some meaning that it was rather designed to exclude." (5.414) At about this time, that is, in 1905, Peirce was "coming to the conclusion that my poor little maxim should be called by another name." (6.482) "So then, the writer, finding his bantling 'pragmatism' so promoted, feels that it is time to kiss his child good-by and relinquish it to its higher destiny; while to serve the precise purpose of expressing the original definition, he begs to announce the birth of the word 'pragmaticism,' which is ugly enough to be safe from kidnappers." (5.414) Pragmaticism was not intended to introduce any doctrine other than pragmatism. It was meant simply to restore an emphasis of the original pragmatism which had been forgotten, and to "close the door against those who would push the doctrine much further than I ever intended." (2.99)

ii. PRAGMATICISM REQUIRES REALISM

Peirce suggested in the way of philosophical nomenclature that "the name of a doctrine would naturally end in *-ism*, while *-icism* might mark a more strictly defined acception of that doctrine." (5.413) Pragmaticism "holds that the immediate interpretant[118] of all thought is conduct," (4.539) and thus "makes the purport to consist in a conditional proposition concerning conduct." (5.535) In a final definition, formulated in 1910, Peirce proposed that "the true meaning of any product of the intellect lies in whatever

---

[116] Cf. James, *Pragmatism*, pp. 59 ff., and this section, above.

[117] "What Pragmatism Is Like" in *Popular Science Monthly*, 71 (1907), 351. James made the same "discovery" about humanism. See his *Essays in Radical Empiricism* (New York, Longmans, 1912), pp. 245-246.

[118] See chap. III, D, ii.

unitary determination it would impart to practical conduct under any and every conceivable circumstance, supposing such conduct to be guided by reflection carried to an ultimate limit." (6.490) The delicate balance of the just proportion of the truth by which pragmaticism is maintained is a delicate balance from which it is possible to fall off on the one side by concentration upon practice, action, contemplation, and on the other by an overemphasis on rationality, relations, prediction. Having demonstrated the relations which hypotheses have to practice, and hence the reality of actuality. it became necessary to show once more, to those who had gone too far in the direction of practice, that pragmaticism is involved also in the reality of generals, and hence the reality of possibility.

What chiefly distinguishes Peirce's doctrine of pragmaticism from the doctrines of the other pragmatists is "its strenuous insistence upon the truth of scholastic realism." (5.423)[119] "So, instead of merely jeering at metaphysics, like other prope-positivists, whether by long drawn-out parodies or otherwise, the pragmaticist extracts from it a precious essence, which will serve to give life and light to cosmology and physics." (5.423) "The most important consequence of it [i.e., pragmatism], by far, on which I have always insisted . . . is that under that conception of reality we must abandon nominalism. That in my opinion is the great need of philosophy."[120] Pragmaticism is a refinement of pragmatism in the direction of more unmistakable realism. "Indeed, it is the reality of some possibilities that pragmaticism is most concerned to insist upon." (5.453) "It is impossible rightly to apprehend the pragmaticist's position without fully understanding that nowhere would he be less at home than in the ranks of individualists, whether metaphysical (and so denying scholastic realism), or epistemological (and so denying innate ideas)." (5.504)[121] "Now whoever cares to know what pragmaticism is should understand that on its metaphysical side it is an attempt to solve the problem: In what way can a general be unaffected by any thought about it?" (5.503) Since pragmatism requires realism, "Its adherent does not shrink from speaking of general objects as real, since whatever is true represents a real." (5.426) "For pragmaticism could hardly have entered a head that was not already convinced that there are real generals." (5.503) But while Peirce was a realist, he was not a victim of the realistic fallacy to which so many

[119] See chap. IV, C, i.
[120] Quoted in Perry, *Thought and Character,* vol. ii, p. 430. For Peirce's emphasis on the importance of nominalism and realism, see my chap. IV, C, i.
[121] See chap. VI, C, iii.

Platonists fall heir.[122] Although generals are real, they are not alone real. "It would also have been well to show that the pragmaticist does not make Forms to be the *only* realities in the world, any more than he makes the reasonable purport of a word to be the only kind of meaning there is." (5.434)[123]

We have seen that pragmaticism is concerned with the reference to conduct which the true meaning of "products of the intellect" carry.[124] But vastly more than actual conduct is involved, and this distinction grows out of the connection between Peirce's pragmaticism and scholastic realism with its requirement of the reality of generals. "Pragmaticism certainly makes the essence of every concept to be exhibited in an influence on possible conduct." (4.534 n.1)[125] As early as 1903, Peirce had discovered that "it was absolutely necessary to insist upon and bring to the front, the truth that a mere possibility may be quite real," (4.580)[126] for the importance of this fact had already occurred to Peirce before he changed the name of his doctrine. (4.581) In order to understand the theory of pragmaticism, "one must understand that there is no other part of it to which the pragmaticist attaches quite as much importance as he does to the recognition in his doctrine of the utter inadequacy of action or volition or even of resolve or actual purpose, as materials out of which to construct a conditional purpose or the concept of conditional purpose." (5.436) ". . . the pragmaticist, then, recognizes that the substance of what he thinks lies in a conditional resolve." (5.499) The influence of the future upon conduct is enormous, since "future facts are the only facts that we can, in a measure, control." (5.461) The reality of generals and possibilities means that general thoughts which refer to occasions not yet actual involve determinations concerning the infinite future, and, indeed, the final lesson of such a realistic doctrine as pragmatism reveals itself to be is that "The rational meaning of every proposition lies in the future." (5.427)

The demonstration that pragmaticism requires realism raises once more the question with which we began,[127] namely, that of the priority of method and system. Peirce's answer is unambiguous: methodology requires metaphysics. Thus this chapter, which is devoted to method, is incorporated

[122] See chap. IV, C, i.
[123] See this chapter, B, iv.
[124] See this chapter, B, v; also C, ii.
[125] See this chapter, B, iv.
[126] See chap. IV, D, i.
[127] See this chapter, A.

as an integral part of the systematic philosophy, because Peirce approached method from a systematic point of view.

iii. CRITICAL COMMON-SENSISM

The development of pragmaticism led Peirce to the formulation of a further complication and refinement in his philosophical method. He came to see that the true philosophy was to be discovered by submitting the instincts of common sense to criticism. "Pragmaticism . . . implies faith in common sense and in instinct, though only as they issue from the cupel-furnace of measured criticism." (6.480) "Common sense, which is the resultant of the traditional experience of mankind, witnesses unequivocally that the heart is more than the head, and is in fact everything in our highest concerns. . . . [for] the dicta of common sense are objective facts, not the way some dyspeptic may feel, but what the healthy, natural, normal democracy thinks." (1.654)[128] Common sense is the inherited wisdom of society, neither acquired nor held consciously, but lying at that deep level of belief from which the instinctive action of habit springs.[129] It is the most powerful force of all philosophy, "so weighty that special experience can hardly attain sufficient strength to overthrow it." (6.574) But for all that it is not fixed and stultified. "Common sense corrects itself, improves its conclusions." (6.573) "Common sense improves; it does not, then, attain infallibility. Then, its decisions are subject to review." (6.574) The good pragmaticist adores power; "not the sham power of brute force, which, even in its own speciality of spoiling things, secures such slight results; but the creative power of reasonableness, which subdues all other powers, and rules over them with its sceptre, knowledge, and its globe, love." (5.520)

The most important thing that any man can do in the pursuit of truth is to discover the beliefs he already has, not those he would be willing to accept, necessarily, but those which have never required any acceptance: the beliefs which constitute an implicitly held philosophy. "For . . . such beliefs are not 'accepted'. What happens is that one comes to recognize that one has had the belief-habit as long as one can remember; and to say that no doubt of it has ever arisen is only another way of saying the same thing." (5.523) Although it must be the case that some beliefs so held are true ones and some are false, to accept the propositions contained in belief in this way is not to accept them uncritically. No man "accepts any belief *on the ground*

---

[128] Cf. the Greek idea of the κοιναὶ ἔννοιαι.
[129] See chaps. V, A, and VI, C, i, and D, iv.

that it has not been criticized." Of course, "to criticize is to doubt, and . . . criticism can only attack a proposition after it has given it some precise sense in which it is impossible entirely to remove the doubt." But doubt is a function that requires reason;[130] hence it must be a conscious affair. So that the procedure to obtain a reasonable yet deeply rooted philosophy would appear to be, first, to bring to the surface those beliefs which have never received criticism and, secondly, to subject them to scrutiny.

These two steps are in fact the ones taken separately by two different schools of philosophy in the endeavor to answer Hume's objections to the traditional methods of obtaining certainty in knowledge. The Philosophy of Common Sense, as expounded by the Scottish school of Reid and his followers, held that first principles, given in belief, were to go unquestioned. The Critical Philosophy of Kant held that criticism must apply to first principles as well as to everything else. Now, it was Peirce's view that these rival schools each had hold of part of a process of inquiry, and that in order to have the whole process it was necessary to put them together. This he proposed to do in his "Critical Philosophy of Common-Sense." (5.505) But in order to achieve this unity, Peirce found it necessary to deviate to a certain extent from both positions, and this he saw that the philosophy of pragmaticism already obliged him to do. (5.439) The deviations from Reid's Common-Sensism and from Kant's Critical Philosophy are brought out clearly in the positive doctrines which Peirce enunciated as the "six distinctive characters" of Critical Common-Sensism. These are (*a*) that there are indubitable propositions and inferences; (*b*) that indubitable propositions are inherent in man from his very beginning; (*c*) that original beliefs are equivalent to instincts; (*d*) that the acritically indubitable is invariably vague; (*e*) that genuine doubt is of immense value; (*f*) that self-criticism is necessary.

(*a*) "Critical Common-Sensism admits that there not only are indubitable propositions but also that there are indubitable inferences."[131] "In one sense, anything evident is indubitable; but the propositions and inferences which Critical Common-Sensism holds to be original, in the sense one cannot 'go behind' them (as the lawyers say) are indubitable in the sense of being acritical. The term 'reasoning' ought to be confined to such fixation of one belief by another as is reasonable, deliberate, self-controlled." (5.440) Now, of course, controlled reasoning is conscious,[132] but "in fact we find a well-

---

[130] See chap. VI, C, ii.
[131] Cf. Thomas Reid, *Essays on the Intellectual Powers of Man*, Essay VI, chap. III.
[132] See chap. VI, D, iii.

marked class of mental operations, clearly of a different nature from any others which do possess just these properties. They alone deserve to be called *reasonings*; and if the reasoner is conscious, even vaguely, of what his guiding principle is, his reasoning should be called a *logical argumentation*. There are however, cases in which we are conscious that a belief has been determined by another given belief, but are not conscious that it proceeds on any general principle. Such is St. Augustine's '*cogito, ergo sum*.' Such a process should be called, not a reasoning, but an *acritical inference*. Again, there are cases in which one belief is determined by another, without our being at all aware of it. These should be called *associational suggestions of belief*." (5.441)

By indubitable proposition, Peirce meant the logico-philosophical aspect of a belief,[133] a proposition which has never needed to be subject to criticism in order to be acted on from habit,[134] an "uncontrolled thought," (5.516) an "ultimate premise . . . held without reference to precise proof" (5.515) by the heart rather than by the head. The "Critical Common-Sensist sets himself in serious earnest to the systematic business of endeavoring to bring all his very general first premises to recognition." (5.517) As to acritical inferences, inasmuch as the great majority of reasonings are unconscious, and consist in "simple Feeling viewed from another side," (5.440) that is to say, in the fixation of one belief by another, Peirce wished to leave the term "reasoning" for this unconscious process, which we have earlier described as "unconscious thought,[135] and to call what we have described as reasoning[136] by the name of logical argumentation.

(*b*) The Scottish philosophers held that it would be feasible "to draw up a complete list of the original beliefs [which] would hold good for the minds of all men from Adam down." (5.444)[137] Peirce's first impression was that "the indubitable propositions changed with a thinking man from year to year," but provisional inquiry showed him that "the changes are . . . slight from generation to generation, though not imperceptible even in that short period," that is, from the earliest man to the present. In other words, while Peirce concurred with Reid and his followers in "the theory of a fixed list [of indubitable propositions or acritical beliefs] the same for all men," (5.509) he yet held that these are altered or amended through the centuries with almost imperceptible slowness. There are beliefs which are as in-

[133] See chap. VI, C, ii.
[134] See chap. VI, C, i.
[135] See chap. VI, D, iv.
[136] See chap. VI, D, iii.
[137] See Thomas Reid, *op. cit.*, Essay VI, chap. IV.

herently part of man as any other inalienable characteristic. Such beliefs, which have been described in (*a*) as indubitable propositions, constitute a set, or system, and while some of them are gradually changed, the change is never sufficient to affect the system seriously. It is this system of beliefs, or indubitable propositions, which constitutes the fundamental philosophy.

(*c*) "The Scotch philosophers recognized that the original beliefs, and the same thing is at least equally true of the acritical inferences, were of the general nature of instincts." (5.445)[138] The original beliefs, which are held as instincts, are not thought of as such but rather as beliefs which we have good reasons for holding. For "it is true that whenever one turns a critical glance upon one of our original beliefs—say, the belief in the order of nature—the mind at once seems vaguely to pretend to have reasons for believing it. One dreams of an inductive proof. One surmises that the belief results from something like an inductive proof that has been forgotten." (5.516) "But little as we know about instincts, even now, we are much better acquainted with them than were the men of the eighteenth century. We know, for example, that they can be somewhat modified in a very short time. The great facts have always been known; such as that instinct seldom errs, while reason goes wrong nearly half the time, if not more frequently. But one thing the Scotch failed to recognize is that the original beliefs only remain indubitable in their application to affairs that resemble those of a primitive mode of life." (5.445) In contradistinction to the Scotch school, the Critical Common-Sensist "opines that . . . while [indubitable beliefs] never become dubitable in so far as our mode of life remains that of somewhat primitive man, yet as we develop *degrees of self-control* unknown to that man, occasions of action arise in relation to which the original beliefs, if stretched to cover them, have no sufficient authority. In other words, we outgrow the applicability of instinct—not altogether, by any manner of means, but in our highest activities." (5.511) Since "The Scotch school appears to have no such distinction concerning the limitations of indubitability and the consequent limitations of the jurisdiction of original belief," (5.445) Critical Common-Sensism is to that extent an advance upon the older philosophy.

(*d*) "By all odds, the most distinctive character of the Critical Common-Sensist, in contrast to the old Scotch philosopher, lies in his insistence that the acritically indubitable is invariably vague," (5.446) "often in some directions highly so. Logicians have too much neglected the study of *vagueness*, not suspecting the important part it plays in mathematical thought. It is the antithetical analogue of generality. A sign is objectively *general*, in so far

[138] See *ibid.*, Essay V, chap. III, and my chap. VI, C, iii.

as, leaving its effective interpretation indeterminate, it surrenders to the interpreter the right of completing the determination for himself. 'Man is mortal.' 'What man?' 'Any man you like.' A sign is objectively *vague,* in so far as, leaving its interpretation more or less indeterminate, it reserves for some other possible sign or experience the function of completing the determination. . . .[189] The *general* might be defined as that to which the principle of excluded middle does not apply. A triangle in general is not isosceles nor equilateral; nor is a triangle in general scalene. The *vague* might be defined as that to which the principle of contradiction does not apply. For it is false neither that an animal (in a vague sense) is male, nor that an animal is female." (5.505)

"Notwithstanding their contrariety, generality and vagueness are, from a formal point of view, seen to be on a par. . . . Evidently no sign can be at once vague and general in the same respect, since insofar as the right of determination is not distinctly extended to the interpreter it remains the right of the utterer. Hence also, a sign can only escape from being either vague or general by not being indeterminate. But . . . no sign can be absolutely and completely indeterminate. . . . Yet every proposition actually asserted must refer to some non-general subject; for the doctrine that a proposition has but a single subject has to be given up in the light of the Logic of Relations." (5.506)[140]

"The Critical Common-Sensist's personal experience is that a suitable line of reflexion, accompanied by imaginary experimentation,[141] always excites doubt of any very broad proposition if it be defined with precision. Yet there are beliefs of which such a critical sifting invariably leaves a certain vague residuum unaffected." (5.507) "One ought then to ask oneself, whether, since much of the original belief has disappeared under an attentive dissection, perseverance might not affect the destruction of what remains of it. . . . But the answer that a closer scrutiny dictates in some cases is that it is not because insufficient pains have been taken to precide the residuum, that it is vague: it is that it is vague intrinsically." (5.508)

(*e*) "The Critical Common-Sensist will be further distingiushed from the old Scotch philosopher by the great value he attaches to doubt, provided only that it be the weighty and noble metal itself, and no counterfeit nor paper substitute. He is not content to ask himself whether he does doubt, but he invents a plan for attaining to doubt, elaborates it in detail, and then puts it

[189] See chap. III, B, i.
[140] See chap. III, B, vi.
[141] See chap. III, D, iii.

into practice . . . ; and it is only after having gone through such an examination that he will pronounce a belief to be indubitable. Moreover, he fully acknowledges that even then it may be that some of his indubitable beliefs may be proved false," (5.451) for "what has been indubitable one day has often been proved on the morrow to be false." (5.514)

Doubt, Peirce discovered in his examination of the Cartesian philosophy,[142] is not an attitude that can be consciously assumed at will. It requires a struggle to attain it; there must be reason to doubt before there can be doubt. But its attainment is all the more valuable for that,[143] and any proposition which survives the test of doubt is more assured of its indubitability. Thus doubt serves to assure the position of those acritical propositions which it does not succeed in overthrowing, although, as Peirce warned, even this test cannot be construed as guaranteeing absoluteness.

(f) The Critical Common-Sensist differs from the Critical Philosophy of Kant and his followers in that the former "criticizes the critical method, follows its footsteps, tracks it to its lair." (5.523)[144] "Now control may itself be controlled, criticism itself subjected to criticism; and ideally there is no obvious definite limit to the sequence." (5.442) Despite the fact that actually the sequence will find a limit in the indubitable acritical propositions and inferences, this is no argument against the necessity of subjecting the critical method itself to scrutiny.

"The Critical Philosopher seems to opine that the fact that he has not hitherto doubted a proposition is no reason why he should not henceforth doubt it. (At which Common-Sense whispers that, whether it be 'reason' or no, it will be a well-nigh insuperable obstacle to doubt). Accordingly, he will not stop to ask whether he actually does doubt it or not, but at once proceeds to examine it. Now if it happens that he *does* actually doubt the proposition, he does quite right in starting a critical inquiry. But in case he *does not* doubt, he virtually falls into the Cartesian error of supposing that one can doubt at will," (5.524) which, as we have already seen, is easily refuted.

It is true, however, that, "as a matter of fact, pragmaticists press their peculiar doubts about first principles a good deal further and with a more straightforward earnestness than Kantians do. For when a Kant expresses a doubt, one has still to learn whether it is the substance of the proposition that he doubts or merely its attachment to one faculty or to another." (5.518)

---

[142] See chap. II, E.
[143] See chap. VI, C, ii.
[144] See Kant, *Kritik der Reinen Vernunft*, A 424, B 452.

Kant maintained that the thing-in-itself can be conceived, a contention which is in fact inconsistent with much of his philosophy. Since the *Ding an sich* "can neither be indicated nor found," "no proposition can refer to it and nothing true or false can be predicated of it. Therefore all references to it must be thrown out as meaningless surplusage. But when this is done, we see clearly that Kant regards Space, Time, and his Categories just as everybody else does, and never doubts or has doubted their objectivity." (5.525) "The Kantist has only to abjure from the bottom of his heart the proposition that a thing-in-itself can, however indirectly, be conceived; and then correct the details of Kant's doctrine accordingly, and he will find himself to have become a Critical Common-Sensist." (5.452) "The kind of Common-Sensism which thus criticizes the Critical Philosophy and recognizes its own affiliation to Kant has surely a certain claim to call itself Critical Common-Sensism." (5.525)

In the doctrine of Critical Common-Sensism we see the unity of method and system in Peirce's philosophy. Discovered through the fusion of two apparently irreconcilable philosophies, one of which has placed its faith in what is believed, the other in what can be analyzed, Peirce found a way to base his system on the instincts and to examine it with the critical method of reasoning. Instinct and reasoning are subjective, or psychological, categories, but their reference is to things external and objective, and independent of the mind. These things are qualities and relations of the universe, to the unity of which all otherwise conflicting functions must be eventually referred.

iv. SUMMARY OF THE CHAPTER

Philosophical method in general decrees that philosophy should be an exact science, drawing upon the special sciences as well as upon common experience for its subject matter. It will never become what it ought to be so long as its followers are busy defending corners instead of pursuing truth.

In the Middle Ages, faith in authority was primary, and reason a secondary adjunct, in the search for knowledge. But philosophy needs no faith except faith in Reason herself. In mathematics, we find reason highly developed; metaphysics might almost be said to be the child of geometry. Thus the analytical method, which is rational, is superior to the historical method. Philosophical method also requires language which furnishes the essential symbols of thought. Philosophy must have its own technical but dull vocabulary.

With these tools, philosophy embarks upon inquiry, defined as the struggle from doubt to belief, undertaken in order to settle opinion. Inquiry enters its first stage with surprise at some wonderful phenomenon, to which some retroductive explanation is forthcoming. The second, or deductive, stage consists in the test of the hypothesis against experiential consequences which ought to follow from its truth. This stage is in two parts: explication of the hypothesis, and demonstration. The third, or inductive, stage sets about to discover whether the consequents accord with experience. This stage has three parts: classification, probation by testing argumentations, and final judgment. Since all such inquiries are of the nature of samples only, philosophy can never be absolute, but must always stand ready to admit its findings to be fallible.

The philosophical systems of the past have been the result of historical evolution, the products of single happy thoughts which have occurred to men, of patchwork reforms and makeshift efforts. These are the wrong ways to construct systems. The right way is slower; it involves preliminary studies, and architectonic surveys of all human knowledge. The classification of philosophy among the other sciences is the next step; and it is found to be the most important one, underlying all the others, which, at the same time, it must take into account. Philosophy itself falls into three divisions: phenomenology, normative science, and metaphysics. We have already treated phenomenology, the study of what appears; normative science studies what ought to be; metaphysics, the universe of mind and matter.

There are two branches of philosophy: the theoretical and the practical. All theory yields practice, and all practice follows from some theory. But the demonstration of their unity may be for theoretical as well as for practical purposes: all sound theory is capable of yielding practical results. The positivists fail to understand the true nature of the relation of theory to practice, by insisting upon the criteria of verifiability and inconceivability—subjective and current tests which are invalid. Future verification may overthrow the present failure to verify; inconceivable hypotheses may prove conceivable when sincere efforts are made to conceive them. Peirce's special interest was in theory rather than practice, and he was interested in practice only for the advantages of the validation of theory to be found in the proper relationship between them.

The name that Peirce gave to philosophical method in particular is pragmatism. What is termed logic is in effect only that half of the topic ordinarily treated under the name of formal logic. Methodology in general and pragmatism in particular comprise the second half, which is ordinarily treated under the name of material logic. Pragmatism follows closely upon Peirce's notions of ontology and epistemology, but more closely, perhaps, upon his psychological ideas. Habitual action from belief shapes conduct in conformity with propositions.

The pragmatic maxim is defined as follows. The practical consequences which might conceivably result by necessity from the truth of an intellectual conception constitutes its entire meaning. The chief purpose of pragmatism is to clarify ideas, not to solve problems. Hence actions demanded by propositions do not have to be actually carried out. The maxim related hypotheses to actual truth, thus requiring that universals be real.

The idea of pragmatism, if not the name, is very old. It has been known to many of the classic philosophers, from Socrates to Duns Scotus, from Spinoza to Kant. Peirce did no more than to abstract the formula, which was indirectly suggested to him by Nicholas St. John Green's championing of Bain's definition of belief as that from which we are prepared to act. Peirce's definition, read to the Metaphysical Club of which Green was a member, was published in 1877.

Through publication the doctrine gained recognition, and soon, by transformation and misunderstanding, it was carried further than Peirce intended its meaning to go. The chief offenders in this regard were Peirce's friend, William James, and F. C. S. Schiller, though there were many others. It became a principle of philosophy where he had intended only a maxim of method. It became a theory in psychology, where he had intended one in logic. It became a matter for nominalistic interpretation, where he had intended one for realism. Hence he found it necessary to abandon the old term to its latest advocates, and to adopt a new one: pragmaticism.

Pragmaticism made it plain that nominalism had to be overthrown. The new term clearly implied scholastic realism, with its requirement of metaphysics, its realm of possibility, its real universals, its representation of reality by truth. At the same time, the realistic fallacy is avoided and possibilities are not held to be alone real, even though the importance of the future is emphasized.

Pragmaticism led to a further refinement of philosophical method. It implies faith in common sense as the inherited wisdom of society, which is self-corrective. Thus our first task in the pursuit of knowledge is to discover what we already believe, without ever having had occasion to doubt. To Hume's objections, Reid and his Common-Sense school answered by faith in such inherited wisdom; and Kant and his Critical Philosophy answered by calling everything into question. Since Peirce held that neither was entirely wrong or entirely right, he countered with his philosophy of Critical Common-Sensism, according to which the fundamental beliefs of man are to be required as a guarantee of their validity to pass the test of genuine doubt. Critical Common-Sensism differs from the older school of Reid by accepting the existence of acritical indubitable propositions and inferences inherent from the beginning of mankind, original beliefs akin to instincts and invariably vague. Critical Common-Sensism also differs from the older school of Kant by insisting upon the immense value of genuine doubt and upon the necessity for self-criticism.

CHAPTER VIII

Science

A. PHILOSOPHICAL PRESUPPOSITIONS

THE EQUIPMENT WHICH PEIRCE BROUGHT TO BEAR UPON THE PHILOSOPHY OF science was that not only of a philosopher but also of a scientist. Unlike the majority of philosophers who have speculated about science, Peirce was, in one long period of his career, a practicing empirical scientist.[1] Although he wrote many papers on specific problems of empirical science, we shall not be concerned with that part of his work here. The presuppositions from which science starts, the logic of its method, and the implications of its conclusions are not treated by science proper and indeed lie outside its province; they must be presumed to be part of philosophy.

Science, including aim as well as method, may be in a certain sense self-contained, but it must start somewhere. Implicit in the means it employs as well as in the end it seeks are certain philosophical presuppositions which are none the less present for being ignored. Certain logical, metaphysical, psychological and pragmatic principles are implicit in science, and hence the postulates from which science takes its beginnings, the rules implied by its method, and the broad import of its conclusions are part of philosophy, and must be available to philosophical examination. Thus, before putting forward Peirce's understanding of science and its method, we shall be obliged to make some remarks concerning the presuppositions to which, by his philosophical principles, his own understanding of science is inevitably committed.

i. FROM LOGIC TO SCIENCE

Since according to Peirce logic and common experience are the topics from which all other branches of philosophy take their start, it must be expected that, broadly speaking, every department of the philosophy of science involves the whole of logic. We may simply say that the philosophy of science

[1] See chap. I, C and D.

presupposes logic. The study of logic began with the refutation of the hypothesis that it might be founded on science,[2] and while the converse is not thereby proved it is nevertheless held by Peirce to be true. Science is similar to logic in that its reasonings from initial assumptions carry their own validity.[3] But logic, Peirce held, is at once more abstract and more developed than any special science. (6.2)

From the strict point of view of logic, we may, without more ado, define science according to the definition required in Peirce's system, and then explain the definition by means of the terms employed. Science consists in a set of asserted modal propositions which represent the system of natural law on the ground of causality. The proposition is an illative argument,[4] and the modal proposition covers "a whole range of possibility."[5] The assertion in this connection would consist in evidence that certain propositions would be "definitely compulsory" on certain occasions.[6] Thus science is a set of illative arguments showing compulsion for certain occasions over a whole range of possibility. What the laws of nature are, on Peirce's assumptions, as well as the elucidation of causality, must be left for later parts of this chapter. But we can here take a glance at the remaining terms "illation" and "system."

Illation, represented by the word "ergo"[7] in the syllogism, is the sign of logical nexus, understanding the relation, "if *A*, then *B*," in a logical rather than a temporal sense. But if, in science, occasion covers the temporal sense of relation in this connection, cause must apply to the other. We shall in fact find that the illative relation in logic becomes translated in science to the relation of cause-and-effect.

The logic of relatives opens up vistas of relations hitherto undreamed. Instead of the confining relation of similarity, to which the older logic was restricted, the logic of relatives comprises many others. (4.5) The relation which is elevated to a position of prominence by the new logic of relatives is that of inclusion, in which the older notion of identity is considered a special case.[8] If all other notions are subordinated to a series of inclusions, the result is a system. The older logic was concerned with genera and species; the new logic is concerned with systems, and in its provisions the

---

[2] See chap. III, A, i.
[3] *Loc. cit.*
[4] See chap. III, B, iii.
[5] See chap. III, B, iv.
[6] See chap. III, C, i.
[7] See chap. III, C, i.
[8] See chap. III, B, vi, (c).

logic of induction "rises from the contemplation of a fragment of a system to the envisagement of the complete system." (4.5)

Later in this chapter we shall see how scientific method is composed of various combinations of deduction, abduction and induction, or the logic of probability.[9] The analytic steps in the scientific method are largely presupposed by the forms of critical logic. It is not too much to say that in one sense at least the method of science is simply an extension of logic, particularly of Speculative Rhetoric, which is the logic of discovery.[10] The discovery of laws and causes, and the prediction of events, by means of a study of facts, is the method of hypothesis and experiment. Logic, in that department of it which consists in the study of experimentation, shows how the method of science approximates toward that ideal form of investigation which consists in the observation of diagrams. This Peirce termed ideal experimentation,[11] and gave by it an aim for the guidance of scientific operations. Thus many of the ideas behind the meaning of science and the method it employs are already contained implicitly in certain of the forms of logic.

ii. FROM METAPHYSICS

There is no such thing as "allaying doubts concerning the first principles . . . by means of scientific experiments," (5.521) inasmuch as "idioscopic inquiry[12] must proceed upon the virtual assumption of sundry logical and metaphysical beliefs." This means that "the special sciences are obliged to take for granted a number of most important propositions, because their ways of working afford no means of bringing these propositions to the test. In short, they always rest upon metaphysics." (1.129)[13] Metaphysics is the prior study, even though it cannot tell us anything specific about actual events. Although particulars are subsumed by universals, it remains true that no number of universals will ever yield a particular. "The logical upshot of the doctrine of Scotus[14] is that real [i.e., actual] problems cannot be solved by metaphysics, but must be decided according to the evidence." (4.28)

If science starts from metaphysics, the question arises, From what metaphysics does science start? Peirce believed that "physical science gives its assent much more to scholastic realism (limited closely to its formal state-

---

[9] See this chapter, C, iii.
[10] See chap. III, D, iii.
[11] *Loc. cit.*
[12] See chap. VII, A, i.
[13] See chap. II, B, i.
[14] See chap. II, C.

ment) than it does to nominalism." (6.361)[15] The argument between the nominalism of Ockham and the realism of Scotus had been won by Scotus, in Peirce's view, and in his scientific work Peirce came to feel that "Had the conceptions of modern science been present to the minds of the disputants, the victory of the Scotists would have been more overwhelming than it was." (2.167)

A companion of Peirce's at college, as we have noted earlier,[16] first pointed out to him that science implies realism, although, being a realist, Peirce would most probably have come to the conclusion by himself sooner or later. Peirce certainly did not fail to elaborate the doctrine of realism[17] and to apply it in other connections. In the Introduction to *Scientific Theism*, F. E. Abbot "has so clearly and with such admirable simplicity shown that modern science is realistic," (4.1) moreover, "that science has always been at heart realistic, and always must be so." (1.20) Although Abbot's whole Introduction is devoted to the theme, one passage will perhaps suffice to show the arguments which convinced Peirce. "Nominalism," wrote Abbot, "teaches that things conform to cognition, not cognition to things; Scientific Realism teaches that cognition conforms to things, not things to cognition. . . . The contradiction is absolute and insoluble."[18] "The principle of cognition on which it [science] proceeds is utterly antagonistic to the nominalism which denies all objectivity to genera and species: it is drawn from Realism alone."[19]

Science, of course, does not and never has consciously operated from a basis of metaphysical realism. We may look once more to Abbot for the true procedure. He said that "science adopted a purely empirical objective method, took Nature for granted, investigated things and their relations by observation and experiment on the hypothesis of their equal objectivity."[20] From the point of view of science, reality is not a metaphysical theory at all; it is a procedural affair: "reality is only the object of the final opinion to which sufficient investigation would lead." (2.693) Peirce has already set forth the metaphysics which he, in common with Abbot declared that science presupposes. The subject matter upon which science operates is the phaneron, or field of phenomenon.[21] Categorically, this means that science seeks in the

---

[15] See chap. IV, C, i, and II, B, iii.
[16] See chap. I, C, ii.
[17] See chap. IV, C, ii.
[18] *Loc. cit.*, p. 11.
[19] *Loc. cit.*, p. 11.
[20] *Loc. cit.*, p. 31.
[21] See chap. IV, A, ii.

area of secondness by tests upon firstness for elements of thirdness.[22] In other words, science operates within actuality but seeks laws of possibility.[23] It learns to distinguish among habits for laws by means of the elimination of chance elements.[24]

In deriving science from ontology, the doctrine of realism, then, seems to be the most likely theory. But we cannot leave ontology for another topic without a word of caution. In actual operation, science must have no artificial obstacles put in its way. No metaphysical theory, not even the one with which it is assumed science starts, can be allowed to block the path of inquiry. Science seems to start from realism, and that also seems to be where it is going; but nevertheless if any facts emerge from inquiry which seem to contradict this derivation, the metaphysics, and not the science, must go. Logically, science starts from metaphysics, but historically, metaphysics—at least the metaphysics of science—is derived from science.

Turning now to that part or branch of metaphysics known as epistemology, we find that there, too, science has been provided for, at least by implication. Science is a special kind of knowledge,[25] and its method is a special kind of knowledge process,[26] learned by means of observed facts gained through brute experience.[27] We saw at the outset of the study of epistemology that an affinity between the mind and the external world was assumed, and that the name given to this assumption is *il lume naturale*. This natural tendency between the ideas which suggest themselves to the mind and the laws of nature is further emphasized in deriving science from epistemology. For, said Peirce, "every scientific explanation of a natural phenomenon is a hypothesis that there is something in nature to which the human reason is analogous." (1.316)[28] "There is a reason, an interpretation, a logic, in the course of scientific advance, and this indisputably proves to him who has perceptions of rational or significant relations, that man's mind must have been attuned to the truth of things in order to discover what he has discovered." (6.476) For every truth, there are an infinite number of errors, and the fact that there are as many truths found as there are is evidence that man must have "a natural bent in accordance with nature's." (6.477)

The foregoing carries with it two corollaries which are consistent with

[22] See chap. IV, B, i, ii and iii.
[23] See chap. IV, D, i.
[24] See chap. IV, D, ii.
[25] See chap. V, A.
[26] See chap. V, A, iii.
[27] See chap. V, A, ii.
[28] See chap. I, B, ii.

Peirce's theories about the knowledge process. The first of these is that science supposes an objective truth to be known. "The laws of nature are true," (5.426) which is to say, they are propositions referable to the universe by the correspondence principle.[29] The second is that if science seeks an objective truth, "only those men can advance science who desire simply to find out how things really are, without *arrière-pensée*." (4.34) The pursuit of pure science must itself be pure.

iii. FROM PSYCHOLOGY

The theory of science and even the theory of scientific method was stated by Peirce independently of the investigating subject, and hence also of psychology. However, since the scientist is also a person, there is a psychology of the scientist, and certain relevancies may be noted between some of the psychological categories, on the one hand, and the activities of scientists, on the other.

The category of belief is to a large extent alien to science. For "the scientific spirit requires a man to be at all times ready to dump his whole cartload of beliefs, the moment experience is against them." (1.55) Belief is out of place in science, which is concerned only with the "provisional establishment of . . . doctrines." (5.60) The kind of belief which is alien to science is, of course, conscious belief involving effort. That there is another kind is evident; for otherwise we would not be carrying a "whole cartload." What unconscious belief has to do with science, we shall learn in the next section.[30] In the conscious realm, doubt is the category that is the most involved in the method of science. The scientific method involves doubt, honest doubt for which we have found reasons. Doubt in the scientific method is the demand for rigorous proof, inasmuch as we can be changed from doubt to belief only by sufficient reason.[31]

We have seen already in studying the relations between epistemology and science that there is a natural light of reason which has correspondence in the objective world.[32] In psychology, this natural light emerges somewhat more candidly as instinct. We are credited with, so to speak, an instinctive attraction for knowledge. In some cases this may be quite specific. Animals as well as men, for instance, "all have from birth some notions however crude and concrete, of force, matter, space, and time; and, in the next place,

---

[29] See 5.153, quoted in chap. V, C, iii.
[30] See this chapter, A, iv.
[31] See chap. VI, C, ii.
[32] See this chapter, A, ii.

they have some notion of what sort of objects their fellow-beings are, and of how they will act on given occasions. Our innate mechanical ideas were so nearly correct that they needed but slight correction." (2.753) "The instincts connected with the need of nutrition have furnished all animals with some virtual knowledge of space and of force, and made them applied physicists. The instincts connected with sexual reproduction have furnished all animals at all like ourselves with some virtual comprehension of the minds of other animals of their kind, so that they are applied psychists." (5.586) In short, "all human knowledge, up to the highest flights of science, is but the development of our inborn animal instincts." (2.754)

Scientific method cannot be accomplished without a high degree of reasoning, a new kind of reasoning, carried on according to an elaborate objective scheme.[33] The highly involved logical pattern which the mind follows in going through the steps of the scientific method is certainly one of the most complex examples of reasoning. Science, through its method, is seeking for general conceptions, which, as the highest function of the mind, approximate most closely to the nature of form.[34]

iv. FROM METHODOLOGY

Although Peirce conceived philosophy as a branch of science,[35] it is clear that scientific method is part of the study of method in general, termed methodology. The method of science is a special case, albeit a highly special one, of the method of philosophy. The science of philosophy is not very greatly developed, but what there is of it must be taken into account in the philosophy of science. "For be this science of philosophy that is founded on those universal phenomena as small as you please, as long as it amounts to anything at all, it is evident that every special science ought to take that little into account before it begins work with its microscope, or telescope, or whatever special means of ascertaining truth it may be provided with." (1.246)[36]

Science cannot proceed, for example, without its well-recognized method. Yet philosophical inquiry is the very essence of scientific investigation, and its analysis reveals the fundamental steps, if not all the details, of scientific method.[37] Again, the distinction between theory and practice, which is so

[33] See chap. VI, D.
[34] See chap. VI, D, iii.
[35] See chap. VII, A, ii.
[36] See chap. VII, A, iv.
[37] See chap. VII, A, iii.

important to philosophy,[38] is of equal importance to science, and the pragmatic maxim[39] is valuable in relating scientific ideas, for science no more than philosophy can operate without clarity in its conceptions.

It is, however, chiefly when we come to the dim but powerful realm of the unconscious that we reach the profoundest effect which the lessons of methodology have to impart to scientific procedure. Critical Common-Sensism presents the problem of the realization of the fundamental beliefs of inherited wisdom with which willy-nilly we start, and the further problem of getting such inherited wisdom up to the surface where it can become available for inspection by the critical faculty.[40] The preliminary work of investigating common sense is laid at the door of philosophy but it is an inquiry which needs must be "concluded before the first outward experiment [of science] is made." (5.521)

The "circumstance which goes toward confirming my view that instinct is the great internal source of all wisdom and of all knowledge[41] is that all the 'triumphs of science,' of which that poor old nineteenth century used to be so vain, have been confined to two directions. They either consist in physical—that is, ultimately dynamical—explanations of phenomena, or else in explaining things on the basis of our common sense knowledge of human nature. Now dynamics is nothing but an elaboration of common sense; its experiments are mere imaginary experiments. So it all comes down to common sense in these two branches." (6.500) For "all science, without being aware of it, virtually supposes the truth of the vague results of uncontrolled thought upon such experiences [as "vague instinctive beliefs"], cannot help doing so, and would have to shut up shop if she should manage to escape accepting them." (5.522) Neither science nor its method knows any *tabula rasa* from which it can start; nor is it free from contamination by acritical indubitable beliefs. The most it can claim in this direction (and it is no small claim, indeed) is that once brought into the open, such beliefs are subjected by science to the closest scrutiny, for which by its method it is ably prepared.

---

[38] See chap. VII, A, v.

[39] See chap. VII, B, iv.

[40] See chap. VII, C, iii.

[41] Peirce did not believe, of course, that the "great internal source" of knowledge is the only one. The existence of the phaneron and its investigation (chap. IV, A) alone prevents that; and there are many other passages in previous chapters which show that the "outer world" is more important in every respect than the "inner world," in Pierce's estimation. Moreover, the great internal source of knowledge is a source and not itself knowledge. Knowledge, we have already learned, is knowledge about the external world. See chap. V.

B. Science in General

i. THE ESSENCE OF SCIENCE

We have just seen that science "is nothing but a development of our natural instincts," (6.604) notably starting from two in particular, feeding and breeding.[42] Physics and the physical sciences in general are based upon "those instincts about physical forces that are required for the feeding impulsion and the other [i.e., the biological sciences] upon those instincts about our fellows that are required for the satisfaction of the reproductive impulse. Thus, then, all science is nothing but an outgrowth from these two instincts." (6.500) But while the instincts may show the occasions which gave rise to science or its historical origins, they do not reveal its logical character or condition of being. Science, like everything else, is ill defined by origins alone. What we wish to discover, then, is a logical definition of science; we want to be able to define science "in such a manner that all its properties shall be corollaries from its definition." (1.232)

Science has been defined by Peirce as "pure theoretical knowledge," (1.637) as the search for truth by a well-considered method, (1.235) a search for "a natural history of [the] laws of nature," (6.12) not only of actual conditions but equally of "permanent possibility." (1.487) While it is true that "science itself, the living process, is busied mainly with conjectures, which are either getting framed or getting tested," (1.234) and that "the life of science is the desire to learn," (1.235) it remains true that "all the followers of science are animated by a cheerful hope that the processes of investigation, if only pushed far enough, will give one certain solution to each question to which they apply it." (5.407) "The only end of science, as such, is to learn the lesson that the universe has to teach it." (5.589) It seeks individual and general facts, laws being in Peirce's conception, as much facts as are individual occurrences. (1.434) "Science, when it comes to understand itself, regards facts as merely the vehicle of eternal truth," and "feeling that there is an arbitrary element in its theories, still continues its studies, confident that so it will gradually become more and more purified from the dross of subjectivity." (5.589)

"Science is not the whole of life," but rather something very special. (5.537) It specializes in generality and specificity of outlook, in completeness of knowledge. But its ideal goal is remote.[43] "Persons who know science chiefly

---

[42] See this chapter, A, iv.
[43] See chap. I, B, ii.

by its results—that is to say, have no acquaintance with it at all as a living inquiry—are apt to acquire the notion that the universe is now entirely explained in all its leading features." (1.116) But as a matter of fact our ignorance is extremely large. For "an infinitesimal ratio [of knowledge] may be multiplied indefinitely and remain infinitesimal still." (1.117)[44] Spencer and others "seem to be possessed with the idea that science has got the universe pretty well ciphered down to a fine point; while the Faradays and Newtons seem to themselves like children who have picked up a few pretty pebbles upon the ocean beach. But most of us seem to find it difficult to recognize the greatness and wonder of things familiar to us. As the prophet is not without honor save [in his own country] so it is also with phenomena." (5.65) Fortunately for all concerned, it is not what science has already accomplished that can be taken as a measure of its value, but rather its direction. "Now, as science grows, it becomes more and more perfect, considered as science," (6.430) and even though it may never become altogether perfect, the direction is one which justifies the energy which is put into scientific endeavors and the expectations which are held for its unlimited future.

ii. CLASSIFICATION AND SYSTEM OF THE SCIENCES

Classification is both a useful and a natural affair; it "is made by every man when he reasons, in the proper sense of that term." (2.204) Although we have already noted that the criterion according to which any classification is made is a philosophical affair,[45] and, moreover, that classification is rudimentary system,[46] the task still remains of choosing a criterion for the classification, or organization, of the sciences. How is the criterion to be chosen? At first, Peirce considered the feasibility of classifying the sciences by their origins. In this connection, he found that "all natural classification is . . . essentially, we may almost say, an attempt to find out the true *genesis* of the objects classified." (1.227) But "Genesis is production from ideas" and ideas have their true nature in logical abstraction rather than in historical origins. Thus the search for classification in genesis led to the notion of abstract order. "A science is defined by its problem; and its problem is clearly formulated on the basis of abstracter science." The possibility of classifying the sciences on the basis of their problems led Peirce to consider another alternative, namely, that of classifying the sciences by their *"techniques,"*

[44] See the list of matters of which we are ignorant, offered as a sample, in 1.119 and 6.464.
[45] See chap. VII, A, iv.
[46] See *loc. cit.*, quoting 3.454.

(2.644) that is, "according to the peculiar means of observation they employ." (1.101) But this, too, proved to be an historical rather than a logical criterion. He fell back upon the idea of classifying by means of degree of abstraction.

The criterion selected was the one found ready to hand in the writings of Auguste Comte.[47] Comte had suggested "that the sciences may be arranged in a series with reference to the abstractness of their objects; and that each science draws regulating principles from those superior to it in abstractness, while drawing data for its inductions from the sciences inferior to it in abstractness." (3.427) "Comte . . . produced a useful scale, as every candid man now confesses. It ran thus: Mathematics, Astronomy, Physics, Chemistry, Biology, Sociology." (1.258) Peirce then proposed to classify the sciences on "the idea that one science depends upon another for fundamental principles, but does not furnish such principles to that other." (1.180) "Of two departments of science *A* and *B*, of the same class, *A* may derive special facts from *B* for further generalization while supplying *B* with principles which the latter, not aiming so high, is glad to find ready-made. *A* will rank higher than *B*, by virtue of the greater generality of its object, while *B* will be richer and more varied than *A*." (1.238) Thus, as Peirce saw it, "the sciences form a sort of ladder, descending into the well of truth, each one leading on to another, those which are more concrete and special drawing their principles from those which are more abstract and general." (2.119) In this classificatory scheme, the sciences must be understood as distinct from one another; (2.41) "the fact that two classes merge is no proof that they are not truly distinct natural classes." (1.224)

"The first great division of science will be according to its fundamental purpose, making what I shall term *branches* of science. A modification of a general purpose may constitute a *subbranch*." (1.238) "I recognize," Peirce announced, "two branches of science: Theoretical, whose purpose is simply and solely knowledge of God's truth; and Practical, for the uses of life." (1.239) This distinction will be easy to make in the following classification of the sciences. For Peirce divided all the sciences into three chief groups: "All science is either, A. Science of Discovery; B. Science of Review; or C. Practical Science." (1.181) Practical science is not subdivided but we know that it is meant to be applied to all the technological applications of scientific knowledge to the practical affairs of life: such as engineering, medicine, navigation, pedagogics, surveying, etc. The practical sciences are "by far the most various of the two branches of science," (1.243) and Peirce confessed that he was "utterly bewildered by its motley crowd." The Science of Review

----

[47] *La philosophie positive,* deuxième leçon.

is half practical, half theoretical; its classification has not been attempted. (1.202) It is "the business of those who occupy themselves with arranging the results of discovery, beginning with digests, and going on to endeavor to form a philosophy of science . . . The classification of the sciences belongs to this department." (1.182)

The great theoretical branch of science is the Science of Discovery. "Science of Discovery is either I. Mathematics; II. Philosophy; or III. Idioscopy." (1.183) We have already considered the science of Philosophy,[48] and we are to consider Mathematics[49] later on in this chapter. The remaining department of theoretical science, then, is Idioscopy, and it is by far the largest branch. By the term "idioscopy" Peirce meant what we mean by the empirical sciences. (1.242) "Idioscopy has two wings: α the Physical Sciences; and β the Psychical, or Human Sciences. Psychical science borrows principles continually from the physical sciences; the latter very little from the former." (1.187) Let us consider the physical sciences first, and then the psychical.

"The physical sciences are: *a*. Nomological, or General, Physics; *b*. Classificatory Physics; *c*. Descriptive Physics. Nomological physics discovers the ubiquitous phenomena of the physical universe, formulates their laws, and measures their constants. It draws upon metaphysics and upon mathematics for principles. Classificatory physics describes and classifies physical forms and seeks to explain them by the laws discovered by nomological physics with which it ultimately tends to coalesce. Descriptive physics describes individual objects—the earth and the heavens—endeavors to explain their phenomena by the principles of nomological and classificatory physics, and tends ultimately itself to become classificatory." (1.188)

The divisions of the physical sciences are in turn subdivided. "Nomological physics is divided into, i, Molar Physics, Dynamics and Gravitation; ii, Molecular Physics, Elaterics and Thermodynamics; iii, Etherial Physics,[50] Optics and Electrics." (1.193) "Classificatory physics seems, at present, as a matter of fact, to be divided, quite irrationally and most unequally, into, i, Crystallography; ii, Chemistry; iii, Biology." (1.194) These are again subdivided, as will later be shown.[51] "Descriptive physics is divided into, 1, Geognosy, and, 2, Astronomy. Both have various well-known subdivisions." (1.198)

---

[48] See chap. VII, A, iv.

[49] See this chapter, D, i.

[50] In considering such studies as Gravitation and Etherial physics as branches of physics, it must be remembered that while Peirce was trying to make a system of the sciences, he had to work with "sciences in their present condition." (1.180) No doubt his own classification as of today would be somewhat different.

[51] See this chapter, D, ii, and iii.

Outline Classification of the Sciences

Theoretical

Science of Discovery

Mathematics
 of Logic
 of Discrete Series
 of Continua and Pseudo-Continua

Philosophy
 Phenomenology
 Normative Science
 Metaphysics

Idioscopy (Empirical Science)
 Physical Sciences
  Nomological Physics
   Molar Physics
   Molecular Physics
   Etherial Physics
  Classificatory Physics
   Crystallography
   Chemistry
   Biology
  Descriptive Physics
   Geognosy
   Astronomy

Science of Review

From digests of science to philosophy of science

Practical

Practical Science

Such sciences as: Pedagogics, gold-beating, etiquette, pigeon-fancying, vulgar arithmetic, horology, surveying, navigation, telegraphy, printing, bookbinding, papermaking, deciphering, ink-making, librarian's work, engraving, etc.

Psychical Sciences
 Nomological Psychics
  Introspectional Psychology
  Experimental Psychology
  Physiological Psychology
   Child Psychology
 Classificatory Psychics
  Special Psychology
  Linguistics
  Ethnology
 Descriptive Psychics
  History Proper
  Biography
  Criticism

(1.180–1.202; 1.243)

"The psychical sciences are: *a*. Nomological Psychics, or Psychology; *b*. Classificatory Psychics, or Ethnology; *c*. Descriptive Psychics, or History. Nomological psychics discovers the general elements and laws of mental phenomena. It is greatly influenced by phenomenology, by logic, by metaphysics, and by biology (a branch of classificatory physics). Classificatory psychics classifies products of mind and endeavors to explain them on psychological principles. At present it is far too much in its infancy (except linguistics . . .) to approach very closely to psychology. It borrows from psychology and from physics. Descriptive psychics endeavors in the first place to describe individual manifestations of mind, whether they be permanent works or actions; and to that task it joins that of endeavoring to explain them on the principles of psychology and ethnology. It borrows from geography (a branch of descriptive physics), from astronomy (another branch) and from other branches of physical and psychical science." (1.189)

The divisions of the psychical sciences are in turn subdivided. Nomological psychics is divided "into, i, Introspectional Psychology; ii, Experimental Psychology; iii, Physiological Psychology; iv, Child Psychology." (1.199) "Classificatory psychics is divided into, i, Special Psychology . . . ; ii, Linguistics . . . ; and iii, Ethnology." (1.200) "Descriptive psychics is divided into, i, History proper . . . ; ii, Biography . . . ; and iii, Criticism." (1.201)

The branches of theoretical branches, of which we have given some of the subdivisions, are again subdivided; but we shall postpone the inspection of them until later in the chapter, when we come to treat the special sciences separately.[52]

iii. THE LEADING CONCEPTIONS

Before going on to consider the empirical sciences and their method in detail, we may conclude this section on science in general by an analysis of what Peirce considered to be the leading conceptions of science. What is, so to speak, the firstness, secondness and thirdness of science in general? "Three of the leading conceptions of science," may be considered to be "the ideas of force, of continuity, and of evolution." (1.154) The quality with which science is chiefly concerned is that of (*a*) evolution, in all its various manifestations. The reaction is that of (*b*) force. And the representation is that of (*c*) continuity. Let us examine Peirce's conception of them.

(*a*) Evolution is a theory which "in general throws great light upon history and especially upon the history of science—both its public history and the account of its development in an individual intellect." (1.103) Before dis-

[52] See this chapter, D.

cussing evolution in its relation to science, let us look at the meaning of evolution itself.

The three theories of evolution were those of Darwin, Lamarck, and King. According to Darwin, evolution is brought about by "successive purely fortuitous and insensible variations *in reproduction*," (1.104) or natural selection, resulting from heredity which allows for sporting plus the "destruction of breeds or races that are unable to keep the birth rate up to the death rate." (6.15) According to Lamarck, evolution is brought about by a succession of minute changes not the result of reproduction but of individual striving. According to Clarence King,[53] evolution is brought about by the large changes in reproduction which have been forced on the organism by correspondingly large changes in the environment. (6.17)[54] Now, Peirce argued, "it seems altogether probable that all three of these modes of evolution have acted. It is probable that the last has been the most efficient." (1.105)

"The theory of natural selection is that nature proceeds by similar experimentation to adapt a stock of animals or plants precisely to its environment, and to keep it in adaptation to the slowly changing environment. But every such procedure, whether it be that of the human mind or that of the organic species, supposes that effects will follow causes on a principle to which the guesses shall have some degree of analogy, and a principle not changing too rapidly." (2.86)

In the wider sense in which the theory of evolution is applicable outside the province of biological species, it can be said that "evolution means nothing but *growth* in the widest sense of that word. Reproduction, of course, is merely one of the incidents of growth. And what is growth?" (1.174) In the same passage Peirce finds that growth is simply diversification, in the Spencerian sense of passage from the homogeneous to the heterogeneous. Evolution may be defined as "continual and indefinite progress toward a better adaptation of means to ends," (1.395) "the working out of a definite end," (1.204) and even though we do not yet know what the end is.

Can we, then, describe growth as the first quality of science? There is an evolution in the way in which qualities determine one another. (1.484) In the evolution of science, the change might take place by minute modifications of judgment. (1.107) This would mean externally and objectively that science "advances by leaps; and the impulse for each leap is either some new observational resource, or some novel way of reasoning about the observations." (1.109)

---

[53] *Catastrophism and the Evolution of Environment*, 1877.
[54] Also 1.104.

However, "the momentous question of evolution has unmistakable dependence on philosophy," (1.249) and must always remain a "theatre of controversy." (5.578)

(*b*) Force is "the great conception which, developed in the early part of the seventeenth century from the rude idea of a cause, and constantly improved upon since, has shown us how to explain all the changes of motion which bodies experience, and how to think about all physical phenomena; which has given birth to modern science, and changed the face of the globe; and which, aside from its more special uses, has played a principal part in directing the course of modern thought, and in furthering modern social development." (5.404) Despite the importance of the conception, "it is surprising to see how this simple affair has muddled men's minds. In how many profound treatises is not force spoken of as a 'mysterious entity' . . . " It is important, then, to get a clear notion of it.

We have already had a hint of the nature of force, in our study of ontological secondness.[55] There it was shown that "pure dyadism is an act of . . . blind force." (1.328) Force is "almost pure binarity." (2.84) "A brute force is only a complication of binarities. It supposes not only two related objects, but that in addition to this state of things there is a *second* subsequent state. It further supposes these two tendencies, one, of the one relate, tending to change the first relation in one way in the second state; the other, of the other relate, tending to change the same relation in a second way. Both those changes are in some way combined, so that each tendency is to some degree followed, to some degree modified. This is what we mean by *force*." "All dynamical action, or action of brute force, physical or psychical, either takes place between two subjects or at any rate is a resultant of such action between pairs." (5.484) For instance, "Every physical force reacts between a pair of particles, either of which may serve as an index of the other." (2.300)

So much for the ontological approach to force. But now let us come down upon the conception from another perspective, that of mathematics and of force itself considered quite simply as it operates. There is one "grand fact which this conception embodies. This fact is that if the actual changes of motion which the different particles of bodies experience are each resolved in its appropriate way, each component acceleration is precisely such as is prescribed by a certain law of Nature according to which bodies, in the relative positions [and velocities] which the bodies in question actually have at the moment, always receive certain accelerations, which, being com-

[55] See chap. IV, B, ii.

pounded by geometrical addition, give the acceleration which the body actually experiences" (5.404) "This is the only fact which the idea of force represents.... Whether we ought to say that a force *is* an acceleration, or that it *causes* an acceleration" makes no essential difference. The point is that the ideas of force and of acceleration are one.

Brute force is "force without law or reason." (1.427) Force is "not only irrational but anti-rational, since to rationalize it would be to destroy its being." (6.342) There is no doubt that "blind force is an element of experience distinct from rationality," (1.220) although this does not mean that there is no relation between force and law, since laws themselves are forces in a sense. (1.175) The sense is that law requires force in order to be effective. "Law, without force to carry it out, would be a court without a sheriff; and all its dicta would be vaporings." (1.212)

"The work of Galileo and his successors lay in showing that forces are accelerations by which [a] state of velocity is gradually brought about. The words 'cause' and 'effect' still linger, but the old conceptions have been dropped from mechanical philosophy; for the fact now known is that in certain relative positions bodies undergo certain accelerations. Now an acceleration, instead of being like a velocity a relation between two successive positions, is a relation between three; so that the new doctrine has consisted in the suitable introduction of the conception of threeness. On this idea, the whole of modern physics is built." (1.359)

(*c*) Continuity is a conception made up of two classical definitions, those of Aristotle and Kant. First of all, it is evident that continuity contains the ideas of "unbrokenness" (1.163) or "fluidity, the merging of part into part." (1.164) This idea is embodied in Aristotle's understanding of continuity, termed by Peirce "Aristotelicity." "The property of Aristotelicity may be roughly stated thus: a continuum contains the end point belonging to every endless series of points which it contains." (6.123) "Aristotle seems to have had it obscurely in mind in his definition of a continuum as that whose parts have a common limit." (4.122)[56]

But clearly this is not a sufficient definition of continuity, since continuity also contains the notion of infinite subdivision. (1.166) Peirce showed that since the totality of points on a line were not a totality of distinct points, and hence could not be said to constitute a collection, the question occurs of what such a totality is. "The answer is plain: the possibility of determining more than any given multitude of points, or, in other words, the fact that there is room for any multitude at every part of the line, makes it *continuous*. Every

---

[56] *Metaphysics*, 1069a5.

point actually marked upon it breaks its continuity, in one sense." (3.568) The property of infinite divisibility is one with which Aristotle failed to reckon. It has been set up by Kant, who defined [the] "continuity [of a line] as consisting in this, that between any two points upon it there are points." (4.121) Peirce "termed the property of infinite intermediety, or divisibility, the *Kanticity* of a series. It is *one* of the defining characters of a continuum."

Peirce held that Kant's definition, like that of Aristotle, "must be accepted as a fact." (3.215) Therefore, he "made a new definition, according to which continuity consists in *Kanticity* and *Aristotelicity*. The Kanticity is having a point between any two points. The Aristotelicity is having every point that is a limit to an infinite series of points that belong to the system." (6.166) In other words, "a perfect continuum is the absolute generality with which two rules hold good, first, that every part has parts; and second, that every sufficiently small part has the same mode of immediate connection with others as every other has." (4.642)

The doctrine of continuity is full of "scientific beauty and truth." (1.171) Continuity exists in nature, as an objective affair. (1.22) The uniformity of nature is related to the notion that "*all things* . . . swim in continua." (1.171) In this sense, a continuum may also be described as "a discontinuous series with additional possibilities." (1.170) We may perceive that where actuality is discontinuous, possibility supplies the continuity. Thus, thirdness alone suffices to yield the conception of continuity. (5.67) "Continuity represents thirdness almost to perfection." (1.337)

Thirdness has especially been important in science under the conception of continuity, (1.340) for "all the great steps in the method of science in every department have consisted in bringing into relation cases previously discrete." (1.359) Continuity "enters into every fundamental and exact law of physics or of psychics that is known." (1.62) Thus, "continuity, it is not too much to say, is the leading conception of science."

C. Scientific Method

i. THE ROLE OF THE SCIENTIST

We have already seen that the scientist is committed to the assumption of an affinity between his own mind and the laws of nature.[57] In scientific method, of course, this assumption becomes a paramount one, and even guides the minutiae of research. "In examining the reasonings of those physi-

[57] See this chapter, A, ii.

cists who gave to modern science the initial propulsion which has insured its healthful life ever since, we are struck with the great, though not absolutely decisive, weight they allowed to instinctive judgments," (1.80)[58] suggesting beyond a doubt that they were, sometimes unconsciously, relying upon "some natural tendency toward an agreement between the ideas which suggest themselves to the human mind and those which are concerned in the laws of nature." (1.81) "Think of what trillions of trillions of hypotheses might be made of which one only is true; and yet after two or three or at the very most a dozen guesses, the physicist hits pretty nearly on the correct hypothesis. By chance he would not have been likely to do so in the whole time that has elapsed since the earth was solidified. . . . Man has not been engaged upon scientific problems for over twenty thousand years or so. But put it at ten times that if you like. But that is not a hundred thousandth part of the time that he might have been expected to have been searching for his first scientific theory." (5.172) The fact that "logical principles are known by an inward light of reason, called the 'light of nature'," (2.23) not only distinguishes it from the theological "light of grace," but also points toward precision in science. It suggests, for instance, Galileo's *il lume naturale*,[59] but with the special meaning that "it is the simpler Hypothesis in the sense of the more facile and natural, the one that instinct suggests, that must be preferred." (6.477) Such precision, however, is not to be allowed to steer scientific investigation toward the interpretation of it held by the positivists. For more than naïve empirical investigation is required. Peirce said that he agreed with Whewell, "that progress in science depends upon the observation of the right facts by minds *furnished with appropriate ideas.*" (6.604)[60]

If there were nothing more required for the scientific method except its subjective elements, it would be a simple affair, indeed, and perhaps, on the principle of the widespread possession of common sense, more persons would be scientists. But the guidance of the natural light of reason has its limits. The evidence that Peirce was not recommending a subjective method for science is contained not only in his objective logical method but also in the contrast which he made between the scientific method and the *a priori* method, "The test of whether I am truly following the method is not an immediate appeal to my feelings and purposes, but, on the contrary, itself involves the application of the method." (5.385)[61] "It is a great mis-

---

[58] See this chapter, B, i.
[59] See chap. V, A; and this chapter, A, ii.
[60] *History of the Inductive Sciences,* 3rd ed. (London, 1837), p. 6.
[61] See also 5.386-387.

take to suppose that the mind of the active scientist is filled with propositions which, if not proved beyond all reasonable cavil, are at least extremely probable. On the contrary, he entertains hypotheses which are almost wildly incredible, treats them with respect for the time being." He does this simply because likely hypotheses are those which fall within the range of our preconceived ideas. The affinity, which undoubtedly exists, "between the reasoner's mind and nature's" (1.121) must be "checked by comparison with observation."

"The man of science has received a deep impression of the majesty of truth, as that to which, sooner or later, every knee must bow. He has further found that his own mind is sufficiently akin to that truth, to enable him, on condition of submissive observation, to interpret it in some measure. As he gradually becomes better and better acquainted with the character of cosmical truth, and learns that human reason is its issue and can be brought step by step into accord with it, he conceives a passion for its fuller revelation. He is keenly aware of his own ignorance, and knows that personally he can make but small steps in discovery. Yet, small as they are, he deems them precious; and he hopes that by conscientiously pursuing the methods of science he may erect a foundation upon which his successors may climb higher. This, for him, is what makes life worth living and what makes the human race worth perpetuation. The very being of law, general truth, reason—call it what you will—consists in its expressing itself in a cosmos and in intellects which reflect it, and in doing this progressively; and that which makes progressive creation worth doing—so the researcher comes to feel—is precisely the reason, the law, the general truth for the sake of which it takes place."[62]

"When a man desires ardently to know the truth, his first effort will be to imagine what the truth can be," for "nothing but imagination . . . can ever supply him an inkling of the truth. He can stare stupidly at phenomena; but in the absence of imagination they will not connect themselves together in any rational way." (1.46) "It is not too much to say that next after the passion to learn there is no quality so indispensable to the successful prosecution of science as imagination." (1.47) But imagination in the mind of the scientist is a peculiar affair. The phenomena of the experimentalist is general and future, "what *surely will* happen to everybody in the living future who shall fulfill certain conditions." (5.425) "The scien-

[62] Review of Karl Pearson, *The Grammar of Science* in *Popular Science Monthly*, 58 (1901), 296 ff.

tific imagination dreams of explanations and laws." (1.48) Imaginative reasoning is "reasoning by diagrams." (4.74)[63]

"A scientific man is simply one who has been trained to conduct observations of some special kind, with which his distinctive business begins and ends." (6.568) But, as a matter of fact, the famed powers of observation possessed by the trained and gifted scientist are exaggerated. Peirce asserted of the scientific men "that the artists are much finer and more accurate observers than they are, except of the special minutiae that the scientific man is looking for." (1.315) The reason for this is that the scientist is not called on for observation alone; a large part of the field of science "is absolutely inaccessible to our powers of observation." (2.730) "We may, however, learn of a fact indirectly. Either the fact was experienced directly by some other person whose testimony comes to us, or else we know it by some physical effect of it." (1.431) Thus the scientist must possess adequate powers of judgment. It is a fact that "scientific men now think much more of authority than do metaphysicians." (1.32)

Despite the reliability, and indeed the necessity, of *il lume naturale*, or common sense, "there is no proposition at all in science which answers to the conception of belief." (1.635) Consequently, the scientist may have preconceived notions but no feeling of loyalty toward them.[64] In general, science is indifferent to the good qualities and good intentions of the scientist. Science is a thing apart from the ulterior purposes of the scientist; (1.45) it is even indifferent to his morality, (1.50) although scientists can hardly be other than moral men. (1.49)

Peirce divided men into three classes according to the three ontological categories: those for whom the chief thing is the quality of feelings, the artists; those for whom it is power over activity, the practical men of business; and those for whom it is reason, the scientists. "For men of the first class, nature is a picture; for men of the second class, it is an opportunity; for men of the third class, it is a cosmos, so admirable, that to penetrate to its ways seems to them the only thing that makes life worth living." (1.43) It is this third class, wholly possessed by a passion to learn, which is the scientific class. The scientist, then, requires as his primary equipment a completely absorbing concern with inquiry. "This is a property so deeply saturating its inmost nature that it may truly be said that there is but one thing needful for learning the truth, and that is a hearty and active desire to learn what is true. If you really want to learn the truth,

[63] See chap. III, D, iii.
[64] See this chapter, A, iii.

you will, by however devious a path, be surely led into the way of truth, at last." (5.582)

ii. THE PRINCIPLES OF INQUIRY

"If we are to define science, not in the sense of stuffing it into an artificial pigeon-hole where it may be found again by some insignificant mark, but in the sense of characterizing it as a living historical entity, we must conceive it as that about which such men as I have described busy themselves. As such, it does not consist so much in *knowing*, nor even in 'organized knowledge', as it does in diligent inquiry into truth for truth's sake, without any sort of axe to grind, nor for the sake of the delight in contemplating it, but from an impulse to penetrate into the reason of things." (1.44) The true purpose of skepticism is to "push inquiry," (1.344)[65] and the "sole object" of inquiry is the "settlement of opinion." (5.377)[66]

The attempt of the positivists to purify inquiry by restricting it marks the death of inquiry.[67] Inquiry cannot be held down to hypotheses whose truth or falsity is capable of being directly perceived. (5.198)[68] The extension of research tends to reduce the area of impossibility, (3.527) an unsafe category in which to regard anything as finally placed, except perhaps logical things. Freedom of inquiry is restricted by reason (2.635) and not without injury to it by anything else. The over-all principle of inquiry is "Do not block the way of inquiry." (1.135) From the principle that inquiry may be restricted by reason but is otherwise free, three subordinate principles of inquiry follow. These may be termed the principles of (*a*) fallibilism, (*b*) pragmatic indifference, and (*c*) economy.

(*a*) We have seen in the logic of probability that "all positive reasoning is of the nature of judging the proportion of something in a whole collection by the proportion found in a sample.[69] Accordingly, there are three things to which we can never hope to attain by reasoning, namely, absolute certainty, absolute exactitude, absolute universality. We cannot be absolutely certain that our conclusions are even approximately true; for the sample may be utterly unlike the unsampled part of the collection." (1.141) Fallibilism, then, is required by logic. It is required also by ontology, since the living spontaneity and irregular departures from law of the ontological

---

[65] See chap. VI, C, ii.
[66] See chap. VII, A, iii.
[67] See chap. VII, A, v.
[68] Also 2.511 n.
[69] See chap. III, C, iii.

category of chance[70] make any absolute formulations impossible. We should not allow ourselves to be bound, or our inquiry restricted, by any "absolute assertion," (1.137) by any statement "that this, that, or the other" can never be known, (1.138) by the postulation of any inexplicable ultimates, (1.139) or by any "last and perfect formulation" (1.140) or a law or truth.[71] Fallibilism is required of science by the method of philosophy:[72] no rational method is absolute but all involve indeterminacy. Thus fallibilism appeared to Peirce to be proved by deduction from his philosophy. But he admitted the prevalence of the opinion that science yielded absolute knowledge, (1.9) holding it to be an error less common in the physical sciences. He proposed to "lop off the heads," (6.603) not of all absolute propositions but only of "all absolute propositions whose subject is not the Absolute."

Of course, all strictures upon the final unreliability of knowledge act as boomerangs; and the question must eventually arise of whether the principle of fallibilism is itself fallible; for if we can doubt the absoluteness of the principle of fallibilism, then the possibility of reaching absolute knowledge is restored. The problem is perhaps irreducible. Suffice to say that Peirce saw its difficulty and retreated a little: he attacked the absolute notion that no hypothesis can ever be more than approximately true, (5.199) and he gave due credit to the critic who accused him of not seeming to be "absolutely sure of [his] own conclusions." (1.10) Nevertheless, the principle of fallibilism demands of all inquiry that it should be remembered that our knowledge is limited in scope and that what we do know we know "only in an uncertain and inexact way." (5.587)

(*b*) The principle of pragmatic indifference may be stated as the independence of theory from practice and the consequent necessity for conducting scientific inquiry on abstract grounds divorced from all considerations of use. We have already noted that all methodological considerations demand the sharp distinction between theory and practice.[73] Pure science "takes an entirely different attitude toward facts from that which practice takes.[74] For Practice, facts are the arbitrary forces with which it has to reckon and to wrestle. . . . Practice requires something to go upon, and it will be no consolation to it to know that it is on the path to objective truth." (5.589) It is "desirable, not to say indispensable . . . for the successful march of discovery . . . in science generally that practical utilities,

[70] See chap. IV, D, ii, (*a*).
[71] See this chapter, A, ii.
[72] See chap. VII, A, iii.
[73] See chap. VII, A, v.
[74] See this chapter, B, i.

whether low or high, should be *put out of sight* by the investigator."
(1.640)

"True science is distinctively the study of useless things." (1.76) Investigators who are concerned with industrial problems can hardly be said
to "rank as genuine scientific men," for example "chemists who occupy
themselves exclusively with the study of dyestuffs." "The genuine scientific
chemist cares just as much to learn about erbium—the extreme rarity of
which renders it commercially unimportant—as he does about iron. He
is more eager to learn about erbium if the knowledge of it would do more
to complete his conception of the Periodic Law, which expresses the mutual
relations of the elements." (1.45) "It would be useless to enumerate the
other sciences, since it would only be to reiterate the same declaration."
(1.670) Practicality is something which in science "must be forgotten and
forgiven." (1.671) For when a proposition "is sunk to the condition of a
mere utensil . . . it ceases altogether to be scientific." This does not mean,
of course, that theoretical science is wanting in practical applications. Quite
the contrary is true; for "a theory cannot be sound unless it be susceptible
of applications, immediate or remote,[75] whether it be good economy so
to apply it or not." (2.7) The point is not that scientific inquiry excludes
practical applications but that such applications must be put out of sight,
as Peirce says, and forgotten, during the course of the inquiry.

(*c*) The principle of economy is one which governs all scientific activity.
"There never was a sounder logical maxim of scientific procedure than
Ockham's razor: *Entia non sunt multiplicanda praeter necessitatem*. That
is to say, before you try a complicated hypothesis, you should make quite
sure that no simplification of it will explain the facts equally well." (5.60)
" 'Try the theory of fewest elements first; and only complicate it as such
complication proves indispensable for the ascertainment of truth.' . . . Realism can never establish itself except upon the basis of an ungrudging acceptance of that truth." (4.35)

In research, economy means weighing the expenditure of such means
as energy, money, time, etc., out of the available fund. For instance, "knowledge that leads to other knowledge is more valuable in proportion to the
trouble it saves in the way of expenditure to get that other knowledge."
(1.122) "It *must* be true that it does not pay (in any given state of science)
to push the investigation beyond a certain point in fullness or precision."
There is a certain residual irregularity which in all observation is due to
chance and not to insufficiency of investigation. (6.46) Absolute exactitude

[75] See chap. VII, B, iv.

in research should be considered the direction of research rather than its finite goal. Thus, "For every line of scientific research there is in any given stage of its development, an appropriate standard of certitude and exactitude, such that it is useless to require more, and unsatisfactory to have less. This is a part of the doctrine of the Economy of Research." (1.85)

The principle of economy is, as we have just noted, also one of simplicity. This means in the process of investigation the advisability of attacking the simplest problems first. (1.63) Such is the task of the analytic method. (1.64) Another movement toward simplicity is the relating of previously separate materials: "all the great steps in the method of science in every department have consisted in bringing into relation cases previously discrete." (1.359) This is made possible by "not trusting to principles and methods which are not logically founded upon facts." (1.110) It is also made possible by confining inquiry to the most universal and regular events. "Science is from the nature of its procedure confined to the investigation of the ordinary course of nature." (1.87) Nothing can be dismissed on the score of extraordinary occurrence, however. For "although science cannot infer any particular violation of the ordinary course of nature, it may very well be that it should find evidence that such violations are so frequent and usual that this fact is itself a part of the ordinary course of nature." (1.91)

The principle of economy, finally, compels the scientist to keep as closely as possible to his method. By this, Peirce did not intend to restrict science to positive experimental evidence, (5.200) since the method of science in turn depends upon other things and is not ultimate. Science is, so to speak, "laboratory-philosophy," (1.129) and in emphasizing the method rather than the results of science, (1.116) Peirce did not mean that only the method is valid. The metaphysical presuppositions are always present, and the conclusions emerge, but as a matter of scientific simplicity, the logical method must be the chief concern of those engaged in inquiry. Let us turn next, then, to an examination of this logical method.

iii. THE LOGIC OF SCIENTIFIC INVESTIGATION

The purpose of the "logic of scientific investigation" (2.751) is to settle "real problems" according to the evidence. (4.28) The difficulty is to determine which generals are real.[76] Surely not all are, nor even all those which are held to be so. In the actual, or, as Peirce called it, the real world,

[76] See 5.430, quoted in chap. IV, C, ii.

"certain combinations occur while others do not occur. Of those which occur in the ideal world some do and some do not occur in the real world; but all that occur in the real world occur also in the ideal world." (3.527) "For the simple reason that the real world is a part of the ideal world, namely that part which sufficient experience would tend ultimately (and therefore definitively), to compel Reason to acknowledge as having a being independent of what he may arbitrarily, or willfully, create." (3.527 n.1) "For the real world is the world of sensible experience, and *it is a part of the process of sensible experience to locate its facts in the world of ideas. . . .* [77] In respect to the ideal world we are virtually omniscient; that is to say, there is nothing but lack of time, of perseverance, and of activity of mind to prevent our making the requisite experiments to ascertain positively whether a given combination occurs or not. Thus, every proposition about the ideal world can be ascertained to be either true or false." (3.527)

We have already noted how a method for the discovery of general ideas and the demonstration of their validity is developed from the activities of symbols in the relations between minds and facts.[78] This is possible because "We usually conceive Nature to be perpetually making deductions in *Barbara*. This is our natural and anthropomorphic metaphysics.[79] We conceive that there are Laws of Nature,[80] which are her Rules or major premises. We conceive that Cases arise under these laws; these cases consist in the predication, or occurrence, of *causes*, which are the middle terms of the syllogisms. And, finally, we conceive that the occurrence of these causes, by virtue of the laws of Nature, result in effects which are the conclusions of the syllogisms.[81] Conceiving of nature in this way, we naturally conceive of science as having three tasks—(1) the discovery of Laws, which is accomplished by induction; (2) the discovery of Causes, which is accomplished by hypothetic inference; and (3) the prediction of Effects, which is accomplished by deduction." (2.713) Put another way, the operation of the scientific method consists in the following three stages: (*a*) This particular entity or thing must belong to that class (abduction). (*b*) Let us look for that class among a fair sample of particulars (induction). (*c*) What is true of the whole class must be true of its particulars (deduction).

Peirce felt that his logic of science would have to be one which would

[77] Italics mine.
[78] See chap. III, D, iii.
[79] See 1.487, quoted in chap. IV, A.
[80] See chap. IV, D, ii, (*b*).
[81] See chap. III, C, i, for the logic of the syllogism.

"preserve all these natural conceptions." (2.713) This would not consist of the imposition of a logic of science upon its method, or of reading into scientific method a logic that was alien to it. There are logical principles at work in science which we never suspected until recently, but which stand revealed in the examination of scientific procedure. What F. E. Abbot has termed "the silent method of science"[82] proves to be a peculiar synthesis of logic and fact.

The unique method of science consists in the welding of experimentation and reasoning and is named by Peirce "indagation." (6.568)[83] "Reasoning is strictly experimentation.[84] Euclid, having constructed a diagram according to prescription, draws an extra line, whereupon his mind's eye observes new relations not among those prescribed quite as surprising as new metals or new stars. Experimentation is strictly appeal to reason. [The] Chemist sets up [a] retort, introduces ingredients, lights [a] fire, [and] awaits [the] result. Why so confident? Because he trusts that what happens once happens always; nature follows general laws, in other words, has a reason. Successful research—say Faraday's—is conversation with nature; the macrocosmic reason, the equally occult microcosmic law, must act together or alternately, till the mind is in tune with nature. This, the distinctively scientific procedure, linked experimentation and reasoning (suppose we say *indagation*), essentially involves special, new experience." Scientific observation consists in not plain unaided perception but rather in "perceiving by the aid of analysis." (1.34)

"Reasoning from familiar experience plays a great role in science: it lays the indispensable foundation, is needful in frequent later conjectures. The part so built is the strongest of the structure, upholding the rest." (6.568) While it is true that we lean on common sense[85] in science and trust to instinctive beliefs,[86] nevertheless "the whole history of thought shows that our instinctive beliefs, in their original condition, are so mixed up with error that they can never be trusted till they have been corrected by experiment." (1.404) Science mainly "advances by leaps;[87] and the impulse for each leap is either some new observational resource, or some novel way of reasoning about the observations. Such novel way of reasoning might, perhaps, be considered as a new observational means, since it draws atten-

[82] *Scientific Theism*, p. 37.
[83] Lat. *indago*, to search out or investigate.
[84] See chap. III, D, iii, and VI, D, iii.
[85] See chap. VII, C, iii.
[86] See chap. VI, C, ii.
[87] See this chapter, B, iii, (*a*).

tion to relations between facts which would previously have been passed by unperceived." (1.109) What a scientific proposition expresses may be real, provided both experience and reason uphold the truth of the predicate. (3.460) Of course, "scientific explanation ought to consist in the assertion of some positive matter of fact," (6.274) but as F. E. Abbot says, quoting from Jevons, we can only get from particulars to particulars through generals.[88] Hence the necessity for reasoning about generals as well as experimentation with facts.

The logic of scientific investigation, or "indagation," viewed from Peirce's realistic position, involves reasoning as inseparable from experimentation. The radical empiricist's scorn for rationality is found to be inconsistent with scientific method. For, as Peirce pointed out, observing consists in "testing suggestions of theories," (1.34) and scientists venture into the laboratory and the field from "an interest in finding out whether or not general propositions actually held good." (1.34) It follows from this, as well as from the principle of economy,[89] that reasoning is the first step to be taken in experimentation. There is one thing which the scientists, or, as Peirce called them, the "laboratory-philosophers ought to grant: that when a question can be satisfactorily decided in a few moments by calculation, it would be foolish to spend much time in trying to answer it by experiment." (4.69)

The element in scientific investigation which links experimentation and reasoning is the hypothesis, or hypothetical proposition.[90] To set up an hypothesis is to "postulate" a proposition which is "no more than to hope it is true." (6.39) "Every concept, every general proposition of the great edifice of science, first came to us as a conjecture." (5.480) "The order of the march of suggestion . . . is from experience to hypothesis." (2.755) "These ideas are the *first logical interpretants* of the phenomena that suggests them, and which, as suggesting them, are signs, of which they are the (really conjectural) interpretants." (5.480)[91] Hypotheses are "spontaneous conjectures of instinctive reason." (6.475)[92] An hypothesis "is a surrender to the Insistence of an Idea. The hypothesis, as the Frenchman says, *c'est plus fort que moi*. It is irresistible; it is imperative. We must throw open our gates and admit it at any rate for the time being." (5.581) Observation consists in yielding to that force. By *hypothesis* is meant "not

[88] *Scientific Theism*, p. 42.
[89] See this chapter, C, ii, (c).
[90] See chap. III, B, iv.
[91] See chap. III, B, i.
[92] See chap. VII, C, iii.

merely a supposition about an observed object, . . . but also any other supposed truth from which would result such facts as have been observed." (6.525) A "working hypothesis" is "a problematic proposition that touches a question of fact, and from which can be deduced definite consequences which the inquirer is engaged in testing by comparing them with observations."[93] An hypothesis, or "retroduction," (1.68) or "abduction," (5.171, 5.590) is simply a proposition which in science you "try first and endeavor to refute." (6.216) An important hypothesis is called a theory. (2.638)

The problem of choosing hypotheses for testing in the method of science presents difficulties. "Now the testing of a hypothesis is usually more or less costly. Not infrequently the whole life's labor of a number of able men is required to disprove a single hypothesis and get rid of it. Meantime the number of possible hypotheses concerning the truth or falsity of which we really know nothing, or next to nothing, may be very great. In questions of physics there is sometimes an infinite multitude of such possible hypotheses. The question of economy[94] is clearly a very grave one." (6.530) On the other hand, it is not advisable to restrict the field of hypotheses to be chosen, for fear of strangling science in its cradle. The safest rule is to say that "Any hypothesis, therefore, may be admissible, in the absence of any special reasons to the contrary, provided it be capable of experimental verification." (5.197)[95] In other words, this means that it is "best to adopt the hypothesis which leaves open the greatest field of possibility." (1.170) This substantially conveys the prohibition against the nominalistic tendency to declare things "absolutely inexplicable. That blocks the road of inquiry."[96] The field of possibility[97] in this connection is "that . . . which, in a certain state of information, is not known to be false." (3.442)[98]

The adoption of an hypothesis is a "provisional adoption . . . because every possible consequence of it is capable of experimental verification, so that the persevering application of the same method may be expected to reveal its disagreement with facts, if it does so disagree." (1.68)

Peirce gave three rules for the choosing of successful hypotheses: "1. The hypothesis should be distinctly put as a question, before making the observations which are to test its truth. In other words, we must try to

[93] Review of David D. Ritchie, *Darwin and Hegel* in *The Nation*, 57 (1893), 393.
[94] See this chapter, C, ii, (c).
[95] "This is approximately the doctrine of pragmatism." See chap. VII, B, iv.
[96] See this chapter, C, ii.
[97] See chap. IV, D, i, (a).
[98] This procedural definition is as such valid, despite the repudiation of it as an anacoluthon in 3.527. The difficulty is solved and the definition saved in 6.367.

see what the result of predictions from the hypothesis will be. 2. The respect in regard to which the resemblances are noted must be taken at random. We must not take a particular kind of predictions for which the hypothesis is known to be good. 3. The failures as well as the successes of the predictions must be honestly noted. The whole proceeding must be fair and unbiased." (2.634) If according to these rules fair hypotheses are chosen, procedure in science is ready to introduce the next step, which consists in the testing of hypotheses.

"The operation of testing a hypothesis by experiment, which consists in remarking that, if it is true, observations made under certain conditions ought to have certain results, and then causing these conditions to be fulfilled, and noting the results, and, if they are favorable, extending a certain confidence to the hypothesis, I call *induction*." (6.526)[99] The difference between induction and hypothesis in scientific investigation is important. The bearing of the two logical steps is closely related but clearly distinguishable. "Induction is the experimental testing of a theory. . . . Abduction consists in studying facts and devising a theory to explain them." (5.145) "The only sound procedure for induction, whose business consists in testing a hypothesis already recommended by the retroductive procedure, is to receive its suggestions from the hypothesis first, to take up the predictions of experience which it conditionally makes, and then try the experiment and see whether it turns out as it was virtually predicted in the hypothesis that it would. Throughout an investigation it is well to bear prominently in mind just what it is that we are trying to accomplish in the particular stage of the work at which we have arrived. Now when we get to the inductive stage what we are about is finding out how much like the truth our hypothesis is, that is, what proportion of its anticipations will be verified." (2.755) Hypotheses lead us to causes; inductions, to laws.[100] "Induction shows that something *actually is* operative; Abduction merely suggests that something *may be*." (5.171)

"Induction consists in starting from a theory [i.e., an "important hy-

[99] See chap. III, C, iii, (*b*). By induction in this connection Peirce did not mean crude induction. He meant rather the quantitative variety. In scientific method crude induction becomes the historical argument, that the future will in every negative way resemble the past. What has not happened in the past is not likely to happen in the future, the argument runs. It leans on deduction through the continuity of experience to demonstrate that nothing can happen in the future that has not happened in the past, thus flying in the face of the fact of novelty. The historical argument is not the method of science but of extreme rationalists who wish to place reason without experiment before reason with experiment, and to lay strictures upon facts in the future, a logically as well as a scientifically impossible task.

[100] See chap. III, C, ii, (*c*).

pothesis"], deducing from it predictions of phenomena, and observing those phenomena in order to see *how nearly* they agree with the theory." (5.170) "When I say that by inductive reasoning I mean a course of experimental investigation, I do not understand experiment in the narrow sense of an operation by which one varies the conditions of a phenomenon almost as one pleases. We often hear students of sciences, which are not in this narrow sense experimental, lamenting that in their departments they are debarred from this aid. No doubt there is much justice in this lament; and yet those persons are by no means debarred from pursuing the same logical method precisely, although not with the same freedom and facility. An experiment, says Stöckhardt[101] . . . is a question put to nature. Like any interrogatory, it is based on a supposition. If that supposition be correct, a certain sensible result is to be expected under certain circumstances which can be created, or at any rate are to be met with. The question is, Will this be the result? If Nature replies 'No!' the experimenter has gained an important piece of knowledge. . . . If Nature says 'Yes' to the first twenty questions, although they were so devised as to render that answer as surprising as possible, the experimenter will be confident that he is on the right track, since 2 to the 20th power exceeds a million." (5.168)

"The justification for believing that an experimental theory which has been subjected to a number of experimental tests will be in the near future sustained about as well by further such tests as it has hitherto been, is that by steadily pursuing that method we must in the long run find out how the matter really stands. The reason that we must do so is that our theory, if it be admissible even as a theory, simply consists in supposing that such experiments will in the long run have results of a certain character. But I must not be understood as meaning that experience can be exhausted, or that any approach to exhaustion can be made." (5.170)

A number of important facts stand out sharply in this presentation. First, it is extremely significant that Peirce pointed out how induction, or the logic of laboratory procedure, must be preceded by abduction, or hypothesis. The real advances of science are carried by abduction; induction in the laboratory is made in order to disprove or allow the abduction. This brings us to the second fact. Peirce did not believe that experimentation could constitute proof in any strict meaning of that term. Only those "who are so impressed with what they have read in popular books about the triumphs of science . . . really imagine that science has *proved* that the universe is regulated by law down to every detail." (6.201) The correct answer given

[101] See Julius A. Stöckhardt, *Die Schule der Chemie*, pt. i, sec. 6.

by Nature in the laboratory question put to her can only indicate a probability in favor of the experimenter's idea, which then can become, as Peirce said, "only somewhat more deeply engrained." (5.168)

Probability thus proves to be an important factor in the method of science. Its determination of chance distributions seems to be as close as science can come to certainty, without either attaining absolutes or impugning the validity of objective law. One of the most wonderful features of reasoning, prominent in the doctrine of science, is the fact that "reasoning tends to correct itself, and the more so, the more wisely its plan is laid." (5.575) The wise laying of such plans is the method of science, starting from hypothesis aided by induction. "That Induction tends to correct itself, is obvious enough . . . [and] a properly conducted Inductive research corrects its own premisses." (5.576)

It is customary in science to make predictions concerning the outcome of events, the success of which is taken as a certain degree of verification. This is accomplished in the following manner: "Qualitative induction[102] consists in the investigator's first deducing from the retroductive hypothesis as great an evidential weight of genuine conditional predictions as he can conveniently undertake to make and to bring to the test, the condition under which he asserts them being that of the retroductive hypothesis having such degree and kind of truth as to assure their truth. In calling them 'predictions,' I do not mean that they need relate to future events but that they must antecede the investigator's knowledge of their truth, or at least that they must virtually antecede it." (2.759) They may be merely "general description[s] of . . . experimental phenomena." (5.427) "A verification of a general prediction is a method which consists in finding or making the conditions of the prediction and in concluding that it will be verified about as often as it is experimentally found to be verified. Its justification is that if the Prediction does not tend in the long run to be verified in any approximately determinate proportion of cases, experiment must, in the long run, ascertain this; while if the Prediction will, in the long run, be verified in any determinate, or approximately determinate, proportion of cases, experiment must in the long run, approximately ascertain what that proportion is." (2.269) Thus, "a hypothesis can only be received upon the ground of its having been *verified* by successful *prediction*." (2.739) The process, termed "predesignation,"[103] is an "argument from a random sample."

When the degree of certainty in favor of an hypothesis proves to be

[102] See chap. III, C, ii, (*b*), (3).
[103] See 2.790 and 2.269, quoted in chap. III, C, ii.

high, and the predictions verified, the investigation is assumed to be at an end. This does not mean that the inquiry is closed forever, and the hypotheses thus verified turned over to belief, for "it is only the premises of science, not its conclusions, which are directly observed." (6.2) "We call them in science established truths [i.e., demonstrated hypotheses], that is, they are propositions into which the economy of endeavor prescribes that, for the time being, further inquiry shall cease." (5.589) The whole structure erected by science is always subject to revision; it is always in process and never complete. Induction and abduction (or retroduction) are steps leading to the formation of a deductive system. "Over the chasm that yawns between the ultimate goal of science and such ideas of Man's environment as, coming over him during his primeval wanderings in the forest, while yet his very notion of error was of the vaguest, he managed to communicate to some fellow, we are building a cantilever bridge of induction, held together by scientific struts and ties. Yet every plank of its advance is first laid by Retroduction [or abduction] alone . . . and neither Deduction nor Induction contributes a single new concept to the structure." (6.475)[104]

Peirce did not dwell upon the deductive steps in scientific method, which, while not responsible for discovery in the sense in which induction and abduction undoubtedly must be admitted to be, are yet necessary to produce the system that holds the inductions together. He was an experimental scientist as well as a philosopher, and he was keenly aware that the first rule of thumb in scientific investigation is "Do not block the way of inquiry." (1.136) "Induction and Deduction are after all not so very unlike." (5.580)[105] But deduction, despite its daily employment by scientists, is yet associated in their minds with philosophy. Now, "to set up a philosophy which barricades the road of further advance toward the truth is the one unpardonable offence in reasoning, as it is also the one to which metaphysicians have in all ages shown themselves most addicted." (1.136) Peirce was not concerned to freeze and thus to arrest the accomplishments of science, but rather to define the method so that the accomplishments could continue to increase. He had faith in the ultimate goal of science as an objective set of absolute and universal truths to be known, and he believed, as does every true scientist, that "Inquiry properly carried on will reach some definite and fixed result or approximate indefinitely toward that limit." (1.485)[106]

[104] See also 5.145.
[105] See chap. III, C, iii.
[106] See 5.409, quoted in chap. V, C, i.

D. THE SPECIAL SCIENCES

i. MATHEMATICS

In treating of the special sciences, we begin with mathematics, since it is "far more developed than any [other] special science." (6.2)

"Every science has a mathematical part, a branch of work that the mathematician is called in to do." (1.133) "There is no science whatever to which is not attached an application of mathematics. This is not true of any other science, since pure mathematics has not, as a part of it, any application of any other science, inasmuch as every other science is limited to finding out what is positively true, either as an individual fact, as a class, or as a law; while pure mathematics has no interest in whether a proposition is existentially true or not." (1.245) "The first questions which men ask about the universe are naturally the most general and abstract ones. Nor is it true, as has so often been asserted, that these are the most difficult questions to answer." (1.52) "Cut off from all inquiry into existential truth . . . mathematics is only busied about *purely hypothetical questions,*" (1.53) and hence is "the most abstract of all the sciences. For it makes no external observations, nor asserts anything as a real fact.[107] When the mathematician deals with facts, they become for him mere 'hypotheses'; for with their truth he refuses to concern himself. The whole science of mathematics is a science of hypotheses; so that nothing could be more completely abstracted from concrete reality." (3.428)

Mathematics is close to logic (1.245)[108] as we shall see, close also to metaphysics, particularly to phenomenology. (5.40) In a sense, it is broader than metaphysics, (4.232) but in another it is answerable to the triad of ontological categories, even to their complex subdivisions, (1.365)[109] and the effort of one mathematician to avoid the triad in geometry ended by surrendering to them. (3.423) Peirce in fact erected his metaphysics upon a phenomenological basis, and his phenomenology consists of a triad of categories numerically entitled.[110]

"Mathematics is the study of what is true of hypothetical states of things. That is its essence and definition." (4.233)[111] This is in agreement with

---

[107] See also 4.232.
[108] See chap. III, A, ii.
[109] See chap. III, B, i.
[110] See chap. IV, B.
[111] See also 4.238.

Plato and Aristotle. (4.232) Mathematics occupies itself in "merely tracing out the consequences of hypotheses"; (4.132) its "only aim is to discover not how things actually are, but how they might be supposed to be, if not in our universe, then in some other." (5.40) "Mathematics studies what is and what is not logically possible, without making itself responsible for its actual existence." (1.184)

"The primary division of mathematics into algebra and geometry is the usual one. But, in all departments, it appears both *a priori* and *a posteriori*, that divisions according to differences of purpose should be given a higher rank than divisions according to different methods of attaining that purpose. . . . For now that everybody knows that any mathematical subject, from the theory of numbers to topical geometry, may be treated either algebraically or geometrically, one cannot fail to see that so to divide mathematics is to make twice over the division according to fundamental hypotheses, to which one must come, at last. This duplication is worse than useless, since the geometrical and algebraical methods are by many writers continually mixed." (4.247) "Let us, then, divide mathematics according to the nature of its general hypotheses, taking for the ground of primary division the multitude of units, or elements, that are supposed; and for the ground of subdivision that mode of relationship between the elements upon which the hypotheses focus the attention." (4.248)

"The hypotheses of mathematics relate to systems which are either [*a*] finite collections, [*b*] infinite collections, or [*c*] true continua;[112] and the modes of reasoning about these three are quite distinct. These, then, constitute three orders." (1.283) (*a*) Finite collections subdivide into (1) the simplest mathematics [i.e., mathematical or symbolic logic] and (2) "the general theory of finite groups." (*b*) Infinite collections subdivide into (1) "arithmetic, or the study of the least multitudinous of infinite collections" and (2) "the calculus, or the study of collections of higher multitude." (*c*) True continua, or "topical geometry," is subdivided into Topics, Metrics and Graphics. Metrics "is the doctrine of the properties of such bodies as have a certain hypothetical property called absolute rigidity, and all such bodies are found to slide upon a certain individual surface called the Absolute. This absolute, because it possesses individual existence, may properly be called a thing. Metrics, then, is not pure geometry; but is the study of the graphic properties of a certain hypothetical thing. But neither

---

[112] Elsewhere Peirce stated his primary triad of mathematical categories as: "a. the Mathematics of Logic; b. the Mathematics of Discrete Series; c. the Mathematics of Continua and Pseudo-continua." (1.185)

ought graphics to be considered as pure geometry. It is the doctrine of a certain family of surfaces called the *planes*. . . . Graphics then is not pure geometry but is geometrical perspective." (4.219) Topics "is the study of the continuous connections and defects of continuity of loci which are free to be distorted in any way so long as the integrity of the connections and separations of all their parts is maintained." Metrics and Graphics, then, are impure subdivisions, and "All strictly pure geometry, therefore, is Topics."[113]

Since "all necessary reasoning, whether it be good or bad, is of the nature of mathematical reasoning," (5.147) it may be well to examine it with some care.[114] "Mathematicians alone reason with great subtlety and great precision." (4.425) "The mathematician does two very different things: namely, he first frames a pure hypothesis stripped of all features which do not concern the drawing of consequences from it . . . and, secondly, he proceeds to draw necessary consequences from that hypothesis." (3.559) Mathematics begins as an observational science.[115] It "advances, just as the physical sciences do, by observation and generalization."[116] What is observed is an image or diagram.[117] "The reasoning of mathematics is now well understood. It consists in forming an image of the conditions of the problem, associated with which are certain general permissions to modify the image, as well as certain general assumptions that certain things are impossible. Under the permissions, certain experiments are performed upon the image, and the assumed impossibilities involve their always resulting in the same general way." (5.8) The image observed is always the image of a diagram: "mathematical reasoning is diagrammatic. This is as true of algebra as of geometry." (5.148) "The algebraic schemata are arrays of characters, sometimes in series, sometimes in blocks, with which are associated certain rules of permissible transformation. . . . By virtue of these rules . . . when one array has been written . . . the mathematician directly perceives that another array is permissibly scriptible." (4.246) In other terms, mathematical reasoning "consists in constructing a diagram according to a general precept, in observing certain relations between parts of that diagram not explicitly required by the precept, showing that these relations will hold for all such diagrams, and in formulating

---

[113] Topics, however, is an extremely undeveloped science. See 4.428.

[114] See Arthur W. Burks, *Logical Foundations*, chap. III, sec. 2.

[115] See chap. III, A, ii. Also, e.g., G. H. Hardy, *A Mathematician's Apology* (Cambridge, University Press, 1940), pp. 63-64.

[116] Review of John Watson, *Comte, Mill and Spencer* in *The Nation*, 60 (1895), 284.

[117] See chap. III, D, iii.

this conclusion in general terms." (1.54)[118] "Thus the necessary reasoning of mathematics is performed by observation and experiment." (3.560)

Mathematical reasoning is deductive. (5.145) But it is also indirect. Indirect reasoning is "the mathematician's recipe for everything," (4.132) for "in solving a mathematical problem, we usually introduce some part or element into the construction which, when it has served our purpose, is removed." (3.561) Since "the mathematician conceives an operation as something itself to be operated upon," (1.83) mathematics leads directly into the method of hypostatic abstraction.[119]

"It may be said that mathematical reasoning . . . almost entirely turns on the considerations of abstractions as if they were objects. The protest of nominalism[120] against such hypostatisation . . . is simply a protest against the only kind of thinking that has ever advanced human culture." (3.509) For "the hypotheses of pure mathematics are purely ideal[121] in intention," (5.126) and "you will find that the typical pure mathematician is a sort of Platonist. Only, he is [a] Platonist who corrects the Heraclitan error that the eternal is not continuous. The eternal is for him a world, a cosmos, in which the universe of actual existence is nothing but an arbitrary locus. The end that pure mathematics is pursuing is to discover that real potential world." (1.646) "The pure mathematician [as we have seen] deals exclusively with hypotheses. Whether or not there is any corresponding real thing, he does not care. His hypotheses are creatures of his own imagination; but he discovers in them relations which surprise him sometimes. A metaphysician may hold that this very forcing upon the mathematician's acceptance of propositions for which he was not prepared, proves, or even constitutes, a mode of being independent of the mathematician's thought, and so a *reality*.[122] But whether there is any reality or not, the truth of the pure mathematical proposition is constituted by the impossibility of ever finding a case in which it fails." (5.567)

ii. PHYSICS

The chief contribution Peirce had to make was in philosophy and not in physics, yet it was due in large measure to physics since Peirce was for

---

[118] See also 3.560.
[119] See chap. VI, D.
[120] See chap. IV, C, i.
[121] By ideal here is not meant mental, but rather perfect and possible. See chap. I, B, ii; also IV, C, ii.
[122] See chap. IV, C, ii.

so long a practicing physicist. Thus, he announced that his "philosophy may be described as the attempt of a physicist to make such conjecture as to the constitution of the universe as the methods of science may permit, with the aid of all that has been done by previous philosophers." (1.7) Since he held that metaphysics can throw light on physics,[123] we shall not be surprised, therefore, to find embedded in his physical ideas some of the philosophical notions with which we are already familiar.

It will be recalled that the support given by physics to scholastic realism was an argument which weighed heavily with Peirce.[124] Then, again, Pierce was the first metaphysician to assign the notion of probability[125] such a high place that his leading notions are indissolubly associated with it. "Law, which requires to be explained, and like everything which is to be explained must be explained by something else, that is, by non-law or real chance." (6.613) There was nothing to do but "follow the usual method of the phycisists, in calling in chance to explain the apparent violation of the law of energy which is presented by the phenomena of growth; only instead of chance, as they understand it, I call in absolute chance."[126] "The idea that chance begets order ... is one of the corner-stones of modern physics." (6.297) Chance at once begets order in the physical world, and prevents it from becoming absolute; (1.404) physical facts suffer "aberrations due to the imperfect obedience of the facts to law." (1.402) The standard absolute uniformities of the older physics were asserted by Peirce to be a thing of the past. (6.101)

All men and even animals "have from birth some notions, however crude and concrete, of force,[127] matter, space, and time." (2.753)[128] Dynamics, for instance, is "nothing but an elaboration of common sense." (6.500)[129] All physics is based on mechanics, or on suggestions from mechanics. Force, time and space all refer to the category of secondness. (6.212)[130; 131] Force is almost pure secondness, but the physical categories of time and space will require further discussion.

"Time," Peirce maintained, "is real." (5.458)[132] It is "a particular variety

---

[123] 5.423, quoted in chap. VII, C, ii.
[124] 6.361, quoted in chap. IV, C, i, (c).
[125] See chap. III, C, iv.
[126] See chap. IV, D, ii, (a) and (b).
[127] See this chapter, B, iii, (b).
[128] See this chapter, B, i.
[129] See also 6.573, and chap. VII, C, iii.
[130] See chap. IV, B, ii.
[131] See also 2.84 and 5.456.
[132] And "not the figment which Kant's nominalism proposes to explain it as being." (6.506)

of objective Modality." (5.459) The temporal order is dependent upon ontological secondness, since comparison between first and last requires a standard, and thus is dyadic. (1.497) But since time has no limits, and is thus infinite, it also involves thirdness.[133] "Time is a continuum," (1.499)[134] and since "continuity and generality are the same thing," (4.172) namely, the "absence of distinction of individuals," time "embod[ies] conditions of possibility."[135] The existence of memory proves not that the continuity of time is subjective, but on the contrary that it is objective and a constituent of the universe, for if it "consists of discrete instants, all but the feeling of the present instant would be utterly non-existent." (4.641) The objectivity of time is given in perception,[136] and we may conclude that "time is the form under which logic presents itself to objective intuition," (6.87) not a product of subjective intuition at all.

But "Time with its continuity logically involves some other kind of continuity than its own. Time, as the universal form of change, cannot exist unless there is something to undergo change, and to undergo a change continuous in time there must be a continuity of changeable qualities." (6.132) Time in this sense may be described as the order of affectibility. (6.128) The theory is that "time has a point of discontinuity at the present," (6.86) yet the present is not discontinuous with past and future. It is impossible to tell about "the present instant were it utterly cut off from past and future. We can only guess; for nothing is more occult than the absolute present." (2.85) The present "is [yet] connected with the past by a series of real infinitesimal steps." (6.109) "The Past consists of the sum of *faits accomplis*, and this Accomplishment is the Existential Mode of Time." (5.459) The future is "not Actual [or existent], since it does not act except through the idea of it, that is, as a law acts; but is either Necessary or Possible, which are of the same mode." In other words, the future "is plainly that Nascent State between the Determinate and the Indeterminate."

It would be impossible to examine time without also introducing events, since one cannot be understood without the other. "Time is that diversity of existence whereby that which is existentially a subject is enabled to receive contrary determinations in existence. Phillip is drunk and Phillip is sober would be absurd, did not time make the Phillip of this morning another Phillip than the Phillip of last night." (1.494) "Events are constituted by regularities," (1.411) and regularities involve time. Events are no more

---

[133] See chap. IV, B, iii.
[134] See this chapter, B, iii.
[135] See also 6.325.
[136] See chap. VI, B, iii, quoting 5.205.

subjective than is time; "only real [i.e., objective] events . . . 'take place,' or have dates, in real time. . . . What, then, is a real event? It is an existential junction of incompossible facts." (1.492)

Events exist in space as well as in time, although absolute position is a fallacious notion. "A thing may be said to be wherever it acts; but the notion that a particle is absolutely present in one part of space and absolutely absent from all the rest of space is devoid of all foundation." (1.38)[137] Space is "so to say, nothing but the way in which actual bodies conduct themselves." (5.530) This contention did not, in Peirce's view, imply the unreality or even the derived reality of space. He declared that "Newton's view that it [i.e., space] is a real entity is alone logically tenable." (5.496) On the whole, however, Peirce decided to "adopt the Leibnizian conception of Space in place of the Newtonian. . . . In that Leibnizian view, Space is merely a possibility limited by an impossibility; a possibility of no matter what affections of bodies (determining their relative positions), together with the impossibility of those affections being actualized otherwise than under certain limitations, expressed in the postulates of topical, graphical, and metrical geometry. . . . Space is thus truly general." (5.530) Space presents a hierarchy of dimensionality, (1.501) embodied, like time, in conditions of possibility. (4.172) Since no two things can be alike in all respects, space provides places in which two things, otherwise alike, can differ as to position. "Thus space does for different subjects of one predicate precisely what time does for different predicates of the same subject." (1.501)[138]

We began the examination of Peirce's philosophy of physics by referring to his metaphysical category of chance; we may fittingly close by discussing his ideas of causality, which he deemed to be predominantly physical. Peirce did not posit cause as fundamental. (6.66)[139] Much that we deem ascribable to errors of observation are due to chance, not cause. (6.46) Peirce finally refused to use cause at all as a philosophical word, and preferred to substitute in most cases "explanation." (6.600) The truth is that existential events do not have causes, only facts do. (6.93)[140] The "idea of second is predominant in . . . causation . . . For cause and effect are two." (1.325)

Cause may be divided, as by Aristotle,[141] into final and efficient cause. For "we must understand by final causation that mode of bringing facts about

---

[137] A clear anticipation of modern physics.

[138] See 6.82-85 for further on the relation of space to particles and events.

[139] The definition of science in general according to logic yet involves the notion of causality. See this chapter, A, i.

[140] Presumably Peirce is referring to facts rather than events in 6.414-415.

[141] *Metaphysica*, 44b1 and 70b26.

according to which a general description of result is made to come about, quite irrespective of any compulsion for it to come about in this or that particular way." (1.211) "Efficient causation, on the other hand, is a compulsion determined by the particular condition of things, and is a compulsion acting to make that situation begin to change in a perfectly determinate way." (1.212)[142] "Efficient causation is that kind of causation whereby the parts compose the whole; final causation is that kind of causation whereby the whole calls out its parts." (1.227) Although "we still talk of 'cause and effect' . . . in the mechanical world, the opinion that phrase was meant to express has been shelved long ago. We now know that the acceleration of a particle at any instant depends upon its position relative to other particles at that same instant; while the old idea was that the past affects the future, while the future does not affect the past." (5.382 n.)[143] The fact is that "science can allow itself to be swayed only by efficient causes." (6.434)

iii. BIOLOGY

Although Peirce divided biology "into, 1, Physiology; and 2, Anatomy," (1.197) and asserted that "Physiology is closely allied to chemistry and physics," and "Anatomy is divided into many distinct fields," it was not the classificatory aspect but the developmental one which interested Peirce here. Biology, at least in its philosophical aspects, centered for Peirce chiefly around the theory of evolution, and indeed he asserted that the purpose of the triad of ontological categories in biology is "to show the true nature of the Darwinian hypothesis." (1.354)[144] "In biology, the idea of arbitrary sporting is First, heredity is Second, the process whereby the accidental characters become fixed is Third." (6.32)[145] From the point of view of chemical protoplasm, feeling[146] is first, reactivity or "contractility" is second, and assimilation, or habit-taking,[147] is third. (1.351) In terms of physiology, these become, first, "the excitation of cells"; second, "the transfer of excitation over fibres"; and third, "the fixing of definite tendencies under the influence of habit." (1.393)

In the process of natural selection, the same three factors emerge: "first, the principle of individual variation or sporting; second, the principle of

---

[142] See this chapter, A, i.
[143] See also 6.600: the past no more determines the future than the future the past.
[144] See chap. II, D, throughout.
[145] See chap. IV, B.
[146] See chap. VI, B, i.
[147] See chap. VI, C, i.

hereditary transmission, which wars against the first principle; and third, the principle of the elimination of unfavorable characters." (1.398) Evolution produces both real and natural classes, (1.216) which have no metaphysical sanctity. (1.204) "For evolution is nothing more nor less than the working out of a definite end," a final cause that is not known. The dissection of a corpse would leave nothing but meaningless parts from the point of view of the whole organism; the final causation of the whole is as necessary to life as the efficient causation of the parts. (1.220)[148] Final causation in the organism takes the form of regularity of rhythm: "A man is a wave, but not a vortex." "The Darwinian controversy is, in large part, a question of logic. Mr. Darwin proposed to apply the statistical method to biology." (5.364)[149] Peirce observed that "growth *appears* to violate the law of energy. To explain it, we must, at least, suppose a simulated or *quasi*, chance, such as Darwin calls in to produce his fortuitous variations from strict heredity." (6.613) But the classifications according to evolution are equivalent to the genealogy of species but not to logical division which has to be set up on some other basis. (1.572)

iv. SOCIAL SCIENCE

Social science was in Peirce's day, as it has remained in ours, a field which successfully defied all attempts to render it scientific. All efforts to elicit from its subject matter theories which are true and practices which can be fruitfully applied had thus far failed. And there was suspicion in the minds of many physically oriented speculators as to whether there was after all such a thing as social science to be developed. Peirce had made up his mind on this question. "That there are social sciences—the natural history of religion, economics, political science, the science of human heredity—there can be no doubt. Whether or not there already exists a general sociology apart from the social sciences, is a question too vague to be answered."[150]

A current of misunderstanding runs through modern social science, akin to that from which the normative sciences suffer. (5.128) Social science has been held to be a science of mind, on nominalistic premises.[151] Now, this subjective status cannot be allowed even to psychology which is "a special science . . . based upon a well-grounded logic." (3.432) Since "the greatest achievements of mind have been beyond the powers of unaided individuals," (6.315), the subject matter of social science is not an individual affair. Social

[148] See this chapter, D, ii.
[149] See also 1.395-399, and chap. II, D.
[150] Review of E. A. Ross, *Foundations of Sociology* in *The Nation*, 81 (1905), 43.
[151] See chap. IV, C, i.

science should investigate the personality of social organizations, such as corporations. (6.271) It should study such phenomena as telepathy. The triad of ontological categories, Peirce claimed, led in this case to a science which should be called "pneumatology." (1.354) If "man [is] a community of cells," then society is a community of men. We are "mere cells in a social organism." (1.647) And "man's circle of society . . . is a sort of loosely compacted person, in some respect of higher rank than the person of an individual organism." (5.421) There is no progress in the conception of truth as that for which one fights, which is the conception dictated by society when it is "broken into bands, now warring, now allied." (1.59) The next logical step toward alleviating such a condition would be "the recognition that a central authority ought to determine the beliefs of the entire community," (1.60) but this would be advisable only where "a less absolute authority," namely, science, prevails.

The upshot of Peirce's conclusions concerning the organization of society is that the application of scientific method to social science is a prime necessity, but one which has been prohibited by the conception of social science as a subjective affair and by the conception of society as associated with final cause. That society is so associated is undoubtedly true. (1.267) That physical science is probabilistic, while social science appears to be absolute because conduct works in absolutes, also is true. And these facts do present difficulties for social science. But Peirce felt that social science exists, nevertheless, on a par with the other sciences, as a possibility, and he would have agreed with his friend, Abbot, who declared, in that splendid Introduction which Peirce never tired of praising, that "Scientific men have quietly assumed the objectivity of relations, and steadily pursued the path of discovery in total disregard of the disputes of metaphysicians—not, however, without a serious loss to science itself, in the growth and spread of the false belief that science can legitimately deal only with physical investigations, and that the scientific method has no applicability with higher sciences."[152]

Certainly the scientific method, as an implicit affair, has worked well enough in the physical sciences. But before the same method can be applied equally well to the social field, the logic of scientific method, or, as Peirce named it, indagation, will have to become explicit and self-aware; its principles will have to be made known abstractly and without regard for any empirical field to which it may be applied. Prerequisite for such a development are "broad and philosophical *aperçus* covering several sciences, by which we are made to see how the methods used in one science may be

[152] F. E. Abbot, *Scientific Theism*, p. 33.

made to apply to another.[153] This involves the development of the philosophy of science, as an integral part of science and a guarantee of the progress of the special sciences, especially of those whose development has been hitherto retarded.

V. SUMMARY OF THE CHAPTER

This chapter deals with the philosophy of science. Science is a system of natural law, illatively expressed in modal propositions. Science is thus an extension of logic. The relation of inclusion in logic yields system in science. Scientific method is an extension of logical method: its analytic steps presuppose the forms of critical logic.

It requires metaphysics, since it assumes metaphysical principles in trying to decide questions according to the evidence. The metaphysics required by science is that of scholastic realism, as Peirce learned from Abbot. The derivation is tacit; science takes nature for granted, seeking within actuality for laws of possibility. This is possible because of an affinity between mind and the world: human reasoning is analogous to nature.

Science is independent of the scientist, but there is also a psychology of the scientist. Belief is alien to science, for the scientist must be ready to abandon all belief, despite the undoubted correspondence of the mind and the objective world. Science is produced by instinct but does not remain dependent upon it. The analysis of scientific reasoning reveals the existence of an elaborate logical method.

We have already examined the broad outlines of this method, as part of the general method of philosophy. The method reveals that it, too, confirms what metaphysics has avowed: dependence upon logic and instinct. In methodology, the latter is termed common sense. Science presupposes the vague results of uncontrolled thoughts, although later subjecting them to criticism.

Science is the result of the development of two instincts: feeding and breeding, physical sciences from the former and biological sciences from the latter. Science is pure theoretical knowledge, not facts; it involves a specialized generality of outlook.

Theory and practice dictate the first grand division of the sciences. Under these come the sciences of discovery, of review, and of practice. The latter two are the most numerous but the former is the most vital. All three branches have numerous subbranches.

All the sciences depend upon three leading conceptions, corresponding to

[153] Review of W. S. Jevons, *Studies in Deductive Logic* in *The Nation*, 32 (1881), 228.

the triad of categories. These are: evolution, force, and continuity. Evolution is growth in its widest sense; force is dynamical action between pairs of particles; continuity is infinite divisibility plus unbroken connexity.

The affinity of the scientist for truth is the first postulate of scientific method. But scientific method is nothing merely subjective; it involves the application of an abstract logical method. For the scientist is not a person who has been granted special powers; he is simply a trained observer in a specialized field who also brings reasoning to bear upon it.

Scientific inquiry is governed by principles rather than by professional men. Inquiry must not be held down by any principles, however, but must be free. Three cautions have been set up to ensure this. They are: fallibilism, pragmatic indifference, and economy. Fallibilism does not allow any absolutes in science—not even the absolute of fallibilism. Pragmatic indifference assures the independence of science from practical considerations. Economy recommends that the simplest principles and operations be tried first in scientific procedure.

The purpose of scientific investigation is to settle real problems according to evidence, by locating facts in the world of ideas. Science has three tasks: the discovery of laws, the discovery of causes, and the prediction of effects. The unique method of science consists of the welding of experimentation and reasoning, termed by Peirce "indagation." Suggestions begin with experience and go on to hypothesis. The hypothesis arises from surrender to the insistence of an idea. The correctly chosen hypotheses, or abductions, are tested by induction. Induction predicts phenomena from an hypothesis, and then examines the phenomena to see how nearly it agrees with the hypothesis. The wonderful feature of inductive procedure is its capacity for self-correction. A scientific theory or law is an hypothesis into which the principle of economy dictates that for the present further inquiry shall cease. But inquiry has as its final goal a unified and fixed limit.

Mathematics is the most abstract and perfect of the sciences. It is the study of what is true of hypothetical states of things. The subdivisions of mathematics are: finite collections, infinite collections, and true continua. Mathematical reasoning is deductive and ideal, a model of reasoning in science.

Physics is most important to philosophy. All physics is based on mechanics. Force, time, and space are its leading categories. We have already discussed force. Time is a real, objective modality, a continuum of the order of affectibility. Time reconciles contrary determinations in existence: Phillip drunk and Phillip sober are enabled to be the same Phillip without contradiction. But things are wherever they act; space is the way in which actual bodies conduct themselves. Cause is the last physical category, divided into efficient and final varieties. Final cause brings about events of a general description; efficient causation is compulsion, bringing about specific determinations. Science is swayed only by efficient causes.

Biology centered for Peirce about the notion of Darwinian evolution. The triad of categories here appears as sporting, the transmission of hereditary characters, and the elimination of unfavorable characters. The organism is a wave but not a vortex. Real classes have no metaphysical sanctity but are produced in evolution. Thus the lesson of Darwin is one of logic, the application of statistical method of biology.

Social science is not subjective, an affair of minds or even only of collections of persons. Social science, or pneumatology, studies communities. But the social field cannot become a science until the logic of scientific method is understood abstractly and applied consciously, a task for the philosophy of science.

CHAPTER IX

Ethics

‹‹‹‹‹‹‹‹‹‹‹‹‹‹‹‹‹‹‹‹‹‹‹‹‹‹‹‹‹‹‹‹‹‹‹‹‹›››››››››››››››››››››››››››››››

A. Philosophy and Ethics

i. from logic

ETHICS, PEIRCE ASSERTED, "HAS A VITAL CONNECTION WITH LOGIC." (2.82) FOR one thing, ethics aids in the understanding of logic. It may be "impossible to be thoroughly and rationally logical except upon an ethical basis," (2.198) but that is far from saying that logic is founded upon ethics. For, although "the logician ought to recognize what our ultimate aim is," (1.611) "good reasoning and good morals [being] closely allied," (1.576) the fact remains that the "proper concern [of logic] is with truths beyond the purview" of ethics. (4.240) When Peirce said that "*logic*, or the doctrine of what we ought to think, must be an application of the doctrine of what we deliberately choose to do, which is ethics," (5.35) he had reference to applied logic and practical ethics. Reasoning, at least of the deliberate variety, (5.114)[1] may be judged as a species of behavior, and "thinking is a kind of conduct." (5.534) Certainly when logic occupies itself with dividing arguments into the good and the bad, (2.203) it is leaning upon ethics.[2] Practical ethics is concerned with the "conformity of action to an ideal." (1.573) But just as there is more to logic than the classification of arguments,[3] so "ethics involves more than the theory of such conformity." (1.573)

But if the proper concern of logic is with truths that lie beyond the purview of ethics, the reverse is not true, for ethics does not concern itself entirely with truths beyond the purview of logic. Ethics is called upon to aid in rendering the universe more reasonable. (1.615) Indeed, ultimately sought goals are inherently logical. "The only desirable object which is quite satis-

---

[1] See also 5.109. Peirce was among the earliest to recognize that there are thought processes over which we exercise no control. See chap. VI, D, iv.

[2] See Arthur W. Burks, *Logical Foundations*, chap. V.

[3] Critical logic, or Critic, is concerned with arguments, but not so Speculative Grammar and Speculative Rhetoric. See chap. III, B and D.

factory in itself without any ulterior reason for desiring it, is the reasonable itself,"[4] and this is "an experiential truth."[5]

Logic, we have been told, rests neither on subjective feeling nor on objective experience,[6] but rather on stubborn fact.[7] We are indeed specifically told that "the social principle is rooted intrinsically in logic." (5.354)

It is not difficult upon reflection to see how this could be true. Ethics recognizes the supreme importance of the good, manifested in lesser goods, and symbolic compulsions are semiotic in character.[8] Certainly, nothing in ethics can controvert logical truth and consistency. The normative, of which the ethical is one branch, is not far removed from the hypothetical; the norm is properly stated as an "if . . . then" proposition. And the study of ends is not clearly distinguishable from preoccupation with the ideal.[9] The notion of ideal ends becomes in practical ethics the method of approximation in action to a limit, as we shall see presently; and this series of approximations must assume the existence of a series of inclusions as a fundamental logical notion.[10] Ethical action depends upon the *logica utens* as the best guide to practice, (1.623) and is aimed at the future. (5.402 n.2)

ii. FROM METAPHYSICS

Since ontology is a continuation of logic, ethics is dependent upon ontology in the same sense in which it is dependent upon logic.[11] Phenomenology, which is one source of the ontological categories, draws no distinctions of good and bad.[12] The phenomenological categories dictate to some extent the ethical ones. Quality[13] becomes the value of the good, the essential ethical value. Reaction[14] becomes the field of moral action and conduct. And representation[15] becomes the moral and ethical law. The ethical realm as part of the ontological realm must be an inflexible one, containing truths to be discovered which are independent of opinion.[16] Moreover, the ethical realm

---

[4] Review of Karl Pearson, *The Grammar of Science* in *The Nation*, 58 (1901), 296 ff.
[5] *Ibid.*
[6] See chap. III, A, i.
[7] See chap. III, A, ii.
[8] See chap. III, B, i.
[9] See chap. III, D, iii.
[10] See chap. III, B, v.
[11] See chap. IV, A, iii.
[12] See chap. IV, A, i.
[13] See chap. IV, B, i.
[14] See chap. IV, B, ii.
[15] See chap. IV, B, iii.
[16] See chap. IV, C, ii.

is a real one, and hence must exist objectively to and independent of the moral person.

Ethics must be subdivided in accordance with the distinction between pure theory and practical application. This accords with the ontological distinction between the fixed order of firstness and thirdness and the flexible field of application, of action and reaction, of secondness.[17] Pure ethics is part of being, while practical ethics, which is a selection from pure ethics, takes place in existence. Destiny[18] relates practical to pure ethics. Moral conduct requires freedom as well as law. Conduct must seek for the moral order in a world of chance and continuity.[19] Thus ethics rests not only on phenomenological experience but also on the categories of ontology.

Epistemology dictates that the universal law of mind is final cause or purpose,[20] and upon this notion the idea of the moral end must rest. The end of mental action is something nonmental. Moral conduct depends upon good habits of behavior,[21] and behavior takes place in terms of belief.[22] Believing is defined in at least one of its meanings as shaping conduct into conformity with a proposition.[23] That conduct is proper at all must be due to a certain insight in human beings which though real is indistinguishable from rational processes.[24] The good, as the object of desire, may be general like desire itself.[25] The person is a connection of ideas; and character is what is potential in the person, defined by the virtues of the person.[26]

iii. FROM PSYCHOLOGY

Ethics is closely derived from some of the psychological ideas, although this does not make it reducible to psychology. For, as we have just seen, it is derivable also from logic and metaphysics, and has its own autonomous realm. In noting the derivation from psychology, we should, moreover, bear in mind not only the particular points of derivation but also the more general aspects of Peirce's conception of psychology, in which all three of the chief categories—the feelings, the sensations of reaction, and the general conceptions—are responses to stimuli which have an independent existence in

[17] See chap. IV, B, i, ii and iii.
[18] See chap. IV, D, i.
[19] See chap. IV, D, ii.
[20] See chap. V, A, iv.
[21] See Chap. V, C, i.
[22] See chap. V, C, ii.
[23] See chap. V, C, ii, quoting 5.480.
[24] See chap. V, C, iii.
[25] See chap. V, C, iv.
[26] See chap. V, E, i.

the actual world. Pierce's psychology is as objective as he could make it, and as a consequence there will be no basis for considering his ethics to be a subjective affair even to the extent to which it is dependent upon psychology.

Ethics begins to take suggestions from psychology in the division of sensations of reaction. "Every man," Peirce said, "has certain ideals of the general description of conduct that befits a rational animal in his particular station in life, what most accords with his total nature and relations." (1.591) Every man, that is to say, has an aesthetic taste and an instinct for consistency in his conduct. These ideals have been "imbibed in childhood" and gradually "shaped to his personal nature." (1.592) By the time he acts from them as an adult it can be said that he acts from impulse and not from reason.[27]

Yet though he act from impulse, it is, so to speak, not naive impulse in the sense of a primitive characteristic which has survived untouched from a simpler species and a primordial age. Right and wrong may be volitional,[28] it is true; but for all that it is reasoning which educates the instinct, and even "reasoning essentially involves self-control"; (5.108)[29] "the *logica utens* is a particular species of morality." Again, Peirce's conception of conscience as a psychological rather than an ethical affair makes him regard it as presupposed by ethics. Conscience in his understanding is a "community-consciousness"[30] and not an individual affair at all. In view of this, it should not be surprising that personality, in which we lead up to the very threshold of ethics, is not considered to be a physiologico-individual thing, either, but consists in a "coördination of ideas."[31] Ethics, then, cannot be predicated upon any narrow understanding of the rights and duties of the individual but must be constructed to include the social aspects of the individual character. We shall grasp these aspects more firmly perhaps from an examination of the methodology.

iv. FROM METHODOLOGY

According to the classification of the branches of philosophy to be found in the methodology, ethics is a normative science and thus studies what ought to be.[32] Ethics is from the same study also involved in the distinction between theory and practice, in which theory is applicable to practice.[33] In ethics this

[27] See chap. VI, C, iii, quoting 1.630.
[28] See chap. VI, C, iv.
[29] See chap. VI, D, iii.
[30] See chap. VI, D, iv.
[31] See chap. VI, E, i.
[32] See chap. VII, A, iv; also 1.191.
[33] See chap. VII, A, v.

distinction leads to one between pure ethics and practical conduct, as we shall note later.[34]

In this chapter, then, we shall present Peirce's explicit ethical theory. We must count pragmatism technically as a theory of the verification of truth, and therefore as a doctrine of methodology. But it is one in which there is considerable emphasis on goodness. Hence pragmatism anticipates the ethics to some extent, and as a consequence the present chapter, in which pragmatism is omitted, must be somewhat thin. But this cannot be taken as any indication of its lack of importance both to the study of ethics and to Peirce's philosophical system. Indeed, we shall treat pragmatism as an antecedent doctrine from which ethics must partly flow.

In this chapter on methodology, we noted that, although pragmatism is the particular theory of philosophical method and does not necessarily involve conduct, it may lead to conduct.[35] It ties up intellectual conceptions of ideals with the attempt to carry them into practice, in this case ethical ideals and moral practice. Actual practice is not required even though moral resolution is involved. It is most important to remember that pragmatism has a direct bearing on conduct but that this does not mean that pragmatism exists for the sake of conduct in the sense given to pragmatism by James.[36] In Peirce's version of pragmatism, conduct is only "recommended."[37] The close connection between the two is obvious, however.

The warning which was announced in the last section against understanding ethics too subjectively is in substance the same point as understanding pragmatism too actively. Theories of practice can be judged to some extent by practice, yet "We must certainly guard ourselves against understanding this rule in too individualistic a sense. To say that a man accomplishes nothing but that to which his endeavors are directed would be a cruel condemnation of the great bulk of mankind, who never have leisure to labor for anything but the necessities of life for themselves and their families. But, without directly striving for it, far less comprehending it, they perform all that civilization requires, and bring forth another generation to advance history another step." (5.402 n.2)

The good pragmatist is a critic, but not an undiscriminating one. He knows that the impulse or instinct from which action takes place is not entirely a product of education in childhood or even of later experiences. He is critical within limits of a common sense which is the instinctive body of beliefs. For belief is an instinctive affair, while doubt must be cultivated. Belief consists

---

[34] See this chapter, B and C.
[35] See chap. VII, B, iv, especially the sixth definition.
[36] See chap. VII, C, i.
[37] *Ibid.*, quoting 5.2.

in indubitable propositions and inferences which are inherent in man, and which are equivalent to instincts.[38] They are the profound sources from which action, and consequently also that part of action which is moral action, takes place. Hence their importance to ethics.

B. Pure Ethics

i. definition and aims

In the matter of deciding where ethics, "one of the very subtlest of studies," (2.120) belongs in the general scheme of things, Peirce followed the tradition of his day in placing it with logic and aesthetics among the normative sciences. (1.191) "A normative science is one which studies what ought to be," (1.281) and a science thus concerned with "the theory of the ideal itself, the nature of the *summum bonum*," (1.573) is "the very most purely theoretical of purely theoretical sciences," (1.281) in that it sets up "norms, or rules which need not, but which ought, to be followed." (2.156) Ethics, Peirce defined as "the science of right and wrong . . . the theory of self-controlled, or deliberate conduct." (1.191) It is "the study of what ends of action we are deliberately prepared to adopt," (5.130) "the philosophy of aims." (4.240) "Ethics—the genuine normative science of ethics, as contradistinguished from the branch of anthropology which in our day often passes under the name of ethics—this genuine ethics is the normative science *par excellence*, because an *end*—the essential object of normative science—is germane to a voluntary act in a primary way in which it is germane to nothing else." (5.130)

By judging ethics to be the theoretical science of ideals, Peirce has admitted then that it is the philosophy of aims. (4.240) But this is not to vary with its normative character, for every science founded in logic must be an exact science. Peirce admitted no conflict between normative and exact science. A normative science, in his view, is one which must answer all the empirical requirements of an exact science, and yet be oriented in the pursuit of an ideal as well. He said of logic, another "normative science," that "it thus has a strongly mathematical character." But to say that a science has a mathematical branch is only to say that it is a science. This, of course, does not mean that the ideal will be found tomorrow, or that it can be worked out mechanically. "Pure ethics has been, and always must be, a theatre of discussion, for the reason that its study consists in the gradual development of a distinct recognition of a satisfactory aim." (4.243)

But what is the ultimate aim of ethical conduct? A great many alternatives

[38] See chap. VII, C, iii.

have been suggested by various ethical theorists. Peirce considered that he had described most of them under the following headings. A man may act for the sake of momentary satisfactions, (1.582) the prompt satisfaction of instincts, (1.583) provision for the satisfaction of future instincts, (1.584) pleasure, (1.603-605) "from persuasion, or from imitative instinct, or from dread of blame, or in awed obedience to an instant command; or he may act according to some general rule restricted to his own wishes, such as the pursuit of pleasure,[39] or self-preservation, or good-will toward an acquaintance, or attachment to home and surroundings, or conformity to the customs of his tribe, or reverence for a law; or, becoming a moralist, he may aim at bringing about an ideal state of things definitely conceived, such as one in which everybody attends exclusively to his own business and interest (individualism), or in which the maximum total pleasure of all beings capable of pleasure is attained (utilitarianism), or in which altruistic sentiments universally prevail (altruism), or in which his community is placed out of all danger (patriotism), or in which the ways of nature are as little modified as possible (naturalism); or he may aim at hastening some result, not otherwise known in advance than as that, whatever it may turn out to be, to which some process seeming to him good must inevitably lead, such as whatever the dictates of the human heart approve (sentimentalism), or whatever would result from every man's duly weighing, before action, the advantages of his every purpose (to which I will attach the nonce-name, *entelism*), or whatever the historical evolution of public sentiment may decree (historicism), or whatever the operation of cosmical causes may be destined to bring about (evolutionism); or he may be devoted to truth, and may be determined to do nothing not pronounced reasonable, either by his own cogitations (rationalism), or by public discussion (dialecticism), or by crucial experiment; or he may feel that the only thing really worth striving for is the generalizing or assimilating elements in truth, and that either as the sole object in which the mind can ultimately recognize its veritable aim (educationalism), or that which alone is destined to gain universal sway (pancratism); or, finally, he may be filled with the idea that the only reason that can reasonably be admitted as ultimate is that living reason for the sake of which the psychical and physical universe is in process of creation (religionism)."[40]

In general, Peirce maintained, there are three broad classes of ends. "The

---

[39] Also 5.355.
[40] C. S. Peirce, review of Pearson's *Grammar of Science* in *Popular Science Monthly*, 48 (1901), 298 ff. See also 1.585 ff.

enumeration [above] has been so ordered as to bring into view the various degrees of generality of motives,"[41] but they fall into one of three groups according as they serve the subjective feelings of the individual, the objective purposes of society, or the rationalization of the universe. (1.590) Of the first two groups, Peirce concluded that they fell far short of constituting the ultimate ethical aim. "All motives that are directed toward pleasure or self-satisfaction, of however high a type, will be pronounced by every experienced person to be inevitably destined to miss the satisfaction at which they aim. On the other hand, every motive involving dependence on some other leads us to ask for some ulterior reason. The only desirable object which is quite satisfactory in itself without any ulterior reason for desiring it, is the reasonable itself."[42] This, Peirce maintained, "is an experiential truth. The only ethically sound motive is the most general one." "The ultimate good lies in the evolutionary process in some way. If so, it is not in individual reactions in their segregation, but in something general or continuous." (5.4)

A good aim is one which can be pursued. (5.133) But an aim which can be achieved in a finite time and space is one which cannot be indefinitely pursued, and is hence a bad aim, for "an aim which *cannot* be adopted and consistently pursued is a bad aim. It cannot properly be called an ultimate aim at all." Hence, according to Peirce, only he who has an infinite aim can be said to be acting in accordance with moral good. The final aim for Peirce is the *summum bonum*, and this direction is by no means confined to human beings, since it is that toward which being itself is aimed.[43] Finally, however, ethics "must appeal to esthetics for aid in determining the *summum bonum*," (1.191) since the ideal of ethics must be drawn from "the science of ideals, or of that which is objectively admirable without any ulterior reason."[44]

ii. PROBLEMS AND METHODS

Ethics is divided by Peirce into the pure and the practical, or normatively practical. Normative science presupposes pure science, and in much the same way normative ethics presupposes pure ethics. The primary question asked by ethics is, "What is good? Now this is hardly a normative question: it is pre-normative. It does not ask for the conditions of fulfillment of a definitely accepted purpose, but asks what is to be sought, *not* for a reason,

[41] *Ibid.*
[42] *Ibid.*
[43] See chap. IV, D, i.
[44] See chap. X, B, i.

but back of every reason. . . . Pure ethics, philosophical ethics, is not normative, but pre-normative." (1.577) It presupposes the answer to the question which governs practical action, in asking "not what *is* but what *ought to be*." (5.39) Thus ethics, pure ethics, if it is to have any utility in the sense of producing something that can be applied to practice as a norm of conduct, must be approached as though it were "as useless a science as can be conceived." (1.667) "A useless inquiry, provided it is a systematic one, is pretty much the same thing as a scientific inquiry. Or at any rate if a scientific inquiry becomes by any mischance useful, that aspect of it has to be kept sedulously out of sight during the investigation or else . . . its hopes of success are fatally cursed." (1.668)

Although the central problem of pure ethics, which is "to ascertain what end is possible," (5.134) should become an exact study, it must not be "thoughtlessly supposed that *special science* could aid in this ascertainment." There is nothing worse, either for the special sciences or for conduct than to look upon the former as a guide to the latter. (1.55) An absolute aim cannot be affected by the findings with regard to contingent facts, for an absolute aim is "that which would be pursued under all possible circumstances." We have seen that in pragmatism the translation of a proposition into action involves an endless future as well as the present.[45] But the future more than the present can be influenced by self-control. Hence pure ethics, which is concerned with possible conduct rather than with practical action, has its emphasis on the future. (5.427) Action is second but conduct third, and while secondness refers to what the actual present is,[46] thirdness is more concerned with how an endless future could be. (1.337)[47] "The pragmaticist does not make the *summum bonum* to consist in action, but makes it to consist in that process of evolution whereby the existent comes more and more to embody those generals which were . . . said to be *destined,* which is what we strive to express in calling them *reasonable*.[48] In its higher stages, evolution takes place more and more largely through self-control." (5.433) Pragmatism thus involves pure ethics in evolution, and takes it out of the sphere both of the immediately practical and of the discretely factual.

It must not be supposed that, because Peirce separated pure from practical ethics, he was also opposed to a connection between them. "The point of view of [mere] utility is always a narrow point of view." (1.641) On the other hand, a pure study which did not issue in practical utility would be

[45] See chap. VII, B, iv.
[46] See chap. IV, B, ii.
[47] See chap. IV, B, iii.
[48] See chap. IV, D, i.

a waste indeed. It so happened that Peirce believed in "the eternal life of the idea [of] Right," (1.219) but, on the other hand, he felt that this "despised idea has all along been the one irresistible power," (1.251) a power that concerns the practical sciences, such as law, politics and economics. That justice, for example, is one of the "great powers in the world is no figure of speech, but a plain fact to which theories must accommodate themselves." (1.348) The exclusion of the findings of pure ethics from such practical pursuits has been an "immense folly." We do not escape the consequences of ignoring pure ethics in everyday conduct, for "notwithstanding the horrible wickedness of every mortal wight, the idea of right and wrong is nevertheless the greatest power on this earth, to which every knee must sooner or later bow or be broken down." (1.217)

The danger of confusing theory and practice in ethics is one which threatens not only them but their interrelations. "The effect of mixing speculative inquiry with questions of conduct results finally in a sort of half make-believe reasoning which deceives itself in regard to its real character." (1.56) "Men continue to tell themselves they regulate their conduct by reason; but they learn to look forward and see what conclusions a given method will lead to before they give their adhesion to it. In short, it is no longer the reasoning which determines what the conclusion shall be, but it is the conclusion which determines what the reasoning shall be. This is sham reasoning. In short, as morality supposes self-control, men learn that they must not surrender themselves unreservedly to any method, without considering to what conclusions it will lead them. But this is utterly contrary to the single-mindedness that is requisite in science. In order that science may be successful, its votaries must hasten to surrender themselves at discretion to experimental inquiry, in advance of knowing what its decisions may be. There must be no reservations." (1.57)

"It is notoriously true that into whatever you do not put your whole heart and soul in that you will not have much success. Now, the two masters, *theory* and *practice*, you cannot serve. That perfect balance of attention which is requisite for observing the system of things is utterly lost if human desires intervene, and all the more so the higher and holier those desires may be." (1.642) The extraordinary behavior of the Greek philosophers comes from the Hellenic error of mixing philosophy with practice. The Greek philosophers endeavored to apply to their own conduct the conclusions of their ethical speculations. (1.616-618)[49] But the philosophical investigator who does not stand aloof from all practical applications will not only obstruct

[49] See chap. VII, A, iv.

the advance of pure ethics but will also endanger his own moral integrity. (1.619) Scientists seek the truth; theologians want to affect the lives of others. Hence the development of pure ethics must be conducted by scientists." (1.620)

"It may very easily happen that the over-development of a man's moral conception should interfere with his progress in philosophy. The protoplasm of philosophy has to be in a liquid state in order that the operation of metabolism may go on. Now morality is a hardening agent. It is astonishing how many abominable scoundrels there are among sincerely moral people. The difficulty is that morality chokes its own stream. . . . We are too apt to define ethics to ourselves as the science of right and wrong. That cannot be correct, for the reason that right and wrong are ethical conceptions which it is the business of that science to develop and to justify. A science cannot have for its fundamental problem to distribute objects among categories of its own creation; for underlying that problem must be the task of establishing those categories. The fundamental problem of ethics is not, therefore, What is right, but What am I prepared deliberately to accept as the statement of what I want to do, What am I to aim at, What am I after? To what is the force of my will to be directed?" (2.198)

iii. THE MEANING OF PRACTICE

The solution of these problems in ethics will have to appeal to a principle already established by Peirce in the course of his methodological investigations. We have learned that pragmatism, as the relation of meaning to practicality, has an important bearing upon ethical problems.[50] In this section, we shall examine further the bearing of this relationship, more specifically from the point of view of meaning. The bearing from the point of view of practice will be treated in the next section.

"One, at least, of the functions of intelligence is to adapt conduct to circumstances, so as to subserve desire." (5.548) "Thereupon it follows that the concept has a capability of having a bearing upon conduct; and this fact will lend it intellectual purport." "Right and wrong are expressly volitional," (1.330) but that volition has an external object toward which it is directed. Since the very "existence of things consists in their regular behavior," (1.411) we may well ask whether volition is not to be judged on the basis of that behavior toward which it leads. The ethical criteria of good and bad are predicates of objects. They are not subjective feelings; or, rather,

[50] See this chapter, A, iv.

like all subjective feelings, they refer to objects. (5.247)[51] They belong in the field of secondness. (5.110)[52]

Now, "moral goodness . . . may be possessed by a proposition or by an argument."(5.141) The maxim of pragmatism can be translated into the moral sphere by qualifying it. We can say that in order to ascertain the ethical meaning of an intellectual conception one should consider what practical consequences to conduct might conceivably result by necessity from the truth of that conception; and the sum of these consequences will constitute the entire meaning of the conception.[53] The moral goodness of a proposition consists in all the good consequences which might conceivably follow from its application. But since this pragmatic conception is couched in terms of *conceivable* consequences, it reaches "far beyond the practical." "Those whose sentiments I share abhor certain doctrines of certain writers upon Ethics[54]—say, for example, those who make action the ultimate end of man." (2.151) Hence the ethical version of the doctrine of pragmatism belongs in the province of pure ethics. In other words, if pragmatism is applicable to all conduct, that is, to conduct understood in the widest sense, (6.481) then it must be applicable to the narrower range of moral conduct as well. From the point of view of pure ethics, pragmatism allows conduct to become an experimental test for hypotheses concerning conduct; the emphasis is placed not on conduct but on propositions. This is not to say that men must act out their lives in order to prove or disprove ethical hypotheses; from the point of view of practical ethics, the moral conduct is more important than the propositions from which it follows. But in the study of pure ethics, conduct plays the role of experimentation, and its allowance or rejection of ethical hypotheses is carefully noted.[55]

Peirce has said that pragmatism makes "purport to consist in a conditional proposition concerning conduct, [and that] a sufficiently deliberate consideration of that purport will reflect that the conditional conduct ought to be regulated by an ethical principle." (5.535) If it is true that "any kind of goodness consists in the adaptation of its subject to its *end*," (5.158) and satisfaction consists in having an action congruous to its end, (5.560) then abduction, which is the logic of pragmatism, (5.195) is "the only possible hope of regulating future conduct rationally." (2.270)[56] Therefore

---

[51] See chap. VI, C, vi.
[52] See chap. IV, B, ii.
[53] See 5.9 and chap. VII, B, iv.
[54] James is the writer referred to here. (5.3) See chap. VII, C, i.
[55] See chapter VIII, C, iii.
[56] See chapter III, C, ii, (c).

the theories that one ought to entertain are only those which are conducive to a certain end. "That ought to be done which is conducive to a certain end. The inquiry therefore should begin with searching for the *end* of thinking. What do we think *for?*" (5.594) This is a question which will have to take us into certain psychological inquiries, and other matters concerning practical ethics, but which will hardly end there. The conclusion will demand a program of moral conduct, and therefore belong in practical ethics, but it will reveal that this demand issues from an ethical principle which was implicit in pure ethics all the while.

C. PRACTICAL ETHICS

i. THE TRANSITION TO MORALITY

In this and the following sections, we shall see how a study of practical action leads inevitably to the principle of pure ethics. If pure ethics is meaningless without some application, application itself requires something to be applied. Peirce named practical ethics "antethics" or "practics," and described it as "the conformity of action to an ideal." (1.573) "Ethics is not practics; first, because ethics involves more than the theory of such conformity; namely, it involves the theory of the ideal itself, the nature of the *summum bonum*; and secondly, because in so far as *ethics* studies the conformity of conduct to an ideal, it is limited to a particular ideal, which . . . is in fact nothing but a sort of composite photograph of the conscience of the members of the community."

In the above sense, morality "is a means to good life, not necessarily coextensive with good conduct. Morality consists in the folklore of right conduct. A man is brought up to think he ought to behave in certain ways. If he behaves otherwise, he is uncomfortable. His conscience pricks him. That system of morals is the traditional wisdom of ages of experience. If a man cuts loose from it, he will become the victim of his passions. It is not safe for him even to reason about it, except in a purely speculative way. Hence, morality is essentially conservative." (1.50)[57] "Some men have not a sense of sin; and there is nothing for it but to be born again and become as a little child." (1.219) "Men of the best heart and purest intentions in the world have been known to commit actions contrary to their own moral principles simply because nothing in their lives had ever called their attention to the moral bearing of the kind of actions in question." (2.153)

[57] See this chapter, A, iv.

The discussion of morality in the abstract, however, despite the personal limitations of individuals, is likely to lead toward some sort of solution and settlement of the moral problem. "In regard to morals we can see ground for hope that debate will ultimately cause one party or other to modify their sentiments up to complete accord." (2.151) Casuistry, or "the determination of what under given circumstances ought to or may be done," (1.577) can be an aid in this regard. The reason for this is that the basis of morality is objective, and constitutes a constant upon the discovery of which men must find agreement. "I dare say that some people's psychical disposition is such that they have no sooner formed a strong desire than their thoughts take a subjective turn and they forthwith begin to think what satisfaction it would give them if that desire were gratified, and such people find it difficult to conceive that there are other people whose thoughts follow a train of objective suggestions and who think very little about themselves and their gratifications." (5.86) "It is true that the majority of writers on ethics in the past have made the root of morals subjective; but the best opinion is very plainly moving in the opposite direction." (2.156) "Lofty moral sense consists in regarding, not indeed *the*, but yet *an*, ideal world as in some sense the only real one; and hence it is that stern moralists are always inclined to dual distinctions." (3.529) "Morality insists that a motive is either good or bad. That the gulf between them is bridged over and that most motives are somewhere near the middle of the bridge, is quite contrary to the teachings of any moral system which ever lived in the hearts and consciences of a people." (1.61)

"The very simplest and most rudimentary of all conceivable systems of quantity is that one which distinguishes only two values. This [is] the system of evaluation which ethics applies to actions in dividing them into the right and the wrong." (4.368) Morality, as the application of ethical principles to conduct, must be an affair of approaching more or less closely to but not of attaining absolute limits. "The rule of ethics will be to adhere to the only possible absolute aim, and to hope that it will prove attainable. Meantime, it is comforting to know that all experience is favorable to that assumption." (5.136) With this understanding, we may now turn to an analysis of the mechanism whereby the purpose of ethics is pursued in morality.

ii. THE PRACTICE OF MEANING

The practice of meaning, so far as human action is concerned, may be summed up in the one word "conduct" and conduct may be described as the "phenomena of controlled action." (1.601) "Self-control of any kind is purely *inhibitory*. It originates nothing." (5.194) Action is controlled so that it may better conform to an ideal; (1.573) but while all actions have motives, only controlled actions have ideals. (1.574) There are three ways in which conduct appeals to a man as ideal: he thinks the conduct fine, he thinks it consistent with his other actions, and he desires its consequences. (1.591) Reflecting upon these ideals, he seeks to make his own actions conform to them with the aid of rules of conduct. He first forms a resolution of how he would act upon a certain occasion. This resolution is a mental diagram or formula, but by a mental act it is converted into a determination. (1.592) A peculiar feeling accompanies the first steps of this process, but later there is no direct consciousness of it. When the determination is sufficiently pent up, we are made aware of its presence as a strain: a need, or desire. (1.593) But, in all events, all action from determination is felt as the pleasures of anticipation and, afterward, of relaxation of need. (1.595)

After the action has been performed, three self-criticisms take place. This is by means, first, of a comparison of the conduct with the original resolution. The resolution was a mental formula; the memory of the action is an image. How does the image conform to the formula? (1.596) The second self-criticism asks how the conduct accords with general intentions. (1.597) The third self-criticism asks "how the image of my conduct accords with my ideals of conduct." (1.598) Each of these self-criticisms is accompanied by a judgment, which, if favorable, is felt as pleasurable. Such self-criticism is "the only respectable kind, which will bear fruit in the future. Whether the man is satisfied with himself or dissatisfied, his nature will absorb the lesson like a sponge; and the next time he will tend to do better than he did before."

"In addition to these three self-criticisms of single series of actions, a man will from time to time review his *ideals*. This process is not a job that a man sits down to do and has done with. The experience of life is continually contributing instances more or less illuminative. These are digested first, not in the man's consciousness, but in the depths of his reasonable being. The results come to consciousness later. But meditation seems to agitate a mass of tendencies and allow them more quickly to settle down so as to be really more conformed to what is fit for the man." (1.599) It is true that "we base our conduct on facts already known, and for these we can only draw upon our memory," (5.460) but "future facts are the only facts that we can, in a measure, control. . . . It cannot be denied that acritical inferences may refer to the past in its capacity as past; but according to Pragmaticism, the conclusion of a reasoning power must refer to the future. For its meaning refers to conduct, and since it is a reasoned conclusion must refer to deliberate conduct, which is controllable conduct. But the only controllable conduct is future conduct." (5.461) Hence ethical reasoning is for the sake of future conduct. "Conduct controlled by ethical reasoning tends toward fixing certain habits of conduct." (5.430)

There are certain implications from this description of the analysis of conduct to problems of belief and of self-control, and in one place or another Peirce has himself drawn them. As to belief, it is "the principle upon which we are willing to act." (1.636) Resolutions are made and judgments determined to a very large extent by the ethos. "Conscience really belongs to the subconscious man, to that part of the soul which is hardly distinct in different individuals, a sort of community-consciousness, or public spirit, not absolutely one and the same in different citizens, and yet not by any means independent in them. Conscience has been created by experience, just as any knowledge is; but it is modified by further experience only with secular slowness." (1.56) The distinction between resolutions and the ethos as determinants of conduct is similar to that described in another sort of way by Peirce as the distinction between categorical and conditional habits. (5.517 n.1)

The inhibition of uncontrolled action makes conduct possible. "It is self-control which makes any other than the normal course of . . . action possible; [which] gives room for an ought-to-be of conduct." (4.540) "In the formation of habits of deliberate action, we may imagine the occurrence of the stimulus, and think out what the results of different actions will be. One of these will appear particularly satisfactory; and then an action of the soul takes place which is well described by saying that the mode of reaction 'receives a deliberate stamp of approval.' (5.538) Another name for this stamp of approval is expectancy, "the act of recognition as one's own, being placed by a deed of the soul upon an imaginary anticipation of experience." (5.540) The only difference between belief and this kind of expectancy is that "the former is expectant of muscular sensation, the latter of sensation not muscular." "It now begins to look strongly as if perhaps all belief might involve expectation as its essence." (5.542)

"Self-control seems to be the capacity for rising to an extended view of a practical subject instead of seeing only temporary urgency." (5.339 n.1) There are modes of self-control which are quite instinctive, others which result from training, still others which follow from the control of self-control, and so on. (5.533) The only distinction between human beings and other animals is that in the case of human beings there is "a greater number of grades of self-control." For even thinking is a faculty which is "a phenomenon of self-control." (5.534) Self-control means that "a process of self-preparation will tend to impart to action (when the occasion for it shall arise) one fixed character, which is indicated and perhaps roughly measured by the absence (or slightness) of the feeling of self-reproach, which subsequent reflection will induce. Now, this subsequent reflection is part of the self-preparation for action on the next occasion. Consequently, there is a tendency, as action is repeated again and again, for the action to approximate indefinitely toward the perfection of that fixed character, which would be marked by entire absence of self-reproach." (5.418) Self-control "is the only freedom of which man has any reason to be proud." (5.339 n.1) The inference which follows from approval must be voluntary. (5.130) We can will nothing where there is no freedom. Peirce maintained that his account of conduct thus "leaves a man at full liberty, no matter if we grant all that the necessitarians ask. That is, the man *can*, or if you please is *compelled*, to *make his life more reasonable*." (1.602)

"We can perceive that good reasoning and good morals are closely allied." (1.576) Nevertheless, "in the conduct of life, we have to distinguish everyday affairs and great crises. In the great decisions," said Peirce, he did "not believe it is safe to trust to individual reasoning." (1.623) In practical matters reasoning can be exaggerated. (1.626) We ought not to hastily change our conduct to fit a philosophy of ethics. (1.633) It is instinct rather than reasoning that must serve as the dependable guide to crises. With dumb animals, instinct guides in little as well as in large affairs. But "while human instincts are not so detailed and featured as those of the dumb animals, yet they might be sufficient to guide us in the *greatest* concerns without any aid from reason." (1.638) "Invariably follow the dictates of Instinct in preference to those of Reason when such conduct will answer your purpose: that is the prescription of Reason herself." (2.177) But when we do reason, we must reason with "severely scientific logic." (2.178) The direction of ethics as a theoretical study is away from instinct and toward reason, but until its findings reach a dependable stage, instinct must still be the guide to conduct, at least in its most vital decisions and actions.

iii. THE UNLIMITED COMMUNITY

We come now to the enunciation of Peirce's great ethical principle: the doctrine of the unlimited community. In order to introduce this doctrine, it will be necessary to begin by bridging the gulf between pure and practical ethics in the way of practice as well as of theory. This is done by examining "the principal end of inquiry, as regards human life. What is the chief end of man? *Answer*: to actualize ideas of the immortal, ceaselessly prolific kind." (2.763) "We are all putting our shoulders to the wheel for an end that none of us can catch more than a glimpse at—that which the generations are working out. But we can see that the development of embodied ideas is what it will consist in." (5.402 n.2) "To that end it is needful to get beliefs that the believer will take satisfaction in acting upon, not mere rules set down on paper, with lethal provisos attached to them." (2.763)[58] Peirce here called our attention to the principle of Locke,[59] that to assent to a proposition is to "receive it for true," (2.649) so that the foundation of assent is the probability of truth. Moreover, truth has a certain force, so that to be put in the way of it is in a sense to be compelled by it.[60] Hence the rules that the believer will take satisfaction in acting upon must rest on logic, and it is from the logic of probabilities that Peirce derives the chief doctrine of ethical action.

The doctrine is derived by going back to the ideal of exact science, and to the conception of probability as the exact science of logic.[61] Probability can be applied to topics to which it has not been applied previously, by virtue of the new maxim of pragmatism. (2.648)[62] It will be recalled that Peirce described probability as the proportion of cases that carries truth with it. (2.650)[83] Probability consists in a relationship, "a fraction whose numerator consists in the number of times in which both A and B are true, and whose denominator is the total number of times in which A is true, whether B is so or not." (2.651) Thus we can say that "if A happens, B happens. But to speak of the probability of the event B, without naming the condition, really has no meaning at all." Probability clearly belongs to "a kind of inference which is repeated indefinitely. An individual inference must be either true or false and can show no effect of probability; and, therefore, in reference to a single case considered in itself, probability can have no meaning." (2.652)[64] Hence "there can be no sense in reasoning in an isolated case at all."

Now, with regard to probability, the individual human being is "an

[58] See chap. III, C, iv.
[59] John Locke, *Essay Concerning Human Understanding*, IV, 15, 1. See also chap. III, C, iv, and 2.48.
[60] See chap. III, D, iv.
[61] See chap. III, C, iv.
[62] See chap. VII, B, iv.
[63] See chap. III, C, iv.
[64] See chap. III, C, iv.

isolated case"; "taking all his risks collectively, then, it cannot be certain that they will not fail." (2.653) No matter how certain human affairs may be, they are in the same predicament as all other actual things. There is always a chance that each one will be destroyed, given a long enough run of time, "and no matter how little that chance may be, as far as this decade or this generation goes, yet in limitless decades and generations, it is pretty sure that the pitcher will get broken, at last. There is no danger, however slight, which in an indefinite multitude of occasions does not come as near to absolute certainty as probability can come." (5.587) The conclusion of this stage of the argument is obvious. "All human affairs rest upon probabilities, and the same thing is true everywhere. If man were immortal he could be perfectly sure of seeing the day when everything in which he had trusted should betray his trust, and, in short, of coming eventually to hopeless misery. He would break down, at last, as every great fortune, as every dynasty, as every civilization does. In place of this we have death." (2.653)

"But what, without death, would happen to every man, with death must happen to some man. At the same time, death makes the number of our risks, of our inferences, finite, and so makes their mean result uncertain. The very idea of probability and of reasoning rests on the assumption that this number is indefinitely great. We are thus landed in the same difficulty as before, and I can see but one solution of it. It seems to me that we are driven to this, that logicality inexorably requires that our interests shall *not* be limited. They must not stop at our own fate, but must embrace the whole community.[65] This community, again, must not be limited, but must extend to all races of beings with whom we can come into immediate or mediate intellectual relation. It must reach, however vaguely, beyond this geological epoch, beyond all bounds. He who would not sacrifice his own soul to save the whole world, is, as it seems to me, illogical in all his inferences, collectively." (2.654)

"Now, it is not necessary for logicality that a man should himself be capable of the heroism of self-sacrifice." (2.654) "But just the revelation of the possibility of this complete self-sacrifice in man, and the belief in its saving power, will serve to redeem the logicality of all men." (5.356) "It is sufficient that he should recognize the possibility of it, should perceive that only that man's inferences who has it are really logical, and should consequently regard his own as being only so far valid as they

[65] Cf. the identity in effect between cool Self-love and Benevolence, in the ethics of Bishop Butler.

would be accepted by the hero." (2.654) "But so far as he has this belief, he becomes identified with that man. And that ideal perfection of knowledge by which we have seen that reality is constituted [66] must thus belong to a community in which this identification is complete." (5.356)

"This would serve as a complete establishment of private logicality, were it not that the assumption, that man or the community (which may be wider than man) shall ever arrive at a state of information greater than some definite finite information, is entirely unsupported by reasons." (5.357) But still it "makes logicality attainable enough. Sometimes we can personally attain to heroism. The soldier who runs to scale a wall knows that he will probably be shot, but that is not all he cares for. He also knows that if all the regiment, with whom in feeling he identifies himself, rush forward at once, the fort will be taken. In other cases we can only imitate the virtue." (2.654)[67] The point is "that no man can be logical whose supreme desire is [limited to] the well-being of himself or of any other existing person or collection of persons." (2.661) "Now, there exist no reasons . . . for thinking that the human race, or any intellectual race, will exist forever. On the other hand, there can be no reason against it . . . and, fortunately . . . there is nothing in the facts to forbid our having a *hope*, or calm and cheerful wish, that the community may last beyond any assignable date. . . . *But all this requires a conceived identification of one's interests with those of an unlimited community*." (2.654)[68]

"Now you and I—what are we? Mere cells of the social organism." (1.673) "The individual man, since his separate existence is manifested only by ignorance and error, so far as he is anything apart from his fellows, and from what he and they are to be, is only a negation." (5.317) "There are those who believe in their own existence, because its opposite is inconceivable; yet the most balsamic of all the sweets of sweet philosophy is the lesson that personal existence is an illusion and a practical joke.[69] Those that have loved themselves and not their neighbors will find themselves April fools when the great April opens the truth that neither selves nor neighborselves were anything more than vicinities; while the love they would not entertain was the essence of every scent." (4.68) What seem to be vitally important topics concern only ourselves and our narrowest interests and thus prove to be the merest trifles. "Not in the contemplation of 'topics of vital importance' but in those universal things with which

[66] See chap. V, C, i.
[67] See chap. VI, C, i.
[68] Italics mine.
[69] See chap. V, C, ii. Also 5.317.

philosophy deals, the factors of the universe, is man to find his highest occupation." (1.673) For "the very first command that is laid upon you, your quite highest business and duty, becomes, as everybody knows, to recognize a higher business than your business, *not* merely an avocation after the daily task of your vocation is performed, but a generalized conception of duty which completes your personality by melting it into the neighboring parts of the universal cosmos."

We cannot leave an account of Peirce's ethics without a word for the problem of evil. The command to love one's neighbors more than one's self, and their neighbors more than them, and so on in an ascending hierarchy of love which eventually must embrace the entire universe of being, makes love the over-all deontological requirement. Hence hatred and evil, in this scheme, must become, as they do, "mere imperfect stages of love and loveliness," (6.287) and through the struggle against evil, which "it is man's duty to fight," (6.479) we are enabled to increase the amount of love in the actual world. "The only moral evil is not to have an ultimate aim." (5.133) Evil is the adaptation of means to ends which are too limited, and it is, after all, as great a thing as the law of growth which imposes fighting upon man. He will not despair to see the things for which he fights perish, since, according to the doctrine of the unlimited community, he must expect it, "accepting his little futility as his entire treasure," (6.479) and understanding that, "though his desperate struggles should issue in the horrors of his rout, and he should see the innocents who are dearest to his heart exposed to torments, frenzy and despair, destined to be smirched with filth, and stunted in their intelligence, still he may hope that it be best *for them*." Thus in Peirce's system, just as logic leads to ethics, so ethics in turn leads to the discernment of reasons and values which lie beyond human comprehension but which demand human allegiance and even sacrifice, and hence to the province of religion.

iv. SUMMARY OF THE CHAPTER

Ethics is founded in part upon logic, but has its own autonomous realm. It has an ontological status, and its subject matter is known as it exists, that is, independently and objectively. Hence ethics is not a branch of psychology, although the psychological categories contribute to the structure of ethics. Moral conduct is to some extent dictated by instinct. Methodologically, ethics is a normative science, a continuation of pragmatism, although existing as a pure study as well as in practical applications. The instinct on which conduct rests is what is called common sense.

Ethics is the study of right and wrong, of deliberate conduct, of ends. It is the science of ideals. Against the claims of many conflicting ends of ethical conduct, Peirce contended that ethics aims at that living reason for the sake of which the universe is in process of creation.

Ethics is divided into pure and practical branches. Pure ethics is prenormative; it asks, what ought to be? Pure ethics has practical application, but theory and practice must be separated if they are to develop their own fields and to serve each other.

In order to throw light upon this relationship, pure ethics must be examined from the standpoint of practice, and practical morality shown to lead to pure ethics. In the first of these problems, the theory of pragmatism, in its bearing on meaning, is helpful. The moral is one subdivision of the meaningful, at least theoretically. The moral meaning of a proposition is its conceivable good consequences in practice. In the second of the problems, ethics is shown to mean nothing in practice except in so far as practice is aimed at an ideal. Morality is the folklore of *right* conduct.

Conduct means controlled, or deliberate, action. This involves a coordination of thinking some action to be fine, consistent and desirous. In addition, ideals must be reviewed, and this is accomplished with the aid of experience. Controlled action, or conduct, is fixed by habits and directed toward the future. Good thinking leads toward great expectations. But in crises of practical action, not thought but instinct must be the guide.

Instinct, as we have noted many times, is a social affair. The aim of man is to actualize ideas of a kind whose ultimate meaning lies beyond even social comprehension. In social action, we are dealing with quantities of individuals and with aggregates of conduct which yield more readily to statistical analysis than to any other method. In terms of probability theory, no single instance is analyzable. This much is obvious: that all actual things of an individual nature have always come to an end: no singular has ever existed which is not subject to defeat and eventual disintegration. Hence we cannot put our faith in limited goals; we cannot trust ultimately in individuals or in institutions. We must place all our interest in an unlimited community which includes all individuals but extends beyond all bounds. Love is the over-all requirement of ethics, and evil is a mere imperfect stage of that love. Ethically, we must be prepared to play whatever role we are assigned in the economy of the universe, whether it be to lead or merely to stand and wait, admiring and imitating as best we can the actions of the moral hero.

CHAPTER X

Aesthetics

A. PHILOSOPHY AND AESTHETICS

i. THE PROBLEM OF AESTHETICS

FROM A CURSORY EXAMINATION OF PEIRCE'S VAST PHILOSOPHICAL REMAINS IT IS apparent that aesthetics is the most infirm of all the divisions of philosophy which claimed his attention. No very extensive passages are devoted to the topic, and everywhere there is evidence of obvious hesitation and a lack of understanding. Peirce read many works on aesthetics in an attempt to discover some clue. Although he confessed "that, like most logicians, I have pondered that subject far too little," (2.197) he gave as his excuse that "the books do seem so feeble. That affords one excuse. And then esthetics and logic seem, at first blush, to belong to different universes.[1] It is only very recently that I have become persuaded that that seeming is illusory, and that, on the contrary, logic needs the help of esthetics. The matter is not yet very clear to me; so unless some great light should fall upon me before I reach that chapter, it will be a short one filled with doubts and queries mainly."

The curious aspect is that the field of aesthetics never failed to arouse Peirce's curiosity, for he returns to it again and again, always with the same energy and enthusiasm with which he endeavored to storm each discipline by turn. Already as a boy in school he "undertook to expound Schiller's *Aesthetische Briefe*" (2.197) to a friend, spending "every afternoon for long months upon it, picking the matter to pieces as well as we boys knew how to do." Later he put himself "through a systematic course of training in recognizing my feelings. I have worked with intensity for so many hours

---

[1] Peirce, who was a conscientious student of Kant from his earliest days (see above, chap. II, A), was probably familiar with Kant's warning that the endeavor to "bring the critical judgment of the beautiful under rational principles, and to raise its rules to the rank of a science" is "a false hope" and "vain." See the *Critique of Pure Reason*, F. Max Muller trans. (New York, Macmillan, 1922), p. 17, n. 1.

a day every day for long years to train myself to this." (5.112) In most cases the sure ability of Peirce in logic combined with his abundant capacity for concentration to make him the master; but such was not the case with aesthetics. Here something was plainly wanting, and none was more aware of the deficiency than Peirce himself. Late in his life he wrote: "As for esthetics, although the first year of my study of philosophy was devoted to this branch exclusively, yet I have since then so completely neglected it that I do not feel entitled to have any confident opinions about it." (5.129) The chapter he had planned to write on aesthetics has not been found; and since the book itself, a work on logic, remained unfinished, it is probable that the aesthetics part was never written. The great illumination which Peirce had feared would not fall upon him did in fact fail to come. He remained in his own estimation "a perfect ignoramus in esthetics" (5.111) and "lamentably ignorant of it." (2.120)[2]

ii. AESTHETICS AS A NORMATIVE SCIENCE

The reputation of a philosophy frequently owes as much to its random suggestiveness as to its complete and systematic form. Peirce's writings are systematic by implication only; but they continue to be immensely suggestive in every line. If the occasional insights which have been gleaned from Peirce have had so much effect, how much more valuable would be the full force of his whole philosophy when viewed in the round? Therefore it is important that we fit together the fragments dealing with the theory of aesthetics, and try to discover where they were meant to lead. In order to reconstruct as much as we can of the projected work on aesthetics, we shall have to fall back upon the scattered and exceedingly brief references to that topic. We shall endeavor to indicate from Peirce's logic and ontology and epistemology the importance of his aesthetics. It will be necessary, however, to depart from our usual practice in this volume, and to show the deductions from other philosophical topics to aesthetics in a manner that will reveal the system of aesthetics. Previously, we have followed the chapter order of development, giving deductions from logic always first, those from ontology second, etc. But here, where we are concerned with adumbrating a topic for which there is little enough ground, we shall find it more helpful to take our order from aesthetics and our deductions from other philosophical topics when and as they are required.

Philosophy is divided, according to Peirce, into three main divisions:

[2] See also Review of F. Paulsen, *Immanuel Kant* in *The Nation*, 75 (1902), 210.

phenomenology, "which simply contemplates the Universal Phenomenon and discerns its ubiquitous elements"; normative science, "which investigates the universal and necessary laws of the relations of Phenomena to *Ends*"; (5.121) and metaphysics, which studies the reality of the phenomenological categories. Psychical as well as physical sciences belong to other divisions of the general classification of the sciences. (1.187)

The normative sciences are: ethics, aesthetics[3] and logic. They bear a "family likeness." (2.156) "All three of them are purely theoretical sciences which nevertheless set up norms, or rules which need not, but which ought, to be followed." "For Normative Science in general being the science of the laws of conformity of things to ends, esthetics considers those things whose ends are to embody qualities of feeling, ethics those things whose ends lie in action, and logic those things whose end is to represent something." (5.129) Peirce followed Uberweg in his use of the term "normative." (2.7)[4] He followed the school of Schleiermacher in doubting whether aesthetics was, after all, a normative science in the same sense as ethics and logic. For these latter require a purpose, whereas the beautiful is so without any purpose. (1.575)

The relations between aesthetics and the other normative sciences are many and complex. For instance, ethics requires some sort of moral principle in order to exercise control over actions. But "this, in turn, may be controlled by reference to an esthetic ideal of what is fine." "It must be an *admirable ideal*, having the only kind of goodness that such an ideal *can* have; namely, esthetic goodness. From this point of view the morally good appears as a particular species of the esthetically good." (5.130) Kant's categorical imperative set up an aesthetic ideal for the guidance of moral action, and Peirce was of the opinion that it could be defended. (5.133) Since fine moral actions are only one variety of what is fine, moral goodness is included in aesthetic goodness. (5.130) Yet the reverse does not hold true, and aesthetics founders when it tries to base itself upon ethics. (2.199)

The relations between aesthetics and logic were not so clear to Peirce, as he himself realized. (2.197) Despite the fact that the best and largest part of his work was devoted to logic, which he argues was founded neither upon subjective feeling (2.19)[5] nor upon philosophy, (2.36)[6] he felt that in any case "logic needs the help of esthetics." (2.197) However, as we shall

---

[3] See chap. VII, A, iv. Also 1.191.
[4] See further, *ibid.*, n. 1.
[5] See chap. III, A, i.
[6] See *ibid.*

note, a further investigation into the ramifications of his philosophy will reveal that logic has important implications to aesthetics.

B. THE THEORY OF AESTHETICS

i. THE THEORY OF BEAUTY

Let us return to a beginning at the phenomenological end. Aesthetics considers objects "simply in their presentation." (5.36) In this sense, aesthetics is merely the product of the awareness of an objective world, considered just as that world is presented to awareness, and is thus made equivalent to the phenomenological level of being. Firstness is what is present to the artist's eye. (5.44)[7] It should be emphasized, however, that phenomenology for Peirce was not equivalent to epistomology, nor yet was it a branch of epistemology. The emphasis is placed not on awareness but rather on the awareness of *objects*. Indeed Peirce's aesthetics hangs upon the objectivity of all aesthetic criteria. Feelings are inherent in the objective world; (1.311) for instance, "it is a psychic feeling of red without us which arouses a sympathetic feeling of red in our senses." "Esthetic Feeling . . . belongs to Category the First." (5.110)[8] A "feeling" is a wave-motion of physical communication from one part to another of an organization, (6.133) capable of exciting sympathetic appreciation in another organization. For Peirce, then, Locke's "secondary qualities" are feelings which enjoy an ontological status in the objective world; they are apprehensible by the senses but independent of such apprehension.

Now, in this objective world of qualities there is one aspect which, more than all others, is in itself to be highly regarded. This is the aesthetic property. Thus the problem of aesthetics becomes that of determining "by analysis what it is that one ought deliberately to admire *per se* in itself regardless of what it may [or may not] lead to." Analysis reveals that "the sensation of beauty arises upon a manifold of other impressions." (5.291) It is not a "first impression of sense" and is therefore in no wise to be construed as a subjective affair. "When the sensation beautiful is determined by previous cognitions, it always arises as a predicate; that is, we think that *something*[9] is beautiful." What, then, is this something which is beautiful? When we state the problem thus baldly we represent it as oversimplified; there are innumerable qualitative differences in the aesthetic field. (5.127)

[7] See chap. IV, B, i.
[8] See *ibid*.
[9] Italics mine.

Perhaps even the term "beautiful" is too limited, since we include in our larger meaning of aesthetic things which are unbeautiful—in a beautiful fashion. (2.199) Peirce finally hit upon the Greek term καλός. "Using καλός, the question of esthetics is, What is the one quality that is, in its immediate presence, καλός?"

After due reflection upon the necessity for ethical action to spring from some aesthetic ideal, Peirce came to the conclusion that "the theory of the deliberate formation of such habits of feeling [i.e., of the ideal] is what ought to be meant by *esthetics*." (1.574) Here the habits are understood to be in the subject and the ideal in the object, where the subject is any organization capable of apprehending the objective ideal. It will be recalled at this point that aesthetics considers "those things whose ends are to embody qualities of feeling." (5.129) Thus one purpose of the aesthetic ideal whose being is independent of the processes of human cognition is to "embody qualities of feeling." The term "body" is used here in its physical sense, such that any physical object is a body. Thus the human apprehension of the aesthetic ideal is one instance of the effect of the ideal, which by no means composes it or limits it to human experience, although the latter may be its only instance at present. For were it not so, Peirce argued, were the only excuse for the being of objects their capacity to arouse feelings in human beings, we would be confronted with "the doctrine that this vast universe of Nature which we contemplate with such awe is good only to produce a certain quality of feeling." (1.614)[10]

"A subtle and almost ineradicable narrowness in the conception of Normative Science runs through almost all modern philosophy in making it relate exclusively to the human mind.[11] The beautiful is conceived to be relative to human taste, right and wrong concern human conduct alone, logic deals with human reasoning." (5.128) The mental conception of these sciences certainly has an element of truth in it, but what is normative can be truly considered mental only by removing the mental from the subjective realm.[12] The aesthetic subject matter is not subjective in the sense that it can be considered to inhere in the mind; only the apprehension and appreciation of that subject matter by human beings is subjective, but that which is apprehended and appreciated has its own independent and objective existence.

Thus the beautiful consists in a common quality of objects which is

[10] The doctrine that one purpose, at least, of the universe is to produce qualities of feeling in any of its parts and not merely in some of its parts, i.e., in those which are human beings, is a more tenable and less subjective doctrine.

[11] See chap. IV, C, i.

[12] See chap. VI, A, iv, and E, ii.

ideal and which, incidentally, is capable of arousing some apprehension of that quality in bodies. The nature of the apprehension of the aesthetic quality of the beautiful by human beings was not considered by Peirce, but he did touch on it incidentally when he pointed out that pleasure is not a simple phenomenon of feeling. (5.112) In opposition to Kant, he maintained that pleasure is a complex affair. (1.333) Pleasure and pain are not mere qualities of feeling; "they are rather motor instincts attracting us to some feelings and repelling others." (6.462) Thus Peirce adduced further evidence from psychology to rule out the notion that aesthetics can be sufficiently explicated on psychological grounds alone.

The objective character of the aesthetic ideal would lead us to suspect, then, that there must be some close relation between the beautiful and the logical, since on Peirce's view the logical is necessarily the relational and the objective. (2.135-139) Such indeed is the case. There is a logic of art, for example. Correspondingly, the imagination works in conjunction with reason, within limits prescribed by logic. "The work of the poet or novelist is not so utterly different from that of the scientific man. The artist introduces a fiction; but it is not an arbitrary one; it exhibits affinities to which the mind accords a certain approval in pronouncing them beautiful, which, if it is not exactly the same as saying that the synthesis is true, is something of the same general kind." (1.383)

"It is true that when the Arabian romancer tells us that there was a lady named Scheherazade, he does not mean to be understood as speaking of the world of outward realities, and there is a great deal of fiction in what he is talking about. For the *fictive* is that whose characters depend upon what characters somebody attributes to it; and the story is, of course, the mere creation of the poet's thought. Nevertheless, once he has imagined Scheherazade and made her young, beautiful, and endowed with a gift of spinning stories, it becomes a real fact that so he has imagined her, which fact he cannot destroy by pretending or thinking that he imagined her to be otherwise." (5.152) The artist, like the geometer, is able to "show relations between elements which before seemed to have no necessary connection." (1.383)

It is important to bear in mind that Peirce's central interest lay in logic. He was concerned with logic for its own sake; but he also discovered that, since it is as basic as ontology,[13] deductions of immense importance could be drawn from it.[14] Aesthetics, like other philosophical branches, is to some extent dependent upon logic. The relation is one of interdependence,

[13] See chap. IV, A, i.
[14] See chap. III, D, iii.

inasmuch as logic also to some extent rests on aesthetics. But the dependence of aesthetics is by far the larger. The nature of logic is essentially representational; as we have seen, its sign always "determines something else (its *interpretant*) to refer to an object to which itself refers (its *object*). (2.303)[15] But the objects represented in logic contain those qualitative ideals which are the elements of the aesthetic property. Thus logic is compelled to take into account, as given, the qualitative ideals of objects.[16]

On the other hand, as we have seen, the dependence of aesthetics upon logic is more important. The logical implications of aesthetic appreciation are iconic.[17] "A diagram, indeed, so far as it has a general signification, is not a pure icon; but in the middle part of our reasonings we forget the abstractness in great measure, and the diagram is for us the very thing. So in contemplating a painting, there is a moment when we lose the consciousness that it is not the thing, the distinction of the real and the copy disappears, and it is for the moment a pure dream—not any particular existence, and yet not general. At that moment we are contemplating an *icon*." (3.362) Works of art, and the beautiful in general, represent the truth of affective relations and are not in any sense arbitrary, except within the narrow limits that logic prescribes. Analytically, the field of aesthetics is a prescribed field, within whose boundaries the laws of logic are applicable to any part or parts.

Such a viewpoint was expressed by Peirce and remains consistent with his metaphysics; but it was nowhere elaborated. We may well ask why. One reason, which has already been given, is that Peirce failed to pursue the topic with the same eagerness with which he had begun it in his youth. (2.201) But another, and in some ways still more important, reason is Peirce's acceptance and defense of the distinction between the normative and empirical sciences. Aesthetics, he held, was one of the three normative sciences, and a normative science is one which "not only lays down rules which ought to be, but need not be followed; but it is the analysis of the conditions of attainment of something of which purpose is an essential ingredient." (1.575) Is this distinction justified? Do the normative sciences differ from the empirical in dealing with a purposive subject matter? The problem is a complex one, and impossible of solution in the brief compass

[15] See chap. III, B, i.

[16] Croce's whole philosophy seems based upon the compulsion of ontology to take the epistemological interpretation of this fact into account. Peirce rejects the interpretation when he states that "although I do not think that an esthetic valuation is essentially involved, *actualiter* (so to speak) in every intellectual purport, I do think that it is a *virtual* factor of a duly rationalized purport." (5.535) The distinction is of immense significance.

[17] See chap. III, B, i.

of this chapter. Suffice to say here that in the case of aesthetics even Peirce had his doubts. He maintained consistently that ethics and logic are purposive, but wavered with regard to aesthetics, since "a thing is beautiful or ugly quite irrespective of any purpose to be so. It would seem, therefore, that esthetics is no more essentially normative than any nomological science," such as for instance optics.

ii. AESTHETICS AS EXACT SCIENCE

The strategy pursued by Peirce was the attempt to get aesthetics over into the field where it could be considered as an exact mathematical science. Yet he could not quite bring himself to accept the full consequences of this program. He was certain that no normative science can "deal entirely with a question of *quantity*," (5.127)[18] and elsewhere equally certain that "it is in esthetics that we ought to seek for the deepest characteristics of normative science, since esthetics, in dealing with the very ideal itself whose mere materialization engrosses the attention of practics [i.e., ethics] and of logic, must contain the heart, soul and spirit of normative science." (5.551)

Peirce was among other things a mathematician with a logical perspective on ontology. He could not bring himself to concentrate upon the normative aspects of any science which he considered to be normative. Logic, his chief interest, although listed by him as a normative science, was not treated normatively; indeed, he was one of the pioneers of symbolic, or mathematical, logic.[19] The truth is that in the studies in which he was profoundly absorbed Peirce made no practical distinction of treatment between those which he considered normative and those which he considered empirical. All were held to be equally normative, in the Greek sense of the setting up of an ἀρετή, or type of excellence; and all were held to be equally empirical in their susceptibility to exact measurement. We may feel aesthetic qualities before we can reason about their logical form, "but what is first for us is not first in nature," (5.119) and the "importance of everything resides entirely in its mathematical form." (5.551)

The failure to get aesthetics out of normative science and over onto its own scientific basis constrained Peirce to continue to look for relations between aesthetics and the other normative studies, more particularly ethics. But the confining of aesthetics to ethics in any way, when the field of aesthetics is considered to be broader than that of ethics, is sure to produce con-

---

[18] Even though normative science is purely theoretical and not practical. (5.125)

[19] See the *Collected Papers*, vol. iii. Also C. I. Lewis and C. H. Langford, *Symbolic Logic* (New York, 1932), pp. 8-26.

fusion. We have seen that aesthetics applies to all objects,[20] and that ethics applies only to objects whose ends lie in action.[21] In his extensive ethical studies Peirce took it for granted that ethics applies only to human beings.[22] But when aesthetics treats of the beauty of everything, nonhuman as well as human, whereas ethics is confined to the conduct of men, the limiting of aesthetics to ethics in any fashion is contradictory with the extent of its application.

There are two ways out of this difficulty. The first solution would be to limit aesthetics; to allow it to apply only to what is humanly beautiful by maintaining that only what is considered beautiful by human beings is to be treated by aesthetics. In this way aesthetics and ethics would cover identical territory; but by the same token they would likewise be reduced to subjective studies and their scientific objectivity entirely removed from them. The second solution would be to accept the wide field of operations of aesthetics and attempt to broaden ethics to meet it. On this proposal, ethics would have to include the moral action of all objects; moreover, both ethics and aesthetics would have to be explicable without reference to their subjective human interpretation. Of these two alternative solutions, the latter alone is consistent with Peirce's general logico-ontological system of metaphysics. No "ideal can be too high for a duly transfigured esthetics." (5.535)

There is no doubt that Peirce came around finally to the objective and rational view of aesthetics, that view which holds it to be capable of development into an exact mathematical science. "An object," he asserted, "to be esthetically good, must have a multitude of parts so related to one another as to impart a positive simple immediate quality to their totality; and whatever does this is, in so far, esthetically good, no matter what the particular quality of the total may be." (5.132) And he went on to maintain that this is equally true of objects which nauseate and scare us, "as the Alps affected the people of old times, when the state of civilization was such that an impression of great power was inseparably associated with lively apprehension and terror"; and the object remains "none the less esthetically good, although people in our condition are incapacitated from a calm esthetic contemplation of it." On this showing of aesthetics it is certain that Peirce's philosophy was consistent and systematic, even on its weakest and most undeveloped side. Others, it is to be hoped, will perhaps

[20] See this chapter, B, i.
[21] See chap. IX, B and C.
[22] Chapter IX. See also the *Collected Papers*, vol. ii, chap. 6.

proceed to develop from this philosophy the important implications to aesthetics, which, Peirce's start has indicated, it is possible to discover.

iii. SUMMARY OF THE CHAPTER

Aesthetics is the least developed of all philosophical topics treated by Peirce. Although it aroused his interest, he never succeeded in developing it in any way which satisfied him.

Aesthetics is a normative science, that one which considers the embodiment of feelings. It seems to include the aim of ethics, since the morally good is a species of the aesthetic ideal. Logic, too, seems to need the help of aesthetics.

Aesthetics considers objects in their presentation. It belongs to ontological firstness, and its subject matter is objective, a psychic feeling from without. In the objective world of qualities, the aesthetic property stands out. The predicate of the beautiful can best be described as καλός. Aesthetics intends the deliberate formation of habits of feeling.

The beautiful has a certain logic. Once set up, it cannot be willfully changed or denied for such quality as it has. The artist is limited by the logic of his aim and material. The appreciation of the beautiful is analyzable into the semiotic relation of the icon.

Although aesthetics is a normative science, it can be brought over into the empirical field of the mathematical sciences. The aesthetic subject matter is susceptible of measurement. The aesthetic object must have parts whose relation to one another imparts a simple, immediate quality to the whole.

CHAPTER XI

Cosmology

A. Introduction

i. from logic

Despite the fact that the bulk of peirce's work is not devoted to speculations concerning the nature of the cosmos as a whole, Peirce said that he "came to the study of philosophy . . . intensely curious about cosmology." (4.2) We may begin to analyze this interest by examining its obligations to other philosophical topics.

Since logic is founded in the stubborn facts which constitute the irreducible elements of experience,[1] we should not be surprised to discover the same logic at the basis of that study of the widest existential universe which is termed cosmology. The universe, in fact, is presupposed by logic; and we may venture to take the use of the term literally even though its actual employment in logic is meant to be figurative. For instance, Peirce said that "the essential office of the copula is to express a relation of a general term or terms to the universe," (3.621) and, further, that "the universe must be well known and mutually known to be known and agreed to exist, in some sense, between speaker and hearer" as the common ground across which communications can travel. The close relation between logic and cosmology becomes more in evidence when we understand that the universe expressed by the copula is indeed—the universe. The very dependability and predominant success of inductive reasoning is largely based upon the constitution of the universe continuing to be what it is.[2] The logic of the universe is our own logic more greatly developed. "Whatever else may be said for or against that hypothesis, that which we of these times ought to try is rather the hypothesis that the logic of the universe is one to which our own aspires, rather than attains." (6.189)

[1] See chap. III, A, ii.
[2] See chap. III, D, iii, quoting 2.749.

In Peirce's view, there is little doubt, indeed, that "the entire universe—not merely the universe of existents, but all that wider universe, embracing the universe of existents as a part, the universe which we are all accustomed to refer to as 'the truth'—that all this universe is perfused with signs, if it is not composed exclusively of signs." (5.448 n.) "The universe is a vast representamen." (5.119) "The conception is that Nature syllogizes from one grand major premiss, and the causes are the different minor premisses of nature's syllogistic development." (6.66) "We usually conceive Nature to be perpetually making deductions in *Barbara*. This is our natural and anthropomorphic metaphysics. We conceive that there are Laws of Nature, which are her Rules or major premisses. We conceive that Cases arise under these laws; these cases consist in the predication, or occurrence, of *causes*, which are the middle terms of the syllogisms. And, finally, we conceive that the occurrence of these causes, by virtue of the laws of Nature, result in effects which are the conclusions of the syllogisms." (2.713)[3]

ii. FROM METAPHYSICS

The way in which Peirce foresaw that cosmology ought to be (although certainly not the way it was) is as an exact science of ontology, or, as he termed it, "mathematical metaphysics." (6.213) It follows from his ontology that the existing universe is the total phaneron[4] and that the ultimate categories of cosmology would have to consist in some complex translation of the phenomenological categories of firstness, or quality; secondness, or reaction; and thirdness, or representation.[5] We shall see that such is the case.

Cosmology accepts ontology at its face value, and clears away from the discussion those topics of perennial debate, topics concerning the nature of knowledge and of reality, and the refutation of subjectivism or objectivism. Cosmology is possible as a separate study only upon the condition of the implicit acceptance of the reality of the world. Of the three fundamental philosophical points of view, represented by idealism, materialism and realism, cosmology as a separate study is irrevocably committed to the last named by its very nature. For, in idealism, the existential universe is held to be an effusion of the subject and inseparable from him, and hence identical with the ontological subject matter. And in materialism, the

[3] See chap. III, C, i.
[4] See chap. IV, A, ii.
[5] See chap. IV, B, i, ii, and iii.

existential universe is held to be identical with the object and inseparable from it, and hence identical with the ontological subject matter. In both idealism and materialism, then, there is no need for a special science of cosmology. But in realism, neither the subject nor that which he knows is identical with the existential universe, which has its own peculiarities of investigation and its own field of laws.

Of the three ontological modes of being, possibility, actuality and destiny,[6] cosmology may be said to lean more heavily on the middle mode than on the former, which belongs more properly to the province of specialized ontology and theology. Destiny is subdivided into freedom and necessity,[7] but these terms, too, refer more particularly to theology. Here we are more concerned with the world of *conditions* that make freedom (or necessity or both) possible than we are with destiny directly.

But the modes of existence refer more directly to the topic here under discussion, and cosmology has direct connections with its categories, chance, law and habit.[8] The ultimate natures of these categories are central to cosmology.

In epistemology, it is only the nature of truth that has important implications to the logic of the cosmos. In epistemology, the truth is defined as "the universe of all universes."[9] "The world is that which experience inculcates." (1.426)[10] But cosmology is not concerned primarily with all universes, only with the existential universe, that "Seme of The Truth, that is, [with] the widest Universe of Reality." (4.553)

Other branches of philosophy have references to cosmology, as, for instance, the very incompleteness of psychology;[11] and the necessity for an application of the method, developed in the methodology.[12] But these will be treated explicitly in footnotes or by inference in the text of this chapter.

B. COSMOGONY

i. THE ORIGINAL CHAOS

If we take a leap into the middle of our topic, and begin with the original chaos from which the existential universe is supposed to have evolved, we are striving for no more than Peirce expected, and evidently received, from

---

[6] See chap. IV, D, i.
[7] See chap. IV, D, i, (e).
[8] See chap. IV, D, ii.
[9] See chap. V, C, iii, quoting 5.506.
[10] See chap. V, A, ii.
[11] See chap. VI, E, ii.
[12] See chap. VII, especially A, iii; and C, ii and iii.

his own act of imagination. "In the beginning was nullity, or absolute indetermination, which, considered as the possibility of all determination, is being." (1.447) "Chaos is pure nothing," (5.431) an "original vague potentiality" (6.203) "where there was no regularity . . . in which nothing existed or really happened." (1.411) Peirce, in other words, tried to "go back to a chaos so irregular that in strictness the word existence is not applicable to its merely germinal state of being; and here I reach a region in which the objection to ultimate causes loses its force. But I do not stop there. Even this nothingness, though it antecedes the infinitely distant absolute beginning of time, is traced back to a nothingness more rudimentary still, in which there is no variety, but only an indefinite specifiability, which is nothing but a tendency to the diversification of the nothing, while leaving it as nothing as it was before." (6.612)

Peirce rejected the notion that "the state of things existing at any time, together with certain immutable laws, completely determine the state of things at every other time," (6.37) since this would require the truth of "the common belief that every single fact in the universe is precisely determined by law." (6.36) Historically, philosophers have always had to introduce a minimal deviation to account fully for the true situation. The argument from determination is inconsistent with a primal indetermination of pure chaos, which Peirce had posited. The reason for Peirce's view is that partial determination is not as potential, as replete with multitudinous possibilities, as is absolute indetermination. To contain the possibility of all future determination, the original chaos was required to be absolutely without determination of any sort or degree.

"We start, then, with nothing, pure zero. But this is not the nothing of negation. For *not* means *other than*, and *other* is merely a synonym of the ordinal numeral *second*. As such it implies a first; while the present pure zero is prior to every first. The nothing of negation is the nothing of death, which comes *second* to, or after, everything. But this pure zero is the nothing of not having been born. There is no individual thing, no compulsion, outward nor inward, no law. It is the germinal nothing, in which the whole universe is involved or foreshadowed. As such, it is absolutely undefined and unlimited possibility—boundless possibility. There is no compulsion and no law. It is boundless freedom." (6.217)

ii. THEORY OF UNIVERSAL ORIGINS

"Now the question arises, what necessarily resulted from that state of things? But the only sane answer is that where freedom was boundless nothing in particular necessarily resulted." (6.218) "That is, nothing according to deductive logic. But such is not the logic of freedom or possibility. The logic of freedom, or potentiality, is that it shall annul itself. For if it does not annul itself, it remains a completely idle and do-nothing potentiality; and a completely idle potentiality is annulled by its complete idleness." (6.219) Peirce did "not mean that potentiality immediately resulted in actuality. Mediately perhaps it does; but what immediately resulted was that unbounded potentiality became potentiality of this or that sort—that is, of some *quality*. Thus the zero of bare possibility, by evolutionary logic, leapt into the *unit* of some quality. This was hypothetic inference. Its form was:

> "Something is possible,
> Red is something;
> Red is possible." (6.220)

We can begin to discern the dim outlines of the "Cosmogonic Philosophy." (6.33) "It would suppose that in the beginning—infinitely remote—there was a chaos of unpersonalized feeling, which being without connection or regularity would properly be without existence. This feeling, sporting here and there in pure arbitrariness, would have started the germ of a generalizing tendency. Its other sportings would be evanescent, but this would have a growing virtue. Thus, the tendency to habit would be started; and from this, with the other principles of evolution, all the regularities of the universe would be evolved." "In looking back into the past we are looking toward periods when it was a less and less decided tendency. But its own essential nature is to grow. It is a generalizing tendency; it causes actions in the future to follow some generalization of past actions; and this tendency is itself something capable of similar generalizations; and thus, it is self-generative. We have therefore only to suppose the smallest spoor of it in the past, and that germ would have been bound to develop into a mighty and over-ruling principle, until it supersedes itself by strengthening habits into absolute laws regulating the action of all things in every respect in the indefinite future." (1.409)[13]

The three categories, which we have seen under various guises:—feeling,[14] habit[15] and regularity,[16] are shown as the first discrete emergents from the

---

[13] See chap. IV, D, ii, (*c*), quoting 1.409.
[14] See chap. IV, B, i.
[15] See chap. IV, D, ii, (*c*).
[16] See chap. IV, D, ii, (*b*).

primal chaos. They are the earliest existents. Peirce, indeed, in another passage, gives them their ontological names in describing the emergence. "Our conceptions of the first stages of the development, before time yet existed, must be as vague and figurative as the expressions of the first chapter of Genesis. Out of the womb of indeterminacy we must say that there would have come something, by the principle of Firstness,[17] which we may call a flash. Then by the principle of habit there would have been a second[18] flash. Though time would not yet have been, this second flash was in some sense after the first, because resulting from it. Then there would have come other successions ever more and more closely connected, the habits and the tendency to take them ever strengthening themselves, until the events would have been bound together into something like a continuous flow" (1.412) of thirdness.[19] "But it does not follow that because there has been no first in a series, therefore that series has had no beginning in time; for the series may be *continuous*, and may have begun gradually." (5.327)

It develops, then, "that primeval chaos in which there was no regularity was mere nothing, from a physical aspect. Yet it was not a blank zero; for there was an intensity of consciousness there, in comparison with which all that we ever feel is but as the struggling of a molecule or two to throw off a little of the force of law to an endless and innumerable diversity of chance utterly unlimited." (6.265) Hence "chance is but the outward aspect of that which within itself is feeling."[20] This equivalence is in many ways one of Peirce's most important ideas. It accounts for cosmogony, since "wherever chance-spontaneity is found, there in the same proportion feeling exists." It accounts, also, for the unity of mind and matter, as we shall see. It accounts for the multifariousness of the world, and for the infinite aims of sentient beings. We feel many things and wish to put in order that which we feel.

But to return to cosmical origins, "variety is a fact which must be admitted; and the theory of chance merely consists in supposing this diversification does not antedate all time." (6.65) "To explain diversity is to go behind the chaos, to the original undiversified nothing. Diversificacity was the first germ." (6.613) "We can hardly but suppose that those sense-qualities that we now experience, colors, odors, sounds, feelings of every description, loves, griefs, surprise, are but the relics of an ancient ruined continuum of qualities, like a few columns standing here and there in testimony that here some

[17] See chap. IV, B, i.
[18] See chap. IV, B, ii.
[19] See chap. IV, B, iii.
[20] See chap. VI, B, i, quoting 6.133.

old-world forum with its basilica and temples had once made a magnificent *ensemble*.[21] And just as that forum, before it was actually built, had had a vague underexistence in the mind of him who planned its construction, so too the cosmos of sense-qualities, which I would have you to suppose in some early stage of being was as real as your personal life is this minute, had in an antecedent stage of development a vaguer being, before the relations of its dimensions became definite and contracted." (6.197)

Substances are "constituted by regularities." (1.411) The flashes of firstness which we have just seen posited as occurring in the primeval chaos of nothing by the sporting of pure arbitrariness occur in pairs of the degree of secondness. "But secondness is of two types.[22] Consequently besides flashes genuinely second to others, so as to come after them, there will be pairs of flashes, or, since time is now supposed to be developed, we had better say pairs of states, which are reciprocally second, each member of the pair to the other. This is the first germ of spatial extension." (1.413)

We have thus seen how from an original indeterminate chaos Peirce has logically derived his three ontological categories, of firstness, secondness and thirdness, or, as they are termed in this connection, chance (or quality or feeling), habit (or growth or evolution), and continuity (or generality or regularity). We now turn to an examination of these as formal cosmological categories, where they appear as independent absolutes.

Peirce called his three categorical absolutes the three universes, and named them separately *tychism*, for chance, *agapism*, for evolution, and *synechism*, for continuity. The three absolute cosmological categories are independent yet also interdependent. (5.91) Their independent being makes possible their interrelatedness, since that which is not at least quasi-independent is not capable of sustaining relationships. We have, then, a "perfect cosmology of the three universes." (6.490) It is left to imagination to "prove all in relation to that subject that reason could desiderate; and of course all that it would prove must, in actual fact, now be true. But reason would desiderate that that should be proved from which would follow all that is in fact true of the three universes; and the postulate from which all this would follow must not state any matter of fact, since such fact would thereby be left unexplained. That perfect cosmology must therefore show that the whole history of the three universes, as it has been and is to be, would follow from a premiss which would not suppose them to exist at all. Moreover, such premiss must in actual fact be true. But that premiss must represent a state

---

[21] See chap. IV, A, ii, quoting 1.418.
[22] See chap. IV, B, ii.

of things in which three universes were completely nil. Consequently, whether in time or not, the three universes must actually be absolutely necessary results of a state of utter nothingness." This conclusion is what in fact Peirce had already derived, as has been shown in this section.

C. The Cosmological Categories

i. tychism

"*Tychism* (from τύχη, chance)" (6.102) is defined as "the doctrine that absolute chance is a factor of the universe." (6.201) It never exhausts the universe, the other two absolutes being present also, (6.202) but it is never absolutely absent, either. "Chance itself pours in at every avenue of sense: it is of all things the most obtrusive. That it is absolute is the most manifest of all intellectual perceptions." (6.612) Peirce was able to discover "four positive arguments for believing in real chance. They were as follows:

"1. The general prevalence of growth, which seems to be opposed to the conservation of energy.

"2. The variety of the universe, which is chance, and is manifestly inexplicable.

"3. Law, which requires to be explained, and like everything which is to be explained must be explained by something else, that is, by non-law or real chance.

"4. Feeling, for which room cannot be found if the conservation of energy is maintained." (6.613)

Absolute chance takes priority over natural laws. Peirce agreed with the contemporary comedian who suspected that the sun, having stood still at the command of Joshua, "might have wiggled a very little when Joshua was not looking directly at it." (1.156) The probability theory in actual application in the sciences, as, for instance, the behavior of particles of gases, is evidence of the existence of real chance. (6.47)[23] But such deviation from natural law is not confined to any one empirical field; spontaneous activity is to be found everywhere. Absolute chance takes priority even over some metaphysical laws. (6.132; 6.47) "By thus admitting pure spontaneity or life as a character of the universe, acting always and everywhere though restrained within narrow bounds by law, producing infinitesimal departures from law continually, and great ones with infinite infrequency, I account for all the variety and diversity of the universe, in the only sense in which

[23] See chap. III, C, iv.

the really *sui generis* and new can be said to be accounted for," (6.59) that is to say, by chance.

In the end, "*tychism* must give birth to an evolutionary cosmology, in which all the regularities of nature and of mind are regarded as products of growth, and to a Schelling-fashioned idealism which holds matter to be mere specialized and partially deadened mind." (6.102) "It is a question whether absolute chance—pure tychism—ought not to be regarded as a product of freedom, and therefore of life, not necessarily physiological." (6.322) This does not mean that matter is dead mind; it means that matter is made up of the same ideas of which mind is composed, only more frozen and inert. It means that chance, which is an exception to law, also leads to law eventually.[24] "No doubt, all that chance is competent to destroy, it may, once in a long, long time, produce." (6.322) "At any time, however, an element of pure chance survives and will remain until the world becomes an absolutely perfect rational, and symmetrical system, in which mind is at last crystallized in the infinitely distant future." (6.33) Thus chance joins evolution and continuity in the task of making over the world to rationalism. "We enormously exaggerate the part that law plays in the universe" (1.406), which is no mere "evolution of Pure Reason." (5.92) *Tychism*, or absolute chance, is thus an ultimate category for the existential universe.

ii. AGAPISM

Agapism, from ἀγάπη, love, (6.287) is the name for evolution, in Peirce's cosmology. Chance accounts for evolution partly, "But as for explaining evolution by chance, there has not been time enough." (5.172) Although "the agapistic ontologist who endeavors to escape tychism will find himself 'led into' . . . 'inextricable confusion'," (6.610) chance does aid in explaining growth (6.64) even if it does not do so fully.

"Evolution means nothing but *growth* in the widest sense of that word," (1.174)[25] the rule of growth through the "law of love." (6.302) "The doctrine of evolution refrains from pronouncing whether forms are simply fated[26] or whether they are providential; but that definite ends are worked out none of us today any longer deny. . . . For evolution is nothing more nor less than the working out of a definite end." (1.204) "Question any science which deals with the course of time. Consider the life of an individual animal or plant, or of a mind. Glance at the history of states, of institutions,

[24] See chap. III, C, iii.
[25] See chap. VIII, B, iii, (*a*).
[26] See chap. IV, D, i, (*e*).

of language, of ideas. Examine the succession of forms shown by paleontology, the history of the globe as set forth in geology, of what the astronomer is able to make out concerning the changes of stellar systems. Everywhere the main fact is growth and increasing complexity. Death and corruption are mere accidents or secondary phenomena." (6.58)[27] Thus, "Philosophy, when just escaping from its golden pupa-skin, mythology, proclaimed the great evolutionary agency of the universe to be Love." (6.287) Evolution is a product of habit; "it is clear that nothing but a principle of habit,[28] itself due to the growth by habit of an infinitesimal chance tendency toward habit-taking, is the only bridge that can span the chasm between the chance-medley of chaos and the cosmos of order and law." (6.262)

Peirce showed that tychastic and anacastic evolutions, or evolution by chance and by mechanical necessity, are degenerate forms of agapistic evolution, or evolution by love. (6.302 f.) Evolutionary love, as Peirce called it, is the one supreme law of the universe. In the human being, it begins with the love of human society, but even society is "itself a poor and little thing enough," (1.647) a thing which evolutionary love has got to transcend.[29] If society is a community of men,[30] then nature is a community of societies of different sorts, and evolutionary love extends beyond man and society to nature in all its manifestations. In order to keep law from being an irrational affair, all laws must be subject to law. "For that purpose that law of laws must be a law capable of developing itself. Now the only conceivable law of which that is true is an evolutionary law. We therefore suppose that all law is the result of evolution." (6.91) Take the laws of empirical science, for example, of dynamics, of chemistry, etc. "Now who will deliberately say that our knowledge of these laws is sufficient to make us reasonably confident that they are absolutely eternal and immutable, and that they escape the great law of evolution?" (1.348) For "the only possible way of accounting for the laws of nature . . . is to suppose them results of evolution." (6.13)[31] This is not so difficult to imagine. "If all things are continuous,[32] the universe must be undergoing a continuous growth from non-existence to existence," (1.175) and since "Reason, or

---

[27] See chap. IV, B, ii.
[28] See chap. IV, D, ii, (c).
[29] See chap. IX, B, iii.
[30] See chap. VIII, D, iv, quoting 1.354.
[31] Of course, "if law is a result of evolution, which is a process lasting through all time, it follows that no law is absolute. That is, we must suppose that the phenomena themselves involve departures from law analogous to errors of observation," (6.101) thus allowing for the retention of cosmological chance as an absolute in the existential universe.
[32] See this chapter, C, iii.

Noῦς," is "a something manifesting itself . . . in nature," (1.615) we must suppose that it, too, undergoes continuous growth.[33]

The law of evolution according to Peirce knows no exception. "In short, if we are going to regard the universe as a result of evolution at all, we must think that not merely the existing universe, that locus in the cosmos to which our reactions are limited,[34] but the whole Platonic world, which in itself is equally real,[35] is evolutionary in its origin, too." (6.200) In the beginning all was vague potentiality,[36] and "it must be by a contraction of the vagueness of that potentiality of everything in general, but of nothing in particular, that the world of forms comes about." (6.196) "The evolutionary process is, therefore, not a mere evolution of the *existing universe*, but rather a process by which the very Platonic forms themselves have become or are becoming developed." (6.194) This does not mean, however, that the Platonic forms developed from the existential universe, for, as we have seen,[37] quite the reverse is true; but both the possible or essential and the existential universes are subject to the evolutionary law.

"The only fundamental kind of causation is the action of final causes," (6.101) and "the *summum bonum* . . . consist[s] in that process of evolution whereby the existent comes more and more to embody those generals which . . . [are] *destined*,[38] which is what we strive to express in calling them *reasonable*." (5.433) For the end of the supreme law of nature, or the final cause, which is the evolutionary law, lies "in the rationalization of the universe." (1.590)

iii. SYNECHISM

"Almost everybody will now agree that the ultimate good lies in the evolutionary process in some way. If so, it is not in individual reactions in their segregation, but in something general or continuous. Synechism is founded on the notion that the coalescence, the becoming continuous, the becoming governed by laws, the becoming instinct with general ideas, are but phases of one and the same process of the growth of reasonableness." (5.4) The procedure of derivation of the continuum is "from the vague to the definite." (6.191) Generals gain control over things by means of habits;

---

[33] See chap. III, B, i, (*b*), for the development of representamens; and chap. VIII, D, iii, for the development of universal classes.

[34] See chap. IV, B, ii.

[35] See chap. IV, C, ii.

[36] See this chapter, B, i.

[37] See chap. IV, C, ii, quoting 6.192.

[38] See chap. IV, D, i, (*e*).

in this case, "Habit is that specialization of the law of mind whereby a general idea gains the power of exciting reactions." (6.145)[39] "Continuity, as generality, is inherent in potentiality, which is essentially general." (6.204)

Synechism is defined as "the doctrine that all that exists is continuous." (1.172)[40] "Now continuity is shown by the logic of relations[41] to be nothing but a higher type of that which we know as generality. It is relational generality." (6.190) Thus we see that its origins in the generality of vagueness are consistent with its logic in the generality of relatedness, which furnishes additional supporting evidence for the consistency of Peirce's system at all points.

"Continuity [then,] is nothing but perfect generality of a law of relationship." (6.172) "Continuity represents Thirdness[42] almost to perfection." (1.337) It thus involves infinity. (1.165) "A true continuum is something whose possibilities of determination no multitude of individuals can exhaust." (6.170)[43] It is thus the emergence of logical unity in cosmology, as the continuum of the existential universe. When we recall that time and space are both coextensive with the existential universe[44] and also realize that as continuous they involve circularity, (6.210-212) we begin to detect the particular character of the existential universe. It is ovate. Matter and even life consist in vortices. (1.220)

The final argument for the ovate world comes from the analysis of the continuum itself conceived as existential. The reasoning here (4.220) is tenuous, but sound. If we conceive of an oval thing, say a filament, then we can say that the particles of the filament lie along the oval. But "If those particles possess each its individual existence there is a discrete collection of them, and this collection must possess a definite multitude. Now this multitude cannot equal the multiplicity of the aggregate of all possible discrete multitudes; because it is a discrete multitude, and as such it is smaller than another possible multitude. Hence it is not equal to the multitude of points of the oval. For that is equal to the aggregate of all possible discrete multitudes, since the line, by hypothesis, affords room for any collection of discrete points however great. Hence, if particles of the filament are distributed equally along the line of the oval, there must be, in every

---

[39] See chap. VI, E, ii, quoting 6.104. The "law of mind" is not a mental law but a law of the spread of ideas taken from the point of view of the ideas themselves and not of the minds (nor the things) to which they spread.

[40] See chap. IV, B, ii, (*b*), quoting 1.411.

[41] See chap. III, B, v, (*a*).

[42] See chap. IV, B, iii.

[43] See chap. VIII, B, iii, (*c*).

[44] See chap. VIII, D, ii.

sensible part, continuous collections of points, that is, *lines*, that are unoccupied by particles. These lines may be far less than any *assignable* mag-
nitudes, that is, far less than any parts into which the system of real
quantities enables us to divide the line. But there is no contradiction whatever
involved in that. It thus appears that true continuity is logically absolutely
repugnant to the individual designation or even approximate individual
designation of its units, except at points where the character of the continuity is itself not continuous." Hence, existence must be said to involve
interruptions in the continuum which are themselves quasi-continuous. The
existential universe is inevitably characterized by continuity.

D. Conclusions

i. mind and matter

In the listing of the categories, Peirce gave for cosmology still other
names for the triad. He said that "Mind is First, Matter is Second, Evolution
is Third." (6.32) This new list, then, identifies mind with chance, or
tychism; matter with evolution, or agapism; and evolution with continuity,
or synechism. In this way he attempted to solve the mind-matter distinction
which was held so prominently in his day. Earlier, he had attacked it under
the guise of Cartesianism, but now he made efforts to show how his metaphysics got rid of the problem altogether.

"It is certainly a desideratum in philosophy to unify the phenomena of
mind and matter." (6.73) We have already examined the nature of mind.[45]
What strikes us most forcefully about the universe of matter is its "un-
speakable variety" (6.464)—and uniformity. It is simple in structure yet
reveals itself to be astonishingly complex upon analysis. Our inability to get
inside objective bits of matter forces us to a consideration of the samples of
matter that we ourselves are. We have seen that subjective feeling corresponds
to objective chance.[46] In the same way, we may on analogy consider the
relations of matter and awareness.[47] "Viewing a thing from the outside,
considering its relations of action and reaction with other things, it appears
as matter. Viewing it from the inside, looking at its immediate character
as feeling, it appears as consciousness." (6.268)

But there is no mental causation, (6.70) just as we saw that there is no

---

[45] See chap. VI, A, iv.
[46] See chap. VI, B, i.
[47] See chap. VI, B, ii.

physical.[48] Matter is interactive with matter, mind with mind, by the law of continuity. (1.170)[49] On the other hand, "mind . . . has a continuous extension in space. . . . Now, in obedience to the principle, or maxim, of continuity, that we ought to assume things to be continuous as far as we can, it has been urged [on the other hand] that we ought to suppose a continuity between the characters of mind and matter, so that matter would be nothing but mind that had such indurated habits as to cause it to act with a peculiarly high degree of mechanical regularity, or routine." (6.277)[50] Thus "what we call matter is not completely dead, but is merely mind hidebound with habits. It still retains the element of diversification; and in that diversification there is life." (6.158) It comes to this, that "wherever diversity is increasing, there chance must be operative. . . . But wherever actions take place under an established uniformity, there, so much feeling as there may be, takes the mode of a sense of reaction. That is the manner in which I am led to define the relation between the fundamental elements of consciousness and their physical equivalents." (6.267)

"Nature only appears intelligible so far as it appears rational, that is, so far as its processes are seen to be like processes of thought." (3.422) Conversely, "the mind of man is adapted to the reality of being." (4.157) The world of mind is the Platonic world of forms; the world of matter is that of existence. But "the old dualistic notion of mind and matter, so prominent in Cartesianism, as two radically different kinds of substance, will hardly find defenders today. Rejecting this, we are driven to some form of hylopathy, otherwise called monism. Then the question arises whether physical laws on the one hand and the psychical law on the other are to be taken—

(a) as independent, a doctrine often called *monism*, but which I would name *neutralism*; or,

(b) the psychical law as derived and special, the physical law alone as primordial, which is *materialism*; or,

(c) the physical law as derived and special, the psychical law alone as primordial, which is *idealism*." (6.24)[51] Peirce condemned neutralism by Occam's Razor, since it supposes more elements than necessary. He condemned materialism, since "it requires us to suppose that a certain kind of mechanism will feel." Elsewhere, and many times, he condemned subjective idealism, under the name of nominalism.[52]

[48] See chap. VIII, D, ii.
[49] See this chapter, C, iii.
[50] See chap. VI, E, ii.
[51] See this chapter, A, ii.
[52] See chap. IV, C, i.

"The one intelligible theory of the universe is that of objective idealism, that matter is effete mind, inveterate habits becoming physical laws." (6.25) Thus the cosmological philosophy ends with an objective idealism, which, however, Peirce insists is harmonious with "a logical realism of the most pronounced type." (6.163)[53]

ii. THE EXISTENTIAL UNIVERSE AND BEYOND

"Philosophy tries to understand. In so doing, it is committed to the assumption that things are intelligible, that the process of nature and the process of reason are one. Its explanation must be derivation. Explanation, derivation, involve suggestion of a starting-point—starting-point in its own nature not requiring explanation nor admitting of derivation. Also, there is suggestion of goal or stopping-point, where the process of reason and nature is perfected. A principle of movement must be assumed to be universal. It cannot be supposed that things ever actually reached the stopping-point, for there movement would stop and the principle of movement would not be universal; and similarly with the starting-point. Starting-point and stopping-point can only be ideal, like the two points where the hyperbola leaves one asymptote and where it joins the other." (6.581)

The universe is infinite, so far as we can tell, infinite in time and space. (6.419 ff.) It extends from an infinite past of absolute chance toward an infinite future of absolute law. It is a sprawling affair, and "ought to be presumed too vast to have any character." (6.422) Any simple explanation of the arrangements of nature, as that it is benevolent or hostile, or "a correspondence between conjunctions of the planets and human events, or a significance in numbers, or a key to dreams," (6.423) which does not yield explanation on mechanical principles, is more than suspect.

There can at any rate be no universe without some order, since " *blind existential being* may possibly not occur at all." (6.346) The order, as closely as Peirce could apprehend it, is that which we have been presenting throughout this work. The final word concerning this existential universe, with its division into chance and order or continuity, is that it is answerable to the over-all law of evolution, and to the provisions of metaphysical realism. The evolution of laws forces the idea that some laws, e.g., the law of evolution, do not change too rapidly.[54] But this requires a division into existence, and a nonexistence which is yet not nothing. "We shall naturally suppose,

[53] See chap. IV, C, ii.
[54] See chap. VIII, B, iii, quoting 2.86.

of course, that existence is a stage of evolution. *This existence* is presumably but a *special* existence. We need not suppose that every form needs for its evolution to emerge into this world, but only that it needs to enter into *some* theatre of reactions, of which this is one." (6.195)

The distinction being considered here is of course that between ontological possibility and actuality.[55] The actual world or existential universe is ontological actuality; the Platonic world of forms or ideas is ontological possibility. The actual world is conceived to be a selection from infinite possibility. "From this point of view we must suppose that the existing universe, with all its arbitrary secondness, is an off-shoot from, or an arbitrary determination of, a world of ideas, a Platonic world." (6.192) "At the same time all this, be it remembered, is not of the order of the existing universe, but is merely a Platonic world of which we are, therefore, to conceive that there are many, both coördinated and subordinated to one another; until finally out of one of these Platonic worlds is differentiated the particular actual universe of existence in which we happen to be." (6.208)

We can detect in this vast universe, with its chance-produced continuum of evolution, certain signs indicating the broad direction. One sign is to be observed in the relations of qualities. We have seen that to conceive the disparateness of qualities as historically absolute is to render them absolutely inexplicable.[56] "Time with its continuity logically involves some other kind of continuity than its own. Time, as the universal form of change, cannot exist unless there is something to undergo change and to undergo a change continuous in time there must be a continuity of changeable qualities." (6.132) Thus "we must not assume that the qualities arose separate and came into relation afterward. It was just the reverse." (6.199) The harmony of the universe does not require that "special ideas shall surrender their peculiar arbitrariness and caprice entirely; for that would be self-destructive. It only requires that they shall influence and be influenced by one another." (6.153)[57] Since all truths form a system[58] and the "universe has an explanation, the function of which, like that of every logical explanation, is to unify its observed variety, it follows that the root of all being is One; and so far as different subjects have a common character they partake of an identical being." (1.487)[59]

The universal mode of action is comparable to that of mind, namely,

[55] See chap. IV, D, i, especially (*a*), (*b*), and (*c*).
[56] See this chapter, B, ii.
[57] See chap. VI, D, i.
[58] See chap. IV, C, ii, quoting 2.447 f.
[59] See chap. XII, B, i.

action by final causation. (1.269) "A purpose is merely that form of final cause which is most familiar to our experience." (1.211) Cosmologically speaking, "A final cause may be conceived to operate without having been the purpose of any mind: that supposed phenomenon goes by the name of *fate*." (1.204)[60] On this note the cosmology closes.

iii. SUMMARY OF THE CHAPTER

Cosmology is concerned with the widest existential universe. It lies behind all logical propositions, and is required as a separate study by metaphysical realism.

The existential universe has evolved from original chaos. This original chaos was a nothingness which anteceded the beginning of time itself, without determination of any sort.

The original chaos leaped into definiteness by a movement akin to hypothetic inference. The sporting of feeling through pure arbitrariness gave rise to the generalizing tendency. Thus feeling, habit and regularity arose from the primal vague potentiality of nothingness. Chance is the outward aspect of feeling. Chance means that diversification does not antedate all time. The sense qualities are like ruined columns, representing some original unity of structure. Substance consists in regularities.

The cosmological categories which thus develop from original chaos are: chance (tychism), evolutionary love (agapism), and continuity (synechism), conceived as absolutes.

According to agapism, evolution is the only law which has no exception in the existential universe. Evolution in this sense is the working out of a definite end. The chief phenomenal facts are increasing complexity and growth, to which death and corruption are accidental exceptions. Evolutionary love is the supreme law of the universe. Not only the laws of nature exemplified in empirical science develop and thus are subject to the law of evolution: the same subordination and growth are true of the Platonic world, the forms of possibility. The existential universe, of course, is a selection from the laws of possibility; but both are under the evolutionary law.

According to synechism, all continuity marks the absolute tendency of actuality toward increasing reasonableness. Synechism is the doctrine that all that exists is continuous. Continuity is perfect generality of the law of relationship. It represents thirdness to perfection. Circularity presents the

[60] See chap. IV, D, i, (e).

most complete form of continuity; hence the existential universe is ovate.

One important conclusion which emerges from Peirce's cosmological speculations is to confirm his early prejudices against the Cartesian dualism of mind and matter. The hint of their unity in cosmology lay in the relation of feeling and chance. There is no mental causation, as there was seen to be no physical. Matter and mind are interactive, and mind has spatial extension. Matter is mind hidebound with habits. The mind of man is thus adapted to the reality of being, and mind and matter are one substance, not two. Thus Peirce arrived at an objective idealism, which is consistent with his metaphysical realism.

The existential universe is infinite, extending from an infinite past of absolute chance toward an infinite future of absolute law. It is too vast to have any character. The universe is thus neither benevolent nor hostile. But there is some order necessary for it: blind existence cannot occur. Existence as we have it is a stage of evolution, an arbitrary determination of the Platonic world which contains the possibility of many such worlds. But the existential universe is directed toward unification; its inherent purpose is the final cause of fate.

CHAPTER XII

Theology

A. RELIGION AND PHILOSOPHY

i. FROM METAPHYSICS

THEOLOGICAL QUESTIONS WERE NOT RESPONSIBLE FOR BRINGING PEIRCE TO philosophy. In his opinion, "Philosophy is a department of pure Heuretic Science[1] even less concerned, for example, about practical religion, if possible, than religion ought to be about it." (5.517) He was more interested in the nature of the world than he was in the problems presented by "God, Freedom and Immortality." (4.2) It so happens, however, that absolute distinctions between ultimate topics do not exist. Peirce as a logician was chiefly concerned with order; and as a scientist, with nature. It was inevitable that he should examine the philosophy of religion, since "Any proposition whatever concerning the order of Nature must touch more or less upon religion." (6.395) And it so happens that "Psychical, or Religious, Metaphysics, concerned chiefly . . . the questions of 1, God, 2, Freedom, [and] 3, Immortality." (1.192)

In general, Peirce was opposed to the formal study of theology. He did "not approve of mixing up Religion and Philosophy." (5.107) "How much theologians may have contributed to the cause of Christianity," or may have held it back, is an open question. (6.3) But, added Peirce, "Theology, I am persuaded, derives its initial impulse from a religious wavering;[2] for there is quite as much, or more, that is mysterious and calculated to awaken scientific curiosity in the intercourse of men with one another as in their intercourse with God, and it [is] a problem quite analogous to that of theology."[3] To Pierce, philosophy was not so much a set of established principles as it was a matter of free inquiry into ultimate problems.[4] "Now the principal business of theologians is to make men feel the enormity of the

---

[1] See this chapter, C, i.
[2] See this chapter, D, i.
[3] See chap. IX, B, iii.
[4] See chap. VII, A.

slightest departure from the metaphysics they assume to be connected with the standard faith." Peirce preferred the theologian who worships the adorable God to him who finds only the evidence of real, or actual, things adorable. (6.396) For instance, he was concerned not so much with the divinity of Jesus as with the religion of Jesus. The evidence of the former is insufficient (6.538) since it must rest on miracles,[5] but, as we shall see,[6] Peirce did embrace an essential Christianity, all the same.

Despite Peirce's antipathy to the theological approach, a certain theology follows from an acceptance of Peirce's philosophy, as he himself asserted; and it will be our task in this chapter to set this theology forth. Although "everything in the psychical sciences is inferential," (1.250) nothing is directly perceived, and logic is present as the structure of all theology, inference does not appear as logic but rather as the experience of value. Theology is thus able to present the unity of inference with feeling, of logic with value.

The logico-ontological triad of categories, which we have traced through various transformations in the chapters of this book, now returns in theology in several last guises. In God, Freedom and Immortality we can still recognize Firstness, Secondness and Thirdness,[7] or quality, reaction and representation. There are additional presentations of the triad, for Peirce asserted, "As soon, however, as I was induced to look further, and to examine the application of the three ideas [i.e., the three ontological categories] to the deepest problems of the soul, nature, and God, I saw at once that they must carry me far into the heart of those primeval mysteries." (1.364) In a formal statement, Peirce finally arrived at his theological triad. This he stated as follows: "The starting-point of the universe, God the Creator, is the Absolute First; the terminus of the universe, God completely revealed, is the Absolute Second; every state of the universe at a measurable point of time is the third." (1.362) "So prolific is the triad in forms that one may easily conceive that all the variety and multiplicity of the universe springs . . . from the λ—an emblem of fertility in comparison with which the holy phallus of religion's youth is a poor stick indeed." (4.310) According to the triad in theology, Peirce held that "Faith requires us to be materialists without flinching," (1.354) for, presumably, actuality holds the evidence for religious belief.[8]

At the same time, however, Peirce did not hold such a view to be inconsistent with a realistic idealism. He held the ideal world to be the whole

---

[5] See this chapter, C, iii.
[6] See this chapter, B, i.
[7] See chap. IV, B.
[8] See this chapter, B, i.

of which the actual world is a part,[9] and this ideal he somehow identified with the infinite being of God. Only in relation to God did he admit degrees of reality.[10] Thus finite creatures are real parts of God, who is the final and absolute reality.

Epistemology has little application to theology, since the former concerns questions of actuality alone, while the latter transcends actuality. We cannot, for example, discuss truth in relation to God.[11] For "there can be nothing of which an Omniscient God would be ignorant, if there were such a Being. But whatever the Omniscient may think is *ipso facto* so. Consequently, the idea of Truth, in the sense of that which is so whether the thinker thinks it so or not, must be foreign to the mind of God. Of such truth Omniscience must be ignorant, and since He is by hypothesis ignorant of nothing, there is no such thing. Another argument is that if there be anything which is *so*, in spite of what be thought [by God], there may be something which cannot be thought. For it is conceivable that all who could think it [including God] were destroyed. But it is inconceivable that there should be anything that cannot be thought, for to conceive this would be to think the very thing supposed to be unthinkable. Hence it is inconceivable that there should be any Truth independent of [his] opinions about it." (2.136)

A similar error is made in the language of psychology, in speaking of the "mind of God." The error arises from the search for the origin of the first two ontological categories, the existence of qualities and their reactions. "This reaction and this existence these persons [those who express the idea to themselves by saying that the Divine Creator determined so and so] call the mind of God. I really think there is no objection to this except that it is wrapped up in figures of speech, instead of having the explicitness that we desire in science. For all you know of 'minds' is from the action of animals with brains or ganglia like yourselves,[12] or at furthest like a cockroach. To apply such a word to *God* is precisely like the old pictures which show him like an aged man leaning over to look out from above a cloud. Considering the *vague intention* of it, as conceived by the *non-theological* artist, it cannot be called false, but rather ludicrously figurative." (6.199) The conception of a theology based on the mind of God runs counter to the cosmology of a Platonic world[13] which retains purpose without having to retain a mind—even a cosmical mind—to contain it.[14]

[9] See chap. IV, C, ii.
[10] See *ibid*.
[11] See chap. V, C, iii.
[12] See chap. VI, A, iv.
[13] See chap. XI, D, ii.
[14] *Ibid*., quoting 1.204.

ii. FROM ETHICS AND OTHER TOPICS

Every topic treated by Peirce points toward an infinite which is ultimately inscrutable; but it is ethics that is the most unfinished of all subjects, and which points most directly toward religion.[15] The hint first came in the idea of pragmatism[16] which Peirce conceived as an extension of "the sole principle of logic which was recommended by Jesus: 'Ye may know them by their fruits,' and it is very intimately allied with the ideas of the gospel." (5.402 n.2) Peirce's ethical doctrine and its logical foundations[17] were not in his opinion far from the ideals of Christianity. His three sentiments, "interest in an indefinite community, recognition of the possibility of this interest being made supreme, and hope in the continuance of intellectual activity . . . seem to be pretty much the same as that famous trio of Charity, Faith, and Hope, which, in the estimation of St. Paul, are the finest and greatest of spiritual gifts." (2.655)[18]

Moral goodness was for Peirce an ethical problem,[19] but the problem of evil was specifically religious. In saying that God is love, the Gospel of St. John[20] meant to convey "that as darkness is the defect of light, so hatred and evil are mere imperfect stages of ἀγάπη and ἀγαθόν, love and loveliness." (6.287) Henry James the elder had already pointed out that "It is no doubt very tolerable finite or creaturely love to love one's own in another, to love another for his conformity to one's self: but nothing can be in more flagrant contrast with the creative Love, all whose tenderness *ex vi termini* must be reserved only for what intrinsically is most bitterly hostile and negative to itself."[21] The Golden Rule says, "Sacrifice your own perfection to the perfection of your neighbor." It is to be found in the Fourth Gospel as a formula of evolution, the import of which derives growth from the kind of love[22] which seeks to satisfy the highest impulses of others. (6.289)

The individual "will see that though his God would not *really* (in a certain sense) adapt means to ends, it is nevertheless quite true that there are relations among phenomena which finite intelligence must interpret, and truly interpret, as such adaptations; and he will macarize himself for his own bitterest griefs, and bless God for the law of growth with all the fighting

[15] See chap. IX, especially B, iii.
[16] See chap. VII, B, iv.
[17] See chap. IX, B, iii.
[18] I Corinthians, 13:13.
[19] See chap. IX, B, i.
[20] St. John, 4:8. See also this vol., chap. IV, B, iii.
[21] *Substance and Shadow: An Essay on the Physics of Creation* (1863), p. 442.
[22] See chap. XI, C, ii.

it imposes upon him—Evil, i.e. what it is man's duty to fight, being one of the major perfections of the universe." (6.479) [23] So, then, religion in Peirce's scheme of things is needed not for the foundation of ethics but rather to complete ethics. Ethics treats of the good and religion of evil; and since ethics is incomplete taken by itself, it develops that "The only moral evil is not to have an ultimate aim," (5.133) the only ethical shortcoming is not to point toward religion.

The last chapter on which we have to draw for Peirce's theological ideas is that containing his system of cosmology. The ideas which we come to in religion are of course closely associated with those which we meet in cosmology, particularly in cosmogony. For the ultimate nature of the world is a problem closely associated with that of God and his relation to the world. There is, Peirce thought, something akin to religion in the occurrence of chance qualities.[24] "When we gaze upon the multifariousness of nature we are looking straight into the face of a living spontaneity." (6.553) [25] "Therefore, if you ask me what part Qualities can play in the economy of the universe, I shall reply that the universe is a vast representamen, a great symbol of God's purpose, working out its conclusions in living realities." (5.119) [26] Thus we see how cosmology rounds out the point which was begun by ethics. For the universal law of cosmology, which is superior to both chance and qualities, is evolution.[27] And "a genuine evolutionary philosophy, that is, one that makes the principle of growth a primordial element of the universe, is so far from being antagonistic to the idea of a personal creator that it is really inseparable from that idea." (6.157) We must leave Peirce's previous topics, then, and turn next to the idea of God.

B. The Sensible Heart

i. the nature of god

Peirce came to the notion of God in two ways. First, through philosophy and, secondly, through perception. We shall treat of the first way in this section, and of the second in the next.

For Peirce, pragmaticism[28] meant believing in God. "If a pragmaticist

---

[23] See chap. IX, C, iii.
[24] See chap. XI, B, ii.
[25] This is indeed close to what was known to the scholastics as the "cosmological argument," i.e., from the existence of things to God's existence.
[26] See chap. XI, A, i, quoting the same paragraph.
[27] See chap. XI, C, ii.
[28] See chap. VII, C, ii.

is asked what he means by the word 'God', he can only say that . . . if contemplation and study of the physico-psychical universe can imbue a man with principles of conduct analogous to the influence of a great man's work or conversation, then that analogue of a mind—for it is impossible to say that *any* human attribute is *literally* applicable—is what he means by 'God'. . . . because the discoveries of science, their enabling us to *predict* what will be the course of nature, is proof conclusive that, though we cannot think any thought of God's, we can catch a fragment of His Thought, as it were." (6.502) Thus "the question whether there really *is* such a being is the question whether all physical science is merely the figment—the arbitrary figment—of the students of nature, and further whether the *one* lesson the Gautama Boodha, Confucius, Socrates, and all who from any point of view have had their ways of conduct determined by meditation upon the physico-psychical universe, be only their arbitrary notion or be the Truth behind the appearances which the frivolous man does not think of; and whether the superhuman courage which such contemplation has conferred upon priests who go to pass their lives with lepers and refuse all offers of rescue is mere silly fanaticism, the passion of a baby, or whether it is strength derived from the power of the truth. Now the only guide to the answer to this question lies in the power of the passion of love which more or less overmasters every agnostic scientist and everybody who seriously and deeply considers the universe. But whatever there may be of *argument* in all this is as nothing, the merest nothing, in comparison to its full force as an appeal to one's own instinct, which is to argument what substance is to shadow, what bedrock is to the built foundations of a cathedral." (6.503)

"So, then, the question being whether I believe in the reality of God," Peirce said, "I answer, Yes. I further opine that pretty nearly everybody more or less believes this, including many of the scientific men of my generation who are accustomed to think the belief is entirely unfounded." (6.496) "The only answer that I can at present make is that facts that stand before our face and eyes and stare us in the face are far from being, in all cases, the ones most easily discerned." (6.162) God, Peirce maintained, is the "*Ens necessarium* . . . really creator of all three Universes of Experience." (6.452)[29]

Of course, to believe in the being of God and to accept any specific description of Him are two different things. All systematic philosophers are forced in the end to a negative theology which refuses to describe God

[29] See chap. IV, B; also chap. XI, C.

for fear of the limitations implied by all distinction and difference. Hence, Peirce's position was one of constant assertion and withdrawal. God, Peirce insisted, is omniscient, but "in a vague sense." (6.508) God has thoughts, probably He refrains from knowing too much, since His thought is itself creative. But, on the other hand, "God probably has no consciousness." (6.489) His knowledge, in fact, "is more like willing than knowing." (6.508) But He cannot have either will or desire, since "whatever he might desire is done. Intention seems to me, although I may be mistaken, an interval of time between the desire and the laying of the train by which the desire is to be brought about. But it seems to me that desire can only belong to a finite creature."[30] Undoubtedly, God is omnipotent and infallible and impeccable; He is not subject to time, (4.67) and possesses "aesthetic spiritual perfection." (6.510) But on the whole such statements are meaningless, and "we only wildly gabble about such things." (6.509) The development of such sentiments is "greatly determined by accidental causes." (5.383) But "whoever cannot look at the starry heaven without thinking that all this universe must have had an adequate cause can in my opinion not otherwise think of that cause half so justly than by thinking it is God." (5.536) In the end, however, the proof of God's existence and the nature of His being must rest upon other grounds than those which rational discourse can discover. We shall turn, now, to an examination of the second way of discovering the notion of God.

ii. MUSEMENT

The philosophy of religion is an important topic; but although theology, "a most interesting study," (1.665) may "lead to some useful result," the fact remains that genuine religion must come from the heart instead of the head. "If . . . a man has had no religious experience, then any religion not an affectation is as yet impossible for him; and the only worthy course is to wait quietly until such experience comes. No amount of speculation can take the place of experience." (1.655) For this purpose, "a Humanism, that does not pretend to be a science but only an instinct,[31] like a bird's power of flight, but purified by meditation, is the most precious contribution that has been made to philosophy for ages." (5.496) Thus "the hypothesis of God's Reality is logically not so isolated a conclusion as it may

---

[30] Letter of March 14, 1909, to Lady Welby, quoted in C. K. Ogden and I. A. Richards, *The Meaning of Meaning* (New York, Harcourt, Brace, 1927), p. 288.
[31] See chap. VI, C, iii.

seem. On the contrary, it is connected . . . with a theory of the nature of thinking." (6.491)[32] While it is true that we know only what we directly experience, we have experiences of more than mere sense perception.[33] "Where would such an idea, say as that of God, come from if not from direct experience?" (6.493) Not from reasoning, or from skepticism. "No: as to God, open your eyes—and your heart, which is also a perceptive organ —and you see Him. But you may ask, Don't you admit there are any delusions? Yes: I may think a thing is black, and on close examination it may turn out to be bottle-green. But I cannot think a thing is black if there is no such thing to be seen as black." As a matter of fact, "The perception of . . . manifold diversity or specificalness in general . . . is a direct, though darkling, perception of God." (6.613)[34] Thus, the Cartesian philosophy aside, it is as easy to believe in God as in one's own existence or that of other persons. (6.436)

"There is a certain agreeable occupation of mind which, from its having no distinctive name, I infer is not as commonly practiced as it deserves to be; for indulged in moderately—say through some five to six per cent of one's waking time, perhaps during a stroll—it is refreshing enough more than to repay the expenditure." (6.458) "I have often occasion to walk at night, for about a mile, over an entirely untravelled road, much of it between open fields without a house in sight. The circumstances are not favorable to severe study, but are so to calm meditation. If the sky is clear, I look at the stars in the silence, thinking how each successive increase in the aperture of a telescope makes many more of them visible than all that had been visible before. The fact that the heavens do not show a sheet of light proves that there are vastly more dark bodies, say planets, than there are suns. They must be inhabited, and most likely millions of them with beings much more intelligent than we are. For on the whole, the solar system seems one of the simplest; and presumably under more complicated phenomena greater intellectual power will be developed. What must be the social phenomena of such a world! How extraordinary are the minds even of the lower animals. We cannot appreciate our own powers any more than a writer can appreciate his own style, or a thinker the peculiar quality of his own thought. . . . Let a man drink in such thoughts as come to him in contemplating the physico-psychical universe without any special purpose of his own; especially the universe of mind which coincides with the uni-

[32] See chap. VI, D, ii, and iii.
[33] See chap. VI, D, iv, quoting 6.492.
[34] This is close to the ontological argument of the scholastics, that God's existence follows from the existence of things.

verse of matter.[35] The idea of there being a God over it all of course will be often suggested; and the more he considers it, the more he will be enwrapt with Love of this idea. He will ask himself whether or not there really is a God. If he allows instinct to speak, and searches his own heart, he will at length find that he cannot help believing it." (6.501)

Such an occupation of mind requires a special name. "Because it involves no purpose save that of casting aside all serious purpose, I have sometimes been half-inclined to call it reverie with some qualification; but for a frame of mind so antipodal to vacancy and dreaminess, such a designation would be too excruciating a misfit. In fact, it is Pure Play. Now, Play, we all know, is a lively exercise of one's powers. Pure Play has no rules, except this very law of liberty. It bloweth where it listeth. It has no purpose, unless recreation. The particular occupation I mean—a *petite bouchée* with the Universes —may take either the form of aesthetic contemplation, or that of distant castle-building (whether in Spain or within one's own moral training), or that of considering some wonder in one of the Universes, or some connection between two of the three,[36] with speculation concerning its cause. It is this last kind—I will call it 'Musement' on the whole—that I particularly recommend." (6.458)

Musement leads to two corollary directions with respect to belief in God. The first is methodological and rational; the second, axiological and evolutionary. We shall examine the former here and the latter in the next section.

As to the former, Peirce concluded, "from what I know of the effects of Musement on myself and others, that any normal man who considers the three Universes[37] in the light of the hypothesis of God's Reality, and pursues that line of reflection in scientific singleness of heart, will come to be stirred to the depths of his nature by the beauty of the idea and by its august practicality, even to the point of earnestly loving and adoring his strictly hypothetical God, and to that of desiring above all things to shape the whole conduct of life and all the springs of action into conformity with that hypothesis." (6.467) But this desire and its effects is, according to pragmatism,[38] what we mean by belief.[39] In other words, the "course of meditation upon the three Universes which gives birth to the hypothesis and ultimately to the belief that they, or at any rate two of the three, have a Creator independent of them . . . I have called the N.A.," (6.483) that is,

[35] See chap. XI, D, i.
[36] See this chapter, B,.i. Also chaps. IV, B, and XI, C.
[37] See chap. XI, C, i, ii and iii.
[38] See chap. VII, B, iv.
[39] See chap. VI, C, ii.

the neglected argument for the reality of God. (6.486) This neglected argument could never have been presented by the theologians, but they might have described it. (6.484) Peirce held the neglected argument to be the first and foremost of the arguments for God's reality.

"If one who had determined to make trial of Musement as a favorite recreation were to ask me for advice, I should reply as follows: The dawn and the gloaming most invite one to Musement; but I have found no watch of the nychthemeron[40] that has not its own advantages for the pursuit. It begins passively enough with drinking in the impression of some nook in one of the three Universes. But impression soon passes into attentive observation, observation into musing, musing into a lively give and take of communion between self and self. If one's observations and reflections are allowed to specialize themselves too much, the Play will be converted into scientific study; and that cannot be pursued in odd half hours." (6.459) For musement leads straight to inquiry.[41] "The student, applying to his own trained habits of research the art of logical analysis—an art as elaborate and methodical as that of the chemical analyst, compares the process of thought of the Muser upon the Three Universes with certain parts of the work of scientific discovery, and finds that [musement] is nothing but an instance of the first stage of all such work, the stage of observing the facts, or variously rearranging them, and of pondering them until, by their reactions with the results of previous scientific experience, there is 'evolved' (as the chemists word it) an explanatory hypothesis." (6.488)[42] This is an instance of abduction.[43] Thus the Neglected Argument or "N.A. is the First Stage of a scientific inquiry." (6.480)[44]

We have now summed up briefly the three arguments for the reality of God, which Peirce held to be paramount. The first, or "humble," argument (6.486) consists in the fact that musement leads to belief in God: the second, or "neglected," argument "consists in showing that the humble argument is the natural fruit of free meditation, since every heart will be ravished by the beauty and adorability of the Idea, when it is so pursued." (6.487) "The third argument . . . consists in a study of logical methodeutic, illuminated by the light of a first-hand acquaintance with genuine scientific thought—the sort of thought whose tools literally comprise not merely ideas of mathematical exactitude, but also the apparatus of the skilled manipula-

---

[40] 24 hours: a night and a day.
[41] See chap. VII, A, iii, quoting 6.469.
[42] See chap. VIII, C, iii.
[43] See chap. III, C, ii, (c).
[44] See chap. VIII, C, iii.

tor, actually in use." (6.488) So much for the methodological and rational conception of God; let us turn now to what is perhaps the leading notion of Peirce's theology: the notion of God as represented in the actual world by evolutionary love.

iii. EVOLUTIONARY LOVE

The second corollary of musement takes us back to the conception of agapism,[45] or evolutionary love. "The movement of love is circular, at one and the same impulse projecting creations into independency and drawing them into harmony." (6.288) This is the view of the New Testament; "the ontological gospeller . . . made the One Supreme Being, by whom all things have been made out of nothing, to be cherishing-love. What, then, can he say to hate? Never mind, at this time, what the scribe of the Apocalypse, if he were John, stung at length by persecution into a rage, unable to distinguish suggestions of evil from visions of heaven, and so become the Slanderer of God to men, may have dreamed. The question is rather what the sane John thought, or ought to have thought, in order to carry out his idea consistently. His statement that God is love seems aimed at that saying of Ecclesiastes that we cannot tell whether God bears us love or hatred.[46] 'Nay,' says John, 'we can tell, and very simply! We know and have trusted the love which God hath in us. God is love.'[47] There is no logic in this, unless it means that God loves all men. . . . This concords with that utterance reported in John's Gospel: 'God sent not the Son into the world to judge the world; but that the world should through him be saved. He that believeth on him is not judged: he that believeth not hath been judged already. . . . And this is the judgment, that the light is come into the world, and that men loved darkness rather than the light.' (6.287)[48]

"That is to say, God visits no punishment on them; they punish themselves by their natural affinity for the defective. Thus, the love that God is, is not a love of which hatred is the contrary; otherwise Satan would be a coördinate power; but it is a love which embraces hatred as an imperfect stage of it, an Anteros—yea, even needs hatred and hatefulness as its object. For self-love is no love; so if God's self is love, that which he loves must be defect of love; just as a luminary can light up only that which otherwise would be dark." (6.287) It will be recalled that Henry James the elder, the Swedenborgian, said that, while it might be a very finite and human

---

[45] See chap. XI, C, ii.
[46] Ecclesiastes, 3.
[47] I John 4:8.
[48] John 3:17-19.

thing to love what one finds of one's self reflected in someone else, still such love is the opposite of true creative love which cares chiefly for what is most foreign to one's self.[49]

"Men who seek to reconcile the Darwinian idea with Christianity will remark the tychastic evolution, like the agapastic, depends upon a reproductive creation, the forms preserved being those that use the spontaneity conferred upon them in such wise as to be drawn into harmony with their original, quite after the Christian scheme. Very good! This only shows that just as love cannot have a contrary, but must embrace what is most opposed to it, as a degenerate case of it, so tychasm is a kind of agapasm.[50] Only, in the tychastic evolution, progress is solely owing to the distribution of the napkin-hidden talent of the rejected servant among those not rejected, just as ruined gamesters leave their money on the table to make those not yet ruined so much the richer.[51] It makes the felicity of the lambs just the damnation of the goats, transposed to the other side of the equation. In genuine agapasm, on the other hand, advance takes place by virtue of a positive sympathy among the created[52] springing from continuity of mind." (6.304)[53]

Here, in a grand effort, if perhaps a trifle obscurely, Peirce has endeavored to bring together into a single strong bond all the various positive and constructive strands of his philosophy. As we have just noted, the begetting-nature of ontological chance combines with the ethical drive toward the unlimited community, with the psychological law of mind, and with the cosmological agapism to produce the religious notion of evolutionary love, the seeds of which Peirce has already been able to observe in the Fourth Gospel. It is, in a way, the culmination of the effective elements of the Peircian philosophy.

"Everybody can see that the statement of St. John [quoted above] is the formula of an evolutionary philosophy, which teaches that growth comes only from love, from I will not say self-*sacrifice*, but from the ardent impulse to fulfill another's highest impulse. Suppose, for example, that I have an idea that interests me. It is my creation. It is my creature; for . . . it is a little person.[54] I love it; and I will sink myself in perfecting it. It is not by dealing out cold justice to the circle of my ideas that I can make

[49] See this chapter, XII, A, ii.
[50] See chap. XI, C, i and ii.
[51] See chap. IX, B, iii.
[52] *Ibid.*
[53] See chap. VI, E, ii.
[54] See chap. VI, E, i, quoting 6.270.

them grow, but by cherishing and tending them as I would the flowers in my garden. The philosophy we draw from John's gospel is that this is the way mind develops; and as for the cosmos, only so far as it yet is mind, and so has life, is it capable of further evolution. Love, recognizing germs of loveliness in the hateful, gradually warms it into life, and makes it lovely." (6.289)[55]

The theory of evolution as promoted through the agency of love is what Peirce meant by agapism—"so far as it may be presumed to bespeak the normal judgment of the Sensible Heart." (6.295) The Supreme Being has not been so much the creator of the universe "as to be now creating the universe." (6.505) "The process of creation has been going on now for an infinite time in the past[56] [and] I think we must regard Creative Activity as an inseparable attribute of God." (6.506) Creation is in fact the "present functions of this Supreme Being toward the universe . . . In general, God is perpetually creating us . . . Like a good teacher, He is engaged in detaching us from a False dependence upon Him." (6.507)

"The gospel of Christ says that progress comes from every individual merging his individuality in sympathy with his neighbors." (6.294) This is the true lesson of the New Testament, which is "certainly the highest existing authority in regard to the dispositions of heart which a man ought to have." (2.655) The "essence of religion" is constituted by "that aspiration toward the perfect." (6.427) Thus, "the belief in the law of love is the Christian faith"; (6.441) "contracted to a rule of ethics, it is: Love God, and love your neighbor; 'on these two commandments hang all the law and the prophets'." Of this, St. John is only the "higher point of view" of "the universal evolutionary formula." This religious outlook is not exclusively Christian; it "was anticipated by the early Egyptians, by the Stoics, by the Buddhists, and by Confucius. So it was; nor can the not insignificant difference between the negative and the positive precept be properly estimated as sufficient for a discrimination between religions. Christians may, indeed, claim that Christianity possesses that earmark of divine truth— namely, that it was anticipated from primitive ages. The higher a religion the more catholic." (6.442) "Its ideal is that the whole world shall be united in the bond of a common love of God accomplished by each man's loving his neighbor." (6.443)

---

[55] "This is the sort of evolution which every careful student of my essay 'The Law of Mind' [e.g., chap. VI, E, ii] must see that *synechism* [i.e., chap. XI, C, iii] calls for." (6.289)
[56] See also 6.613.

C. Religion and Science

i. the challenge of science

The existence of science has been construed as the latest and most serious rival to the authority of organized religion that has come into the world. Peirce as a scientist, but also as one deeply imbued with the religious spirit, was keenly aware of the differences between science and religion and the difficulties in the path of a reconciliation. Yet he felt sure that they were not fundamentally opposed, and he set about to show this in his system.

The difficulties, of course, are serious; there can be no doubt about it. In the first place, since religious truth is always held to be final, and science is always developing and enlarging or otherwise changing its truths, a conflict on this score was inevitable. The result is that "the seminarists and religionists generally have at all times and places set their faces against the idea of continuous growth. That disposition of intellect is the most catholic element of religion. Religious truth having been once defined is never to be altered in the most minute particular; and theology being held as queen of the sciences, the religionists have bitterly fought by fire and tortures all great advances in the true sciences." (1.40) Again, religion is, so to speak, insistent upon a two-valued morality, while science is many-valued. "Religion recognizes the saints and the damned. It will not readily admit any third fate." (1.61) "Religion is a practical matter. Its beliefs are formulæ you will go upon. But a scientific proposition is merely something you take up provisionally as being the proper hypothesis to try first and endeavor to refute. . . . It is a damnable absurdity indeed to say that one thing is true in theology and another in science. But it is perfectly true that the belief which I shall do well to embrace in my practical affairs, such as my religion, may not accord with the proposition which a sound scientific method requires me provisionally to adopt at this stage of my investigation." (6.216)

"Now, as science grows, it becomes more and more perfect, considered as science; and no religionist can easily so narrow himself as to deny this. But as religion goes through the different stages of its history, it has, I fear we must confess, seldom been seen so vitalized as to become more and more perfect, even as judged from its own standpoint. Like a plucked flower, its destiny is to wilt and fade. The vital sentiment that gave it birth loses gradually its pristine purity and strength, till some new creed treads it down. Thus it happens quite naturally that those who are animated with the spirit of science are for hurrying forward, while those who have the interests of religion at heart are apt to press back." (6.430) But when challenged by the truths of science, the conservatives of the church at first draw back, recoil, "with horror from the alleged heresies—about the rotundity of the earth, about its rotation, about geology, about Egyptian history, and so forth—and they have ended by declaring that the church never breathed a single word against any of these truths of science. Perhaps it [will] be just so with fallibility. For the present those knowing in divine things insist that infallibility is the prerogative of the church,[57] but maybe bye and bye we shall be told that this infallibility had always been taken in an *ecclesiastical sense*. And that will be *true*, too. I should not wonder if the churches were to be quite agile in reformed teachings during the coming thirty years.[58] Even one that mainly gathers in the very ignorant and the very rich may feel young blood in its veins." (1.151)

In addition to these differences, religion and science in their capacity as organized institutions exercise unfortunate effects upon each other. We have seen that the existence of science makes religion into a fighting machine occupied with the defence of an established set of beliefs. But the opposite, in quite another way, also is true. Theology has had a deplorable effect upon the morals of science. (6.3) Scientists run into difficulties with the idea of God, which is perhaps sufficiently enormous to benefit from being kept vague.[59] They define God too precisely. "Men who are given to defining too much inevitably run themselves into confusion in dealing with the vague concepts of common sense." (6.496) Belief in God is a matter of the utmost common sense,[60] and for this reason perhaps should not be defined too exactly. Here religion has the advantage over the method of science.

The difficulties, admittedly, are serious; but Peirce conceived of an interpretation of both science and religion which would reveal them to be supplementary rather than conflicting. Before going on to examine the specific religious beliefs which are challenged by science, as we shall undertake in the next three sections, let us glance at the broad possibilities of reconciliation.

Religion is not opposed to science. "God's beneficence is in nothing more apparent than in how in the early days of science Man's attention was particularly drawn to phenomena easy to investigate and how Man has ever

[57] See chap. VIII, C, ii, (a).
[58] Written c. 1897.
[59] See chap. VII, C, iii, (d).
[60] See this chapter, B, ii.

since been led on, as through a series of graduated exercises, to more and more difficult problems." (2.769) "In the light of the successes of science to my mind there is a degree of baseness in denying our birthright as children of God and in shamefacedly slinking away from anthropomorphic conceptions of the universe." (1.316)[61] For pure science, nature is simply the worshipful, revealed through facts. "Moreover, in all its progress, science vaguely feels that it is only learning a lesson. The value of *Facts* to *it*, lies only in this, that they belong to Nature; and Nature is something great, and beautiful, and sacred, and eternal, and real—the object of its worship and its aspiration." (5.589) Thus it is that "Faith requires us to be materialists without flinching." (1.354) The "spirit in which every branch of science ought to be studied" is that of "joy in learning ourselves and in making others acquainted with the glories of God." (1.127)

The religious spirit is at the basis of scientific endeavor. But although science, philosophical science, should "ultimately influence religion . . . it should be allowed to do so only with secular slowness and the most conservative caution." (1.620) "Religion, from the nature of things, refuses to go through her successive transformations with sufficient celerity to keep always in accord with the convictions of scientific philosophy." (6.432) "Am I to be prevented from joining in that common joy at the revelation of enlightened principles of religion which we celebrate at Easter and Christmas because I think that certain scientific, logical, and metaphysical ideas which have been mixed up with these principles are untenable? No; to do so would be to estimate those errors as of more consequence than the truth— an opinion which few would admit." (6.427)

"The day has come, however, when the man whom religious experience most devoutly moves can recognize the state of the case. While adhering to the essence of religion, and so far as possible to the church, which is all but essential, say, penessential, to it,[62] he will cast aside that religious timidity that is forever prompting the church to recoil from the paths into which the Governor of history is leading the minds of men, a cowardice that has stood through the ages as the landmark and limit of her little faith, and will gladly go forward, sure that truth is not split into two warring doctrines, and that any change that knowledge can work in his faith can only affect its expression, but not the deep mystery expressed." (6.432)

"Such a state of mind may properly be called a religion of science. Not that it is a religion to which science or the scientific spirit has itself given

[61] See also 5.47 n.
[62] See this chapter, D, ii.

birth; for religion, in the proper sense of the term, can arise from nothing but the religious sensibility. But it is a religion, so true to itself, that it becomes animated by the scientific spirit, confident that all the conquests of science will be triumphs of its own, and accepting all the results of science, as scientific men themselves accept them, as steps toward the truth, which may appear for a time to be in conflict with other truths, but which in such cases merely await adjustments which time is sure to effect. This attitude, be it observed, is one which religion will assume not at the dictate of science, still less by way of a compromise, but simply and solely out of a bolder confidence, in herself and in her own destiny." (6.433)

ii. FREE WILL

The question of the freedom of the will, which is the question of freedom versus fate, is a difficult one to settle. (5.565) We have already noted that there is a certain amount of freedom allowed in actuality, by ontology[63] and cosmology.[64] The free will is also provided for in psychology; for since the will is general,[65] and since no number of particulars will specify a universal, the will cannot be determined by any specific things and must therefore remain undetermined, i.e., free. A still more potent suggestion issues from psychology, from the conflict between desire[66] and will. "Though 'desire' implies a tendency to volition, and though it is a natural hypothesis that a man cannot *will* to do that which he has no sort of desire to do, yet we all know conflicting desires but too well, and how treacherous they are apt to be; and a desire may perfectly well be discontented with volition, i.e., with what the man *will* do. The consciousness of that truth seems to me to be the root of our consciousness of free-will." (1.331) Now, "the question of free-will and fate in its simplest form, stripped of verbiage, is something like this: I have done something of which I am ashamed; could I, by an effort of the will, have resisted the temptation, and done otherwise?" (5.403) Although necessitarianism is a prevailing belief, the fact is that the necessitarian accepts the freedom of the will himself, at least "when he is not theorizing" (1.323) consciously.

"Have your necessitarianism if you approve of it; but still I think you must admit that no law of nature makes a stone fall, or a Leyden jar to discharge, or a steam engine to work." (1.323) And if law is not determina-

---

[63] See chap. IV, D, ii, (a).
[64] See chap. XI, C, i.
[65] See chap. VI, C, iv, quoting 2.696.
[66] See chap. VI, C, iv.

tive of events at the physical level, it is not likely to be of the higher. Freedom of the will is a brute fact "whether it show brute *force* or not." (1.428) Moreover, even if the physical and other higher levels below that of the ethical and religious were determined, that would in no wise indicate the determination of the will. For the material of lower levels does not determine the form of the higher. It is just the error of supposing it does that has been committed most frequently. But freedom, spontaneity or "Originality is not an attribute of the *matter* of life, present in the whole only so far as it is present in the smallest parts, but is an affair of *form*, of the way in which parts none of which possess it are joined together. Every action of Napoleon's was such as a treatise on physiology ought to describe. He walked, ate, slept, worked in his study, rode his horse, talked to his fellows, just as every other man does. But he combined those elements into shapes that have not been matched in modern times. Those who dispute about Free-Will and Necessity commit a similar oversight." (4.611)[67]

Previous discussions of the problem of the freedom of the will had frequently assumed their irreconcilability. But all universal propositions are hypotheticals.[68] "Accordingly, if the unexpressed condition is some state of things which does not actually come to pass, the two propositions may appear to be contrary to one another. Thus, the moralist says, 'You ought to do this, and you can do it.' This 'You can do it' is principally hortatory in its force: so far as it is a statement of fact, it means merely, 'If you try, you will do it.' Now, if the act is an outward one and the act is not performed, the scientific man, in view of the fact that every event in the physical world depends exclusively on physical antecedents, says that in this case the laws of nature prevented the thing from being done, and that therefore, 'Even if you had tried, you would not have done it.' Yet the reproachful conscience still says you might have done it; that is, that 'If you had tried, you would have done it.' This is called the paradox of freedom and fate; and it is usually supposed that one of these propositions must be true and the other false. But since, in fact, you have not tried, there is no reason why the supposition that you have tried should not be reduced to an absurdity. In the same way, if you had tried and had performed the action, the conscience might say, 'If you had not tried, you would not have done it'; while the understanding would say, 'Even if you had not tried, you would have done it.' These propositions are perfectly consistent, and only

---

[67] For a modern version of this argument, see N. Hartmann, *Ethics*, vol. iii (London, Allen & Unwin, 1932).

[68] See chap. III, B, iii.

serve to reduce the supposition that you did not try to an absurdity." (5.339)

Man, however, should not be proud of his freedom. Self-control[69] "is the only freedom of which man has any reason to be proud; and it is because love of what is good for all on the whole, which is the widest possible consideration, is the essence of Christianity, that it is said that the service of Christ is perfect freedom." (5.339 n.) "My account of the facts, you will observe, leaves a man at full liberty, no matter if we grant all that the necessitarians ask. That is, the man *can*, or if you please is *compelled*, to *make his life more reasonable*. What other distinct idea than that, I should be glad to know, can be attached to the word liberty?" (1.602) But liberty can exist without denying the knowledge which God has of future events. For "those who admit Free-Will suppose that God has a direct intuitive knowledge of future events even though there be nothing in the present to determine them. That is to say, they suppose that a man is perfectly free to do or not do a given act; and yet that God already knows whether he will or will not do it. This seems to most persons flatly contradictory; and so it is, if we conceive God's knowledge to be among the things which exist at the present time. But it is a degraded conception to conceive God as subject to Time, which is rather one of His creatures." (4.67)[70] Time is an affair of actuality; but God comprises possibility as well.[71]

iii. IMMORTALITY

Although Peirce felt that science had advanced no arguments against the freedom of the will that were cogent, he came to an altogether different conclusion concerning immortality.

"What is the bearing of positively ascertained facts upon the doctrine of a future life? By the doctrine of a future life, I understand the proposition that after death we shall retain or recover our individual consciousness, feeling, volition, memory, and, in short (barring an unhappy contingency), all our mental powers unimpaired. The question is, laying aside all higher aspects of this doctrine, its sacredness and sentiment—concerning which a scientific man is not, as such entitled to an opinion—and judging it in the same cold way in which a proposition in physics would have to be judged, what facts are there leading us to believe or to disbelieve it?" (6.548)

[69] See chap. IX, C, ii.
[70] See chap. VIII, D, ii, quoting 4.67.
[71] See chap. IV, D, i.

"Under the head of direct positive evidence to the affirmative would be placed that of religious miracles of spiritualistic marvels, and of ghosts, etc." (6.549) Of miracles we shall have more to say in the next section. Of the arguments adduced in favor of the return of dying persons, by the modern spiritualists, "I have examined with care [and] I am fully satisfied that these arguments are worthless, partly because of the uncertainty and error of the numerical data, and partly because the authors have been astonishingly careless in the admission of cases ruled out by the conditions of the argumentation." Additional argument against the return of the dead is amusingly furnished by the evidence of the stupidity of ghosts and spirits. "They seem like the lower animals. If I believed in them, I should conclude that, while the soul was not always at once extinguished on the death of the body, yet it was reduced to a pitiable shade, a mere ghost, as we say, of its former self. Then these spirits and apparitions are so painfully solemn.[72] I fancy that, were I suddenly to find myself liberated from all the trials and responsibilities of this life, my probation over, and my destiny put beyond marring or making, I should feel as I do when I find myself on an ocean steamer, and know that for ten days no business can turn up, and nothing can happen. I should regard the situation as a stupendous frolic, should be at the summit of gayety, and should only be too glad to leave the vale of tears behind. Instead of that, these starveling souls come mooning back to their former haunts, to cry over spilled milk." (6.550)

"Under the head of positive evidence apparently unfavorable to the doctrine, we may reckon ordinary observations of the dependence of healthy mind-action upon the state of the body. There are, also, those rare cases of double consciousness where personal identity is utterly destroyed or changed, even in this life. If a man or woman, who is one day one person, another day another, is to live hereafter, pray tell me which of the two persons that inhabit the one body is destined to survive?" (6.551) However, it is true that the case is by no means proved against the independence of mind from the body. For instance, "When a part of the brain is extirpated we find the result is that certain faculties are lost. But after a time they are recovered. How can this be? The answer given is that other parts of the brain learn to perform these functions. But after all, we do not know more than that if anything happens to the hemispheres, memory is deranged. It is a most wonderful thing if all we remember is really preserved in the cells of the cerebrum." (6.520)

"Conclusions men reach they know not how are better than those fortified

---

[72] This is not true of the older poltergeists and leprechauns.

by unscientific logic. By logic, *Aquinas*, if not *Calvin*, persuaded himself that one of the chief joys of the blest will be to peer over heaven's parapet and watch the damned writhing in torments and rage below: by instinct, or half-conscious inference a poor peasant girl will inwardly reject the doctrine, for all revered pastor may say." (6.570)

"However, there can be no doubt, I think, that upon death we soon lose consciousness, at least for the time being." (6.520) This fact prompts the further question, " 'If the power to remember dies with the material body, has the question of any single person's future life after death any particular interest for him?' " (6.521) "Common sense is coming to reject the doctrine, good sense does reject it," (6.578) "that soul (such as we can know) is able to feel and act independently of its animal body." (6.577)

"You will observe that the essential immortality of the soul is not exactly the Christian doctrine, which is that the body is reproduced, and with it presumably the memory. There is nothing at all to prove it except that it was a belief clung to by St. Paul and founded by him upon the resurrection of Jesus." (6.520) "*Some* kind of a future life there can be no doubt of. A man of character leaves an influence living after him. It is living: it is personal. In my opinion, it is quite proper to call that a future life.[73] Jesus so spoke of it when he said he would always be with us. It is in some respects more fit to be made the subject of a promise than any other kind of future life. For it is something we all desire; while other kinds present nothing alluring that is not excessively vague or else unwholesome and antipractical. In the next place its vivacity and endurance are proportional to the spirituality of man. How many instances have we seen of that! Beyond that, I simply am content to be in God's hands. If I am to be in another life it is sure to be most interesting; but I cannot imagine how it is going to be *me*. At the same time, I really don't know anything about it." (6.519)

iv. MIRACLES

Not least among the problems presented by religion to theology or the philosophy of religion is the question of whether or not there exist such things as miracles. Central to the problem of miracles, so far as natural science is concerned, is whether the existence of a miracle involves an interruption of the course of nature. (6.511) Some of the most respected theologians "are decidedly of the opinion that God never interfered with what they call the *cursus naturae*. . . . Miracles are for them simply what no man

[73] See chap. IX, B, iii.

can do without special aid from on high, or which at least are signs of some special authority, without being in reality deviations from the regular uniformities of the world." Peirce felt that his doctrine of tychism[74] might "somewhat weaken that view." "The fathers of the church had introduced no more metaphysics into their definitions of a miracle than had the simple folks who had witnessed miracles, or thought they had witnessed them. For both classes a miracle was nothing more than a great wonder." (6.540)

"The miracle remained nothing more than a great wonder, until the scholastic doctors, in their desire to give exactitude to theology, began to define it metaphysically. Aquinas said that a miracle was an interruption of the order of nature;[75] and that remained the regular definition for the scholastics. When Hume took up the subject of miracles, he endeavoured to conform to the definition of the theologians" (6.541) by defining it as a violation of the law of nature:[76] "something the like of which was perfectly unexampled in experience." The Humean tradition had an immense effect; yet "It was while Hume was engaged in writing his first treatise, and long before he touched upon miracles, that Bishop Butler . . . remarks that if we could know what the laws of nature really are it would perhaps be seen that they positively require the occurrence of miracles. . . ."[77] On the surface of it, at any rate, this view creates no objection to Hume's real argument; but it clearly does show that to look upon the order of nature as being of the nature of a 'law' is to adopt a view which is really favorable to miracles, rather than the reverse. But when we come to penetrate the spirit of Butler's remark, we recognize that it has, hidden in the depths of it, an idea which has only to be developed to refute all such reasonings as that of Hume about miracles, and the similar but far more extravagant conclusions of the 'higher critics' of ancient history, and which is in remarkable consonance with the higher teachings of modern science." (6.547) Nevertheless, the popular tradition has tended to follow Hume's lead, so that "At present, historical criticism has almost exploded the miracles, great and small." (6.36)

While it is true that "Of any miraculous interference by the higher powers, we know absolutely nothing; and it seems in the present state of science altogether improbable," (2.750) the fact remains that "Science can no more deny a miracle than it can assert one." (1.90) Although "His [i.e., Hume's] argument has a certain weight" (6.514) and the proof of miracles

[74] See chap. XI, C, i.
[75] But see 6.511.
[76] *Inquiry*, X, I, 90.
[77] *Analogy of Reason with Nature*, pt. ii, bk. iv.

is "simply a question of evidence," it is possible that miracles have occurred and may be occurring still. What about the surprising discoveries of science? What about the isolated occurrence of genius which seems to equal the isolated occurrence of miracles? The question must continue to remain in abeyance, with insufficient evidence presented on either side.

It may be, of course, that "when a miracle occurs there is no violation of the real *cursus naturae*, but only of the apparent course of things." (6.101) A miracle may prove to be only a certain kind of habit, a "miraculous habit." (2.667) Peirce declared that, in all events, it seemed plain to him that "miracles are intrinsic elements of a genuine religion." (6.446)

D. Religion Today

i. the problem of the church

Whether we like it or not, the fact remains that the Christian religion has declined considerably. The signs are incontrovertible. "All those modern books which offer new philosophies of religion, at the rate of one every fortnight on the average, are but symptoms of the temporary dissolution of the Christian faith." (1.659) Then, again, "It is hardly necessary to insist here that the highly cultured classes of Christendom—excepting always those families which are so important as to be an object of solicitude on the part of the priests—are nowadays nearly destitute of any religion." (1.660)

"Undoubtedly the external circumstance, which more than all others at first inclined men to accept Christianity in its loveliness and tenderness, was the fearful extent to which society was broken up into units by the un-mitigated greed and hard-heartedness into which the Romans had seduced the world. And yet it was that very same fact, more than any other external circumstance, that fostered that bitterness against the wicked world of which the primitive gospel of Mark contains not a single trace." (6.311) "After a religion has become a public affair, quarrels arise, to settle which watchwords are drawn up. This business gets into the hands of theologians: and the ideas of theologians always appreciably differ from those of the universal church." (6.438) For "the Church requires subscription to a plat-form—a Creed. And how has that platform been made? With strict party regularity, no doubt. Yet whether it be that of Trent, Lambeth, Geneva, or what, there is not a plank in it that has not, as a matter of historical fact, been inserted with a view of proclaiming the damnation and of procuring the persecution of some body of convinced Christians." (6.450) "Now the principal business of theologians is to make men feel the enormity of the slightest departure from the metaphysics they assume to be connected with the standard faith," (6.3) as we have already noted, an attitude hardly conducive to either the preservation or the discovery of religious truths.

The decline in religion is especially marked by the attitude toward the Heavenly Father "that an earthly father would resent as priggish." (6.437) "We only say that the man who would allow his religious life to be wounded by any sudden acceptance of a philosophy of religion . . . is a man whom we should consider *unwise*." (1.633) We cannot change essential religion just to suit the purposes of orthodox theology. "But no man need be excluded from participation in the common feelings, nor from so much of the public expression of them as is open to all the laity, by the unphilosophical narrowness of those who guard the mysteries of worship." (6.427) "To those who for the present are excluded from the churches, and who, in the passionate intensity of their religious desire, are talking of setting up a church for the scientifically educated, a man of my stripe must say, Wait, if you can; it will be but a few years longer; but if you cannot wait, why then Godspeed! Only, do not, in your turn, go and draw lines so as to exclude such as believe a little less—or, still worse, to exclude such as believe a little more—than yourselves. Doubtless, a lot of superstition clings to the historical churches; but superstition is the grime upon the venerable pavement of the sacred edifice, and he who would wash that pavement clean should be willing to get down on his knees to his work inside the church." (6.447) "For my part, I should think it more lovely to patch up such peace as might be with the great religious world." (6.446)

"A religious organization is a somewhat idle affair unless it be sworn in as a regiment of that great army that takes life in hand, with all its delights, in grimmest fight to put down the principle of self-seeking, and to make the principle of love triumphant." (6.448) The man who wishes to struggle for this end "will see that though his God would not *really* (in a certain sense) adapt means to ends, it is nevertheless quite true that there are relations among phenomena which finite intelligence must interpret, and truly interpret, as such adaptations; and [as we have noted] he will macarize himself for his own bitterest griefs, and bless God for the law of growth with all the fighting it imposes upon him—Evil . . . being one of the major perfections of the Universe." (6.479)[78]

"The *raison d'être* of a church is to confer upon men a life broader than their narrow personalities, a life rooted in the very truth of being." (6.451)

[78] See chap. IX, B, iii.

Christianity had to be "diluted with civilization." (5.445) "Man's highest developments are social; and religion, though it begins in a seminal individual inspiration, only comes to full flower in a great church coextensive with a civilization.[79] This is true of every religion, but supereminently so of the religion of love. Its ideal is that the whole world shall be united in the bond of a common love of God accomplished by each man's loving his neighbor. Without a church, the religion of love can have but a rudimentary existence; and a narrow, little exclusive church is almost worse than none. A great catholic church is wanted." (6.443) "Like every species of reality, it [i.e., religion] is essentially a social, a public affair. It is the idea of a whole church, welding all its members together in one organic, systematic perception of the Glory of the Highest." (6.429) "Yet it is absurd to say that religion is a mere belief. You might as well call society a belief, or politics a belief, or civilization a belief. Religion is a life, and can be identified with a belief only provided that belief be a living belief—a thing to be lived rather than said or thought." (6.439)

"The invisible church does now embrace all Christendom. Every man who has been brought up in the bosom of Christian civilization does really believe in some form of the principle of love, whether he is aware of doing so, or not." (6.444) "Let us, at any rate, get all the good from the vital element in which we are all at one that it can yield: and the good that it can yield is simply all that is anyway possible, and richer than is easily conceivable. Let us endeavor, then, with all our might to draw together the whole body of believers in the law of love into sympathetic unity of consciousness. Discountenance as immoral all movements that exaggerate differences, or that go to make fellowship depend on formulas invented to exclude some Christians from communion with others." (6.445) Toward the end of developing a common religion, prayer, and especially common prayer, (6.518) is efficacious. (6.515) Despite everything that happens, "we see social, political, religious common sense modifying itself insensibly in course of generations, ideas of rights of man acquiring new meaning, thaumaturgic elements of Christianity sinking, spiritual rising in religious consciousness." (6.573) "Do you know what it is in Christianity that when recognized makes our religion an agent of reform and progress? It is its marking duty at its proper finite figure. Not that it diminishes in any degree its vital importance, but that behind the outline of that huge mountain it enables us to descry a silvery peak rising into the calm air of eternity." (1.675)

[79] See for analogy, A. J. Toynbee, *A Study of History* (Oxford, 1935), vols. i-iii.

Peirce was concerned more with religion than with theology, but since he looked to the heart as well as the head for guidance, we must term his remarks theology, for he does not regard religious intuition as subject to reasoning. From ontology comes a theological triad of God the Creator, God the revealed, and the Universe. Truth in epistemology is for theology identical with God's opinion. Yet we cannot speak of the mind of God without delimiting him.

From pragmatism, Peirce concluded that this was the sole principle of logic recommended by Jesus. The love of one's fellows makes self evil and evil itself a negative affair. The ethics of the unlimited community perhaps best points toward this religion of love. From cosmology comes the notion that the universe is working out God's vast design. Both spontaneity and growth illustrate the religious elements in actuality.

To the question whether God exists, Peirce replied yes, without qualification. But we cannot describe God; his omniscience is "vague"; he has no unfulfilled desires, which is to say, no desires. Perhaps it is easiest to say that he cannot be approached rationally at all.

The best approach to the religious experience is through musement. This reverie consists in the drinking in of the most obvious experience of grandeur, as for instance from the stars at night. This experience, like all others, is the experience of something real. Musement has its rational and methodological aspect. This consists, first, in that such meditation, particularly upon the three "universes" of ontology and cosmology, is a neglected argument for God's existence: whatever we experience must exist. Secondly, musement is in a sense the earliest stage of scientific inquiry, the observation of facts leading to the formation of an hypothesis. Both arguments, however, are conducive to the conclusion that the natural universe is sacred, and that God exists.

Musement also has its axiological and evolutionary aspect. The movement of love is circular: God is love, as the Fourth Gospel testifies. Darwin is reconcilable with Christianity in that evolution works toward love; indeed, growth comes only from love. The theory of evolution promoted by love is the normal judgment of the sensible heart. Ultimately, the world will be united by each man's loving his neighbor.

Science has been construed as the most serious rival to religion. Let us examine its claims. Of course, there are great arguments for science which prove obvious upon comparison with religion. Religion is final; science, tentative. Religion is practical; science, theoretical. Religion decays through its successive stages; science grows more perfect. Science and religion seem to exercise unfortunate effects upon each other. These difficulties, however, are not inherent but rather belong to wrong interpretation. Science is concerned with the study of nature, a wholly religious affair. The success of science proves we are children of God, and faith requires us to be materialists without flinching.

Science should be allowed to influence religion only with secular slowness. What we need is a religion of science; and scientists who adhere to religion without its timidity, conscious that there are not two sets of truths but only one.

Science appears to question certain religious beliefs. It questions free will, but there is such a thing as free will not inconsistent with necessity, since the determination at lower levels leaves the higher levels free. It questions immortality; but while there is probably no personal immortality in the sense of the survival of consciousness or memory, and the soul can hardly survive the animal body, our influence lives after us, and we are entitled to call that immortality of a sort. But we know little about the question. Science challenges miracles; but if we conceive of the miracle as a great wonder and not as an interruption in the order of nature, miracles probably have occurred and still do occur.

The most urgent problem for the philosophy of religion is the problem of the church. The Christian religion has declined, since the cultured classes no longer believe in it, and theological works are on the increase. The theologians have ruined the church by narrowing the creed and holding stubbornly to it, thus excluding brotherhood instead of including it. A church should fight to make the principle of love triumphant. It must make life broader for men, by becoming diluted with civilization, by making worship public, and by including rather than excluding. If we can learn to put love above duty, then there is hope for the future of Christianity.

◀◀◀◀▶▶▶▶

PEIRCE'S PLACE IN THE HISTORY
OF PHILOSOPHY

CHAPTER XIII

Realism From Plato to Peirce

We BEGAN THIS STUDY OF PEIRCE WITH A FIRST PART DEVOTED TO AN OUTLINE OF his life and the influences which helped to establish his viewpoint. Now we have come to the end of the second part, in which was presented an account of Peirce's systematic philosophy. In the present, and last, part we shall once again step outside the confines of his philosophy and attempt to see it in perspective against the background of philosophical tradition. Within the severe limits of the space allotted we shall try in this chapter to suggest the line of development in which Peirce's ideas belong, beginning with Plato and ending with a comparison between Peirce and the leading Platonist of the day. Then in the next, and final, chapter we may quickly glance over some of the influences which Peirce's writings have already exerted in the brief period that has elapsed since his death.

A. PLATO AND THE TRADITION OF CLASSIC REALISM

i. THE THREE PHILOSOPHIES

In the miniature theater of ideas that was the Greek world, we may discern the origins of all modern philosophies. Attic Greece survived for only a short period, but that length of time sufficed to set the problems which the next twenty-three centuries have struggled over and which, in slightly altered form, are still with us today. A survey of the history of philosophy reveals that from one point of view there are only three radically different metaphysical positions which it is possible for anyone at any date and place to assume. Many more than three exist, of course, but all are variations of the basic three. These three philosophies are furnished us, with their respective strengths and weaknesses clearly set forth, in the writings of Plato. It is clear in the *Dialogues* that Plato himself wavered between two of these positions, defending one or another against his opponents, the Sophists, who maintained the third position.

We may sketch first the two Platonic positions, since the Sophists held a negative philosophy. The Platonic positions are (*a*) realism and (*b*) extreme realism; the Sophistic position is (*c*) nominalism. We can do little here except set forth a few of the premises of these philosophies; the division of the Platonic writings according to consistency with these premises would show the full extent of the diversion. Needless to add to readers of this book, the terms "realism" and "nominalism" were not employed by the Greeks and only became current in philosophy during the Middle Ages. But in so far as they are accurate descriptions of abstract and timeless metaphysical positions, they may be applied backward in time as well as forward.

(*a*) Realism is predicated upon the equal reality of the ideas and of actuality. There are ideas apart from the things that partake of them.[1] The idea is like the day, which is one and the same in many places at once and yet continuous with itself.[2] The ideas are not mere abstractions; they are essences,[3] essences being only another name for intelligible and incorporeal ideas.[4] By participation in the ideas, things are what they are: the beautiful is beautiful because it shares in the idea of beauty.[5] Being.is defined as the power to affect or be affected, to do or to suffer.[6] The good is the brightest and best of being.[7] Nonbeing both is[8] and is real.[9] It is all things other than being, or in other words, than relations.[10] Thus relations are real and objective. There is motion, but there is also rest.[11] Motion, or becoming, is not identical with being but partakes of it. Everything is not in flux.[12] There is an order of being, or eternity, as well as another of becoming, or time.[13] Names are intended to show the nature of things.[14] Knowledge relates to being and differs from opinion;[15] knowledge is true opinion.[16] Knowledge also differs from belief, for there can be false belief but not false knowledge.[17] And so on.

[1] *Parmenides*, 130.
[2] *Parmenides*, 131.
[3] *Parmenides*, 133.
[4] *Sophist*, 246.
[5] *Phaedo*, 100.
[6] *Sophist*, 247.
[7] *Republic*, 518.
[8] *Sophist*, 258.
[9] *Sophist*, 257.
[10] *Sophist*, 258-259.
[11] *Sophist*, 255.
[12] *Cratylus*, 440.
[13] *Timaeus*, 37.
[14] *Cratylus*, 422.
[15] *Republic*, 477.
[16] *Theaetetus*, 187-188.
[17] *Gorgias*, 454.

(*b*) Extreme realism is predicated upon the superior reality of the ideas. Mind is the cause of all things.[18] The ideas are related to the divine element in us, that is, to the soul.[19] The world of sense is composed of shadows which are less real than the ideas.[20] The lovers of fine sights and sounds are incapable of seeing or loving absolute beauty.[21] Matter is the mediating principle, the nurse of generation.[22] It is the principle of evil in the world.[23] Reality must be distinguished from appearance.[24] Sense perception leads to opinion but not to knowledge.[25] Dialectic alone rises to the principle which is above hypotheses.[26] Knowledge of some kind is the only good.[27] The first knowledge is to know oneself.[28] Knowledge of the self is knowledge of the soul.[29] And so on.

(*c*) Nominalism is predicated upon the superior reality of actuality. Man is the measure of all things.[30] Feeling and appearance coincide with being. Everything is corporeal and material.[31] Everything is also relative; all is becoming, motion, transition and flux.[32] Knowledge is perception. Falsehood is impossible; [33] it may be neither spoken nor said. There is no principle in name.[34] Names as truths are nonsense.[35] Justice is the interest of the stronger.[36] One law is as good as another.[37] Good is what is pleasing; evil is what is disliked.[38] Truth and beauty are determined by taste. And so on.

Peirce was a realist, as was Plato some of the time. Sophism, or nominalism, was attacked by Peirce under its contemporary disguises. He knew it much in the forms in which we know it today, and he expressed his opposition to it, as we have noted throughout this volume, though it was called materialism, positivism or relativism. Peirce also was clear about his opposition to extreme realism, and here he parted company with Plato. For Plato

---

[18] *Phaedo*, 97.
[19] *Phaedo*, 79.
[20] *Republic*, 514-517.
[21] *Republic*, 476.
[22] *Timaeus*, 49-51.
[23] *Statesman*, 273.
[24] *Republic*, 602.
[25] *Republic*, 480.
[26] *Republic*, 533.
[27] *Euthydemus*, 292.
[28] *Phaedrus*, 229-230.
[29] I *Alcibiades*, 130.
[30] *Theaetetus*, 152.
[31] *Sophist*, 246.
[32] *Theaetetus*, 152.
[33] *Cratylus*, 429.
[34] *Cratylus*, 384.
[35] *Cratylus*, 429-430.
[36] *Republic*, 338.
[37] *Cratylus*, 429.
[38] *Republic*, 493.

was often confused as to whether he was advocating realism or extreme realism. Extreme realism, despite the name given to it, is closer to nominalism than to realism. Instead of anchoring its premises in the objective world of matter, it does so in the subjective world of concepts. The modern name for it is subjective idealism, or simply idealism, and as such Pierce voiced time and again his opposition to it.

ii. FROM SPEUSIPPUS TO HUME

The tradition of nominalism was carried forward after Plato chiefly by the Stoic and Epicurean schools. Realism struggled with extreme realism for the inheritance of the Platonic philosophy. Speusippus, who was Plato's successor in the Academy, carried Platonism to neo-Pythagorean excesses of extreme realism. Aristotle was a Platonist—in fact he was the leading Platonist[39]—but he was constantly at war with the extremism of Speusippus. Aristotle left Athens with the conviction that, while Plato's nephew had inherited the Academy, it was he and not Speusippus who would continue the spirit of Plato's philosophy. A careful investigation is sure to support the critical opinion which holds that Aristotle was a realist who wished to correct extreme realism as this position was found not only in the philosophy of Speusippus but also, earlier, in the writings of Plato himself.

The struggle between realism and extreme realism was settled by means of a temporary geographic truce, a dividing of spheres of influence. The influence of Aristotle went to the Hellenistic world of Egypt, where it furthered the development of the sciences. The influence of the Platonists of the persuasion of extreme realism spread to the Roman world of Christianity, where as neo-Platonism it was incorporated into the rapidly crystallizing theology. Of course, this does not mean that the division was sharp and fast; but it is a predominantly true description. The adventures of Platonism as the theology of extreme realism, up to the eleventh century, are enmeshed entirely in the history of Christianity. Roughly, the first thousand years of Christianity were governed by extreme realism, overclouding the elements of realism that were unquestionably present both in the doctrine of Christ and in the dogma of certain of the Church Fathers. The latter half of this period was deeply influenced by the Platonism of Augustine, which carried to its fullest length the theological implications of extreme realism.

Historically, the use of the terms "realism" and "nominalism" and the

[39] See, e.g., Werner Jaeger, *Aristotle*, R. Robinson trans. (London, Oxford Press, 1934), chap. V.

controversy concerning them date from Porphyry's isagoge, or sixth century *Introduction to the Categories* (of Aristotle), where the question of whether Aristotle is to be interpreted realistically or nominalistically was first introduced.[40] The problem does not seem to have received explicit treatment until the eleventh century, when it was suggested perhaps by the lectures of Berengar devoted to a better understanding of the Sacrament of the Eucharist. Berengar raised the question of whether the claret and wafer were more than claret and wafer. It was not a far step from the assertion of the sole reality of physical claret and wafer to the assertion of the sole reality of *all* physical particulars, a step that was taken by Roscellinus. The scholastics, dating from Roscellinus, defined nominalism as the view that universals are *flatus vocis*, mere names without corresponding reality, and the argument for and against their reality was waged furiously.

Between the eleventh and thirteenth centuries, a number of developments of the utmost significance occurred. The limitations put upon the discovery of universal principles by the extreme realism of the Roman Church was found too confining, and this, together with other forms of the denial of the reality of the vivid actual world, conspired to occasion the rise of an official philosophy of nominalism. Empiricism, which is in essence realistic, was brought about by nominalism through the false supposition that because the Church depended upon realism, realism must be limited to the dogma of the Church. Any revolt against the limitations of extreme realism was almost sure to be led by some variety of nominalism. Nominalism was ushered in, then, by a questioning of the Sacrament of the Eucharist, by the Aquinate introduction of Aristotle as a weapon to be turned against Plato, and finally by empiricism.

Aquinas introduced Aristotle as an authority in theological matters and endorsed the natural sciences in an effort to save Church dogma. But by separating revealed and natural theology, he placed revelations beyond rational justification, which is to say also beyond faith. The power of the Church fell apart in a welter of the varieties of nominalism that were exhibited everywhere in current theory and practice.

Meanwhile the tradition of realism was maintained implicitly in the practice of science in the Hellenistic and afterwards in the Moslem world. It migrated from Alexandria to Byzantium, and was brought to Europe by the contact between Mohammedans and Christians, by travelers, chiefly as a result of the Crusades.

The only successful effort to synthesize the new knowledge gained through science with the old system of philosophy was made by the Arabian

[40] Migne, vol. lxiv, p. 82 A.

philosopher Avicenna. According to him, universals (i.e., Plato's *Ideas*) have their being ontologically *before* (independent of) things, are known epistemologically *in* things, and as knowledge are derived psychologically *after* things. This solution of the realist-nominalist controversy was adopted by the leading scholastics: by Albertus Magnus and by Thomas Aquinas; but despite this fact it failed to permeate their philosophies or to have any influence whatsoever in later times. The leading realist of medieval philosophy was Duns Scotus. The leading nominalist was William of Ockham. Scotus opposed the nominalism of Ockham with a severe Platonic realism. Plato had intended to be understood as meaning that universals and individuals share an equal reality. But he had been interpreted by the neo-Platonists as meaning that universals enjoy a superior reality (the realistic fallacy). It was not until Duns Scotus that the error was corrected, and the emphasis on the reality of the individual restored *without losing realism*. Scotus was a penetrating realist, even though his effect has not been strongly felt on subsequent metaphysics. Despite the occasional appearance of realistic philosophers, realism as a movement had to wait until later to be revived.

The history of the succeeding centuries, up through the nineteenth, must be written entirely in terms of the enormous and widespread success of nominalism. It should perhaps be noted here that philosophy is not the exclusive property of the philosophers. Only explicit philosopy is their province and not even all of that. For nominalism as a doctrine dropped out of the writings of the times with the rise of nominalism in events. According to nominalism, philosophy is a controversy over words, and so the real questions of philosophy gravitated toward more important topics, toward what according to nominalism is really important: the objective manipulation of materials and the study of the confines of knowledge. The shift of importance from salvation to material wealth, and from the Christian life to the ethics of expediency, together with the interests of the natural world, whether pursued through art, exploration or commerce, gave undeniable evidence of the deep and implicit acceptance throughout Europe of the nominalistic philosophy.

B. Reid and the Origins of Modern Realism

i. from hume to reid

The story of Peirce's metaphysics is part of the story of how, in recent centuries, realism, shorn of its theological associations and entanglements and restored to the same kind of pristine meaning which it had in Greek philosophy, has come once more to be a powerful force. In order to illustrate Peirce's position in the history of philosophy, we shall be obliged to go back a little in time, and to pick up the thread of realism where it emerged by reaction from the nominalism of the eighteenth century, and follow it through until it issues in Peirce's own times. For Peirce, powerful, original and systematic thinker though he was, resembled other great men in that he did not stand alone but belonged to a definite tradition.

Nominalism extends to all distinctions made on the basis of reality. Nominalism, by questioning the reality of universals, introduced a distinction with regard to reality that threw all subsequent philosophers who were not realists into one of two camps. There were nominalists who held that real knowledge is limited to knowledge of the subject, and later there were also nominalists who held that it is limited to the object. Subjective nominalism assumes either that we are cut off from knowledge of the objective world or that the objective world does not exist, and thus supposes knowledge to be confined to the nearest analogies of physical particulars in us: our sense impressions. Objective nominalism, which supposes that knowledge consists in the knowledge of physical particulars alone, is the purest kind. The first group included the rationalists, the empiricists and the idealists, who held that reality resides in subjective thoughts, sensations and ideas, respectively. The second group included materialists, who held that real knowledge is knowledge of the actual physical world. When Hume came upon the scene, it was dominated by the nominalism of the first variety: the rationalism of Descartes and Leibniz. Locke, in restricting certain knowledge to sensations and in making a real distinction between primary and secondary qualities, and Newton, in demonstrating the mechanistic and atomistic character of the physical world of matter and energy, gave support to the current acceptance of the consequences of the nominalistic postulate. Their conclusions offered no relief from the narrow choice between a reality which must be the property of the mind and one which must belong to the external world. Thus Hume came of a long line of nominalistic philosophers who had blessed the absolute distinction between mind and matter, and he was left with the then familiar but baffling problem of having to explain their interrelations.

Hume was a subjectivistic empiricist. Not content with the synthetically concocted excuse of occasionalism, which seemed to satisfy the Cartesians, nor with the ingenious yet none the less preposterous hypothesis of preestablished harmony, which seemed to satisfy Christian Wolff and the other followers of Leibniz, Hume set about frankly to face the situation. For a constructive philosopher the predicament might have proved disastrous, but for a skeptic it was made to order. Taking the subjective end of the knowledge relation as the given and all else as unreliable, Hume found himself in a locked internal world, fed only by perceptions consisting of lively impressions and of weak ones called ideas.[41] In this world, where causality was utterly inexplicable,[42] he found nothing dependable to which he could cling except the temporal succession of events.[43] There exists, he claimed, a succession of impressions and ideas which is the self.[44] The self, then, can only be a notion acquired from the repetition of the ideas of reflection, such as, for instance, hearing, feelings of pain, thoughts, and willing. The idea of substance is a matter literally of custom or habit.[45] There is no external world of substance, causality being a result of customary succession.[46] Mental association is a connection of a sort, but there is nothing necessary about the casual succession of contiguity.[47] That is to say, there is a psychological necessity to succession but not a logical one. Hume's version of the representative theory of perception contains no evidence that the impressions and ideas resemble what they represent. We may call our perceptions by the names of substance and accidents if we choose, but they are perceptions all the same. Hume clung to the criterion of human nature and what could be comprised within it as final, so that his doctrine may accurately be described as a kind of absolute humanism. Skepticism, in one direction at least, could go no further.

This is not the whole story of philosophy so far as it concerns Hume, but these were at least some of the difficulties which his position presented to other men whose thoughts were running on the same problems.

To the untenability of Hume's ultimate position, there were two philosophical reactions. Kant gave one kind of answer; Thomas Reid, the Scottish philosopher, another. Kant continued the criticism when he asked "How are synthetic judgments *a priori* possible?"[48] By synthetic judgments he meant assertions of positive fact; and by *a priori*, general truths independent of experience;[49] so that the question might be framed, how

[41] David Hume, *A Treatise of Human Nature*, bk. I, pt. I, § II; also I, III, VIII.
[42] *Ibid.*, I, III, VI; also I, IV, I.
[43] *Ibid.*, I, III, VI.
[44] *Ibid.*, I, IV, VI.
[45] *Ibid.*, I, I, VI.
[46] *Ibid.*, I, III, XIV.
[47] *Ibid.*, I, III, XIV.
[48] *Kritik der Reinen Vernunft*, B 19.
[49] Cf. C. S. Peirce, *Collected Papers*, 2.690, 5.92, 5.348.

can the universal principles of human reasoning refer to external fact? Kant no more than Reid meant to be a nominalist, and this is clear from the changes Kant made in the second edition of the *Critique*. Kant was avowedly influenced by Hume,[50] but Rudolf Metz, in his excellent study of British philosophy, passes the following judgment: "Like Kant, Reid was awakened from his dogmatic slumber by Hume, but the powerful influence which both experienced was made fruitful and directed into a new great movement of thought by the German thinker only. From Reid and his followers came no creative renewal of thought."[51]

Of course there can be no question of a single source for any philosophy as powerful as that of modern realism. Reid's influence is not the only one, but it is the strongest. While Kant's influence was widespread and profound, it produced no thinker of the rank of Kant. Although Reid's influence was longer in getting started, yet it produced an effect upon philosophy that has eventually been very important. Since the Kantian tradition is already well known, we shall confine our attention to Reid and his effect upon subsequent thought.

The corrective necessary for re-establishing a tenable theory of the relations between the human nature of the subject and the external world in which he lives and moves and has his existence could hardly be expected to come from the external world, since that world had by definition been denied all value as evidence. It must, then, come from within the subject. Hume himself had left a hint when he declared that, although the senses had to be corrected by reason, we trust them by a natural instinct, for what we doubted was never the senses but only their relations and situation.[52] Reid accepted the absolute cleavage between body and mind, and, like his predecessors, Descartes and Spinoza and Leibniz, held it to be the most important in philosophy.[53] If, however, as Hume had shown, philosophy belongs to the internal world of human nature, then we must put our trust in human nature, or philosophy will break down altogether.[54]

Trusting human nature in this sense means having faith in its profoundest faculties. Not only is the common consciousness of mankind to be trusted, with all its vast store of belief, but even such relatively superficial faculties as sensation are also.[55] We do not have to depend upon the external

[50] Cf. Norman Kemp Smith, 1930, *A Commentary to Kant's 'Critique of Pure Reason'* (London, Macmillan, 1930), p. xxv ff.

[51] *A Hundred Years of British Philosophy* (New York, Macmillan, 1938), pp. 29-30.

[52] *Treatise of Human Nature*, bk. i, pt. iv, §II.

[53] *Essays on the Intellectual Powers of Man* (Cambridge, Mass., Bartlett, 1850), p. 5.

[54] *Essays on the Intellectual Powers of Man*, Essay VI, chap. III, §III (8).

[55] *Ibid.*, II, X, I and II.

world to demonstrate its own existence, since we have sensation. Sensation carries with it an immediate belief in the reality of its object,[56] and this is our criterion of the objectivity of truth, and of the reality of the external world.[57] The group of primitive judgments present to the consciousness of mankind is called common sense, and it is upon common sense that all certainty rests.[58] In this faculty the philosopher does not exceed the ordinary man.[59]

Among the primitive judgments, or principles, of common sense, Reid lists some which sharply mark his departure from the nominalists who preceded him. Against Hume, he maintained as a first principle that the thoughts of which we are conscious are the thoughts of an ego,[60] so that, since we have thoughts, there must be an ego, or mind. Against Hume he also maintained as a first principle the existence of everything of which we are conscious,[61] and went on to assert that "there is a certain regard due to human testimony in matters of fact, and even to human authority in matters of opinion."[62] It is also a first principle that "the natural faculties, by which we distinguish truth from error, are not fallacious."[63] Thus from the confines of the internal world, and despite the acceptance of the body-mind distinction of the nominalists, Reid restored the reality of the mind and of that which the mind knows, the external world, including, besides substance, all possibilities. In the same fashion, Reid substituted for Hume's theory of perception the doctrine of immediate perception.[64] Every feeling suggests an object felt, because we are bound to look upon all feelings as signs.[65] Thus Reid broke the ground for a realistic version of logical symbolism, as well as for a realistic ontology, epistemology and psychology.

In classifying Reid with the realists, we have in mind chiefly the implications of his common-sense viewpoint and its effect upon subsequent philosophers. To trust the senses for a faithful account of the external world is a hallmark of realism. Yet when dealing specifically with the metaphysical problem of realism itself, Reid sometimes wavered. He certainly did

[56] *Ibid.*, II, IV, II; also II, V, III; and II, X, I.

[57] *Ibid.*, II, XI, I.

[58] *Inquiry into the Human Mind on the Principles of Common Sense* (Edinburgh, 1764), p. 52.

[59] *Essays on the Powers of the Human Mind* (Edinburgh, 1819), vol. ii, p. 316.

[60] *Essays on the Intellect*, p. 360.

[61] *Ibid.*, p. 360.

[62] *Ibid.*, p. 373.

[63] *Ibid.*, p. 367.

[64] *Essays on the Intellectual Powers of Man*, Essay II, chap. III, §3.

[65] *Essays on the Powers of the Human Mind*, ii, p. 304 ff.

deny the reality of universals *ante res*.[66] Elsewhere, however, he defended the reality of all possibilities.[67] With this qualification, the assertion can be made that the tone, as well as the import, of Reid's speculations throws the balance of his philosophy definitely on the side of realism.[68]

ii. FROM REID TO PEIRCE

It can hardly be claimed that Reid was one of the world's great philosophers. But he was a key figure in that he opened the path toward a secular realism, which has been followed since his work by most of the great British and the greatest of American realists. The nineteenth century was a bad period for Reid's reputation, although it was in that century that his influence was felt on the most important of American realists, Charles S. Peirce. Peirce freely acknowledged the influence of Reid, and combined the Critical Philosophy of Kant with Reid's Common-Sensism into what he termed Critical Common-Sensism.[69] Peirce understood very well his opposition to the nominalism of Hume and his own realistic premises. He said that "instead of being a purely negative critic, like Hume, seeking to annul a fundamental conception generally admitted, I am a positive critic, pleading for the admission to a place in our scheme of the universe for an idea generally rejected." (6.605) Peirce was a metaphysical realist[70] who felt no doubt about the possibility of reconciling the critical faculty with the common-sense beliefs of the ordinary man.[71] While considering the body of common sense to be general, and hence vaguer than Reid had supposed,[72] Peirce thought that the part of it which could pass through the scrutiny of scientific examination, which would be, incidentally, the greater part, would be all the stronger for having a high probability on its side.[73]

The epistemological realism of the early twentieth century specifically repudiated Reid as its influence, and sought rather to take its start from opposition to the Kantian position, attempting to transfer his critical attitude from its subjectivist-idealist basis to an objectivist-realist one. This gave rise to a kind of objective idealism that is equivalent to realism. Peirce, in

---

[66] *Essays on the Intellect*, Essay V, chap. III, §II.

[67] *Ibid.*, Essay IV, chap. I, §II, and Essay IV, chap. I, §IV.

[68] See also *Contemporary British Philosophers* (Second Series), ed. by J. H. Muirhead (New York, Macmillan, no date), pp. 193-223.

[69] *Collected Papers*, vol. v, bk. iii.

[70] *Ibid.*, 1.20, 5.432.

[71] *Ibid.*, 5.505.

[72] *Ibid.*, 5.446.

[73] *Ibid.*, 5.451.

fact, acknowledged his obligation to Reid and to Kant.[74] But in England, G. Dawes Hicks specifically repudiated the influence of Reid, whom he accused of having "disposed of the 'way of ideas' in far too rough and ready a fashion to satisfy the demands of exact and methodical inquiry.[75] Hicks, however, arrived at substantially the same conclusions, at least with respect to the broad outlines of realism. The point of view of Reid is best carried on by the teaching of John Cook Wilson, who expressed Reid's realistic position by attacking the coherence theory of truth, the subjectivist theory of knowledge, and the influence of psychology on logic; and who, moreover, sought to show the correctness of common sense in his method of inquiry by preferring to express himself in the speech of ordinary men and by avoiding all parade of learning and high-sounding terminology.[76]

Cook Wilson's realism is similar to the doctrines of the American neorealists in that he and his followers denied the objectivity of qualities and values, which were held to be added by the subject to the process of perception. With the later British realists, the theory of realism with respect to values as well as universals returns to the fore, and the influence of Reid is once more explicitly felt. In what proved tactically the most important book defending the position of axiological realism, G. E. Moore gave credit to the work of Reid for having pointed out that perception requires that the thoughts and feelings of other persons as well as mere material objects have an existence objective to and independent of the perceiving subject.[77] He has held strongly to the same status for value.[78] Moore is the product of Cook Wilson multiplied by Reid. Like Wilson, he is devoted to careful and incisive analysis, and very hesitant about reaching conclusions. Of late, the influence of Wilson upon his thought has predominated over that of Reid, and he has become almost exclusively a philosophical analyst. But his earlier work is marked by the adherence to Reid's position, and, indeed, by the candid defense of Reid's Common-Sensism. In one essay, written some years ago, Moore adopted the Scottish philosophy, declaring for a body of original knowledge, common to philosopher and plain man, from which all special philosophical knowledge must take its start.[79] Like Reid, he went so far as to draw up a list of commonplace principles, and attempted to show their inescapability.

[74] *Collected Papers*, 1.522.
[75] *Critical Realism* (London, Macmillan, 1938), p. xiv.
[76] R. Metz, *Hundred Years of British Philosophy*, p. 523.
[77] *Philosophical Studies* (London, Kegan Paul, 1922), p. 57.
[78] *Ibid.*, chap. VIII.
[79] "A Defense of Common Sense," in *Contemporary British Philosophy* (ed. J. H. Muirhead), vol. ii.

Moore's ideas exerted considerable effect upon the thinking of Bertrand Russell, who readily acknowledged the teacher.[80] Moore, of course, made his pupil over into a realist; and Russell came heavily into debt to the Scottish school. He named his philosophy "logical atomism"[81] but pointed out that the theories of American neorealism were close to what he intended.[82] Gradually, however, other eighteenth century influences were brought to bear upon him, especially that of Hume, and nominalism overcame for a while the realism of Reid. It won by means of the analytical method; Hume, so to speak, disguised as Cook Wilson, vanquished Reid. We can see the transition taking place clearly, with Russell clinging desperately to certain of the realistic presuppositions, but gradually going over to nominalism in the course of his many volumes.[83] The way was open for the logical positivists to have their day with him. There are recent signs, however, of a return to realism on the part of Russell, albeit disguised by the language and peculiar interests of the logical positivists.[84] Reid is undoubtedly once more asserting his influence, if only implicitly and in the form of early prejudices.

Of Moore's influence on others we may cite three examples from the work of G. F. Stout, S. Alexander, and John Laird. Stout's realistic epistemology acknowledges great respect for the opinions of the ordinary man, and the ascendancy of Reid and Moore is most apparent in his appeal to common sense. As for S. Alexander, in a recent Preface to his metaphysical system, he recounts how a reading of Moore's essay on "The Refutation of Idealism"[85] was clarified for him by his own conclusion that, since the cause of a thing cannot be the mental state which apprehends it, the presentation of the object must be not a mental picture but the thing itself or a selection from it.[86] John Laird's realism was due to the combined forces of Reid and Moore,[87] both of whom were instrumental in teaching him that the reality of the external world involves its independence of the process of knowing. Laird's work is more comprehensive, if not more systematic, than that of any of the other English realists I have mentioned,

---

[80] *The Principles of Mathematics* (London, Allen & Unwin, 1937), p. viii.

[81] *Our Knowledge of the External World* (New York, Norton, 1929), p. 4.

[82] *Ibid.*

[83] E.g., *Mysticism and Logic* (New York, Norton, 1929), p. 123.

[84] *An Inquiry into Meaning and Truth* (New York, Norton, 1940), especially chap. XXV.

[85] Reprinted as chap. I of *Philosophical Studies*.

[86] Samuel Alexander, *Space, Time and Deity* (2 vols.), (London, Macmillan, 1934), 2nd. ed., vol. i, pp. xiv f.

[87] *A Study in Realism* (Cambridge, University Press, 1920), pp. 2 ff. and 13 ff.

in explicitly setting forth the reality of value, a position for which he gives due acknowledgment to both Reid[88] and Moore.[89]

We can hardly close the account of modern realism without devoting a few words to the philosophy in which Reid's tradition has been brought up to date. That has been done in the organic philosophy of Whitehead. Whitehead is a systematic philosopher who has acknowledged the realistic basis of his system.[90] Realism is implicit in his distinction between "actual entities" and "eternal objects,"[91] and in the earlier attack upon nominalism, under the guise of "the bifurcation of nature into two systems of reality,"[92] which he castigates as "vicious."[93] There are many influences on the realism of Whitehead, chiefly, perhaps, those of Plato and modern physics. But we must recall that the development of Whitehead's philosophy of organism followed his writing of the *Principia Mathematica* with Russell, and that this book was an outgrowth of *The Principles of Mathematics* in which, as we have already noted, Russell freely acknowledged his great obligation to Moore. We may safely surmise that Reid's effect has been felt on Whitehead indirectly through Russell, and, even more indirectly, through Moore's effect on Russell. But in spite of this indirection the effect is plain enough. Whitehead's own refutation of Hume is often reminiscent of Reid, as for example in the criticism of the sensationalist theory of perception.[94] In general, Whitehead takes his start from opposition to Descartes and the nominalistic English philosophers; may we not suppose that in thus going over ground already familiar to Reid, the Scottish tradition of realism is showing not only its vitality, but also its validity and truth?

The conclusion of this brief section, then, is that the theory of metaphysical realism obtained its start in modern times through Reid's objections to Hume, and through his own subsequent affirmative philosophical speculations, and has been carried down in an unbroken tradition, in both Great Britain and America, from the publication of Reid's *Inquiry* in 1764 to the present day, having included on its way the most painstaking of philosophical critics as well as the most comprehensive of system makers. Philosophy is but one of the many studies in which realism is now in the ascendant. Others include such diverse fields as relativity physics and

---

[88] *The Idea of Value* (Cambridge, University Press, 1929), pp. 221 ff.
[89] *Ibid.*, pp. 362 and 365.
[90] *Science and the Modern World* (New York, Macmillan, 1931), p. 132.
[91] *Process and Reality* (New York, Macmillan, 1930), p. 32 *et passim*.
[92] *The Concept of Nature* (Cambridge, University Press, 1926), p. 30.
[93] *Ibid.*, p. 185.
[94] *Process and Reality*, e.g., pp. viii and 220-223.

quantum mechanics,[95] pure[96] and applied[97] mathematics, and mathematical logic.[98] Convincing evidence could be brought forth that even the course of actual events is directed toward realism; but we have reached the end of our particular argument.

C. WHITEHEAD AND THE CONTEMPORARY REALISM

In the previous portions of this chapter we have attempted to place Peirce in the proper perspective of the history of philosophy up to his own times. In the next chapter we shall further attempt to evaluate Peirce's position by carrying the story forward, showing both what his influence has been in recent years and also what it could mean to the future. This section, therefore, is by way of a digression, since it compares Peirce with a later philosopher upon whom he has exercised no influence. It will show that the living tradition of realism resembles the realism of Peirce in certain immutable respects to the same extent to which antecedent realism does. These considerations are not so unrelated to our main topic as would at first appear, since they demonstrate how two philosophers who have been subjected to the same influences, who have felt the same forces at work, and lived in similar intellectual worlds, may, without knowledge of each other, come to strikingly similar conclusions. A great thinker is at once a miracle and a man of his times. It is no derogation of the originality of two great philosophers to show that many of the same currents met in their work.

We may safely assert that Peirce had not read Whitehead, since he died before the latter's important work in philosophy was published. The reverse is not so clear; but since there is no reference in Whitehead's books to Peirce, it is likely to be true; for Whitehead could not have read Peirce without being excited by him sufficiently either to quote him or to refer to him in some way. Yet the similarities between their philosophies are simply astounding. This should not be so difficult to understand when we recall that many of the traditions which strongly bore on both men were

[95] See, e.g., Max Planck, *The Philosophy of Physics* (London, Allen & Unwin, 1936).

[96] See, e.g., G. H. Hardy, *A Mathematician's Apology* (Cambridge, University Press, 1940), especially pp. 63 f.

[97] See, e.g., R. A. Fisher, *Statistical Method for Research Workers* (London, Oliver and Boyd, 1938), chap. I.

[98] All texts in logic written from the standpoint of the *Principia* are realistic in their presuppositions. See, e.g., Morris R. Cohen and Ernest Nagel, *An Introduction to Logic and Scientific Method* (New York, Harcourt, Brace, 1934).

the same. Both were deeply affected by the reaction to Hume[99] and Descartes,[100] by the realistic English tradition since Reid,[101] and by modern science.[102] Both men were in full revolt against the nominalistic philosophy and both inveighed against its effect on the modern world.[103] They shared a common sympathy for the realistic outlook,[104] and described their metaphysics as varieties of realism,[105] yet were equally sure that, in Whitehead's expression, "The really profound changes in human life all have their ultimate origin in knowledge pursued for its own sake."[106]

The group of nine nominalistic doctrines which Whitehead has repudiated happen also to be those which Peirce in one place or another denounced. We may list them here, together with the references in Peirce where similar repudiations may be found.

"(i) The distrust of speculative philosophy."[107] Peirce's whole system of philosophy is speculative in the sense in which speculation refers to theoretical considerations. See especially Chapters III and IV of this volume.

"(ii) The trust in language as an adequate expression of propositions." Peirce trusted language to express philosophy provided the syntax of no single language be identified with the forms of logic. (2.68; 2.338) But the close identification between language and at least one form of the expression of propositions was implicitly accepted by Peirce. See Chapter III, B, iv, of this volume.

"(iii) The mode of philosophical thought which implies, and is implied by, the faculty-psychology." Peirce's own psychology differs from the faculty-psychology. His philosophy implies, and is implied by, his own psychology. See Chapter VI of this volume. Also Chapter III, A, i.

"(iv) The subject-predicate form of expression." Peirce substituted for the subject-predicate form, which is consistent with the substance philosophy, the propositional function of mathematical logic which is consistent with the relation philosophy.

[99] A. N. Whitehead, *Process and Reality* (hereafter *PR*), pt. ii, chap. V; C. S. Peirce, *Col. Pap.*, 5.300, 5.310, 6.500, 6.537, etc.
[100] Whitehead, *Modes of Thought*, p. 204; *PR*, pt. ii, chap. V; Peirce, this vol., chap. II, E.
[101] See this chapter, B, ii.
[102] Whitehead, *PR*, pt. iv; Peirce, this vol., chap. II, B, and chap. VIII.
[103] Whitehead, *PR*, Preface, p. viii; Peirce, this vol., chap. IV, C, i.
[104] Whitehead, *Science and the Modern World* (hereafter *SMW*), Chap. V; Peirce, this vol., chap. IV, C, ii.
[105] Whitehead, *SMW*, chap. IV; Peirce, this vol., chap. IV, C, i.
[106] *Introduction to Mathematics*, Home University Library (London, 1911), p. 32; Peirce, this vol., chaps. VII and VIII.
[107] All nine of the following doctrines are to be found in Whitehead, *PR*, Preface, p. viii.

"(v) The sensationalist doctrine of perception." Peirce's doctrine is that of immediate perception. See Chapter VI, B, iii, of this volume.

"(vi) The doctrine of vacuous actuality." This is repudiated in Peirce's philosophy by the assertion that actuality is a selection from possibility of which it is a part. Actuality as Peirce conceived it is thick, since it must contain elements of all three ontological categories; there are qualities, re-actions and representations in it. See Chapter IV, C, ii, and D, i, of this volume.

"(vii) The Kantian doctrine of the objective world as a theoretical con-struct from purely subjective experience." Peirce accepted the reality of the objective world, and specifically repudiated the Kantian view. See Chapters II, A; V, B, i; and IV, C, ii, of this volume.

"(viii) Arbitrary deductions in *ex absurdo* arguments." Peirce's constant reference to the phenomenological ground and his insistence that philosophy should hang from more than one thread preclude any adherence to this method. See Chapters II, E, iv; IV, A; and VII, A, of this volume.

"(ix) Belief that logical inconsistencies can indicate anything else than some antecedent errors." Peirce's whole philosophy rests upon his logic, in which the law of contradiction and excluded middle is supported. See Chapter III, B, v, of this volume.

Ontologically, the two systems in many respects are much alike. There is the same attack upon the fallacy of "simple location."[108] There is the same distinction between the logical and the actual world: between "gen-erals" and "facts" for Peirce; [109] between "eternal objects" and "actual entities" for Whitehead.[110] Whitehead's "prehension"[111] is Peirce's "precision."[112] Both regard feeling as an objective affair.[113] Whitehead's "novelty"[114] is Peirce's "spontaneity."[115] Both have an immense respect for common sense, which they regard as the ultimate touchstone of scien-tific endeavors.[116] They also share an unusually high regard for vagueness when considered as a stubborn fact of generality and not as a negligible property of confusion.[117]

---

[108] Whitehead, *SMW*, p. 84; Peirce, *Col. Pap.*, 1.38.
[109] Peirce, this vol., chap. IV, B.
[110] Whitehead, *PR*, pt. i, chap. II, sec. II.
[111] Whitehead, *Ibid*.
[112] Peirce, *Col. Pap.*, 1.549.
[113] Whitehead, *PR*, pt. ii., chap. VII, and pt. iii, chap. IV; Peirce, this vol., chap. IV, B, i.
[114] Whitehead, *PR*, pt. ii, chap. III, sec. VII.
[115] Peirce, this vol., chap. IV, A, ii.
[116] Whitehead, *The Aims of Education*, chap. VIII; Peirce, this vol., chap. VII, C, iii.
[117] Whitehead, *Modes of Thought*, pt. ii, Lecture IV; Peirce, this vol., chap. VII, C, iii.

In cosmology, the same astonishing parallel between the outlooks of the two philosophers seems to hold. For instance, both emphasized cosmology,[118] and regarded their philosophies as culminating in it. For both, substance is a common-sense notion which must be subordinated to the superior category of relatedness.[119] Whitehead's "creativity"[120] is Peirce's "evolutionary love."[121] Both denied that universals are exceptions to the primary law of evolution.[122] Both believed that this existence is but one stage among a number of evolutionary stages, and spoke of it as "this cosmic epoch."[123] Both subscribed to the theory that this cosmic epoch is characterized by ovals.[124]

Again, in theology, the comparison is instructive. Both men were realistic Protestants, who saw the true religion in the possibilties if not in the fulfillment of the church.[125] Both men wished to return to the origins of Christianity in the New Testament.[126] Both men thought of God in one of his main aspects as pure creativity,[127] and divided God into a "primordial" and a "consequent" side[128] so that the primordial side is not subject to time,[129] while the consequent is.

The comparable elements in the systems of Peirce and Whitehead are by no means exhausted by what has been given here. It has not been possible to do more than suggest the wide range of similarities of specific influences and abstract categories. The difference in philosophical terminology obscures the underlying generality of outlook, which contains further identities. But at least enough has been shown to offer some evidence against the explanation of mere chance coincidence. While coincidence is still a possible explanation, the odds against its validity are large. It is perhaps safer to suppose that the great tradition of the Greek realists is being reborn in modern times, guided by the explicit inconsistencies of the nominalistic philosophies and the implicit realism of modern physical science. That such a revival has not yet been popularly recognized

[118] Whitehead, *PR*, subtitle and *passim*; Peirce, this vol., chap. XI.

[119] Whitehead, *PR*, Preface, p. ix; Peirce, this vol., chap. III, B, vi.

[120] Peirce, this vol., chap. XII, B, iii.

[121] Peirce, this vol., chap. XII, B, iii.

[122] Whitehead, *PR*, pt. i, chap. II, and Part II, chap. IX; Peirce, this vol., chap. XI, C, ii.

[123] Whitehead, *PR*, Part II, chap. III; Peirce, *Col. Pap.*, 6.196, 6.208.

[124] Whitehead, *PR*, Part IV, chap. III; Peirce, this vol., chap. XI, C, iii, quoting *Col. Pap.*, 1.220; 4.219-220.

[125] Whitehead, *SMW*, chap. XII; Peirce, this vol., chap. XII, D, i.

[126] Whitehead, *Religion in the Making*, chap. II, sec. IV; Peirce, this vol., chap. XII, B, i-iii.

[127] Whitehead, *PR*, Part V, chap. II, sec. IV; Peirce, this vol., chap. XII, C, ii.

[128] Whitehead, *PR*, Part V, chap. II; Peirce, *Col. Pap.*, 1.362, and this vol., chap. XII, C, ii.

[129] Peirce, *Col. Pap.*, 4.67 and this vol., chap. XII, C, ii.

may point less to its weakness than to its eventual tremendous effects. Much of the credit for such a revival will be due to Whitehead and Peirce.

We have reached the end of our study of Peirce's philosophy. We have examined something of the forces, both historical and logical, that formed his mind and his philosophy. We have noted, too, how Peirce constructed his system, starting from logic and the facts of actuality, and resting each separate division upon these and upon previous divisions. The system aims to be self-consistent, and though the final judgment of its validity must rest upon this criterion plus the further one of its continual allowance by fact, the judgment of its worth is not concerned with these criteria alone. It is perhaps more concerned with the suggestiveness of the system to further feeling, reasoning and action—we may call them enjoyment, study and activity, recognizing in them the earliest of the categories with which we started this book. The tentative products of such suggestiveness, in its earlier phases, will be indicated, so far as is possible, in the next, and final, chapter.

CHAPTER XIV

The Early History of Peirce's Influence

A. An Estimate and a Hope

WE HAVE REACHED THE END OF OUR LONG AND PERHAPS IN SOME RESPECTS TEDIOUS account of Peirce's philosophy, of the tradition that formed his ideas, of the environment that partly explains his outlook, of the development of the ideas in his mind, and, finally, of the system of philosophy itself. And now we may safely end on the note with which we started in the Preface: an attempt to evaluate the influence which Peirce has exercised. Hence this chapter, which is partly in the nature of an appendix, will try to point out the effect Peirce has had upon some leading American thinkers.

We cannot make our description of Peirce's influence exhaustive. Undoubtedly, Peirce has exercised certain influences which are wholly unsuspected; while others remain merely obscure. Although, as we shall shortly see, the leading American philosophers of pragmatism, James and, after him, Dewey, were strongly bent in a certain direction by their particular understanding of what Peirce wrote, the work of Peirce has hardly reached its true reputation and dominant status in the general opinion. Indeed, the situation is worse than that; for, as many professional philosophers in America will readily admit, Peirce is still only a name. The situation that prevails is much the same as it was in Peirce's own day, when many eminent gentlemen could boast the occupancy of chairs of philosophy while Peirce was dismissed from one teaching position after another, if indeed he was able to secure one at all.

But now that the fog, which frequently prevents contemporaries from appreciating one another and usually obscures the peaks altogether, has cleared away, it is becoming easier to observe Peirce in something approaching his true perspective, to see the gigantic proportions of his accomplishment and to begin to feel its weight and importance. In all likelihood, those who have begun to know about Peirce and to comprehend the value of his work are at best mere pioneers, men with crude intellectual weapons,

blazing the path for his fuller recognition at the hands of future generations. Peirce is rapidly beginning to be acknowledged as the greatest of
America's philosophers, as a system maker worthy to rank with the best
that Europe has produced. He is in all probability destined to become the
source of a native philosophical tradition, the classic philosopher who will
give America its self-respect by making it intellectually a thing of its own
apart from its debt to Europe. He may thus appear to future historians
as the focal point, the origin and very center, of the American culture, which
must always remain related to that of Europe yet which could contribute
something of its own to the world and thus be independent of the European
tradition.

In this sense the importance of the recognition of Peirce concerns him
less than it concerns America and through America the world of the present
and of the future. For if Peirce's contribution contains anything of value
and validity, then it is sure to be an universal one. In the midst of a period
when true philosophy had fallen into neglect, due to the prevailing philosophy which regarded it as the private consolation of those who had failed
to measure up to the requirements of the hurly-burly world, and who had
therefore retired to the harmless dignity of their own impotent dreams,
Peirce dared to see its enormous possibilities. He remembered what it had
once been in the civilization of the Greeks; he saw what modern science
was achieving; and he had the temerity to suppose that philosophy would
in years to come be required by science to resume its ancient eminence,
to be charged once again with its old vigor, and to take on once more in
men's minds the dimensions which it has perforce in their affairs.

In short, he felt that he could bring philosophy back into prominence
as an abstract study of principles, a study that must be pursued for its own
sake if it is to have as a result its full effect upon practice. He was not
unmindful of the importance of practice, but since practice can only be the
practice of theory, he was chiefly concerned with the state of theory. If philosophy had fallen into the discard, that was in large part at least the fault of
philosophers who preferred to give their allegiance to science. Peirce was a
scientist who preferred philosophy. If we choose to follow him, we shall find
that by his aid we are able to regard philosophy as just what it is: at once
the most theoretical and practical of studies.

If we try to recall those philosophical topics on which Peirce has thrown
fresh light, or to which he has made original contributions, we are em-
barrassed by their abundance. Among them we may mention: in logic,
the basing of logic on experience, the beginnings of symbolic or mathe-

matical logic, the revival of abduction, the objective validity of probability, the revival of rhetoric as the study of communication, the provision for a science of method; in ontology, the proof that at least three categories but no more are necessary—quality, reaction and representation as the primary ontological categories, the arguments for realism and against nominalism, the distinction between being and existence, the establishment of chance and of habit as ontological categories; in epistemology, the perceptual judgment, the importance of falsity, the objectivity of truth; in psychology, the definition of mind as a function of truth, the identity of consciousness and feeling, all modifications of consciousness as inferences, belief as a conscious habit, the generality of desire, images as signs, reasoning as the relating of logic and action, the existence of subconscious reasoning, personality as a bundle of habits; in methodology, the abstract theory of inquiry, pragmatism, pragmaticism as the realistic understanding of pragmatism, the unity of the critical philosophy of Kant with the common-sense philosophy of Reid; in science, the abstract formulation of science, the system of the sciences, the principles of scientific method, the realistic logic of the method; in ethics, the distinction between practical morality and theoretical ethics, the doctrine of the unlimited community; in aesthetics, the possibility of making aesthetics a science; in cosmology, the doctrine of origins in absolute chaos, chance love and continuity as cosmological categories, matter as frozen mind, the direction toward absolute law; in theology, musement as proof of God's existence, evolutionary love, the defense of free will, the interpretation of miracles, and the function of the church. These and other doctrines of Peirce are capable of exciting investigation in the many fields to which they are relevant. The possibilities·as yet have hardly been touched.

The remainder of this chapter will be devoted to showing how Peirce has been understood—or misunderstood—from his flourishing to the present day. But the thought that it will be wisest to remember in closing is that Peirce was a systematic philosopher, yet, unlike most of the systematizers of philosophy who went before him, he regarded his system as something quite open and incomplete, to be changed or amended or otherwise improved by those investigators who come after. He could not have been consistent and have objected to the abandonment of his system altogether, provided it be found to be that much in error. Yet while he retained a broadness of mind, and so much pure and detached interest in the search for truth, it remains undeniable that he must have felt that some part of his work was fated to become integrated with the corpus of human knowledge. And when we read the whole body of his contribution to philosophy, it is difficult to avoid sharing this hope with him.

B. The Influence of Peirce on His Contemporaries

When this chapter was begun in the year A.D. 1939, one hundred years had elapsed since the birth of Peirce and twenty-five years since his death. Peirce's influence was described as "early" because, as was becoming increasingly evident, it had just begun. Certainly early figures like Royce and James had frankly borrowed from Peirce, while certain others had borrowed without acknowledging their source. The break between Peirce's earliest disciples and his later ones lay in the fact that the first group *avowed their debt to Peirce*, while the latter *claimed Peirce* as a sort of primitive precursor of their particular school. The orientation is distinctly different. In this latter group belonged Dewey and some of the logical positivists. Thus, although the tendency was to pay increased attention to Peirce, it was not of the sort properly to enhance his reputation, a task which awaited a new and much more detached viewpoint: a perspective from which one not only could see the whole of his philosophy but could see it *as* a whole.

Peirce repudiated the interpretation put upon his work by many of his followers during his lifetime. He specifically called out and condemned James, Dewey, Carus, Schiller, Papini, and others. From this group we may select two typical ones with divergent views, in order to show how the understanding of Peirce almost immediately went astray, or, from another point of view, how philosophers who had little in common with Peirce's position were yet able to draw upon him.

i. on james's pragmatism

We have already paid some attention to the difference in meaning which Peirce and James attached to the doctrine of pragmatism.[1] But since this was done chiefly from the point of view of Peirce, it may be useful to give a further word here to the difference, this time taking our emphasis from James rather than from Peirce.

In a volume devoted to the topic of pragmatism[2] James first acknowledged Peirce as his source and then proceeded to expatiate on what his own version of pragmatism implies. Pragmatism for James is a theory of truth;

---

[1] See chap. VII, C, i.
[2] William James, *Pragmatism* (New York, Longmans Green, 1940), Lecture II.

it is a way of discovering truths. It is anti-intellectualistic, and so looks away from abstractions, absolutes, fixed principles and closed systems. It is practical, and so looks toward facts, concreteness and action. According to Jamesian pragmatism, "the only test of probable truth is what works best in the way of leading us." His pragmatism "can see no meaning in treating as 'not true' a notion that has been pragmatically successful." On the ethical side we may note the same divergence. In real life when truths clash with "vital benefits" it is the truths that must go. If actions which seem demanded clash with principles, then, said James, he takes a moral holiday. For justification, the moral holidays are either just brazenly taken or else as a philosopher James said he tries to justify them by some other principle.

In dealing with the fundamentals of metaphysics, the slightest change may produce repercussions in implications that will result in causing the final doctrine to square off in direct contradiction, and in having men who follow such implications anxious to get at each other's throats. Could we expect a theory of methodology, despite an identity of names, to have much in common, when we find such divergence in metaphysical views? Peirce, as we have noted often, was a confirmed realist. James, on the other hand, was a nominalist. For him, "Empiricism lays the explanatory stress upon the part, the element, the individual, and treats the whole as a collection and the universal as an abstraction."[3] The divergence between the two pragmatists is made clear by a comparison of their psychological theories, or, better still perhaps, by an examination of Peirce's review of James's *Principles of Psychology*.[4] By the slightest shift in emphasis, James brought the Peircian doctrine of pragmatism around to mean its direct opposite. James asked practical consequences to determine his truths and to determine them immediately. He did not care about truths but only about practice. Furthermore, he did not care about practice as a *theory* of practice but only as concrete and forceful actions. And he thought that a limited number of practical consequences are adequate for the determination of truths. Success is borne out by what is immediately successful, regardless of what may be its later failures. But how are we to know what "works best" if we do not allow it to work indefinitely? No matter how long we allow it to work, the day after we stop our judgment of workability, it may break down, perhaps forever. Workability, like success, may support a certain theory in today's practice, and let it down, if not directly disprove it, in tomorrow's. But James evidently took no such difficulties into account.

[3] *Essays in Radical Empiricism*, II.
[4] *The Nation*, 53 (1891), 15 and 32.

On the ethical side, we may apply the same arguments as those used against pragmatism. What are "vital benefits" and how are they to be determined? Are they individual or social, temporary or permanent, hedonistic or stoical? The notion of the moral holiday, with its post-rationalized justification, opens the door to any and every kind of action, whether antisocial or whatever. One wonders why rational justification is required at all. Certainly, if moral holidays are to be recommended regardless of what principles they come into conflict with, the brazen way of just taking them would seem to be the best. But we must not convict James on the findings of his theory, for James himself was, if the evidence of his other writings and of his friends is to be considered, a sincere seeker after the truth, whose superabundant vitality carried him into excesses of philosophical approval of activity for its own sake. He did not mean the harm which his own version of pragmatism and its ethics would indicate. There is no doubt of the great value of James's philosophical endeavors. He succeeded in instilling into a mordant and abandoned profession a new life and direction and purpose. He showed that philosophy is not a dull and useless discipline, confined to the classrooms and divorced from the most immanent and significant of public affairs in the rough-and-tumble world. But unfortunately this contribution, the value of which it is hard to underestimate, does not free James from the charge of having perverted Peirce's pragmatism from a realistic to a nominalistic metaphysics, by elevating practice as concrete and actual above principles whose abstract nature he deplored.

Finally—and this is the chief point of this section—James's contribution does not free him from the charge of having departed to a considerable extent from the position of Peirce. Peirce's pragmaticism, as we have seen, was intended as a guide to meaning, not as a guide to action. It is speculative and inquisitive, and not irrational and peremptory. It is realistic, and not nominalistic. It led to a concern with logic, metaphysics and theoretical science, and not to a preoccupation with psychology as containing the presuppositions of philosophy. In ethics the contrast is equally marked. Peirce's ethics demands the utmost sacrifice of the individual in terms of an infinite ideal; it is uncompromising and absolute and knows nothing of moral holidays. In short, James's philosophy represents an outlook more fashionable than Peirce's, and to some perhaps more valid, but of which it is the very antithesis. Not even by the utmost exertion of tolerance and sympathy can James's philosophy be said to be an extension or development of Peirce's, although no doubt certain aspects of it, and particularly the notion of pragmatism, were suggested to James by Peirce.

ii. ON ROYCE'S IDEALISM

The idealistic elements in Peirce's philosophy certainly must have exercised a profound influence upon Royce's ideas. Royce admitted as much in a number of places. In his letters to William James, for instance, he acknowledged the strong influence that Peirce's thought exerted upon him, both in the articles which Peirce had published in *Popular Science Monthly*[5] and in the lectures arranged for Peirce by James in Boston.[6] The statements of indebtedness contained in the Prefaces to both volumes of *The World and the Individual* constitute final proof that Royce himself was mindful of the debt. But where Peirce's idealism was of the objective variety, Royce identified the real with consciousness.[7] Where Peirce's idealism is reconcilable with a Scotist realism, to which during the thirty years that he was writing on philosophical questions he had never failed in his allegiance, (6.605) Royce's idealism is subjective and reconcilable rather with the Hegelian philosophy. We have already taken note of Peirce's rejection of Hegel's logic.[8] While giving some credit to Royce, (1.343; 3.563) Peirce himself was not unmindful of these differences, for in a lengthy review of Royce's chief metaphysical work, *The World and the Individual*,[9] he stated what he thought to be Royce's main thesis as follows:

"The design of the whole now comes out—to introduce into the Hegelian philosophy of religion such rectifications as must result from recognition of scientific conceptions worked out during the century now completing itself since that philosophy first appeared."[10]

Peirce then proceeded to argue as though Royce's second purpose in writing his book was to refute certain contentions of the realists—and of one realist in particular! Peirce's arguments against Royce may be summed up, since they illustrate concretely the divergence between Royce and Peirce.

Royce defined an idea as "any state of mind that has a conscious meaning." It should not be necessary to indicate that this reduces all ideas to concepts, and allows them no objective being whatsoever, a position utterly foreign to Peirce's metaphysics. Peirce contended that Royce had carried the spirit of his pragmatic maxim further. "Royce holds that the internal meaning of an idea is a Purpose, instead of regarding it, with his predecessor, as a germinal purpose. This purpose, obscurely recognized, since not all to which it will

---

[5] Perry, *Thought and Character*, vol. i, p. 788.
[6] *Ibid.*, vol. ii, p. 421.
[7] *Ibid.*, vol. i, p. 792.
[8] See chap. IV, B, iii.
[9] New York, Macmillan, 1901. Reviewed by Peirce in *The Nation*, 75 (1902), 94-96.
[10] Peirce's review, p. 94.

lead is foreseen; partially fulfilled in being recognized, since a purpose strives first of all to understand itself; but mainly unfulfilled, since it would not remain a purpose after fulfillment—is the internal meaning, or signification, or depth, of the idea. The purpose is vague—anything that refers to the future is more or less vague; and a sincere purpose to do a thing 'right now' actually does it. The purpose is to do a thing under certain circumstances. Completely to define these circumstances, it would be necessary to give a biography of the purposer from birth, without any omission. The purpose is to do something in order to produce certain results. Completely to define the result accomplished must involve a complete representation of the agent's future life. In short, the complete fulfillment of any purpose, which alone is the external meaning of the idea, is no less than the entire life of the thinker."[11]

The confusion of the idea with the conceptual holding of the idea involves a confusion of the internal and external meanings of the idea, and gives to the pragmatic spirit a subjective interpretation which it cannot possibly render valid. Another confusion resulting from these two is that between being and signification. "All reasoning goes upon the assumption that there is a true answer to whatever question may be under discussion, which answer cannot be rendered false by anything that the disputants may say or think about it; and further, that the denial of that true answer is false. This makes an apparent difficulty for idealism. For if all reality is of the nature of an actual idea, there seems to be no room for possibility or any lower mode than actuality, among the categories of being. . . . But what, then, can be the mode of being of a representation or meaning unequivocally false? For Hegel, the false is the bad, that which is out of harmony with its own essence; and since, in his view, contradiction is the great form of activity of the world, he has no difficulty in admitting that an idea may be out of harmony with itself. Professor Royce, however, seems almost to resent the idea that anybody could suppose that he denied the validity of the distinction of truth and falsehood. He is fairly outspoken in denouncing sundry doctrines false (a word Hegel hardly uses), even if we do not quite hear his foot come down; and nothing does he hold more false than the usual form of stating the distinction now in question, namely, that a true proposition corresponds to a *real matter of fact*, by which is meant a state of things, definite and individual, which *does not consist merely in* being represented (in any particular representation) *to be as it is*."[12]

Royce's announced maxim of procedure in refuting a proposition is to

[11] *Ibid.*
[12] *Ibid.*

state that proposition in its "most extreme form," a maxim which he proceeds to put into effect, according to Peirce, by "assuming that realists hold that no idea in the slightest degree determines the real object of it, whether causally or in any other manner. Whether this does not overstep the limits or admissible interpretation, seeing that a realist who meant this would deny that any promise can really be kept, or that any purpose can influence the real result, the reader must say. At any rate, it would not seem to be a difficult position to refute."[13]

Royce assumed that all causal action is reciprocal, which is denied by the past, which can influence the action of the future while the future cannot influence the action of the past. Royce's extreme realist would probably admit that the real object of an idea cannot have influenced the idea, although Peirce himself did not. Royce contended that the realist holds that the relation between an idea and its object is such that, no matter how the idea may be metamorphosed, it is logically possible for the object to remain unchanged. But no two things in the world are that independent of each other. "The truth is that Professor Royce is blind to a fact which all ordinary people see plainly enough; that the essence of the realist's opinion is that it is one thing to *be* and another thing to be *represented*; and the cause of this cecity is that the Professor is completely immersed in his absolute idealism, which precisely consists in denying that distinction."[14] The difference between absolute idealists of the Hegelian variety and realists, Peirce concluded, lies in this, "that realists do not admit that matters of fact can be apodeictically demonstrated."[15] Realism can never be refuted by the Hegelian philosophy, of which Peirce held Royce to be a disciple.

In the domain of ethics, a certain superficial similarity between Royce's doctrine and Peirce's is to be noted. Peirce's essay on "The Doctrine of Chances" in which he outlines his theory of ethics was published in 1878.[16] Royce's work, *The Philosophy of Loyalty*,[17] was not published until 1908. But since Royce does not mention either Peirce or his doctrine in that book, the tracing of a direct influence is not to be considered as anything more than tentative.

That Royce's ethics is nearer to that of Peirce than is James's, however, is hardly to be denied. Royce first defined loyalty as "The willing and practical and thoroughgoing devotion of a person to a cause."[18] In a final defini-

---

[13] *Ibid.*
[14] *Ibid.*
[15] *Ibid.*
[16] In *Popular Science Monthly.*
[17] New York, Macmillan.
[18] *The Philosophy of Loyalty*, pp. 16 f.

tion, he said, "Loyalty is the Will to Believe in something eternal, and to express that belief in the practical life of a human being.[19] If we accept, as indeed we must, the idea that Peirce's "unlimited community"[20] provides a "cause" and moreover an "eternal" one, and if we further admit that "interest" of such strength as to demand personal sacrifice[21] is identical with "devotion" or "loyalty" expressed in the "practical life of a human being," then there is no essential difference thus far at least and in its main features between the ethical conceptions of Royce and those of Peirce.

By main features here is meant the ethical goal and its pursuit. The ethics of the two men do differ, however, with respect to the way in which they were arrived at. It might be possible to argue that method is unimportant while doctrine is not, that since both men came to the same position by different means, the fact that the means were different is not so significant as the fact that the position is the same. To some extent, of course, this contention is valid. The fact is, however, that most great ethical systems do hold essentially the same position. That the individual person should strive with all his being toward as wide a community as possible has always been contended, and marks the moral lesson of most great ethical teachings. Yet, while Royce's method of arriving at his conclusions is to some extent the orthodox one of depending upon subjective elements, such as his "will to believe," Peirce strove to place the whole topic upon objective considerations, and indeed argued his conclusion from probability theory, on strict logical formulae. From the point of view of immediate action, it may seem necessary to know only what we must do in order to do what is right. But certainly from the standpoint of philosophy, it is just as important to want to know why. Philosophers may continue for thousands of years to appeal to our intuitions of what is right without adding one single bit of evidence to their contentions. Peirce did try, and to some extent succeeded, in going further by utilizing an exact logico-mathematical method for the purpose at hand. He did show us that we should act in much the same way as Royce contended that we should. But he went a little beyond in that he did offer some evidence why we should act in that way, by demonstrating that only so could our actions be considered logical. Thus despite the similarity in ethics, Peirce's formulation would appear to be somewhat more valuable than Royce's.

[19] *Ibid.*, p. 357.
[20] See this vol., chap. IX, C, iii.
[21] *Ibid.*

iii. ON DEWEY'S LOGIC OF INQUIRY

(a) Particular and Act

It is an historical fact that the work of Peirce exercised a profound influence upon the outlook of James and Dewey; and indeed both men gratefully have acknowledged their debt. But in an essay on "The Pragmatism of Peirce" Dewey tells us that James gave to pragmatism an emphasis which Peirce had not intended. Although Dewey was correct in his criticism of James, the argument of this section will be to the effect that Dewey himself fell into the error of enlarging one aspect of Peirce's pragmatism to the neglect of others, an overemphasis which resulted in the setting up of a logic that is foreign to the conception of Peirce.

Dewey quotes James's California address in which the latter stresses the fact that according to pragmatism it is the *particular* aspect of experience rather than the *active* aspect that is important. But Peirce is "less of a nominalist"[22] than James and so "the curious fact is that Peirce puts more emphasis upon practise (or conduct) and less upon the particular; in fact, he transfers the emphasis to the general."[23] There is such an extraordinary shift here in what is considered to be important that it is well worth noting. Dewey sees, correctly, that James's doctrine of pragmatism implies nominalism while that of Peirce implies realism (although later he says they are both realists),[24] but he holds that it is the emphasis of Peirce upon practice that brought about his emphasis on the general.

We may very well ask whether every occurrence of practice does not imply extreme particularity. There is indeed nothing more particular than an act, for every act is highly concrete and of the utmost specificity. There is nothing more down-to-earth than an act, and no two acts are absolutely alike. To change from emphasis on the particular to emphasis on action is not to have gained the slightest in generality. Moreover, what Dewey calls practice, or conduct, implies the particularity not of all things but only of certain things, namely, those things which are capable of conscious forethought; for, as we shall presently note, practice, or conduct, is to become, in logic, inquiry, and inquiry in Dewey's sense is meaningless unless it is taken to include consciousness. The notion that the shift from the particular to the act marks a gain in generality is the error which pervades Dewey's whole account of

---

[22] John Dewey, "The Pragmatism of Peirce," in Charles S. Peirce, *Chance, Love and Logic*, p. 303.
[23] *Ibid.*
[24] *Ibid.*

logic and makes his philosophy over into one which is in opposition to that of Peirce.

We can see the extent to which the transformation of a philosophy can go when we read further the interpretation Dewey puts upon Peirce's definition of the real. Peirce was engaged in a perpetual struggle against the philosophy of nominalism, as the errors attributed to it in innumerable references throughout the *Collected Papers* show. And so in defiance of nominalism he defined the real as "that whose characters are independent of what anybody may think them to be," a proposition carefully intended to remove the criterion of reality from the human province. Human beings may learn about reality, they may acquire certain habits whose value depends upon certain characters which the real possesses, yet reality is unaffected thereby.

Now, the odd thing is that Dewey quotes this same definition of the real but manages to return reality even under this definition to its old nominalistic reliance on cognition. For he goes on to observe that "it is only the outcome of persistent and conjoint inquiry which enables us to give intelligible meaning in the concrete to the expression 'characters independent of what anybody may think them to be'."[25] The fact is, however, that intelligible meaning is not confined to the concrete. Indeed, Peirce's intention is far from such an interpretation. Peirce's definition of the real was intended not only to make reality independent of cognition but also to free it from any necessity to be held down to the concrete. The concrete is real for Peirce, but so, assuredly, is the abstract. It is not only actuality but possibility as well which in Peirce's metaphysics shares the ascription of reality. But if "persistent and conjoint inquiry" were to be required to give intelligible meaning to Peirce's expression, then Peirce would have been a subjectivist like Dewey, which he emphatically was not. Dewey insists that "Peirce was a realist—in opposition to idealism,"[26] whereas Peirce opposed his realism chiefly to nominalism, although to be sure he was no subjective idealist, either. Peirce did call himself an objective idealist, but he intended realism by the phrase.[27]

The point to be stressed is that inquiry, the term used by Dewey in his essay to give meaning to Peirce's definition of reality, presupposes an inquirer, and since inquiry in this self-conscious sense is indulged in only by human beings, we may take it that reality is dependent upon our inquiring

[25] *Ibid.*, p. 308.
[26] Letter of February 16, 1939.
[27] *Collected Papers*, 6.24.

into it. And if this is true, then we are landed back in a subjective cognitional criterion of reality which is assuredly nominalistic and essentially foreign to, and even contradictory with, the definition of reality which Dewey admits is Peirce's own.

(b) Logic and Methodology

Peirce defined logic as the general theory of signs.[28] Since "a sign is something which stands in some respect for something to somebody,"[29] he considered that there are three branches of logic, corresponding to the three references of the sign. These are: Speculative Grammar, or "the general theory of the nature and meaning of signs";[30] Critical Logic, "which classifies arguments and determines the validity of each kind"; [31] and finally Speculative Rhetoric, which "studies the method that ought to be pursued in the investigation, in the exposition, and in the application of truth."[32] Speculative Grammar, then, deals, according to Peirce, with the general theory of *relations*; Critical Logic, with the relevancy of arguments to *truth*; and Speculative Rhetoric, with the *communication* of reasoning.

Dewey informs us in the Preface to his recent and definitive work on logic that Peirce was his most important influence,[33] and, more specifically, that so far as he knew Peirce alone had called attention to the principle of the continuum of inquiry.[34] So primary did Dewey consider this principle that he gave "the theory of inquiry" as the subtitle of his book. For Dewey, then, logic is the theory of inquiry, a phrase quite freely taken from Peirce. The fact is, however, that for Peirce "the logical study of the theory of inquiry"[35] constitutes only one of three branches of logic, namely, that branch which he has termed Speculative Rhetoric, or methodeutic, and thus by no means the whole of logic. From Peirce's point of view, Dewey's selection of one department of logic, the methodological, to stand for logic in general, including Speculative Grammar and Critical Logic, would be equivalent to the attempted reduction of both the theory of relations and the relevancy of arguments to truth to the communication of reasoning. Such a reduction, tantamount to a reduction of logic to methodology, is one which Peirce would never have countenanced.

---

[28] *Ibid.*, 1.191, 2.227, 2.93.
[29] *Ibid.*, 2.228.
[30] *Ibid.*, 2.206.
[31] *Ibid.*, 2.205.
[32] *Ibid.*, 1.192. Cf. also 1.559, 2.229, 2.93.
[33] *Logic*, p. iv.
[34] *Ibid.*, p. iii.
[35] *Collected Papers*, 2.106.

There is, of course, no evidence that Peirce would have been willing to endorse Dewey's interpretation, and much evidence against it. Certainly if Peirce had understood by logic nothing more than methodology he would not have set up the other two branches. Moreover, he would not have considered methodology to rest upon the others, as he most assuredly did.[86] Peirce never supposed that the theory of relations and the relevancy of arguments to truth were subdivisions of the study of inquiry; rather are all three, as we have noted, divisions of the theory of signs.

But perhaps the most ample illustration of the philosophical distance that separates Dewey from Peirce will be given if we follow through with the implications of Dewey's definition of logic, as the latter has himself developed them. Dewey tells us that his theory of logic "is that all logical forms (with their characteristic properties) arise with the operation of inquiry and are concerned with control of inquiry so that it may yield warranted assertions. This conception implies much more than that logical forms are disclosed or come to light when we reflect upon processes of inquiry that are in use. Of course it means that; but it also means that the forms *originate* in operations of inquiry. To employ a convenient expression, it means that while inquiry into inquiry is the *causa cognoscendi* of logical forms, primary inquiry is itself *causa essendi* of the forms which inquiry into inquiry discloses."[87] There are more implications here than there is space in which to discuss them. We will pass over such interesting questions as, for instance, why Dewey finds the highly ontological terminology of the scholastics so convenient, and proceed to consider the three most important points. He is very insistent in this passage not only that (1) logical forms originate in the process of inquiry but (2) that such origination is the cause of the forms, and, further, (3) that the logical forms are concerned with the control of inquiry. Let us examine these points separately.

(1) Acceptance of the contention that logical forms originate in the process of inquiry gives us an odd picture of the world as it must have been before the inception of inquiry. It raises the puzzling question, which is perhaps unsolvable, of how a world in which there must have been no logical forms (since there had been no inquiry) succeeded in developing creatures like ourselves who were capable of inquiring and thus of originating logical forms. It raises the further puzzling question of how logical forms survive and somehow seem to maintain a real status, beyond the inquiry which produced them. Suppose, for example, that, while inquiring into the problem

[86] *Ibid.*, 1.191, 2.206-207.
[87] *Logic*, p. 4.

of constructing a vehicle, some primitive man discovered the principle of the wheel. How did it happen that long after his death and the consequent termination of that particular inquiry men were still able to use the notion of "wheel" in constructing actual wheels?

(2) The statement that inquiry causes the being of the forms involves the assumption that what changes is responsible for what does not change, that history is causative of logic. On the basis of this assumption, Dewey would be responsible not only for the *assertion* that inquiry causes the being of the forms, he would also be responsible for the *being* of the forms, since it was *his* inquiry which determined the fact that inquiry determines the being of the forms. It would appear from Dewey's detailed treatment of the logical forms that they have for him very much the status we had assigned to them; yet on his hypothesis the continuation of their being now seems to hang upon the continuation of his inquiry into them.

The only escape from such an egocentric predicament, given, of course, Dewey's faith in inquiry as a first principle, consists in the appeal to a social interpretation of inquiry. This step Dewey does, in fact, take, when he discusses the continuum of inquiry.[38] "There is continuity of inquiry. The conclusions reached in one inquiry become means, material and procedural, of carrying on further inquiries."[39] Remembering that inquiry causes the being of the forms, it is horrible to contemplate what would happen in the world were the continuum of inquiry to falter. The result proves, however, to be other than we had supposed; for Dewey holds onto the subject regardless of the fate, subjective or objective, of the logical forms. All that would happen is that it would "make us believe our belief invalid if not imaginary."[40]

(3) If the logical forms which have originated in inquiry are concerned with the control of inquiry, then the process seems endless indeed. Inquiry must interfere with the situation into which inquiry is being made,[41] so that the only purpose of the inquiry becomes that of discovering the extent to which it interferes. Thus inquiry into the nullifying effects of inquiry nullifies that inquiry, and so on in an infinite regress of inquiries and nullifications which would seem to render the whole process nugatory.

But if, according to Dewey, logical forms depend for their being upon inquiry and have no existence without it, the same must hold true, it de-

[38] *Ibid.*, pp. 8-9.
[39] *Ibid.*, p. 140.
[40] *Ibid.*, p. 226.
[41] " . . . the position here taken is that inquiry effects existential transformation and reconstruction of the material with which it deals." *Ibid.*, p. 159.

velops, for all objects. Dewey tells us that "things exist *as* objects for us only as they have been previously determined as outcomes of inquiries."[42] Objects as well as forms, then, are the straight results of inquiry, and so the objective world does not exist for us when we are not inquiring into it. We know now why there were no logical forms in the world before the inception of inquiry: there was no objective world. Dewey is not willing to consider the possibility of an objective world of things which are changing and perhaps having an effect upon *him* even when he is not having any effect upon *them*. Yet the fact remains that there must be a world of things which have form and are objective to us whether we are aware of such a world or no.

The intense subjectivity of Dewey's position persistently confuses logic with human thinking. He confines the whole business of logic to the matter of solving problems. Although explicitly rejecting the psychological implications of this understanding of logic,[43] he is nevertheless involved in them. The assertion that judgment is perforce the result of inquiry[44] reaffirms the subjective character of the latter: by inquiry Dewey evidently intends conscious activity. But logic is not problem-solving except in its applied psychological aspects, and only applied logic is definable as an activity. Dewey would equate the proximate human purposes served by logic in the process of thinking with the final nature of logic itself.

(c) Subjectivism and Historicism

How far Dewey has strayed from Peirce's central position is clear in many passages. First of all, Peirce argued strenuously, against Wolf and Mill, that logic must not be confused with psychology. The rejection of the definition of logic as "controlled" inquiry is contained in the mere existence of thought processes which are not controlled.[45] In conscious thought the case is even worse, for then, says Peirce, logic has no criterion other than that of clarity, or the negative caution of inconceivability, which is, to say the least, vague.[46] The foundation for the independent being of relations, on which an objective logic might rest, given by Peirce in "The Order of Nature,"[47] was, according to Peirce's own account, "stripped by Dewey of all rational precision."[48] As

---

[42] *Ibid.*, p. 119. Cf. also p. 520.
[43] *Ibid.*, p. 423.
[44] Cf. the effect of inquiry, *ibid.*, p. 159, with the definition of judgment, p. 283.
[45] *Collected Papers*, 2.47.
[46] *Ibid.*, 2.50.
[47] *Ibid.*, vol. vi, bk. ii, chap. I.
[48] *Ibid.*, 5.508.

a matter of record, Peirce himself regarded Dewey's work in logic as something apart from logic itself. Dewey, he said, "seems to regard what he calls 'logic' as a natural history of thought."[49] Such a history would form a valuable part of knowledge, but Peirce recognized that the history of thought is natural history and not logic, and he observed that the mere appropriation of the name "logic" for "the new natural history" was a confirmation of his opinion that there is an urgent need for the construction of a sicence of logic.[50]

Logic for Peirce is the general theory of signs, and while all thoughts are signs,[51] only some signs are thoughts.[52] Sign is the wider category. The theory of signs is for Peirce an observational science,[53] and objectivity can go no further than what is implied in that assertion. Peirce learned from Duns Scotus[54] that a realist may hold the reality of actual particulars to be equal to that of generals without losing the generality of his realism. Thus Peirce cited everyday experience "such as presses in upon every man, at every hour of his life" as the starting point for logic, and immediately added that "it is open to no other doubt than that it may not have been correctly formulated in general terms."[55] His definition of the real as "that whose characters are independent of what anybody may think them to be" means for the true realist that general theories as well as particular facts stubbornly resist any effort to think them otherwise by insisting upon being just what they are. Peirce is both clear and emphatic on this score. Indeed, he erects as the cornerstones of his system, on a par with the firstness of feeling, the secondness of resistance, or objectivity, and the thirdness of generality, or relationship.[56] These elements *participate* together in activity, in all inquiry, specifically in scientific method, but they do not *originate* in this way. Thus the foundation of Peirce's system requires the distinction between the separate categories and their fusion in activity, while in Dewey's system the activity itself is central and the categories emerge from it, a difference which leads to profound ontological implications of a radically opposite nature.

[49] *Nation*, 79 (1904), 220.
[50] See this vol., chap. III, D, and chap. VIII, C.
[51] *Col. Pap.*, 1.538, 5.253.
[52] This is evident from Peirce's whole categoreal scheme of logic, in which, among the subdivisions of classes of signs, only a comparatively few stand for thoughts. *Ibid.*, vol. ii, bk. ii.
[53] *Ibid.*, 2.227.
[54] *Ibid.*, 1.6. See also C. R. S. Harris, Duns Scotus (Oxford, 1927), vol. ii, p. 24.
[55] *Collected Papers*, 2.75.
[56] *Ibid.*, vol. I, bk. iii, chap. II.

(d) Further Inconsistencies

The emphasis of Dewey's logic upon controlled inquiry leaves no doubt as to its pervasive nominalistic cast. In the notion that being is exhausted by conscious activity, as in the conception of a controlled inquiry which either constitutes or causally originates objects and their interrelations, we have one variety of subjective nominalism, a reduction of ontology to epistemology which has divided the world between subject and object and, while requiring both, somehow assigned the primary reality to the subject.[57] But, as we have seen, Dewey regards Peirce, from whom he has derived so much, as a realist, and there is no doubt that Dewey wishes to be included in that great tradition of realists who have sublated the realism-nominalism controversy.[58] As a result, although his essential ontological position remains that of nominalism, Dewey has followed Peirce into a great many important realistic inferences. It will mark the influence of Peirce upon Dewey more precisely if we indicate some few of these.

Dewey is at one with the realism of Peirce (and consequently at odds with his own basic nominalism) in understanding that form and matter are relative terms;[59] that temporal events can be understood only in abstraction from time;[60] that the scientific objects are of this abstractive character;[61] that probability has an objective and independent status;[62] that the rational is experienced;[63] that ideas, or universals, are identical with possibilities;[64] that the distinctions between actuality and possibility,[65] or potentiality,[66] and between inference and implication[67] are required for the realistic character of logical distinction; that common qualities are general qualities;[68] that positivism is wrong in holding verification above directive powers;[69] that the mere observation of facts leads nowhere;[70] that scientific method necessarily

---

[57] Cf. further on this point, J. W. Friend and J. Feibleman, *The Unlimited Community*, chap. II.

[58] Dewey, *Logic*, pp. 262-263.

[59] Dewey, *op. cit.*, p. 405. Cf. Peirce, *Collected Papers*, 6.353.

[60] Dewey, *op. cit.*, p. 450. Cf. Peirce, *op. cit.*, 6.93.

[61] Dewey, *op. cit.*, pp. 117, 376. Cf. Peirce, *op. cit.*, 6.361.

[62] Dewey, *op. cit.*, p. 474. Cf. Peirce, *op. cit.*, 6.534.

[63] Dewey, *op. cit.*, p. 38. Cf. Peirce, *op. cit.*, 6.327-328.

[64] Dewey, *op. cit.*, p. 109. Cf. Peirce, *op. cit.*, 5.103.

[65] Dewey, *op. cit.*, pp. 288, 352, 399. Cf. Peirce, *op. cit.*, 1.475.

[66] Dewey, *op. cit.*, p. 388. Cf. Peirce, *op. cit.*, 6.185.

[67] Dewey, *op. cit.*, p. 54. Cf. Peirce, *op. cit.*, 2.433, 2.444.

[68] Dewey, *op. cit.*, p. 269. Cf. Peirce, *op. cit.*, 5.291, 5.119.

[69] Dewey, *op. cit.*, p. 519, Cf. Peirce, *Nation*, 32 (1881), 227.

[70] Dewey, *op. cit.*, p. 70. Cf. Peirce, *Collected Papers*, 1.34.

involves the existence of universals and that scientific laws are possibilities;[71] and finally that science has the properties of a logical system.[72]

The advocacy of such realistic elements as those listed above when combined with insistence upon a basic nominalistic metaphysics leads to contradictions in the matter of first principles. For example, Dewey denounces "that type of modern rationalism which selected the relational function and made relations the center and heart of all knowledge,"[73] a good description, incidentally, of what Peirce called "thirdness" and of which, he urged, knowledge must consist. Yet Dewey in another place recognizes that progress depends upon high degrees of abstraction and that "possible ways of performing physical operations" are "there awaiting occasion" whether "actualized at a given time" or not.[74] To transfer a problem explicitly from the metaphysical to the logical realm of discourse does not dispense with its implicit metaphysical assumptions, which continue to exist at the metaphysical level.[75] Yet Dewey employs this method in order to attack the necessity for metaphysics. The description of the universal as the abstract possibility of a way of interaction resulting from a comparison of kinds[76] does not get rid of the vexed question of its ontological status. Twist and turn as we might in the effort to describe things, hitherto distinguished, as combinations of operations of inquiry—even of *possible* combinations of operations of inquiry—we will yet find that problems concerned with primitive postulates have not been proved pseudo problems or otherwise dissipated.

We may conclude from the foregoing observations that Peirce was a realist who insisted upon the absolute particularity of the actual while maintaining the independence from actuality of the generals which the actual illustrates. Dewey evidently is, by his predilections, a realist of the Peircian persuasion, but, led by an interest in the metaphysical importance of actuality to substitute activity itself for the place occupied by the particular in Peirce's philosophy, he came to hold an explicit nominalistic position which is essentially alien to the point of view we associate with the name of Peirce. The derivation is an instance of the kind of effect which a great philosopher may expect his influence to exercise. Followers tend to mold their own ideas into discrete bodies of theory based on the overemphasis of selected items. The promise of tradition (sometimes partially fulfilled) is that these over-

[71] Dewey, *op. cit.*, p. 427. Cf. Peirce, *op. cit.*, 1.129.
[72] Dewey, *op. cit.*, p. 18. Cf. Peirce, *op. cit.*, 5.407.
[73] Dewey, *op. cit.*, p. 517.
[74] Dewey, *op. cit.*, p. 416.
[75] Dewey, *op. cit.*, p. 390.
[76] Dewey, *op. cit.*, pp. 440-441.

emphases will constitute themselves into an aggregate, thus allowing the systematic ideas of the philosopher to make a proper place for themselves in the world.

C. RECENT INFLUENCES

i. ON THE POSITIVISTS

It is a sign of the strength of Peirce's philosophy that so many diverse schools claim him, albeit only as a forerunner, predecessor or pioneer.

Peirce has been accused of not being a good pragmatist, since his pragmatism follows from realism and is not therefore a pure method, metaphysically free, like the pragmatism of James and Dewey.[77] One writer on American pragmatism has gone so far as to exclude Peirce altogether from his account.[78] Peirce has been praised for the objectivity of his philosophy and its categories.[79] He has been accepted by the idealists.[80] On the whole, the pragmatists, the positivists, the idealists, the realists—equally wish to make him an honorary member. The pragmatist claim has already been examined in the previous section. We may glance for a moment at that of the positivists.

Typical of the positivist point of view is the work of Justus Buchler.[81] It is also the most ambitious. Dr. Buchler's approach is not altogether novel, however. He sees in Peirce only what would be seen by a disciple of Dewey who had been strongly influenced by the logical positivists. In line with this perspective, Dr. Buchler makes a distinction between two strains of Peirce's thought: the logical and empirical, on the one hand, and the metaphysical, on the other. He proposes to treat of the former and exclude the latter. Accordingly, he devotes the first part of his book to Peirce's epistemology, the second part to his theory of meaning, and the third part to his logic.

A number of things must be said about this plan and its execution. By "metaphysics" Dr. Buchler evidently means ontology, since he gives epistemology, considerable space, more, in fact, than a work on empiricism justifies. Peirce himself devotes many more pages to ontology than to epistemology. The distinction inherent in Dr. Buchler's plan assumes that an exposition of Peirce's metaphysics would add nothing to our understanding

---

[77] W. H. Hill, "Peirce's 'Pragmatic' Method" in *Philosophy of Science*, 7 (1940), 168.

[78] Eduard Baumgarten, *Der Pragmatismus* (Frankfort, 1938).

[79] Eugene Freeman, *The Categories of Charles S. Peirce* (Chicago, Open Court, 1934).

[80] F. I. Carpenter, "Charles Sanders Peirce: Pragmatic Transcendentalist" in *The New England Quarterly*, 14 (1941), 34.

[81] *Charles Peirce's Empiricism* (New York, Harcourt, Brace, 1939).

of his logic and empiricism, a questionable assumption indeed. From the point of view of treatment, Dr. Buchler's work fails to exhibit that consistency the absence of which in Peirce he so laments. The parts break down into a series of little essays on empirical topics, into sections which are not interconnected. Moreover, there is hardly any development in the exposition. The side of Peirce with which Dr. Buchler treats is, in a sense, the one which has been the most exploited: the contribution to empiricism, scientific method, meaning and inquiry. Yet there is, surprisingly, no space given over to that classification of the sciences which Peirce evidently considered so fundamental a part of his achievement.

The side of Peirce's philosophy with which Dr. Buchler does not concern himself—the ontological, the rational, and the speculative—has not been fully considered as yet by anyone. Attention to it might have indicated to Dr. Buchler that his particular interpretation of the empirical side was not altogether in agreement with what Peirce meant. Whole areas of Peirce's writings are devoted to his realistic metaphysics; more particularly to his triad of ontological categories and their implications. His brand of realism is consistent with the logic from which it sprang—a logic not unlike *The Principles of Mathematics* of the earlier Russell—and inconsistent with the view that a fair presentation of his logic can be made which opposes it to his metaphysics.

Dr. Buchler's implicit instrumentalism, in selecting Peirce's empiricism without its foundations, seems thus to be at odds with the explicit realistic metaphysics of Peirce. The theory of inquiry which Dewey and his followers consider to be another name for logic is, according to Peirce, only one of three branches of logic. Moreover, it is not an independent branch, but rests upon the other two. Dr. Buchler continues the error, made popular by Dewey, of considering the last third of Peirce's logic to be the whole of logic. This was clearly not Peirce's understanding. The theory of inquiry is only the *application* of logic; logic itself is much broader.

Evidently, each of us is going to have his own Peirce. The Peirce of Dr. Buchler is a confused thinker who did much useless work in metaphysics, but who had some brilliant logical insights which were altogether unconnected with his other work. But the thesis can be defended, as against this view, that although Peirce's writings were unsystematic his principal ideas were not. And therefore his metaphysics can be exhibited to form a unity with his empiricism. The proper evaluation of the work of a great man demands that we make our earliest approach in a sympathetic frame of mind, not in a critical one. The criticism must come later; but first we must ask and answer the problem of what the man was trying to do. Although all philosophers have inscribed some contradictions, it is unfair to assume that they intended them or that they cannot be explained as attempts to arrive at a consistent position.

In this light it is evident that Peirce was endeavoring throughout his life of work to restore realism to its position as the truth of philosophy. In the course of these labors, it was necessary from time to time to avoid the fallacy of the realm of essence by emphasizing the empirical basis of the realistic logic, and also to avoid the fallacy of nominalism by emphasizing the reality of universals. Thus Peirce did not have two philosophies which were contradictory, but only the one which he attempted to clarify and defend in two ways. Partisans have a tendency to seize upon one of these extremes at a time and to present an indulgent countenance to what they deem the gross and obvious errors of the other. They agree in that they feel an extreme must be chosen; but neither was the choice of Peirce. It is by no means enough that Peirce has, like most great philosophers before him, bequeathed a new terminology to old controversies of ontology, and served as the precursor of new discoveries in logic which he anticipated more than he affected. For Peirce's philosophy, with all its immense potentialities, yet remains to be evaluated as a whole.

Other positivists have been even more succinct in their denial to Peirce's philosophy of his own claims for it. For Karl Britton, Peirce was not a realist, and would never have accepted his own claim that his philosophy reposed entirely upon his logic. Furthermore, he would never have accepted his own contention that he could find a place for himself in the Christian church.[82]

Charles W. Morris has seen the culmination of Peirce's work as converging with that of Dewey and Mead in modern scientific empiricism.[83]

For Ernest Nagel, the same Peirce who rejected "positivisms of the type of Comte and Pearson" would have "endorsed the happy marriage of the cultivation of logic and the empirical temper which distinguishes this [i.e., the logical positivist or empiricist] movement."[84] The title of Nagel's paper as well as its sin of omission is somewhat misleading. Central to the logical positivist philosophy are many notions which are in conflict with the very

[82] Karl Britton, "Introduction to the Metaphysics and Theology of C. S. Peirce" in *Ethics*, 49 (1939), 435.

[83] Charles W. Morris, "Peirce, Mead and Pragmatism" in *The Philosophical Review*, 47 (1938), 109.

[84] Ernest Nagel, "Charles S. Peirce, Pioneer of Modern Empiricism" in *Philosophy of Science*, 7 (1940), 69.

foundations of Peirce's ideas. Would Peirce have endorsed the antimetaphysical stand of the logical positivists? Would he have accepted the unity of science on the basis of the sole reality of physical science or its entities or its concepts? Was Peirce, in short, the pioneer of a movement which denies the very existence of most of his interests? This is hardly acceptable. All that can fairly be said is that Peirce had an interest in empiricism and in logic, and that the positivists of today have the same interest, although from an altogether different metaphysical basis (for the denial of metaphysics implies a certain unexpressed metaphysics), which brings them round to a position opposed to Peirce's own.

ii. ON THE REALISTS

Among the realists, Peirce has as yet exercised no tremendous effect, although it is hard to see how the realists of the future will be able to escape his influence.

The editors of the *Collected Papers*, Charles Hartshorne and Paul Weiss, have been touched by Peirce's realism. The influence on Hartshorne is apparent in the books and essays he has published in recent years.[85] Hartshorne is struck by the fact that a logician and metaphysician of Peirce's stamp should have interested himself in such theological questions as God and the ultimate nature of the universe, and it is chiefly the theological aspect of Peirce's thought that concerns him.

Paul Weiss has done much to earn for Peirce the kind of attention he deserves, and has continually stressed the many-faceted suggestiveness of the great philosopher.[86] The effect of Peirce on Weiss's own metaphysics is apparent throughout.[87]

Arthur W. Burks, in an unpublished thesis entitled "The Logical Foundations of the Philosophy of Charles Sanders Peirce" (Ann Arbor, Michigan, 1941), which deserves to be better known, has shown the importance of Peirce the logician to Peirce the systematic philosopher.

Other students of Peirce are beginning to make themselves known,[88] and

---

[85] See *Beyond Humanism* (Chicago, Willet & Clark, 1937); *Man's Vision of God* (Chicago, Willet & Clark, 1941); "Charles Sanders Peirce's Metaphysics of Evolution" in *The New England Quarterly*, 14 (1941), 49; "A Critique of Peirce's Idea of God" in *The Philosophical Review*, 50 (1941), 516.

[86] E.g., "The Essence of Peirce's System" in *The Journal of Philosophy*, 37 (1940), 253.

[87] *Reality* (Princeton, 1938).

[88] E.g., Thomas A. Goudge, "Peirce's Treatment of Induction" in *Philosophy of Science*, 7 (1940), 56; Julius W. Friend and James Feibleman, *The Unlimited Community* (London, Allen & Unwin, 1936).

the increase of Peirce's effect upon the world of philosophy, and through philosophy upon the world of affairs, is beginning to become apparent.

D. Conclusion

Speaking very broadly, there are in the main, and with respect to method of presentation, two philosophical traditions: the open, or exploratory, and the closed, or systematic. The open may be exemplified by Plato's writings; the closed, by Aristotle's. Plato's work has been more suggestive and has on the whole opened up more avenues to research. The vitality of the Platonic tradition today is evidence that it will continue to do so. Aristotle's work, though perfectly formulated and systematized, seemed to end all investigation for some centuries, and was chiefly responsible for the fact that Aristotle's name for so long served as the authority on all important questions. But perhaps this is in the end a detrimental eminence, since it has a tendency to terminate inquiry by assuming that the leading questions have all been answered.

Perhaps the chief contribution of Peirce is his open system. He has managed to combine the best features of his two Greek models in that he has designed a system but managed to keep it open. The English tradition followed Plato in being merely inquisitive; the Germans followed Aristotle in being merely systematic. Peirce followed the scientific method in being inquisitively systematic. For, although he had a system, he did not regard it as in any sense the final word, and assumed that it would be modified and expanded by later investigators. He was a critic but he was more than that; he was, again, "a positive critic, pleading for the admission to a place in our scheme of the universe for an idea generally rejected." (6.605) That idea is metaphysical realism as applied to the philosophical and empirical sciences.

Peirce's philosophy is hodogetic; it is a system for showing the way, a system whose chief feature is its direction. That is why it is safe to say that the history of his influence up to date is only the early history of his influence, and that the greater part of his effect will be felt by those who follow after us in the indefinite future.

Index of Topics

Index of Names